BUSINESS COMMUNICATION

Strategies and Skills   FOURTH EDITION

BUSINESS COMMUNICATION

Strategies and Skills

FOURTH EDITION

RICHARD C. HUSEMAN
*University of Central
Florida*

JAMES M. LAHIFF
University of Georgia

JOHN M. PENROSE, JR.
*San Diego State
University*

THE DRYDEN PRESS   Chicago Fort Worth San Francisco Philadelphia Montreal Toronto London Sydney Tokyo

Acquisitions Editor: Robert Gemin
Developmental Editor: Kathi Erley
Project Editor: Paula Dempsey/Susan Jansen
Design Manager: Rebecca Lemna
Production Manager: Bob Lange
Permissions Editor: Cindy Lombardo
Director of Editing, Design, and Production: Jane Perkins

Text and Cover Designer: Frances Hasegawa
Copy Editor: Jean Berry
Indexer: Lois Oster
Compositor: Impressions Publishing Services
Text Type: 10/12 Garamond Light

Library of Congress Cataloging-in-Publication Data

Huseman, Richard C.
    Business communication : strategies and skills / Richard C.
Huseman, James M. Lahiff, John M. Penrose, Jr. — 4th ed.
      p. cm.
    Includes bibliographical references.
    ISBN 0-03-033067-X
    1. Business communication. I. Lahiff, James M. II. Penrose,
John M. III. Title.
HF5718.H84 1990
658.4'5—dc20   90-35560
                                                          CIP

Printed in the United States of America
12-039-98765432
Copyright © 1991, 1988, 1985, 1981 by The Dryden Press, a division of Holt,
Rinehart and Winston, Inc.

Address orders:
The Dryden Press
Orlando, FL 32887

Address editorial correspondence:
The Dryden Press
908 N. Elm Street
Hinsdale, IL 60521

The Dryden Press
Holt, Rinehart and Winston
Saunders College Publishing

THE DRYDEN PRESS *Series in Management*

Since the first edition of *Business Communication: Strategies and Skills* was published in 1981, the U.S. workforce has increased from 77 million people to 124 million. During the same period, the gross national product grew from $1,549 billion to nearly $5,000 billion.

Besides such obvious changes, more subtle forces are reshaping the social, business, and political environments in which we must function. One constant, however, is that businesspeople, from CEOs to line workers, recognize the importance of communication to themselves and their organizations: they need to be able to communicate effectively. The primary mission of this fourth edition is to develop readers' abilities to communicate and, consequently, to work effectively with others.

EMERGING FORCES IN THE BUSINESS ENVIRONMENT

Two forces that now affect the business community are likely to intensify. First, society has grown more aware of the ethical implications of actions and communication. Newspapers and television regularly announce breaches of ethics by business executives. Adherence to ethical guidelines has become a yardstick by which individuals and organizations will and should be evaluated.

The internationalization of business is a second force reshaping the business environment. The international business community has eagerly awaited 1992 and the opportunities inherent in the move toward a united Europe. The dissolution of national boundaries in Europe will affect the conduct of business and, therefore, business communication.

Even more significant are events that occur with little advance notice. Russia, China, and Eastern Europe strive for equilibrium amidst gale-force winds of democratization; Central America may be on the verge of a new age. The changing shape and size of the international business community presents new challenges and offers greater rewards to organizations that most effectively convey their message.

NEW FEATURES IN THIS EDITION

This fourth edition features many improvements in addition to extensive updating of material. Two of these features are responses to national awareness of the importance of ethics and of the internationalization of business. Ethical considerations, which must pervade all aspects of our communicative behavior, are not isolated in a single chapter. Rather, ethics is integrated throughout the book. Each chapter includes an "Ethical Dilemma" designed to stimulate class discussion and critical thinking. By the end of their business communication course, students should recognize that ethics and communication are unalterably entwined.

While analyzing each Ethical Dilemma, readers should keep these questions in mind:

- Are any laws being broken?
- Is the situation fair to all parties involved?
- Would I feel guilty if my friends and family learned that I was involved in a similar situation?

Ongoing international dynamics herald a new openness to business abroad. As never before, the careers of today's business students are likely to include the opportunity to work abroad. Organizations that ignore the forces of internationalization risk a future of stagnation. Hence Chapter 21 is devoted to international business communication.

Both written and oral presentations can be bolstered significantly through the use of visual aids. Until the development of the personal computer, only individuals with artistic ability were able to create effective visual aids. At best, the process was laborious and expensive. Now anyone can learn to lay out, design, and deliver tables, graphs, or charts that enhance any type of presentation. Heightening the impact of communication through the use of visual aids is the subject of Chapter 16.

Systematic planning is a prerequisite for successful business writing. Chapters 5 through 9 provide extensive coverage of the planning and revising process as it relates to specific written strategies. Because many organizations seek new business primarily through proposals, Chapter 9 includes a section on the writing of effective proposals.

LEARNING TOOLS

The fourth edition offers learning tools as follows:

- Learning Objectives to help readers focus on the important features of each chapter.
- Opening vignettes that serve as a bridge between the chapter objectives and content.
- Marginal notes to assist readers in identifying significant ideas.
- Checklists to facilitate the review of information.
- Annotated letters to illustrate both effective and ineffective writing strategies.
- Many new cases and exercises to give additional opportunities for discussion and analysis.
- Highlighting of key terms in the text.
- A glossary to provide easily located definitions of important terms.

INSTRUCTIONAL PACKAGE

The fourth edition is accompanied by a comprehensive package of teaching and learning materials. The *Instructor's Manual* contains the following elements:

- Chapter Outline
- Student learning objectives
- Chapter synopsis
- Teaching suggestions
- Answers to review questions
- Case notes
- Exercises for Students
- Readings on Teaching Methods
- Transparency Masters emphasizing key learning points from the text.

The *Test Bank* contains approximately 2,000 true/false, multiple choice, and essay questions and answers. Each chapter of the test bank will also include one mini-case problem followed by several multiple choice questions. This unique test item allows you to test the students' grasp of concepts without grading time-consuming essay questions. A computerized test bank is available featuring the true/false and multiple-choice items.

A computerized interactive letter-writing and grammar tutorial is available for the text.

An interactive workbook/study guide containing grammar and writing practice, key terms from the text, and other applications is available to students.

ACKNOWLEDGMENTS

Many individuals have contributed to this and previous editions. For their help in co-authoring and updating chapters, special recognition is due John Lough (Ch. 17) and Susan Tucker Kinney (Ch. 21) of the University of Georgia, Houston Carr (Ch. 20) of Auburn University, and Richard David Ramsey (Appendix) of Southeastern Louisiana University.

The following reviewers merit special thanks for their assistance in improving the fourth edition:

Anita Bednar, Central State College
Charlotte Gale, Widener University
Richard Haughey, The Citadel
Louise Holcomb, Gainesville College
Carolyn Hollman, New Hampshire College
Doris Johnson, West Valley College
Lorraine Krajewski, Louisiana State University in Shreveport
Tom Lombard, College of Lake County
Marcia Mascolini, Western Michigan University
Paula Nossett, Vincennes University
William Sharbrough, The Citadel
Charlotte Thralls, Iowa State University
Ron Weidenfeller, Grand Rapids Junior College

For their help on previous editions, we thank E. Paul Alworth, Lois Bachman, Martha Bickley, Frankie Clemons, Betty Cochran, Marian C.

Crawford, William Damerst, Nancy Darsey, George H. Douglas, Ron Dulek, Nancy Elliott, Lilian Feinberg, Alton V. Finch, Michael Finnigan, Marie E. Flatley, Barbara Miller Gentile, Theresa Gilbert, Lee Goddard, Hal W. Hepler, Herb Hildebrandt, Betty Jacquier, Charles Jamison, Betty S. Johnson, Ron Kapper, Paul J. Killorin, Retha Hoover Kilpatrick, Judith Remy Leder, David O. Lewis, Robert Lorenzi, Iris Mauney, Robert Ochs, Virgil R. Pufahl, Mary Ellen Raleigh, Richard David Ramsey, Diana C. Reep, Jeanette Ritzenthaler, Joan C. Roderick, Ron Schlattman, Arthur Smith, Ted Stoddard, James Stull, Ron Weidenfeller, and Charlotte West.

We would like to thank the following people at Dryden for their help and support: Paula Dempsey, Susan Jansen, Becky Lemna, and Bob Lange. A special thank you is extended to Butch Gemin and Kathi Erley for their help in conceptualizing and incorporating new elements in the text. A very special thank you is due Jean Berry, whose superb copyediting created a smooth flow throughout the text.

Students have also offered helpful ideas, and many of their contributions are reflected in the additions, deletions, and updating found in this edition. We are grateful for all of the suggestions as well as for those we have yet to receive.

We have attempted to produce a book that will be of value to students now and throughout their careers. By mastering the contents and learning to apply the principles presented, they will have constructed a foundation for long-term personal and professional development.

Richard C. Huseman
James M. Lahiff
John M. Penrose, Jr.

November 1990

ABOUT THE AUTHORS

Richard C. Huseman, Ph.D. (University of Illinois), was recently named Dean of the School of Business at Central Florida University. He had previously taught for 26 years at the University of Georgia, where he served as Chairman of the Department of Management. He is the author of more than 100 articles and scholarly papers. His major area of interest is communication and human performance. In addition to this text, he has co-authored the following: *Readings in Interpersonal and Organizational Communication, Interpersonal Communication in Organizations,* and *Readings in Organizational Behavior.* His book *Managing the Equity Factor . . . Or After All I've Done For You . . .* (1989) is a popular explanation of the role communication plays in relationships, both on and off the job, and has been translated into Russian, German, Chinese, and Greek. In addition to his academic duties, he has been active as a trainer and consultant for numerous private corporations, including IBM, AT&T, and 3M. He participated in more than 250 training programs at the supervisory, middle management, and executive levels.

James M. Lahiff, Ph.D. (Pennsylvania State University), has taught at the University of Georgia since 1969. He is on the faculty of the Management Department in the College of Business. His teaching specialties include organizational communication, personnel interviewing, and time management. His articles have appeared in many academic and practitioner-oriented publications. In addition to this text, he has coauthored several other books on communication. His most active professional affiliation is with the Association for Business Communication. He has headed a variety of ABC committees and has made many presentations at ABC meetings. He has done training and consulting for many organizations in both government and the private sector.

John M. Penrose, Ph.D. (University of Texas at Austin), is Professor of Information and Decision Systems in the College of Business Administration at San Diego State University. From 1972 to 1988 he was on the faculty of the Graduate School of Business at the University of Texas at Austin, where he served as coordinator of the 11-member business communication faculty. He has also served on the faculties of Southern Illinois University at Edwardsville and Ohio University. He is the author of many journal articles, book chapters, and six textbooks in business communication. He was president in 1989 of the Association for Business Communication and serves on the editorial boards of three scholarly journals. As a consultant to business, he has worked with numerous business and nonprofit organizations as a trainer and expert on technical writing, written and oral strategies, and organizational communication.

CONTENTS

PART TWO **STRATEGIES FOR WRITTEN
COMMUNICATION 59**

PART FIVE   **CAREER STRATEGIES   559**

CHAPTER **22**   *Writing a Resumé*   *561*

INTRODUCTION

An Overview of Communication in Business

Chun-Sheng Yu, a graduate of the College of Foreign Affairs in Beijing, left China in 1959. Yu was more confident than most of his fellow refugees that the United States would offer him the chance for a good life because he was an interpreter with the U.S. State Department, he spoke English well, and he had traveled in the United States frequently on vacation. Yu, his wife, and their five children settled in Atlanta. Yu's skills and personality enabled him to advance to management positions, and he soon became a respected member of the Atlanta political community. By the time he had sent all five children to college, he began making plans to spend his retirement years in Fort Myers, Florida.

In 1989, however, Yu faced a crisis. Students and citizens in the Republic of China were peaceably striking in Tiananmen Square, calling for democratic social and economic reform, when they were stormed by soldiers of the People's Liberation Army. Thousands were killed. A wave of students seeking the freedom of expression so violently denied them in the wake of the massacre began to arrive in the United States. Yu took an early retirement and organized a citizens' support group to work in concert with other groups across the nation to provide emotional and physical support to the refugees. At a rally sponsored by the Federation of Independent Chinese Student Unions in the United States, he met Cheng Mei.

Cheng Mei arrived in the United States with few belongings and unable to speak English, but hoping to continue her education. When she met Yu she was

Learning Objectives

1 *To recognize how organizations depend upon communication.*

2 *To identify some of the monetary and nonmonetary costs of communication.*

3 *To recognize the increasing importance of business communication.*

4 *To understand the value of training in sending and receiving messages.*

5 *To understand the environment of business organizations.*

6 *To recognize the effect of environment on business communication.*

7 *To become aware of the challenges inherent in international business communication.*

8 *To appreciate the impact of technology on business communication.*

living at a temporary shelter in Atlanta. Yu helped her to learn English and to understand the ways of the people in her new country, about which she knew little. When it was time to leave the shelter, Mei found a job at a fast food restaurant that paid enough to provide her with food and a room in a poor part of town. She could not count on friends made in support groups for financial assistance because there were many other refugees to be helped. She wondered how she would ever save enough money to pay tuition.

Mei has made little progress understanding what the United States is really like. She and Yu have lost touch. The contrast between his experience and hers suggests two questions: How important to his success in his new country were Yu's language skills and his understanding of cultural differences between China and the United States? Could Mei's marginal existence in her new home be a function of her inability to communicate effectively?

Newcomers' communication problems are understandable. More difficult to understand is that millions of people born in the United States who know English as their first language struggle to communicate effectively both on and off the job.

THE PERVASIVE NATURE OF COMMUNICATION

When a former president of Shell Oil Company said, "This business of communicating has become as important as finding more oil," he succinctly stated a belief held by many.[1] Regardless of the type of organization in which you work now or will work in the future, the business of communicating is all important. Communication is significant to organizations and to individuals alike.

Even the monster in the classic *Frankenstein* became aware of the significance of communication. While hiding in the woods, the monster observed the family of a shepherd for several days.

> I found that these people possessed a method of communicating their experiences and feelings to one another by articulate sounds. I perceived

[1]Robin D. Willits, "Company Performance and Interpersonal Relations," *Industrial Management Review* 7 (July 1967): 91–107.

that the words they spoke sometimes produced pleasure or pain, smiles or sadness, in the minds and countenances of the hearer. This was indeed a godlike science and I ardently desired to become acquainted with it.[2]

Regardless of where communication occurs or who is involved, the basics of the transaction are identical. To illustrate, Frank Rhodes owned and operated a small wholesale janitorial supplies company. The workforce consisted of five warehouse workers, one secretary, and three outside salespeople. He regularly encountered problems caused by salespeople failing to complete their order forms, warehouse workers losing bills of lading, and the secretary misfiling important papers. Frank found that the more closely he observed his workers and the more he talked with them, the less frequently such problems occurred. No matter how hard he worked at it, however, problems involving information seemed to arise. Sometimes a message did not go where it was supposed to. Other times information was distorted by the time it reached the intended recipient.

Much of the information exchanged on the job has little to do with the job itself but it is vital to the individual. Human beings are sometimes referred to as social animals, for they need to communicate even when there is nothing urgent for them to express. In fact, much conversation may appear purposeless on the surface but actually satisfies the need to interact with others. To recognize the importance of such communication, we need only to consider what is generally regarded as the ultimate punishment for troublesome prison inmates: solitary confinement. The person placed in solitary confinement is absolutely deprived of the opportunity and right to communicate with others.

Although human communication often appears purposeless, it is not.

Because communication is recognized as crucial, many organizations train employees to become better communicators. Training programs may be structured around many different aspects of communication. For example, an American Management Association catalog of course offerings included the following communication courses or courses that list communication as a key topic:[3]

Organizations devote much effort to improving communication.

- Interpersonal Skills Lab
- Effective Executive Speaking
- Projecting a Positive Executive Image
- Negotiating to Win
- How to Sharpen Your Business Writing Skills
- Recruiting, Interviewing, and Selecting Employees
- Communicate to Get the Response You Want
- Written and Verbal Techniques for Successful Communication
- Improving Your Managerial Effectiveness
- Effective Functioning as an "Assistant To"
- Managing through Influence
- Advanced Management Skills for Supervisors
- Assertiveness Training for the New or Prospective Manager

[2]Mary W. Shelley, *Frankenstein* (London: Oxford University Press, 1969), 112.

[3]*American Management Association Course Catalog,* March–October 1982 (New York: American Management Association, 1982).

- How to Write and Implement Business Plans That Work
- Understanding the Computer: An Introductory Program for Business Executives
- Coaching and Counseling for Productivity
- Developing Your Skills as a Personnel Assistant
- AMA's Career Development Seminar for Executive Secretaries and Admimistrative Assistants
- Training the Trainer
- AMA's Management Course for Controllers and Treasurers
- Principles of Professional Selling

- Field Management of Salespeople
- AMA's Executive Course for the General Sales Manager
- Telephone Selling Skills That Increase Sales
- Marketing Communications
- How to Manage Your Advertising
- Basic Public Relations Skills
- Fundamentals of Customer Service
- Managing Your Customer Service Operation
- Handling Customer Complaints and Inquiries

The list suggests just how varied the nature of communication courses is as well as the many organizational activities in which communication is vital.

THE COST TO ORGANIZATIONS OF COMMUNICATION

Monetary Costs

The government requires much information from business organizations.

Business organizations must provide a great deal of information to federal, state, and local governments. This is difficult for the best of communication systems, and the expense involved is high. For example, over 5 million business firms and associations reported detailed information on income and finances to the Internal Revenue Service in 1989. The federal government requires lengthy reports and applications from thousands of businesses, nonprofit organizations, and state and local agencies that must comply with regulatory requirements or that receive federal grants or contracts. In all, American organizations and individuals spent over 1.7 billion hours to meet federal information collection requirements during 1989. This is equivalent to employing 850,000 people full time.

The expense of federal government paperwork has been documented.

Not surprisingly, the single largest paperwork agency in the federal government is the Department of the Treasury, which includes the Internal Revenue Service (IRS). The IRS Form 1040 and related schedules impose an annual burden of more than 297 million hours. The Department of Defense required 263 million hours of paperwork in 1989. Demands for information increase each year:

> Despite efforts by the Federal government to reduce the amount of paperwork necessary for its operation, changes in the governmental laws and services continue to increase paperwork burdens. In an attempt to tighten

controls on the Department of Housing and Urban Development (HUD), the government increased paperwork responsibilities by 3 million hours and the courts are likely to require further changes. As the result of a court order, the Department of Labor's Occupational Safety and Health Administration (OSHA) increased paperwork requirements by 48 million hours in order to inform employees of potential chemical hazards and to train them to avoid exposures. The Environmental Protection Agency's (EPA) paperwork burden increased by 13.5 million hours as a result of new regulations related to asbestos and chemicals.[4]

Research has shown that we spend approximately 75 percent of waking time involved in some form of communication. The time spent on one or another phase of communication in a typical manufacturing plant comprises approximately half of an average workday. The cliché "time is money" is true. The tremendous cost of business communication partially accounts for the intense interest in it.

Consider the cost of a single letter to a business organization. From dictation to mailing it was $10.26 in 1989. This represents an increase of 54.8 percent over the 1981 cost of $6.63 and an increase of 20.4 percent over the 1985 cost of $8.52. When investigators conducted the first Dartnell survey on this subject in 1930, the cost of a business letter was $.30.[5] Even more expensive are face-to-face sales calls. The cost rose from $96.79 in 1977 to $251.63 in 1987.[6] Projections for 1991 suggested a cost of approximately $305 per call.

Nonmonetary Costs

Monetary costs are important to an organization, but many other less tangible costs of communication are also important. For instance, although it is difficult to compute the cost of communication failures, such failures often cause long-felt repercussions.

To illustrate, when Fred Adkins misunderstood the tolerances required for the pipe fittings he was machining, his mistake was not noticed until he had completed half the order. The completed fittings had to be scrapped. To replace them, other orders were delayed, and the work schedules for some other lathe operators were disrupted. The customer waiting for the fittings was also inconvenienced and may be hesitant to place another order with Fred's employer. Fred believed that his supervisor had given him incorrect instructions, which the supervisor denied. For the next week Fred was disgusted with his boss and with his job. His friends

[4]Office of Management and Budget, *Information Collection Budget of the United States Government,* 1989, (Springfield, Va.: National Technical Information Services, 1989); Commission on Federal Paperwork, *Final Summary Report,* October 3, 1977, 5.

[5]*Dartnell Institute of Business Research Target Survey* (Chicago: Dartnell Corporation, 1986).

[6]Roy G. Ljungren, *The Business-To-Business Direct Marketing Handbook* (New York: American Management Association, 1989), 35; Nina Streitfeld, "How to Communicate in Other Cultures," *Public Relations Journal* 42 (February 1986): 34–35.

at work sympathized with him, and shop productivity temporarily dropped. After several weeks, things returned to normal, but Fred continued to talk occasionally about finding another job.

The repercussive nature of communication failures may make it difficult to determine the exact financial costs involved. No doubt exists, however, that ineffective communication results in errors, misunderstanding, poor performance, and negative feelings.

INTERNAL AND EXTERNAL COMMUNICATION

When a major corporation installed an 800 number to provide the news media with a daily recorded update on the status of the company, the majority of the calls came from the company's own managers stationed all over the world. They wanted to know what was going on and what was being said by the home office.[7] This should have caused top management to question how effectively the company was addressing the information needs of its employees.

Messages sent and received within an organization comprise its **internal communication**, which may be formal or informal. **Formal communication** messages are sent through channels developed by management. Much communication in any organization, however, does not go through regular channels. This **informal communication** consists of exchanges between individuals who, although not formally connected, interact by telephone conversation, social or chance meetings, and even on the golf course.

Much of the communication conducted by an organization is with individuals or groups outside the organization. **External communication** may involve any of the many different segments of the public with which the organization interacts. Most organizations have their greatest number of public contacts through **advertising**, which is a highly structured form of external communication. Examples include television commercials, printed ads, and brochures sent by the company to persons on a select mailing list. Most external communication is less formal than advertising; for example, management might informally keep the neighboring community aware of how the company contributes to the local economy. Annual reports, news releases, and public speeches by executives are other examples of external communication.

Advertising is the most structured type of external communication.

Not all external communication is planned.

External communication is not always planned and purposeful. Employees play many different roles in the course of a day, and the roles are sometimes difficult to separate. For that reason all employees are unofficial spokespersons for their employers. Even though you may seldom talk to outsiders about your work or about your employer, you are still representing the organization.

[7]William J. Corbett, "Internal Communication: Where It All Starts," *International Public Relations Review* 12 (1988):15–25.

GROWTH OF BUSINESS ORGANIZATIONS: IMPLICATIONS FOR COMMUNICATION

Most business organizations are much larger today than they were even a generation ago. Much organizational growth has occurred through mergers and acquisitions. Even a decade ago, many organizations were small enough to allow managers to know personally a sizable share of the employees; expansion has now made close contact more difficult. As an organization grows, so do its communication problems. Organizational development through planned expansion or consolidation may result in one or more levels being added to the organization or even a major restructuring of the entire organization. Figures 1.1 and 1.2 illustrate how the increased distances among the different levels of management and the distribution of responsibilities greatly complicate transmission of information, which in turn may prevent the organization from performing efficiently.

Organizational growth often leads to communication problems.

International Expansion

The growth of business organizations is not limited to the size and complexity of the organization. Growth also occurs geographically, from across the street to around the world. International growth makes communication all the more important and at the same time frequently more difficult.

When two people attempt to communicate, each may assume that the other person "shares the code" and that the message sent is very close to the message received. However, individuals from different cultural backgrounds frequently do not share the code and, therefore, must be careful not to miscommunicate. Many language and cultural influences can disturb the process of effectively getting a message across to people from a culture different from the sender's.

Even individuals who share the same language may have difficulty communicating. For example, if British service station attendants wanted to lift your bonnet, they would actually be asking to look under the hood of your car. If you told them that they could look under your hood, they might expect to find a gangster in the car. To most Americans, bonnets are something grandmothers wore at Easter. To buy bonnets, they went to a department store and rode the elevator to the ladies' hat section. In Great Britain grandmothers would have ridden the lift.

Sharing the code involves more than a shared language base; it involves the sharing of a culture. For example, women in the rural United States spoke of their decorative headgear as Easter bonnets, not simply as bonnets. They wore functional bonnets throughout the summer to protect against the sun. Such bonnets were invariably homemade rather than purchased at a store with a lift, or elevator. To these women, a lift was a set of metal arms at the rear of tractors used to raise and lower implements. An elevator was a mechanism used to convey grain from a low elevation to a higher one.

Sharing the code also means sharing the culture.

FIGURE 1.1   ■   *Organization in Biblical Times before Expansion*

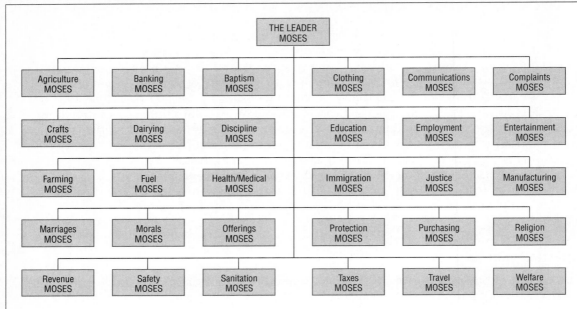

Source: Adapted by permission of the publisher from *Organization,* by Earnest Dale, pp. 11, 13. © 1967 AMACOM, a division of American Management Association, New York. All rights reserved.

Specialization of Tasks

In recent years many companies have become more diversified in the products or services they provide. Such diversification is intended to make a company more profitable by making it less susceptible to the ups and downs of one segment of the economy. As organizations grow, whether through diversification or other means, management seeks ways of creating greater and greater efficiency. One way to increase efficiency is to make the individual worker's duties more specific. As duties are narrowed down, the consequences are that (1) the use of sublanguage or jargon increases and (2) individual workers become competent and more productive faster because less training is required for them to master their highly specialized jobs.

The use of jargon will facilitate communication between specialists.
Business communication is affected significantly by the use of **jargon**, a verbal shortcut that allows specialists to communicate more easily among themselves. An accountant, for example, uses certain terms that are understood by other accountants and, in doing so, is able to be briefer and more specific. Consequently, jargon saves time and achieves understanding readily — as long as both individuals are specialists of the same sort.

Problems occur when a specialist uses jargon to communicate with someone outside the discipline. Economists, for example, sometimes use

FIGURE 1.2 ▪ *Organization in Biblical Times after Expansion*

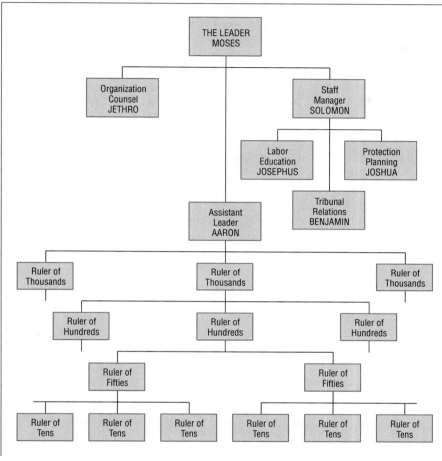

the term "negative saver" to describe people who spend more than they earn. This term may convey the intended meaning to other economists but not to the general public. The longer specialists work within their chosen fields, the more inclined they become to communicate with everyone else through jargon. When that happens, misunderstandings and frustrations inevitably follow.

At one time management researchers viewed specialization as a solution to many of the problems confronting business organizations. Through specialization many companies become more productive and more efficient.

Jargon is functional only when the communicators possess similar occupations.

Years ago, a single carpenter built most of a house alone. This was both time consuming and expensive, however, and work teams were developed. Individual workers became highly specialized. Rather than work on a single house from start to completion, an individual did one job and moved on to the next building. Through specialization it became possible to construct large housing developments using many workers in the time span formerly associated with building a single house.

Without good communication, specialization will be ineffective.

Managers now realize that specialization is not the panacea they once thought. When management narrows jobs and turns people into specialists, these people become more dependent upon the efforts of other specialists. For specialization to be effective, whether in construction or in any other endeavor, there must be good communication among the specialists.

THE DEVELOPMENT OF COMMUNICATION SKILLS

Without training, one cannot reach full potential as a communicator.

Many people consider oral communication to be as natural as breathing, eating, and sleeping. They maintain that with maturity humans naturally develop into proficient communicators. Each day we can observe examples of the falsity of that position.

Business leaders frequently bemoan the lack of communication skills among many college graduates. Workers often cite the inability to communicate as a prime shortcoming of their superior. The ability to communicate ranks high among attributes that employers seek in all potential employees.

Brenda Fernandez, for example, enjoyed working with numbers and was pleased when she was hired as a payroll clerk. She had always thought that a payroll clerk spent most of the day working with numbers. After a few months on the job, she said, "I like my work, but it's different from what I expected. At least half of my time is spent getting and giving information. Mathematical ability is important to this job, but the ability to communicate with others is just as important."

Many communication problems are the fault of the receiver.

Through training, listening ability can be improved.

Until recently most people did not realize that effective communication requires that both the speaker and the listener have good communication skills. We spend almost 50 percent of our average workday listening to others. Listening ability can be improved, and several tape-recorded courses are available for this purpose. Listening is also the subject of many training courses conducted in business and governmental organizations.

Some companies also provide remedial reading instruction for employees who are unable to read and to comprehend at an acceptable level. Certain employers consider reading to be so important that they provide this instruction completely at company expense. The worker attends these classes at full pay.

Improper reception of information can be costly to an organization.

Companies and individuals daily pay the price for problems caused by a lack of skill in receiving information. For example, the drill press operator who did not listen carefully to the supervisor's explanation of how to work with a new alloy ruined $300 worth of drill bits and wasted $1,000 worth of raw materials. Several weeks after the human resources manager announced in a memo the provisions of a new group health insurance plan, it became apparent that several maintenance workers had misunderstood them.

Geoffrey Nightingale, managing director of Burson Marsteller's Syner Genics Division, recommends the following rules for overcoming barriers to effective organizational communications:[8]

1. Always establish the context before trying to communicate anything. If the context is wrong, your communication will not make sense, no matter how bright and attentive you believe your audience to be. If the context is right, if it makes sense, you have the audience standing right up there alongside of you as you communicate.
2. There can be no communications without both give and take. An internal communications system that allows for one-way communications only cannot possibly be effective. Set up a formal system that encourages two-way communications. Design and install programs and activities that ensure two-way communications take place. And train your managers to become "active listeners" in their dealings with employees and others.
3. Too much communications is no communications at all. Get rid of the clutter, the "sacred-cow" reports, bulletins, newsletters. Consolidate and streamline. Make sure priority information gets priority treatment.
4. Foster the belief at all levels within your organization that behavior — what a person does, how he or she acts, what the company rewards and what it punishes — is much more important in terms of communicating, than what is formally written or what is said. If you're looking for a crusade, this is it. Make a personal commitment to see to it that the behavior of management matches their words and, then, follow that commitment through.

THE RELATIONSHIP BETWEEN COMMUNICATION AND ORGANIZATIONAL EFFECTIVENESS

A survey of 1,300 consumers, business executives, and investment professionals reported in *PR News* confirms the correlation between outstanding management and good communication skills. "All good companies seen as winners were also seen as good communicators," observed James Foster, president of Brouillard Communications. The companies identified by the study as being the top three superior achievers were IBM, Merck, and General Electric. *Fortune* magazine, on the other hand, has ranked both IBM and General Electric top in their industries in sales while Merck ranked third.[9]

---

[8]Geoffrey Nightingale, "Communicating from a Standing Position," *International Public Relations Review* 12 (1988).

[9]"Excellence and Communications," *International Public Relations Review* 12 (1988): 12–13.

The widespread recognition of the importance of communication has spawned much research in business communication. The researchers have discovered that effective communication enhances much of what is considered important in business organizations.

Improved communication usually leads to better morale.

Management considers worker morale to be an important indicator of a healthy organization. Better communication is usually accompanied by better morale. Managers who are concerned about low morale should create additional communication opportunities for workers.

A relationship exists between communication and such factors as job satisfaction and relationships with coworkers.

A close link exists between job satisfaction and morale. Research in business organizations has revealed that interpersonal relationships among workers greatly influence job satisfaction. When workers believe they are actually a part of their work group, they will be more satisfied than if they feel left out. Workers are also more likely to be satisfied with their jobs if they are satisfied with the amount of information that they receive on the job. Communication is therefore a vital part of the manager's job.

MBWA: A Style of Managing

Communication occurs in a variety of settings and under varying circumstances. The variability in the communication process dictates that a manager must adopt any one of several roles to remain effective. These include **interpersonal roles**, which focus on interpersonal relationships; **informational roles**, which recognize the manager's vital position in the receipt and dissemination of information; and **decisional roles**, which focus on the essential managerial activity of decision making.

The one element common to these roles is that effective communication is necessary if the manager is to perform effectively. Tom Peters and Nancy Austin have written in *A Passion for Excellence:*

> The number one managerial productivity problem in America is, quite simply, managers who are out of touch with their people and out of touch with their customers. And the alternative, "being in touch," doesn't come via computer printouts or the endless stream of overhead transparencies viewed in ten thousand darkened meeting rooms stretching across the continent.[10]

In an earlier book, *In Search of Excellence,* Tom Peters and Robert Waterman introduced the concept of **management by walking around (MBWA)**.[11] This managerial technique enables managers to increase their contact time with subordinates, suppliers, and customers. Informal communication becomes the stimulus for managerial decision making as well as the vehicle for feedback to all of the individuals who contribute to organizational success.

[10]Tom Peters and Nancy Austin, *A Passion for Excellence* (New York: Random House, 1985), 8.
[11]Tom Peters and Robert Waterman, *In Search of Excellence* (New York: Harper & Row, 1982).

Just as managers have different styles of communicating and different roles to play in the organization, they also can practice MBWA in a variety of ways. Some managers, like those at Westinghouse, choose to have a program of MBWA. Westinghouse sent 30 hourly employees to New York to assess workmanship on the subway generating equipment for the city's transit system. The purpose of this close contact with their product was not only to increase reliability for the equipment that Westinghouse manufactured but also to put the employees closer to the user of the product to gain firsthand insight into how to improve the equipment. Others, like Milliken and Company's chairman Roger Milliken, spend as much as 80 percent of their time listening to customers, much of it away from the office.[12]

An example from *A Passion for Excellence* illustrates how one manager uses MBWA to improve the effectiveness of his organization. Apple's John Couch was the developer of much of the software for the Apple Macintosh, which is noted for its user-friendly characteristics. How was John Couch able to understand what the computer consumer needed when others did not? While working for Apple, he also sold computers — incognito — on weekends in his father's computer outlet and learned of the frustrations that consumers were having with computers. This touchstone with the consumer provided Couch the insight to design a user-friendly system. Other software engineers may sit at the drafting table and do what they are trained to do best, but John Couch preferred to get in touch. He was, simply put, managing by walking around.[13]

Informality is a hallmark characteristic of MBWA.

A Changing Workforce

Some dramatic changes in the workforce have had an impact on communication in organizations. The sheer growth in the size of the workforce has been impressive, as has its growing diversity. In 1970 the civilian labor force in the United States totaled 82.8 million workers; in 1988 it was 121.5 million.

The composition of the labor force has shifted. For example, in 1975, 46.3 percent of all women held a job while 77.9 percent of all men worked. By 1987, the figures were 56.1 percent and 76.4 percent. They are expected to be 60.3 percent and 76.1 percent by 1995.[14] The proportion of African-Americans, Hispanics, and Asians in the workforce will also increase as it increases in the general population (see Figure 1.3).

Such changes plus many others contribute to the turbulence in today's business organizations. Much organizational turbulence, however, can be controlled and managed through effective communication.

An increasingly diverse workforce provides new challenges for the communicator.

---

[12] *The Wall Street Journal.*

[13] Peters and Austin, *A Passion for Excellence.*

[14] U.S. Department of Labor, Bureau of Labor Statistics, *1989 Information Please Almanac,* 59–62.

FIGURE 1.3   ▮   *A Changing Population*

Sometime in the next century whites in the United States will no longer be the majority.

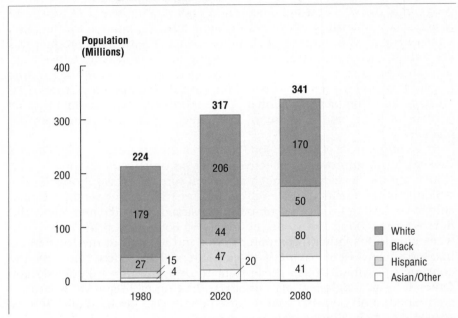

Source: Permission to reprint from the *1988 Statistical Fact Book,* p. 160, granted by the Direct Marketing Association.

✓▮ *CHECKLIST for MBWA Characteristics*

___▮ **MBWA is informal.**

___▮ **Its focus is internal (employees) as well as external (customers, suppliers, and competitors).**

___▮ **It involves actively listening to what others are saying.**

___▮ **It is demanding in terms of time and energy.**

___▮ **It is a mindset that the manager must adopt, not just a "gimmick" to solve particular problems.**

The Interpersonal Environment

Turbulence within organizations causes repercussions that extend beyond organizational boundaries. Pressures emanating from the organizational environment affect the interpersonal environment and thereby influence our relationships and interactions with others.

Some of the changes in the workforce have resulted in a greater diversity of workers who possess fewer shared goals and interests. This heterogeneous workforce represents differing frames of reference. With reduced commonalities communication problems are more prevalent.

Communication problems are intensified in a heterogenous workforce.

Changing lifestyles affect us both interpersonally and organizationally. For some workers, a growing interest in leisure-time activities may result in a declining interest in their jobs. On the other hand, the word **work-aholic** has become a common part of our language to describe people who become obsessed with their work to the point that other aspects of their lives suffer.

Personal problems, even though removed from the workplace, have an effect on job performance. For example, a person going through a divorce may seek to alleviate pressures through altered on-the-job behaviors. Because family problems in general affect one's work, repercussions from such problems will affect the work environment.

Personal problems affect job performance.

Coping with stress is one of the challenges of modern living. Some sources of stress are occupational; others are not. Regardless of source, however, the effects are far-reaching. The term **burnout** is used to describe exhaustion caused by excessive demands on one's energy or strength.

Social phenomena such as divorce, leisure-time pursuits, or burnout profoundly affect every dimension of life. Such phenomena intensify communication problems of both an interpersonal and an organizational nature.

THE EVOLUTION OF COMMUNICATION TECHNOLOGY

Our society is communication oriented. In the fiscal year 1989, the United States Postal Service (USPS) delivered over 160 billion pieces of mail, an increase of more than 29 billion pieces in just five years. By the year 2001, the annual volume will have leaped to a staggering 250 billion pieces. The USPS, the nation's largest civilian employer, now has about 770,000 full-time employees and could have more than one million in 2001. Despite this increase in volume and staff, Postmaster General Anthony Frank predicts that automation can lower total expenses by $3.5 billion. Notwithstanding the present strength of our postal system, competitors such as Federal Express, grossing $1.4 billion in 1988, and United Parcel Service, grossing $7.5 billion, have grabbed large pieces of the delivery pie. And coming up fast are electronic messaging services—telex, fax, and E-mail.[15]

Reporting on the use of different communication technologies in the United States, Dan Brown and Jennings Bryant have noted that, from 1975 to 1987, the number of telephones in use jumped up 69 percent with

[15]Abner A. Layne, "The High-Tech Needs of the Postal Service," *High Technology Business,* June 1989, 14–19.

BOXED IN	*AN ETHICAL DILEMMA*

Cory works in the quality control department at Grady Memorial Hospital. In the two years she has been there, her work responsibilities have grown steadily. At first she was proud of the confidence her superiors showed in her, but now she sees her role in a different light.

"I am tired of being taken advantage of!" Cory complained to her brother Justin. "I hardly have time to audit my assigned charts and now they want me to do physical checks of patient schedules. Just because the hospital is having problems with accreditation, they think it's OK to work me to death."

Knowing that Cory is a hard worker and had been putting in many hours of overtime, Justin suggested that she cut back on less important duties.

"To the hospital, all my duties are important," Cory replied. "But the one place I could easily save time without anyone noticing is the chart audits. Besides, I know which staff are competent and never make mistakes. I could just sign off those charts without checking them, and that would leave me time to complete my other assignments."

Cory feels boxed in. What would you do?

current ownership in approximately 98 percent of all U.S. households.[16] By 1988 Americans were making over 800 million calls a day on the 155 million phones they owned. As prices fell from $4,000 in 1984 to $400 in 1989, the number of cellular phones in operation increased proportionally. Over all, 1.6 million portable phone users spent $3 billion in 1988.[17]

Brown and Bryant further related that in about the same time period (1975 to 1987) the number of households with radios increased 18.3 percent to account for a 99 percent penetration rate. Approximately 98 percent of all households currently have a television set, and the average person watches television 7.1 hours each day. In 1987, consumers purchased 13,306,000 VCRs compared with only 402,000 a decade earlier. In the decade from 1976 to 1986, the number of cable television systems swelled by 106.5 percent and the number of cable subscribers multiplied by 242 percent.[18]

Evolution versus Revolution

Each technological change that we have witnessed has heralded the coming of a "new age" in communication—the end of communication as we know it, the beginning of an "information revolution." In Brown and

[16]Dan Brown and Jennings Bryant, "An Annotated Abstract of Communication Media in the United States," in *Media Use in the Information Age,* eds. Jerry L. Salvaggio and Jennings Bryant, (Hillsdale, N.J.: Erlbaum, 1989), 259–302.

[17]*High Technology Business,* June 1989, 61.

[18]Brown and Bryant. "An Annotated Abstract."

Bryant's examination of this phenomenon, they note that with the advent of radio in 1922 and again in 1946 with television, oracles predicted the end of the newspaper. More recently, we heard prophecies of the demise of motion picture attendance as home videos replaced the need to leave the home for movie viewing. Although we have seen a 47 percent decrease in the number of newspaper firms (1909–1986) and a stabilization of average weekly movie attendance (1975–1985), during the same time frames we have also witnessed an increase in newspaper circulation of 259.5 percent and an increase in box office receipts of 90.8 percent. While eight-track cassettes have gone the way of the pony express, audiocassettes have increased in sales from 15 million to 2.97 billion (1973–1987).[19]

What we typically see happening is not extinction of media dimensions, but evolution of their forms and how they fit together. This is occurring at faster rates than in the past. The telephone took 70 years and newspapers more than 100 years to reach 50 percent market penetration, but television took just 8 years and VCRs 11 years to do as well. Rather than replacing older forms of technology, new information tools are supplementing and complementing them. Printed media continue to flourish but now we collect, order, edit, print, and sometimes deliver information via computer electronics. We can anticipate further changes in the use of printed media not only as a result of technological changes, but also in response to growing environmental concerns pertaining to the destruction of trees, energy shortages, and the disposal of wastes.

The Computerization of the Business Organization

Many authorities predicted that modern technology would eliminate jobs and reduce the volume of paperwork in business organizations. Advanced high-speed printing machines and modern photocopiers have instead contributed to the already high volume of written communication. These devices so simplify the preparation process that paperwork is now disseminated more widely than ever. Some authorities are calling the proliferation of paperwork an **information explosion**.

Computers that process and store tremendous amounts of information have truly detonated the information explosion. Equipped with a high-speed printer, a computer can turn out reams of paper daily and, in the process, inundate management with information.

As costs of computer hardware and software dropped, as software increased in ease of use, and as people became familiar with its use and capabilities, incorporation of computer technology into the business arena skyrocketed. Estimates for the number of microcomputers in U.S. businesses rose from 2.6 million in 1982 to 4.6 million in 1984 and the number was projected to reach 13 million by 1990.[20] A study estimates that the true cost of a PC, including training and support, is about $18,000. A

Modern technology has contributed greatly to organizational effectiveness, but problems remain.

Because of computerization, a greater need exists for skilled communicators than ever before.

[19]Ibid.

[20]Tor Guimaraes and Vasudevan Ramanujam, "Personal Computing Trends and Problems: An Empirical Study," *MIS Quarterly,* June 1986, 178–179.

company with 200 PCs will have made an investment of $3.6 million. Data for 1989 indicate that 59.3 percent of surveyed small manufacturers own microcomputers (a 31 percent increase in 6 years), 53.1 percent own minicomputers (a 6 percent increase), and 43.2 percent own mainframes (a 15 percent increase). Only 2 percent of all companies surveyed indicated that they owned no computers.[21]

Despite predictions to the contrary, computerization has neither eliminated jobs nor reduced paperwork. Peter F. Drucker, a management authority, has said:

> At present the computer is the greatest possible obstacle to management information because everybody has been using it to produce tons of paper. Now, psychology tells us that the one sure way to shut off all perception is to flood the senses with stimuli. That's why the manager with reams of computer output on his desk is hopelessly uninformed.[22]

Modern technology has contributed greatly to management's access to information. It has also enhanced management's ability to transmit information quickly and economically. Modern technology has not, however, replaced the human communicator. If anything, computerization has increased the importance of the human communicator's role, for it is the manager who must ultimately determine the information to be retrieved and those to whom it should be sent.

Growing numbers of organizations now employ a **director of communication**, a job title virtually unheard of until recently. The director of communication is responsible for managing the flow of information within the organization and for solving communication problems. No matter how sophisticated technology becomes, individuals who are skilled in communication and aware of the vital components in the communication process will always be needed.

The chapter thus far has presented numerous examples of the progress and changes evidenced in information transmission during the past 20 years. Organizations have continued to invest increasing amounts or resources — as much as 10 to 15 percent of revenues — in the development of data processing and information management systems.[23]

The diffusion of technology into the organization has not always been an orderly or well-planned operation, and it is still common to see archaic conventions in operation next to high-tech practices. A major corporation may print out lengthy files from its database and send them through the mail to be keyboarded into an associate's database when the files could have been easily transmitted through telecommunications. Today's competition does not allow for inefficiency in organizational operations; businesses must eliminate out-of-date operations and utilize existing technology to perform productively.

---

[21]Paul Pittman, James Cox, and John Blackstone, Working Paper, 1989.

[22]Peter F. Drucker, *Technology, Management and Society* (New York: Harper & Row, 1970), 174–175.

[23]William E. Cwiklo, "Learning How to Look Ahead: Information Management Planning," *Inform*, October 1989, 10–14.

Telecommunications

Given the importance of time, accuracy, and money in today's business environment, an improved process of mail communication was inevitable. The traditional method of typing a letter and sending it by U.S. mail provides the sender with a confirmed hard copy for transmission but is costly in terms of staff and delivery time. If a document requires input from reviewers in other locations and is sent by Federal Express, transmission and manpower costs will quickly add up in addition to the elapsed time (see Table 1.1).

In about 30 minutes a **facsimile (fax) machine** can send a ten-page document to four different locations. With turnaround, all participants can have a copy of the completed document in a reasonable period of time at a reasonable cost (see Table 1.2). Fax machines use an electronic scanner to transmit graphic images.

The telephone also transmits messages quickly, and it provides a means of immediate feedback to the sender. The cost to the company is typically about $700 to $1,000 per employee to install and an additional $100 to $200 per month to maintain. However, experts estimate that about 50 to 70 percent of all calls are not completed, resulting in games of telephone tag. Telephone discussions are often subject to miscommunication. Additionally, staff must usually prepare follow-up documents.[24]

Computer-based **voice mail** systems process voice messages rather than text messages. The sender records the spoken message into the machine for the receiver to listen to, thereby saving transcribing time. It serves to eliminate telephone tag, to save time by broadcasting messages to a group, and to lower secretarial costs. Disadvantages include high initial costs (capital investment of $150 to $200 million), the resistance of individuals both to deliver and to listen to recorded messages of substantial length, and the lack of a permanent document. Only about 1,500 to 2,000 voice mail systems were in operation in North America at the beginning of the decade[25] (see Table 1.3 on page 24).

The generic name for noninteractive communication of text, data, image, or voice messages utilizing telecommunications links is **electronic mail (E-mail)**. Despite "noninteractive" in the definition, E-mail is a means of communication between people and can be responded to immediately upon retrieval of a message. More than 1,485,000 business people sent more than 3 billion E-mail messages in 1988. That figure was expected to climb to 10 billion by 1991.[26] The rate on costs of this technology vary based on time of day and speed of modem.

Both facsimile and voice mail are examples of electronic mail. The benefits of electronic mail include speed (though not as fast as a tele-

[24]Stephen A. Caswell, *E-Mail* (Boston: Artech House, 1988), p. 15.
[25]Caswell, *E-Mail*, p. 17.
[26]"Boss USPS Has Flourishing Rivals," *High Technology Business*, June 1989, 17.

TABLE 1.1 ▪ *Document Preparation Cycle for Physical Delivery*

Step	Transmission Cost	Work Time (hours)	Elapsed Time (days)
Prepare draft 1		4	
Send draft	$50		1
Make comments		4	
Return draft	50		1
Create draft 2		3	
Send draft	50		1
Make comments		2	
Return draft	50		1
Create draft 3		2	
Send draft	50		1
Make comments		2	
Return draft	50		1
Prepare draft 4		1	
Send draft	50		1
Make comments		1	
Return draft	50		1
Prepare final draft		1	
Send final draft	50	—	1
Totals	$450	20	9

Source: Stephen A. Caswell, *E-Mail,* p. 16, © 1988 Artech House, Inc., Norwood, MA. Reprinted with permission.

phone), low cost, more precision, and more control. When preparing for a meeting, background material (which often constitutes 80 percent of the discussion time) can be distributed ahead of time using E-mail, freeing up the meeting time for more crucial issues.

Videotext is an interactive two-way system for sending and receiving graphic or textual information through a computer interface by electronic means. Examples of videotext include *CompuServe®*, *The Source®*, and *Dow Jones News/Retrieval®*, which offer access to a variety of services for the business user.

The Extended Office

Telecommunications has yielded the means for releasing individuals from the confines of the office while providing them with a way to continue operations from virtually any place and at any time they choose. Freed from the headaches and costs of office dress, commuting, business lunches, and idle chatter, employees can perform more work in less time and feel better about it. Employers save as well in the form of less required office space and more efficient communications with employees. Society in gen-

TABLE 1.2   ▮   *Document Preparation Cycle for Facsimile*

Step	Transmission Cost	Work Time (hours)	Elapsed Time (days)
Prepare draft 1		4	
Send draft	$15		
Make comments		4	
Return draft	15		1
Create draft 2		3	
Send draft	15		
Make comments		2	
Return draft	15		
Create draft 3		2	
Send draft	15		1
Make comments		2	
Return draft	15		
Prepare draft 4		1	
Send draft	15		
Make comments		1	
Return draft	15		
Prepare final draft		1	
Send final draft	15	—	1
Totals	$135	20	3

Source: Stephen A. Caswell, *E-Mail,* p. 17, © 1988 Artech House, Inc., Norwood, MA. Reprinted with permission.

eral profits from having fewer people in automobiles on congested highways, using precious fuel and contributing to air pollution.

To illustrate, Jennifer Chiu is a morning person. By 6 a.m., she is in her home office, reviewing her E-mail and either typing in responses or forwarding messages for further action. She works steadily until 10:30, when she breaks to dress for lunch with a client. From her car, she makes calls to her boss and checks on the status of a job she sent to marketing. Having spent so much time alone this week, Jennifer thoroughly enjoys her client's company at lunch and her warmth contributes to making a big sale for her company. She spends the afternoon completing a major report and faxes it into the office before closing time. Following a two-mile run and a light supper, she takes advantage of lower phone rates and begins downloading needed information from a large commercial information network. She calls it a day at about 9 p.m., having put in nearly 13 hours of steady work. She sleeps well, knowing that one more equally productive day will allow her to enjoy a peaceful four-day weekend in the country.

Initially, telecommuting was an executive-dominated process or a way programmers might choose to do business. Today thousands of employees from such major firms as J.C. Penney, Pacific Bell, and Travelers are par-

TABLE 1.3 ▪ *Cost Comparison of Voice Mail as a Telephone Answering Service*

	Phone Mail	Message Center	Group Secretary
Number of hours during the day when callers can leave messages or users can get their messages	24 hours	9–12 hours	8–9 hours
Delay between time message is left by caller and time message is received	No delay	1–4 hours	Short delay
Accessibility of messages from various locations	From any touch-tone telephone	From one location	Accessible at or near secretary's desk
Cost per month per user	$7–$20	$40	$100

Source: Stephen A. Caswell, *E-Mail,* p. 18, © 1988 Artech House, Inc., Norwood, MA. Reprinted with permission.

ticipating in company-supported telecommunications. Additionally, self-employed individuals, particularly single parents and handicapped people who would otherwise face daily impediments to employment, are enjoying the flexibility of this alternative work style.

Current estimates indicate that around 5 million people are full or part-time telecommuters. To support these figures, there were expected to be 5 million cellular phone subscribers by 1991, with projected growth to 10 million by the end of 1993.[27]

SUMMARY

Communication has always been an important activity in business. It is vital to the goals of the organization and to the individuals within the organization. Management constantly seeks ways to improve internal and external communication, many times by providing communication training for employees.

The exact cost of communication to an organization is difficult to calculate. To arrive at the intangible costs of communication is even more difficult. Communication failures in organizations, however, have many repercussions and affect individuals far removed from the site of the problem.

[27]"Keeping Pace with Cellular Phone Growth," *Management Review,* October 1989, 12–13.

The tremendous growth of organizations makes managing more difficult and necessitates improved communication. As workers become more specialized, they become more dependent upon others and must exchange more information. Most individuals are not naturally skilled in sending and receiving messages, but these abilities can be learned. Business organizations must provide the government with a great deal of information, and this responsibility is met only through communication. Research in business organizations has shown that effective communication enhances workers' attitudes and encourages behavior that business considers desirable.

The evolution of communication technology has brought about significant changes in the way individuals communicate among themselves in almost every organization. Advances in telecommunication are having an impact not only on our methods of communication but in the very way we organize for work.

Key Terms

- **internal communication**
- **formal communication**
- **informal communication**
- **external communication**
- **advertising**
- **jargon**
- **interpersonal roles**
- **informational roles**
- **decisional roles**
- **management by walking around (MBWA)**
- **workaholic**
- **burnout**
- **information explosion**
- **director of communication**
- **facsimile (fax) machine**
- **voice mail**
- **electronic mail (E-mail)**
- **videotext**

Review Questions

1. What is meant by the pervasive nature of communication?
2. Why are humans sometimes referred to as social animals?
3. Which type of costs, monetary or nonmonetary, can be more accurately computed? Why?
4. Define internal communication.
5. Define external communication.
6. Compare formal channels to informal channels.
7. Explain how task specialization affects communication between individuals within an organization.
8. Define jargon.

9. Give one example of the effect that government monitoring of business has on business communication.

10. In what ways does computerization aid business communication? How does computerization complicate business communication?

11. List and describe some of the latest advances in telecommunications technology. Discuss the possible impact on the way organizations do business.

CASE | *A Costly Misunderstanding*

Larry R. Smeltzer, Arizona State University

Kenneth Newson is a middle-level manager in a large chemical company. With over 15 years of managerial experience, Kenneth has experienced many difficult communication situations. His effective communication skill is one reason for his steady record of increased responsibilities and promotions.

Kenneth recently decided to invest a rather large sum of money he had been saving. He thoroughly reviewed several alternatives including stocks, bonds, treasury certificates, and real estate. He was especially interested in a new small apartment building located near his home.

Jacobs, the real estate agent, was very persuasive as he explained the tax advantages and potential income of a newly built apartment building. Kenneth had confidence in the real estate agent and agreed to buy the building at the asking price on three conditions: first, landscaping had to be completed; second, a fence had to be built around the back patios; and third, mail boxes must be installed along the street. Based on his managerial experience, Kenneth insisted that each of these items be written into the contract.

Approximately 45 days after Kenneth took possession of the building from the builder, the mail boxes had been installed but neither the fence nor the landscaping had been completed. Kenneth called Jacobs to ask about the delay. Jacobs replied that the contractor told him the job had been completed. Kenneth then called the builder directly, and again he was told the conditions of the contract had been met.

Kenneth was furious. He did not feel that the two pine trees in the front yard were "landscaping"; furthermore, short fences between the patios but no back enclosure did not meet the terms of the agreement. He believed that nearly $1,000 worth of services and goods were still to be supplied. The contractor replied that everything agreed on had been provided and that additional work could not be expected because of the low purchase price of the building. No agreement could be reached, and Kenneth filed a suit against the contractor for breach of contract.

Case Questions

1. Kenneth, Jacobs, and the building contractor are all experienced, well-meaning business people. What caused the misunderstanding here?

2. How could the parties involved avoid the extra expense of a lawsuit?

3. How would you define *fence* and *landscape*? Are these difficult terms to define? Why or why not?

What Happened to My Luggage? | CASE

David B. Parsons, Lakehead University, Thunder Bay, Ontario, Canada

In June 1990, John and Anne Davis flew from Calgary to Winnipeg, where they were to catch a connecting flight to Thunder Bay. Once they arrived in Thunder Bay, they planned to rent a car and drive 450 kilometers to an isolated northwestern Ontario logging town to attend John's sister's wedding.

In the luggage hold of the aircraft were not only their clothes but also wedding presents and the bridal gown, which John's mother had worn at her own wedding. Approximately ten minutes before the flight was due to land, Jim Richards, a flight steward, noticed wisps of smoke coming through the floor in the rear galley.

Having been notified of the problem, the captain asked all passengers to leave the plane when it landed because a minor technical problem had to be corrected. John and Anne left the plane and waited the scheduled three hours in the terminal for their flight to Thunder Bay. What they didn't know was that all the luggage in the hold was either destroyed or severely damaged by a flash fire that had erupted in the luggage hold during the flight.

When John and Anne landed in Thunder Bay, their luggage and that of 40 other passengers failed to appear on the conveyor belt. When John and Anne explained their dilemma to the airport manager, they were told to report their luggage as lost. The Thunder Bay airport hadn't been informed about the fire in Winnipeg. Consequently, John and Anne had to leave for the wedding without their luggage, the gifts, or the gown. They did not find out about the destruction of their belongings for six days after the incident.

Case Questions

1. Should the passengers have been told about the fire while the plane was in the air? Explain your answer.

2. Should the passengers whose luggage was destroyed in the fire have been told about it while they waited in the airport for their connecting flights?

3. Should the Winnipeg airport have informed the airports of destination about the damaged and destroyed luggage?

4. Assuming the role of John or Anne Davis, write a letter to the airline expressing your concerns about the way the situation was handled.

The Nature of Communication

Item: A student concerned about her grade in a psychology class has a conference with her professor. Although the professor has given no tests, the students have turned in a number of short papers on various aspects of psychology. At the conference the professor assures the student she is doing good work. When the final grades come out the student receives a C. Later, when she meets with the professor again and says that she thought she was doing good work and expected an A, the instructor replied that a C was good in his class.

Item: The owner of a restaurant telephones her supplier and tells him that she wants her order of Thanksgiving turkeys cut in half. When the order arrives, she is shocked to receive the same number of turkeys that she ordered last year — with each bird cut neatly in half.

Item: An employee in an organization is told that his work is outstanding and he is going to receive the highest raise among the five people in the office. Later the employee finds out that his raise was just a few dollars more per month than the others. Even more significant is that the person who got the lowest raise says the supervisor has promised to have a private office built for her. The other four will continue to work in one large open area. What are the rewards for outstanding work?

CHAPTER 2

Learning Objectives

1 To understand the nature and purpose of communication.

2 To learn how reinforcing and aversive stimuli can affect behavior in the communication exchange.

3 To understand the role and importance of superior–subordinate communication.

4 To comprehend the myths and realities of communication.

5 To improve your ability to exchange information through an awareness of the variables in the communication process.

6 To master encoding and decoding skills to avoid communication breakdowns.

7 To identify your major strengths as a communicator.

As these situations show, there are many ways of communicating. Often what we hear is not what the other person said. What we say can frequently be interpreted in an entirely different manner by the listener.

Most of this book will focus on developing effective communication skills. This chapter provides a theoretical framework for the chapters that follow.

THE NATURE AND PURPOSE OF COMMUNICATION

A basic goal of any organization is survival. If campus organizations fail to meet the needs of their members, they cease to exist. Many student government organizations on campuses in the United States have gone out of business because members found the organization no longer met any particular goals. In private business a major goal is making a profit. When businesses fail to make a profit, they eventually cease to function.

The major factor enabling organizations to meet their goals and continue to exist is the behavior of their people. The judgments, decisions, and efforts put forth by employees determine to a large extent the profitability of a business. Admittedly, some other factors—such as government intervention and regulation, competing businesses, and natural disasters—also influence profits, but the behavior of people in organizations has great influence. The fundamental question is one of motivation. How do we motivate others to behave in the desired manner?

Just as the behavior of others affects us, our behavior affects others. For example, have you ever found an item at a garage sale that really caught your interest? "That's a good deal for the price," you said to yourself, "but it's more than I have to spend." The transaction may have occurred as follows:

> "That item over there that you have marked $10—does it work?"
> "Sure it works; it's almost brand new."
> "If it works I'd be interested in it for $5, but I don't think it's worth much more than that."
> "You kidding? Those sell for $20 new and that's if you can find one. I got a new one for Christmas. That's why I'm selling this one. I'd have to have at least $8 for it."
> "Yeah. It's probably worth that, but I only have $7.25 with me. If you'll take that, I'll buy it."
> "Okay."
> "Wow!" you thought. "I'd have paid the whole $10 if I'd had to. What an opportunity!"
> "I'd have let that old thing go for $5. Hope that person comes back," the seller thought.

Just as your behavior influenced the seller, so did the seller's behavior influence you. Interpersonal behavior elicits responses. Communication is not one-way.

The Influencing of Behavior

To understand how we influence the behavior of others we need a brief examination of reinforcing and aversive stimuli.[1] Reinforcing stimuli are pleasant, and in many cases we seek them out. Reinforcing stimuli are experienced through our senses in such forms as the taste of good food or drink, the sight of an attractive man or woman, or the smell of perfume or cologne. This type of stimulus is positive and can have a motivating effect on behavior. It is sometimes called positive reinforcement.

Aversive stimuli have quite the opposite effect on our behavior. Aversive stimuli are also sensory experiences and can include the taste of rotten food, a nasty smell, or the sight of something or someone we find ugly. These stimuli influence our behavior in a negative way in that we seek to avoid aversive stimuli. They are sometimes called negative reinforcement.

Perhaps some of the most forceful stimuli, both reinforcing and aversive, come to us as auditory verbal stimuli, those that arrive through the sense of hearing. For example, the statement "You are doing good work" can be a reinforcing stimulus that will encourage long, hard work. Likewise, "You really muffed that one" can have an aversive effect that will cause the person to reduce effort and perhaps skip a day of work. Frequently, aversive stimuli may cause an employee to quit the job altogether.

What is reinforcing to one person may be aversive to another. For example, drinking blood is aversive to most people in this country, but in some parts of the world it is reinforcing. Or perhaps more realistically, some find drinking alcoholic beverages aversive, while others find this activity reinforcing. Any stimulus can be reinforcing or aversive depending on the person and the situation. The basic question is, how does a stimulus become reinforcing or aversive?

Any stimulus paired or linked with a (positive) reinforcer becomes a reinforcing stimulus. Any stimulus paired or linked with an aversive (negative) stimulus becomes an aversive stimulus. An example of a reinforcing stimulus is found in advertisements in statements such as "Eating yogurt leads to a long life." An example of an aversive stimulus pairing is part of the learning process of a young child who puts a finger on the hot stove; the pain in the finger (stimulus) is associated with the stove, which is now avoided (aversion).

Many important pairings take place in conversations. The statement, "Karen thinks you are doing a bad job," will cause you to react less favorably to Karen the next time you see her. Likewise, the statement, "John says you are one of our best sales reps," will be reinforcing to how you behave with John.

This discussion of stimuli makes three important points. First, it is the behavior of people that enables most organizations to meet their goals.

Communication is the major way we influence the behavior of others.

---

[1]For a more detailed discussion of reinforcing and aversive stimuli, see David Thompson, *Managing People — Influencing Behavior* (St Louis: Mosby, 1978).

✔️ *CHECKLIST for Influencing Behavior*

——◢ Behavior is influenced by reinforcing and aversive stimuli.

——◢ Reinforcing stimuli have a positive impact on behavior.

——◢ Aversive stimuli have a negative impact on behavior.

——◢ Auditory stimuli are some of the most forceful.

——◢ A paired stimulus produces either a reinforcing or an aversive reaction.

Second, behavior is greatly influenced by reinforcing and aversive stimuli. Third, some of the most powerful reinforcing and aversive stimuli come to us through the auditory sense, the sense of hearing. Communication is the major way we influence the behavior of our business colleagues. Indeed, the verbal and nonverbal communication of managers influences profits more than any other factor.

Superior–Subordinate Communication

Internal communication flows either horizontally or vertically within the organization. **Horizontal communication** is the communication between peers (people on the same level in the organization). **Vertical communication** is between superiors and subordinates. From the superior to the subordinate is called downward communication and from the subordinate to the superior is called upward communication.

Perhaps the most influential element of the relationship between superiors and subordinates is the communication climate. Several factors affect upward communication. The subordinate's willingness to communicate accurate information to a superior is affected by the subordinate's desire to climb the organizational ladder. Believing that the superior may "kill" the messenger who brings bad news, the subordinate may distort the message to disassociate himself or herself from the bad news. This distortion is a result of the subordinate's upward mobility aspirations. The end product of this behavior is that superiors are often either poorly informed or uninformed about organizational ills.

Subordinates may also distort upward communication if they perceive their superior as having little or no influence with persons higher in the organization, or if they do not trust their superior. If a subordinate thinks the boss cannot influence other superiors, the subordinate is more likely to distort the information passed on to the superior.

Other barriers to upward communication include physical distance between the superior and the subordinate, too many layers of the organization that require the information, and the lack of tradition of upward communication. These barriers give rise to the principle of information inertia: once information has come to rest at a certain level of the organization, it will tend to remain there.

Downward communication is usually job-related and not personal. A major shortcoming of superiors in downward communication is this depersonalization of the superior–subordinate relationship.

Downward communication is usually job related.

SEVEN MYTHS AND REALITIES ABOUT THE NATURE OF COMMUNICATION

To understand the nature of communication, we must confront some of the common misunderstandings, or myths.

Myth: We communicate only when we consciously and deliberately choose to communicate.

We may think we control our communication. For example, we decide to send a letter to a prospective employee making a job offer or we decide to call a staff meeting to discuss an important problem. In such instances we consciously and deliberately control the way we communicate. However, we are often surprised when our communication brings a different result than we had anticipated. The prospective employee may reply that he has already accepted a job at a lower salary with a lesser firm. Why? Several days had passed after his employment interview without any word from the company. He assumed he was not going to get an offer or, at least, he was not the company's first choice. He had received a message of disinterest just as if it had been communicated face-to-face.

Reality: We communicate many times when we are not consciously aware that we are communicating.

Continuing the example, the reason that several days passed before the applicant received the job offer was that one secretary was ill and the other was busy typing a lengthy report. The reality of the situation is that the employer offering the job communicated a message he was unaware of. Indeed, all of us frequently communicate messages that we do not intend to communicate.

Myth: Words mean the same thing to our listener as they do to us.

The basis for this myth is that we assume words have the same meanings for everyone. In a large organization, for example, one of the sales representatives phones in a special order and asks that it be shipped right away. On the following Monday, the customer reports that the order has not been received. The rep learns that it was not shipped until Friday. She complains to the shipping department supervisor, who replies, "We did ship it right away." To the rep, "right away" meant the same day. To the person who receives dozens of calls daily demanding "Ship it now" or "Ship it yesterday," the phrase "right away" meant within the week.

To illustrate further, when the word "apple" is spoken, some will hear or see a red apple, some a yellow apple, and still others perhaps will think of an apple pie. Why does the same word mean different things to different people?

> Reality: Words do not really have meanings; meaning is dependent on our experiences and perceptions.

In the example, "right away" meant different amounts of time to the sales representative and to the shipping supervisor because of their different perceptions. Because of the myth that words have specific meanings, we assume that others will get exactly the same message from words that we do. The reality is that words mean different things to different people.

Words have denotative and connotative aspects. Denotative meanings are those that are commonly agreed upon or standard, such as the definitions in dictionaries. Thus, "chair" yields the denotative meanings of a support one sits on, usually alone, probably having a back and four legs. However, when you internalize—that is, add your own meaning to words—you are introducing the connotative aspect. "Chair," for example, might bring to mind a dentist's chair or a barber chair if your day's activities include them. We seldom share the same connotative meanings.

> Myth: We communicate primarily with words.

People tend to believe that a communicated message is one that is either spoken or written. For example, assume you go to your professor's office to discuss a topic for your term paper. The professor says, "The outline looks good. Go ahead with the paper." You feel somewhat uneasy, however, because she looked over the outline very quickly and several times glanced at her watch, as if she had something more important on her mind. Nevertheless, you proceed with the paper.

> Reality: The majority of the messages we communicate are based not on words but rather on nonverbal symbols.

The professor in the example communicated nonverbally. In recent years we have become much more aware of nonverbal communication. Books such as *Body Language* and *How to Read a Person like a Book* show that our tone of voice, eye contact, body movement, or even the clothes we wear communicate much more than the words we use. Albert Mehrabian, an expert on nonverbal communication, has calculated that as much as 93 percent of our attitudes are formed by nonverbal messages, while only 7 percent are the result of verbal stimuli.[2]

Frequently our nonverbal communication undermines our verbal communication. For example, at a lecture the speaker begins by saying, "I am pleased to be here and to talk about my favorite topic — human motivation." However, his nonverbal communication denies it: he wears a wrinkled suit, he looks at his notes instead of the audience, and he speaks in

---

[2]Albert Mehrabian, "Communication without Words," *Psychology Today* 2 (September 1968):53–55.

a monotone. The real message that has been communicated is that it is going to be a long and boring afternoon.

When there is a contradiction between what is communicated verbally and what is communicated nonverbally, why do we usually choose to believe the nonverbal message? It is easier for people to manipulate words than to manipulate nonverbal behavior. Most of us believe that nonverbal messages more accurately reflect what a person really is thinking. There really is some truth in the old adage, "Actions speak louder than words."

Myth: Nonverbal communication is the silent language.

The term body language is often misused in place of nonverbal communication. Many think nonverbal communication is never heard — that it is only seen.

Reality: Nonverbal communication is received through all the five senses.

Gestures, body positions, and the way we walk are silent nonverbal messages — and so are tone of voice, the clapping of hands, and the touch of a handshake. Nonverbal messages can be felt, heard, smelled, and tasted, as well as seen.

Myth: Communication is a one-way activity.

The basis for this myth is the assumption that our message moves uninterrupted to the receiver and ends there. All of us at one time or another have had people communicate in this fashion, talking at us rather than with us. For example, a supervisor uses a tone of voice that makes you reluctant to ask any questions or to respond other than with a passive, affirmative nod. If you fail to carry out an assignment correctly, the boss may say, "I *told* you exactly how to do it." All of us have been guilty of *telling* people rather than *communicating with* people.

Reality: Communication is a two-way activity.

Most of us have played a parlor game similar to "Pass the Message" in which people sit in a circle and one member of the group whispers a message to the person on the right. The message is passed in turn from one person to the next. Each repeats the message only once, and no one can ask any questions about the message. When the message finally reaches the last person, that person states the message aloud. Usually there is little, if any, resemblance to the original message. This game is a classic example of one-way communication. The message is passed quickly but inaccurately.

Using the same group of people, the game can be played so that each member, after hearing the message, is allowed to ask questions about the message. There are two dramatic differences from the first version of the game. First, it takes longer to play the game. Two-way communication always takes longer than one-way communication. The second and more important difference is that the message is passed along much more accurately. The major reason for the increased accuracy is **feedback**.

Feedback is simply the reaction that the listener has to the sender's verbal and nonverbal message. A major function of feedback is that it allows senders to see how well they are accomplishing the objectives of the original communication. In brief, what distinguishes effective from ineffective communication is the ability to accurately interpret the feedback provided by the other party.

Myth: The message we send is identical to the message received by the listener.

We all have a tendency to assume that the message we send is received by our listener exactly as we sent it. For example, suppose you send a letter to a friend in another state inviting that person to be your guest during homecoming next month. When you receive no response to your letter, you become irritated. Why did your friend not respond? Perhaps the problem is not that your friend did not reply, but that the post office lost your letter. Perhaps you inadvertently left out a page of the letter when you sealed the envelope and your friend never received the message.

Reality: The message as it is finally received by the listener is never exactly the same as the message we originally sent.

The message that we send may be perfectly clear to us but not to our listener because of some influence that neither we nor our listener can control, such as a lost letter. Also, as was suggested earlier, no two of us have had exactly the same set of experiences. The message received by one person can therefore never be exactly the same as the message sent by another.

Myth: You can never give someone too much information.

People in organizations sometimes say, "Nobody ever tells me; I just work here." Indeed, there are times when people do not receive the information that they need to perform their jobs properly. In an effort to keep employees informed, some organizations have adopted communication policies that send an abundance of information on all types of topics to all employees. We frequently assume that the more information we provide employees, the more productive they will be.

Reality: There are times when people can be given too much information and thus suffer from an information overload.

A problem more common than most of us realize is **information overload**, that is, having too much information to make intelligent use of it. In the past 50 years the development of copying machines and other types of mechanical reproduction has vastly increased our ability to generate and transmit information. But our capacity as humans to handle and process information has remained virtually unchanged. We speak at about the same rate as we did 50 years ago. We listen and understand at about the same level as we did 50 years ago. It is not surprising, therefore, that information overload is a major problem for people in many organizations. We need to be concerned not so much with the quantity of communication as with the quality of communication.

As these seven myths and realities about the nature of communication indicate, communication can be a confusing activity.

VARIABLES IN THE COMMUNICATION PROCESS

Communication can be defined broadly as the transmission of a message between two or more people. Many writers also discuss intrapersonal communication—occurring within the individual—but our concern here is to examine interpersonal communication.

Communication is the transmission of a message between two or more people.

The six major variables in the interpersonal communication process are (1) sender/encoder, (2) message, (3) channel, (4) receiver/decoder, (5) perception, and (6) feedback. The way these six variables interact is illustrated in Figure 2.1, a model of the communication process. Too many of us take the art of communication for granted because we are ignorant of the mechanics involved. This model is intended to increase awareness of the variables responsible for successful communication.

The communication process includes six variables.

The Sender/Encoder

The sender has the responsibility for formulating the message in a way that accurately conveys an idea to the receiver. Because communication is essentially a process of creating understanding, concerted effort on the part of the sender and receiver is needed to arrive at a similar meaning. The sender, however, bears the major burden. The sender must mentally see the communication from the receiver's viewpoint. The sender's task is to search for and use communication symbols and communication skills that will bring about understanding in the mind of the receiver.

The sender's basic task is to search for and use communication skills that will bring understanding to the receiver.

Specifically, the sender should use verbal and nonverbal symbols that are on the receiver's level and should secure feedback from the receiver.

The Message

The message consists of the verbal and nonverbal symbols that represent the information we want to transmit. Each message we send is an attempt to convey an idea to the receiver. Some of the messages we attempt to communicate are relatively simple. An example of a simple message is a stop sign. Although we may not always obey the sign, the message is clear and straightforward. Other messages are more complex and thus are more difficult to impart to the receiver. For example, we may wish to convey to a group of employees that we want simultaneously to increase production and improve quality control. Achieving understanding of that message by the entire group of employees could be difficult because the two components of the message—improve quality control and increase production—seem incompatible on the surface.

FIGURE 2.1　▪　*A Communication Model*

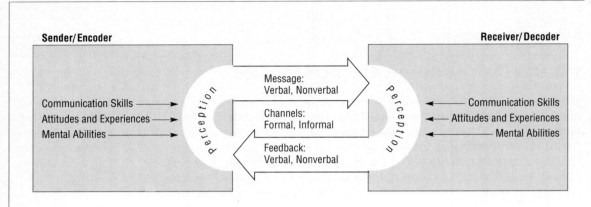

The Channel

What is the appropriate channel for any given message? Should it be communicated face to face or on paper? The decision as to whether to use an oral or a written channel can be based partially on answers to the following questions:

1. Is immediate feedback needed? Is it important to get the receiver's reaction to your message? Oral communication provides the quickest feedback. Although feedback can be gained from written communication, it generally comes slowly. For many messages there is a need for immediate feedback, and oral communication provides that opportunity.
2. Is there a question of acceptance? Frequently there may be resistance to the message we are attempting to communicate. If acceptance is likely to be a problem, oral communication is better than written communication. When people receive a written communication, they feel they have had no chance for input. In face-to-face communication, the message can be adapted to the receiver to seek feedback.
3. Is there a need for a documented record of the communication? Many times in organizations the messages we send may need to be verified or monitored at a later date. Frequently the receiver of a message is expected to be accountable for information contained in the message. If accountability is important, written communication is superior to oral communication.
4. Is there a need for detailed accuracy? If the message being communicated contains detailed or exacting information, or if it explains a complicated procedure, the written method is a superior means of communication.

Frequently there is a need for both written and oral communication.

No one communication method is universally superior to another method. In many cases the message can best be communicated by a combination of written and oral channels. Frequently individuals will follow a conversation with a written summary. In other cases people will hand carry a written communication so that they can provide a few words of explanation and ensure acceptance of the written statement.

Whatever your choice of communication channel, be sure to weigh both its benefits and its costs. For example, most managers are always short on time, a precious resource. The high cost of time can determine which channel of communication is most appropriate. A company directive announcing an increase in employee health benefits should obviously not be communicated face to face to two thousand employees; it would take too much time. A written memo is the more appropriate channel of communication in light of the number of people and the nature of the message. On the other hand, relaying a new business strategy against competitors to the director of marketing would definitely call for a face-to-face conference to ensure complete understanding of the company's revised approach. Determination of the communication channel depends on its cost (time, people, equipment) and the derived benefits (more effective message and more efficient means of message dissemination).

Formal communication includes downward, upward, and horizontal channels.

Downward Channels

There are five major types of downward communication.[3]

Downward channels of communication include several types of information.

- *Job instructions* explain how a task is to be done. The instructions come from written specifications, training manuals, training sessions, or on-the-job training.
- *Job rationale* tells workers how their task relates to other jobs in the organization. Specialization in many organizations has made it difficult for workers to see this.
- *Policy and procedure* communications explain to workers the regulations and personal benefits that are provided by their employer. An example of policy is "Employees receive a three-week paid vacation after three years with the company." Policy and procedure communication may be thought of as "the way we do things around here."
- *Feedback* includes messages that inform employees about whether their work is being performed satisfactorily. Feedback should be provided daily as well as in the form of systematic performance-appraisal reviews.
- *Indoctrination* communications seek employee support of a particular organizational objective. For example, "Acme Company would like all employees to participate in the blood drive."

[3]Daniel Katz and Robert Kahn, *The Social Psychology of Organizations* (New York: Wiley, 1978), 440.

✔️ *CHECKLIST for Selecting the Appropriate Channel*

☑ **Is immediate feedback needed?**

☑ **Is there a question of acceptance?**

☑ **Is there a need for a documented record of the communication?**

☑ **Is there a need for detailed accuracy?**

Much of the message is lost as it is passed down the organizational structure.

As messages travel downward in organizations, they tend to become distorted. In many cases much of the message never gets through to the intended receiver. One study of downward communications in 100 firms attempted to determine how much of what top management said actually penetrated the organizational structure.[4] The results of that study were:

Level	Percentage Understood
Vice President	65
General Supervisor	56
Plant Manager	40
Foreman	30
Production Line	20

Upward Channels

Upward channels are important because they are the major means of getting information to higher organizational levels where important decisions are made. Essentially, upward communication means following the chain of command. The individual employee communicates a request or a problem to the immediate supervisor; if the immediate supervisor is not able to respond or make the decision, the message is passed to the person at the next higher level.

Upward channels of communication contain several types of information.

Communication moving upward in the organization consists of the following types of information:[5]

- What the employee has done.
- What those under the employee have done.
- What the employee's peers have done.
- What the employee's problems are.
- What the problems of the employee's department are.
- What the employee thinks needs to be done.
- What the employee's perceptions of his or her job performance are.
- What organizational policies and practices need adjusting.

[4]Ray Killian, *Managing by Design . . . for Executive Effectiveness* (New York: American Management Association, 1968), 254.

[5]Katz and Kahn, *The Social Psychology of Organizations*, 446–448.

Horizontal Channels

Four major purposes for using horizontal channels have been identified: (1) task coordination, (2) problem solving, (3) sharing information, and (4) conflict resolution.[6] Because horizontal communication occurs among employees of about the same level in the hierarchy, it has a different tone from communication between superiors and subordinates. The tone is likely to be consultative, persuasive, or suggestive rather than directive.

Horizontal channels of communication have four important uses.

Informal Channels

Informal communication in organizations is referred to frequently as the grapevine. While many writers assume that grapevine communication is inaccurate, at least one researcher maintains that between 75 percent and 95 percent of grapevine information is correct.[7] In addition, informal channels usually provide information faster than formal ones and play an important role in coordination of organizational tasks.

Informal channels of communication are frequently referred to as the grapevine.

Informal messages are also called by other names: non-job-oriented, task, social, or maintenance communication. At times communication can follow the chain of command but still be informal; this is especially true when the topic is not related to the organization or the job. An example is when various levels of employees discuss nontask topics on the golf course or at the company picnic.

The Receiver/Decoder

The receiver can be viewed in many ways. How much does the receiver know about the topic? Is the receiver likely to be receptive to the message and the sender? What experience has the receiver had with the sender? These questions and many others determine the impact of the message upon the receiver.

The basic skills employed by the receiver are listening and providing feedback to the sender.

Specifically, the receiver is primarily concerned with two types of behavior: listening and providing feedback to the sender.

Perception

One of the most important variables in communication is **perception** — our unique understanding of the way things are. As shown in Figure 2.1, perception is an integral part of both the sender's and the receiver's involvement in the communication process. As a perceiver, each of us is a product of all of our experiences. Our attitudes toward the surrounding environment also modify our perception of what is being communicated.

Perception greatly affects how we send and receive messages.

---

[6]Gerald M. Goldhaber, *Organizational Communication*, 3d ed. (Dubuque, Ia.: William C. Brown, 1983), 162–163.

[7]Keith Davis, "Care and Cultivation of the Corporation Grapevine," *Dun's Review* (July 1973): 46.

Of course, our mental abilities, or intelligence, greatly determine our capacity to discern the communication experience accurately. Finally, communication skills, whether in the area of speaking or listening, will influence the way we send a message and the way we receive feedback about that message. In all likelihood each sender and receiver will bring different attitudes, experiences, mental abilities, and communication skills to bear on the communication process. This does not mean that an understanding cannot be reached. Rather, an awareness and sensitivity to these differences in perception can facilitate an open and productive communication experience.

The position a person occupies in an organization strongly influences perception. In one study, 76 percent of the foremen "always or almost always" sought ideas from subordinates in seeking solutions to job problems. However, only 16 percent of the workers thought their foremen actually sought their opinions.[8] There can be little question that perception greatly influences the way we send and receive messages.

Feedback

Feedback is the reaction the receiver has to the message.

Feedback is the reaction that the receiver has to the message. Feedback may be verbal or nonverbal; it can be written or oral. Feedback provides guidance for the next message that we send to the receiver. In brief, we can evaluate the effectiveness of our communication by the feedback we receive. The ability to interpret feedback accurately is an important skill to master.

COMMUNICATION BARRIERS

Several barriers to communication affect the six major variables in the communication process. One of the earliest and most complete lists of these barriers includes seven major categories.[9]

- *Meaning barriers:* problems with meaning, significance, and the sending and reception of the meaning of the message.
- *Organizational barriers:* problems with physical distance between members; specialization of task functions; power, authority, and status relationships; and information ownership.
- *Interpersonal barriers:* problems with the climate of the relationship, values held, and negative attitudes held by the participants.
- *Individual barriers:* problems with individual competencies to think and act, which would include physical ailments or handicaps, and problems with individual skills in receiving and transmitting

[8]E. Jacobson, "Foremen–Steward Participation Practices and Work Attitudes in a Unionized Factory," unpublished doctoral thesis (Ann Arbor: University of Michigan, 1951).

[9]Lee Thayer, *Communication and Communication Systems* (Homewood, Ill.: Irwin, 1968), 195–203.

information, which would include poor listening and reading skills and psychological considerations.

■ *Economic, geographic, and temporal barriers:* problems with time and dollar costs, different locations, and the effects of time upon reception of the message.

■ *Channel and media barriers:* problems that confront the issue of how to best communicate a message. (For example, is it best to transmit a message face to face rather than in writing?)

■ *Technological barriers:* problems with too much information for the capacity of the recipient.

ENCODING–DECODING SKILLS

The process of translating an idea into a message is called **encoding**. Imagine that you want to write a letter to a company about possible summer job openings. You have certain ideas you want to communicate in the letter. For example, you should offer reasons why you chose that particular company. Also, you should provide some general information about your qualifications in the letter accompanying your resumé. As these ideas form in your mind and you put them on paper, the encoding process is occurring. Encoding includes your decisions whether to use verbal or nonverbal channels; which communications channels, such as writing or speaking, are within your selection; which words to use and with how much emphasis; and when and how to deliver the message.

The process of translating a message into an idea is called **decoding**. Imagine the personnel manager of the company you have written as she opens your letter of inquiry. She notes that you are asking about a summer job. At the same time she makes decisions about you and your qualifications. She decodes information about your work by how neat and attractive the layout of your letter and resumé are. She decodes information about your work experience, courses you are taking, and interests you seem to have. All the decisions the personnel manager makes about your messages are the end result of the decoding process.

Perhaps the descriptions of encoding and decoding make them appear to be simple processes. They are not. Anywhere in the encoding–decoding processes, breakdowns in communication can occur. Three main encoding–decoding skills can help overcome common breakdowns: (1) analyzing the other person, (2) getting and giving feedback, and (3) understanding perception.

Encoding–decoding skills help avoid communication breakdowns.

Analyzing the Other Person

As a sender, we should know that different receivers react to the same message in different ways. Imagine a football coach criticizing a player's performance: "Wilson, you couldn't stop that halfback with a cannon." How will Wilson react? Some people will try harder because their pride is hurt, or they want to avoid future criticism. Other people might stop trying altogether and quit the team. Many of us at one time or another have "quit the team," whether quitting involved football, playing the piano, attending a class, or any other activity where someone important criticized our work. Still others have succeeded in an activity in part because someone prodded them to improve. We react differently to the same message.

Receivers of our messages are unique. They are of different races and sexes. They have different family backgrounds and come from different parts of the country or the world. Their personalities are different. Therefore, they will react in individualized ways to what we encode.

As a receiver we should analyze the sender's frame of reference, too. Consider this telephone exchange:

> Martha: Jim, I've *got* to have that report on my desk by 9 a.m. tomorrow.
>
> Jim: Impossible. I'll be up all night working on it.
>
> Martha: I'm sorry, but I've got to have it by nine.

As Jim puts his phone back on the receiver, he thinks, "This is terrible. . . . I can't believe how unfair she is. . . . She'll get her report all right . . . but it's the last time." At the same time Martha is thinking, "If he doesn't get that report to me by nine, I'll never be ready for the board meeting. . . . It's unfair. . . . Why can't they give us more time?"

The receiver analyzes the sender's frame of reference—and responds accordingly.

It's easy for Jim to be angry. Martha hasn't told him why the 9 a.m. deadline is so important. Would he feel different if Martha had justified the deadline? Perhaps not. He would need to work all night anyway. However, Jim needs to understand why Martha acts in such an adverse manner. She is pressuring him, but she also has pressures on her.

When receiving messages, we must analyze our senders. They are just as individual as we are and consequently, they encode messages in different ways.

Getting and Giving Feedback

Feedback lets the sender know how he or she is performing.

Feedback is important because it is the only way we can know how we are performing. Think a minute about the varied ways Boris Becker gets feedback during a match on center court at Wimbledon. First, he gets immediate visual feedback about his shot: he sees the ball land either in or out on the opponent's court. Even if something blocks his vision, Becker can also hear the call of the line judge if the ball lands out or wide. If he makes a particularly spectacular shot, he hears the roar of the crowd and perhaps even the groan of his opponent.

Feedback is crucial to organizational success.

If Boris Becker were alone on center court at night with portable lights only for his side of the court, his serve would vanish across the net. No visual contact, no line judge, no opponent, no crowd: in essence, no feedback. Although Becker may be confident enough in the accuracy of his serves to continue serving into a darkened court, most of us would quit immediately. Feedback is a critical element that motivates people to continue. As a member of the organization, you need to ensure that you, your peers, your boss, and your subordinates receive adequate feedback.

As a sender, we need to create a climate in which the receiver will feel comfortable and be willing to provide feedback. Immediate feedback seldom occurs when we use written communication. That is one of the disadvantages of writing letters or memos instead of speaking face to face with our receiver. In verbal situations we must try to get as much immediate feedback as possible to determine whether we have created the understanding we want.

The recipient of a message has certain obligations, too. As receivers, we should try to apply the guidelines to better listening that are presented in Chapter 13. We should avoid giving false feedback and should seek agreement on message meaning.

Many managers ask questions such as these to get feedback about instructions or directions: Do you understand? Repeat that to me, will you? Got any questions? What'd I forget to tell you?

For each of these questions, think about three things. Will the question get useful feedback? How will the receiver react to each question? Is the receiver likely to return false or expected feedback?

For example, "Do you understand?" is a very common question that might follow this set of instructions: "Here, type this double-spaced except for tables. I need one-inch margins all around, two inches at the bottom. Don't forget the enclosures. Do you understand?" We say it almost unconsciously. At the same level of consciousness our secretary responds, "Yes."

In some organizations "Repeat that" is used as a matter of policy, especially in areas where misunderstood instructions might endanger the safety of employees. Yet what would you think if your own supervisors asked you to repeat them every time they gave you instructions?

There is no one sure way of getting accurate and willing feedback. In many situations, though, if we ask questions or perhaps pause momentarily, our receiver will give us the feedback we need.

Feedback is the way we tell senders about the understanding or misunderstanding they have created. There are several characteristics of effective feedback:

Getting useful feedback involves more than phrasing questions. Feedback is a receiver's responsibility.

- *It is specific rather than general.* To be told, "You are dominating," is not as constructive as to be told, "You did not listen to what others said and thereby curtailed their suggestions."
- *It is descriptive rather than evaluative.* By avoiding evaluative language, such as, "You handled that badly," you reduce the need for the individual to react defensively.
- *It takes into account the needs of both the receiver and the giver of feedback.* Feedback can be destructive when it serves only your needs and fails to meet the receiver's needs.
- *It is directed toward behavior the receiver can do something about.* Frustration is increased when people are reminded of some shortcoming over which they have no control.

▪ *It is well-timed.* In general, feedback is most useful at the earliest opportunity after a given behavior — depending on the other person's readiness to hear it. There are occasions when a cooling-off period should occur.
▪ *It is two-way.* You get feedback about the feedback.
▪ *It is tailored to the individual.* A successful communicator recognizes the different needs and abilities of each person and interacts with each accordingly. You must guard against the desire to remake others in your own image. Changes in behavior must be within the framework of each individual's personality and skills.

Understanding Perception

Perception occupies a central role in the communication process. Perception is the process of assigning meaning to a message and illustrates the reality that meanings are in people. Consider the following statement: "Ned is a moderate, middle-aged smoker." Now estimate how many cigarettes Ned smokes on an average day (10? 20? 50?). Estimate his age (30? 40? 50? 60?). If the statement had been "Carol is a moderate, middle-aged smoker," would you estimate that Carol smokes as many cigarettes as you estimated for Ned? Is Carol as old as you estimated Ned to be? In your estimates, you were perceiving the words moderate and middle aged. You assigned meaning to the message.

Misperception is the major cause of communication breakdowns. We are simply not careful when we perceive other people and their messages. For instance, Chevrolet was a victim of misperception when it attempted to market its Nova line in Latin American countries. Sales were dismal, and company officials were baffled. The cause of the low sales came to light when Chevrolet officials realized that, in Spanish, "no va" means "does not go."[10] Chevrolet's lack of analyzing the cultural dimension of its marketplace plus the misperception of the Latin American consumers cost Chevrolet many sales.

Perception is the filter through which all communication passes, as Exhibit 2.1 showed. The element that separates communication from miscommunication is perception. Accurate perception results in communication; misperception results in miscommunication. Unfortunately, we misuse our perceptual skills in several ways.

First, our experiences influence our perceptions of messages. Consider this old riddle: A father and his son are driving to work one morning. A terrible accident occurs. The father is killed instantly, and the son is badly injured. An ambulance arrives at the accident scene. The attendants place the son in an ambulance and rush him to the hospital. When they carry him into the emergency room, the nurse says, "He's in terrible shape. We've got to get him to surgery." They rush him down the hall to surgery.

[10]David A. Ricks, *Big Business Blunders* (Homewood, Ill.: Dow Jones–Irwin, 1983), 38.

The surgeon walks in, takes one look at him, and says, "I'm sorry. I can't operate on him. He's my son." How can this be?

Perhaps he is the father's stepson. Perhaps the "father" is a Catholic priest. Perhaps the boy was adopted. Other explanations abound. Yet actually the surgeon was the boy's mother. Why couldn't we think of this correct answer? Simply because our experiences have convinced us that surgeons are male.

Receivers interpret messages according to their past experiences.

In another case of perception, read aloud the sentences in the two triangles pictured in Figure 2.2. Did you notice that "the" was repeated by mistake in the first triangle and "a" was repeated in the second? If not, then your experiences ("I've read this before") are controlling your ability to perceive and, in this case, to read.

Second, we often fill in missing information about messages we receive. Consequently, we sometimes perceive them wrongly. For example, what appears in Figure 2.3 is the Roman numeral nine. Your instructions are to add one line to this Roman numeral and make six out of it. Possibly, you placed an *S* in front of the *IX* and created *SIX*. If you tried to create a Roman numeral six, then you filled in missing information. Reread the instructions. They do not specify that you must use Roman numerals.

Receivers fill in missing information.

Many times when we are faced with an unclear message, we fill in information and hope for the best. In our earlier example of the sales representative who asks for an order to be shipped right away, the shipper assumed the rep meant by the end of the week. Without feedback and further information, the shipper simply assigned his own meaning to the sales rep's message.

Third, we often perceive messages so that they are consistent with our own attitudes and beliefs. Tom and Bill are playing tennis:

Receivers interpret messages according to their own attitudes and beliefs.

Tom: You play much tennis?

Bill: Every day.

Tom: Wow. Don't you miss a lot of class?

Bill: Yeah, I only went to Math 104 twice last quarter.

Tom: How'd you do?

Bill: Flunked.

Tom: You failed?

Bill: Yeah. Prof gave really tricky tests. Besides that, I don't think she liked me.

We are often inclined to interpret messages so that they satisfy our impression of the world and see the world through rose-colored glasses, shaded the hue of personal attitudes about ourselves, others, and life in general.

COMMUNICATION STYLES

Effective communication often depends on assuming the appropriate communication style for the occasion. The trick is to correctly analyze the occasion and to have the ability to modify your communication to meet that situation.

FIGURE 2.2 ▪ *A Test of Visual Perception*

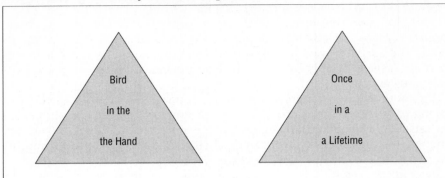

FIGURE 2.3 ▪ *A Test of Mental Perception*

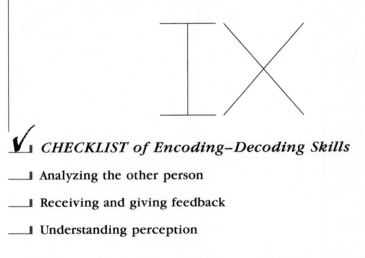

✔ CHECKLIST of Encoding–Decoding Skills

___▪ Analyzing the other person

___▪ Receiving and giving feedback

___▪ Understanding perception

There is no agreed-upon number of categories of communication styles. Some authorities find as few as one, while others list as many as eight. Most of the styles cluster around four dimensions: blaming, directing, persuasive, and problem solving.[11]

A person who uses the **blaming style** is trying to find fault or discover who is to blame for a problem. At the extreme, the tone is accusatory and negative. "This is what you did wrong" is a typical blaming expression. This tone evokes a negative feeling in the receiver, and the results are not likely to be positive. Usually this style is to be avoided; it might be selected when all other styles have failed or when the facts of the situation are absolutely clear.

[11]Much of this discussion is taken from Sandra O'Connell, *The Manager as Communicator* (San Francisco: Harper & Row, 1979).

| BOXED IN | *AN ETHICAL DILEMMA* |

Anne Barrington runs a successful commercial construction company. It hasn't always been easy. Following her graduation with a degree in construction engineering, she took a job with a national firm specializing in the construction of major shopping malls. After five years of extensive travel and highly stressful situations, Anne returned to her hometown to establish her own company. Through shrewd planning and careful bidding she was able to land some very profitable contracts. Lately, however, increasing materials costs, rising interest rates, and competition from a new local firm have caused profit margins to fall to a precarious level.

Anne's top estimator, Jack Cleveland, is feeling the pressure. Anne and Jack have spent many hours discussing a proposed school district project now open to bids. Among local contractors, only Barrington Construction Company or the new competitor is likely to be awarded such a large job, which involves six buildings. During one session with Jack, Anne stated emphatically, "We simply *must* get this one if we are to survive!"

Jack will write the final bid; success or failure is in his hands. Failure would mean an end to his career with Barrington Construction. Jack has an old friend who, if approached in the right way, could be used to get inside information about the local competitor's planned bid. Jack's perception of his mission is clear: land the contract at all costs.

Jack feels boxed in. What would you do?

The second style is the **directing style**. A directing person tells others, particularly subordinates, how to do their jobs or how to solve problems. Discussion is minimized; communication is predominantly one-way. "This is the way you'll do it" exemplifies a directing tone. Don't confuse the directing style with the more positive instructional tone that involves more feedback. Keep in mind the unidirectional aspect of the directing style.

The directing style can be effective in certain situations. The school teacher who finally becomes exasperated with note passing in the fourth-grade class orders "Be quiet!" and reestablishes authority. The acceptance of the command may not be heartfelt, but the command is followed.

The **persuasive style** employs information sharing and acceptance techniques. Instead of directing the audience to do something, the sender presents the message for their evaluation and active acceptance. The goal of the message may be to have the receivers want to do what you present, but because *they* chose to. Because the recipient makes the decision, much greater acceptance of the action is likely than with the blaming or directing approaches. Frequently the truly persuasive person is able to establish a need in the receiver and present a plan of action that meets that need. The action is the original goal.

The **problem-solving style** seeks mutual acceptance from both sender and receiver of the final action; compromise is usually frequent. Two-way communication is required. Ideas are jointly explored and evaluated. Personalities may emerge but are not used in deciding the final action, as they are in the other three styles. Discussions between the parties may lead to fruitful plans of action and mutual respect. On the other hand, they may also lead to disagreements, confusion, and frustration when consensus is evasive. This style is especially valuable when group behavior change is sought.

The blaming and problem-solving approaches, from the sender's viewpoint, are almost opposites; and the directing and persuasive approaches are bipolar. Further, the blaming and directing techniques have little feedback whereas the persuasive and problem-solving methods build on this interaction, as Figure 2.4 illustrates. Another diagrammatical technique that outlines other relationships between the four styles places them on a continuum from blaming to problem solving, as shown in Figure 2.5.

SELF-ASSESSMENT

If you know which style is your dominant style, you can better prepare for the occasion with the correct style — whether it is your first choice or another one. The self-assessment instrument in Figures 2.6 and 2.7 measures the tendency to use blaming and problem-solving styles. Having evaluated these, you should be able to determine your abilities on the styles between these extremes.

If your score for the left column in Figure 2.7 is between 21 and 28, you are probably a moderate blamer; a score of 29 or higher suggests you rely somewhat heavily on the blaming style.

If your score for the right column is from 21 to 28, you fall in the moderate problem-solving style category. A score of 29 or higher indicates a strong leaning toward problem solving as your dominant technique.

Blaming is not always bad and problem solving is not always good. There are occasions when you need to be directive and perhaps even blame. Problem solving can be both tedious and time consuming; it is not a panacea for all ills. Become familiar with the four styles and with your own strengths and weaknesses, then try to select the appropriate style for the occasion.

SUMMARY

The behavior of people enables organizations to achieve their goals, and communication is the major way to influence behavior. Communication within the organization flows both horizontally and vertically.

Several myths exist about the nature of communication. The realities are these: We frequently communicate messages we are not aware of communicating. Words do not have meanings; rather, meanings are within people based on their experiences. The majority of the messages we communicate are based on the nonverbal aspects of communication. Some

FIGURE 2.4 ▪ *Four Communication Styles Compared by Degree of Interaction*

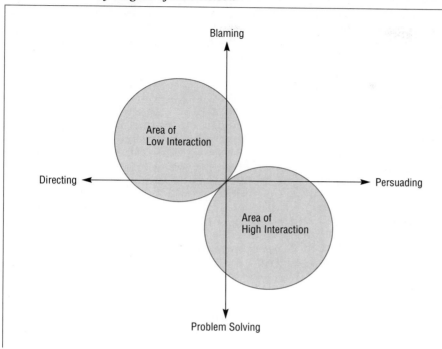

FIGURE 2.5 ▪ *Four Communication Styles Compared by Extent of Participant Involvement*

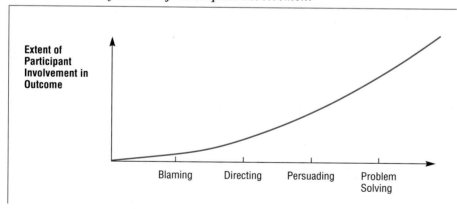

nonverbal communication is silent, but much of it is not silent. Communication is a two-way activity in which feedback from the other party is crucial. The message finally received by the listener is never identical to the message sent. People can be given too much information. An information overload can be just as much of a problem as not having enough information.

FIGURE 2.6 ▪ *Self-Assessment of Communication Style*

Indicate the degree to which you do the following:

	Very Little	Little	Some	Great	Very Great
1. Make judgments early in the conversation.	_____	_____	_____	_____	_____
2. Share my feelings with others.	_____	_____	_____	_____	_____
3. Talk about the issues.	_____	_____	_____	_____	_____
4. Have analyzed others' motives.	_____	_____	_____	_____	_____
5. Talk about the person.	_____	_____	_____	_____	_____
6. Use clear and precise language.	_____	_____	_____	_____	_____
7. Decide on the action before the conversation.	_____	_____	_____	_____	_____
8. Encourage the other person to discuss feelings.	_____	_____	_____	_____	_____
9. Am open for new information.	_____	_____	_____	_____	_____
10. Ask questions which seek agreement with me.	_____	_____	_____	_____	_____
11. Talk the majority of the time.	_____	_____	_____	_____	_____
12. Ask questions which get others to describe events.	_____	_____	_____	_____	_____
13. Talk half the time or less.	_____	_____	_____	_____	_____
14. Others defend their position to me.	_____	_____	_____	_____	_____

Source: Figure from *The Manager as Communicator* by Sandra E. O'Connell, p. 25. Copyright © 1979 by Sandra E. O'Connell. Reprinted by permission of Harper & Row, Publishers, Inc.

The six major variables in the communication process are the sender/encoder, the message, the channel, the receiver/decoder, perception, and feedback. Channels may be downward, upward, or horizontal. Several barriers to communication affect the six major variables.

Encoding/decoding skills that can help overcome communication breakdowns include analyzing the other person, getting and giving feedback, and understanding perception.

Effective communication often depends on assuming the appropriate style. Most authorities recognize these styles: blaming, directing, persuasive, and problem solving.

FIGURE 2.7 ▪ *Score Sheet for Self-Assessment*

Item No.	Score	
1	_____	
2		_____
3		_____
4	_____	
5	_____	
6		_____
7	_____	
8		_____
9		_____
10	_____	
11	_____	
12		_____
13		_____
14	_____	
Totals	_____	_____

Total column 1 _____
Total column 2 _____

Interpretation of scores: very little = 1 point, little = 2 points, some = 3 points, great = 4 points, and very great = 5 points

Source: Figure from *The Manager as Communicator* by Sandra E. O'Connell, pp. 25–26. Copyright © 1979 by Sandra E. O'Connell. Reprinted by permission of Harper & Row, Publishers, Inc.

Key Terms

▪ **horizontal communication**

▪ **vertical communication**

▪ **feedback**

▪ **information overload**

▪ **perception**

▪ **encoding**

▪ **decoding**

▪ **blaming style**

▪ **directing style**

▪ **persuasive style**

▪ **problem-solving style**

Review Questions

1. How can reinforcing or aversive stimuli have an impact on behavior?

2. In the superior–subordinate communication relationship, what do subordinates want from their superiors? Discuss why most downward communication is job related.

3. Discuss the seven myths and realities about the nature of communication. Support your discussion with an example of each.

4. What is the sender's major responsibility in the communication process?

5. Comment on the statement, "The more information we provide employees, the more productive they will be."

6. What important criteria determine whether an oral or a written channel of communication is the most appropriate form of a message?

7. What are downward, upward, and horizontal channels of communication? Suggest several situations in which these channels should be used.

8. Name the encoding and decoding skills that both sender and receiver should master to prevent communication breakdowns. Within the context of a business setting, give an example of each.

9. What are the characteristics of good feedback? Who bears the primary responsibility for good feedback? How can good feedback facilitate an accurate and willing information exchange?

CASE | *The Wonderful Opportunity*

Dan Viamonte, Professor, North Texas State University, Radio/TV/Film Department

Bob Anderson had been a trade specialist with the state Agricultural Development Division for almost two years. He was attracted by the philosophy of the new administration to attract international trade. Although Bob's background was in music, he had acquired some business experience with a small food-processing company in the western part of the state.

During the past year, Bob attended several statewide training sessions designed to inform and develop interest in international trade. Many food producers, packaging firms, and brokers were not accustomed to dealing with foreign markets.

Bob traveled throughout the state in the months that followed, trying to establish a network of participants eager to supply quality food products. The task was difficult. Trade opportunities went to other states. Somehow the typical obstacles and problems the growers and trade brokers faced were not easily dealt with, and the Agricultural Development Division was not helping to solve them.

At one of the regional trade meetings sponsored by the state, Bob met Dr. Beldon, a former college professor who was now an international trade consultant representing business associates from the Middle East. They both agreed that the state had tremendous resources at its command but lacked the critical sophistication, contacts, cultural understanding, and experience to negotiate with the Middle Eastern markets. Bob was very excited about this new foreign market opportunity and returned to his office vowing to get something started.

Three days later, Bob called Dr. Beldon and shared a rumor that the governor was planning an unofficial business trip to the Middle East within two months. Would some of Dr. Beldon's associates be willing to prepare letters of introduction? Dr. Beldon responded that, coincidentally, several major agricultural businessmen from the Middle East had decided to tour parts of the United States on their way to an international trade show in Japan. Although this was short notice, Bob suggested that perhaps the Agricultural Development Division could invite the Middle Eastern businessmen next week to tour the state's facilities and meet with interested agribusinessmen. It would also be an excellent opportunity for the governor to meet with delegates from three Middle Eastern countries.

Dr. Beldon had some reservations about Bob's enthusiasm. He had been involved in several unpleasant experiences before with previous state officials. He knew that the foreign businessmen could be persuaded to come, but they would require assurances that they could meet with people who were authorized to negotiate. Once they heard that the governor was interested they would be disappointed if he did not appear.

Bob sensed that Dr. Beldon was worried. He assured him that all would work out well. He promised to send an official letter of invitation to the foreign businessmen the very next day but realized that he had to get approval from his superiors.

Bob was surprised to discover that several of his peers were skeptical about the value of a meeting with businessmen from the Middle East. The director of the Agricultural Development Division seemed interested but warned that these things had to be handled carefully. It was suggested that the Agricultural Development Division send an official letter to the department requesting a state agricultural tour.

Not knowing quite how to resolve this impasse, Bob ignored several telephone messages from Dr. Beldon. With only a few days remaining before the Middle Eastern businessmen had to leave the United States for Japan, Bob received an urgent message from the governor's office. Who was Dr. Beldon? What trade delegation was he talking about? Was the governor planning to attend some agricultural exposition in Japan?

Dr. Beldon, in a final attempt to ensure that his telex to the Middle Eastern associates in New York was correct, had placed a direct telephone call to the governor. He spoke with several members of the governor's staff and tried to explain the urgency of the situation. Nobody seemed to know anything about the proposed meeting. He was told that someone from the staff would talk to the governor that evening. The governor was attending a regional conference of governors outside the state but would be checking in with his office later that evening. Two hours later, the governor's chief assistant returned Dr. Beldon's call and explained that some mix-up had occurred. The governor was not aware of any trade delegation visiting the state. The staff person had just talked with the director of the Agricultural Development Division at his home and had been told that no such contact had been authorized. Perhaps Dr. Beldon had misunderstood Bob Anderson's enthusiasm.

Everyone in the governor's office agreed it was a wonderful idea and suggested that perhaps at some later date a meeting could be arranged with the businessmen to discuss the state's interest in agriculture. Apologies were given for any inconvenience or embarrassment that may have been caused.

Case Questions

1. What assumptions did Bob Anderson make?

2. What channels of communication did Bob Anderson establish to ensure the success of the venture? What could he have done to improve communication lines?

3. Why did the director of the Agricultural Development Division tell the governor's staff that no such contact had been authorized?

4. What reservations did Dr. Beldon have concerning this proposed meeting?

5. How would you have written a letter of introduction for the governor?

6. Why was there confusion about the governor's trip?

7. How might this whole situation have been handled to ensure that the growers, packagers, and brokers could meet with the businessmen from the Middle East directly?

CASE | *Whom Can You Trust?*

David B. Parsons, Lakehead University, Thunder Bay, Ontario, Canada

Joan Duncan is a registered nurse. One day she took her son to the family physician because he was experiencing difficulty in breathing. After diagnosing a bronchial infection, Dr. Smithers prescribed an antibiotic. Duncan decided to have the prescription filled at the pharmacy in the neighborhood mall.

Being a registered nurse, Duncan read the prescription before she took it to the pharmacy. She told the pharmacist that her husband would pick up the prescription later in the day.

When Mr. Duncan brought the prescription home, Mrs. Duncan read the instructions on the label. Immediately, she realized that the pharmacist had indicated the wrong dosage and frequency of administration on the label.

Therefore, she phoned the pharmacy to question the apparent discrepancy between the doctor's orders and the instructions on the bottle. Making certain that she was speaking to the pharmacist, she asked him to check the prescription order. The pharmacist's first response was the Connors Drug Mart does not make mistakes and that the instructions on the label were correct.

However, Mrs. Duncan insisted that the pharmacist check the original order. Reluctantly, and somewhat indignantly, he agreed to do so. When he returned to the phone, he admitted that, in fact, the instructions were wrong. However, he passed off the error as a typographical mistake, refusing to admit that someone on his staff had made a medication error.

After discussing the situation with several friends who also deal with this pharmacy, Mrs. Duncan discovered that they had also experienced similar problems. For example, just the week before, Mrs. French had been dispensed and had used the wrong eye drops. Fortunately, no serious complications had arisen.

Case Questions

1. How would you describe the communication problem involved in this situation?

2. Assuming the role of Mrs. Duncan, write a letter of concern to the physician, to the pharmacy, or the Society of Professional Pharmacists.

3. What would be the appropriate steps to take to correct this problem?

PART TWO

STRATEGIES FOR WRITTEN COMMUNICATION

A Systematic Approach to Effective Written Communication

One of the first things Brad Whitlow did after he was elected president of the Student Government Association was to appoint a committee to investigate student grievance procedures on the campus. During his three earlier years on campus Brad had observed an absence of uniformity concerning how grievances were resolved. The handling of grievances seemed to depend as much on who the aggrieved knew as on the relevant facts of the situation. Eventually a student–faculty committee developed a grievance procedure for all undergraduate students. It was published in the student handbook:

> In order to provide a mechanism by which students may air their problems concerning academic courses, the university has established the following grievance procedure for all undergraduate students. First, the student should attempt to resolve his grievance with the course instructor. If not satisfied, then he may petition the head of the department in question, who will respond to the grievance in writing. If the student is not entirely satisfied, then his grievance may be submitted to the Undergraduate Petitions Committee, a three-man panel composed of two faculty members and one student who will render a final decision concerning the grievance.

Jim Malone received his final term grades, and one of them was an unpleasant surprise — a grade two letters lower than he had expected. He called the course instructor, who declined to see him. Angered

Learning Objectives

1 *To know 10 characteristics of effective writing.*

2 *To recognize writing that does not have the 10 characteristics.*

3 *To understand how the 10 characteristics work in combination to make writing effective.*

4 *To learn techniques to build the 10 characteristics into your own writing.*

by this response, Jim called the dean of student affairs and was told to consult the student handbook.

Reread the grievance procedure. As you do, make a mental list of the things you find wrong with it. Remember that whatever you think is wrong probably is. After all, it was written for students — you're the audience.

This chapter introduces 10 characteristics that make written communication effective. Each one will be discussed — and then the grievance procedure will be rewritten to incorporate it. The goal is to help you see how written communication, if approached systematically, can be improved.

CHARACTERISTIC 1: TACTFUL

People who possess tact know the right thing to do or to say in a given situation. This is especially important in business communication. Unfortunately, too many of us assume that what is inoffensive to us is inoffensive to everyone else. Not every person enjoys off-color jokes, nor does everyone appreciate ethnic jokes or religious anecdotes. As Chapter 2 pointed out, one skill the effective encoder of messages has is the ability to analyze the receiver. An outcome of such an analysis should be more tactful writing.

Appeal to the Reader's Intelligence

Writing at too high or too low a level may insult the reader.

Write *to* your reader, neither above nor below. Tactlessness occurs when writers seek to impress rather than express. The reader becomes baffled and loses interest or, even worse, misinterprets the information and responds inappropriately.

Shortly after his election, a first-term governor sent a memo to his department heads. As a group the department heads, entrenched in their jobs for many years, had much more experience in state government than the governor. They received the following memo:

> Until further notice, no department shall employ personnel to fill budgeted positions which have been vacant for a period of one month prior to the date of this memorandum unless the filling of such positions is essential to the continued operations of the department and the prior approval of the State Budget Bureau has been given.

The memo precipitated an uproar from department heads who felt their authority was being usurped. This follow-up memo was then sent to the department heads:

> That previous memo was not intended as a limitation on the authority of any department head, either appointed or elected. You were asked, however, not to fill any position unless that position is essential to the contin-

ued operation of your department. You are in the best position to determine essential needs.[1]

The tone of the initial memo was authoritarian and brusque; the second was more tactful. There was a significant yet subtle change in content, and the change in tone was even greater. Had the writer exercised more tact in the first memo the relationship between the novice governor and the powerful department heads would not have been jeopardized.

This series of memos illustrates one type of demeaning communication. There are others. "You're looking much better than usual" is not likely to be well-received, even if it slips out without malicious intent. And as blatant an insult as "I really thought you could handle the job but I guess I was wrong!" is sure to bring out a negative reaction. Demeaning language is to be avoided in spoken communication just as judiciously as in written communication.

Appeal to the Individual

Tactful writing appeals to the individual rather than to categories. Consider the following:

> People such as you like a good bargain. That's why we're offering you these fantastic discounts on . . .

As the sender of this message, you might be assuming that all customers like good bargains. However, many of your customers will think of themselves as being different from other customers. "People such as you" puts the customer in the same category with everyone else. The extent to which you offend one, two, or several customers with your categorization is the extent to which your potential sales could decline. In a different type of categorization, imagine being a personnel manager who receives several hundred resumés from potential employees each year. Many of these resumés are accompanied by a cover letter with the salutation "Dear Personnel Manager." Some managers react quite differently to this salutation than to one containing the manager's name.

The reader may consider it insulting to be categorized.

Avoid Sexism

We can insult at least half our readers by using sexist language. The student grievance procedure at the beginning of this chapter, taken literally, was written only for males; the petitions committee is "three-man." Whether you as the sender are offended by sexist language is irrelevant. Someone in your audience could be.

One problem in removing sexist language is that changing *he* to *he or she* (or perhaps *s/he*) and *him* to *him or her* can become cumbersome

Sexist language may insult the reader.

[1]Harry Murphy, "Carter's Ship Backs Off as Memo Runs Aground," *Atlanta Constitution*, January 31, 1971, A-6.

unless it is done sparingly. With this problem in mind, here are some ways of removing sexist language from your writing:

1. Use the word *person.* For example:

   Sexist: When you schedule a meeting with a businessman, be aware of the importance of time.

   Nonsexist: When you schedule a meeting with a business person, be aware of the importance of time.

2. Use plurals. For example:

   Sexist: An employee will be promoted based upon his ability and seniority.

   Nonsexist: Employees will be promoted based upon their ability and seniority.

   Sexist: A good manager develops his subordinates.

   Nonsexist: Good managers develop their subordinates.

3. Use the words *you* or *your.* For example.

   Sexist: An employee should punch his time card promptly each morning.

   Nonsexist: Punch your time card promptly each morning.

Many commonly used words in business communication are potentially sexist. Here are some examples of those words and their more contemporary replacements.[2]

Don't Say	*Say*
Businessman	Business person, business executive, manager
Chairman	Chairperson, moderator, chair
Manmade	Manufactured, handmade
Salesman	Salesperson, sales agent, sales representative
Spokesman	Spokesperson, representative
Workmen	Workers
Foreman	Supervisor
Stockboy	Stock clerk

Finally, avoid falling victim to sexual stereotypes when writing about people who have assumed roles once reserved for a single sex. Such terms as *male nurse, female attorney*, and *woman manager* merely call attention to the sex of the role occupant rather than the role itself.

Avoid Offensive Language in General

Sexist writing is not the only offensive use of language.

Other uses of language are just as offensive to some readers as sexist terms.

[2]Carolyn Crawford Dolecheck, "Are You Teaching Affirmative Action Writing?" *ABCA Bulletin* 41, no. 4 (December 1978): 21.

Humor in bad taste

Even a weak joke is not a good opening for a collection letter; for example:

> Maybe you've heard this one: Why are little birds so sad in the morning? Answer: Because their little bills are all "overdew." It may remind you that we have a little bill that is overdue. If you feed it a check . . .[3]

An accusatory tone

When your writing contains an accusation, whether implied or expressed, you risk offending your reader. Compare these two sentences:

> Perhaps you didn't follow the instruction manual that accompanied your Expresso Coffeemaker. (accusatory)

> Please recheck the instruction manual that accompanied our Expresso Coffeemaker. (nonaccusatory)

Focus on the Receiver's Perception

As you work toward increasing tact in your writing, remember that your own perception of tact is not what counts. All that really counts is the meaning your receiver assigns to the message.

To make the grievance procedure paragraph at the beginning of this chapter more tactful, we need to remove the sexist language (*his* and *man*):

> In order to provide a mechanism by which students may air their problems concerning academic courses, the university has established the following grievance procedure for all undergraduate students. First, the student should attempt to resolve the grievance with the course instructor. If not satisfied, the grievance may be filed with the head of the department in question, who will respond to the grievance in writing. If the student is not entirely satisfied, then the grievance may be submitted to the Undergraduate Petitions Committee, a panel composed of two faculty members and one student who will render a final decision concerning the grievance.

CHARACTERISTIC 2: PERSONAL

What you write should convey a "you" attitude, which means focusing on the receiver's needs and interests — not on yourself. In terms of writing technique, this means deemphasizing the use of *we* and *I* and emphasizing *you* and *your*. Here are some examples:

The "you" attitude puts the reader first.

We and I	You
We've mailed a check.	You'll receive your check in the mail.
Our savings accounts pay 6 percent interest.	You'll earn 6 percent interest from your savings account.
I want to express my appreciation for . . .	Thank you for your help with . . .

[3]Herta A. Murphy and Charles E. Peck, *Effective Business Communication* (New York: McGraw-Hill, 1976), 457.

✔ CHECKLIST for Tactful Writing

☑ **Appeals to the reader's intelligence.**

☑ **Appeals to the individual rather than to categories of readers.**

☑ **Avoids sexism.**

☑ **Is not offensive.**

Using *you* and *your* makes the reader the center of attention in the message. Writing with the "you" attitude can be done on two levels. The first is fairly mechanical and easy. Go through your draft and spot each *I* reference. Then work on the elimination of these words. You won't be able to remove all the references, but the tone improves with each removal. Now go through that same draft and insert some *you* references. Up to the point when the use of *you* becomes bothersome and noticeable, it is a valuable interest developer. Once or twice in a letter the person's name can be spliced into the message for special emphasis.

The second level of applying the "you" attitude is more elusive and difficult. This level goes beyond the mere substitution of pronouns and seeks a between-the-lines tone that the message is to the reader rather than from the author. This is the level and tone you should strive toward. Compare these two short messages:

> The company wishes to encourage employees to take part in the suggestion system that it has provided; the system has produced many money-saving ideas in the past.

> Employees are the heart of XYZ Company, and each employee's ideas are enthusiastically sought and carefully evaluated. Many employee-volunteered ideas have produced time- and effort-saving changes.

Neither passage has an *I* or a *you*, but the second one has a tone that is directed to the employee rather than from the company.

Tactful and personal writing are related. As you have probably already discovered, using the "you" attitude is also a convenient way to avoid sexist language. However, tactful writing sometimes requires that you avoid the "you" attitude in order not to offend the reader. Consider the following:

We and I	*You*
We didn't receive a check.	You didn't send your check.
Employees who are late 3 days with no excused reason will be dismissed.	If you are late 3 days with no excused reason, then you will be dismissed.

In the first example, "You didn't send your check" contains an accusatory tone. The *we* and *I* approach implies that the check did not arrive for reasons other than the reader's not having sent it. The second example is less explicit in its absence of tact. The "you" version communicates an expectation that every reader is considering taking 3 free holidays. The more appropriate *we* and *I* version successfully communicates the company's policy but avoids the implication that all employees are irresponsible.

Generally, you'll want to put the reader first. Write from his or her point of view. However, if making the reader the center of attention might bring offense, then shift to the *we* and *I* approach.

If the "you" attitude might offend the reader, we and I should be used instead.

Here, then, is a further revised (but not perfect) version of the grievance procedure paragraph at the beginning of the chapter.

> In order to provide a mechanism by which you can air your problems concerning academic courses, the university has established for you the following grievance procedure. First, you should attempt to resolve your grievance with your course instructor. If not satisfied, your grievance may be filed with the head of the department in question, who will respond to your grievance in writing. If you are not entirely satisfied, request your grievance be submitted to the Undergraduate Petitions Committee, a panel composed of two faculty members and one student who will render a final decision concerning your grievance.

CHARACTERISTIC 3: POSITIVE

Effective written communication has a positive tone. How people react to your writing depends in part on the climate of communication you establish with them. Such a climate can be positive or negative. Compare the two messages in Figure 3.1. Both messages have the same meaning, yet they convey different ideas about the relationship the doctors want to establish with patients.

A positive tone develops a positive relationship.

When writing for business, we want to create as positive a climate and as much good will as possible. We need to avoid using negative words such as *delay, can't, impossible, inconvenience,* and *trouble.*

Here are some examples:

Negative: You *failed* to enclose a check with your order; therefore, it is *impossible* to send you the merchandise.

Positive: As soon as your check arrives, we'll send your order via parcel post.

Negative: There can be *no* exceptions to this policy.

Positive: This policy must apply equally and fairly to everyone.

Negative: The oven *doesn't* come with a 40-inch cooktop.

Positive: The oven is available with either a 30-inch or a 36-inch cooktop.

Negative: The paint is guaranteed not to *dull, chip,* or *scratch* for two years.

Positive: The paint is guaranteed to stay bright and smooth for two years.

Negative: We *regret* having *forgotten* to include your refund check.

FIGURE 3.1   ▪   *Two Doctor's Office Messages*

NO SMOKING	*Please refrain from smoking.*

Positive:	You will receive your refund check by the end of the week.
Negative:	We *cannot* meet until Monday morning.
Positive:	We can meet on Monday morning.

The tone we employ sets the climate for our communication. A positive climate means we use a positive tone.

Reversal words change the direction or tone of a message.

Other than careful word selection, there are two other ways to enhance a positive message; both relate to emphasis. The first approach employs the concept of **reversal words**. These words change the direction or tone of a message from positive to negative or from negative to positive. When they occur at a transition point they identify the upcoming change. This identification can be valuable when you are moving from bad news to good news, for the reader knows that the negative is finished.

The change from a positive message to a negative message is unpleasant. For this reason, try not to add extra emphasis to the negative information by saying, in effect, "Brace yourself, here it comes."

In summary, we might wish to use reversal words between negative and positive thoughts, but we should always avoid reversal words prior to negative thoughts. Examples of reversal words and phrases are *however, on the other hand, but,* and *unfortunately.* Of these, *unfortunately* should especially be avoided because it is a negative word that is used only before a negative thought.

The second approach to gain maximum benefit from your message is emphasis through location. In **place emphasis** we place our information at either the beginning or the end of the message because those are the locations of maximum emphasis. The opposite of this works, too; putting negative information in the middle of a message — away from the beginning or ending emphasis locations — draws as little attention to it as possible.

The technique of using repetition for emphasis is called **mass emphasis**. A positive message might be repeated in both similar and different ways throughout the piece of writing.

CHARACTERISTIC 4: ACTIVE

Of the two sentences that follow, which seems more emphatic to you?

Effective business writers use the active voice.

The active voice is used by effective business writers.

The first sentence is written in the active voice, meaning that the subject performs the action expressed by the verb. The second sentence is in the passive voice; the subject receives the action expressed by the verb. The active voice helps make sentences come alive. Because people usually talk in the active voice, they are more accustomed to dealing with it. Active is strong because the subject is acting. Passive is weak because the subject is being acted upon. Consider the following:

The active voice emphasizes ideas.

Passive: A refund will be sent to you.
Active: You will receive a refund.
Passive: The report was written by Jim.
Active: Jim wrote the report.
Passive: The product's safety has been shown by laboratory tests.
Active: Laboratory tests have shown the product's safety.

Sometimes you'll want to use the passive voice, especially if you want to de-emphasize a point. Again, we are concerned about tact in writing:

The passive voice de-emphasizes ideas.

Passive: Your payment has not been received.
Active: You didn't send in your payment.
Passive: Your credit was checked.
Active: We checked your credit.

The passive voice need not always be used to de-emphasize an idea. We can rewrite "Your credit was checked" in the active voice and still be tactful: "To assure that the use of credit is in the best interest of the applicant, we do check all credit references."

Using the active voice guideline, we should make two changes in the grievance procedure paragraph at the beginning of the chapter. "Your grievance may be filed" should be changed to "You may file your grievance." And "Your grievance may be submitted" should read "You may submit your grievance."

CHARACTERISTIC 5: UNIFIED

Each sentence in business communication should contain only one idea. When writing a sentence, the goal is to make sure that two unrelated ideas do not appear. Meeting this goal is easy if you write nothing but simple sentences. Limiting yourself to simple sentences, however, will result in a choppy writing style characteristic of a first-grade reader: "See Dick. See Jane. See Spot run."

Sentence unity requires limiting each sentence to one idea.

Experienced writers combine simple, compound, and complex sentences to vary the rhythm. Yet using compound and complex sentences brings the danger of lack of unity:

Poor: Thank you for placing your order, and your new Beachcraft Towels should reach you by July 15. (compound sentence)
Better: Thank you for placing your order. Your new Beachcraft Towels should reach you by July 15. (two simple sentences)

Poor: When you start the engine, adjust the motor speed immediately, and check your owner's manual if you have any further problems. (compound-complex sentences)

Better: When you start the engine, adjust the motor speed immediately. If you have any further problems, please check your owner's manual. (two complex sentences)

Paragraph unity requires limiting each paragraph to one central idea.

Unity applies in much the same way to writing paragraphs. In this case our goal is to be sure that no paragraph contains more than one central idea. However, many times our thoughts get mixed together:

We need to talk about expansion plans tomorrow. The report is due next month, and I'm afraid we're running short on time. I can't figure out last month's profit statement. Need to go over it with you. We're over budget. Enclosed is a bill from the printer. Impossible! Did you authorize this?

You can see that this writer is dealing with three separate ideas—expansion plans, the profit statement, and the printer's bill. The paragraph can be improved by making three paragraphs out of it:

We need to talk about expansion plans tomorrow. The report is due next month, and I'm afraid we're running short on time.
   I can't figure out last month's profit statement. Need to go over it with you. We're over budget.
   Enclosed is a bill from the printer. Impossible! Did you authorize this?

Besides reading more smoothly, the material is presented so as to tell the reader that these are three important ideas, as opposed to only one.
   Perhaps the best way to make sure that your paragraphs are unified is to begin each of them with a topic sentence. Then do not write any other sentence not related to the topic sentence. Save unrelated ideas for future paragraphs.
   The grievance procedure material at the beginning of the chapter is so brief that paragraph unity is not a problem. In practice, however, you will find that many paragraphs are quite lengthy and require careful attention to unity.

CHARACTERISTIC 6: COHERENT

Writers should achieve a logical connection between ideas and a smooth flow of ideas within a document. Referred to as **coherence**, this is important to both sentences and paragraphs If sentences or paragraphs are coherent, the ideas in them are clearly tied together and easy to understand.

Sentence Coherence

Coherent sentences and paragraphs are understandable because they stick together.

Sentences often lack coherence because we use pronouns such as *this*, *that*, and *it* ambiguously.

Unclear: Your Grasscutter electric mower will operate quietly and quickly, this will save you money.

Clear: Your Grasscutter electric mower will operate quietly and
           quickly. Its speed will save you money.
Unclear: They rented furniture for their apartment that cost $100 per
           month.
Clear: For their apartment, they rented furniture that cost $100 per
           month.

Dangling constructions also make sentences incoherent:

Unclear: Being a preferred customer, I am sure you'll be interested in
           this.
Clear: Because you are a preferred customer, I'm sure you'll be
           interested in this.
Unclear: Having been run through the adding machine, the clerk
           rechecked his figures.
Clear: After running figures through the adding machine, the clerk
           rechecked them.

Paragraph Coherence

Paragraphs can be coherent if we make a conscious attempt to use certain
devices to help the reader along. Unfortunately, we too often assume the
reader can read our mind along with our writing, and we produce paragraphs like this:

> You'll want to own a Washamatic clothes dryer for several reasons. It costs
> only 9 cents for the average load and has a one-year guarantee on all
> parts. It comes in three brilliant colors — harvest gold, fresh green, and
> sunflower yellow.

Four devices for improving paragraph coherence are parallel structure, linking words, enumerating, and signposting.

One device for improving the coherence of this paragraph is the use of
parallel structure. **Parallel structure** consists of the repetition of sentence
patterns. It adds clarity and readability to ideas.

> You'll want to own a Washamatic clothes dryer for several reasons. It costs
> only 9 cents for the average load. It comes with a one-year guarantee on
> all parts. And it comes in three brilliant colors — harvest gold, fresh green,
> and sunflower yellow.

Parallel structure simply emphasizes all three of the reasons equally.
   Another way to improve coherence is to use **linking words**, which serve
as transitions or bridges between ideas. In the following paragraph, "also"
and "in addition" are linking words.

> You'll want to own a Washamatic clothes dryer for several reasons. It costs
> only 9 cents for the average load. Also, it has a one-year guarantee on all
> parts. In addition, the Washamatic comes in three brilliant colors — harvest
> gold, fresh green, and sunflower yellow.

Other examples of linking words are *however*, *and*, *consequently*, and
therefore.
   A third device for enhancing paragraph coherence is called **enumerating**.
Here we give a specific numeric or chronological label to each of our
ideas:

> You'll want to own a Washamatic clothes dryer for several reasons. First, it costs only 9 cents for the average load. Second, it has a one-year guarantee on all parts. And, third, the Washamatic comes in three brilliant colors — harvest gold, fresh green and sunflower yellow.

Finally, we can **signpost**, that is, assign brief headings to our major ideas:

> You'll want to own a Washamatic clothes dryer for several reasons:
> Cost — only 9 cents for the average load.
> Guarantee — one year on all parts.
> Colors — three brilliant colors: harvest gold, fresh green, and sunflower yellow.

If you examine the grievance procedure paragraph at the beginning of the chapter, you will find that coherence was achieved when we made other wording changes. Coherence can also be brought about through careful outlining, which will contribute to improved clarity as well. Coherence and clarity tend to go hand in hand.

Coherence through Careful Outlining

The better you organize your written material, the easier it will be to understand. And the better you outline your ideas, the more organized they will become as you put them on paper. Outlining is one key to reader understanding.

Outlining will be discussed in detail in Chapter 9 in relation to report writing. However, you can use an outline for any lengthy written communication — memos, letters, policies, and procedures.

An outline is a convenient way to organize paragraphs and groups of paragraphs into a logical arrangement. Imagine that you need to write a memo to employees about timeliness. They are late reporting to work in the morning, they take extended breaks, and their 30-minute lunch breaks often last from 45 minutes to one hour. Somehow, you need to communicate to them and influence them to abide by company policies. The first step in writing this memo is to outline your ideas on paper. You might, for example, follow the AIDA (Attention, Interest, Desire, Action) sequence, a formula for persuasive writing discussed in more detail in Chapter 7 on persuasive letters, and construct an outline similar to this:

I. Attention
   A. Some statistics about output per hour
   B. Some statistics about lost output because of lost time
II. Interest
   A. Employees' role in company success
   B. Reference to time policies
      1. Tardiness
      2. Break time
      3. Lunchtime
III. Desire
   A. Consequences of conforming to time policies
   B. Consequences of not conforming to time policies

IV. Action
   A. Simple call for conformity
   B. Expression of appreciation for conformity

Because we have outlined four basic ideas (Attention, Interest, Desire, and Action), at least four paragraphs are needed in our memorandum. Also, we might easily have two paragraphs under Interest and perhaps two under Desire. In any case, we are planning our memo logically. If the material is well organized, our chances of having it understood are increased.

✔ CHECKLIST for Coherent Writing

—❙ Carefully outline your ideas before putting them in writing.

—❙ Use parallel structure to emphasize all points equally.

—❙ Use linking words to provide transitions between points.

—❙ Enumerate — that is, give a specific numeric or chronological label to the points being made.

—❙ Signpost — that is, assign brief headings to major points.

CHARACTERISTIC 7: CLEAR

Clarity in writing applies to word choice, to sentence and paragraph structure, and to the overall organization of whatever you write, be it a letter, a memo, or a report. Clarity is a general concept meaning that what we write is understandable to the reader. Readability, the ninth characteristic, is important to clarity. Unity and coherence are also important. Clarity also involves several additional techniques we have discussed: choosing your words carefully, using topic sentences in your paragraphs, and outlining your ideas before you begin writing.

Clear writing exhibits readability, unity, and coherence.

Avoiding Technical Jargon

Every field has its own special language. A blow to the head is a subdural hematoma to a doctor. What the military calls a protective reaction strike is nevertheless the dropping of bombs. And if you do poorly in school, you will probably be called an underachiever. Figure 3.2 humorously illustrates the principle of avoiding jargon except with fellow specialists. Read the material from *Consumer Reports* in Figure 3.3 and notice the impact of the technical jargon.

Technical jargon may be impressive but meaningless.

FIGURE 3.2 ▪ *Technical Jargon as a Barrier to Communication*

Writing clearly means avoiding jargon. Why didn't he just say: "All the fish died!"

Source: Copyright International Paper Company

FIGURE 3.3 ▪ *Some Technical Jargon Translated*

Hey there, plainspeak fans . . .
A number of our readers have been bemused by the following gem, enclosed with one of their monthly credit-card statements:

> Any holder of this consumer credit contract is subject to all claims and defenses which the debtor could assert against the seller of goods or services obtained pursuant hereto or with the proceeds hereof. Recovery hereunder by the debtor shall not exceed amounts paid by the debtor hereunder.

Well, that's easy enough to understand — if you're a lawyer. If you're not, a translation (as it applies to credit sales) might go something like this:

> When you buy a product on credit, you incur a debt. Your creditor may sell that debt to a third party. That third party can't duck responsibility for making good to you on an unsatisfactory product by claiming that he or she is not the one who sold it to you. But you can't get more back than you've paid for the product.

The insert, as is shown above, was sent out by the Mobil Oil Credit Corp. But the legalese wasn't Mobil's fault. As the insert also noted: "The Federal Trade Commission rule on preservation of consumer claims and defenses requires that creditors give you this notice."

Source: Copyright 1978 by Consumers Union of United States, Inc., Mount Vernon, N.Y. 10550. Reprinted by permission from *Consumer Reports,* March 1978.

Avoiding Unfamiliar Words

Jargon basically consists of words that are unfamiliar to all but specialists. Other unfamiliar words, although not jargon, create just as much mis-understanding. Try this paragraph:

Using familiar words can improve reader understanding.

> Fully cognizant of the inoperative nature of his vehicle, George's initial response was to institute repairs. Prior to modifying the timing, he found a defective wire in the anterior portion of the engine.

See whether these changes make the paragraph more understandable:

> Knowing well that his car was not working, George's first response was to begin repairs. Before changing the timing, he found a faulty wire in the front part of the engine.

Even the simplest ideas can be made almost unintelligible with unfamiliar words. See if you can translate these old sayings into their familiar form:

- He who expresses merriment subsequent to everyone else expresses merriment of most superior quality.
- Precipitation entails negation of economy.
- Pulchritude is not evinced below the dermal surface.

To help make your writing clear, use words that will be familiar to your reader. Here are some examples:

Don't Say	Say
Prior to	Before
Subsequent to	After
Accomplish	Do
Reimburse	Pay
Determine	Find out
Transmit	Send
Advantageous	Helpful
Locality	Place
Facilitate	Help
Encounter difficulty in	Find it hard to
Pursuant to your request	As you asked

Using Topic Sentences

A unified paragraph has only one central idea, which is usually expressed in the topic sentence of the paragraph. The topic sentence should be placed at either the beginning or the end of the paragraph. In business communication it usually appears at the beginning. However, you might place your topic sentence at the end of the paragraph if (1) the main topic of your paragraph will be unclear unless the reader is first exposed to some details or (2) you are attempting to persuade the reader, and his or her

The topic sentence presents the main idea of the paragraph.

reaction might be unfavorable. In the second case, presenting details first will help you support the position you take in the topic sentence.

These two examples should help you understand how the topic sentence (in italics) can make writing clearer:

> *Burns Brick Company has several employee relations problems.* The turnover rate is 39 percent, up 10 percent from last year. Absenteeism has increased almost 25 percent this year. And the number of grievances has more than doubled during the past 6 months.

> The turnover rate at Burns Brick Company is 39 percent, up 10 percent from last year. Absenteeism has increased almost 25 percent this year. And the number of grievances has more than doubled during the past 6 months. *Obviously, the company is faced with several important employee relations problems.*

By using topic sentences and by ensuring that every sentence in the paragraph is related to the topic sentence (unity), the reader better understands our written message.

CHARACTERISTIC 8: CONCISE

You can become a concise writer if you will avoid wordy expressions, trite phrases, useless repetition, and abstract words. **Conciseness** is simply saying what you want to say in the fewest possible words. The opposite of conciseness is wordiness.

Avoiding Wordy Expressions

Wordy expressions are simply deadweight in a sentence. Many sentences beginning with *there are*, *it is*, or *there is* are wordy sentences. You can say the same thing without phrases that make your sentences begin slowly:

Don't Say	*Say*
There are three fine restaurants on Broad Street.	Broad Street has three fine restaurants.
It is important that all employees read the company handbook.	All employees should read the company handbook.
There is little time left us to make a decision.	We have little time left to make the decision.

In just these three examples we have saved seven words at no expense to understanding.

"More matter, with less art" were Queen Gertrude's words to the rambling, wordy Polonius in Shakespeare's *Hamlet*. As she encouraged him to speak more concisely, we encourage you to write more concisely with the following changes:

Wordy	*Concise*
A long period of time	A long time (or two weeks)
At the present time	Now (or the present date)
Consensus of opinion	Consensus
Due to the fact that	Because
During the month of November	During November
For the purpose of	For
For the reason that	Because
In many cases	Often
In some cases	Sometimes
In the near future	Soon
In the event that	If
In the state of Illinois	In Illinois
In view of the fact that	Because
With regard to	About
With reference to	About
The jar which is blue	The blue jar

Avoiding Trite Phrases

Trite phrases are worn-out, commonplace expressions. Because they are overused, trite phrases have lost their meaning and can reduce your credibility as a writer.

Some trite phrases can simply be deleted from a sentence; others have fresher replacements. Here are some examples:

Don't Say	*Say*
Advise	Tell
Enclosed please find	Enclosed is
Numerous and sundry	Many
Permit me to say	(nothing)
It has come to my attention	I have learned
Under separate cover	Separately
Please be advised	(nothing)
Up to this writing	Until now
In accordance with your request	As you requested
Kindly	Please

Avoiding Useless Repetition

Sometimes we repeat ideas for effect — to impress them in the reader's mind. Television advertisements repeat the product's name many times so that we will not forget it. When you write, you might also repeat ideas.

Yet one careless mistake we sometimes make is useless repetition of the same idea, as the following examples show:

- The two cars were *exactly* identical.
- His pay raise was small *in size*.
- We join *together* in wishing you well in your new job.
- If you can't use the new typewriter, return it *back* to me.
- What we need are some *new* changes.
- Please see me at 3:30 p.m. *in the afternoon*.

The words in italics can be omitted from each sentence with no loss of understanding.

Avoiding Abstract Words

Abstract words contribute to unclear writing because they are so vague that the reader is not sure what we are trying to say. Concrete words, the opposite of abstract words, have clear, specific meanings. They help readers create the image that we want created in their minds.

"Vehicle" is an abstract word. When we say, "A vehicle was parked at the curb," the reader is not sure just what kind of vehicle we mean—truck, bus, car, or other vehicle. To create a more vivid image for the reader, we should move from the abstract to the concrete:

Vehicle→Car→Pontiac→1991 Pontiac→1991 Pontiac Grand Prix→Brown and gold 1991 Pontiac Grand Prix

Saying "A brown and gold 1991 Pontiac Grand Prix was parked at the curb" creates a much clearer image.

Here are some examples of the use of abstract versus concrete language:

Abstract	*Concrete*
Your savings account will earn the *highest possible interest*.	You savings account will earn the *maximum 6.5 percent* interest *each year*.
The *majority* of our stockholders voted for the new plan.	*Sixty-four percent* of our stockholders voted for the new plan.
Your new, *lightweight* Electro Typewriter can be carried easily from *room to room*.	Your new Electro Typewriter is *feather light. Weighing only 12 pounds*, it can easily be carried from *office to office*.
You will receive your refund check *soon*.	You will receive your full $132.19 *by July 15*.

In summary, you can write concisely if you avoid using wordy expressions, trite phrases, useless repetitions, and abstract words. Writing more concisely usually means using fewer words, thus saving the reader time and energy. When abstract words are replaced, however, conciseness may require increasing the number of words to create a more vivid image.

✔ CHECKLIST for Being Concise

⬜ **Avoid wordy phrases.** Wordy phrases add dead weight to a sentence.

⬜ **Avoid trite phrases.** Trite phrases can make you appear shallow.

⬜ **Avoid useless repetition.** Repeat ideas only for effect, not because you were carelessly repetitious.

⬜ **Avoid abstract words.** Abstract words create unclear images in the reader's mind.

CHARACTERISTIC 9: READABLE

Saying that something is readable means that it is understandable because of its clear style of writing. Many of us purposefully choose long words and write lengthy, complicated sentences in order to show off our command of the language. Any idea, no matter how simple, can be written in such a way as to make it difficult or even impossible for our readers to understand. The writer of the following paragraph could not have been interested in achieving understanding.

> This chapter's primary purpose is to facilitate and otherwise enhance an individual's proficiency in translating cognitions into appropriately presented written material which effectively satisfies a minimum of 10 salient criteria.

When readers become aware of our writing style, they no longer concentrate on the meaning of our message. The best writing style is one that does not draw attention to itself.

What is your impression of the original form of the grievance procedure paragraph? It is more complicated than it needs to be, yet the style of writing is fairly typical of much communication in business, including handbooks for students.

Readability has been a popular topic since the late 1940s when mathematical formulas were developed to judge the degree of complexity of written material. One of these formulas is Robert Gunning's Fog Index.[4]

Applying the Fog Index

Gunning's Fog Index is intended to gauge the grade level of written material: what level of education will the audience need to have in order to understand something that is written? It works best with text of at least

---

[4]Robert Gunning, *The Technique of Clear Writing* (New York: McGraw-Hill, 1952). Gunning's Fog Index is only one of many formulas for measuring readability. You might be interested in another: Rudolph Flesch, The Art of Readable Writing (New York: Harper & Row, 1949).

200 words. Only prose can be evaluated. The Fog Index does not work on nonsentence material, such as letterheads, inside addresses, or balance sheet information.

Try your hand at using the Fog Index by applying it to the grievance procedure paragraph at the beginning of the chapter. The steps to take are as follows:

1. *Count the number of words in the passage.* There are 100 words in the grievance procedure material.
2. *Count the number of complete thoughts in the passage.* A simple or complex sentence has one complete thought; a compound sentence has two thoughts. We counted four complete thoughts.
3. *Compute the average sentence length.* To do this, divide the number of words in the passage (100) by the number of complete thoughts (4); the answer is 25.
4. *Compute the percentage of "hard words."* These words have three or more syllables. Some types of longer words should not be computed:
   a. Proper names (Kennedy, Carolina)
   b. Combinations of short, easy words (bookkeeper, homemaker, however)
   c. Verb forms made three syllables by adding *ed* or *es* (created, trespasses).
   To compute the percentage, divide the number of hard words (we counted 15) by the total number of words in the passage (100). The answer is 15 percent.
5. *Add the average sentence length and the percentage of hard words.* The average sentence length (25) plus the percentage of hard words (15 — with no decimal point) equals 40.
6. *Multiply the answer in Step 5 by 0.4.* The answer, 16, is the Fog Index.

Interpreting the Fog Index

The readability index corresponds to a grade level.

We can interpret the Fog Index by comparing it to a grade level. For example, if the index is 6, then the material is written at the sixth-grade level. Our index of 16 for the material from the grievance procedure means that it is written at the level of a senior in college.

Is this level appropriate? Hardly. Gunning states that anyone who writes at a level greater than 12 is inviting misunderstanding.[5] Many publishers urge authors of college textbooks to write at the ninth-grade level.[6]

Using Readability Formulas

Readability formulas are only guides to better writing.

In determining the readability of the material from the grievance procedure, you might have realized two things that raise a readability index — long sentences and long words. Use the Fog Index with care. Applying

[5]Ibid., 38.
[6]*Chronicle of Higher Education*, October 15, 1974, 11.

the formula too strictly in your own writing might result in short, choppy sentences that could become monotonous and perhaps offensive to your readers. Also, longer words often add precision to what we are saying. Yet the readability formula can serve as a guide in your writing — a warning that you may be trying to impress rather than communicate for understanding.

Try to write at a level at or below your audience's educational level. Always avoid writing above their level. When writing below their educational level, never allow your message to sound as if you are writing down to your audience. Your goal is quick understanding and easy comprehension. Insulting members of your audience by writing too far below them, however, is quite detrimental.

If the Fog Index is low, that does not necessarily mean the material sounds childish or immature. One mark of an effective writer is the ability to write clearly at a low index while maintaining an intelligent tone. Journalists, for example, sharpen these skills. *Time* and *Newsweek* do not sound immature to most of us, yet they regularly average a level of advanced high school (grades 10 to 12).

Using the Fog Index goes beyond applying the formula. There are three steps: (1) quantitative evaluation through the Fog Index formula; (2) interpretation and analysis of the index score; and (3) revision as necessary. Once you have determined your typical index level or the level for a specific piece of writing, compare it to the educational level of your intended audience. If your level is higher than their educational level, make adjustments in your writing.

Gunning shares 10 suggestions for clearer writing, many directly influencing the Fog Index:

- Keep sentences short. Aim for an average of 20 words or fewer.
- Use the simple over the complex; this suggestion applies to sentences as well as words and thoughts.
- The familiar word is best.
- Avoid unnecessary words.
- Use action verbs; avoid the passive voice.
- Write the way you talk. Your writing should have a conversational tone rather than a stilted or affected tone.
- Use terms your reader can picture. Avoid abstract words.
- Try to relate to your reader's experience.
- Vary your words, sentence length, and sentence construction to sustain interest.
- Write to express ideas, not to impress the reader.

For its many values, the Fog Index has several shortcomings. First, it is oblivious to the connotations of words; only the number of words and the number of difficult words are noted. Second, the index works only with text. Third, the index is English-language oriented. Finally, reader interest in the material is not determined. An interested reader will put up with difficult writing more than will a disinterested reader.

Readability tests, such as the Fog Index, are widely used both in business and in government. The federal government, for example, sometimes requires organizations producing equipment for the government to apply readability tests to the users' manuals that accompany the equipment.

Measuring readability must be kept in perspective. A readability test is simply a tool intended to give feedback to writers. When you write, you should not limit your attention to achieving a low readability score. You should still focus your primary attention on meeting the needs of your readers.

The grievance procedure paragraph has been revised once again, this time to improve readability:

> So that you can air your problems about your courses, the university has adopted the grievance procedure below for you. Please help us by following each step. Try to resolve your grievance with your instructor. After talking with your instructor, if still unsatisfied, you may file your grievance with the head of the department in question. The department head will respond to you in writing. If you want further consideration, you may submit your grievance to the Undergraduate Petitions Committee. This committee is made up of two faculty members and one student. Its decision will be final.

The Fog Index of the revised material is as follows:

1. 97 words
2. Seven complete thoughts
3. Average sentence length = 13.9
4. Percentage of hard words = 8
5. 13.9 + 8 = 21.9
6. 21.9 × .4 = 8.8

CHARACTERISTIC 10: MECHANICALLY SOUND

Correct grammar enhances understanding.

Mechanically sound writing is free of two kinds of defects—errors in grammar and format problems. You may have wondered how an English teacher you once had could have been so cruel as to reduce your grade on a theme by three points for every comma splice. Phrases such as dangling construction, faulty reference, and subject-verb agreement may annoy you. Yet one reason correct grammar is so important is that, at the very least, it helps ensure reader understanding. Consider these examples:

- City Council Bans Gambling behind Closed Doors (a newspaper headline)
- Your speech will be followed by dinner, to begin promptly at 7:30 p.m. (from a letter to an invited speaker)
- An audience of nearly 200 heard her lecture on "The Future of Endangered Species." A number of them have already perished. (from a newspaper article)

Correct grammar enhances credibility.

Written communication can often be understood in spite of grammatical errors. However, a second reason for correct grammar is it improves your

BOXED IN | *AN ETHICAL DILEMMA*

Shortly after Paula Winston was hired as the copywriter at Champion Appliance, she began to think about someday becoming advertising manager. Owner Warren English promoted her to the position two years later, when his cousin retired.

Warren founded Champion in 1978 by opening one appliance store. It prospered in a highly competitive field, and eventually he owned six stores in a single urban area. Warren attributes the company's success to aggressive advertising. Champion has also benefited from rapid population growth in the area where the stores are located.

As advertising manager, Paula meets regularly with Warren to discuss ads for the following week. Warren usually decides the products to feature and the prices. Paula and her one subordinate, a copywriter, then prepare the ads, subject to Warren's approval. Paula is also responsible for local radio and television advertising.

Paula has questioned some of the claims that Champion regularly makes in its advertisements. Champion had always billed itself as "The House of Lowest Prices and Highest Quality." When Paula suggested this was not entirely true, Warren became upset. Paula maintained, "Our prices are the lowest and our quality is the highest, but only in some cases." She feels that the ads should specify which products are truly the lowest priced and which are truly of the highest quality. She also feels that advertising "Same Day Delivery" is misleading because purchases have to be made before noon to ensure delivery that day.

Warren and Paula no longer discuss ad content during their meetings. Instead, they argue about ethics, and Warren always wins. Paula maintains that some of the advertising is deceptive. Warren's position is that Champion's ads are "no worse than anyone else's." Today Paula described the phrase "Guaranteed Quality" as meaningless and deceitful. Warren threatened to fire her unless she does what she is told.

Paula feels boxed in. What would you do?

credibility as a writer. No matter how good your ideas are, if they are presented on paper with poor grammar, many readers will discount the ideas because the grammar detracts from them. Advertisers know that the package sells the product. Many business people are just as concerned about correct grammar as your English teacher was. Grammar is the package that helps sell your ideas. (The Appendix contains material to help you refresh your grammar skills.)

As you read the following chapters about letters, memos, policies and procedures, and reports, you will find that there are certain formats for each. Business letters, for example, typically have a heading, inside address, salutation, body, and complimentary closing. As a writer of business letters, you are expected to adhere to this format.

Format is the physical arrangement of written material.

One format requirement for procedures is that they be written in step-by-step fashion. We should alter the format of the grievance procedure so that it has an orderly appearance. Our new product is this:

> So that you can air your problems about your courses, the university has adopted the grievance procedure below for you. Please help us by following each step:
>
> 1. Try to resolve your grievance with your instructor.
>
> 2. After talking to your instructor, you may, if still unsatisfied, file your grievance with the head of the department in question. The department head will respond to you in writing.
>
> 3. If you want further consideration, you may submit your grievance to the Undergraduate Petitions Committee. This committee is made up of two faculty members and one student. Its decision will be final.

In Figure 3.4 we evaluate this final draft of the grievance procedure against the 10 characteristics of effective written communication.

SUMMARY

Compare our final grievance procedure product with the handbook material at the beginning of the chapter. We haven't done a perfect job, but we've come a long way from writing for ourselves toward analyzing and writing for our readers.

As you work your way through the remaining chapters in this section, look for ways to incorporate these 10 characteristics into your writing. We hope you've learned to apply these ideas to other people's writing. Now you should apply them to your own written communication.

Key Terms

reversal word		linking words
place emphasis		enumerating
mass emphasis		signpost
coherence		conciseness
parallel structure		

Review Questions

1. How do we interpret Gunning's Fog Index?

2. What do we mean by tactful written communication?

3. What are some ways of avoiding sexist language when we write?

4. Why should we adopt the "you" attitude when we write?

5. Why is correct grammar important to mechanically sound written communication?

FIGURE 3.4 ▪ *Evaluation of Grievance Procedure Final Draft*

_____ Tactful	We've removed the sexist language. The material does not insult the reader's intelligence.
_____ Personal	Very "You" oriented.
_____ Positive	As positive as possible for a grievance procedure, in which we must use some negative words.
_____ Active	Only one sentence in passive voice.
_____ Unified	Sentences appear to have only one major idea.
_____ Coherent	All sentences and paragraphs are clearly tied together. Enumerating is used to enhance coherence.
_____ Clear	Much more understandable than the material at the beginning of the chapter.
_____ Concise	Deadweight has been removed.
_____ Readable	The material now has an index of 9.1.
_____ Mechanically Sound	Meets all the format specifications for a procedure. Grammar correct.

6. When should you use the passive voice? Active voice?

7. How can we ensure paragraph unity?

8. What are some ways of improving paragraph coherence?

9. How can we enhance the clarity of our writing?

10. Suggest some ways of writing concisely.

11. What is meant by positive tone?

Exercises

1. Evaluate part of the student handbook for your college or university against the 10 characteristics of effective written communication, as we have done in this chapter. Then rewrite the part you have evaluated and try to improve it.

2. Compute the Fog Index of three randomly selected paragraphs from *Time* and *Reader's Digest.* Compare the average index for the two magazines. Are there readability differences? If so, why?

3. Select an essay or column from *Time, Newsweek,* or some other national news magazine. Rewrite the material using each of the four devices for improving paragraph coherence.

4. Write a 300-word essay on something you consider to be a major problem of the day. Describe the problem as you see it and suggest solutions. *Intentionally*

ignore or violate five or more of the characteristics of effective written communication. (There will be an exchange of papers among students, each of whom who will then identify mistakes and rewrite another student's article.)

5. Imagine that you end a particularly bad day by getting a parking ticket. When you parked the car, you had tried to insert a coin, but the meter would not accept it. You were aware of the city's policy of ticketing cars at expired meters even though the meter is broken. However, parking spaces are not plentiful and parking meters have been poorly maintained. Moreover, you had been parked only long enough to buy some stamps at the nearby post office. You are upset. Write a completely tactless letter to the Chief of Police. (Letters will be read aloud in class and desirable changes suggested. An award may be given for the most tactless letter.)

6. Examine the following memorandum about customer refunds. It was circulated among employees only. Customers did not see it.
   a. Compute and interpret readability.
   b. Find at least five other writing problems in the memo.
   c. Rewrite it so that all writing problems are removed.

Customer Refunds
Teaneck Department Store will refund a customer's money in the event that the customer is dissatisfied with his merchandise. If the merchandise is being returned by the customer, it should be accompanied by a sales slip. The merchandise should be examined by the salesman for potential abuse. Subsequent to merchandise inspection, the salesman should fill out a retail credit check form and acquire the appropriate approval (in the form of a signature) from his supervisor. The customer should be asked to sign the credit check and then refund the money. The credit check should be placed beneath the cash drawer.

7. Rewrite the following sentences so that they conform to the 10 characteristics of effective written communication. Each sentence contains at least one error.
   a. Our regional director, a girl with substantial years of experience, will audit your accounts.
   b. If you don't pay promptly, a substantial discount won't be received by you.
   c. In view of the fact that you've had the merchandise for only 6 months, it goes without saying that your warranty covers the repair.
   d. If the employee has a grievance, the employee should take his grievance to the grievance committee.
   e. Smelling of liquor, the policeman arrested the driver.
   f. It is believed by the Board of Trustees that the new plan will work.
   g. Despite your delay in paying the bill, we will not cancel the account.
   h. I can say at this time that a lawyer could provide a solution to this problem, but that he would necessarily need to be a tax specialist.
   i. There can be no exceptions to this policy.
   j. A full report will be sent to you by the department chairman.
   k. Decentralization of the word processing center was suggested by the report to improve work flow and reduce noise.
   l. You are not allowed to miss work if you don't have a good reason.
   m. At the present time the consensus of opinion is that employee turnover will increase during the month of May.

n. Your performance was totally unsatisfactory.

o. The purposes of the meeting was: (1) to communicate personnel policies; (2) encouragement of participation in inservice training programs; and (3) introducing several new employees.

p. The report was intended for Fred and I, not for John and Susan.

q. Each of the following pages have been proofread by the editorial staff.

r. In accordance with your request, attached herewith is the surplus inventory report.

s. Smoking is not permitted anywhere except in the lobby.

t. We beg to inform you that unless you act soon, the contract will expire.

Schmitz Clothing Company | *CASE*

Dr. Beryl D. Hart, West Liberty State College

Schmitz Clothing Company, your employer, is a West Virginia clothing manufacturer that specializes in tailor-made dress shirts for both men and women. The firm has been in business for 15 years. Some of the company's shirts are sold through specialty men's stores across the United States. However, most are made to order and sold directly to customers who appreciate high-quality tailoring.

This morning you received a letter from an influential customer, Yvonne Cocoa of Huntington, West Virginia. Her November 1 order for 10 tailor-made dress shirts, which she wants to give to her husband for Christmas, totaled $550. Her letter reported that when the shirts were delivered by carrier, the box was damaged and all of the shirts were stained with blue. Naturally she is furious. She has requested immediate replacements so she will have them in time for Christmas. You have been with the company for all of its 15 years, and this is the first time the carrier has lost or damaged an order. After inspecting the shipping cartons, the carrier reported they were in bad condition and agreed to pay the company $250.

Your dilemma is that you cannot duplicate the entire shipment in the 5 weeks until Christmas. You will try to complete half of the order.

Case Questions

1. Considering the above information and the feelings of the customer, determine how you will write the letter. Use the effective letter writing principles that you have learned.

2. What is the purpose of the letter? What will be your opening paragraph? What will be your explanation? What will be your closing paragraph?

Letter Parts and Appearance

Meg Jenkins was flattered to be asked to speak to the Student Management Association at her alma mater. She gave much thought to what she would say to this group of business majors. She entitled her remarks, "My Three Biggest Surprises."

First, she had been surprised by the length of time it took to find a job. She advised her listeners to start looking as early as possible. They should try to meet business people while they were still students. They should expect to experience rejection. Plenty of doors were likely to be closed in their faces before they landed the right job.

Second, she was surprised by the variety of her communication responsibilities. For her first six months on the job, Meg was completely responsible for her own letters and reports. She was told simply to remember that any letters she sent out influenced the way the readers perceived the company. Any reports or memoranda she prepared influenced the way people perceived her. She was glad that she had not sold her business communication textbook. She relied on it even more than she had as a student.

Third, she was surprised that, even when a subordinate prepared a document for her signature, she was still ultimately responsible for it. Meg learned this the hard way. A secretary left a word out of a sentence, thereby changing its meaning. Meg failed to proofread carefully and problems resulted. Meg also sent a report to her boss that he returned because he felt that it was "sloppy and ill-appearing."

CHAPTER 4

Learning Objectives

1 To be able to evaluate the quality and appropriateness of business stationery.

2 To know the information to include in the standard parts of a letter.

3 To know the information to include in additional parts of a letter.

4 To understand how to position the letter parts on stationery letterheads and second pages.

5 To recognize the four major letter formats and understand the advantages and disadvantages of each.

6 To know how to enhance the appearance of letters of varying lengths by adjusting the margins.

Meg ended her remarks to the group of business majors by reminding them that, no matter what their career goals, their ability to communicate would greatly influence their success.

If, when talking with someone, you closed your eyes, you would miss a large part of the message. The same principle applies to business writing. The reader has access to many cues in addition to the verbal message. These cues, which together constitute appearance, create the first impression that the reader forms of the message and of its writer.

Too often business people overlook the importance of appearance in written communication. The effect of hours of effort spent developing a logical and coherent message may be neutralized by a displeasing appearance. Such factors as quality and color of paper, spacing, margins, and size of type will influence a reader's receptivity to a message.

The appearance of a message should not call attention to itself, but it should meet reader expectations.

The content of a message is certainly more important than its appearance, but an appropriate appearance increases the likelihood of its being read. A written message must meet certain expectations if it is to be read and seriously considered. A cardinal rule in business writing is that appearance should not call attention to itself. Instead, it should subtly facilitate communication.

STATIONERY

Stationery should not detract from the message.

One of the first things a reader notices when opening a letter is the stationery on which it is typed. One characteristic of stationery is that it is both seen and felt.

Paper and Envelopes

Stationery should be the quality used in most business organizations. Good paper will meet public expectations and enhance the image of the organization. The same quality should be used for envelopes.

The most common paper size is 8½-by-11-inch sheets, but some executives use Monarch-size sheets of 7¼-by-10½ inches. Half sheets, 8½-by-5½ inches, are often used for brief internal messages such as memos or notes. Stationery weight is expressed in pounds. Business stationery ranges from 16 to 20 pounds. If lighter than 16 pounds, it is too fragile, and if heavier than 20 pounds, it is too bulky and hard to fold, as well as expensive.

Business stationery is often personalized with a watermark.

White continues to be the standard color for business stationery, although greater use is being made of pastels. Colored paper is used more often in sales letters than in other types of correspondence. Many companies personalize their stationery with a watermark, which is impressed on the paper during production. A watermark is a faint design that can be seen when the paper is held up to the light. The company logo, or some other identifying symbol, is often used as a watermark.

In most routine business communication the role of the envelope is innocuous. In direct mail advertising, however, the envelope greatly influences the effectiveness of the advertising enclosed. The perfect envelope is the one that is always opened. Research in direct mail advertising has shown that the right envelope can double or triple the number of responses. Envelopes that resemble those used by Federal Express and other overnight mail companies are more likely to be opened than are plainer envelopes. Envelopes that are opened the quickest are those that appear to have been sent by the Internal Revenue Service.[1] For purposes other than sales, a company's envelopes should be consistent with its desired image.

The *1989 Zip Code and Post Office Directory* urges the use of all capital letters for envelope addresses.

The Printed Letterhead

The printed heading on stationery is called a **letterhead**. A letterhead lends legitimacy to any business organization. Virtually all business organizations, whether one-person operations or much larger, use letterhead stationery.

At one time the letterhead took up a large part of a sheet of stationery. Often it included names of company officers and pictures of the plant along with routine identifying information. A modern letterhead has no extraneous details and usually occupies about two inches at the top of the sheet.

The modern letterhead includes the company name, address, and ZIP code. Most firms also give their telephone number, including the area code. Telefax numbers now appear in many letterheads. Companies engaging in international business often show the country in which they are located and include a code address for cablegrams.

STANDARD PARTS OF A BUSINESS LETTER

Compare letters from a number of companies and you will notice obvious differences. They may vary considerably in such stylistic features as size of type, margins, and general appearance.

All, however, will contain the same basic parts. Regardless of the purpose of the letter, the reader has certain information needs that the following parts satisfy:

The eight standard parts of a business letter satisfy the reader's information needs.

[1]Erik Larson, "In Direct-Mail Biz, Envelopes Are What Are Run Up Flagpole," *The Wall Street Journal*, May 5, 1985, 1 and 30.

- Return address of sender
- Date letter was written
- Inside address of receiver
- Salutation

- Attention line
- Body of letter
- Close
- Signature block

Return Address

The return address of the sender consists of the street number and name or a post office box number, city, state, and ZIP code. On letterhead stationery, this is usually printed at the top. On plain paper, it is typed at least 1½ inches from the top of the sheet. It can be positioned horizontally in either of two ways: (1) begin each line at the center of the sheet or (2) position the return address so that the longest line ends at the right margin. It thus establishes the top and right margins.

Date

The date is an important part of any business letter.

All letters and reports should be dated. The date tells the reader something about the context in which the letter was written. It also simplifies filing; correspondence in a file folder is usually arranged chronologically. The standard form for dates is month, day, and year — for example, November 19, 1991. Companies with international business and foreign companies often use a day, month, year sequence, such as 19 November 1991. The date should be typed three line spaces below the sender's address, whether or not there is a letterhead.

Inside Address of Receiver

The inside address includes the name, title, and address of the person to whom the letter is being sent. Be very careful that all of this information is correct. Letter writers create unnecessary obstacles to their intended goal when they misspell receivers' names or use incorrect job titles.

Information in the receiver's address is arranged from specific to general.

Information in the receiver's address is arranged in descending degrees of specificity. The most specific information, the receiver's name, if known, is presented first and followed by the receiver's professional title, the name of the organization, mailing address, city, state, and ZIP code. It is customary, although not mandatory, to abbreviate the names of states, districts, and territories. The U.S. Postal Service recommends the abbreviations presented in Table 4.1. The two-letter state abbreviation should be separated from the ZIP code by a single space.

Inside addresses are typically arranged in this manner:

Dr. John Robinson
Affirmative Action Officer
Central States College
Administration Building
Macon, MO 63552

Modern Office Supply
2226 Main Street
Buckeye, NM 88212

The first line of the inside address determines the left margin for the letter.

TABLE 4.1 ▪ *Recommended Abbreviations for State, District, and Territory Names*

Alabama	AL	Kentucky	KY	Ohio	OH
Alaska	AK	Louisiana	LA	Oklahoma	OK
Arizona	AZ	Maine	ME	Oregon	OR
Arkansas	AR	Maryland	MD	Pennsylvania	PA
California	CA	Massachusetts	MA	Puerto Rico	PR
Panama Canal Zone	CZ	Michigan	MI	Rhode Island	RI
Colorado	CO	Minnesota	MN	South Carolina	SC
Connecticut	CT	Mississippi	MS	South Dakota	SD
Delaware	DE	Missouri	MO	Tennessee	TN
District of Columbia	DC	Montana	MT	Texas	TX
Florida	FL	Nebraska	NE	Utah	UT
Georgia	GA	Nevada	NV	Vermont	VT
Guam	GU	New Hampshire	NH	Virgin Islands	VI
Hawaii	HI	New Jersey	NJ	Virginia	VA
Idaho	ID	New Mexico	NM	Washington	WA
Illinois	IL	New York	NY	West Virginia	WV
Indiana	IN	North Carolina	NC	Wisconsin	WI
Iowa	IA	North Dakota	ND	Wyoming	WY
Kansas	KS				

Salutation

Many writers of business letters today fret over what constitutes an appropriate **salutation** — the word or phrase of greeting that precedes the body of the letter. William Safire, a columnist for *The New York Times*, raised the question of how to begin a business letter and was inundated with suggestions.[2] The volume of responses was the greatest ever elicited by one of his columns, suggesting the importance that people attach to the question.

Ten percent of Safire's readers felt that a letter need not have any salutation. The other 90 percent expressed a variety of preferences. Gentlepeople, Gentlefolk, Gentlepersons, and even Gentle/wo/men were among the suggestions. Salutations such as Dear Colleague, Dear Professional, Dear Compatriot, and Dear Executive were preferred by some of the respondents. Suggested single-word salutations ranged from Greetings to Hail to Howdy.

By asking yourself how well you know your correspondent, you should be able to select an appropriate salutation. Some frequently used saluta-

How well the writer knows the correspondent will affect the style of the salutation.

[2]William Safire, "The Mulvihill Perplexity," *The New York Times Magazine*, June 25, 1989, 10.

tions in business letters are Dear Mr., Dear Ms., or Dear Mrs. The better you know the correspondent, the more informal you may be. By the time you have written several times and perhaps talked on the telephone with the person, you will probably be on a first-name basis.

In the past, salutations of Gentlemen, Sirs, and Madam were not only acceptable but widely used. These terms are used less today, even when a letter is addressed to a company. Instead a writer, unaware of an individual's name, may address a job title or use a subject line:

Purchasing Agent	Twin Cities Software, Inc.
Kennan Paper Company	14162 Perimeter Road
Hoffman, NC 28347	Groton, VT 05046
Dear Agent:	SUBJECT: Cash Discounts

The following are examples of plural salutations:

▌ Dear Mr. Dooley and Mr. Paterno
or
Dear Messrs. Dooley and Paterno

▌ Dear Mrs. Ross and Mrs. Warwick
or
Dear Mmes. Ross and Warwick

▌ Dear Ms. Landers and Ms. Manners
or
Dear Mses. Landers and Manners

When little is known about the intended recipient, determining an appropriate salutation can be troublesome. Salutations to women, to mixed-sex groups, or to organizations present special challenges. These challenges are best met by learning as much as possible about the correspondent. When you are responding to a letter, the correspondent's signature block should be your guide.

Mistaking the sex of the correspondent is sometimes possible. Names such as Jerry, Terry, Stacy, and Kelly are used interchangeably. The problem is even more widespread in England, where the bearers of names such as Leslie, Sydney, and Marion may be either male or female. Greeting a male with "Dear Ms." or a female with "Dear Mr." does little for the goodwill that letter writers strive to achieve. If you are uncertain as to an appropriate salutation, you may omit the salutation by following the simplified letter format described later in this chapter.

A letter writer may choose between open and mixed punctuation.

A business letter writer has the choice of two styles of punctuating the salutation and the close of a letter. Open punctuation omits punctuation following the salutation and the close. Mixed punctuation uses a colon following the salutation and a comma following the close.

Open:	Dear Sir	Sincerely
Mixed:	Dear Ms. Ladd:	Cordially,

A recipient's title should be used in the salutation (Dear Captain Watson). Deciding how to address high-level officials in government or dignitaries in the church is sometimes difficult. Table 4.2 illustrates appropriate forms of address and salutation for some of them.

Some writers use what we call a **salutopening** instead of a traditional salutation. A salutopening presents the first few words of the opening paragraph and the reader's name in place of the salutation.

Yes, Ms. Jefferson:

You are right to expect extended service . . .

The sentence continues into the letter body, which is a double space below the name line.

Salutopenings eliminate the artificiality of greeting strangers as "Dear." Conventional salutations, however, continue to be used much more frequently than salutopenings.

Attention Line

The **attention line** indicates the specific person who should read the letter. The letter is not addressed to that person, however, nor is that person named in the salutation. In fact, the attention line and the salutation are rarely used simultaneously. Either may be used with or without a subject line.

Allied Lenses, Inc.
1418 Industrial Drive
Carbondale, IL 62901

Attention: Mr. Robert Jenkins

Subject: Insurance plans for lenses

Some writers use an attention line when they know the receiver's name but do not know the receiver's sex. For example:

Quality Printing Co.
124 East Frontage
Lobo, TX 79855

Attention: W. C. Brown

The attention line is placed below the inside address of the receiver. A salutation, if also used, is below the attention line.

The Body

The main message of a letter is contained in the body. The body should answer all significant questions but should be no longer than necessary. Many writers believe they are obligated to fill an entire sheet even when a shorter message would do.

Use short paragraphs. They make it easy for a reader to scan a letter and identify important points. Some authorities consider an average of four to six lines per paragraph to be reasonable.

TABLE 4.2 ▪ *Forms of Address*

Addressee	Address (envelope and letter)	Salutation
U.S. Officials		
The President	The President The White House Washington, DC 20500	Dear Mr. (or Madam) President
The Vice President	The Vice President United States Senate Washington, DC 20510	Dear Mr. (or Madam) Vice President
Senator	The Honorable (full name) United States Senate Washington, DC 20510	Dear Senator (surname)
Representative	The Honorable (full name) House of Representatives Washington, DC 20515	Dear Mr. (or Madam) (surname)
Canadian Officials		
Member of House of Commons	Mr., Ms., Miss, or Mrs. (full name), M. P. House of Commons	*Formal:* Dear Sir (or Madam) *Informal:* Dear Mr., Ms., Miss, or Mrs. (surname)
Canadian Minister	Mr., Ms., Miss, or Mrs. (full name) Canadian Minister to (city or country)	*Formal:* Sir: (Madam:) *Informal:* Dear Mr., Ms., Miss, or Mrs. (surname)
Members of Provincial Governments	Mr., Ms., Miss, or Mrs. (full name), M.L.A. Member of the Legislative Assembly (name) Building (city, province)	*Formal:* Dear Sir (or Madam) *Informal:* Dear Mr., Ms., Miss, or Mrs. (surname)
Mayor	His or Her Worship (full name) City Hall (city, province)	Dear Sir (or Madam)
Religious Leaders		
Minister, Pastor, or Rector	The Reverend (full name) (title, name of church) (local address)	Dear Mr., Ms., Miss, or Mrs. (surname)
Rabbi	Rabbi (full name) (local address)	Dear Rabbi (surname)

The body begins a double space below the salutation or attention line. Use a single space within paragraphs and double space between paragraphs.

Addressee	Address (envelope and letter)	Salutation
Catholic Bishop	The Most Reverend (full name) Bishop of (diocese) (local address)	*Formal:* Your Excellency *Informal:* Dear Bishop (surname)
Catholic Priest	The Reverend (full name), (initials of order, if any) (local address)	*Formal:* Reverend Sir *Informal:* Dear Father (surname)
Protestant Episcopal Bishop	The Right Reverend (full name) Bishop of (name) (local address)	*Formal:* Right Reverend Sir (or Madam) *Informal:* Dear Bishop (surname)
Protestant Episcopal Dean	The Very Reverend (full name) Dean of (church) (local address)	*Formal:* Very Reverend Sir (or Madam) *Informal:* Dear Dean (surname)
Anglican Archbishop	The Most Reverend Archbishop of (archdiocese) (local address)	*Formal:* Most Reverend (full name) *Informal:* Dear Archbishop
Anglican Bishop	The Right Reverend (full name) Bishop of (name) (local address)	*Formal:* Right Reverend Sir *Informal:* Dear Bishop
Anglican Canon	The Reverend Canon (full name) (local address)	*Formal:* Reverend Sir *Informal:* Dear Canon
Methodist Bishop	The Reverend (full name) (local address)	*Formal:* Reverend Sir *Informal:* Dear Bishop (surname)
Miscellaneous		
President of University or College	Dr., Mr., Ms., Mrs., or Miss (full name) President, (name of institution) (local address)	Dear Dr. or President (surname)
Dean of College or School	Dean (full name) School of (name) (name of institution) (local address)	Dear Dean (surname)
Professor	Professor (full name) Department of (name) (name of institution) (local address)	Dear Professor (surname)

The Close

The close should match the salutation in formality or informality. An exception is form letters, especially sales messages, which frequently do not match salutations and closes. For example, one may contain the salutation Dear Resident and close with Sincerely.

The close and the salutation should be of equal formality.

The words most commonly used in closing letters are truly, sincerely, respectfully, and cordially. Each may be used with *yours* and sometimes with *very.* Some common and appropriate closes are:

BOXED IN *AN ETHICAL DILEMMA*

In the ten years that Bob Harmon has owned and operated Bob's Quality Hardware, he has attracted a loyal clientele. His customers have come to trust the quality and the reasonable prices available at Bob's store, which is one of approximately 700 in a national franchise operation.

The franchisor recently began a nationwide sweepstakes contest with a grand prize of an expensive luxury automobile. All customers on the franchisees' mailing lists were sent cards with identification numbers. To learn if they have won they can compare the number with the winning number posted in each participating store. No purchase is necessary.

The letters sent to Bob's customers along with the identification numbers seem to suggest that this is a local contest and that the winner will come from Bob's clientele. For example, the statement, "As a Quality Hardware customer, you have an excellent chance of winning a $30,000 luxury automobile," fails to indicate that the contest is actually national in scope, and that the winner could come from any one of the many different locations. At the bottom of the identification-number card is a statement that the odds against winning the prize are approximately 1,000,000 to 1, but the print is so small that Bob thinks that most readers would not notice it.

Bob complained to the franchisor and was told that he did not have to participate if he did not want to. If he chooses not to participate, however, he will have to direct customers to the nearest participating Quality store, which is 30 miles away.

Bob feels boxed in. He doesn't like the idea of having to send his participating customers to a competitor nor does he want to endanger the trust he has worked so hard to develop. What would you do?

- Yours truly
- Cordially
- Sincerely yours
- Sincerely
- Respectfully
- Respectfully yours

A double space separates the close from the last line of the letter body.

Signature Block

The writer's name and job title comprise the signature block.

The **signature block** consists of the writer's name and job title. The job title can be typed on the same line as the name if both are short. Otherwise it is typed directly below. In some organizations, the name of the company is also included in the signature block. This is to clarify the company's legal responsibility for the letter. It is no longer considered necessary, and the practice is diminishing.

Through the signature block, correspondents may indicate how they prefer to be addressed:

Sincerely   Yours truly

PHOENIX INDUSTRIES
                             Wanda L. Sinclair, Editor

Kenneth E. Booth
Director of Public Relations

The signature block is separated from the close by four lines of space. If the company name is included, however, it is separated from the close by only two lines, and the four lines of space follow.

ADDITIONAL PARTS OF A BUSINESS LETTER

The standard parts just described are routinely found in business letters. You should also be familiar with some additional parts that you may need to use on occasion.

Subject Line

The subject line alerts the reader to what the message is about. Subject lines assist in the proper filing of correspondence as well as in its transfer to an appropriate recipient. Regular use of subject lines enhances efficiency and paper management. The subject line is placed two lines below the salutation either along the left margin, indented the same as paragraphs, or centered on the page.

Reference Initials, Enclosures, and Copies

The sender's initials in unspaced capital letters precede the typist's initials, which are lowercase. A colon, dash, or diagonal separates the two sets of initials. The sender's initials are often omitted, however, because the name is typed in the signature block. Reference initials appear at the left margin a double line space below the last line of the signature block.

If something in addition to the letter is included in the envelope, an enclosure notation should be made one or two line spaces below the reference initials. The word enclosure may be spelled out or abbreviated *Encl.* or *Enc.* If more than one enclosure is sent, the number should be indicated. Enclosures may be listed although this is not required.

If someone other than the intended receiver will be sent a copy of a letter, that person should be identified at the very end of the letter. List the names of those who are to receive copies after the single letter *c*. This notation refers to copies made by any means such as carbon or photocopies.

Persons who will be sent a copy of the letter should be identified.

JTD:nvp   pnp

Enclosures 3   Enclosures: 1. Brochure
                                          2. Registration Form

c: Mr. Jenkins
   Ms. Phillips   c: B. Kelly

Blind copies are copies of which the addressee is unaware.

Copies of letters may be sent out without the receiver or addressee being made aware that this is being done. Such copies are called **blind copies** and noted with *bc*. This notation is typed on the copies but not on the original and appears directly below the usual copy notation.

Information about copies is typed at the very end of the letter and appears one or two spaces below the reference initials, enclosure notation, or signature block.

Postscripts

A postscript conveys thoughts added to a letter after it has been completed. If a message is planned and well-organized, a postscript would not be necessary. Postscripts are not often used today; when used, they are usually for emphasis. A postscript is often preceded by "P.S.," but this is not necessary. A postscript should appear at the bottom of the letter, one or two spaces below the last line typed on the page.

Second-Page Headings

Subsequent pages of a letter should be headed by the receiver's name, page number, and date.

When a letter continues beyond one page, each subsequent page should be headed by the receiver's name, page number, and date. The first page may be typed on letterhead stationery, but subsequent pages should be on plain paper.

Two or more lines of the body must be carried over to warrant a second page; never begin a second page solely for the signature block. These second-page headings are commonly used:

Wilcox Tool Company   -2-   May 14, 1991

Mr. Frank Settles, July 31, 1991, page 2

Ms. Tanya Berancourt
March 15, 1991
Page 2

The date that appears in the heading of the second and subsequent pages should be the same as the date on the first page. This is true even though subsequent pages may be typed on a different date from the first page.

Second-page headings should be typed one or two inches from the top of the page. The body of the letter should resume four spaces below the heading.

LETTER FORMATS

By varying margin sizes on the basis of message length the writer is able to enhance appearance.

Planning is necessary so that letters will appear attractive and organized. An unattractive or disorganized appearance is likely to detract from the message itself. The placement of the letter on the page is an important determinant of appearance.

A letter that is balanced on the page is more attractive than one that is not. By surrounding your message with ample margins you can achieve a framing effect. Side margins are commonly 1½ inches, and top and bottom margins are approximately 2 inches. By varying the top and side margins on the basis of the message length, you can produce a letter with eye appeal. Space may be varied above and below the date; the spacing between other letter parts is constant.

Companies differ in the format of letters. In general, however, writers single-space within the parts of a letter and double-space between the parts. Some organizations provide employees with a manual or style sheet prescribing a certain format. The writer has four main formats from which to choose: full-block, modified-block, traditional (a modification of full-block), and simplified.

In the **full-block format**, every line begins at the left margin including the date, close, and signature block. Because of the focus on the left margin, a typist need not make many adjustments on the typewriter; thus it is fast. Critics of this format contend that it results in an unbalanced, left-leaning appearance. The full block format is shown in Figure 4.1 on page 102.

The full-block format contributes to fast typing.

In the **modified-block format**, the date begins at the center of the page. The close and the signature block are normally aligned with the date. This format is shown in Figure 4.2 on pages 103–104.

In the **traditional format**, each paragraph is indented five spaces. Except for that, traditional is identical to modified-block. They are the most popular formats both in the United States and abroad. The traditional format is shown in Figure 4.3 on page 105.

The traditional format is characterized by indented paragraphs.

In the **simplified format**, developed by the Administrative Management Society, neither a salutation nor a close is used.[3] A subject line replaces the salutation. As in the full-block format, all lines begin at the left margin. The simplified format is becoming increasingly popular because it contributes to greater keyboarding efficiency. The simplified format is shown in Figure 4.4 on page 106.

The simplified format is becoming increasingly popular.

Most of the business letters you will send or receive use one of the four formats just discussed. Writers will sometimes devise special formats to get the reader's attention by using devices such as unusual margins, color, and boxes that enclose important information. Sales letters frequently have unusual formats, but even they are comprised of the standard parts.

Special letter formats are sometimes devised to attract the reader's attention.

The parts of a letter and appropriate spacing are illustrated in Figure 4.5 on page 107.

---

[3] *The Simplified Letter*, a brochure published by the Administrative Management Society, Willow Grove, Pa.

FIGURE 4.1   ∎   *Full-Block Format*

INTERNATIONAL PUBLISHING COMPANY
Mercantile Building, Suite 20
Miami, FL 33101

January 5, 1991

Professor Laurence Gray
Mobile Technological College
Post Office Box 1412
Mobile, AL 36601

Dear Professor Gray:

All lines begin at the left margin.

As a prominent educator in the field of business communication, you have corrected the writing faults of numerous students of business administration. Because you are well aware of current trends in business communication, would you please share some of your thoughts with us at International?

The full-block format facilitates fast typing.

Over the years, surveys have shown a wide variety of writing problems experienced by students. What are the most common problems that your students display in the writing they do for you? As a professor, how do you help your students overcome these problems? Lastly, what do you especially look for when selecting a text on business communication?

A major complaint is that the full-block format looks unbalanced.

By spending a few minutes writing a one-page response to these questions, you will help us produce textbooks that directly meet your needs. As a token of our appreciation, we will be pleased to send you a complimentary prepublication copy of the <u>International Directory of Business Communicators.</u>

By responding today, you will benefit from the <u>Directory</u> within ten days.

Sincerely,

Beverly A. Dolan

(Ms.) Beverly A. Dolan
Customer Service Agent

jo

FIGURE 4.2 ▪ *Modified-Block Format*

MOBILE TECHNOLOGICAL COLLEGE
Post Office Box 1412
Mobile, AL 36601

January 8, 1991 ———————————— *Date begins at*
center of page.

International Publishing Company
Mercantile Building, Suite 20
Miami, FL 33101

Attention: Beverly A. Dolan

During my career as a business communication educator I have
become aware of certain recurring problems that students experience
in their business writing. I am pleased to be asked to share my
thoughts on this subject.

Students are never taught to recognize good writing, and this ——————— *Although not*
constitutes a major problem. While they may learn some basic   *indented here,*
principles of effective communication, they complete their   *paragraphs may*
education still unaware of the characteristics of good writing.   *be indented in*
                                                                     modified-block
                                                                     format.

It seems to me that another problem lies in the unrealistic
expectations so many students possess. Too many foresee their
future business roles as positions of authority, in which someone
else will be responsible for correcting their writing faults. Such
unrealistic expectations result in some students not taking their
business communication course as seriously as they should.

I try to correct these and other such problems by bringing into ——————— *Modified-block*
the classroom many samples of good writing, without limiting it   *format is more*
to business writing. In the process, I point out the universal   *balanced than*
characteristics of superior writing.   *full-block.*

The best way to combat unrealistic expectations seems to be to use
many realistic case studies and, when possible, to bring in former
students to discuss their experiences involving business communication. It has been my experience that former students are almost
always much more appreciative of their communication training than
is the current crop of students.

(Continued)

FIGURE 4.2 ▪ *Continued*

International Publishing Company
January 8, 1991
Page 2

When I select a business communication textbook, I look for one
that presents a balance of theory and practical information in a
readable fashion. Interesting anecdotes, believable problems, and
margin notes also contribute much to student learning. Regardless of
the textbook used, I always recommend The Elements of Style by
William Strunk, Jr. and E. B. White as a supplement.

I hope that you find my comments helpful, and I look forward to
receiving the Directory.

Cordially,

Laurence Gray

Laurence Gray
Professor of Business

*Close and signature
block begin at
center of page.*

FIGURE 4.3 ▪ *Traditional Format*

1628 Ludington Street
Mobile, AL 36603
January 14, 1991

Ms. Beverly A. Dolan
International Publishing Company
Mercantile Building, Suite 20
Miami, FL 33101

Dear Ms. Dolan:

    Several days ago in class, Professor Gray told us of your
interest in business communication problems. He described the way
in which he had responded to your letter, and because I do not
agree with what he told you, I am presenting my own point of view.

    It seems to me that most of what we learn in business
communication class is useless. When I graduate from college, I
don't plan to spend my time organizing and writing letters and
reports. That's what secretaries are for. The way I see it, I'll
dictate the main ideas and my secretary will do the rest.

    Professor Gray considers spelling to be a major problem, but
I do not see it that way. I have lost plenty of points in my
business communication assignments because of misspelled words. He
shouldn't take off points for spelling because, after graduation,
I'll make sure that I have a secretary who is a good speller.

    Things like communication principles, neatness, and correct
spelling are truly irrelevant for me. I intend to deal with
important activities such as business strategy and long-range
planning. In case you're curious, I have already accepted a job
offer and will begin work in early June for Multinational
Industries.

    I wrote this letter so that you would get a student's point
of view. Please consider it as you plan your textbooks. I am
sending copies of this letter to the officers of Multinational.

            Sincerely yours,

            Stanley H. Sedgwick

            Stanley H. Sedgwick

cc: Buckminster Sedgwick
     Peter Sedgwick
     Suzanne Sedgwick

Each paragraph is indented five spaces.

Except for indenting paragraphs, this is like the modified-block format.

FIGURE 4.4   ∎ *Simplified Format*

PRO-AM SPORTSWEAR • *Ivy, VA 22945*

January 16, 1991

Jerry Dolan
Customer Service Agent
International Publishing Company
Mercantile Building, Suite 20
Miami, FL 33101

PROBLEMS IN BUSINESS COMMUNICATION

The impact of communication on any business organization is
indisputable, so it was with great interest that I received your
recent letter. I am glad to have the opportunity to express some
of my thoughts on the subject.

The skills and qualities emphasized in business communication
courses are the skills and qualities in shortest supply in the
current work force. It is common for people who hold degrees,
whether associate, bachelor's, or master's degrees, to have
severe difficulties in communicating.

Students who are unable to make presentations or conduct meetings
are receiving degrees in business. It is important that business
communication courses develop these abilities that are so crucial
to a person's success in business.

The communication course I took as an undergraduate contributed
more to my own success than did any other single course. To this
day, I continue to refer to the textbook used in that course. Over
the years I have participated in training programs on communication
to reinforce those principles learned so long ago.

I have enclosed two brochures we use to communicate our fringe
benefits to our employees. What do you think of the brochures?

Harrison Burke

HARRISON BURKE
President

kt
Enclosures 2

A subject line is used instead of a salutation.

All lines begin at the left margin.

Simplified format makes typing efficient.

No complimentary close is used.

FIGURE 4.5 ▪ *Spacing Layout*

RELIABLE TRUCKING, INC. —————————————————— *Letterhead*
4100 Madison Road   Cincinnati, OH 45227

February 2, 1991 ——————————————————————— *Date*

Precision Plastic Parts ——————————————————— *Receiver's address*
P.O. Box 1542
Hammond, LA 70402

Attention: Traffic Manager ——————————————— *Attention line*

Dear Manager: ————————————————————————— *Salutation*

REVISED PICKUP SCHEDULE ——————————————————— *Subject line*

Your recent letter was forwarded to me by Brenda Bishop, Vice
President of Operations. Because your continued satisfaction is
important to us, we intend to accommodate your need for a different
daily pickup schedule for the spring and summer months.

On February 18 and 19 our customer service agent, Carmella Bryant, ————— *Body*
will be in the Hammond area. One week before that she will phone
you to arrange a specific time to meet with you.

We appreciate your contacting us well in advance of the time when
your pickup needs will change. Carmella will be able to offer
several different pickup and delivery options, one of which is sure
to be appropriate.

I have enclosed a brochure describing some additional services we
will soon introduce in the Hammond region. Please contact me if I
may be of further service.

Sincerely, ——————————————————————————————— *Close*

Shane R. Ellington

Shane R. Ellington ———————————————————————— *Signature block*
Operations Supervisor

af —— *Reference initial*

Enc. ——————————————————————————————————————— *Enclosure*

cc: B. Bishop ————————————————————————————— *Copies*
     C. Bryant

SUMMARY

The appearance of a letter can enhance or detract from the image of the
organization or individual that sends it. Such factors as stationery and
letterhead are a significant part of the visual dimension.

The eight standard parts of the business letter are the return address,
date, inside address of receiver, salutation, attention line, body, close, and
signature block. Each part has a definite and important function.

Proper spacing adds to the appearance of a letter. By adjusting the vertical space above and below the date, a typist can center the letter on the page and thereby make it more attractive. Ordinarily the body is single-spaced within paragraphs and double-spaced between paragraphs.

The four main letter formats are full-block, modified-block, traditional, and simplified. Each possesses distinct characteristics and conveys a definite image. Occasionally writers devise special formats, especially in sales letters, to attract attention.

Key Terms

- letterhead
- salutation
- salutopening
- full-block format
- modified-block format

- attention line
- signature block
- blind copy
- traditional format
- simplified format

Review Questions

1. What are the most visible characteristics of business stationery?
2. What information is usually contained in a letterhead?
3. How must letter writers compensate for the absence of letterhead stationery?
4. How can writers achieve a framing effect in their letters?
5. What are the eight basic parts of business letters?
6. Where is the writer allowed some flexibility in spacing between letter parts to adjust the length of the letter?
7. For what reasons might a writer use a subject line?
8. What four words are most commonly used in closing letters?
9. What are the differences among the four main letter formats?
10. What is a blind copy? What is its purpose?

Exercises

1. Locate Dun & Bradstreet's *Principal International Businesses* in your library.
   a. Using the white section, choose four companies from four different foreign countries. Write the mailing address of each.
   b. Using the yellow section, choose four companies, each classified by a different SIC (standard industrial code) number and write the mailing address of each. Also, separate from the addresses, indicate the SIC index of each and what it signifies. (The SIC number identifies the function and product or service associated with a particular company.)

2. Bring in copies of two mass-produced letters that you or your parents received. The letters may be of any type — sales, sweepstakes, fund-raising, and so on. Using Figure 4.5 as a model, identify the various parts of the letters.

3. As a class project, divide into small groups and calculate the total number of different salutations in the letters in Exercise 2. Which salutation was used most frequently? Which was used least frequently?

4. Share with the class a copy of a letter that you think has eye appeal. Identify the characteristics that you think make it attractive.

5. Interview one or more of the following about the letter format that they prefer. Find out why it is preferred and write a brief analysis of what you learned from your interviews.
   a. An office manager.
   b. The supervisor of a typing pool.
   c. A typing teacher

6. Using *America's Corporate Families and International Affiliates*, a common library reference book, identify a U.S. company with one or more subsidiaries. Write the mailing addresses of the parent company and of its subsidiaries.

7. Interview someone who has worked abroad for a multinational company. Determine the ways business communication in a foreign culture differs from business communication as practiced here.

The Dilemma of Length versus Format | CASE

Richard Pompian, University of Texas

Mark Rothmark is a recent college graduate who is employed as a personnel consultant by a management consulting firm. The personnel director at Smith & Smith Mfg. Co. asked the consulting firm for a study of employees' information needs, and Mark was assigned to the project. The personnel director believed that company employees were spending more time finding out the latest gossip about each other than working.

Mark knew that his supervisor, son of the owner of the consulting firm, liked one-page letters and memoranda. Mark is generally a pretty good writer. Although he had a lot of information to convey about the project, he tried to put everything in a one-page letter even though, in this instance, he was not instructed to do so. He was not able to.

Mark showed the letter to his boss before sending it. The boss called it "terrible, very poorly written" and told Mark to redo it. Mark is trying to figure out what to do because he thinks the writing is well organized and clear. He realizes, however, that the problem may be with the format.

Case Question

1. What specifically could be done to make the letter in Figure 4A more attractive and inviting to read? Give at least six suggestions. Where and how should your suggestions be implemented?

FIGURE 4A ▪ *Letter from Mark Rothmark, Consultant*

GANDLOPE CONSULTANTS / P.O. Box 1144 / Hinsdale, IL 60521

June 25, 1991

Ms. C. M. Robins
Director of Personnel
Smith & Smith Mfg. Co.
2000 Smith Bros. Road
Mildred, MI 47047

Dear Ms. Robins:

This is in response to your April 30 request for a study to determine employee information needs. We find that your employees' high morale and efficiency have partially been lost as a result of the many personnel transfers occurring recently. We therefore recommend that a company newspaper be established as soon as possible. As you know, many of your employees have been transferred to other plants or departments because the company has grown so much and so quickly over the past year. This growth was due in part to the high morale of the employees, who had formed tightly knit and efficient work units. The many transfers have caused those efficient work units to break up, in turn causing a number of problems for the company. Morale has declined somewhat as a result of the dissolution of the "family structure" that was created. Employees have been accusing the management of becoming "cold and impersonal" as a result of the breakups. Declining morale has led to declining production. The decline in production has been aggravated because employees frequently call or visit ex-members of the group on company time. The entire situation sets a poor example for newly hired workers, who see the workplace as a "goof-off" opportunity (which will further hurt production). Means must be found to reestablish employee morale, eliminate or reduce time away from the workplace, improve current production, and set an appropriate example for new employees. Although nothing short of a full-scale employee relations program can be expected to meet your needs fully, I am proposing a company newspaper as part of the program, one that can be implemented very quickly.

I believe that the newspaper will help combat many of the problems indicated above. In order to help solve your current problems and meet the needs outlined above, the company newspaper should help reestablish the "family atmosphere" that led to your early success; reestablish respect for management by showing that

(Continued)

CASE | *But We Already Paid the Bill*

David B. Parsons, Lakehead University, Thunder Bay, Ontario, Canada

Angela and Don Johnson had always wanted to start an educational library for their children. When Hawkeye Publishing Company advertised a series of nature books, the Johnsons decided to subscribe. Three weeks later, a book on insects

FIGURE 4A ▪ *Continued*

```
        Smith & Smith Mfg. Co.
        June 25, 1991
        Page 2


        management still cares about the employee; provide sufficient news
        about transferred employees so that remaining employees do not
        spend so much time inquiring about or making contact with those
        transferred; and through all of the above, convince new employees
        to take their work seriously.  If you can accomplish those four
        objectives, you should be on your way to increased productivity.
        The newspaper could be a 17" x 11" sheet folded to 8-1/2", printed
        on both sides in one or two colors.  Editorially, I recommend that
        the newspaper focus on news and events directly related to the
        employees' interests.  Management notices and general news about
        the company should be included, but the paper must not be allowed
        to become a "puff sheet" for management. Instead, it must be "of,
        by, and for the employees" in order for it to accomplish its
        objectives.

             The paper must be published frequently in order for it to
        become part of the work environment.  I recommend that it be
        published once a week if possible, and no less than twice monthly.
        If it cannot be published at least twice monthly, I withdraw my
        recommendation, for the paper will contain "stale news" and not
        have the intended effect.  A survey of employees indicates that
        they would like to see the following items: employee transfers,
        employee promotions, personal and family news, community announce-
        ments, company news, and "getting ahead" articles.  I will furnish
        additional information if you are interested in following up.

        Sincerely,
```

Mark R. Rothmark

```
        Mark R. Rothmark, Consultant

        c: M. Gandlope
```

*P.S. I will call you next Thursday
about this matter.*

arrived. The Johnsons thoroughly enjoyed the book, which was filled with fascinating information such as why fireflies glow and beautiful pictures of each insect.

The Johnsons immediately sent Hawkeye a check for $16.95, on which they recorded their account number. At the end of the month, they received the cancelled check from their bank as proof of payment. At the same time, they also received another bill for the same book and a gentle reminder to pay the overdue account. Angela Johnson wrote Hawkeye a letter explaining that they had paid the bill, and she enclosed a photocopy of the cancelled check.

One month later, the Johnsons received another bill and another collection letter. One sentence in the letter infuriated the Johnsons: "*Should we not hear from you within two weeks, we will have no recourse but to take the necessary action to collect this delinquent account.*"

Considering that her previous letter and photocopy of the cancelled check had not settled the matter, Angela Johnson decided to write two separate letters, one to the Subscriber Service Department and one to the Credit Department. The only reply she received was another collection letter and bill. At this point, Angela didn't know what step to take to solve her problem.

Case Questions

1. Why do such communication problems exist?

2. Write a letter to the Subscriber Service Department.

3. Write a letter to the Credit Department.

4. How important is the need to analyze the audience in each situation?

5. What do you think Angela's next move should be?

Good-News and Neutral Letters

Once referred to as "the people's literature," personal letters appear to be a dying form. In 1989 North Americans sent more than 164 billion pieces of mail through the U.S. Postal Service, but only six percent were personal. A sizable portion of the six percent was greeting cards with printed messages sent by people unable or unwilling to write their own.

The exchange of personal letters was once considered an enjoyable experience for writer and recipient alike. Garrison Keillor has described the joy of receiving a letter, ". . . a sweet gift — a piece of handmade writing, in an envelope that is not a bill, sitting in our friend's path when she trudges home from a long day spent among wahoos and savages, a day our words will help repair."[1]

Many famous Americans have taken their letter writing seriously. John Steinbeck often wrote six or seven letters in the morning as a warm-up exercise for his work, which resulted in 29 books. H.L. Mencken disliked the telephone intensely and wrote letters instead, among them more than 700 to the woman who eventually became his wife. Edith Wharton wrote more than 40 books and thousands of letters; more than 4,000 are known to exist. Former president Ronald Reagan, a constant writer of letters, signs himself "Dutch" to his closest friends.[2]

Learning Objectives

1 To recognize the relationship between planning and effective communication.

2 To learn the steps in the planning process.

3 To recognize the importance of revising writing.

4 To identify the characteristics of good-news and neutral letters and when each is appropriate.

5 To recognize the strategic decisions that must be made in planning good-news and neutral messages.

6 To make effective requests by letter.

7 To develop appropriate written responses to requests.

8 To identify the advantages and disadvantages of form letters and when they are appropriate.

[1]Keith Graham, "Is Writing on the Wall for the Personal Letter?" *Atlanta Constitution*, August 23, 1989, B4.

[2]Graham, "Is Writing on the Wall?" B1.

These writers of personal letters represent another era and reflect a more relaxed lifestyle. The custom of exchanging letters with friends is not likely to revive. The advent of electronic communication has caused a decline in the use of letters for business purposes also. However, letters will continue to be an important vehicle for business messages.

THE IMPORTANCE OF APPROPRIATE LETTERS

The most frequent contact many people have with certain business organizations is through the written word. Printed advertisements and, perhaps, correspondence constitute whatever link is formed between the public and the organization. Letters that are readable and thorough contribute to building and maintaining good will. Letters that are vague and poorly organized have the opposite effect. Letter by letter, a company's written communication influences public perception of the company.

A company's written communication influences public perception of the company.

To illustrate, when Robert Hill was no longer able to find air filters for his 20-year-old mower, he wrote to the manufacturer, who replied with the letter in Figure 5.1. Robert did not like the letter for several reasons. The suggestion for finding some air filters was pretty well buried. Besides, having owned a Kleenkutter for 20 years, he hardly had to be sold on the product. Robert said to his wife, "They must think I'm an idiot, telling me to read the owner's manual. In 20 years of operating this mower I've practically memorized it." Robert did not like the tone of the letter and resented that the writer ignored his status as a long-time satisfied user.

We seldom receive a letter that has no effect on us: some letters are pleasing; others are displeasing. Robert was definitely displeased. Sometimes we are impressed with the cleverness of a letter we receive; we marvel at the writer's ability to select just the right word. Sometimes we are so aware of the writer's flair that we may remember a certain phrase but forget the purpose of the letter. At other times a letter may be so dull that we remember nothing about it at all. We may even throw it away after reading the first line.

Writing letters that work is not easy, but the process can be made easier through a systematic approach. This chapter, building on the basic techniques presented in Chapter 3, provides a systematic approach to writing good-news and neutral letters of various kinds.

THE PLANNING PROCESS

Planning provides focus to a message.

Sometimes referred to as prewriting, planning contributes significantly to a message that is clearly written and easily understood. Written messages that were not planned are identifiable by their lack of clear focus.

FIGURE 5.1 ▪ *An Inappropriate Letter*

STELLAR LAWN PRODUCTS, INC.
645 High Street
Troy, MI 48007

March 1, 1991

Mr. Robert Hill
1215 Oakdale Drive
Trenton, NJ 08600

Dear Mr. Hill:

We are pleased to learn of your satisfaction with the Q-11
Kleenkutter. Although our products may cost a little more than
the products of some of our competitors, they are designed to last
longer and perform better.

> *Opening ignores the customer's complaint.*

Since the Q-11 was finely tuned at the factory, it should
require very little in the way of maintenance. When servicing is
required, however, one must be sure to follow all of the instructions provided on pages 12-19 of the owner's manual. For the best
in servicing and repair, it is advisable that you deal with a
registered company technician.

> *The company's self-interest is emphasized in trying to convince the customer to use registered technicians.*

Since the Q-11 went out of production 15 years ago, it has
become difficult to find some of the parts for it, but air filters
designed for the Q-13 or Q-14 are readily available and may be
adapted to the Q-11. Any one of our registered technicians is
able to do this, and the cost would be moderate.

> *The main message is finally stated.*

The next time you visit a Kleenkutter dealer, why not inspect
the Q-14, our newest and most efficient mower? You'll find that
it has the same basic design as the Q-11 with some advanced
features intended to simplify its operation.

> *Sales promotion is unlikely to influence an already frustrated customer.*

Yours truly,

William W. Dunbar

William W. Dunbar
Customer Service

Managers sometimes claim not to have enough time to plan their written messages. Careful planning will actually result in a savings of time, however, both for the sender and for the receiver. To illustrate, Brenda Robb, as a part of her internship with a large midwestern bank, was assigned to a project measuring the volume of bank correspondence that required additional follow-up messages. She learned that written follow-up was necessary for nearly ten percent of the letters sent by the bank. She also discovered that writers who wrote without planning were much more likely to send follow-up letters. They were needed either to explain the initial message or to provide information that should have been included originally.

The **planning** process involves these four steps: (1) Determine the objectives. (2) Consider the audience. (3) Choose the ideas to include. (4) Select the appropriate medium.

Determining the Objectives

Unless a message has an obvious purpose, it is unlikely to elicit the response sought by the writer. Some messages, such as sales letters, seek overt responses. Most sales letters seek to get the reader to purchase the good or service, or at least to request a brochure on the item that is being offered. Other messages seek covert responses, such as a changed attitude toward the notion of leasing rather than purchasing an automobile. Whether the desired response is covert or overt, however, the objective must be clear in the writer's mind if it is to be transferred to the mind of the reader.

Considering the Audience

The more that you, the writer, know about your readers, the more able you will be to frame your message to elicit the desired response. Audience characteristics that require careful analysis include expertise, hierarchical position, age, educational level, occupation, and attitudes.

Audience Expertise

How much do the various receivers know about the topic? When writer and reader(s) possess the same degree of expertise, problems in achieving understanding should be minimal. When the audience is large and the range of expertise is broad, multiple messages may be the most appropriate approach, because a single message is unlikely to appeal to a widely diverse group of readers.

Hierarchical Position

Is your written message being directed at a subordinate or a superior? If a subordinate, will that individual have any choice about accepting the message? If a superior, how familiar is the superior with you and your work? If you do not already have credibility in the eyes of the superior, you must devote some effort to creating it.

Audience Age

Writers frequently reveal their age by the examples and illustrations they use in their communication. Effective business communicators are careful to select examples and illustrations on the basis of the age of the intended receivers. Professors who fail to update their notes ignore the need to appeal to the interests of their receivers and persist in using examples that hold little meaning for students. What does the Bay of Pigs mean to you?

How about the War on Poverty? Such topics, meaningful and interesting to the middle-aged professor, are ancient history to the average college student.

Educational Level

Effective communicators may acknowledge the educational level of their audience, but they need not communicate on that same level. The writer or speaker who is easily understood is most likely to get a quick and favorable response. As discussed in Chapter 3, mathematical formulas are available for determining the readability level of written material.

Occupation

Language and occupation influence each other. For that reason a knowledge of the occupation(s) represented in any group of listeners or readers will help you tailor your message to them. As long as you limit the use of jargon to audiences that share the same occupation, the practice is beneficial to all concerned.

Audience Attitudes

The five audience characteristics just discussed will influence the attitudes that the audience will hold toward you and your message. Is the overall attitude positive, negative or neutral? If your message is to be appropriate, you must consider the attitudes of the receiver when drafting your message. The frustration experienced by employees who claim that nobody ever listens to them results to some extent from unawareness of audience attitudes on the part of management.

Choosing the Ideas to Include

Novice writers sometimes try to create a polished and finished message at the start. Resist this urge and concentrate on generating as many ideas as possible on the subject. Only then should you edit the list to include the most important ideas based on objectives and audience.

Pam MacDonald, for example, was asked by the director of human resources to report on whether their bank should become involved in providing day care for the children of employees. Having already received a cost study, he wanted Pam to research the nonmonetary aspects. She generated the following ideas:

- Effect on maternity leaves
- Turnover
- Morale
- Productivity
- Recruitment
- Development of children
- Image of the bank

The report she eventually wrote centered on these ideas.

Selecting the Appropriate Channel and Medium

Business communicators have two basic channels and a wide variety of media from which to choose when determining how to convey a message. Messages may be either written or oral. Communication should be in writing when any of the following circumstances is important:

- Information is detailed and complex.
- The audience is geographically dispersed.
- A permanent record is important.
- Immediate feedback is not necessary.

Memos, letters, reports, and proposals are some of the commonly used media of business communication.

✓ CHECKLIST for the Planning Process

☐ **Determine the objectives.**

☐ **Consider the audience.**

☐ **Generate a list of ideas and choose the most important ones.**

☐ **Select the appropriate channel and medium.**

THE WRITING AND REVISION PROCESS

The moment of truth arrives as you complete the final step of the planning process. You have selected the appropriate medium, in this case the letter, and it is now time to create a first **draft** — that is, to write a preliminary version of your message.

Stories abound about writers who are whirlwinds at planning but who freeze up when it is time to begin the draft. This is sometimes attributed to **writer's block**, a widely researched condition that prevents a communicator from writing. No one seems to be completely immune. You may have already found yourself frozen in front of a word processor or vacantly staring at a writing pad. Some writers seek inspiration by sharpening pencils, rearranging their desks, or taking a break, all to no avail. If you carefully plan your message, however, writer's block should not be a problem.

If the initial draft satisfies you, your standards are probably too low. Should you be tempted to skip the revision stage, remember that careless writing is costly to the business organization. It can also be costly to employees in terms of jobs lost and promotions denied.

A **revision** is simply an altered version of the draft. The changes made may be additions, deletions, or substitutions. Some revisions entail significant changes or major rewrites. Others consist of little more than correcting a few errors in grammar or word usage.

All written messages do not deserve the same amount of attention. Some messages are less important than others and can be written, by the experienced writer, with little or no modification. As a novice business communicator, however, you should plan to revise everything you write. For that reason, when you begin to write you should do it rapidly, realizing that this is not the final version. Make sure that you allow yourself enough time to both write and revise. Keep in mind, as you write, the objectives and intended audience that you previously identified.

✓ *CHECKLIST for Revising Content*

——◗ Include all necessary information.

——◗ Make sure the information is accurate.

——◗ Be sure it is clear and well-supported.

——◗ Include answers to likely questions of readers.

✓ *CHECKLIST for Revising Language*

——◗ Adhere to rules of grammar and punctuation.

——◗ Be sure the language is tactful and clear.

——◗ Use the active voice where appropriate.

——◗ Use a professional tone.

——◗ Use concise and readable language.

Approaches to revision vary with the writer and the situation. Some prominent authors anticipate eight to ten major revisions before satisfying both themselves and their publishers. Mark Twain reportedly advised deleting every third word, on principle, to achieve more vigorous writing.[3]

Business writing is unquestionably improved through careful revision. Important reports and ultra-sensitive letters routinely go through multiple revisions. Word processors have simplified the task of revising immeasurably, but the process remains mentally taxing.

Revising is an especially demanding task because it requires objectivity. Students have been known to ask, "How do you improve on perfection?" Try to place yourself in the role of the intended receiver and read the message from that person's viewpoint. If possible, have a colleague read your initial draft and make suggestions.

Some writers equate revising with proofreading. From the standpoint of the business communicator, however, the revision process extends beyond proofreading. It requires focusing on content, language, and organization.

Revising is a skill that is developed through practice. The accompanying checklists are intended to help you, but they are not exhaustive. The more familiar you are with the characteristics of effective writing, as presented in Chapter 3, the better able you will be to perform a revision likely to strengthen the original draft.

[3]Kenneth Roman and Joel Raphaelson, *Writing That Works* (New York: Harper & Row, 1981), 97.

✔ *CHECKLIST for Revising Organization*

___◗ **Introduce ideas in logical sequence.**

___◗ **Include a topic sentence in each paragraph.**

___◗ **Be sure that purpose and structure are clear.**

___◗ **Smooth out transitions to make reading easier.**

WRITING GOOD-NEWS AND NEUTRAL LETTERS

In many letters you will transmit either good news or routine, neutral information. These letters are relatively easy to write because of the nature of the message. Some typical situations in which such a letter is written are: placing an order, receiving an order to be filled promptly, making an adjustment requested by a customer, granting an application for credit, and supplying information. When writing a good-news or neutral letter, present your ideas in a direct or **deductive arrangement**:

Neutral and good-news letters should be arranged deductively: the main idea should precede the secondary details.

1. *Start with the main idea.* Because you are conveying positive or neutral information, resistance or disagreement is unlikely. Get right to the point. Such an approach elicits the goodwill of the reader while saving time—both yours and the reader's.
2. *Present the secondary details.* In a good-news or neutral letter, secondary details are usually explanatory. If you are acknowledging an order, the secondary details may pertain to method and time of shipment. In a letter of adjustment, the secondary details may explain why the problem occurred in the first place. Respond to whatever questions the reader may have asked. At the same time anticipate and respond to other likely questions.
3. *Close on a positive note.* The letter should end in as straightforward a fashion as it began. If you are acknowledging an order, a reference to future business would be appropriate. Be brief and direct. Avoid clichés such as "Do not hesitate to contact me if I can be of further help." Either omit the close, or, better, end with a brief and direct statement such as "Write me again when I can help."

A good-news letter differs from a neutral letter primarily in the first paragraph.

The main difference between a good-news letter and a neutral letter is found in the first paragraph. A **good-news letter** begins with the good news, the main point of the letter. For example, to respond to a customer's request for a full refund on the purchase price of a five-pound package of grass seed, Rhonda Davis arranged her ideas in this sequence:

Main idea:	Here is a check for the refund you requested.
Secondary details:	Slight soil irregularities occasionally minimize the effectiveness of any grass seed.
Close:	Your satisfaction is important to us.

The **neutral letter**, as the name suggests, presents a message that is neither good nor bad. It begins with the main idea, which is neutral rather than good news. Frank Lofton, to request information for a term paper, arranged his ideas in this sequence:

Main idea:	Please send information on the products manufactured by Amco, Inc.
Secondary details:	(1) I want the material for a term paper. (2) I am especially interested in products developed in the last 10 years.
Close:	Thanks for your help.

In responding for Amco, Beth Johnson also used a direct approach. She presented this sequence of ideas in her letter:

Main idea:	I am enclosing a brochure describing each of our products.
Secondary details:	(1) The products described on pages 3–8 and 11 were developed during the past 10 years. (2) We are pleased that you selected Amco as a subject for your paper.
Close:	Good luck with your paper.

CHARACTERISTICS OF GOOD-NEWS LETTERS

In a good-news letter, you are complying with the wishes of the other party. The reader will be pleased with the message, so get right to the main point. Among the more common types of good-news letters in business are those in which the writer approves an adjustment, grants a routine request, extends credit, or acknowledges the receipt of an order. Responses to such letters are usually positive.

Directness is appropriate when relaying good news.

Approving Adjustments on Claims

When merchants are able to approve an adjustment sought by a customer, they should respond promptly and directly. This approval is positive, and the letter should also include an attempt at another sale. Figure 5.2 is an example of such a letter.

Letters granting an adjustment should be prompt and direct.

When a customer seeks an adjustment on the basis of an error made by a business, most firms grant the adjustment immediately. Many cases are not that clear-cut, however. Sometimes neither party appears to be at fault. A third party may be responsible, or responsibility may be impossible to determine.

Many firms, not wanting to lose a customer, will assume responsibility even though responsibility may be unclear. For example, a woman who ordered a dozen plants through the mail received only two that appeared healthy; the others had died. She had not done business with the company before. She requested replacements for the plants. Figure 5.3 shows the company's response.

Many firms will assume responsibility for an error even when responsibility is unclear.

FIGURE 5.2   ▪   *Adjustment Approval Letter*

DELUXE, INC.
P.O. Box 413
Milton, MA 02186

November 20, 1991

Mrs. Lois Hammond
2314 N. 21st Street
Metairie, LA 70006

Dear Mrs. Hammond:

The good news is stated immediately, without fanfare.

You will receive a brand-new Deluxe Glide steam iron later this week. We are happy to be of service to you.

The writer expresses appreciation and a desire to improve customer service.

Thank you for returning the other iron to us. Our technicians are analyzing its performance in order to learn how to improve our inspection procedures. By calling the problem to our attention, you are helping us to serve you better.

The excellent service makes the reader receptive to this sales promotion.

You should receive our summer sale catalog next week. It is full of high-quality products that we are pleased to stand behind.

Sincerely,

R. A. Sumner

R. A. Sumner
Customer Service

Granting Routine Requests

Writers granting routine requests should give an immediate, enthusiastic yes answer.

Directness is a desirable characteristic in any good-news letter. When you can answer yes to a request, you should do so enthusiastically. Because yes is the answer that the reader is hoping for, say it immediately, as in Figures 5.4 and 5.5. The plant manager in Figure 5.5 is obviously enthusiastic and sincere about donating scrap metal to a charity drive.

When granting routine requests, you should always view the reader as a potential customer. This does not mean your good-news letter must

FIGURE 5.3 ▪ *Claim Approval despite Unclear Responsibility*

Worldwide Flowers P.O. Box 40080 Lafayette, LA 70504 (318) 504-3750

February 12, 1991

Ms. Margo Boggs
1987 Maple Avenue
Iowa City, IA 52240

Dear Ms. Boggs:

A dozen healthy plants are being mailed to you today at no —————— *Honors the customer's request immediately.*
expense to you.

Under normal circumstances, plants from Worldwide Flowers are —————— *Assures this new customer that such problems rarely occur.*
extremely resistant to those conditions likely to harm lower-
quality plants. In the five years we have been shipping plants in
our patented stay-moist containers, more than 99 percent of the
plants shipped have arrived in greenhouse condition.

To ensure that plants will arrive in good condition, it is —————— *Reminds reader how to handle newly arrived plants.*
important to remove them from the carton and transplant them
within 24 hours of receiving them. Doing this will result in
healthy plants that will add much to your gardening pleasure.

From now on you will receive our "Green Thumb" newsletter —————— *Points to the future positively.*
each month. It features unadvertised specials that are likely to
enhance your garden at a fraction of the usual price.

Yours truly,

Winnie P. Ivy

Winnie P. Ivy
Sales Correspondent

always be sales-oriented; it does mean your letters should display characteristics that are likely to instill a positive image of your firm.

There are certain pitfalls to avoid if you are to convey a positive image. The writer of the letter in Figure 5.6 on page 126, unfortunately, did not avoid them in responding to an inquiry about when a specific course would next be offered. The writer could have made a better impression and conveyed the information more efficiently by using a direct arrangement. Here is a better version of the letter:

The direct arrangement is appropriate for granting a routine request.

FIGURE 5.4 ▪ *Routine Request Grant*

Agrees to reader's request.

Extends an additional offer.

Provides helpful secondary details.

Uses positive ending.

*Electro Flex, **INC.*** 2162 Industrial Blvd. Ypsilanti, MI 48197

March 19, 1991

Mrs. Rachel Levine
Barrow Elementary School
Ypsilanti, MI 48197

Dear Mrs. Levine:

Yes, I will be happy to give your sixth-grade class a tour of our plant on the afternoon of March 27.

Your students will especially be interested in the assembly line, but I will also show them one of our research labs, if they care to see one.

The enclosed brochures will acquaint your students with our full line of products. If you will have them read and discuss the brochures before your visit, it may make the tour more interesting.

I look forward to meeting you and your class in the lobby of Building B at one o'clock next Wednesday afternoon.

Sincerely,

Lance Elrod

Lance Elrod
Industrial Relations Manager

Encls.

Our course, Auto Repairs for the Layperson, will begin on September 8. The class will meet on Monday and Wednesday evenings from 7:00 to 10:00 during the fall quarter.

You may register by completing the attached form and returning it to me by September 6. By enclosing tuition payment of $75.00, you will avoid delays often encountered when paying tuition on the first night of the quarter. Many have already expressed interest in Auto Repairs for the Layperson.

Congratulations on taking a significant step in your personal development. Please call me if I can be of assistance.

FIGURE 5.5 ∎ *Request Acceptance*

FOREMOST MANUFACTURING, INC.
Midville, OH 43601
(614) 549-0102

November 1, 1991

Ms. Estelle Rawls
Tri-County Connection
P.O. Box 245
Midville, OH 43601

Dear Ms. Rawls:

Yes, we will gladly contribute the scrap materials from our mill for the next four weeks to the Tri-County Charity Drive.

Many of the poor and elderly of the community will benefit from the Tri-County blanket-making project. It is certainly worthwhile, and we are pleased to be a part of it.

We will deliver the remnants to your temporary warehouse on each of the next four Fridays at 2:00 in the afternoon.

Yours truly,

Frank Zeeman

Frank Zeeman
Plant Manager

Presents good news with enthusiasm.

Recognizes the worth of the project.

Describes future action.

Extending Credit

Few business organizations insist on cash payment from customers. The extension of credit has become the rule rather than the exception. Consumers are applying for credit in increasing numbers, and the degree to which it is extended grows proportionately.

When a person seeks credit and a business organization sees fit to extend it, the situation calls for a good-news letter. As with all such letters, directness is appropriate. What applicants want to know is whether or not

FIGURE 5.6 ▪ *Ineffective Routine Response*

Mᴵᴰ-Cᴼᵁɴᴛʏ Tᴇᴄʜɴɪᴄᴀʟ Cᴼᴸᴸᴇɢᴇ
P.O. Box 4104
Madison, NJ 07940

March 5, 1991

Mr. Fred Bradwell
1240 Elm Street
Madison, NJ 07940

Dear Mr. Bradwell:

Thank you for your letter of February 28, in which you requested information concerning Auto Repairs for the Layperson.

This is one of our most popular courses, and you are one of many who have expressed an interest in it. The practical nature of the course and the present shortage of auto mechanics seem to explain the popularity of this course.

You will be happy to learn that we will offer Auto Repairs for the Layperson in the fall quarter. Classes begin on September 8 and will meet Monday and Wednesday evenings from 7:00 to 10:00.

I have enclosed the necessary registration form. Please complete the form and return it to me as soon as possible, along with the tuition payment indicated on the registration form.

Sincerely,

Debra J. Bennett

Debra J. Bennett
Associate Director

Encl.

Margin annotations:

Unnecessary—letter is a response to a request.

Irrelevant information, not oriented to the reader.

Should be in the first paragraph—it is what the reader wants to know.

Necessary but vague—give specific date.

---

they are going to be given credit. The main purpose of such a letter is to extend credit to the reader; however, this is not the sole purpose. In writing such a letter the writer should try to do the following:

1. Tell the person seeking credit that it will be granted.
2. Compliment the person for meriting the faith implicit in any credit approval.
3. Explain the terms of the credit plan.

| BOXED IN | *AN ETHICAL DILEMMA* |

Rod Simmons had always taken pride in being able to work effectively with anyone. That changed when he was promoted to the position of national sales manager two years ago. Brian Ingles, one of six regional managers reporting to him, has since caused 80 percent of Rod's headaches.

Rod is upset primarily by Brian's work habits and attitudes. He feels that Brian's region consistently exceeds its sales quota only because of the quality of the sales representatives, who are top-notch. Privately, he says that Brian's region meets its goals "in spite of Brian, not because of him."

Rod has been resigned to enduring Brian indefinitely. A few days ago, however, he received a request for a letter of recommendation. Brian apparently is being considered for the position of national sales manager with another major firm.

Rod recognized a golden opportunity. Drafting a letter of recommendation, he emphasized the quotas met and exceeded by Brian's team. Commenting on Brian's work habits, he used "careful thinker" to describe what is actually a major weakness — Brian's refusal to make decisions. He described Brian as a "person of strong principles" rather than argumentative, which he is. "Forceful" and "meticulous attention to detail" glossed over Brian's tendency to be not only argumentative but a nitpicker.

Rod decided, before mailing the letter, to sleep on it. This morning he has reread the letter and is still pleased with it. It emphasizes Brian's good points and soft-pedals his shortcomings in such a way that he is presented as an ideal candidate for the job. Rod is delighted at the prospect of being rid of Brian. Yet, at the same time, he is beginning to feel pangs of guilt. He wonders, Am I doing the right thing? can I in good conscience mail the letter?

Rod feels boxed in. What would you do?

4. Point toward future business with the customer and express appreciation for the credit request.

A letter offering to extend credit to an applicant should contain positive phrasing. It should welcome the applicant to a preferred group of customers, and it should express acceptance and trust of the new charge customer. This is an example:

> We are pleased to send you a Rusk Brothers credit card. Thank you for thinking of us when you decided to open a charge account. It is through your intelligent use of credit in the past that you have earned this account.
>
> Bills are mailed on the 20th of each month and are payable by the 15th of the next month. There is a finance charge of 1½ percent on the unpaid balance each month.

In extending credit the writer should express acceptance and trust.

✔ CHECKLIST for Adjustment Approval

___I Indicate immediately that the adjustment is being granted.

___I Grant the adjustment wholeheartedly.

___I Play down the negative aspects by avoiding negative words.

___I Briefly explain the reason for the problem or imply it when describing the measures.

___I Specify any action the reader must take.

___I Look forward to future business in the close.

> The enclosed brochure describes many of the special services we offer our charge customers. As a charge customer you may easily shop by telephone, and you will receive advance notification of sales.
>
> We appreciate the opportunity to serve you, and we hope to merit your patronage for a long time.

A company that extends credit takes a risk. Through a careful selection of applicants the risk is reduced but still present. However, once the decision to extend credit is made, the company has determined that the customer has the capacity to use credit wisely. At this point the letter writer should not mar a pleasant occasion with overtones of distrust and apprehension. Contrast the positive tone of the previous example with the negative tone of this one:

> We are pleased to grant you credit as you requested January 3. Bills are sent monthly on the 20th and must be paid by the 15th. It is our policy to charge 1½ percent interest on the unpaid balance on the 15th. Therefore, if you are wise and wish to protect your credit rating, you will be sure to pay your bill by the 15th. We appreciate the opportunity to serve you.

The first letter was optimistic and hopeful; the second was neither. In each case the applicant's request was honored, but the impression created was quite different. In extending credit a company has an opportunity to develop a positive relationship with a customer. An effective letter will capitalize on this opportunity.

This is how a furniture factory informed a retailer that credit was being granted and the goods were being shipped:

> The Deltina cane-back chairs you ordered on May 1 are being shipped to your store via Statewide Motor Company. They should arrive in Augusta by May 5. The amount of this merchandise has been debited to your new account.
>
> Your excellent record with other creditors allows us to extend to you our regular terms of 2/10, n/30. As a new customer you may carry as much as $1,000 worth of our products on account.
>
> Included with your order are some suggested window and floor displays that other dealers have found helpful in attracting customers. Once cus-

tomers pause to look at the chairs, they recognize their stylishness and proven durability.

Use the enclosed order forms for placing your next orders. You can always count on prompt deliveries and our full cooperation.

Unlike the earlier credit-extending letter, this one was written to a dealer. A dealer is generally interested in the sales potential of a product and ways to display a product; a consumer will be more interested in price and durability.

In writing to extend credit you should certainly adapt your message to the interests of the customer. Whether writing to a dealer or to a consumer, however, the same principles apply. In either case the structure of the message is the same.

A credit extension message should be adapted to the interests of the reader, whether dealer or consumer.

Acknowledging Orders

Many business organizations live or die according to the volume of orders received. The link between orders received and business success is a clear one; the link between acknowledgments and success is less clear. For that reason, business people have a tendency to play down the importance of letters of acknowledgment.

Many people look upon acknowledging orders as nothing but a time-consuming chore. Some organizations send only preprinted postcards in acknowledgment. Other sellers, reasoning that the promptly shipped order will soon be delivered to the buyer, send no acknowledgment. Although the postcard is preferable to no acknowledgment at all, a letter is desirable and personal.

Some acknowledgment of an order is desirable: a letter is preferable.

Letter writers should recognize that orders are routine for the seller, but may not be routine for the buyer. Future business with the buyer often depends on the way the seller handles the present order.

One practice that suggests the seller is uninterested in the customer is the tendency to overuse an order-acknowledgment message. Whether the message is in the form of a letter or a postcard, it should be changed at regular intervals. When a seller persists in sending the same message for a long time, customers may begin to feel they are being taken for granted. Customers most likely to feel this way are those who are most important — your best customers.

At regular intervals a company should change the order acknowledgment letters it uses.

To illustrate, Francis Genet has worked as a purchasing agent for three companies for a total of 18 years. During that time he has observed a wide variety of business practices on the part of suppliers. One of the most irritating practices, he believes, is the repeated use of the same acknowledgment letter. "In some cases," Francis says, "a company will send out the same letter for years. After a while you start thinking that your business means nothing to the supplier."

No matter how small the order being acknowledged, its potential may be considerable. If handled properly, today's new customer may be tomorrow's major purchaser. Customers — whether old and valued or brand new — are receptive to a statement of appreciation and an assurance that

✔ CHECKLIST for Credit Extension

___ Indicate at the start that credit is being extended.

___ If goods are being shipped, give the details immediately.

___ Specify the goods and the method of shipment.

___ Mention how the reader earned the credit.

___ Resell the reader on the wise choice.

___ Point to future orders in the close.

___ Avoid sarcasm, name-calling, and threats.

✔ CHECKLIST for Order Acknowledgment

___ Tell the buyer that the order was received and is being filled according to directions.

___ Identify the order clearly enough to prevent the reader from confusing it with another order.

___ Give the buyer the details of shipment — how it is being shipped and when the buyer should receive it.

___ State the financial arrangement if it was not made clear prior to shipment.

___ Express appreciation for the order.

___ Encourage more orders in the future.

the order will be sent promptly. Consider the impression likely to be made by each of these kinds of acknowledgments: letter, preprinted fill-in postcard, and completely preprinted postcard.

Letter of Acknowledgment

A good letter of acknowledgment gets down to business immediately:

Individualized letters of acknowledgment provide a personal touch and are appreciated.

Your order for one X-365 workbench is being processed and will be shipped within 48 hours.

Since you included a check for the full purchase price, we are pleased to pay all of the shipping expenses. We know you will be pleased with the workbench, just as thousands of other customers have been. We believe, Mr. Morris, that you will find the table surface truly resists all types of scratches, dents, and burns. This feature, plus the stability ensured by the four sturdy legs, means you will enjoy it for many years to come.

When you decide to order tools, remember that Harris, Inc., carries a full line of manual and power tools. These tools, like the workbench, are designed to provide good service and take hard use. The drawers and shelves of the workbench were designed especially for Harris tools.

Use the enclosed order blank and postage-paid envelope for placing your next order. We look forward to serving you again.

This letter immediately identifies the item ordered and commits the company to a shipping date. It seeks future orders and remains personal throughout.

Preprinted Acknowledgments

A preprinted fill-in postcard, such as the one in Figure 5.7, informs the buyer that the order has been received and action is being taken. If the buyer happens to have placed several orders with Harris recently, however, this postcard does not show which order is being filled. Although such a postcard is impersonal, it does answer the buyer's most likely question about whether the order is being filled.

Certain merchandise occasionally may be out of stock, especially when the seller does a sizable volume of business. In acknowledging the out-of-stock status of an order the seller must inform the buyer that the merchandise will be available soon.

Many organizations that receive a tremendous volume of orders do not acknowledge orders unless shipment will be delayed. Major retailers such as Sears fill most orders almost immediately—the goods arrive as quickly as any acknowledgment would.

When a delay does occur, Sears acknowledges it with the form in Figure 5.8. The customer's address, along with the information identifying the order, is written on the front of the postcard. Without this information customers who have placed several orders do not know which order was delayed. On the other side of the card is a sales message.

Any of the three kinds of acknowledgements is better than no acknowledgment. Even when an order is filled promptly, unless an acknowledg-

Even the most impersonal order acknowledgment is preferable to none, because it tells the buyer that the order is being filled.

FIGURE 5.7 ▪ *A Preprinted Postcard*

Dear _____ :

    Your order for _____ has been received and will be shipped within 48 hours by United Parcel Service. You should receive it no later than _____.

    Thank you for your business.

            Robert Bates
            Harris, Inc.

FIGURE 5.8 ▪ *Postcard Informing the Consumer of a Delay in Shipment*

SEARS, ROEBUCK AND CO.
Customer Relations Dept.
925 S. Homan Ave.
Chicago, Illinois 60607

```
┌──────────────┐
│    Sears     │
└──────────────┘
```

THANK YOU . . . . .
. . . for your order.
The merchandise you ordered
is temporarily out of stock.
We expect to make shipment
by the date shown.
Should you write about this
order, please return this card
with your letter.

```
┌──────────────┐
│    Sears     │
└──────────────┘
```

Shop and Save

the convenient Catalog way . . . Place
orders by phone or in person at your
nearest Sears Retail Catalog Order
Department, Sears Catalog Sales Office,
or Sears Catalog Merchant.

Source: Courtesy of Sears, Roebuck and Co.

ment is made, the customer is left wondering until the shipment actually arrives.

The benefits of a personal letter of acknowledgment must be weighed against its cost. Such letters are expensive, but they can be justified if an opportunity for significant further business exists.

In many cases a form letter will suffice, but it is unwise to rely solely on forms to acknowledge orders. An organization will be most effective in acknowledging orders if it uses a combination of completely preprinted forms, fill-in forms, and personal letters.

CHARACTERISTICS OF NEUTRAL LETTERS

A neutral letter conveys neither good news nor bad news. Such letters are usually met with cautious interest on the part of the receiver. As with the good-news letter, a neutral letter should be direct. Some of the more common types of neutral letters make routine claims, request routine information, request credit, or place orders.

Making Routine Claims

Consumers evaluate stores partly according to how the stores treat them. The way a store responds to a request for an adjustment is greatly influenced by the manner in which the customer seeks the adjustment. Although the letter in Figure 5.9 does make a claim, it does not do so effectively. This letter is wordy and rambling. It is arranged in an **indirect sequence**, from general (seen on television) to the specific (a full refund).

The indirect sequence is not appropriate for good-news and neutral letters.

When writing to make a routine claim, you should use the **direct sequence**, from specific points to general ones. As you expect the claim to be readily satisfied, tell the reader the action you seek and the reasons for the request. If persuasion seems necessary to get a claim satisfied, the persuasive sequence presented in Chapter 7 is appropriate. The approach in making a routine claim is straightforward, as in this letter:

> Will you please send another Flora and Fauna Dictionary to replace the one I am returning in the attached package?
>
> This book arrived with many of the illustrations blurred, especially those between pages 200 and 300. I have enclosed the invoice that accompanied the book.
>
> If an unsoiled copy is unavailable, I shall appreciate a full refund.

Requesting Routine Information

When you read an advertisement in a magazine about a product in which you are interested, you may have some unanswered questions. Like many other consumers, you may write directly to the company for answers. Business organizations receive and send numerous requests for routine information. The more specific a request is, the more likely it is to elicit the desired response.

Requests should be specific.

In requesting routine information, state the request in the first sentence. In that way you will leave no doubt about what information is desired. Next, provide whatever other details might be necessary. Last, point to the future by stating what you want the reader to do. Note the differences between the letter in Figure 5.10 and the following one:

> Can the gas water heater (model HN422) be installed in a horizontal rather than vertical position? I would like to install it in the space under my workbench. It would be in a clean environment, and there would be no tools or equipment in direct contact with it. The room in which I hope to install it is heated. Since I am in the midst of remodeling my house, I would appreciate a prompt reply.

FIGURE 5.9   ▪   *Ineffective Routine Claim*

286 Greencrest Drive
Athens, OH 45701
September 1, 1991

Appliance City
1012 Main Street
Athens, OH 45700

Dear Sales Manager:

Unnecessary information that does not clarify the problem.

When I saw your humidifier advertised on television, I thought it was just what I needed. You said that it would solve the problems of dry air and static electricity, and both of these are real problems in my house.

Wordy and beside the point.

One thing I didn't anticipate was the way its color would clash with most of the furnishings in my house. I thought that gray would blend in with the surroundings, but it doesn't.

States the problem, but gives no relevant specifics such as model or size.

After using it for one week, I've decided that I can't get used to it. None of the colors in which it comes would be any better for my house.

Finally requests a specific action.

I would like to return my humidifier to you. If I do so, would you please send me a full refund? I would certainly appreciate it.

Sincerely,

Kenneth Adams

Kenneth Adams

Requesting Credit

Requests for credit should get to the point immediately.

When you request credit by letter, the sequence of ideas is identical to those in the standard order letter. As with an order letter, you should get to the point immediately and then provide the necessary details.

Please open a charge account for me. My name and address follow:
Marcia O. Bonner
1400 Tiffany Avenue, Apt. 980
Orlando, FL 32802

FIGURE 5.10 ▪ *Request for Routine Information*

```
                              1813 Violet Avenue
                              Midview, TN 38238
                              June 14, 1991

Mayor Heather Lange
City Hall
Midview, TN 38238

Dear Mayor Lange:

    On the six o'clock news last night, they showed a brief
portion of the speech you gave yesterday.

    It sounded interesting, and I would like to learn what else
you said in your speech.

    Please send me a copy of the speech you gave.

                    Yours truly,

                    Robert J. Rasmussen

                    Robert J. Rasmussen
```

*Unclear purpose—
most politicians give
more than one speech
each day.*

*Presents no new
information.*

*The request doesn't
indicate whether note
cards or a handout
would suffice if no
copy of the speech is
available.*

Prior to moving to Orlando I lived for three years at

> 1011 Live Oak Lane
> Building C
> New Orleans, LA 70113

While living in New Orleans I had charge accounts with Axel's Emporium, Carson's Department Store, and Michelle's Boutique.

I have worked for B&J Electronics for the past five years as a sales representative. I earn more than $25,000 per year.

My Orlando bank is Sun City Bank & Trust, where I have a checking and savings account. In New Orleans I banked at Tri-State Bank.

✔ CHECKLIST for a Routine Claim

— When making a claim, write promptly.

— Request a specific action in the first sentence.

— Explain why such action would be desirable.

— Express confidence in the reader's judgment and appreciation for the action you are seeking.

— Avoid sarcasm, name-calling, and threats.

✔ CHECKLIST for an Information Request

— Make a specific request immediately.

— Ask whatever specific questions are necessary to get the desired information.

— Avoid wordiness by asking direct questions. "Will the machine . . ." is preferable to "I am interested in . . ."

— Make a positive and an appreciative reference to the action desired of the reader.

Most requests for credit are made on application forms.

Most requests for consumer credit are made by completing an application form furnished by the organization from which credit is sought. Even the person who writes a letter requesting credit will probably be asked to complete such a form. The information requested, however, will be very similar to that provided in the letter.

A person opening a new business will most likely request credit by letter. The sequence of ideas is identical to those presented by an individual consumer.

> Please open a credit line of $1,500 for my company, Schief Clothiers, Inc., formerly known as Threads Unlimited.
>
> On July 1, 1990, I purchased Threads Unlimited from the estate of Waldo Gillis. I plan to feature your Falcon line of sportswear as our highest quality offering.
>
> I have 12 years of experience in men's clothing, the last four of which were spent owning and operating Suit City in Boise, Idaho. The Greater Boise Credit Bureau has my complete credit history on file.
>
> The grand opening of Schief Clothiers will be held September 1–3, Labor Day weekend. By that time, I hope to have a complete inventory of Falcon sportswear.
>
> Please send me a confirmation of a $1,500 line of credit and the payment plan you offer. Also indicate the date by which I must place an order so that I will receive it by late August.

✔ *CHECKLIST for a Credit Request*

——◗ **Make request immediately.**

——◗ **Provide necessary details regarding type of account and line of credit desired.**

——◗ **Describe your recent credit history.**

——◗ **Provide current banking and credit references.**

Placing Orders

When you order something from a supplier of any sort, the process is simplified if you have an order blank from the company. When you do not, you should follow the good-news and neutral letter format.

In your letter, indicate exactly what you are ordering, the instructions for shipping, and the manner in which you intend to pay.

> Please send me one X-365 workbench. I have enclosed a check for the total amount, $249.95.
> Since I intend to give the workbench as a birthday gift, it is important that it arrive before May 30. If, for any reason, the workbench is unavailable, please notify me immediately.

Robert Palmer works as an assistant purchasing manager for a large company. For many of the purchases he makes, he simply completes an order blank. Frequently, however, he must write letters of order. When Robert writes a letter of order, he provides enough information so that the seller does not have to request additional details. The following excerpt from one of his letters shows his approach.

> Please ship the following goods to reach our Silvertown plant by December 2, 1990.

Quantity	Catalog Code	Unit Price	Total Price
12	A-812–0610	$167.99	$2015.88
12	A-842–1914	79.99	959.88
		Total	$2975.76

> Charge these goods to our account on the regular 1/10, net 30 terms.
> It is important that the goods arrive by December 1. We appreciate the promptness with which you always fill our orders.

Whether using an order form or writing an order letter, you must include all of the necessary details. Delays often occur because information in the order letter is incomplete.

Using Prewritten Messages

In many situations a reply tailored to a specific individual is not needed. The expense of an individualized letter simply cannot be justified in other instances. Still other situations are so routine that it is impractical to com-

In the absence of an order blank, the good-news and neutral letter plan should be followed in placing orders.

✔ CHECKLIST for an Order Letter

____❙ Start with your main point. "Please send" or "Please ship" are appropriate openings and are likely to result in a fast response.

____❙ Provide all the details necessary for the seller to fill the order now. If details such as catalog number, size, color, and price are omitted, further correspondence will be necessary and a delay will result.

____❙ Indicate the payment plan you will follow.

____❙ Include shipping instructions if you have a preference.

____❙ Close with your expectations of an appropriate delivery date.

Form messages allow for immediate responses to predictable requests.

pose individual letters. A suitable alternative is often a **form letter**—a very general letter that may be sent to many people without change.

Two approaches may be used with form letters. One is to prepare individual paragraphs in advance for use in situations that frequently occur. The other approach uses complete letters prepared in advance for use in certain routine situations. These prewritten messages allow an organization to respond more quickly to much of the correspondence it receives.

Form Paragraphs

After determining the kinds of information usually sought in incoming routing correspondence, writers can save time by preparing appropriate paragraphs in advance. Some organizations have a manual of form paragraphs, and each paragraph has a reference number. The correspondent need only indicate to the typist the numbers of the paragraphs to be used and the sequence in which they are to appear.

To illustrate, Coach Hank Sloane found that interest was growing in his summer basketball camps as he became better known through his successful basketball teams. The great number of inquiries about the camps made it difficult for him and his secretary to keep up with their work. On the basis of a careful record of the kinds of inquiries he received, Hank prepared a series of paragraphs that answered the most commonly asked questions. He numbered the paragraphs and, after reading a letter, he would tell the secretary which paragraphs to send in response.

When asked by a potential participant about the size of the camp and the possibility of tuition grants, for example, he told his secretary to send paragraphs 2 and 5. This is the letter that resulted:

Yes, there are openings available in the July basketball camp. Enrollment is limited to 25 participants per session. As a participant, you will receive intensive coaching that will help you sharpen your skills.

Yes, partial grants are available for a limited number of participants. Please complete the enclosed application and return it to me in order to be considered for a grant. The enclosed brochure describes our camp in greater detail.

Form Letters

Inquiries are sometimes so predictable that it is more efficient to go beyond form paragraphs and prepare complete form letters. The only types of information that need be added to a form letter are name, address, and date.

Most form letters in business cover routine matters, but there are some exceptions to this rule. According to one newspaper columnist, for example, a television network responded to viewers' complaints about a sports commentator with the form letter in Figure 5.11.

Another unusual instance in which a form letter was used occurred during the 1985 football season. Many fans of the Atlanta Falcons were irate when National Football League officials penalized their team when Billy "White Shoes" Johnson danced in the end zone after he scored touchdowns. So many fans wrote to the National Football League office that the NFL supervisor of officials responded with this form letter:[4]

> We have received a number of postal cards from your area asking that Billy "White Shoes" Johnson be permitted to "do his dance."
>
> Please be advised that we will forward your suggestion to the Rules Committee for its review prior to the start of the 1986 season. This is a routine procedure we follow whenever we receive suggestions from clubs, fans, and members of the media.
>
> However, for the remainder of the 1985 season, the officials will continue to enforce the rules prohibiting such actions. We will have to see what develops in 1986.

Form letters are even more efficient than form paragraphs because they are completely prepared in advance. They are more economical than form paragraphs, and they can be dispatched more quickly. An organization's best writers should be assigned to develop the necessary form letters, for these letters are circulated widely.

This prepackaged approach to written communication has some disadvantages. Form paragraphs and form letters are intended for use in highly specific situations, but they are sometimes used in situations for which they were not designed. Care must be exercised to prevent this tendency, because an inappropriate form letter may be more irritating to the receiver than no response at all. Another disadvantage of the prepackaged approach is that form paragraphs and form letters tend to become outdated quickly. Organizational policies and practices are constantly changing, and management should ensure that its prepackaged messages reflect the changes.

Form messages tend to become outdated quickly.

Appropriateness of Prewritten Messages

Careful thought should be given as to when form letters are appropriate. Most form letters are used in situations that occur so frequently that the cost of individual letters would be prohibitive.

Form letters should be used with discretion.

[4]Chris Mortensen, "NFL Can't Calm White Shoes' Dance Fever," *Atlanta Journal Constitution,* November 2, 1985, 3-D.

FIGURE 5.11 ▪ *Form Letter*

*Main idea—
appreciation to a
viewer for having
written.*

*Secondary details
that support
employing the subject
of the complaint
while acknowledging
its validity.*

*Closes on a positive
note and looks to
the future.*

XYZ *SPORTS,* **INC.**
P.O. Box 4440 • Grand Central Station • New York, NY 10017

November 8, 1991

Mr. T. V. Viewer
1412 Any Street
Any City, NY 10001

Dear Mr. Viewer:

I appreciate your taking the time to write to express your
feelings about _____. While your comments and pointed criticisms
do not pass by unnoticed, I would like to state the feelings of XYZ
Sports regarding this matter.

Mr. _____ is an expert commentator with a vast knowledge and
total recall of many sports and sports personalities. We feel his
intelligence and keen mind far outweigh his sometimes controversial
statements. The precision and articulation of Mr. _____'s sports
presentations rank him among the best of all sports broadcasters.

Nevertheless, we do not like to alienate our viewers. In the
interest of improving all of our telecasts to the greatest possible
extent, we take into consideration your comments and the comments of
all viewers in connection with future programming. We look forward
to winning your full support.

Yours truly,

I. M. Worthy

I. M. Worthy
Public Relations

Source: Jeff Denberg, ''Three's a Crowd,'' *Atlanta Journal,* December 17, 1979,
13-B.

Department stores, for example, often use form letters to extend credit
privileges to those who have sought them. Colleges may use form letters
to acknowledge applications for admission. These are among the many
situations in which form letters may be used effectively. An organization
should be careful in sending out form letters, because there are always

possible exceptions to their use. For example, a company may routinely use form letters to acknowledge orders. This is good procedure, but a form letter certainly would be inappropriate to acknowledge the initial order from a new customer whose business has been long sought.

Consider two college students who received identical form letters denying them permission to substitute one course for another.

> Bill Thompson, an excellent student, asked permission to take another accounting course in place of a required cost accounting course. He had two years of cost accounting experience. Also, the required course was scheduled for a time when Bill had to be at work. He was the sole support of his wife and two small children.
> Brad Hennessey, an average student, requested permission to make a similar substitution. The required course was offered at a time that would conflict with his duties as volunteer photographer for the school yearbook. Although photography was only a hobby, he hoped to make it his profession eventually.

When Bill received a form letter, he felt that he had been treated with cold indifference. His excellent grades and personal requirements certainly deserved more personal treatment and consideration. Brad, on the other hand, did not find the form letter offensive. Form letters constitute an aid to communication as long as they are used with discretion.

A major criticism of form letters is that they are too impersonal. Through the use of word-processing equipment, it is now possible to individualize form letters somewhat. Automatic typewriters that are controlled by magnetically recorded instructions make it possible to insert special wording for a personal touch. Although the best form letters are not as effective as individual letters, they are expedient. Most readers prefer a prompt and clear reply and thus will overlook any impersonality.

Personal matters deserve personal, rather than form, letters.

As the volume of business communication increases, there will be still greater reliance on form messages. As long as management exercises good judgment, form letters are an effective communication tool.

SUMMARY

Letters provide a personal link between individuals and the organizations with which they do business. For that reason what people think about an organization is determined partly by the letters they receive from it.

Letters that are planned are more likely to elicit the desired results than are letters that are written without the benefit of planning. When planning a letter the writer should consider its objectives, the audience, the ideas to be included, and the most appropriate medium to convey the information.

After finishing the planning the writer drafts the letter. A draft is a preliminary version of a document. Focusing especially on content, language, and organization, the writer revises the draft until it meets the most important criteria.

When writing a letter that transmits either good news or neutral information, the writer should get directly to the main point. The main point should be followed by secondary details, and the letter should end on a positive note. Besides adhering to this sequence, the writer must also attend to the characteristics of effective writing presented in Chapter 3. The writer should be very specific throughout.

Some of the purposes of good-news letters are to approve an adjustment, to grant a routine request, to extend credit, or to acknowledge the receipt of an order. Among the many possible purposes of a neutral letter are making a claim, requesting routine information, requesting credit, or placing orders.

Prewritten messages are often used in order to expedite routine correspondence. In some situations, an organization may profit from the use of prewritten paragraphs. For other instances, completely prewritten form letters may be appropriate. Prewritten messages are often used in situations that occur so frequently that the cost of individual letters would be prohibitive. This prepackaged approach to business communication is less personal than individually written messages, but it is expedient. Through the use of good judgment, business people can use prewritten messages as an effective communication tool.

Key Terms

- **planning**
- **draft**
- **writer's block**
- **revision**
- **deductive arrangement**

- **good-news letter**
- **neutral letter**
- **indirect sequence**
- **direct sequence**
- **form letter**

Review Questions

1. Describe the four steps of the planning process.
2. What types of letters do you think merit the most careful planning?
3. What are the main differences between writing a draft and revising?
4. What are the main areas on which the writer should focus when revising?
5. What is meant by the term good-news letter?
6. State the arguments for and against an organization's acknowledging every single order received.
7. In what ways is a completely preprinted postcard as effective as an individual letter for acknowledging orders?
8. Describe the outline for a letter in which credit is extended to a new customer.
9. In extending credit to a new customer, should the writer state the penalties for late payment? Why?
10. If the seller is clearly at fault and is giving the adjustment sought by the

buyer, why is it desirable to explain the problem that necessitated the adjustment?

11. Why is the direct or deductive arrangement most appropriate for good-news and neutral letters?

12. What criteria determines the appropriateness of a form letter for a particular situation?

13. Why has the wider use of the telephone not made letters less important?

Exercises

1. While perusing a small, little-known trade publication you find an article on a new diet plan that has become very popular in Japan with business executives. Called the Kyoto Plan, it is a regimen of diet plus exercise. At present you are self-employed as a sales representative for a number of different brands of exercise equipment, most of which you sell to health clubs. You are curious as to whether the Kyoto Plan diet would be tolerable to U.S. adults and whether the required exercises would be viewed positively by the same audience. Write for answers to your questions as well as for a more thorough picture of the plan. Since you are unable to learn the names of any of the operatives of the plan, you should send your letter to Kyoto Plan, Inc., 14-5-201, Nihombashi Kodenma-cho, Chuo-Ku, Tokyo 103, Japan.

2. You are employed at a television station in a large urban area. The programming at the station, which is not affiliated with any network, consists mainly of popular reruns. The station has been inundated with phone calls and letters following an announcement that "The Beverly Hillbillies" will be moved from its 6:30 p.m. daily time slot to 11:30 p.m. The reason is that advertisers are reluctant to pay high, early-evening rates for that program. Advertising rates for the 11:30 slot are much lower. The station vice president asks you to prepare a form letter to send to viewers who complain that the new time will be too late for children to watch. Many of these viewers also complain about the shortage of programs on your station that are "fit for a family to watch."

3. You own and operate a medium-size printing plant. After several years of seeking business from Foster's Department Store, you finally receive an order for five reams of letterhead stationery. Compose a letter to the office manager (Walter Davis, Foster's Department Store, P.O. Box 1010, Amston, CT 06231).

4. Select a foreign country in which you are interested and write a letter to its embassy in Washington, D.C. (get the address from a library). Request information on points of interest for a first-time visitor. Indicate the time of year you hope to visit there and inquire about what the weather will be at that time.

5. Extensive market research has shown a rapidly growing market for fiberglass insulation in Latin America. As assistant vice president for development, you have been assigned to locate a suitable site in Colombia at which to build a manufacturing plant. The plant would employ approximately 120 people, 100 of them unskilled workers, within the first year. A city with a population of 50,000 to 100,000, with good road, rail, and air facilities would appear to be ideal. Your employer, Fiberall, Inc., is interested in securing local tax waivers for as long a time as possible. Another important factor is the educational opportunities available in the area. Write to Mr. Omar Cortez, Director, Colombian Development Office, Carrera 13 No. 2700, Bogotá, Colombia.

6. As circulation manager of *Contemporary Living* you have received several complaints in the past month about improper billing. The cause of the problem is a new computer system; it had been malfunctioning, but the situation has now been corrected. Write a response to a subscriber who has complained about incorrect billing. The letter should be sent to Robert Strong, 1210 4th Avenue, Vilas, CO 81087.

7. As the owner of a chain of three sporting goods stores, you are always looking for new products to give your business an edge on the competition. While vacationing in the French Alps you learn of a new type of ski, aerodynamically designed and constructed of a newly developed alloy that is lighter and stronger than anything now on the U.S. market. Upon returning from vacation you write to the company in order to get all of the particulars on the skis. You would like to become the U.S. distributor. If your request for a U.S. distributorship is denied, you hope at least to establish a relationship with the company and sell its skis at your stores. Write to Francois Levant, President, Levant Aero Products, 184 Rue du F.g. Saint Antoines, 75012 Paris, France.

8. Select a letter to the editor from a newspaper and revise it in accordance with the discussion here and in Chapter 3. Indicate your reasons for the changes you make.

9. You have been assigned to write a research paper on water pollution in the northeastern states. You are especially interested in the industrial causes of the problem as well as legislative changes that are currently being considered. Write a letter to Senator Justin Davis, Chairman of the Fish and Wildlife Committee and an acknowledged expert on the subject of pollution. His address is Room 410, Senate Office Building, Washington, DC 20000.

10. For many years, it was the policy of Classic Mail Order House to send a personal note to any customer whose order would be delayed more than a week. This chore has become too time-consuming. You have been asked to draft a form letter that could be sent to customers in the case of delayed orders.

11. You are planning a week's vacation two months from now, and you are considering taking a Windjammer Cruise. You have learned the schedule and rate information from advertisements, but you have several questions: How many tourists will there be on the ship? How many of them are likely to be single like yourself? You are aware that each tourist must perform some work on the ship each day, and you do not object to that. You wonder, however, how many hours per day and what kinds of duties you would have to perform. Write a letter seeking the above information to Windjammer Cruises, P.O. Box 1111, Miami, FL 33101.

12. Assume that you are public relations director of Windjammer Cruises. Respond to the request for information in Exercise 11. Use your imagination in responding, but remind the writer that the fare for singles is $56 higher than for double occupancy. The single-occupancy fare is $251. Write this letter to Bill Hawkins, 1220 Lake Shore Drive, Apartment 1119, Chicago, IL 60607.

13. As an automobile dealer you offer periodic service specials to persons who purchased cars from you by mailing coupons that feature a special price list for various maintenance and repair services. Gary Brightson (1910 W. Boulevard, Indianapolis, IN 46206) brought his car in for a tune-up and presented an outdated coupon. According to the year-old coupon the cost of the tune-up was $32. The present tune-up special costs $39.50. As service manager write a letter

to Gary Brightson and explain the reason why he still owes you $7.50. There is no expiration date on the coupon, only the date on which the coupon was sent out.

14. Inspired by the success of the San Diego Chicken, you purchased an appropriate costume and have become the Rochester Rooster. For $25 you will make an appearance at any sort of gathering. For $50 you will present a 20-minute act including singing and dancing. You are not especially talented, but people don't seem to expect much talent from a rooster. Recently you were hired by Big Bill Bluss, President of Bluss Imports (4848 Lake Freeway, Rochester, MN 55901) to appear at the store and present a birthday gift to one of his long-time employees. When you arrived, a birthday party was in progress and the partygoers insisted that you entertain. Because you could not exit gracefully, you presented your complete show. Write a letter to Big Bill requesting $50 rather than the agreed upon $25.

15. As the Rooster (from Exercise 14) you come in contact with a wide variety of audiences. At a recent appearance at a St. Patrick's Day party, sponsored by the Kelly Construction Company, the participants were overly enthusiastic. Several partygoers poured green food coloring on you in an attempt to dye your costume, and several others plucked three of your longest tail feathers. Write a letter to Sean Kelly, President, Kelly Construction Company, P.O. Box 1702, Boston, MA 02109 and request payment of $47 — $25 for dry cleaning and $22 for costume repair.

16. As credit manager for Walsh Specialties (P.O. Box 143, Conyers, GA 30207), you approve Harold Smith's request for credit. He has just opened a lamp store called Let There Be Light (P.O Box 840, Atlanta, GA 30304) in an Atlanta shopping center. You are sending him the following items on terms of 3/10, n/30:

3 solid brass shell floor lamps @ $65	$195.00
6 solid brass 6-way lamps @ $75	450.00
1 Cathay table lamp @ $40	40.00
1 clear glass hexagon table lamp @ $35	35.00
	$720.00

These lamps are fashionable as well as functional and have been popular in all parts of the country. Harold recently came to Georgia from Durham, North Carolina, where he had operated and sold a similar business. A credit report described Harold as "generally prompt in meeting financial obligations." As with all new accounts, you limit his credit to $1,000 until he proves himself to be a responsible individual. Write to Smith confirming the order and extending credit up to $1,000. Point out the 3 percent discount available for payment within 10 days. Mention the desirability of maintaining a good credit record. Also, tell him to watch for the new Walsh catalog, which he will be receiving in approximately 30 days.

17. You have always wanted to learn French and you are considering taking a one-week French Immersion vacation at the Club Miami (P.O. Box 1900, Miami Beach, FL 33139). You have read the brochures but you still have several concerns. The literature states that a variety of teaching techniques are used. You wish to learn what the teaching techniques are. Are the teachers from France or from the United States? Is the focus solely on language or is the French culture also emphasized? A daily jogger, you are interested in whether there will be time and facilities available. Write to the special events director of the Club Miami to get the necessary information.

18. As special events director of the Club Miami, respond to the letter described in Exercise 17. Teaching is accomplished through lectures, group seminars, daily audiovisual language labs, and daily French film classics. The French culture receives considerable emphasis throughout the program. The instructors are U.S. citizens, but each has lived in France for at least one year. Two hours are scheduled each afternoon for recreation and there is a park with jogging paths nearby. Remind the reader that beginning on September 1, the fee for the French Immersion vacation will increase from $375 to $450.

19. You have just opened a sporting goods store (The Right Stuff), and you want to send a note of appreciation to each customer who makes a purchase of $75 or more. Besides thanking the customer, you want to mention that you intend to offer frequent unadvertised specials. Also, entry forms will be available at your store for all of the road races and various softball, soccer, and tennis tournaments held in the community. Prepare an appropriate letter.

CASE | *Not So Picture Perfect*

PJ 158

Randy E. Cone, University of New Orleans

You are Assistant Customer Service Manager for a nationally known film-processing company, and you have worked in that capacity for about two years. Your duties are many and varied but involve primarily helping the Customer Service Manager (your supervisor) resolve conflicts and disagreements between retailers and customers (photographers). You enjoy your work and hope to ultimately be promoted to Customer Service Manager when your supervisor — an older person of great influence in the company — retires in one year.

In the last three months, though, you have been confronted with a situation that you feel really tests your mettle. A number of letters and telephone calls have reached you, complaining about the contents of a form letter that your supervisor routinely sends to customers on the relatively rare occasions when their film has been lost. Irate and often profane as the photographers have been when writing or calling your office, you have to agree with them. In your opinion, the letter *is* awful and is doing a lot to create ill-will toward your company. You have shielded your supervisor from those complaints partly because you know your supervisor took pride in that letter.

In short, the letter is replete with negative words and poor excuses. It begins immediately by saying that the writer is "sorry not to have good news but we regret to advise you that as of the above date, we have not been able to find your lost film. Even though we take great pains to care for each and every roll of film entrusted to us, yours has apparently gone astray somewhere. We will continue looking for it, but we must admit that we sincerely doubt if we will ever find your missing film. Here is another roll; and though it will probably never be possible to take the same pictures again, we hope you will use the film to take pictures of a like interest. Once again, we are very sorry for the loss of your treasured film." The letter is reproduced on sophisticated equipment and doesn't appear to be a form letter. Your supervisor, in fact, personally signs each one before mailing.

Case Questions

1. Rewrite the letter so that the customer-photographer whose film has been lost will regain confidence in your company.

2. How will you convince your supervisor that yours is the letter that should be sent to these often angry customers?

Easy to Judge, Hard to Correct | *CASE*

Lynne K. Anderson, Tidewater Community College, Chesapeake, Va.

Professor Karen Cook teaches a course in business letter writing at Coastal Community College. Instead of giving a final exam, she asks students to collect letters from businesses and organizations throughout the area served by the college. They organize the letters into a report consisting of a title page, letter of transmittal, table of contents, the letters themselves, and critiques of each of the letters based on the criteria developed throughout the course. Finally, each letter is assigned a grade by the student.

Every quarter many of the students' reports include letters that were written by employees of the college. Invariably these letters receive grades of C, D, or even lower.

Karen concurs with these grades. The letters very often are typed with many unnecessary indentations, thereby adding to the cost of producing them. They are full of *I* and *We* with little emphasis on the reader. Some of the letters are so disorganized that they leave the reader wondering why they were written. Tired phrases abound; an insincere "thank you" is tacked onto the end of many letters even when there really is nothing for which to thank the reader. Fill-ins on form letters are not aligned and often are done in a different size type from the form itself.

It would be a simple matter to recommend an in-house seminar for the staff on improving letter-writing skills. However, the college already employs an administrative assistant to the president who screens and approves all of the form letters that go out from the college. This assistant does not screen communications that are not mass produced. This assistant's background and experience are unrelated to business communication.

Case Questions

1. Would you recommend that Professor Cook change the content of her course to be more in line with the letters sent out by various staff people in the college?

2. Should she request that students not include college letters in their term projects?

3. Should she agree with the students' critiques of college letters and still do nothing to suggest improvements?

4. What other alternatives does she have?

Bad-News Letters

When Sandi Torres began her senior year in college, she decided it was time to establish a credit rating. She applied for charge accounts at the four major stores in the area. All four of the stores had advertised widely that it was easy to establish credit with them. Sandi soon discovered that the advertisements were not completely accurate.

Three of the four stores rejected Sandi's application outright because of her lack of full-time work experience. The fourth store granted her a probationary charge account, but only after her parents agreed to cosign her application. What upset Sandi most, however, was the manner in which her applications were rejected. All three of the letters of rejection were curt and impersonal, not at all likely to motivate applicants to reapply for credit later.

No one enjoys receiving bad news; Sandi certainly did not. It is possible, however, to convey negative information in such a way that it will be accepted with understanding.

Business organizations are routinely besieged with requests ranging from the acceptable to the extremely unreasonable. Regardless of the merit of a request, they should respond to it with restraint and with an interest in keeping the goodwill of the person making the request.

Sandi's experience taught her some of the many different ways of saying no. In addition, she discovered that the way she was turned down affected the way she felt about the business.

CHAPTER 6

Learning Objectives

1 *To recognize the strategic decisions that must be made in planning messages of refusal.*

2 *To learn the sequence of thoughts to be conveyed in a letter of refusal.*

3 *To learn the reasons for the thought sequence presented in a letter of refusal.*

4 *To identify the characteristics of effective letters of refusal.*

5 *To learn to write refusals that readers will understand as well as letters that will accomplish the intended purpose.*

The letter of refusal is difficult to write because it denies the reader's request. The reader is unlikely to respond favorably to such a message, and so the directness of the good-news letter is inappropriate. Most authorities suggest that **bad-news letters** be written in an indirect or inductive manner.

The indirect sequence of ideas makes the message more palatable to the reader because it allows writers to convey their thought processes on the subject prior to presenting their decision. The reader can look into the mind of the writer and, ideally, is convinced of the reasonableness of the decision.

Bad-news letters are made more palatable by the indirect sequence and positive words.

The indirect sequence will be either strengthened or weakened by the wording used in the letter. In many bad-news letters the wording throughout is negative, and the overall impression on the reader is negative. Even though the purpose of such a letter is to convey something other than what the reader wishes to receive, it can be done in a positive manner.

PLANNING THE BAD-NEWS LETTER

In recent years the expression "winging it" has become a part of the vocabulary of most of us. Students wing it when they come to class not having prepared the day's assignment. Business people wing it when they make presentations or perform any of their other duties without benefit of customary preparation. People who wing it are gambling that their performance will be acceptable; many times the gamble pays off and their performance does meet minimum standards.

A lack of planning dooms many bad-news letters.

For anyone who is not content with merely meeting minimum standards, however, planning must become routine. This is especially true for challenging tasks—such as conveying bad news. Unless this is done properly, it threatens the relationship that exists between the writer and the reader. In the absence of careful planning it is unlikely to be done properly.

Careful attention to planning differentiates effective business communication from ineffective communication. The following paragraphs describe two different reactions to bad-news letters. Which letter do you suspect was the better planned?

> When Alex MacEnzie's application for a charge account was turned down by a local clothing store, he was irate. He ripped up the letter of rejection, vowing never again to set foot in that store.
>   When Evan Slade received word that he had been denied a charge account with a local building supply company, he was displeased but philosophical. Because he recognized that the goods sold by that company were of high quality and priced fairly, he intended to continue doing business there.

Chapter 5 described the four steps in the planning process. Now we will tailor those steps to situations in which the writer must convey bad news, using the following example:

Bob Costner, fraternity president, recently had to face the task of writing a bad-news letter when the fraternity was sponsoring a sale of 5-pound cans of pecans. Bob had placed an advertisement in the local newspaper that resulted in more than 4,000 orders for the pecans. Unfortunately the fraternity had greatly underestimated the demand and had purchased only 1,000 cans of pecans. Because no more would be available this year, the situation called for a bad-news letter. Bob planned the letter according to the four steps of planning described more thoroughly in Chapter 5.

Determining Objective(s)

Writers must decide what it is they intend to accomplish with their message. Some bad-news letters have more than one objective. If so, decide which is the most important. Although it is not necessary to belabor the bad news, you must ensure that the reader will receive the intended message. Bob felt that the main objective of his letter would be to inform the readers that their orders could not be filled. Another objective would be to retain the goodwill of those whose orders could not be filled.

Considering the Audience

Unless the writer looks at the issue from the standpoint of the readers it is unlikely that the letter will have the desired effect. The audience for Bob's letter consists of local townspeople who were anticipating a genuine bargain. The price of the pecans was approximately half of the usual retail price. Not only was the audience pleased with the notion of a bargain, it was also pleased with the fact that the pecans were guaranteed to be fresh. Virtually all who had placed orders were permanent residents of the community and, therefore, potential customers for future fraternity projects.

Choosing the Ideas to Include

After identifying the objective and the audience to be reached, the writer is ready to determine the ideas that should be included in the message. Sometimes writers list ideas before specifying the objective; this practice usually results in a message with an unclear purpose. Writers who do not identify the audience prior to choosing ideas produce messages that do not appeal to the needs or interests of the readers. Bob felt that these ideas should be included in his letter:

▪ Thanks for your order.
▪ Unfortunately we won't be able to fill it.
▪ We would like to consider you as a possible customer for future fraternity projects.

Selecting the Appropriate Channel and Medium

In selecting the appropriate channel and medium the writer must consider the best way to reach the intended audience. Seeking to maintain a positive relationship with the disappointed individuals, Bob decided to send out letters. He felt that mail would be the most effective medium because his audience was geographically dispersed.

The letter that resulted from this planning is presented later in the chapter.

STRATEGY FOR THE BAD-NEWS LETTER

The general strategy for a letter of refusal is to induce the reader to read the entire letter so as to understand the reasons for the refusal. In this way the writer may be able to retain the reader's approval and business. A continuing relationship might be possible if the reader suspends judgment until the entire message is understood.

The writer should prepare the letter so that it has as little negative effect as possible. Before beginning to write, writers must place themselves in the reader's position. They must decide how to lead the reader to accept their decision.

Imagine that you are the plant manager of an electrical parts manufacturing company. You receive a letter from a sixth-grade class requesting a plant tour for a 40-member group. According to company policy, tours are available only to persons 16 years of age and older and group size is limited to 10. The company benefits from this policy because it greatly restricts the number of individuals likely to take a plant tour. There is, therefore, less disruption of plant operations. Those excluded from such tours may benefit by not being exposed to the potential dangers of the plant's machines, noise, and fumes.

If possible, the letter writer should point out how the reader may benefit from a refusal.

An effective letter writer will strive to point out how the reader will benefit even though the request is denied. In some cases the writer may be able to make a helpful suggestion or offer an alternate plan. The plant manager, for example, might recommend a film that would introduce the students to manufacturing processes and could substitute for a tour.

Occasionally it may be impossible to point out any benefit. However, a writer who looks at the situation from the reader's point of view will generally find a way either to show a benefit or suggest some alternative.

The key to writing letters of refusal that accomplish the intended purpose is to know the facts of the situation. Situations that require such letters are sometimes similar, but they are rarely identical. By knowing the relevant facts, a writer can develop a line of reasoning that the reader is likely to understand and accept.

STEPS IN TRANSMITTING BAD NEWS

Situations requiring letters of refusal vary greatly. However, following certain steps will produce letters that are appropriate and effective.

Neutral Opening

A neutral opening should indicate an area of agreement between writer and reader.

Start with a neutral comment that includes some form of agreement. Your opening comment should let the reader know the subject of the letter, but it should not imply either a yes or a no. After reading the first paragraph, the reader should be aware that the letter is a response to a request. Ideally the writer will indicate some form of agreement with the reader. For example, when a customer wrote to complain about auto repair service, the dealer began his response by stating, "You are certainly right to expect service work that is done properly the first time." This opening accomplishes two things. It indicates the subject of the letter and it points out an area of agreement.

The opening should be consistent with the message that is to follow. Readers who are led to expect acceptance and are then denied it tend to be unhappy and unlikely to continue any relationship with the writer. "We at Baily Motors take pride in the service we provide our customers" would be inappropriate if the writer did not intend to comply with the reader's wishes.

The opening should be objective. Express neither pleasure nor displeasure in responding to the request. "We at Baily Motors are always pleased to hear from our customers" suggests that the writer is enjoying the difficulties the customer is experiencing.

The subject of the letter should be indicated in the opening. "For the past 50 years Baily Motors has been a leader in sales and in service" will leave the reader uncertain as to the subject of the letter. That opening would probably lead the reader to expect a sales letter.

The opening should be written in a positive manner. Don't signal that a rejection is coming. Words such as "however," "although," or "but" signal rejection, as do negative words such as "won't," "can't," and "unable."

Positive Explanation

Present an explanation in a positive manner. The reader will be interested enough to continue reading your letter if you have succeeded in your neutral statement. Next you should give the reasons for your decision. The reasons precede the actual denial of the request. By getting the recipients to read the reasons, you increase the likelihood that they will understand those reasons. It may be true that understanding does not guarantee acceptance, but acceptance seldom occurs without understanding.

Explain rather than apologize. When a writer apologizes, the reader begins to suspect that the decision was not well thought-out. Another shortcoming of writing in an apologetic fashion is that it emphasizes the negative rather than the positive. "We at Baily Motors regret to tell you" reeks of insincerity and negativism.

Whenever possible, cite reasons other than company policy. When the writer must fall back on policy as a reason for not complying with the reader's wishes, it appears that the writer made no attempt to recognize the reader's uniqueness. "For 50 successful years Baily Motors has had a policy that prohibits" is not an adequate explanation.

Communicate on the reader's level. Few things irritate people more than being talked down to. When a writer says, "Our experience in 50 years of serving the public has taught us," it sounds like a parent addressing a child. Readers will not respond favorably.

Provide enough information so that the reader will understand, but not so much that it numbs the reader's mind. An overly brief explanation suggests a lack of concern. When a writer says "Our present exchange policy, which has been in effect for 58 years, originated when a man tried to exchange a saddle," it is overexplanation.

Whenever possible, emphasize reasons that might possibly benefit the reader. To inform a customer that a service contract would not pay for certain auto repairs, one correspondent wrote:

> Your service contract pays for all necessary engine repairs as long as the car is brought in for inspection every 6 months. In the absence of a 6-month inspection, the contract ceases to provide coverage. Regular inspections are intended to identify minor automotive problems before they become major and costly ones. Regular inspections help us to balance our work load so that each workday is quite predictable.

The writer not only explained how customers benefited from service contracts but also how the auto dealer benefited. By describing how the dealer will benefit, the writer comes across as candid and honest, and it makes the whole message more believable. Although the explanation is based on organizational policy, the writer never refers to policy. Policies are cold and impersonal, and it is difficult for people to relate to them. On the other hand, when the writer presents reasons that are clearly stated and plausible, the reasons are better received.

In some instances, the only reasons for refusing a request are, plainly and simply, company reasons. In these instances the writer should not go to great lengths to dream up imaginary benefits for the reader. Instead, just state the company's reason or reasons and let it go at that.

The Refusal

In the third part of the bad-news letter the writer gets to the heart of the matter, the actual refusal. If the reasons were explained clearly, the reader can probably infer a refusal even before actually reading it. Ideally the refusal flows logically from the reasons.

Sometimes it is not necessary to state the refusal directly if it can be implied. When a personnel director writes to tell job applicants that they are unsuitable for the position, a statement such as "We need a person who has had actual supervisory experience" will transmit the bad news. It is unnecessary to say "You do not meet our requirements" or any highly directed equivalent.

De-emphasize the refusal. Convey it without belaboring it. In most well-written bad-news letters, the refusal is embedded in a paragraph — the refusal is neither at the beginning nor the end of a paragraph.

Phrase the refusal in a positive manner. Telling the reader, "Since you forgot to oil the motor, we are unable to give you a refund," conveys the message; however, its accusatory tone may alienate the reader. "We would refund the purchase price if the maintenance instructions had been followed" is preferable.

Use the passive voice when stating the rejection. The active voice is overly blunt and calls undue attention to the refusal. For example, instead of "The admissions committee voted against your application for membership," "Your application for membership was denied by the admissions committee" is more muted but still conveys the refusal.

If there is any chance that the message may be misunderstood, the refusal should be stated directly. The clearer the relationship between the reasons and a refusal, the less necessary it is to state the refusal explicitly.

Positive Note

A letter of refusal should end on an upbeat and should leave the reader favorably disposed toward the writer (and the business). After conveying the refusal, the writer should try to regain some of the goodwill that may have been lost. This can be done in a number of ways. A department store, for example, may suggest its layaway service when it rejects a person's credit application.

Write about something of interest to the reader other than the refusal. Rather than remind the reader of the refusal, offer a counterproposal or some other helpful suggestion.

End in an unapologetic manner. The tendency to apologize suggests that you may have some doubts about the decision, which may encourage the reader to persist in seeking some adjustment or action.

Write positively without relying on clichés. Clichés are tired, overused expressions that may suggest an absence of thought on the part of the writer. Clichés often also suggest insincerity.

The purpose of the ending is to show the reader that you remain interested.

ADJUSTMENT REFUSALS

Customers who request adjustments generally consider themselves and their requests reasonable. Most companies take pride in their equitable adjustment policies. No matter how liberal a company's attitude toward claims is, however, certain requests are bound to be refused. Writing an adjustment refusal letter is a delicate process; the writer implies that the request, viewed by the customer as reasonable, actually is not.

Adjustment refusals are difficult to write because the writer is denying a request that the customer considers reasonable.

In writing an adjustment refusal you should follow the four steps described for refusals. As with all letters of refusal the two main purposes are (1) to state the refusal and (2) to maintain a positive relationship with the reader. The second purpose is especially important when customers seek adjustments, because they are more likely to remain customers if they are treated well. The writer must strive to maintain a positive relationship.

Imagine that you are the sales manager of a company that manufactures sporting goods. A retailer writes to ask if she might return a sizable number

✔️ *CHECKLIST for Transmitting Bad News*

___▪ **Start with a neutral comment that includes some form of agreement. The opening should be consistent with the main message, objective, relevant to the interests of the reader, and written in a positive manner.**

___▪ **Present an explanation in a positive manner. The explanation should explain rather than apologize, cite reasons other than company policy, communicate on the reader's level, and provide enough information so that the reader will understand.**

___▪ **Convey the refusal. When stating the refusal, the writer should embed the refusal in the paragraph, phrase the refusal in a positive manner, and state the refusal in the passive voice.**

___▪ **End on a positive note. The writer should write about something of interest to the reader, end in an unapologetic manner, write positively without relying on clichés, and make the reader aware of the writer's concern rather than of the refusal.**

of skateboards that she purchased from your company. Although interest in skateboarding had been high across the nation, the sport never grew very popular in Green Bay, where the retailer's store is located. Because interest in skateboarding is declining nationally, the skateboards would take up valuable warehouse space for some time. You decide that it is unwise to grant her request, and you write her accordingly. Figure 6.1 shows how one correspondent did it.

In refusing adjustment requests the writer should take the indirect approach.

As mentioned earlier, the indirect approach is appropriate for most bad-news letters. The manager of a convention hotel used the following approach in responding to a request for an adjustment. The president of a national student government association had written to complain about the quantity of food the hotel provided for its Keynote Night banquet.

> Pleasing our customers is the foremost goal of the Elliot Plaza. Our success depends upon your satisfaction, and we appreciate your comments regarding the banquet service provided for your group.
>
> Having catered banquets for more than 200 groups during the past year, we have established a reputation for offering quality meals at reasonable prices. Our standards ensure that food will be served in generous portions. Our records show that the dinner prepared for your group was identical to portions served similar-sized groups, most of which have praised our food service. We would certainly make an adjustment if our standard servings had not been available for your group.
>
> Many organizations are already reserving rooms for holiday banquets, and most of them are repeat customers. We would appreciate the opportunity to count you and your group among them.

When a rock concert promoter was forced to make a substitution for a warm-up group she had advertised, she received a complaint following

FIGURE 6.1 ▪ *Adjustment Refusal*

OMNI SPORTS, INC.
P.O. Box 3546
Athens, OH 45701

March 15, 1991

Ms. Grace Trent
Games Aplenty, Inc.
3612 Main Street
Green Bay, WI 54301

Dear Ms. Trent:

You were right to expect our Rollfree skateboards to be a popular item among your customers. After all, they have been shown to be superior both in durability and in safety. Sales figures have shown the Rollfree to be one of the most popular skateboards in the country.

One of the many challenges in the leisure goods field is the speed with which consumers' interests change. The public's changing tastes frequently leave us with excess inventory. We're always willing to make adjustments if there are quality problems in our merchandise. In the absence of such problems, all sales are final.

Some analysts already predict a resurging interest in skateboarding. This resurgence and Rollfree's upcoming national advertising campaign should help boost your sales. Also, I am sending you separately some new mats for newspaper advertisements that have stimulated sales in cities like Green Bay.

Sincerely,

Ramon Evans

Ramon Evans
Sales Correspondent

mb

Neutral comment that confirms the store's good judgment.

Reasons for the decision with an implied refusal.

Ends on hopeful note with focus on the future.

the concert. She sought to reject the request for a refund without sacrificing future business by writing the letter reproduced in Figure 6.2.

Although a small number of requests for adjustments may border on the fraudulent, most do not. Sometimes correspondents who regularly handle adjustments grow cynical, and cynicism is reflected in their letters. Such letters often may read like this:

The writer should avoid cynicism in letters of refusal.

You claim that the hair dryer did not work as advertised. We cannot understand how this quality-checked appliance could possibly malfunction. According to you the dryer never worked as it was supposed to.

FIGURE 6.2 ▪ *Request Denial*

Neutral statement that confirms the original expectation.

Explains the cause of the unusual occurrence and subtly justifies the decision.

Describes the organization's policy and conditions that would warrant a refund.

Compliments the complainant's good judgment and looks ahead to doing business again.

Star Productions, Inc.
2006 Mainline Avenue, Suite 2000
Newark, NJ 07102

October 12, 1991

Randolph Scott
1646 12th Street
Perth Amboy, NJ 08861

Dear Mr. Scott:

We can certainly understand why you had expected Abject Failure to be the warm-up act at the concert last Friday. We begin to advertise a concert only when all of the acts on the program have agreed to perform.

Occasionally something happens that we cannot control. Two members of Abject Failure were hospitalized the night before the concert, and there was little time to advertise the change. Most of the spectators seemed to think that the Scavengers did an excellent job as the replacement warm-up group. Our surveys show that most spectators attend concerts to see the headliners. Since the headline acts appeared as advertised, everyone seemed pleased with the concert.

We take our responsibilities to the public very seriously. If ever an advertised headliner is unable to appear, you can be sure that you will receive a full refund.

Loyal fans like you may soon be able to see Abject Failure headlining a concert here. Our schedule for the next three months is enclosed. You're sure to find some of these concerts to your liking.

Yours truly,

Whitney Dallas

Whitney Dallas
Promotion Specialist

nf

Enc.

Letters written by cynical correspondents are tinged with distrust and suspicion. They may convey the message but lose a customer. An effective bad-news letter clearly conveys the message yet retains the trust and business of the customer.

Occasionally a writer faces a situation in which the indirect approach is either inappropriate or unworkable. If a customer has already received a written refusal and explanation yet persists in requesting an adjustment, the direct approach may be suitable for a second letter. If the reader

BOXED IN | *AN ETHICAL DILEMMA*

One of the things that Beth Sommers likes about her job as assistant credit manager at United Hardware Wholesalers is the diversity of duties. Another is that she has personally gotten to know most of the major customers. Among her favorites is Walt Gibson, owner of a large hardware store in a nearby suburb. Although he is not United's largest customer, Walt has dealt regularly with United during the five years Beth has been there. Walt is occasionally a month late in paying his bill, but so are many other customers.

For the past year Walt has been asking for an increase in his credit line from $5,000 to $10,000. Beth's boss, Ralph Bell, has always answered that they would consider an increase "one of these days." Several times, however, Ralph has told Beth not to increase Walt's credit because it is "only a matter of time before some national hardware chain moves into Walt's suburb and drives him out of business." In fact, Ralph would like to reduce Walt's line of credit so that United will not lose money when the inevitable happens.

Now Walt has made a formal request in writing to United for an increased credit line, saying that it is impossible to maintain an adequate inventory without it. Ralph instructs Beth to write to Walt and tell him that his request is "under advisement" and that a decision will be made "in the near future."

"That ought to hold him for six more months," Ralph says.

Beth realizes that Walt will never be granted more credit by United. She is uncomfortable leading him to believe that a higher credit line is a possibility. She thinks that this is no way to treat a long-time customer. She doesn't want to write what she considers a misleading letter.

Beth feels boxed in. What would you do?

---

ignores the first letter refusing adjustment and simply repeats the request, the writer is justified in becoming more blunt.

To ensure that the message is unmistakably clear the writer might present the denial in the first sentence. (For example, "Until you complete the travel expense form properly, you will not be reimbursed for your business trip.") This approach may make the reader realize that the problem is serious. It is a risky approach, however, and may alienate the reader. For this reason the direct approach should be used only after careful consideration of how the reader is likely to respond.

After buying a lightweight suit on sale, Bob Norris had second thoughts and wrote to the store:

> Two weeks ago I purchased a lightweight suit at your half-price sale. Now I realize that the color isn't right for me and I'd like to return it. I wore the suit only once.
>
> As you can see from your records, I am a longtime customer of Grenier's. In fact, almost once a month I make the 60-mile drive to shop

A direct approach is sometimes taken in bad-news letters, but only after careful consideration.

at your store. Since I plan to go shopping within the next two weeks, please inform me promptly of your decision.

The store conveyed the bad news of an adjustment refusal in this way:

As a smart shopper you know that taking advantage of sales makes sense. You saved 50 percent by buying your suit at our recent end-of-the-season sale. Your willingness to drive 60 miles to shop at Grenier's shows that you appreciate quality, too.

Customers like you benefit from our end-of-the-season sales in several ways: not only do you enjoy tremendous savings, you also have the opportunity to select from the newest styles. Our end-of-the-season sales allow us to change our stock often and to be up-to-date.

You can be sure that any clothing you buy at Grenier's will be brand new and that you are the original purchaser. We feel that we owe that to our customers. Although sales items are nonreturnable, the purchase price would, of course, be refunded on any defective merchandise.

We appreciate your loyalty and we hope to continue to earn it.

After reading the letter, Bob:

▪ Knew that he couldn't return the suit.
▪ Understood why the store was unable to take it back.
▪ Believed that the store was aware of the facts.
▪ Believed that he had been treated fairly.
▪ Intended to continue shopping at Grenier's.

These are the kinds of responses sought by the writer of a letter refusing a requested adjustment.

✔ CHECKLIST for an Adjustment Refusal

___▪ Make your opening comment neutral and relate it to the subject of the letter.

___▪ Imply neither yes nor no in the opening.

___▪ Keep the opening brief.

___▪ Convey a positive tone rather than an apologetic one in presenting the reasons for your decision.

___▪ If possible, show how the reader may actually benefit from the decision because of the reasons.

___▪ Present the reasons so that the reader anticipates a refusal.

___▪ Make your refusal clear, but don't overemphasize it.

___▪ Avoid mentioning the refusal in the ending. End the letter on a positive note.

CREDIT REFUSALS

Some authorities maintain that every single business letter is a sales letter. No matter what the stated purpose of a letter, the writer must also try to sell the reader on the organization.

When you write a refusal of credit, you face a real challenge. Although you are denying a request, you should take a positive approach and try to retain the goodwill of the reader. Many people today regard credit as a right that cannot be denied them. This attitude complicates the task facing the writer.

Denying a person credit while keeping that person's business is a challenge to the writer of credit refusals.

Many writers seem to ignore the challenge of a letter of refusal. Writers who believe that you cannot deny credit and at the same time keep a friend write uninspired letters, such as this:

> Thank you for applying for a charge account at Wilson's Department Store. We regret to state that we are unable to extend credit to you at this time.
> We appreciate your patronage.

A credit refusal like this suggests that the company has little hope of retaining the applicant's business. The letter is cold and impersonal. The writer presents the obvious message but pays no heed to the applicant's feelings or continued patronage. The person who receives such a letter is likely to become frustrated and angry.

By changing the thrust of the letter, the writer may be able to turn a negative situation into a more positive one. The applicant might be persuaded to become a cash customer. A department store stressed in its refusal letter the advantages of shopping there:

When denying credit, the writer might strive to sell the reader on becoming a cash customer.

> Thank you for your recent application for a charge account at Astor Brothers.
> Much information is considered before opening a new charge account, and your application was carefully considered. Once you are employed on a full-time basis, it may be possible for you to receive an Astor Brothers credit card.
> Until that time please allow us to serve you on a cash basis. As our fall fashions are about to arrive, you may also enjoy our convenient layaway plan.

Of the many possible reasons for refusing a request for credit, a poor credit record is number one. Other common reasons may be that the applicant has too small or unsteady an income or, perhaps, no credit experience upon which to base a decision.

Whether the credit applicant is an individual consumer or a business organization, the letter of refusal is organized in the same way. In either case the writer will probably refer to the advantages of paying cash or making cash-on-delivery purchases. The writer should follow the four steps for transmitting unpleasant news. The letter to the organizational applicant may be somewhat more forthright. A letter that refuses credit to a business follows the usual pattern of neutral comment, explanation, refusal, and positive ending. In Figure 6.3 the writer incorporates a bid for cash business in the ending.

The writer follows the same steps rejecting credit to an organization, or an individual.

FIGURE 6.3   ▪   *Credit Refusal to a Business*

NATIONAL HARDWARE SUPPLY   4000 Industrial Parkway   Tell City, IN 47586

February 28, 1991

Mr. Paul Friendly
Friendly Hardware
1002 S. Adams Street
Letts, IA 52754

Dear Mr. Friendly:

Thank you for your order for four dozen Evenflow seed and
fertilizer spreaders. Your large order suggests that you are
expecting a profitable spring. We are glad to hear that.

Your credit references unanimously agree that you are a person
of integrity and sound business principles. At this time the
information about your hardware operation, however, is somewhat
less positive. It is obvious that the competition for hardware
customers is indeed intense, and this always has an adverse impact
on one's financial position. Current economic conditions lend
additional uncertainty to the general business environment.

The upturn in the economy that is expected this spring will most
likely improve your position considerably. For the present,
however, we'll be pleased to continue serving you on a cash basis.
You, in turn, will continue to receive a 2 percent discount for
cash purchases. Another advantage of cash payment is that orders
may be of any size; no minimum order is required.

By reducing your present order by as much as one-half, you will
still have adequate stock to meet the early spring demand.

Please send us your instructions on the enclosed order form.
Your shipment will be sent as soon as we hear from you.

Sincerely,

Rankin Jones

Rankin Jones
Credit Analyst

na

Enc.

Introduces the subject objectively.

Simultaneously presents a positive personal profile of the customer and a rationale for the decision.

Points out positive aspects of the refusal.

Ends on a positive note and requests specific action.

The refusal should be de-emphasized.

   Those who seek credit cannot be expected to be pleased when their applications are rejected. Many people think a rejection of credit is a rejection of personal worth. Refusing credit is a delicate matter meriting thoughtful consideration. Writers often err by emphasizing the refusal rather than developing a cash customer. By de-emphasizing the refusal and stressing the advantages of cash payment, a writer can often retain customers who might otherwise be lost.

   Beyond this, a person who is refused credit has a legal right to know the reason for the refusal. If it is based on information provided by a credit-reporting agency, the writer should say so. Although the writer is not required to give the specific reasons in the refusal letter, according to the Fair Credit Reporting Act, customers are entitled to an explanation if they request one within 60 days of receiving the credit refusal. In order to avoid having to write an additional letter of explanation to rejected credit applicants, many organizations include the reasons in the initial credit refusal letter. Some organizations use forms such as the one in Figure 6.4 for refusing credit applications.

Sometimes the volume of credit applications is so great that they cannot be handled individually. Using a refusal form serves a useful purpose in that the reader receives the necessary information more promptly than might otherwise be the case.

PROBLEM ORDERS

The success of any business organization depends to a considerable extent on the speed with which the organization can satisfy its customers. The term **turnaround time** is often used to describe how long it takes for business firms to provide customers with their goods and services.

Even the most efficient organization sometimes experiences delays in handling orders. Regardless of who is responsible for the delay, it often calls for a letter in which the writer must convey information likely to displease a customer.

Items Not in Stock

When an item is temporarily out of stock but will be available soon you should so inform the customer. Because the customer will experience a delay, you will be transmitting bad news. At the same time you want to retain the customer's business. Here is an example of a letter of refusal that suffers from misplaced focus:

> Thank you for your order of April 7. Unfortunately, we are presently unable to fill your order for one Classic circulating fan.
>
> We pride ourselves on our speed in filling orders, and we usually order in ample quantities. Skyrocketing energy costs combined with customer recognition of a genuine bargain may help explain why customer demand has outdistanced our supply.
>
> We're working hard to remedy the situation, however, and by May 15 you should be enjoying the economy and comfort that accompany a Classic circulating fan. If, due to the delay, you wish to cancel this order, please notify us promptly. We hope you won't do that, however, since we know you'll agree that a Classic circulating fan is worth waiting for.

This letter is ineffective for several reasons. The first paragraph shows no attempt to indicate an area of agreement between writer and reader. The writer presented the bad news immediately, so it is unlikely that the disappointed reader will finish the letter. When notifying a customer of a delay in an order, you should focus on the order rather than on the delay. The example focuses on the delay in the first paragraph.

FIGURE 6.4   ■   *Example of Credit Refusal Form*

Date _____ 19_____

☐ Statement handed to Applicant

☐ Mailed

by: _____
Authorized Signature

Telephone: 546-1866

We would like to thank you for your recent loan application. We have given it careful consideration. However, we regret to inform you that your application has been declined.

We have provided the reason(s) for our decision in the section below. This notice is given in accordance with the various consumer credit laws and regulations applicable to our bank.

Description of account, transaction, or requested credit: _____

Description of adverse action taken: _____

Reason(s)

☐ Credit application incomplete
☐ Insufficient credit references
☐ Unable to verify credit references

☐ Length of employment
☐ Temporary or irregular employment
☐ Unable to verify employment

☐ Insufficient income
☐ Excessive obligations
☐ Unable to verify income

☐ Too short a period of residence
☐ Temporary residence
☐ Unable to verify residence

☐ No credit file
☐ Insufficient credit file
☐ Delinquent credit obligations

☐ Garnishment, attachment, foreclosure, repossession, or suit
☐ Bankruptcy
☐ Inadequate collateral

☐ We do not grant credit to anyone on the terms and conditions you request.

☐ Other-(specify) _____

DISCLOSURE OF USE OF INFORMATION OBTAINED FROM AN OUTSIDE SOURCE.

☐ Disclosure Inapplicable
☐ Information obtained in a consumer report from: Credit Bureau of Athens, 400 College Avenue, Athens, Georgia 30601.

☐ Information obtained from an outside source other than a consumer reporting agency. Under the Fair Credit Reporting Act, you have the right to make a written request within 60 days of receipt of this notice, for a disclosure of the nature of the adverse information.

The Federal Equal Credit Opportunity Act prohibits creditors from discrimination against credit applicants on the basis of race, color, religion, national origin, sex, marital status, age, (provided that the applicant has the capacity to enter into a binding contract); because all or part of the applicant's income derives from any public assistance program; or because the applicant has in good faith exercised any right under the Consumer Credit Protection Act. The Federal Agency that administers compliance with this law concerning this creditor is: COMPTROLLER OF THE CURRENCY, CONSUMER AFFAIRS DIVISION, WASHINGTON, D.C. 20219

Knowing that the company takes pride in filling orders quickly provides little consolation for the customer who is not benefiting from this speed. If anything, the customer will be skeptical of an organization that boasts at such an inopportune time. The second paragraph, therefore, serves no useful purpose.

The third paragraph states that the situation will be remedied soon and reminds the reader of the product's superiority. This statement is completely appropriate. Suggesting that the order could be canceled, on the

✔ *CHECKLIST for a Credit Refusal*

——◣ Begin with a neutral idea with which the reader will agree.

——◣ Explain the reasons for the decision.

——◣ State the refusal briefly and without using negative language.

——◣ If possible, offer an alternative, such as paying cash or using COD purchasing.

——◣ Close with a look toward the future and without apologizing.

other hand, is not in the company's best interests. The customer may choose to cancel the order, but the writer need not suggest it. The request that the customer not cancel is weak and unnecessary. By ending the letter with a reminder of the delay, the writer incorrectly makes it the parting thought.

A letter of refusal should not end with a reminder of the bad news.

A letter that informs a reader that an order will be delayed has two main purposes: (1) to convince the reader to wait for the order and (2) to retain the reader's business in the future. These purposes are accomplished better in this way:

> Your order for a Classic circulating fan identifies you as a person who recognizes both quality and value.
>
> A growing volume of orders for the Classic indicates that the public has also become aware of the superiority of the Classic. Production is increasing, but the quality you associate with the Classic is being maintained.
>
> You will be enjoying the comfort and economy of a Classic circulating fan by May 15, well before the onset of hot weather. The Classic will make the heat and humidity of summer disappear in a breeze.

When Bob Costner learned that his fraternity would be unable to fill many of the orders for pecans, as described earlier in this chapter, he wrote this letter:

> Dear Patron:
>
> Do you realize how many friends you have? It was only after the TZ fraternity house was swamped with orders for pecans that we realized the number of our friends.
>
> In each of the past five years our pecan sales have increased by approximately 10 percent. For that reason we felt comfortable in increasing our total order by 10 percent this year. We intended to keep our order realistic so that we would not have to pay for shipping any unsold pecans back to the wholesaler. Such shipping expenses would eat into the amount earned for the Family Shelter, this year's project. We are still wondering if it was the quality of the pecans, the fair price, or the importance of the Family Shelter that caused the avalanche of orders. Whatever the reason, we received orders for 300 percent more pecans than last year.
>
> As we have always done with this project, the orders were filled in the sequence in which they were received. Each of the other patrons is receiving this letter.

This has been a learning experience for us. When you place your order with us next year, we plan to have enough fresh pecans on hand to fill it.
Sincerely,

Discontinued Items

In the best of all possible business worlds, as soon as a company stopped handling a certain item, all orders for that item would cease immediately. What actually happens is that orders continue to trickle in for the item long after its discontinuation.

The writer should offer an appropriate substitute, if possible, for a discontinued item.

In response to an order for a discontinued item, you must inform the customer of the discontinuation while offering an appropriate substitute. Do not, however, offer a substitute that is not clearly appropriate. It is better to lose one sale and to retain the goodwill of a customer than to provide a substitute with which the customer will be displeased.

When a retailer ordered some T-450 tapes from a wholesaler who had stopped carrying the T-450, the wholesaler offered an appropriate substitute.

> Thank you for your order of March 17. Your customers apparently associate high quality with the Superchron name as do most people who take pride in their video investment.
>
> As a result of its ongoing research program, Superchron has now developed a videotape that is significantly superior to anything formerly available. This new product offers 30 percent higher picture quality and 50 percent longer life than does the T-450. By refining high-energy tape particles, Superchron has created the T-900, a tape that is mirror smooth and which provides perfect pictures for replay after replay. Although you may be able to order some T-450 tapes directly from the Superchron Company, your customers will prefer the T-900 once they learn of it.
>
> Your customers will agree that the T-900 is worth an additional $1.50 for a 60-minute cassette. Call me at (601) 592–1313 any weekday between 9 and 5. I'll fill your order that same day at a price of $15.25 per tape on orders of one dozen or more.
>
> The savings your customers will enjoy through the longer life of the T-900 will make them glad you acquainted them with the T-900.

Too Small an Order

Many different types of misunderstandings may occur in the process of placing and filling orders. One instance happens when a customer places an order for a quantity too small to merit the discount expected by the customer.

In order to stimulate sales, the Green-Gro Company offered a 5 percent discount on purchases of 100 or more 50-pound bags of lawn fertilizer. When a retailer requested the 5 percent discount on an order of only 50 bags, the wholesaler responded this way:

> This year marks the 12th year you have purchased your supply of Green-Gro products from us. The growth of your orders over these years suggests that your customers enjoy dealing with you as much as we do. Your adherence to sound business practices in placing orders, making prompt payment, and customer follow-up have been appreciated.

✓ *CHECKLIST for a Problem Order*

▁▁▙ Begin with a noncommittal statement to which the reader is likely to respond positively.

▁▁▙ Present the reasons for the decision.

▁▁▙ If possible, show how the reader would benefit from the decision.

▁▁▙ Present the refusal without belaboring it.

▁▁▙ Avoid additional references to the refusal and point to future business in the closing.

> For the first time ever, the Green-Gro Company has offered a special 5 percent discount on its lawn fertilizer, and we are passing this discount on to our customers. The one stipulation made by the Green-Gro Company is that orders must be for at least 100 50-pound bags in order to get the special discount.
>
> By increasing your order to 100 bags, you will be ready for the upcoming seasonal rush and you will qualify for the special discount. Regardless of the size of your order, you will still receive our regular terms of 2/10, n/30.
>
> You will be receiving our new catalog within three weeks. It features several new garden products that your customers will soon be seeking.

Many problems in ordering can be resolved face to face or over the telephone. When a letter is necessary, however, remember to use the indirect arrangement.

When refusing or modifying problem orders, the writer should use the indirect arrangement.

FAVOR REFUSALS

Business organizations routinely receive requests for favors of various types. Some of the favors may be business-related, such as a special discount or preferential treatment for a particular order. Other favors may be sought by complete strangers. Charities may seek contributions. Students may write for information for research papers. A list of the types of favors sought from business organizations would be endless.

It is easy to write a letter granting a favor—that's good news! Denying a favor is somewhat more difficult, but it is best accomplished through a carefully considered letter of refusal. If it is possible to offer a counterproposal, the writer will soften the refusal.

A counterproposal will soften the impact when a request for a favor is refused.

One of the authors of this book asked several business organizations to provide some actual letters to serve as examples in this book. Although Delta Air Lines would not grant the request, it made a generous and attractive counterproposal. The letter in Figure 6.5 follows the four steps: neutral comment, explanation, refusal (with a counterproposal), and a positive ending.

Sometimes you receive a request that you are unable or do not choose to honor, and no counterproposal is possible. Nevertheless, you should

FIGURE 6.5 ▪ *Letter Offering a Counterproposal to a Request*

 . DELTA AIR LINES, INC.
GENERAL OFFICES/HARTSFIELD ATLANTA INTERNATIONAL AIRPORT/ATLANTA, GEORGIA 30320 U.S.A.

September 5, 1987

Mr. James M. Lahiff
Associate Professor
Department of Management
College of Business Administration
University of Georgia
Athens, Georgia 30602

Dear Mr. Lahiff:

This is just the helpful sort of reply to your good letter (of August 30th)
that you imagined you'd receive. College students are likely correct in
their complaints that classrooms are "far-removed" from the real world. And
too many of us "out here" in the private sector must share the blame.

Unfortunately, Delta's correspondence must be considered as confidential
between the company and those to whom we address letters. So, we can't
"lift" from our files, forwarding copies of actual letters. However, we
might be able to draft several "sample-type" examples, if you'd give us some
subject ideas, and if you agree that such samples would suffice.

I have a special place in my heart for the University and its excellent
College of Business Administration. My late son, Lane, graduated from your
college, magna cum laude, in 1975. He thought very highly of Georgia and
its faculty.

You see, Professor, because of your nice comments about Delta and my special
affiliation with you all, I can't let you down! Let's hear from you soon
and we'll supply your sample business letters.

Thank you so much for your interest in Delta, and with best wishes, I am

Sincerely,

James L. Ewing, III
Staff Director—National Media Relations

JLE/dw

Source: Courtesy Delta Air Lines.

follow the four steps. Try to convey the refusal clearly while retaining the reader's goodwill. This is how one corporation responded when solicited for a financial contribution:

> You and the other members of the Committee to Preserve the Strand should be commended for your efforts to have the theater designated as a historic site. The lives of future generations will be enriched through the success of such projects.
>
> We at the regional headquarters of Turflo are impressed with the large number of worthwhile projects such as yours. Several times each week we receive requests for financial support, and invariably the causes are worthy ones. Determining the worthiest recipients is a task precluded by our own time constraints.
>
> One way in which we try to meet our social responsibility is through our financial support of three major health-oriented organizations and the United Way. By targeting our contributions in this way we balance our support between social action goals and quality of life improvement.
>
> Your efforts to preserve a genuine landmark deserve widespread support. Best wishes on this project.

SUMMARY

Many of the requests made of any business organization must be refused. Because the letter of refusal conveys bad news, you should plan it carefully. Organize it in an indirect fashion proceeding from the general to the specific. This increases the chance that the reader will suspend judgment until the entire message is understood.

In writing a letter of refusal, begin with a neutral statement that makes the reader aware of the subject but implies neither an acceptance nor a refusal. Next, provide the reasons for your decision. By the time you state the refusal, the reader probably has already inferred it; the refusal should flow logically from the reasons. The ending should be positive and should not refer to the refusal.

When writing any bad-news letter, two concepts are especially important: (1) Present your ideas in an indirect sequence. In that way the reader will be more likely to read and understand your reasoning. (2) Use positive wording. Even though the message is not what the reader is hoping for, you may be able to salvage the relationship with the reader.

Refusing an adjustment request is a delicate process because the writer implies that the reader's request was unreasonable. A poorly written adjustment refusal can irritate and frustrate the reader.

Many people consider credit to be a basic human right, which makes writing a credit refusal difficult. Try to convey the message while retaining the friendship of the reader. A refusal of credit to a business organization is usually somewhat more forthright than one sent to an individual.

Problems in handling orders often require letters in which bad news must be conveyed. When ordered items are temporarily out of stock or discontinued, the writer is challenged to satisfy the customer in some other way.

Sometimes favors are requested that cannot be granted. When you must deny a request for a favor, try to provide a counterproposal. This, of course, is not always possible. Regardless, follow the four steps presented in this chapter.

Key Terms

▪ **bad-news letter**   ▪ **turnaround time**

Review Questions

1. What are the four steps of planning?

2. Explain the indirect sequence.

3. Why should you withhold the actual refusal until well into the letter?

4. What are the functions of the neutral comment at the beginning of a letter of refusal?

5. Why should you present the reasons for your decision before the actual decision?

6. If the main purpose of a letter is to refuse a request, why should the refusal be sandwiched between neutral and positive statements?

7. Explain the purpose of a positive ending.

8. When are direct adjustment refusals appropriate?

9. What is meant by the expression, "Every business letter is a sales letter"?

10. What are the advantages of providing the reasons for refusing credit in the initial credit-refusal letter? Are there any disadvantages?

Exercises

1. You are reservations manager for the Extravagancia, a 900-room oceanfront hotel in Florida. The Extravagancia has an annual occupancy rate of 88 percent, and it is strongly oriented toward families. In fact, 90 percent of its guests bring at least one child with them.

In recent years there has been a growing influx of college students who spend their spring break at the Extravagancia. Boisterous college students have upset some of the more sedate guests in several instances.

You have decided to discourage the college trade, but you realize that today's undesirable college students will be tomorrow's desirable customers. For that reason you do not want to alienate the students when you decline to allow them to stay at the Extravagancia.

Today you received the season's first request for a reservation from a college student. Send your response to Billy Joe Harrison, 120 Finnegan Hall, Central State University, Eclipse, VA 23349.

2. As a commercial rental agent in Atlanta you have profited considerably from the sizable influx of business firms into Atlanta. Much of the next great wave of business rental activity is expected to be provided by foreign companies opening facilities in Atlanta. Rather than waiting to be approached for your services, you have decided to develop a form letter to be sent to those foreign

firms that announce an intent to open a branch of any sort in Atlanta. Among the services you provide to your clients are: selection of most ideal site; negotiation on monetary and nonmonetary terms of lease; identification of the image provided by various business locations; assessment of convenience of location; and evaluation of quality of building management at various possible locations. Competition is very keen among 20 major rental agents in Atlanta, and you want your letter to give you a competitive edge. Write the form letter.

3. You have just received a request from the seniors at Martin High School to allow them to conduct a sales campaign among the employees and on the premises of Rampart Insurance Company. The proceeds will be donated to a nearby children's hospital. Company policy prohibits such soliciting, and the firm's liability insurance policy would not cover solicitors. Write a letter of refusal to Robert Hocking, president of the senior class, Martin High School, Beaufort, SC 29902.

4. You are employed by Quikheat, an electrical appliance company. Approximately 10,000 toasters produced by one of your competitors, Solarist, have been declared unsafe by a governmental agency. Solarist has been ordered to repair them at no expense to the owners. This widely publicized order has been misunderstood by many Quikheat owners, who have been writing to learn what they must do to get their toasters repaired. Prepare a form letter explaining the situation for Quikheat owners who write to you.

5. Each year for the past 20 years your electrical parts company has offered free calendars to customers and to people in the local community. These calendars have become very popular because of the interesting artwork. They have also become increasingly expensive, and for this reason you decide to discontinue the practice. Instead you send greeting cards, and soon you are swamped with letters and postcards from persons asking why they did not receive a calendar. Write a form letter in response to such inquiries.

6. When you received a check from Gilson Hardware Company on November 10, you discovered that Gilson deducted the 2 percent discount that is available only for payment within 10 days of delivery. Gilson received an order of 12 lawn mowers from your company on October 12 and was billed $1,788.00. The check dated November 8 is for $1,752.24. Gilson Hardware has been a good customer for 10 years. Write a letter to Gilson Hardware Company (1400 Clayton Street, Farley, MO 64028) requesting a check for $35.76, the amount incorrectly deducted from the original check.

7. You are the admissions director for Scotsdale College, a private, liberal arts institution that is widely respected for its strong curriculum. Late in May you receive an application from a German student for admission for the fall quarter. Although he has excellent grades and outstanding test scores, you are unable to accept him. It is a policy of the school that no more than 25 percent of the student body may be comprised of non-U.S. citizens, and that quota has already been met for this year. You feel that this individual would be a real addition to your institution, and you would like him to consider reapplying for the next school year. Convey this information in writing to Boris Langer, Zwickhauer Strauss 23, D5400 Koblenz, West Germany.

8. Imagine that you are the manager of Vittles Super Store, a huge ultramodern supermarket that includes a pharmacy, bank, beauty salon, florist, and bakery. The store is located in a college town and you employ 120 parttime employees, almost all of them college students. Last year, the first year of operation, you encountered many personnel problems during the week of spring break. A number of employees who were given the week off did not return when they were scheduled to. Several phoned from out of town to tell you that they were quitting. Some simply did not show up again. About 60 percent fulfilled their obligations completely. You have decided to avoid problems this year by allowing no one to take time off during spring break. It is only 6 weeks from now, and some employees are already asking to be away. Write a letter to all employees in which you convey your decision.

9. One of your many duties as personnel manager at Steadfast, Inc. is to administer the Educational Assistance Plan (EAP). The EAP provides for the reimbursement of tuition expenses to any employee who earns a grade of *C* or better in any preapproved college course. Jack Sommers, an hourly employee, has submitted a request form to the EAP for reimbursement for a preapproved psychology course that he recently completed. You call the registrar at the college and learn that Jack earned a *D* for the course. This was the first college course that Jack has taken. Write a letter in which you deny Jack's request for reimbursement.

10. You are the promotion manager for the Multi, a large arena in a metropolitan area. Following a concert by the most popular group in the nation, the Gazelles, you receive this letter:

> My friends and I camped in front of your box office the night before tickets for the Gazelles' show went on sale. This was our first visit to the Multi. There were about 20 people ahead of us, but we were sure that we'd have seats down front.
> Imagine our surprise when we went to the concert and found ourselves in the 16th row. Not only that, but most of the people in front of us bought their tickets on the day of the concert.
> We were so mad that we went home after the concert and broke all our Gazelles' records. We'll never attend another concert at the Multi. We may reconsider, however, if you will refund the price of our tickets. After all, fair is fair, and we should have been in the front row. I am enclosing our ticket stubs.

There had been a malfunction in the computerized ticket operation that hadn't been discovered until the day of the concert. That is how the last purchasers got the best seats.

Write a letter to Donny Zigler, 1219 Southview, Delano, TN 37325. Deny his request for a refund, but sell him on the idea of returning to the Multi for future concerts. Even though he was not in the first row, his seat was in the $22 section as he had requested.

11. You are the owner of Trash Master Inc., a refuse collection firm that picks up trash from both residential and commercial customers. Trash Master is 15 years old, the oldest such firm in town. Until 3 years ago you had no competitors. Since then Trash Wiz, a national firm, arrived in the community and has taken 15 percent of your customers.

You have resisted raising your rates for the past 3 years but you must now do so. Your own rapidly increasing expenses dictate that rates must be raised by 15 percent. For residential customers the new monthly rate will be $9 for the usual twice-a-week pickups. The rates for commercial customers vary according to the number and size of the pickups. For example, fast-food restaurants will pay $50 per month for daily pickups. There are several differences between Trash Master and Trash Wiz: (1) Trash Master is locally owned and operated. (2) Trash Master offers residential customers two pickups per week while Trash Wiz, which uses containers one-and-one-half times larger than those used by Trash Master, offers a single weekly pickup. (3) Trash Wiz has curbside pickup only, while Trash Master customers need not carry their trash containers down to the street. (4) As a result of the rate increase, Trash Master residential rates will be 20 percent higher than those of Trash Wiz, while the commercial rates of the two will be the same.

Write (a) a letter to all of your residential customers, announcing the rate increase while trying to retain their business, and (b) a letter to your fast-food clients.

12. As manager of customer services for British Isles Airways you spend much of your time handling complaints. You are presently trying to reach a settlement for a piece of luggage that has been lost somewhere in the BIA system for 35 days. According to the BIA policy, after 35 days luggage is declared officially lost and the owner is compensated for it. Also, according to BIA policy, compensation for lost luggage may not, in the absence of sales receipts, exceed $400. The owner of this average-sized suitcase is demanding $750, claiming that amount as the value of the contents of the suitcase. In accordance with BIA policy an itemized list of contents has been submitted, but the owner, Susan Jeffries, was unable to provide any sales receipts for the items lost. In your letter you should deny her request for $750 while retaining her goodwill. Her address is 79/82 Middle Abbey Street, Dublin, Co Dublin 1, Ireland.

13. In this morning's mail you received an almost new ½-horsepower electric motor and a request for a complete cash refund. In the accompanying letter the customer noted that the motor would no longer work after only 12 hours of use. An enclosed receipt showed that the motor had been purchased one month ago. The motor is protected by a 12-month warranty. A technician tested the motor and discovered water inside it, making it appear that the motor broke because it had been either hosed down or immersed in water. The operating instructions expressly stipulate that the motor must not come in contact with water and that such an occurrence is not covered by warranty. As a customer service representative for Dynamotors Inc., write to the customer (George Adam, 1044 Norman Lane, Lebanon, IN 46052). Deny the requested cash refund and give your reasons. Indicate that the company will repair the motor for $12 if the customer so desires. In any case the motor will be returned to George COD.

14. In cooperation with the city of Los Angeles' attempts to reduce traffic on the freeways during rush hours, Lamicraft Inc. has introduced a flextime work schedule. The flextime plan allows employees some discretion in setting their work hours so that all employees do not leave at the same time. The plan has been well-received. The company has also organized carpools. The two programs together have noticeably reduced the volume of traffic in the area in which Lamicraft is located. Tammy Parker, a mail clerk, has rearranged her schedule so that she arrives and departs one hour later than she formerly did. Her absence during the first hour of each work day has caused problems that you had not anticipated. Many people, including your boss, have been upset that she was not on the job first thing in the morning. You know that Tammy has been especially pleased with her new work schedule as well as with the carpool she has joined. She is an excellent worker and you want to retain her.

As her boss you are to write a letter to her informing her of the necessary change.

15. Eighteen members of a German tour group of 40 complained individually to Liberty International Inns, Inc., about the poor service, dirty rooms, and discourteous treatment they received at a Liberty Inn while visiting the United States. Each one of the 18 writers is requesting a 50 percent refund as a result of the unpleasant experience. Evaluate the form letter sent by the president of Liberty International to each complainant:

> Thank you for your letter regarding your recent stay at the Liberty Inn in the Big Apple. We are always happy to hear from our customers and we thank you for letting us serve you.
>
> We think that your complaints might have some merit; however, we can't truly imagine how any of our well-trained employees could make such mistakes. The overcharges might have been caused by the high rate of turnover we have experienced among our bookkeepers. The job market is so good for bookkeepers right now that they don't seem to stay on the job very long.
>
> We at Liberty International take pride in the courteous and efficient manner in which we treat our guests. The fact that we do a good job is evident from the 86 percent annual occupancy rate we have enjoyed for the past three years. Incidentally, according to the research of the H.A.A., that is the highest occupancy rate in the entire lodging industry.
>
> When you look at the wide variety of organizations that stay with us on a regular basis, everything from NFL teams to MADD conventions, it's obvious that we must be doing something right. Just last week, for example, our site in the Windy City hosted the national convention of Trekkies.
>
> We hope that you will give us another try because we expect that you will become as satisfied as our regular customers.
>
> Even though we have been unable to verify your complaints, we have decided to give you the benefit of the doubt. It is contrary to our policy to provide refunds for such complaints; however, on your next visit to the United States, please be our guest at any Liberty Inn, absolutely free for two nights.
>
> Thanks again for your letter.

16. You are a building supply wholesaler. You receive an order from King Hardware for one dozen Vent Lights, a plastic-domed ventilating skylight that wholesales for $185 each. The balance due on the King account is already $1,400, and $2,200 for the Vent Lights will raise the balance over the $3000 credit limit allowed Ken King, owner of the store. Write to him (225 Main Street, Joplin, MO 64810) and refuse the order as requested. You might suggest that the order be reduced in order to stay below the credit limit, or you might ask that part of the bill be paid in cash. Whatever you do, remember that you want to retain his business.

17. Write a letter to Tom Healey, President, Fort Smith Tire Co., Fort Smith, AR 72901. He recently ordered a large number of tires from you, including two dozen G78–14 Ponzi belted whitewall blems at the low price of $20 each. Upon receiving his order he observed that the Ponzi tires had some obvious defects, ranging from faded whitewalls to irregular tread patterns. Healey wishes to return the Ponzi tires to you at your expense. Being new in the tire business, Healey did not realize that *blem* means blemish and that such tires ordinarily possess visible imperfections which in no way affect safety or wear. Healey claims that he thought that *blem* was part of the name of the tire. It is against your policy to take back blems because you sell them so cheaply. In your letter decline to take the tires back but point out the desirability of blems to many buyers. Try to build a positive relationship with this new dealer.

18. You have owned and operated Quality Discount, a successful mail-order business, for the past 20 years and have developed a clientele of many loyal customers. In seeking ways to cut expenses you have adopted a policy of mailing (or giving) catalogs only to customers who did at least $200 business with you the previous year. This policy has upset some of your older customers who no longer buy much from you but still enjoy paging through your lavish full-color catalog.

Write a letter to Florence Watkins (410 Shady Lane, High Point, NC 27260) in which you deny her request for a free catalog. Explain the policy and offer to send her a catalog for $5, which is what it costs you. Should she spend more than $200 this year at your business, the $5 would be credited to her account.

An Embarrassment of Riches | CASE

R. Eugene Hughes, West Virginia University

Hi-Tk is located in an older midwestern city generally associated with smoke-stack industries. The company's decision to locate here was influenced by the city's proximity to potential customers and by the efforts of the city's Economic Development Authority (EDA). As part of the EDA's location package, one of the city's technical schools (Middle-City Technical Center) offers an intense one-year basic program in electromechanical servosystems.

Recently, Hi-Tk has met its hiring needs by employing graduates from two-year technical programs and eight to ten graduates (approximately 60 percent of each class) of MCTC's yearly graduating class. All newly hired employees enter one- or two-year training programs specific to the separate design/production areas of the company.

The ability of this hiring program to meet Hi-Tk's needs in the future is doubtful, based on new production goals that will require increased levels in hiring in each of the next five years. Negotiations between Hi-Tk and MCTC have produced an agreement to increase the number of students who can be enrolled in MCTC's program. The time necessary to implement MCTC's new program and the reluctance of Hi-Tk to hire all of its graduates point to a probable shortfall of new-hires in the first 36 months of Hi-Tk's growth plan.

Beth Carol, the personnel manager for Hi-Tk, seems to be faced with an embarrassment of riches. Word has filtered out into the community that Hi-Tk is considering a major increase in production, and the personnel department has been swamped with applicants. Review and evaluation have identified a number of applicants who have the necessary qualifications for immediate entry into one of Hi-Tk's training programs. A somewhat larger number of applicants might easily be qualified by successfully completing the one-year basic program offered by MCTC. The largest number of applicants, however, do not seem to possess the education or work experience required for entry into MCTC's program. This latter group is of special concern to Beth because of MCTC's success rate with students admitted to the program as "special students." Although special students do not meet the normal requirements for admission to the program, those who have been admitted have generally completed the program and successfully entered the labor market.

Beth is satisfied that the combination of "qualified" and "easily qualified" walk-in applicants has the potential to meet the expected near-term (24 to 36 months) hiring shortfall. In fact, Beth is convinced that the applicant pool will be sufficiently large that some hiring selectivity can be exercised. Beth's satisfaction with these circumstances is tempered, however, by her realization that the enlargement and maintenance of the pool of labor depend on her ability to successfully communicate with each applicant.

As she begins to outline her communications strategy, Beth realizes that the three groups must be defined more precisely. She notes in her outline:

- Qualified group. Hiring needs for this group represent a 24-month time period.
- Easily qualified group. Even with successful completion of MCTC's program, Hi-Tk cannot promise these individuals a job.
- Doubtful group. Hi-Tk does not make decisions regarding entry into MCTC's program.

Successful completion of MCTC's program does not assure employment of the individual by Hi-Tk.

Reflecting on what she has written, Beth concludes that at least four general subject letters will be needed. She lists the four as:

1. Accept.
2. Accept — but not now.
3. Reject — but express interest if/when qualified.
4. Reject — but with referral.

Not sure that these four subject areas are complete or adequate, Beth begins to match the letters with the three groups of applicants.

Case Questions

1. Has Beth adequately identified and described the groups and individuals with whom she must communicate?

2. Are the four general letters sufficient to successfully communicate with the separate groups and individuals identified in Question 1?

3. Has Beth given adequate consideration to the communication medium and the personalization of the communications?

4. Prepare a communications plan that will accomplish Beth's goals (enlarge and maintain Hi-Tk's pool of applicants). Such a plan will include a draft of all appropriate and necessary communications to accomplish this goal.

Children Are Customers, Too | CASE

David B. Parsons, Lakehead University, Thunder Bay, Ontario, Canada

Jane and Billy Harris, 11-year-old twins, saved up $130 from their paper route to buy their mother a cordless telephone for her birthday. Filled with excitement, they walked down to their local department store to look at its selection of cordless telephones. They decided to buy a white Sanyo model that cost $129.84, including sales tax.

The salesclerk, however, not only refused to wait on them until all of the adults had been served, but he also questioned their ownership of the $130. Blinking back tears, the children told him they had earned the money delivering papers. The clerk then sold them a floor model in an unsealed box.

One week after their mother had opened her present, the telephone's antenna would not extend properly, a problem created by the abuse the telephone had taken while on display. The children decided to return the telephone and ask for a replacement or a refund. The clerk refused to replace the damaged telephone or to refund their money, accusing the children of breaking the antenna through carelessness.

The children returned home, hurt and bewildered, after being thoroughly intimidated by the rude and abusive clerk. After hearing the details of the entire incident, Mrs. Harris decided to write two letters, one to the salesclerk (whose name was on the receipt) and one to the store manager.

Case Questions

1. Identify and discuss the communication barriers involved in this situation.
2. Write the letter to the salesclerk.
3. Write the letter to the store manager.

Persuasive Letters

The letter promised, "Take one look at Baden Springs and you'll never forget it." Gwen had received similar letters before and promptly discarded them; however, she decided to take advantage of this offer. For attending a brief orientation session at Baden Springs she would be reimbursed for the gasoline she used to make the 80-mile trip, and she was guaranteed a prize. "You have definitely won one of the following prizes: (1) a new limited-edition sports car; (2) a large-screen color television set; (3) two acres of lakefront property; or (4) a name-brand digital watch."

Gwen was unprepared for what she encountered at Baden Springs. The orientation, which more closely resembled brainwashing, was hard sell throughout and lasted two hours, hardly what Gwen would call brief. Following the session she set out to investigate the property alone. No matter where she went, one of the counselors was always nearby. Selling, rather than counseling, appeared to be their main function. All of them had the same message: buy today because the price was going up soon.

By midafternoon Gwen decided that she had had enough. It took an hour to be reimbursed for the gasoline expense and to collect her prize. On the way home she was ticketed for speeding, and a flat tire made the trip even more memorable. Two days later the digital watch she received stopped running. At about the same time she discovered that she had contracted poison ivy.

As the letter had promised, Gwen did not forget Baden Springs. From then on, whenever she saw an

Learning Objectives

1 *To understand the goals of persuasion.*

2 *To get and hold the receiver's attention.*

3 *To understand the motivation factors involved in persuasion.*

4 *To identify the characteristics of the persuasive letter and when it is appropriate.*

5 *To relate the four steps of the planning process to writing persuasive letters.*

6 *To learn to organize persuasive messages for greatest impact.*

7 *To write sales letters using the AIDA steps.*

8 *To develop a collection campaign in which the twin goals of payment and goodwill are achievable.*

9 *To write effective letters of request.*

advertisement trying to entice people to "relax for a day at
Baden Springs," she recalled how turned off she had been by the
unrelenting pressure and the strident sales pitches made by the
so-called counselors. Gwen sometimes wondered whether she
might have bought a piece of lakefront property had the
persuasion been more subtle and the persuaders more soft
sell.

━━━━━━━━━━━━━━

Throughout our waking hours we are inundated with messages attempting
to persuade us. Television, radio, magazines, and newspapers bombard
our senses with a multitude of appeals. We are urged to buy products and
services, prevent forest fires and tooth decay, and, whatever we do, vote
on election day. Inconsistencies abound. Advertisements in newspapers
and magazines extol the rewards of smoking, whereas television commercials point out its harmful effects.

Some of the more blatant attempts to persuade are found in advertising,
but we receive many other persuasive messages as well. Ministers, priests,
and rabbis urge us to live a better life and suggest ways we might do so.
Police officers remind us to watch our speed. Our friends seek favors from
us.

Our responses to persuasive messages vary. We barely pay attention to
some, and so advertisers continue their search for better ways to get and
hold our attention — bright colors, attractive people, catchy music, pleasing situations. Other messages attract our attention but have very little
effect. Some products we simply do not want or cannot afford to buy, but
the commercials for them are nevertheless entertaining.

Other messages change our behavior. We purchase the product or service. We slow down as we drive, especially when we near the place where
we earned our last speeding ticket. We do help our friends in need, perhaps
at great inconvenience to ourselves.

GOALS OF PERSUASION

Although for some of us the process of persuasion is so mysterious that
it is threatening, persuasion is nothing new. Aristotle, Plato, and Cicero
wrote about persuasion almost two thousand years ago. Popular treatments
of persuasion abound today in such books as Vance Packard's *The Hidden
Persuaders*,[1] Michael Gilberts' *How to Win an Argument*,[2] and Fisher and

---

[1]Vance Packard, *The Hidden Persuaders* (New York: D. McKay, 1957).
[2]Michael Gilbert, *How To Win an Argument* (New York: McGraw-Hill, 1979).

Ury's *Getting to Yes.*[3] David Ogilvy's *Confessions of an Advertising Man*[4] and *Ogilvy on Advertising*[5] look at the commercial aspects of persuasion. Each of these writers takes a different approach to persuasion, but they are all concerned with one central idea — shaping the behavior of others.

How the behavior of people enables an organization to meet its goals was discussed in Chapter 2. The essence of persuasion is to shape the behavior of others so that goals can be reached more easily. Simply defined, **persuasion** is the art of getting people to do something that they would not ordinarily do if you did not ask. By asking in a persuasive manner, we shape behavior.

The primary goal of persuasion is to shape behavior.

Persuading and threatening are two distinct approaches to shaping behavior. Effective persuasion results in willing compliance. Threats may elicit grudging compliance. People usually become defensive when threatened, and whatever the outcome, their relationship with the threatening party is adversely affected.

When shaping others' behavior, you will often want to influence not only what they do, but also when they do it. The next time you receive an invitation to enter a sweepstakes from a mail-order advertiser, see if there are extra rewards for winners who enter the contest by an early deadline. Television commercials offering such consumer goods as tapes, records, books, and kitchen gadgets may provide a toll-free number for you to call in your order. They may also remind you to call immediately: "The supply is limited, so act now!" Many salespeople in department stores are instructed never to let a customer leave without having signed on the dotted line. In each case the persuader is aware that delay in shaping behavior could mean no shaping at all.

Some persuaders also want to influence how (or where) you perform the behavior. Although the League of Women Voters simply encourages you to vote, politicians are obviously interested in controlling the way you cast your ballot: "Don't forget to vote in the October 3 primary. And when you do, vote for George Jenkins." Some owners of fast-food restaurants would prefer that you never prepare meals in your kitchen and now offer every meal of the day. When they tell you, "You deserve a break today," they clearly want to influence where it is you take that break.

Goal clarification is a vital prerequisite to persuasion. Many persuasive efforts fail because their goals have never been clarified. Shaping the behavior of others should be based on the more specific goal of influencing at least one of the following:

- What the behavior should be
- When the behavior should occur
- How (or where) the behavior should be performed

[3]Roger Fisher and William Ury, *Getting to Yes* (New York: Penguin Books, 1983).
[4]David Ogilvy, *Confessions of an Advertising Man* (New York: Atheneum, 1963).
[5]David Ogilvy, *Ogilvy on Advertising* (New York: Crown, 1983).

THE PERSUASION PROCESS

After selecting your specific goals, you are prepared to develop your persuasive message. As in any form of communication, certain factors will influence the success of your persuasive attempt. The four important factors are (1) the sender of the persuasive message, (2) the receiver of the persuasive message, (3) the persuasive message itself, and (4) the channel through which the persuasive message is sent.

Sender

The more credible the source, the more persuasive the message will be.

"Consider the source," we often say if we doubt the truthfulness of a message. The source of a persuasive message has an enormous impact on how well the message shapes behavior. This impact is one reason why baseball players sell aftershave lotion on television and why the picture of an Olympic champion is on the front of thousands of breakfast cereal boxes. You are more apt to respond favorably to persuasive messages when the sender is someone you respect or admire. Your response is based on the key sender concept of source credibility.

To understand how credibility works, try this exercise: think of the best supervisor you have ever worked for (if you have never had a job, then think about the best teacher you have had). Respond to the following statements about that person by answering *yes* or *no:*

1. This person really knew the work. (expertise)
2. This person always told the truth and kept his or her word. (trustworthiness)
3. This person was active and energetic. (dynamism)
4. This person would always level with me. (objectivity)
5. This person was always interested in my personal welfare. (goodwill)

How many *yes* responses did you give? The more you gave, the more credible the person is. **Credibility** — the quality of inspiring belief — is based on the overall image of the message sender.

The exercise you just completed points out five important components of credibility. A receiver's image of you involves how competent, trustworthy, dynamic, objective, and well-intentioned the receiver perceives you to be. The more favorable this perception is, the more likely you are to shape the receiver's behavior.

The relative importance of these components varies from one situation to another. Here are some persuasive situations that might apply to you now. Which components of credibility do you think are most important in each situation?

▪ You're turning in a term paper to your instructor one day late. The lateness is not your fault, and you want to avoid losing points because of tardiness.
▪ You're trying to convince a friend not to drop out of school.
▪ You're asking someone for a date.

▪ You're running for an office in school government.

As a sender of persuasive messages you should evaluate your own credibility. What is the receiver's perception of you? The word "source" may refer to more than you as an individual. When you communicate in business, the credibility of your organization may be just as important as your own personal credibility. The first step in shaping the behavior of others is to consider your credibility as a sender of persuasive messages. Both within and outside of business your receivers will usually consider the source before they act.

Receiver

An important encoding skill is the ability to analyze your receiver, as was pointed out in Chapter 2. In persuasive situations this ability is critical. Two sets of factors to consider in analyzing the receiver of your persuasive message are attention and motivation. Before motivating the receiver you must first gain the receiver's attention.

Attention Factors

In any persuasive situation—a letter, speech, or advertisement—your first function is to get and hold your receiver's attention. Knowing several things about receivers will help you to do this.

First, people pay attention to the unexpected. Several years ago a man toured the country giving speeches on driving safety to high school assemblies. He began every speech this way:

The unexpected will get attention.

> Look around you. Look at the person on each side of you. Ten years from now one of the three of you will be dead.

The original, startling, and personal way he used those statistics caught the receivers' attention.

There are many examples of using the unexpected. The New York Racing Association, seeking buyers for its horse manure, advertised:

> Our horses leave a lot to be desired.

The owner of a service station and restaurant along a busy highway posted a sign outside his establishment reading:

> EAT HERE AND GET GAS

An orphanage for boys began its solicitation letter with:

> How much is a homeless boy worth?

People heed the unexpected, and once they do, they're easier to persuade.

Second, people pay attention to what is pleasing. Many persuaders use reinforcing stimuli to get the receiver's attention. Look at the advertisements in one of your favorite magazines. You will immediately notice that many products are shown in elegant surroundings—physically attractive men and women, cheerful settings, pleasing colors. Such attention-getters

Reinforcing stimuli will get attention.

are used in television commercials as well. Besides the surroundings, reinforcing words and phrases are often used to get attention:

Make Anyone Do Anything You Mentally Command — With Your Mind Alone

One Pill Blocks 600 Calories

How to Find Someone to Love

Instant Memory — The New Way to Remember

Once attention is gained, the real persuasive message begins.

Emphasizing the relevant will get attention.

Third, people pay attention to messages related to their own goals and objectives. Receivers will heed your persuasive message if it concerns something important to them. People who have dentures are more likely to watch denture-cleaner commercials on television than are people who have their natural teeth. The latter pay more attention to toothpaste commercials. Pet owners pay more attention to pet food commercials than do viewers who have no pets.

The three attention factors are thus the unexpected, the reinforcing, and the relevant. Which factors you use in developing a persuasive message depends on your analysis of the receiver. Will he or she respond more favorably to an attention getter that is not expected, one that is reinforcing, or one that emphasizes his or her important goals?

You should also consider your own credibility when choosing an attention factor. Low credibility can weaken any attempts at getting attention to persuade.

Motivation Factors

Once you have gained the receiver's attention, you need to know what will make that person respond favorably to your persuasive attempt. Many theories have been developed to explain what motivates people both at work and in their personal lives. One of these theories, developed by Abraham Maslow almost 40 years ago, states that people do things to satisfy certain needs.[6]

▪ Physiological needs: lower order survival needs, such as food, sleep, and air.
▪ Safety and security needs: lower order needs for personal security (for example, a safe home) and financial security (for example, a steady income or a savings account).
▪ Belonging needs: higher order needs to be included in other people's activities and affection.
▪ Esteem and status needs: higher order needs to feel self-respect and respect from others.
▪ Self-actualization needs: higher order needs for self-realization or fulfillment in a vocation or avocation. .

[6]Abraham Maslow, *Motivation and Personality* (New York: Harper & Row, 1954).

FIGURE 7.1   ■   *Maslow's Hierarchy of Needs*

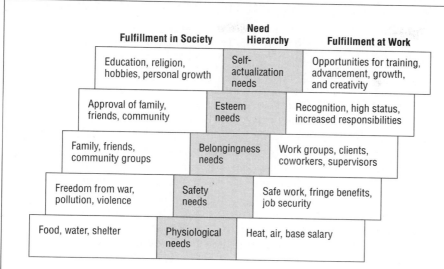

The first two needs are lower order and the last three needs are higher order. Maslow maintained that you progress from the first need to the fifth; that is, you first satisfy your physiological needs. You then satisfy the safety and security needs, and so on, until you reach the self-actualization needs. This progression from lower to higher order needs is the reason why Maslow's theory is sometimes called Maslow's **hierarchy of needs**. It is illustrated in Figure 7.1.

To incorporate Maslow's theory into your attempt to persuade, you must (1) estimate the receiver's level of needs at the time of your attempt; (2) create a message relevant to those needs; and (3) tell the receiver that the behavior you desire will satisfy the needs. The following three persuasive messages involve the same product, yet are adapted to different needs.

Your new Phantom will be the safest car on the highway. Heavy-duty bumpers, specially molded fenders, and our exclusive invisible roll-bar frame will protect you better than any other car on the market. (safety and security needs)

The Number 1 car in America—that's the Phantom. More than 30 million people drive Phantoms. Maybe you should think about owning one, too. (belonging needs)

For the discriminating driver, Phantom's Marquis de Luxe is a step above luxury. It's a sign you've arrived. (esteem and status needs)

Direct and Indirect Rewards

Maslow's hierarchy is only one way to analyze what motivates your receiver. Another way is based on the assumption that people do things for reasons. In your persuasive message you show how these reasons can be rewarded in two ways—direct and indirect.

Direct rewards come from the actual, shaped behavior.

Direct rewards come from actually buying the product or using the service; that is, these rewards come directly from the consumer's involvement with the behavior the persuasive message prompts. Think for a few moments about the rewards a consumer gets from purchasing a washing machine. There's the convenience of not having to visit a laundromat once or twice a week. It's more economical because it costs less to use a home washer than a coin-operated machine. Perhaps the clothes are washed better because the consumer can control the cycle, temperature, and water level of each wash. Clothes might even wear longer, because the home washer treats them more delicately than the commercial laundromat washer. These rewards all come directly from the consumer's having bought a washer. In that sense they are direct.

Indirect rewards come from other people as a result of shaped behavior.

Our consumer might also receive some indirect rewards from having purchased the washer. Indirect rewards come from other people as a function of the consumer having performed the behavior. Assume that the clothes washer is the top of the line of a name brand and that our consumer is the first person in the neighborhood to own this superior machine. Among the indirect rewards our consumer might receive are status, prestige, respect, and approval from others in the neighborhood. You don't give these rewards to yourself. Doctors and lawyers have status only because others in the community assign that status to them. You may have heard conspicuous consumption used as an explanation for why many people purchase expensive consumer goods — large automobiles, color television and stereo combinations, and so on. These people buy expensive items so that others will notice their accomplishments and assign them various kinds of indirect rewards.

You can choose from a multitude of both direct and indirect rewards when analyzing your receiver. Here are some examples:

Direct Rewards	*Indirect Rewards*
Comfort	Affection
Convenience	Appreciation
Enjoyment	Approval
Entertainment	Belonging
Health	Friendship
Less work	Pay increase
Money saved	Popularity
Personal improvement	Prestige
Problem solved	Promotion
Safety	Recognition
Satisfaction	Reputation
Sense of achievement	Respect
Variety	Status

Which of these rewards can you find in the persuasive message that follows? (You should find at least eight.)

Lonely? Never again!

Are you a wallflower at parties? Are you afraid to approach strangers? Do you have trouble with conversation openers? Starting today, you can meet and date dozens of interesting, attractive people.

WINNING PEOPLE will show you more than 50 proven techniques for being successful with the opposite sex. For example, you will find out: How to tell immediately if someone is attracted to you. . . . How to be the life of the party without making a fool out of yourself. . . . How to say you find someone attractive without appearing weak or foolish . . . and much, much more. WINNING PEOPLE will teach you how to win others and, in doing so, become a winner yourself.

For persuasive messages like this one, the writer carefully analyzes the characteristics of the intended receivers. These messages are put together to bring certain rewards to the receiver's mind as the message is read. The words are not selected haphazardly. Rather, they are carefully chosen to meet the needs of the receiver.

The more you learn about the needs and interests of your receivers, the more likely you are to persuade them. One authority on advertising described the effects of different approaches to persuasion in this way:

I have seen one advertisement actually sell not twice as much, not three times as much, but 19½ times as much as another. Both advertisements occupied the same space. Both were run in the same publication. Both had photographic illustrations. Both had carefully written copy. The difference was that one used the right appeal and the other used the wrong appeal.[7]

Message

A third variable in the persuasion process is the message. The type of persuasive message you create depends, in part, on the channel (for example, sales letter, speech, advertisement) you intend to use. In constructing a persuasive message you should pay careful attention to both the organization of that message and the kinds of persuasive appeals you use within it.

No matter what channel you use, your message should contain at least three essential ingredients: (1) an attention step; (2) a need step (in which you emphasize needs or direct and indirect rewards); and (3) an action step (in which you specify the behavior the receiver should perform).

The organizational pattern provides the skeleton for your persuasive message, but the persuasive appeals you use flesh out the skeleton and give the message substance. These appeals are like tools in a toolbox. You pick the ones most appropriate for your specific persuasive task. The two kinds of appeals used in persuasive messages are emotional and logical.

[7]John Caples, *Tested Advertising Methods* (Englewood Cliffs, N.J.: Prentice-Hall, 1975), as quoted in David Ogilvy, *Ogilvy on Advertising* (New York: Crown, 1983).

Emotional Appeal

Emotional appeals are directed to the receiver's emotions or feelings.

Most widely used in shaping consumer behavior, **emotional appeals** are directed to the feelings (rather than the intellect) of the receiver. Such appeals promise the direct and indirect rewards described earlier. Some examples of how emotional appeals work are given in Table 7.1.

Some emotional appeals are technique oriented. For example, the bandwagon technique appeals to a need to belong. This emotional appeal says, in essence, "Everybody is doing it." For years a certain automobile was advertised as the number-one car in America (meaning, of course, that everyone was buying this car). A well-known car rental agency advertises: "We're number one."

Logical Appeals

Logical appeals, directed to the receiver's rational thinking, are used most often in persuading other business people.

Appeals may be directed toward the receiver's rational thinking. These **logical appeals** are used most often when persuading other business people. One reason is that people in business (for example, purchasing agents) must be able to clearly justify the behavior that the persuasive message suggests. This need to justify behavior calls for appeals such as the examples in Table 7.2.

Most persuasive messages are positive — that is, the message describes a reward to be attained through some positive action. Occasionally, however, a persuader will use a negative appeal to arouse emotions of fear or of self-interest. Avoiding social disapproval is sometimes the reward when a negative appeal is used.

TABLE 7.1 ▪ *Examples of How Emotional Appeals Work*

Shaped Behavior	*Rewards*	*Message*
Purchase of a pair of sunglasses	Personal improvement, prestige	How good-looking can you get? Watch for those second looks as you stroll the beach in your new Sundowners. They're a sure sign you live the good life.
Joining a computer dating service	Belonging, friendships, problem solving	Why spend time waiting when you'll find that perfect someone at Date-A-Match? Love is just around the corner at 100 Houston Drive.
Signing up for a cruise	Entertainment, friendships, enjoyment	There's dining, dancing, swimming . . . or, if you'd like, lounging on our spacious sundeck with the most interesting people you'll ever meet.

TABLE 7.2 ∎ *Examples of How Logical Appeals Work*

Shaped Behavior	Rewards	Message
Using a collection agency for overdue accounts	Convenience, saving money	Let us show you how we can help you reduce your uncollectible bills by 25 percent. Our service also means you won't have to spend your own time dealing with delinquent accounts.
Purchasing a new typewriter	Convenience, efficiency	The Porta-Type memory typewriter is so light (only 15 pounds) that you can easily move it from office to office. Its computerized memory system will eliminate all those retyping chores from the briefest letter to the longest report.
Purchasing a prefabricated building	Money saved, durability	The aluminum siding on Brock buildings means you'll get years of economical and long-lasting service.

Insurance companies try to sell policies by pointing out that, in the event of your death, your family will be left destitute unless you have insurance. This is a negative appeal. The persuader is predicting an unfortunate occurrence unless some action is taken. A company advertising a mouthwash may play on your fear of rejection. Health care organizations publicize the fact that smokers do not live as long as nonsmokers. In other words, unless you quit smoking you will die at an earlier age. Collection letters, described later in this chapter, may sometimes include negative appeals.

Negative appeals may suggest an unfortunate occurrence unless some action is taken.

The appeals used in persuasion can be either positive or negative. Positive appeals are used more frequently, but in some situations negative appeals are appropriate.

Many persuasive messages contain a mixture of emotional and logical appeals. If you carefully analyze television commercials and magazine advertisements, you will notice that emotional appeals are made more frequently, especially to consumers. You will also begin to recognize the various organizational formats used in constructing persuasive messages.

Emotional appeals are used more often than logical appeals in consumer advertising.

Channel

As a business communicator you will probably use the persuasion process in many different situations. Some typical uses are these:

∎ *Written*
In a collection message
In a job application letter
In a sales letter

In a magazine or newspaper advertisement
In a claim letter
In a request for a favor

■ *Face to face*
   In a public speech
   In an interview
   In a small group conference

In everyday conversation
■ *Orally*
   On the telephone.

Sometimes you have a choice between oral or written channels. For example, if you want to persuade a credit customer to mail an overdue payment, should you telephone or write a brief collection message? If you want immediate feedback and better acceptance, perhaps the oral channel is preferable. But if you need documentation, or if your message is fairly detailed, a written message might be better. Chapter 2 discussed when to use each type of communication.

Several factors discussed in this chapter should also enter into your decision. First, you might show more goodwill through an informal telephone conversation. Or perhaps you would be more objective in a letter. Also, your decision should be based partly on your analysis of the customer. An unexpected telephone call might get attention, but it might be better to communicate in a letter so that you can more easily control both the organization and the types of appeals you use in your message. As a persuasive source, you should weigh the channel benefits carefully when beginning your effort to shape behavior.

PLANNING TO PERSUADE

The four steps in the planning process introduced in Chapter 5 can be tailored to the planning of persuasive messages. Ray Williams' experience will be used to demonstrate.

> Ray Williams took an expensive leather jacket to Peerless Cleaning, a company that specialized in leather goods. He was upset when it was returned with a large spot on the back. He made repeated visits to the cleaner, who was unable to remove the spot. In fact, the local manager denied any responsibility for it. Ray knew that the spot was not on the jacket when he initially took it to Peerless. He decided that he must write a letter to persuade someone in upper management that Peerless, not he, caused the spot and was therefore responsible for it.

Determining Objectives

The first step in planning is to recognize the reason for writing. Decide whether you are seeking a covert or an overt response. Are you trying to change the way the reader feels about a problem or issue, or are you asking the reader actually to do something about it? Ray decided to seek $295, the full purchase price of his leather jacket, from the cleaning company. The jacket was only 6 months old, and this had been its first cleaning.

Considering the Audience

When trying to persuade, think of the audience as being actively involved in the communication process. Even when using a written message to persuade, imagine the reader responding either positively or negatively

| BOXED IN | *AN ETHICAL DILEMMA* |

During the past 10 years the fortunes of Imperial Caterers have soared. The business that Ray Hilton started as a sideline consumes all of his time. In fact, most of his efforts are now devoted to administrative detail. The assistant managers he hired several years ago, Bruce Thornton and Ernest Nettles, are responsible for managing the catered events.

Bruce and Ernest are both competent but have very different personalities. Bruce is outgoing and gregarious; Ernest is quieter and serious. Customers are equally pleased with the services provided by the two; however, they are initially more impressed with Bruce. For that reason customers who know Bruce request him for their catered affairs. Several have expressed disappointment when Ernest has been sent when Bruce was expected. These customers have agreed that Ernest handled his duties well. No business has been lost.

Ray was pleased when Northern Industries, a major local employer, approached him about catering a company event. Ray had been calling on the company, seeking its catering business, for a long time. Ray and the Northern representative sat down together and worked out the arrangements for the event. The representative then asked if Bruce could be scheduled to manage it. Not wanting to jeopardize a new account, Ray said, "I don't see why not," although he knew that Bruce was already committed elsewhere on that day.

Ray's contracts for catered meals cover many details, but not the name of the on-site manager. He words his contracts to allow himself flexibility on that point. He reasons that his two assistants are equally competent and it should not make any difference which one is assigned to a job.

The Northern Industries event is only days away. Ray is beginning to have second thoughts about misleading the Northern representative. He can't decide whether it really matters. Ray feels boxed in. What would you do?

to each of your statements. Knowing the needs and interests of the audience, whatever its size, makes it more likely that the audience will respond as desired. Ray decided to send his letter to the vice president of customer relations at Peerless Cleaning. He believes that this person, although far removed from day-to-day cleaning operations, will be vitally interested in keeping customers satisfied.

Choosing the Ideas to Include

At this stage, based on your impression of the intended reader or readers, decide which ideas have the most reader appeal. Ray felt that the following ideas might be included in his letter:

He is a long-time customer of Peerless. The spot had to have been caused by the cleaner. The jacket was practically new. This is his first problem with Peerless, but he is familiar with the company's reputation for customer satisfaction. He hopes to be able to continue to do business with Peerless; however, this depends on how the problem of his jacket is resolved.

Selecting the Channel and Medium

Communicators have many different channels and media available. They must decide which is most likely to help accomplish the predetermined objective. Ray decided to write a letter.

WRITING PERSUASIVE LETTERS

The persuasive letter seeks to modify others' actions and thought.

The **persuasive letter** is one in which you seek to modify the thought and action of others in a certain direction. The types of persuasive letters most frequently encountered in the business setting are sales letters, collection letters, and letters of special requests. Whether you are writing an individualized persuasive letter or a letter that will be widely distributed, the same basic principles apply. Whenever you seek to persuade someone, you should follow four steps:

1. Get the reader's *attention*. (A)
2. Stimulate the reader's *interest*. (I)
3. Awaken a *desire* in the reader. (D)
4. Encourage the reader to take a specific *action*. (A)

These steps are known as the **AIDA sequence**. They are discussed and developed in the section on sales letters under "Writing."

Persuasive writing is not limited to letters, of course. Persuasion is frequently employed in memos and reports. Many reports, for example, include recommendations that are presented persuasively.

SALES LETTERS

Millions of unsolicited sales letters are mailed each year to consumers. Many of these letters are routinely discarded and disparagingly referred to as junk mail. What may be junk mail to many consumers is called direct mail advertising by advertisers, and it is big business. Approximately $15.5 billion is spent annually on direct mail advertising, almost as much as is spent on television advertising.[8]

Direct mail advertising is considered to be more precise than either television or newspapers, which are ordinarily directed at the general population. Direct mail advertising can be tailored and sent to a narrow

---

[8]*Advertising Volume in the U.S., 1948–1985* (New York: TV Bureau of Advertising, 1986).

segment of the population. Another attractive feature of direct mail advertising is it can be scientifically tested. Sales results can be easily related to a specific letter, and various versions of a letter can be compared for effectiveness.

Large organizations often send sales letters by the thousands. Composing an individual letter for each reader is impractical, and so a form letter may be developed. Figure 7.2 is an example of a form sales letter developed for college students. A credit account application ordinarily accompanies such a letter.

Writing good sales letters is an art. For some people it is a full-time occupation—and a well-paying one at that. Some of the best-known practitioners of direct mail advertising are paid up to $25,000 to develop a single packaged sales letter that will produce the desired results. Because such letters are mailed in tremendous quantities, a response rate of 1 to 2 percent is considered good.[9]

You may never become a part of the direct mail advertising business, but much of your writing will be aimed at persuading your reader. The obstacles you face will be similar to those encountered by the direct mail writer. In the split second that a reader may actually look at your sales letter before discarding it, you must grab the reader's attention.

When you try to persuade someone, you are trying to sell that person on an idea or a course of action. By becoming familiar with the strategy of the sales letter you can become a more effective persuader.

The principles governing sales letters pertain to all persuasive writing.

The reception a sales letter gets is considerably different from the reception for other types of letters. The good-news and neutral letter is easy to write because it tells readers what they want to hear. The letter of refusal, on the other hand, delivers an unfavorable response. No one wants that type of news, but a well-written letter of refusal will be read because it contains information that interests the reader.

Sales letters generally fall into two categories, unsolicited and solicited. The unsolicited sales letter does not have the advantages of other types of letters. It does not present information that the reader is likely to consider good news. In fact, the reader may not even be interested at first. To succeed, the writer must create a message that, although unsolicited, will stimulate a relatively uninterested reader.

The solicited letter is easier to write because the reader has expressed interest, sought information, or made specific inquiry. The writer is responding to some needs of which the reader is already aware.

Preparation

Before beginning to write persuasively you should learn as much as possible about the idea, service, or product to be offered. You should thoroughly understand all aspects of a product before trying to sell it. You should certainly have the following information about the product:

[9]Jim Powell, "The Lucrative Trade of Crafting Junk Mail," *The New York Times*, June 20, 1982, F-7.

FIGURE 7.2 ▪ *Form Sales Letter Directed to College Students*

Richard V. Skagen
National Credit Marketing Manager
Sears, Roebuck and Co.

Dear Mrs. Lewis,

You are invited to apply for a Sears Credit Card
-- one of the most useful and valuable credit cards a
student can have.

It's easier to get a Sears Credit Card than you
might think. And there are so many advantages to
having a Sears Credit Card especially right now, while
you're at school. Among them:

. Your Sears Credit Card is good at over 3400
  Sears Stores coast to coast. Wherever you
  live, travel or move, you have credit available at a nearby Sears.

. Your Sears Credit Card opens the door to a vast
  range of over 100,000 products and services --
  and everything Sears sells is backed by our
  famous guarantee, "Satisfaction Guaranteed or
  Your Money Back."

. You can choose from Cheryl Tiegs™ Signature
  Sportswear, famous Kenmore Appliances, DieHard®
  Batteries, Junior Bazaar Sportswear, Free Spirit
  Bicycles and ROEBUCKS® authentic western wear.

. You can take advantage of Sears special sales
  -- even though you may be short of cash. With
  a Sears Charge Account you can stretch your
  payments over many months if you wish.

. You can save time and unnecessary travel by
  shopping from Sears catalogs. Just mail or
  phone in your order and say, "Charge it."

(over please)

(Continued)

Source: Sears, Roebuck and Co.

FIGURE 7.2 ▪ *Continued*

> There are never any hidden charges. All Sears
> finance charges are always fully disclosed.
> And there's no annual fee, unlike some other
> credit cards.
>
> To apply for your Sears Credit Card, just fill in
> and mail the enclosed form -- the postage is already
> paid. Or, if it's more convenient, bring in your
> application to the Credit Department of the Sears
> Store in your area. Sears believes responsible young
> adults deserve credit.
>
> Why not fill it in right now, and begin enjoying
> the many benefits of your Sears Credit Card as soon as
> possible.
>
>   Sincerely,
>
>   Richard V. Skagen
>   National Credit
>   Marketing Manager
>
> P.S.   I strongly urge you not to pass up this
>   opportunity. In addition to its immediate
>   usefulness, your Sears Charge Account will help
>   establish the credit background you'll need
>   after you leave school.

- Exactly what it can do
- Materials from which it is made
- The expertise that developed it
- Outstanding features of the product

- Ways it differs from its competitors
- Price of the product

- Extent of the maintenance required and the expertise required to perform it
- Warranty, if any, that accompanies the product

Without this basic information you are unlikely to sell the product successfully. This information by itself, however, is not usually enough because physical characteristics are only one dimension of a product.

The writer of a sales letter should become familiar with the product and the intended customers.

Buyers will be as interested in the benefits they will derive from a product as in its physical characteristics. For that reason you should learn as much as you can about those to whom the letter will be sent. The more you know about the readers, the more likely you are to appeal to their interests and the more successful the resulting letter will be. You will understand the readers better if you have this type of information about them:

- Income level
- Whether homes are owned or rented
- Urban or rural location
- Occupations represented
- Educational level attained
- Marital status
- Family size
- Age of family members

At times you may have to write a sales letter with little specific advance knowledge about the readers. In those instances, the product or service itself may indicate the kind of person who will read the letter. For example, if you are trying to attract customers for a lawn-care service, the letter will be geared to homeowners who live in the suburbs.

After you are fully aware of the product or idea and the potential customers, you can plan the sales message. You must determine how best to link the intended customer with what is being offered. In other words, exactly how will the reader benefit from the physical characteristics and capabilities of the product? For example, the physical characteristics of a certain brand of running shoes are lightweight rubber, canvas, and color. The benefits to the purchaser of such shoes, however, would be factors such as these:

- The purchaser saves money because the shoes last longer than other running shoes.
- The shoes make the runner faster because they are very lightweight.
- The shoes improve the runner's appearance because they are stylish and available in many different colors.
- The shoes provide more comfort because of the specially designed arch.
- The shoes provide more safety through the unique double-deep tread.

Potential buyers are interested in the physical features of a product, but they are more interested in how they would benefit from them. David Ogilvy recognized this fact when he said, "Advertising which promises no benefit to the customer does not sell." He also referred to a study that showed "advertisements with headlines that promise a benefit are read by an average of four times more people than advertisements that don't."[10] The likely benefits, or psychological features, convince the reader to buy.

Writing

Whether you are trying to sell something or trying to convince the reader to pursue a certain course of action, the four steps in the AIDA sequence discussed earlier have proven to be effective. Although the terminology has varied somewhat, persuasive writers have used these same steps for years. Here they are applied to sales letters.

Attracting the Reader's Attention

The first sentence of an unsolicited sales letter must grab readers while leading them on to the remainder of the letter. In order to accomplish this, the letter should identify one of the most significant features of the product it is trying to sell. If possible, it should suggest how the reader stands to benefit from using the product.

The first sentence of a sales letter must attract the reader's attention.

Many writers attempt to include in the first sentence the aspect of the product that will interest most readers. The manufacturer of an energy-efficient water heater, for example, considered economy to be the most important characteristic of the product. For that reason economy was emphasized in this opening:

Want to cut your water heating expense by 30 percent?

An auto dealer who believed that the product's new styling was its most interesting aspect stressed this newness:

Test drive the all-new C-7 now. Be the first in the neighborhood to own one.

There is no one right method of getting the reader's attention. Only after becoming familiar with both the product and the intended reader will you be ready to select an appropriate method. Some of the more common methods used are these:

▪ Make a thought-provoking statement: "The best thing about our new line of purses is something you can't see."
▪ Present a startling fact: "Ninety-five out of 100 families would be bankrupt if they missed just three paychecks."
▪ Offer a bargain: "Imagine, two pairs of shoes for the price of one!"
▪ Describe something that currently is happening: "Today more than 500 families enjoyed the *Press Journal* with breakfast."
▪ Present a direct challenge: "Try to tear the enclosed piece of rubberized plastic and you'll understand why our seat covers won't wear out."

[10]Ogilvy, *Ogilvy on Advertising,* 60

▪ Tell an interesting anecdote: "Until I was 25 years old I thought you had to be rich to afford a new car. The day I visited Bill Smith's Auto Market was the day I learned otherwise. That was also the day I bought my first new car."

Originality is an important characteristic of a sales letter.

An opening is more likely to attract attention if it is written in an original manner. When the writer uses clichés and timeworn phrases, the reader is likely to discard the letter. The reader is more likely to continue reading if the opening paragraph is short. Brevity and conciseness are vital to an effective opening in an unsolicited letter.

While striving to make your approach unique, you risk making an error that may cause the reader to lose interest. These are some of the most common errors to avoid:

▪ Avoid asking a foolish question. The writer will lose the reader's attention with a question that has an obvious answer, such as "How would you like to double your income and shorten your work week?"
▪ Avoid emphasizing the writer instead of the reader. Readers want to know how they will benefit. "It looks like WKUR will be number one in the ratings soon" virtually ignores the reader.
▪ Avoid presenting an irrelevant statement. A sales letter that begins, "There's at least one thing in life that you needn't be a millionaire to enjoy," sounds intriguing until the reader discovers that the product is a new deodorant soap. A direct link between the opening statement and the product being sold should always be made.
▪ Avoid phrasing an idea in an unoriginal way. Do not use clichés such as "a stitch in time saves nine" or anecdotes that are already widely known.

Stimulating the Reader's Interest

The interest section of the sales letter should make the reader want the product.

Having attracted the reader's attention, you must now strive for a receptive reaction. In this section of your letter you usually introduce the product and provide the reader with good reasons for buying it. Some authorities recommend that at this point the reward that will be derived from the product should be emphasized rather than the actual product. For example, instead of selling the reader on a lawn mower, stress the pride associated with having an attractive lawn. In this way the reader goes beyond the product to the pleasure that results from its use. In the interest step, therefore, you are both describing the product and suggesting its value to the reader.

Once you have the reader's attention, you must link the attention-getting step to the interest step. Unless the interest step flows naturally from the attention step, the reader will probably stop reading the letter. In this letter the writer failed to link the steps:

Some things are unforgettable, and the new DMS electronic typewriter is one of them. More than 50 years of technology have produced a machine that allows revision without retyping. It features more automatic functions than any other typewriter. Because of its incredible memory it can retype virtually anything that you have typed before, and it does it automatically.

✓ CHECKLIST for Attention Getting

▢ Present what the reader will view as the major benefit of the product that you seek to sell.

▢ Relate the product to the reader rather than to the writer (the "you" attitude).

▢ Write an original opening statement.

▢ Make the first paragraph interesting enough to appeal to the reader and so short that the reader will have to read subsequent paragraphs to get the important details.

The key idea of the attention-getting step is that the typewriter has a memory ("unforgettable"). The writer does not return to that point, however, until three sentences later. There is no continuity between the attention and the interest steps.

To stimulate the reader's interest, the writer should emphasize a **central selling point** of the product. A central selling point is the prime reason why a person would want what a seller is offering. Any product or service has many possible central selling points. What kind of person is the customer? What are the customer's needs and interests? Answering these questions will help you identify a likely central selling point.

Developing Desire within the Reader

In the desire section the writer moves the reader from the "like to have" category to the "really need" position. By relying on an appropriate emotional or logical appeal, the writer helps readers justify the desire for the product. The product being sold will usually suggest whether to use logical or emotional appeals. Sometimes a combination of the two is preferable.

The desire section of the sales letter should make the reader feel a need for the product.

One automobile dealer may try to sell a car on the basis of its complete warranty. This appeal is logical. Another dealer may try to sell the product through an emotional appeal: the reader will be the first one on the block to own this distinctive new model.

If price is mentioned, it will appear in the desire section. Rather than emphasize it, however, the writer should bury it within a paragraph.

Sales letters must usually be longer than other types of business letters. The greater length is required to develop a successful persuasive appeal. However, sales letters sent to dealers are usually shorter than those sent to consumers because appeals to dealers are more direct, generally emphasizing the profit to be made.

Encouraging the Reader to Take a Specific Action

The writer has pointed out the most significant features of the product as well as how the reader will benefit from its use. All that remains is for the reader to take the desired action. The writer must now tell the reader what action to take. If you want the reader to complete an enclosed form and

The action close should indicate the specific action the reader should take.

✓ CHECKLIST for a Sales Letter

____❙ Begin with a brief statement or question that is likely to attract attention.

____❙ Be sure the opening statement clearly relates to the product offered.

____❙ Gain the reader's interest by emphasizing a central selling point that appeals to him or her.

____❙ In the desire section try to develop a need within the reader by providing additional evidence of the product's value. Also remind the reader of the central selling point.

____❙ Minimize price resistance by de-emphasizing it. Mention some of the strong points of the product while referring to price.

____❙ Indicate briefly and specifically what the reader should do, and restate the reasons the reader should take the desired action.

mail it, say so as specifically as possible. Some otherwise good sales letters are rendered ineffective by the lack of a clear action closing.

An example of a sales letter in which the four steps are used is presented in Figure 7.3. The steps are not always as separate and distinct as this. In some sales letters the interest and desire steps may be indistinguishable. You may not recognize the point at which one step ceases and another begins, but the sequence of ideas is obvious. Following this idea sequence is more important than keeping the steps separate.

A letter sent to office managers by a large office equipment supply company is shown in Figure 7.4.

COLLECTION LETTERS

An effective collection letter will collect the money due and also maintain the customer's goodwill.

In most organizations relationships between salespeople and customers are carefully cultivated. These same relationships are often threatened by the company's efforts to collect unpaid bills. Collecting the unpaid balance should not be the only goal of the collection process. Another important goal is to retain the goodwill and the business of the delinquent customer. Many collection letter writers alienate the same customers in whose loyalty the company has heavily invested. Much of what has been accomplished through advertising, public relations, and skilled sales personnel can be undone through inept collection procedures.

Collection letters become more direct in tone as the account becomes further past due.

Virtually every type of business relies at least occasionally on collection letters to prod past-due accounts. These letters comprise the collection campaign, and they are written and mailed in a predetermined sequence. The early letters, sent when an account is slightly late, are mild in tone. As the account becomes more delinquent, the letters become more direct. Collection letters should never, however, become as direct as this one:

FIGURE 7.3 ▪ *Sales Letter for a Trade School*

TROTTER INSTITUTE   *P.O. Box 1981   Baltimore, MD 21233*

July 30, 1991

Mr. Charles Dunbar
286 Greencrest Street
Anita, PA 15711

Dear Mr. Dunbar:

Did you know that you don't need a college degree to get a good job? — *Gets attention by suggesting a benefit for the reader.*

You've probably read newspaper articles about how job opportunities are declining today. At the same time, however, there are occupations in which opportunities are expanding. The U.S. Bureau of Labor Statistics reports that in the next 10 years the demand for electronics technicians will increase by 21 percent. That means that for every 10 electronics technicians now working, two more will be needed. As an electronics technician, you can expect to have your choice of many high-paying jobs with excellent working conditions. — *Stimulates interest by emphasizing the reward to be derived from the product.*

One of the best aspects of an electronics education is that you don't even have to leave home to get one. The Trotter Institute of Electronics offers a one-year correspondence course that leads to a Certificate of Electronics. You could soon be on your way to a career in electronics. — *Points out desirable features; introduces but de-emphasizes price by linking it with another product strength.*

You probably think that any course offered by the Trotter Institute would have to be expensive. You're in for a surprise! You get textbooks, assignments, and consultation with our excellent instructors for only $450.00, and this includes employment counseling after you graduate. You can see now that getting a better job is easier than you thought.

To prepare for a better job with a great future, complete the enclosed registration form. Within 10 days you'll be progressing toward an interesting and rewarding new career. — *Encourages specific actions and reminds the reader about benefits.*

          Yours truly,

          Michael J. Langford

          Michael T. Langford
          Admissions Counselor

Enc.

Your bill is overdue. Pay us immediately or I'll see that you never get credit in this town again.

Reasons for Collection Problems

A blacksmith shop in a one-story building in northern Wisconsin displayed this sign prominently: "Interested in credit? See our credit manager. Please take elevator." With a credit policy like this a company would have no collection problems.

FIGURE 7.4 ▪ *Sales Letter for Office Equipment*

ACE *OFFICE EQUIPMENT*, INC. ● 2814 17th Avenue Gary, IN 44407 ● (800) 555-2101

May 31, 1991

William C. Sams
Office Manager
Calumet Insurance Agency
5146 N. 56th Street
Calumet Park, IL 60643

Dear Mr. Sams:

Identifies the problem and documents how widespread it is.

Blurred vision and headaches are considered to be normal occupational hazards for video display terminal (VDT) operators. In fact, research by the National Institute for Occupational Safety and Health shows that up to 90 percent of VDT operators complain of such problems.

Explains how the problem makes the office manager's job more difficult.

Other studies have shown that such complaints lead to a variety of adverse effects. Sore, burning eyes will make it difficult for your VDT operators to concentrate; consequently, productivity is diminished. Absenteeism and insurance claims often increase. The lowered job satisfaction that accompanies such conditions leads to higher rates of turnover.

Describes an expensive solution.

Some specialists suggest that rearranging the office layout to avoid glare from windows and installing customized lighting systems is the only way to prevent these problems. However, there is another, less disruptive and less expensive solution. The Contrast Control® antiglare filter can be mounted on any VDT screen in seconds. Its thin-film optical coating will eliminate over 90 percent of the glare that results in eye fatigue and irritability.

Presents a simple and inexpensive solution and documents its effectiveness.

Describes an additional important benefit.

You'll be amazed at the way your VDT operators will respond to this tangible evidence of your concern. You'll be even more amazed at its low price.

Suggests a specific action.

Call us today on our toll-free line for additional details and a price list. Act now to protect the health and productivity of your valued employees.

Sincerely,

Diane C. Fast

Diane C. Fast
Sales Associate

The underlying reason for collection problems is that we extend credit. If a business were to revoke the credit privileges of all its customers, collection problems would disappear, but this almost surely would be accompanied by a decline in sales and profits. People expect credit. It has become a part of life both for the creditor, which is the organization extending credit, and for the debtor, which is the customer purchasing on credit.

In the quest for greater profits business organizations often extend credit to customers who, in an earlier time, would probably have been refused credit. As the number of these questionable accounts increases, so do collection problems increase.

Debtors become delinquent in paying their bills for many reasons, and many of these reasons are completely valid. Some credit managers refer to nonpayers as deadbeats, and they impute the motives and character of these debtors. Although some customers may use credit in bad faith, their number is small.

Many collection problems may be explained by such factors as illness, loss of job, or some other unexpected occurrence. In some cases collection difficulties can be traced to a debtor's misunderstanding the terms of the credit agreement. By taking greater care in explaining the operation of a charge account, companies can prevent some future collection problems. No matter how much care is taken in extending credit, however, there will be some problems.

The Collection Campaign

Company efforts to collect past-due accounts can best be described as campaigns. As in any campaign there is a series of stages. The stages in the collection process are (1) reminder, (2) strong reminder, (3) inquiry, and (4) urgency. You must approach each stage somewhat differently. The assumptions you make about a debtor change as the account becomes more overdue, and you write differently on the basis of the new assumptions.

Although we divide the campaign into four stages, this division does not mean that only four letters will be sent to a delinquent debtor. For any single stage, more than a single letter is usually sent.

Reminder

When a customer is first recognized as delinquent, collection efforts are restrained and mild. The assumption guiding the collection correspondent at this point is that the customer has merely overlooked the bill and needs only a reminder. When the account is about two weeks late, many companies merely send a duplicate of the original bill with some reminder that it is overdue.

The approach in the early stages of collection is low key. This approach continues into the first actual collection letter. Many people require only slight prodding, and the initial letter should only prod:

The first collection letter is a reminder.

> Have you overlooked your unpaid balance with us? Please accept this friendly reminder and send us your check for $97.50.

The number of reminders that are sent to a delinquent customer varies from one company to another. A creditor will likely send several reminders to a customer who has a good credit history. To a customer who is viewed as a poor risk, the creditor might send only one reminder and then move to the strong-reminder stage. The process moves to the next stage quickly when it appears that the customer is not likely to respond.

Strong Reminder

In a strong reminder the writer may call the customer's attention to the value of the company's services.

The second stage consists of a strong reminder, yet the assumption remains that the customer has simply forgotten to pay the bill. Some companies use this occasion to remind the customer of the value of the company's services and to point out that the customer is held in high regard despite the oversight. This letter from a department store exemplifies such an approach:

> You will like the wide array of merchandise we now have in stock. You are sure to find something that suits your taste and your needs throughout each department.
>   At the time you come in, you may pay your bill of $180, which is 60 days past due. Then, let us help you look and feel great this summer.

Besides reminding the customer of the past-due account, the writer has reassured the customer that credit will not be a problem. The customer is reminded that this store is a reasonable place to do business.

Inquiry

In the inquiry stage the writer asks the customer why the bill is past due.

If the reminders do not have the desired effect, you as the writer must take a stronger position. Rather than continue to attribute the past-due status of the account to oversight, you now assume that some other reason has kept the customer from paying. This stage is called inquiry because you ask why the past-due account is not being paid. If it is not possible to elicit payment through this letter, you seek at least an explanation. If the customer responds with an explanation, there is a good chance that a payment plan will eventually result. In short, you seek customer action, preferably to pay the bill, but at least to give an explanation.

When you write a letter in the inquiry stage, you should also appeal to the reader's pride, sense of equity, or self-interest.

By appealing to the reader's pride, you encourage self-esteem. You may point out the pride of satisfying financial obligations. Some writers emphasize pride in terms of avoiding the embarrassment of a bad credit record.

An alternative is an appeal to the reader's sense of equity. The thrust of an equity appeal is that the creditor provided what the customer had requested. In all fairness, the customer should acknowledge the creditor's trust by paying the bill.

Some readers may not be swayed by appeals to their pride or to their sense of equity. They may, however, respond to an appeal to their self-interest. Many people take credit for granted. If you can remind the reader of how valuable credit is, you may get a positive response. When readers realize how credit contributes to their self-interest, they may be more inclined to pay their bills and protect their credit rating.

This is how one writer approached the inquiry stage:

> Because payments have not been received on your clothing account for either July or August, the account is delinquent.

In the past you have met your obligations promptly. We believe that something unusual has temporarily disrupted your payments. May we assist you in solving the problem?

Please send the balance due of $180 or let us know of your plan for satisfying the account.

Usually only one letter is sent in the inquiry stage. By this time the account will be approximately 90 days late. As in the example, the writer seeks to reestablish contact with the customer by making a reply easy. By suggesting that an unusual situation has caused the delinquency, the writer makes it easy for the customer to save face. At no point, however, should the writer suggest the possibility that there was any problem with the merchandise.

Urgency

The collection process moves into the urgency stage if the inquiry did not result in positive action by the customer. At this point the account has been delinquent for at least 120 days. A very small percentage of accounts remain delinquent for this long; however, the collection writer must be prepared to deal with the problem.

At this stage you must impress upon the customer the seriousness of the situation. To signify the gravity of the situation a higher level executive will often sign the letter instead of a collection correspondent. You should convey the idea that this is the end of the line, although hope for a reasonable solution still exists. Avoid threats, however, for they may have an adverse effect on goodwill and usually elicit defensiveness rather than compliance.

In the urgency stage the writer indicates that payments must be made at once.

At this point you might refer to the possibility of legal action, although not in specific terms. If several letters comprise the urgency stage, you should not mention a specific date for action until the final letter. One writer wrote the final letter in the urgency stage in this way:

Based on your credit record we were sure that you would have contacted us regarding your delinquent account. The time has come for us to take stronger action in order to collect the $180 balance of your account.

We will expect full payment of your account within the next five days. We hope to avoid having to present your account to the Interstate Collection Association. Neither of us wishes to get involved in court actions, but it is a definite possibility.

Please send your check for $180 by October 31. By doing so you will avoid legal entanglements that will be expensive and damaging to your credit record.

In the urgency stage the tone of the letter is more demanding that persuasive. You should emphasize the need to pay rather than the reasons the customer has not paid. In that way you avoid the stridency that destroys goodwill, but leave no question in the reader's mind about the need for immediate action.

A series of collection letters used by a department store follows. Each letter represents one of the four stages of a collection campaign.

✔️ *CHECKLIST for a Collection Letter*

____ Be aware of the assumption under which each letter should be written.

____ Get what is owed without sacrificing the goodwill of the customer.

____ As a collection campaign progresses, letters should become more demanding and stress collection rather than any additional sales.

____ Keep the reminder letter low-key and matter-of-fact.

____ In the strong reminder letter you may make the customer aware of the benefits of having credit.

____ Appeal to some interest of the reader in the inquiry stage when seeking a payment or an explanation.

____ In the urgency stage you should convey the seriousness of the situation and the fact that time is running out.

Reminder — A Gentle Prod

This is a gentle reminder that a portion of the unpaid balance on your account is overdue. This is more than likely an oversight that you will correct by making a payment within the next few days. Perhaps you have mailed your remittance already. If so, we would like to thank you for your patronage.

Strong Reminder — A Direct Prod

Most of our customers appreciate a reminder when their account is overdue.

Therefore, we would like to remind you of your overdue account. Listed below is your present balance as well as the minimum amount due if you prefer monthly payments.

You may have already mailed a payment within the past few days. If not, won't you please do so?

Inquiry — To Reestablish Communication

We recently wrote to you regarding the past-due balance on your charge account. With your revolving charge account you have the option of a 30-day account or monthly payments of as little as 5 percent of the balance. At any time, of course, you may pay more or all of your balance.

Please contact us immediately if you are unable to pay the $225 now due. Together we will be able to resolve your problem.

Use the enclosed envelope for your prompt reply.

Urgency — A Genuine Crisis

Twelve years ago this October you opened a charge account with us. Since that time we have worked hard to meet your needs. Apparently we have succeeded because you have been a regular customer.

Because you have been such a loyal customer, it's all the more surprising that we have not heard a word from you. It's a mystery to us why you have allowed your account to become overdue after such a good credit history.

We are waiting for your check for $260 and we must have it. If your credit record is to be protected, you must act now.

Please send us a check today, or at least contact us so that a payment plan can be arranged. By acting immediately your valuable credit record may be saved.

Collection strategies differ somewhat from one organization to another. In general, however, the collection correspondent's approach follows the progression from reminder to stronger reminder to inquiry to urgent appeal. Collection campaigns require thorough planning so that past-due bills are collected without sacrificing the goodwill of the customer.

SPECIAL REQUESTS

Large organizations may send sales letters by the hundreds of thousands. If research shows that a particular sales letter is effective, it may be used for a long time. The same is true of collection letters. Another kind of persuasive letter, however, is not normally used in mass mailings; this is a letter in which you ask a favor of someone. You will write many such letters during your career.

Because the reward for complying with such a request is small or nonexistent, writers tend to dispense with the proven sales approach. In this example the writer seems to think that the reader is either going to comply or not and that persuasion will have no effect:

The Public Library Guild is in the midst of its annual drive for volunteers.

Your name has been submitted as a possible volunteer. Please join us for an orientation session at the Woodword Library on Wednesday, September 8 at 7 p.m.

Through the involvement of volunteers professional librarians are freed from clerical duties and can concentrate on performing the duties for which they were actually hired. Volunteers help make the Woodword Library run more efficiently.

Please let us know that you are interested in enhancing the quality of the services provided by the Woodword Library. Your help will make a difference.

The first paragraph is more likely to elicit a response of "who cares?" than the reader's attention. In the second paragraph an invitation is extended; however, the writer made no attempt to motivate the reader to accept it. The writer points out in the next paragraph that volunteers allow professional librarians to perform their intended duties but does not explain why this is important. The closing paragraph implies that the reader's unwillingness to volunteer would be evidence of disinterest in the library's services. Such a close is unlikely to make the reader receptive to future contact with the writer.

When a writer takes a fatalistic approach and assumes persuasion will have no effect, the resulting letter will be bland and a positive response is unlikely. By adhering to the persuasive sequence, this writer was much more effective:

> You have demonstrated, through your civic mindedness in the past, the effect one dedicated person can have on a project. Now you have the opportunity again to significantly improve the services provided by one of our most important institutions.
>
> Thomas Carlyle described the founding of a library as "one of the greater things we can do." Our entire community has enjoyed the benefits of the Woodword Library, yet one obstacle prevents its continued development. A reduced budget has resulted in staff reductions, and our professional librarians must now spend most of their time on clerical tasks.
>
> Misusing professional librarians is a waste of tax money. Equally important, librarians are less accessible to those who come to learn and grow. You can help the library serve the public by performing some of the clerical duties necessary for efficient operation. There will be an orientation for new volunteers on Wednesday, September 8 at 7 p.m. in the conference room of the Woodword Library. As a Woodword volunteer you will enjoy being part of a team so clearly devoted to the public good.

The writer recognized past contributions of the reader and then described a problem that the reader could do something about. By following the AIDA steps, the writer presented the reader with good reasons for helping prior to actually requesting assistance.

Too many writers try to avoid wasting the reader's time by leading off with the request. When a letter begins, "Please send me a packet of the materials that you used to try to enlist public support for the recent bond referendum," the reader may immediately begin to think of reasons for not complying and may never read the rest of the letter. In contrast, this is the opening of a letter in which the recipient is asked to give a public speech:

> Effective public relations practitioners are able to influence the attitudes of the public on virtually any issue. You demonstrated this ability by persuading more than 40 percent of the voters to support the recent bond referendum.

The writer presented a statement with which most public relations practitioners would agree and followed that with an acknowledgment of the reader's abilities. Because no request has yet been made, there is nothing for the reader to refuse. The writer has established a common ground with the reader; the reader will continue reading:

> Most students preparing for a career in public relations are unaware of all that such a career entails. Their knowledge of the field is limited to the advice of professors, many of whom are long removed from the public arena. It is only through greater contact with successful practitioners that students will become more attuned to the realities of public relations.

The writer has laid out the problem, which is of concern to practitioners such as the reader. As a practitioner the reader is uniquely qualified to alleviate the problem:

> By speaking to the Mid-City Public Relations Society on Wednesday, March 15, you will contribute greatly to the development of public relations students. The meeting will begin at 7:00 and will be held at the Downtowner. All of our 75 members hope you will share your expertise with us.

In this paragraph the writer provided the reader with an opportunity to make a valuable contribution. This is a request that the reader will find hard to refuse.

Note the subtlety of the letter in Figure 7.5. At no point is an actual request made, yet it is certainly a request for support. It was sent on the letterhead stationery of a prestigious law firm and signed by the chairman of the board of trustees of St. Jude's House. The writer emphasized the attention and interest steps with some specific examples. The examples will stimulate the desire of the reader to provide continued support. The same organization took a different approach in another letter, shown in Figure 7.6. It follows the AIDA sequence and is more explicit.

Many of the requests you write will be briefer and more explicit than either of these examples. However, the sequence of ideas will be the same. Note that Ray Williams followed the AIDA sequence in his letter about a jacket damaged by the dry cleaners:

> Imagine that one of your most prized possessions was ruined through no fault of your own.
>
> When you are putting yourself through college you think twice before parting with your hard-earned money, especially for luxuries, such as the leather jacket I purchased six months ago for $295. This jacket is the most expensive piece of clothing in my wardrobe. Because I was so proud of it, I gave it the best of care.
>
> Last month when the weather became too warm for leather, I took my jacket to the Peerless location in Abeline. Because I was aware of Peerless' excellent reputation in cleaning leather, I did not object to the premium price.
>
> When I picked up my jacket and discovered a large spot on the back, I was upset. I was even more upset when the Peerless manager was unable to remove the spot and then denied any responsibility for it.
>
> Please recognize that I have been too careful with my jacket to allow it to get soiled. If such had occurred I would certainly have recognized it. Since my jacket, which had been in perfect condition, is now unwearable, I believe that I am entitled to $295, the price I paid for it.
>
> For three years I have been a satisfied customer of Peerless. For even longer than that I have been aware of the excellent record of Peerless for customer satisfaction. I look forward to hearing from you.

Among the countless purposes for writing letters of special request, some of the more common ones are recruiting a guest speaker, seeking financial contributions, recruiting a chairperson or a member for a committee, requesting a letter of recommendation, and seeking cooperation for a survey. Competition is keen for the attention and cooperation of the reader. Letters that follow the persuasive strategy are more likely to elicit the desired response.

SUMMARY

Four factors are important to building an effective persuasive message: sender, receiver, message, and channel. Being aware of these factors and understanding the process of persuasion will enable you to write and speak more persuasively.

FIGURE 7.5   ■   *Letter Making a Special Request: Subtle Appeal*

Dear St. Jude's Benefactor:

In an effort to give you a report in the most human terms of the return on your monetary investment in St. Jude's House, it seemed appropriate to share the following vignettes with you.

Mr. D., a long-time resident of St. Jude's House, simply could not function outside a structured environment. He is now employed by a hospital, pays his own way, and was recently able to spend his vacation in his hometown—sober!

St. Jude's director has supper once a month with a former resident with eight years' sobriety, and he is a working, taxpaying citizen now. College educated, he came to us at St. Jude's after living in cardboard cartons under a bridge and delivering handbills to finance the next drink.

Mr. C., a former resident of St. Jude's House, has remained sober for over four years. He now is an active member of Alcoholics Anonymous. He has secured a high-paying job as a computer programmer. His last four Christmases were sober ones, the first in over twenty years!

Ms. B. has a long history of nonalcoholic drug abuse. She was admitted to St. Jude's House because we needed bed occupancy. Although she is on legal probation, last month she obtained a job as a clerk typist, the first job she has had in a very long time.

Mr. A., a person we have worked with over the last five years, had a kidney transplant. He was the donor—he saved his brother's life! He now has something to be proud of, and he is sober for the first time in twenty years! Both are recovering well.

Mr. E. is in his late twenties and has been an alcoholic since he was fourteen. After two aborted residences, he is now settling in and making use of the community that St. Jude's makes available to him. His progress is good and his outlook positive for the first time since he was fourteen.

Mr. F. was once a prominent Atlantan. He now suffers brain damage from his alcoholism, but he has been able to "hang in" at St. Jude's House. He now works as a parking lot attendant. Although his family feels this job is beneath him, he is beginning to come to grips with the fact that he will never be able to return to his earlier profession. But he can pay his own way and become a valued member of his community. He now has self-respect.

(*Continued*)

Source: Reprinted with permission of St. Jude's House, Inc.

Sales letters, collection letters, and letters of request play an important role in business communication. Regardless of the type of persuasive message, however, careful planning is extremely important. Determining objectives, considering the audience, choosing one's ideas, and selecting the appropriate channel and medium are all crucial to the success of any persuasive message.

FIGURE 7.5 ▪ *Continued*

St. Jude's Benefactor
October 11, 1991
Page 2

    Although I have only scratched the surface of the human drama
that unfolds day in and day out at St. Jude's House, I hope this
insight will indicate the tremendous return on your financial help
at St. Jude's House. Your money is wisely garnered and spent.
Human suffering is alleviated, and the hope you provide is the
most touching thing in the world!

                         Sincerely,

                         E. Reginald Hancock

                         E. Reginald Hancock
                         Chairman of the Board of Trustees
                         St. Jude's House

ERH/sts

cc: Reverend Canon Herbert J. Beadle
     St. Jude's House Board Members

Although some sales letters are solicited by the reader, most are not. The writer of a sales letter usually faces the challenge of securing a positive response from a reader who has expressed no interest in the product or in the ideas of the writer.

A definite strategy underlies most effective sales letters. Before writing such a letter you should learn as much as possible about the product to be sold and about the intended reader. Determine what the reader is likely to consider the most attractive feature of the product and make this the central selling point. Refer to this point throughout your letter.

FIGURE 7.6 ▪ *Letter Making a Special Request: Explicit Appeal*

October 18, 1991

Dear St. Jude's Benefactor:

In past years, you have generously supported St. Jude's House, and I hope you will do so again this year.

As responsible, affluent citizens we are all asked to respond to many good causes. These range from our church, handicapped children, the elderly, finding a cure for cancer and MS, Jerry Lewis Telethons, the Atlanta Symphony, the High Museum, and more. Depending on our loyalties and dispositions, we make our charitable gifts. Whose heartstrings have not been touched by a little blonde, blue-eyed girl about 5 years old with her legs in braces? It's easy to give to her.

Now, contrast that with a sloppy, falling down, filthy, bug-ridden, sour-smelling drunk who has not shaved in weeks. Some think that if he were not so damned sorry, he could stay off booze and earn a good living. Of course, this overlooks the fact that he or she is a victim of a disease, too, called alcoholism.

All those other diseased folks are going to get their share of the funds. But who is going to help that dirty drunk, who will cheat, lie, and steal for another shot of red-eye? St. Jude's does by providing a home, hope, and health for the alcoholic whose family and friends have given up. The result in many cases is little short of miraculous.

It doesn't take much to give to those other needful people. I think it takes real guts, real character, to work for and give to St. Jude's House.

St. Jude's is not perfect. Anyone who knows the frustration of fighting alcoholism will appreciate that, but we do save lives and we do give men and women an opportunity to regain their respect and return to our community. Moreover, while at St. Jude's, these men and women pay for a substantial portion of the cost of the house and, with the help of job location assistance, find jobs where they become taxpayers, no longer a drain on the taxpaying citizens of the city and country.

(Continued)

Source: Reprinted with permission of St. Jude's House, Inc.

In writing a sales letter you should develop your ideas in this sequence: (1) attract the reader's *attention*, (2) stimulate the reader's *interest*, (3) develop a *desire* within the reader, and (4) encourage the reader to take a specific *action*.

Although collection policies may differ among organizations, the collection process almost always progresses through four stages: (1) re-

FIGURE 7.6 ■ *Continued*

```
        St. Jude's Benefactor
        October 18, 1991
        Page 2


            St. Jude's makes no pretense to being a large institution.
        It is modest in its size and scope, but it is the best thing that
        ever happened to many people who have been victimized by alcoholism.
        We receive no government aid and are not a United Way agency.
        Rather, we have served for 18 years because of the faithful support
        that you and our other friends have given us. In this fall of 1991,
        we ask again for your support and pledge our continued work to the
        alcoholics who turn to us for help.

            Please help in whatever way you can and know that we are
        grateful.

                            Sincerely yours,


                            E. Reginald Hancock

                            E. Reginald Hancock
                            Chairman of the Board of Trustees
                            St. Jude's House


        ERH/sts
```

minder, (2) strong reminder, (3) inquiry, and (4) urgency. Regardless of the stage of an overdue account, you must strive to maintain goodwill while collecting the unpaid balance.

In both the reminder and strong-reminder stages you should assume that the customer has simply overlooked the unpaid balance. The letters written in these stages are based on the assumption that, when reminded, the customer will pay. In the inquiry stage you should seek an explanation of the circumstances that prevent payment. This letter is more direct than the previous ones. You become insistent in the urgency stage. The theme may be that the customer can avoid greater problems only by paying now.

We often must write to request a favor that has no clear reward. Such letters of request are usually more personal than sales or collection letters, but they too follow the AIDA sequence.

Key Terms

- **persuasion**
- **credibility**
- **hierarchy of needs**
- **emotional appeal**

- **logical appeal**
- **persuasive letter**
- **AIDA sequence**
- **central selling point**

Review Questions

1. What is the primary goal of persuasion? What more specific goals does this goal encompass?

2. What is meant by source credibility? How can we use it in constructing persuasive messages?

3. What factors can you use to gain and hold the attention of a receiver?

4. Compare and contrast Maslow's theory of motivation with the direct and indirect reward approach to motivating receivers.

5. How do the four steps in the planning process relate to the four steps in writing a sales letter?

6. Explain the difference between the interest step and the desire step.

7. Four common errors in seeking attention are presented in this chapter. Describe another error and provide an example of it.

8. Describe the four stages of a collection campaign.

9. In which ways is the reminder stage in the collection campaign similar to the strong-reminder stage? How are they different?

10. What is meant by central selling point?

Exercises

1. According to the local newspaper, Professor Reginald Smith of Sydney, Australia, has been selected as visiting professor for the upcoming school year by Randall College, located in your city. The article states that this will be the first visit to the United States for the professor, his wife, and their two children. Because you are about to be temporarily transferred to another city by your employer, you hope to lease your condominium to someone for the next 12 months. It appears to you to be a match made in heaven.

Keeping in mind that the professor may not be familiar with the way things are done in the United States, write a "sales" letter to him in which you introduce yourself and try to interest him in leasing your condo.

2. Assume that you are a correspondent for the Ultimate Watch Company. Your company is about to introduce its first chronograph, a wristwatch designed especially for runners. These are its main features: displays hours, minutes, and

seconds on a digital face; functions as a stopwatch with time in minutes, seconds, and hundredths of seconds; has fewer moving parts than any other chronograph; is shock- and water-resistant; carries a two-year warranty. Write a sales letter that will be sent to all of the subscribers to several running magazines.

3. You are sales manager of Columbia Cable Television Corporation. You must persuade the public to subscribe to Living Room Theatre, a channel featuring movies 24 hours a day. Many of the movies are recent films; none is more than one year old. The cost of Living Room Theatre is $5.50 per month or $55 per year if paid in a single payment at the time of subscribing. There are no commercials on this channel, and free maintenance is provided to any subscriber. Living Room Theatre has just become available in Huntington, West Virginia. Write a sales letter in a form that could be sent to all the residents of that area. (If you wish to name some of the movies scheduled to be shown in the near future, use your imagination.)

4. Jeff Walker now qualifies for promotion from the position of mechanic helper to apprentice mechanic. He qualifies as a result of his two years of experience plus the evaluation exam on which he scored an 88. (The minimum passing grade is 70.) If he accepts this promotion he must agree to work the third shift, 11:00 p.m. to 7:00 a.m., for the next three months. After three months he would be scheduled on the regular three-shift rotation. As a mechanic helper he has worked the day shift for the past two years. The required three-month period of third shift is a probationary period during which Jeff will have the opportunity to work, under the supervision of a mechanic third class, on the production machinery that is down (idle) at night. As an apprentice mechanic, Jeff would earn 90 cents more per hour plus a 25 cent hourly differential for night work. Jeff is 23 years old, single, and an active participant in community bowling and softball leagues. As personnel manager of Barr Bushings, Inc., you have had some problems in getting employees to accept similar promotions because of the long stint on third shift. Write a persuasive letter to Jeff Walker.

5. Select a product and assume that you are employed by its manufacturer. Prepare a collection campaign including one letter representing each stage of the collection process. Prepare the four collection letters as form letters that could be sent to any customer.

6. Make the same assumptions as in Exercise 5. This time, however, prepare four letters to be sent to dealers rather than consumers.

7. William Rogers has been a good customer of Meteor Finance Company for eight years. In the past 10 months, however, his account has been overdue twice. At present the account is 60 days delinquent. He has missed his last two monthly payments of $120 each.

a. Write a paragraph in which you appeal to his sense of pride.
b. Write a paragraph in which you appeal to his sense of equity.
c. Write a paragraph in which you appeal to his self-interest.
d. Write a paragraph in which you appeal to something other than pride, equity, and self-interest.

These paragraphs are not intended to appear in a single letter. Therefore, it is not necessary to relate one paragraph to another.

8. As owner-publisher of *Global Running* magazine you have observed a significant decline in running as a pastime during the past two years. During the same period the number of subscribers has declined 45 percent. Walking appears to be the sport of choice for an ever-increasing segment of the population. For that reason, you have started *Healthful Walking* magazine and are planning to discontinue *Global Running* in February.

In recent years favorable publicity for walking has emphasized that, unlike running, it is not harmful to ankles, knees, or the skeletal system. It has been shown to strengthen the cardiovascular system, and people of any age can do it. Different age groups have different interests, and when you write to present subscribers about discontinuing publication of *Running*, you plan to tailor your message to three age groups: 16–30, 31–50; and over 50. Prepare a letter for one of the age groups. Offer either to send a refund for the unfulfilled portion of their *Running* subscriptions or to substitute issues of *Walking*. Those who elect to receive *Walking* will receive double the number of issues remaining on their *Running* subscriptions.

9. Find a sales letter from a mass mailing. Identify the four steps of persuasion in it and the main appeals used in the letter. Rewrite the letter. Either emphasize a different appeal than is emphasized in the original letter or introduce a new appeal to emphasize.

10. Your favorite coursework, with the exception of business communication, is international business. You have become aware of the importance of understanding people from other cultures, and, with that in mind, you have decided to embark on a project. Every other week during the summer your community is visited by a group of 30 to 40 German tourists. These tours are sponsored by the German-American Friendship Association and are conducted by a major U.S. bus company. Although each group spends 2½ days in your community, the members rarely meet any of the residents, nor, to your way of thinking, do they get much of a feel for the area. The individual tour guides, who are invariably from northeastern cities, are basically unfamiliar with your area, and their knowledge is limited to what is provided them by their employer in the tour guide manual. Write a letter to the German-American Friendship Association and offer your services as a guide for the 2½ days each group spends in your community. Suggest also that the association seek out knowledgeable individuals in each community to serve as guides. You feel that better understanding between people would result and that the tours would be more enjoyable for the tourists. Your fee for serving as a local guide would be $100 per day. The address of the German-American Friendship Association is 2 Hamburg 13, Hafenstrasse 28, West Germany.

11. You have been assigned a research paper on universal life insurance policies. Universal life insurance is regarded by many as the most promising new approach to life insurance in years. Use the *Business Periodical Index* to locate several articles on universal life insurance. After learning what it is, write a letter to Commissioner of Insurance, State of Wisconsin, Madison, WI 53703, requesting information for your research paper. Be specific in the type of information you seek.

12. You own a sporting goods store and have completed a mailing list of the members of the various bicycle clubs in your area. Prepare a sales letter to be sent to the club members in late October when a typical Minnesota winter is about to begin. Try to sell the readers on continuing to enjoy the benefits of cycling exercise by purchasing a new Exer-Bike. The Exer-Bike is manufactured in the United States, weighs only 22 pounds, and sells for $110. It is a stationary

bike, 40 inches long and 30 inches high, and the handlebar is 22 inches long. The handlebar is easily adjusted, without tools, for persons of any height.

13. You volunteered to take pictures at your cousin's wedding to save the newlyweds the expense of hiring a photographer. You took approximately 150 pictures and gave them to a local camera store for processing. More than half of the photographs were badly blurred. Because you are an accomplished photographer, you know that you are not at fault. The owner of the camera store disclaims responsibility, because he merely sent the films to another city for processing. The store owner has offered to give you free film equivalent to the amount of film that was blurred. Write a letter to the photo laboratory that processed the film. You have suffered considerable embarrassment, and you believe that the photo laboratory should pay you at least $100 in damages. You intend to give whatever payment you get to your cousin. Write your letter to Slic Pics Inc., P.O. Box 1212, Hilda, MO 65670.

14. In an effort to conserve energy, two years ago you replaced the caulking compound in all of the windows in your eight-room house. Now the caulking compound is badly mildewed and looks unsightly. You complain to the owner of the store where you bought the compound, but he is not sympathetic. "It's not advertised as mildew-resistant," he says. Write a letter to the manufacturer in which you request that a representative be sent to inspect your house and remedy the situation. Write your letter to Home Products, Inc., P.O. Box 290, Pottsburg, FL 32216.

15. While you await your flight home after a two-week tour of Europe, an announcement is made that the flight is overbooked. You volunteer to take a later flight in exchange for the airline's offer of a free six-course dinner at an elegant French restaurant. The airline guarantees that you will have a seat on the next flight, which is scheduled to depart 10 hours later. When you arrive for the later flight, having enjoyed a sumptuous meal, you learn that, in order to get enough volunteers for a later flight, the airline paid some passengers as much as $400 in exchange for their seats. You are upset with what you regard as unequal treatment, and you feel that you should get additional payment. Write a letter to Jean-Paul Langlois, Vice President of Customer Service, Air Marseilles, Inc., Marseilles, France.

The Nirvana Alarm Clock | *CASE*
Robert Underwood, Ball State University

At your new job with a local advertising agency, you have been given the assignment of writing a persuasive letter to market the Nirvana Alarm Clock. According to the list provided to you, these are the features of the clock:

1. Automatically resets the alarm for the next day.
2. Has a sturdy, nontip base.
3. Has a 5-decibel buzzer.
4. Has a snooze alarm.
5. Is available in the following seven colors: red, pink, blue, black, purple, green, and orange.

6. Is constructed of durable polystyrene.
7. Has a luminous face and projects the correct day and time on the ceiling.
8. Measures 6 by 6 by 2 inches.
9. Costs $21.95, plus $3.00 for shipping and handling.
10. Comes with an unconditional 2-year guarantee.

Thousands of these clocks have been sold nationally, but your target market will be college students. Write a sales letter built around a central theme. You might not want to include all of the features listed.

Case Questions

1. What would be your central theme for this letter?

2. Which characteristics of the clock would be of most interest to a college student? Which characteristics would be of least interest to a college student?

3. List two attention-getters that you could use to begin your letter.

CASE | *Ten Percent Is Not Always Ten Percent*

David B. Parsons, Lakehead University, Thunder Bay, Ontario, Canada

Dr. Tom Rathwell was hired by Lakehead University to teach business and technical writing. The university's policy is to pay all moving expenses through a purchase order, but Tom had to get three estimates on what it would cost to move his belongings from Toronto to Thunder Bay. The three estimates he received were $3,700, $4,200, and $4,500.

To save the university money, Tom decided to accept Olsen Van Line's estimate of $3,700. However, Olsen's contract included a 10 percent adjustment clause that stated that the company would increase the estimate up to 10 percent to cover any discrepancy between the estimated weight of Tom's furniture and the actual weight.

When Tom's furniture arrived in Thunder Bay, he was presented with a bill for $4,300, an increase of almost 15 percent. When Tom pointed out the fact that he was being overcharged, the driver told him that the only way he would get his furniture was to sign the bill. Needing his furniture and wishing to avoid a confrontation with the driver, Tom signed. Now, however, Tom is writing a letter to Olsen's, requesting that they return the $230 that they overcharged the university.

Case Questions

1. Why would Olsen's overcharge Tom Rathwell by $230?

2. What is his primary purpose in writing this letter? What might be some secondary purposes?

3. Considering the nature of the situation, who would Tom write to at Olsen's and how would he analyze his audience?

4. Write the letter to Olsen's.

The Broken Heel | *CASE*

Anita S. Bednar, Central State University

You recently represented your company at a conference in Ft. Worth, Texas. The conference was held in the Imperial Hotel, a three-star hotel that you had stayed in before. The service had always been excellent—good food, friendly professional atmosphere, and fast check-in and checkout. You were pleased when the business meeting was scheduled for the Imperial again this year.

Unfortunately, some construction was underway at the hotel; in fact, a contractor was refurbishing most of the meeting rooms. Plastic sheeting was being used as dividers, and this made hearing the speakers nearly impossible. Going from one meeting room to the next, you stepped in a space that was normally covered by carpet and broke the heel of your shoe. You had to hobble around for a couple of hours before buying new shoes to wear during the remainder of the three-day conference. The shoes cost $65.

When you arrived home from the meeting, you attempted to have your shoe with the broken heel repaired. The Tyler Shoe Shop did repair the heel for $10.50, but did not match the heel on the other shoe. One of your colleagues suggested that you write the Imperial Hotel for some kind of reimbursement. You decide that you will.

Case Questions

1. Should this be considered a persuasive letter or a routine claim letter?

2. Should you ask the Imperial Hotel to reimburse you for your new shoes, the repair of the broken heel, or both?

3. To which of the following should you send the letter?
    The general manager of the hotel
    The convention director
    The reservation clerk

4. How much detail should you give about the circumstances?

5. Should you use your personal stationery or your company letterhead?

6. Should you also complain about the disruption of the meetings because of the construction going on?

7. What kind of goodwill statement can you include?

Memoranda

In his new position with a large insurance company, Ted Landers was surrounded by unfamiliar faces. Before long, however, he was invited to join a group of employees his own age who often got together after work on Fridays. Their conversations usually ended up on job-related matters. They talked a lot about their bosses' personalities and idiosyncracies. One was said to be "a fanatic" on punctuality, another a "neatness freak," and Mr. Jenkins was described as "laid-back" about his duty to enforce the company's dress code.

Ted noticed that the labels assigned to bosses were usually related to something they had recently done. The exception was Mr. Beckwith, who was termed a "hothead" because of an incident three years before.

Soon after he became claims manager, Mr. Beckwith concluded that the employees in the claims department were either wasting or stealing many office supplies. He wrote a memo criticizing them for "misuse of company property" and sent a copy to each person in the department. The memo said, among other things, "If you were rightfully using stationery, at the rate it is disappearing this department's productivity would be 50 percent greater than it is."

Someone showed Ted a copy of the memo. It was, just as it had been described, strongly worded and laced with accusations. It was definitely a memorable memo. After three years people were still using it to evaluate the writer. Ted vowed privately that he would begin considering the consequences whenever writing a memo.

Some people call it "memoitis," and others talk about "memomania." Many refer to it in terms that would never appear in textbooks. Managers who overuse memos are called "memomaniacs." What they are all talking about is the excessive use of memoranda. In many organizations employees complain that they are swamped with memos. "If I read every memorandum that I received, I wouldn't have time for anything else," is a frequent complaint.

Complaints about the excessive use of memoranda are not new. Nearly 40 years ago Robert Benchley described the problems in this way:

> When the mail is disposed of we have what is known as Memorandum Hour. During this period everyone sends memoranda to everyone else. If you happen to have nothing in particular about which to dictate a memorandum, you dictate a memorandum to someone, saying that you have nothing to suggest or report. This gives a stimulating exchange of ideas, and also helps to use up the blue memorandum blanks which have been printed at some expense for just that purpose.[1]

Such statements are exaggerations. It is true that memoranda are widely used, but mostly for good reason.

CHARACTERISTICS AND USES OF MEMORANDA

The memorandum is used primarily for internal communication.

A **memorandum** is a message written for use within the organization. Traditionally letters are used for external communication; ordinarily the memorandum is intended solely for internal communication. Researchers recently found that approximately 90 percent of the writing done by business people is in the form of letters or memos. The same researchers also found that business people write more memos than letters.[2]

The main explanation for the popularity of memoranda is that within large organizations there is a great need for communication. As organizations grow, problems of coordination become more severe. Memoranda can help to keep the various parts of the organization in touch with one another. They have many different uses: to convey information from one department to another, to communicate between branches, or to file as records and reference. In fact, the memorandum is the most widely used form of written communication within the organization.

Memoranda influence the personal and professional lives of most business people simply because they are the primary means of updating employees on what is going on in the organization. Policy and procedural changes as well as details of internal operations in general are usually conveyed via memoranda.

---

[1]Robert Benchley, *The Benchley Roundup* (New York: Harper & Row, 1954), 28.
[2]William H. Baker and Larry D. Hartman, "A Follow-Up Study of Business Students with Good and Poor Writing Abilities," paper presented at a meeting of the Association for Business Communication (Las Vegas, 1989).

Because memos are highly visible in most organizations, employees have definite opinions about them. In a poll of 1,000 executives conducted by Robert Half International, a personnel consulting firm, the following major complaints were registered:[3] 76 percent felt that most memos are too long; 58 percent believed that copies are distributed too broadly; 55 percent believed that most memos are too self-serving; and 20 percent think that memos are too often written in haste or anger. Not too surprisingly, four out of ten executives said that memos were a waste of time. The management of United Technologies Corporation felt strongly enough to purchase the full-page ad in *The Wall Street Journal* shown in Figure 8.1.

THE ADVANTAGES OF MEMORANDA

Because memoranda are intended for internal communication, it might appear easier to talk to the other person than to write a memorandum. This is sometimes true, but using a memorandum has distinct advantages:

Memoranda have several advantages over oral communication.

1. A memorandum provides a written record. Unlike a conversation, a memorandum can be filed for future reference. It serves as a written record for the writer or for the reader or for both. The more important the subject of the memorandum, the more likely that copies will be filed. By referring to the memorandum at a later date, both receiver and sender are reminded of specifics, such as date, individual responsibilities, and deadlines.
2. A memorandum is suitable for transmitting complex information. When a spoken message contains a lot of very specific detail or is in some other way complex, the listener has difficulty remembering it. Complicated instructions are easily misunderstood under the best of circumstances, but when they are spoken, the chances for error are manifold. Consequently, a memorandum becomes an accurate memory jogger.
3. A memorandum can reach many persons simultaneously. If you must transmit some information to a number of coworkers, contacting each one individually is time consuming. Schedule conflicts may make it difficult to assemble the group for a meeting. A memorandum, however, can reach a large number of individuals easily.

At one time memoranda were considered to be economical. They were routinely handwritten and usually designated for individuals who were difficult to contact by telephone or face to face. Many memoranda are now dictated and typed, however, and the expense is almost as great as for actual letters. There is a savings in postage and envelopes, perhaps, but little more than that.

Memoranda were once economical but now may cost almost as much as a letter.

3Marcy Eckroth Mullins, "USA Snapshots," *USA Today*, March 25, 1987, 1-A.

FIGURE 8.1   ▪ *A Public Statement on Memorandum Writing*

Memo To Those Who Write Memos:

Art Buchwald tells of the kid who visited his father's office. When asked what his father did, the kid said, "He sends pieces of paper to other people and other people send papers to him." When you draft a memo, remember other people love to "correct" drafts. The more textually taut you keep it, the less chance for others to pounce on it. The Lord's Prayer has 71 words. The Ten Commandments have 297. The Gettysburg Address has 271. The legal marriage vow has two. General McAuliffe at the Bulge made his point in one: "Nuts!" For practice, send your memo to yourself as a straight telegram at your own expense. Chances are, the less your telegram costs, the more effective your memo is.

A message as published in the *Wall Street Journal*
by United Technologies Corporation, Hartford, Connecticut 06101

Source: Courtesy of United Technologies.

THE SIGNIFICANCE OF MEMORANDA TO THE WRITER

In larger organizations the impression you make on your coworkers is determined partially by the memoranda you write. Your manner of communicating influences what others think of you. The further removed the other person is from you, the stronger the effect of your memoranda. For example, when Brenda Thornton sent a memorandum suggesting a change in pricing procedures, her superior, Bill Hawley, did not have the authority to act on it. For that reason she provided more detailed information than Bill, who was familiar with the topic, would have required. Bill forwarded the memorandum to his superior, Max Whitcomb, who had never met Brenda and knew little about her. His perception of her was created largely by her thorough memorandum.

People are judged in part by the memoranda they write.

When you are working in a large organization, the impression you make upon others goes beyond those with whom you personally interact. It extends to all who read your memoranda. For some, their sole link with you may be through your memoranda. In the example, Brenda's managerial potential was recognized in part through her effective use of the medium.

THE SIGNIFICANCE OF MEMORANDA TO THE ORGANIZATION

Occasionally a memo intended for a small number of receivers within the organization is released to the public, either inadvertently or intentionally. Such occurrences, while rare, have sometimes been covered by the mass media. For example, in September 1989, when Bryant Gumbel, "Today Show" host, wrote a memo to his boss in which he evaluated other people on the show, its release triggered a public outpouring of feelings, many negative toward Gumbel.[4] The incident led to a live on-the-air public apology by him.

In another instance, Georgia Pacific Corporation's bitter takeover battle with Great Northern Nekoosa Corporation was further inflamed by Great Northern's contention that it had "uncovered" one of Georgia Pacific's internal memos. In it Georgia Pacific is alleged to have been planning an action contrary to what it had been publicly proclaiming.[5]

Fortunately most of the memos you will write during your career will be unlikely to result in such major repercussions. Nevertheless, you should write them with care.

PREPARATION OF MEMORANDA

The memorandum has evolved to simplify communication within the organization. Some of the niceties of letter writing are sacrificed for the sake of conciseness.

[4]Barrett J. Mandel and Judith Yellen, "Gumbel's Bumble Redux," *Working Woman*, September 1989, 136–138.

[5]Bill Hendrick, "Memo Heats Up the Battle between Great Northern, Georgia-Pacific," *Atlanta Journal and Constitution*, December 15, 1989.

BOXED IN *AN ETHICAL DILEMMA*

The Cumberland Corporation has experienced problems in retaining good employees since Uniframe Inc. opened a plant in the same town two years ago. Uniframe recently announced the addition of a third shift. This meant to Ben Thomas, plant manager at Cumberland, that he could expect even greater problems in retaining his best workers.

Today Ben received in his company mail packet a memo from division headquarters that was actually intended only for the vice presidents. It details a sizable layoff scheduled in two months to last for an indefinite period. Readers are cautioned to honor the secrecy of the memo because Cumberland must complete several major orders before the layoff.

Ben knows that he should not have received the memo in the first place. He also knows that, unless he alerts good, loyal workers to the coming layoff, they will miss the chance to be hired by Uniframe. To whom does he owe the greatest allegiance: his loyal employees or the company?

Ben feels boxed in. What would you do?

Format

The format of the memorandum ensures consistency in internal communication.

The format of the memorandum is intended to simplify and speed up internal communication by ensuring consistency. A typical form for memoranda appears in Figure 8.2.

Some organizations provide employees with preprinted forms that have the basic elements of any memorandum printed at the top of the page:

To:
From:
Date:
Subject:

By providing this format, a company can ensure that certain types of information always appear in the same place in memoranda. Finding a particular memorandum in a file is easier if all the memoranda are uniform in the placement of this information. You will know precisely where to look to find the subject of each memorandum.

Some organizations provide more structured forms to further simplify the process of memorandum preparation. Some structured forms consist of an original and two color-coded carbon copies and include space for the recipient to reply. This is the usual sequence of steps in using such a form:

1. The initiator writes the message, addresses the form, and removes one of the copies to keep as a reminder.
2. The recipient replies in the space provided, removes the second copy, and returns the original to the initiator.

FIGURE 8.2   ▪   *Example of a One-Page Memorandum*

```
                          MEMO



        TO:         All Department Heads

        FROM:       Wayne Kasten,
                    Compensation Manager

        DATE:       December 2, 1991

        SUBJECT:    Holiday Schedule for Salary
                    Submission

            Because of the abbreviated work
        schedule for December 23 through Decem-
        ber 27, all salary request forms must be
        received at this office no later than
        December 16.  Any adjustments in pay that
        are requested between December 16 and
        December 23 will be represented in the
        January payroll.
```

3. The initiator now has the message and its reply on one form and can take whatever action is necessary.

Although such forms are intended primarily for internal communication, in exceptional instances they are sometimes used more broadly. Some organizations use such forms for routine correspondence with people outside the organization. For example, suppose that you order a lightweight tent from a sporting goods company. Although the company does not have the model you ordered in stock, a comparable model is available. The company might use such a form to notify you and await your response.

Memoranda vary considerably in length. Some, such as Figure 8.2, are brief, perhaps no more than a few sentences, while others may be three or four pages long. Some companies provide half-sheet memorandum forms for short messages, thus reducing the expense of paper. (Others feel that the savings from smaller forms are offset by the problems in filing and finding these smaller forms.) When a memorandum is more than one page long, each subsequent page should have a heading showing the addressee's name, the page number, and the date, similar to the continuing page of a letter. In some organizations the subject of the memorandum is also included, as shown in Figure 8.3.

Planning and Writing

Generally, business writers agonize less over wording and other stylistic matters when they write memoranda than when they write letters. Intended for internal communication, memoranda are usually less formal and more direct. Exceptions occur, however. For example, after Becke Longman's research convinced her that a training program was the most likely solution to the materials waste problem, she devoted three days to preparing the report for her boss. She knew that he would not be willing to spend the sizable amount of money necessary for the program unless she could show that the training program would be likely to solve the problem. In short, she had to persuade him.

Regardless of the situation in which the memo is written, planning is essential. The four steps of the planning process, described in Chapter 5, are crucial to the success of any kind of business communication. The characteristics of effective business writing presented in Chapter 3 also pertain to memos.

As in letters, ideas in a memo conveying good or neutral news should be arranged in the direct or deductive manner described in Chapter 5. Figure 8.4 on page 231 is an example of such a memo.

Bad-news memos, like bad-news letters, are made more acceptable by using the indirect sequence.

Memos must sometimes provide negative information. Ideas in bad-news memos should be arranged in the indirect sequence described in Chapter 6. Ed Percivel used this sequence when he notified the members of the maintenance crew, all of whom were avid hunters, that they would have to work on the first day of hunting season. His memo is presented in Figure 8.5 on page 232. Ed followed the bad-news sequence. What do you think of his approach? Should he have mentioned that he realized that it was the first day of hunting season?

✓ CHECKLIST for Planning a Memo

____�] **Determine your objective(s). Why are you writing?**

____⏋ **Consider your audience. To whom are you writing?**

____⏋ **Select your main ideas. What do you especially want the reader to remember?**

Purposes

Memoranda are prepared for many different purposes. Among their routine purposes are: (1) requesting information, (2) giving instructions, (3) serving as covers for other messages, and (4) making announcements.

FIGURE 8.3 ▪ *Example of a Two-Page Memorandum*

MEMO

TO: All Exempt Employees

FROM: Bill Wendall, Chairperson, Evaluation Committee

DATE: September 30, 1991

SUBJECT: Explanation of Delphi Technique to Measure Clarity
           and Equity of Personnel Procedures

    On October 1, 1991, 20 percent of the exempt employees will
be invited to participate in an evaluation of personnel procedures
within the company. This memo is an explanation of the Delphi
technique, which will be used in investigating the subject.

Purpose of Delphi Technique

    The Delphi technique is a method of combining the knowledge
and abilities of a diverse group to reach conclusions when true
values are not known. Exempt personnel from all departments will
be involved in presenting their thoughts on all aspects of personnel
procedures. It is expected that such company practices as recruitment, selection, performance evaluation, and promotion will be
among the topics considered.

    This study is intended to result in some modifications in
current personnel practices within the company. It is expected
that subsequent personnel operations will better meet the needs of
exempt employees once the personnel practices needing improvement
are identified.

Advantages of Delphi Technique

    The Delphi technique is an upward communication format that has
several advantages over the questionnaires used in previous surveys.
The Delphi technique is less structured than the questionnaire and thus
allows for greater input from employees. Feedback is more immediate
than it is from questionnaires, and unlike questionnaires the Delphi
technique allows respondents to refine their thinking.

    In earlier studies within the company, interviews and group
meetings have been used to elicit employee attitudes and opinions.
The Delphi technique is not only less expensive, but it also provides
the anonymity that is lacking in interviews and group meetings.

(*Continued*)

Requests for Information

Memoranda requesting information are a part of organization life. Sometimes the request will require hours of research by the reader. At other
times the reader may be able to write a paragraph in reply on the original
memorandum and return it to the sender. An example of a memorandum
requesting information is presented in Figure. 8.6 on page 233.

The three steps in preparing memoranda requesting information are:

1. State the key idea, the request.

FIGURE 8.3   ▪   *Continued*

```
Memo to All Exempt Employees
(Explanation of Delphi Technique)
September 30, 1991
Page 2



     The feedback present in the Delphi technique exposes all of the
members to other points of view and stimulates everyone's thinking.
The participants' anonymity means that the respondents need not take
conventional viewpoints nor follow a policy dictated by their super-
iors.  The Delphi technique allows a participant to safely abandon
long-defended stands, and the participant cannot be pressured into
following the opinion of a well-known expert in the field.

Procedures

1. On October 1, 1991, 20 percent of the exempt employees will receive
   several open-ended questions concerning personnel practices. Parti-
   cipants will be asked to comment on those practices and to list the
   strengths and weaknesses of the practices.  Participants may also
   suggest possible changes. Responses to these questions should be
   sent to me no later than October 8.

2. On about October 22, the participants will receive returns from the
   first round of questions.  Responses will be arranged according to
   the frequency in which they were given.  Participants are urged to
   reconsider and possibly modify their previous statements.  Sugges-
   tions previously given will be voted on according to desirability
   and feasibility.  Participants should return their responses to me
   no later than November 1.

3. On about November 15, the participants will receive returns from
   the second round of questions.  Responses will again be arranged in
   order of frequency.  Participants may modify their previous respon-
   ses if they wish and return their responses to me by November 25.

4. On about December 2, participants will receive results of the third
   round in summary form.  Appropriate action will be taken shortly
   thereafter.

     If you are selected to participate, you will be able to do so at
your convenience.  Each round will require only 30 to 90 minutes of
your time.  Through the cooperation of those selected to parti-
cipate, company personnel practices will become more attuned to the
needs of the employees.
```

2. Present the details.
3. Remind the reader of the request and provide additional specific information.

The effectiveness of a memorandum requesting information is determined largely by the clarity and reasonableness of its message as well as by the writer's explanation of purpose. The readers of the message in Figure 8.6 knew what they were to do and why they were to do it. They also rec-

FIGURE 8.4   ▮   *Memo Conveying Good News*

```
                          MEMO



        TO:        All Employees

        FROM:      Gabe Harrison, President

        DATE:      November 15, 1991

        SUBJECT:   Successful Halloween Fund-Raiser

                For the third consecutive year, the
        proceeds from our haunted house project
        have exceeded our goal.  This year's goal
        of $6,000 had seemed unrealistically high;
        however, the project's final accounting
        shows receipts of $6,875.

                Thanks to the involvement of every
        Harrison International employee, the pro-
        ject was a complete success.  We should
        all be pleased with the knowledge that
        our efforts have provided this year's
        beneficiary, the Mid-Town Shelter, with
        the resources necessary to complete its
        renovation.
```

ognized that their task would be accomplished easily and would result in benefits for them.

Giving Instructions

In giving instructions through a memorandum you must try to cover the subject so that the reader will not have any unanswered questions. At the same time you should avoid overwriting or belaboring the obvious. Figure 8.7 on page 234 shows a sample memo of this type.

Transmittals

A **transmittal memorandum** introduces the reader to a longer, accompanying message. At times you may go beyond a mere introduction and interpret the message for the reader or at least describe the main points of the message. Regardless of its length or brevity, however, the transmittal memorandum introduces something.

When her boss asked her to learn the reasons for the high turnover among custodial workers, Sharon Wilcox did extensive research and pre-

A memorandum of transmittal covers another message.

FIGURE 8.5 ▪ *Memo Conveying Bad News*

```
                              MEMO


          TO:        All Members of Maintenance Crew

          FROM:      Ed Percival, Personnel Director

          DATE:      October 30, 1991

          SUBJECT:   Weekend Maintenance Schedule
                     Change for November 10-11

              You have been involved for the past
          two years in providing your expertise to
          Engineering regarding the long-awaited new
          generator.  After more than a year of plan-
          ning and construction, we are almost ready
          to put the new generator on line.  The
          installation will be completed over the
          weekend on November 10-11.

              All production will cease at 6:00 a.m.
          on November 10, and all maintenance person-
          nel will be expected to work on the 10th and
          11th.  Because it so rarely happens that
          all production equipment is down at the same
          time, it is important that we take advantage
          of the opportunity to perform as much rou-
          tine and nonroutine maintenance as possible.

              The work we will be able to accomplish
          over that weekend should ensure that the
          maintenance schedule for the rest of the
          year, including the holiday season, will
          not necessitate any unexpected weekend work.
```

pared a memorandum on the subject. The transmittal memorandum she wrote to accompany the report appears in Figure 8.8 on page 235.

Announcements

Memoranda are used to announce a great variety of matters of interest to one or to many.

Memoranda may be used to announce such matters as personnel transfers, meetings, or policy changes. **Announcement memoranda** are sometimes disseminated widely within the organization; in other instances they are sent only to a select few. They are often posted prominently on company bulletin boards.

SUMMARY

Much of the communication within any organization is in the form of memoranda. A memorandum is a message written for use within the organization. Some distant advantages of the memorandum are that it: (1) provides a written record; (2) is suitable for transmitting complex infor-

FIGURE 8.6 ▪ *A Memorandum Requesting Information*

```
                              MEMO


        TO:        Faculty, Business Education
                   Department

        FROM:      Y. A. Young, Chairman,
                   Business Education Department

        DATE:      January 8, 1991

        SUBJECT:   Film Catalog for Faculty Use

                In order to reduce the time it takes
        to screen and select appropriate films,
        we are putting together a catalog of films
        that have been used effectively in business
        education classes.

                Please submit to this office the
        following information, using a separate
        sheet of paper for each film:

        1. Film title and approximate length.
        2. One-paragraph description of the main
           points made in the film.
        3. One-paragraph description of how the film
           relates to the course in which it was used.

                Please provide this information by Jan-
        uary 31.  Shortly thereafter you will receive
        your copy of the completed catalog. Through
        the cooperation of all faculty members in
        this project, all of us will benefit.
```

mation; and (3) can reach many persons simultaneously. The format of the memorandum is intended to simplify and speed up internal communication by ensuring consistency.

Because much time is devoted to the preparation and reading of memos, business people have strong feelings about them. The most common complaint is that memos are too long. Because memos are designed primarily for internal communication, some writers do not attach as much importance to them as to external communication. Planning is crucial for any and all types of business communication.

Key Terms

▪ **memorandum**   ▪ **announcement memorandum**

▪ **transmittal memorandum**

FIGURE 8.7 ▪ *A Memorandum Giving Instructions*

```
                              MEMO


        TO:        Faculty, Sinclair College

        FROM:      J. R. Easton, Assistant Circu-
                   lation Manager, College Library

        DATE:      March 15, 1991

        SUBJECT:   New Procedure for Reserving
                   Books for Class Use

              A new procedure for putting books
        on reserve will begin at the start of the
        summer quarter.  Follow these guidelines:

        1.  Submit a list of books on the attached
            form to the Reserve Department at least
            four weeks before the start of the quar-
            ter in which the books will be assigned.
        2.  Do not include more than ten books on
            a form.
        3.  Include the following for each entry:
            a. Call number
            b. Book title
            c. Author's name
            d  Course number and name
            e. Type of reserve desired — two-hour
               or overnight
            f. Anticipated class size
            g. Instructor's name, campus address,
               and office telephone number

              By following these procedures you will be
        contributing to library efficiency.
```

Review Questions

1. What is a memorandum?

2. What are the advantages of the memorandum?

3. For what reasons do business people express strong feelings on the subject of memoranda?

4. What might a writer do to overcome the complaints most frequently made about memoranda?

5. What might an organization do to overcome the complaints most frequently made about memoranda?

6. In what ways does a memorandum differ from other business communication formats? In what ways are they similar?

7. How do the steps to the planning process apply to the memorandum?

8. Describe a situation in which a memo might be used for external communication.

FIGURE 8.8 ∎ *A Transmittal Memorandum*

```
                          MEMO


         TO:      James Bellamy,
                  Personnel Director

         FROM:    Sharon Wilcox,
                  Logistical Support Coordinator

         DATE:    August 1, 1991

         SUBJECT: Research Report on Turnover
                  among Custodial Workers

              Here are the results of the research
         I conducted pertaining to turnover among
         custodial workers.

              My report is divided into four parts,
         and each part is preceded by a brief
         abstract of its contents.

              Part I clarifies the problem and its
         effects on operations; Part II presents
         a compilation of the custodial supervisors'
         perceptions of the problem; Part III pre-
         sents a compilation of the custodial work-
         ers' perceptions of the problem; Part IV
         presents conclusions based on the findings
         of the survey.
```

If Wilcox thought Bellamy might not remember the problem (much less her assignment to do the research), she might have begun the memo as follows: "I have done some research on the high rate of turnover among custodial workers."

9. When preparing a memo for internal communication, what assumptions can the writer ordinarily make about the reader(s)?

Exercises

1. Think about a problem you have either experienced or observed at the college you attend. Write a memo in which you suggest one or more changes that are intended to overcome the problem. Explain why you think that these changes would be helpful. Direct your memo to the individual who would have the authority to make the changes you suggest.

2. As manager of Tri-State Merchants Mall, which consists of 150 retail establishments, you are responsible for identifying and soliciting promotions that are likely to attract more shoppers to the mall. You have been approached by Statewide Auto Association about holding an auto show at the mall. The show would feature most of the latest model automobiles and could be held in the enclosed pedestrian area of the mall. Salespeople from the local dealers would be available to assist interested shoppers.

Mall policy is that decisions on large promotions must be made by the members of the Promotions Committee, 10 merchants who represent all of those at the mall. In order to make the best decision about the proposed auto show, the committee will need more information. Write a memo to Brian Benson, head of the Promotions Committee, in which you ask him to do some research on the effects of auto shows on shopping centers: Do auto shows attract customers who would not otherwise come to a shopping center? What possible disadvantages accompany having an auto show in an enclosed shopping center? Would additional liability insurance be desirable for such an event? Include several other questions that you think would be appropriate for such a situation.

3. Assume that your employer will soon begin doing business in a specific foreign country and that 25 employees, including you, may be transferred there. Read one or more articles on that country from recent newspapers or magazines. Describe in a memo what you have learned about current conditions in the country and the possible effects of current conditions on business operations. Prepare the memo for your boss, Bill Irving, president, C & C Industries.

4. Write a memo to the branch managers, all of whom are U.S. citizens, of the foreign production sites of 3T, Inc. Urge the managers to set up speakers bureaus and to encourage their staff members to become involved. You feel it is especially important for those staff members who are U.S. citizens to participate as speakers. You view a speakers bureau as an opportunity for employees to develop their communication skills while educating their listeners about 3T, Inc. Also, you feel that exposing the community to U.S. citizens would be good advertising for the United States.

5. You are employed by HH Manufacturing as a plant manager in a foreign country (you select the country). You receive a request from your boss, Morris Corrales, for a list of the national holidays celebrated in that country. These are days on which most business organizations in that country would ordinarily be closed. He wants this information in order to facilitate the scheduling of visits and meetings during the upcoming year. Get the necessary information from a library and prepare an appropriate memo. Morris Corrales is based at the home office in Marinette, WI 54143.

6. As director of the college library you have received a growing number of complaints about the way the periodical room is managed. Twelve patrons have complained that magazines are allowed to pile up on tables before being shelved; eight complained that magazines are often put back on the wrong shelves. Also, many magazines are reported to be torn, and no apparent attempt is made to repair them. Some students have been observed cutting articles out of magazines in violation of library policy. Write a memo to Curtis Farnsworth, periodical room manager, in which you describe the complaints and make recommendations.

7. You are the manager of 3T's production facility in Manila. Write a memo for your boss, Marie Desmond, on the activities of the speakers bureau that you began one year ago. She wants to know the number of employees who are participating in it, topics covered, number of speeches given, and nature of the audiences. Your research reveals that eight of your 14 staff members are participating as speakers. A total of 36 speeches have been given. Three topics have been covered during the year: the history and future of 3T, Inc.; the

contributions of 3T to the community; and the American way of life. There have been five presentations of history and future, three on 3T's contributions to the community, and 28 on the American way of life. Twelve of the presentations were made to adult church groups, five to neighborhood social clubs, and 18 to high school classes. Ten of the 18 were given at private schools and the rest at public schools. Of the eight participating employees, three spoke only once and three gave five speeches. One person spoke six times and one gave 12 speeches. You conducted an informal and anonymous survey of the six nonparticipants to learn their reasons for not joining the bureau. Three mentioned a fear of speaking in public as their main reason. Two did not consider it a part of the job, and one had no particular reason.

8. You are the manager for international production for a large multinational organization. Write a memo to the managers of the branches located in foreign countries. Point out the importance of their active participation in the culture in which they are presently living. Also, point out that they represent the United States as well as the company. Request from these managers a brief report on the extent to which their staff members who are U.S. citizens have become involved in the respective foreign cultures.

Analysis of the Membership of a City Chamber of Commerce | CASE

Anthony S. Lis, University of Oklahoma

You are the vice president for membership of the Chamber of Commerce in a city with a population of over 85,000. Chamber members total 153.

Within the city limits are located a state comprehensive university with an enrollment of over 16,000, a state mental health hospital with over 1,000 patients, a 230-bed municipal hospital, and two manufacturing plants employing over 900 workers combined.

The Chamber of Commerce secretary has given you the following data about the composition of the membership of your organization:

		Sex		Govt./Ed.		Retail		Mfg		Service		Other	
Age Group	Total	Male	Female	M	F	M	F	M	F	M	F	M	F
35 and under	3	3	0	1	0	2	0	0	0	0	0	0	0
36–44	37	22	15	4	1	11	9	3	1	4	4	0	0
45–54	68	41	27	4	2	26	13	8	1	3	11	0	0
55–64	36	21	15	4	0	9	10	7	2	1	3	0	0
65 and over	9	9	0	0	0	4	0	1	0	1	0	3	0

The column group header above reads *Employment* spanning Govt./Ed., Retail, Mfg, Service, and Other.

Case Questions

1. Prepare an appropriate table giving the percentages for the various characteristics according to the sex and the employment categories.

2. What conclusions can be drawn on the basis of the data about the nature of the current membership?

3. What recommendations could you as the vice president for membership offer to the board of directors concerning any appropriate and desirable changes in the membership?

4. In your opinion, how should any changes be implemented?

5. Should the members of the Chamber of Commerce be told about this study and any changes that you will be proposing? Why?

6. Prepare a two-page memorandum to the board of directors with an appropriate table and your recommendations for changing the composition of the membership.

CASE | *Is There a Better Way?*

David B. Parsons, Lakehead University, Thunder Bay, Ontario, Canada

Jim Walker has been the staff development officer for Memorial Hospital for only three weeks. He is a firm believer in following the regulations. A conscientious individual, he has worked hard to familiarize himself with the hospital's policies, including the procedures for ordering supplies and equipment.

Consequently, he was shocked and quite upset when he received the following memorandum from the hospital's purchasing officer.

> To: Staff Development Officer
> From: Purchasing Officer
> Subject: Improper Buying Practices
>
>   Please find attached an example of a purchase that was made without first obtaining a purchase order.
>   I require an explanation, as this practice is contrary to hospital policy.
>   I await your reply.

As far as Jim knew, both he and his staff had been submitting the correct purchase orders. Furthermore, he could not understand how a purchase could be made without the authorization of the purchasing department.

What upset Jim most was the implied message of the memorandum. He was not surprised by the tone because he had heard about the purchasing officer through the grapevine.

Case Questions

1. Discuss the tone of the memorandum.

2. Describe the implied message in the memorandum.

3. Was the memorandum the best medium of communication to use in this situation?

4. If you were Jim, what action would you take?

5. How would you analyze the memorandum, apart from the tone?

Short Reports and Proposals

In his business communication classes, Enrique Fernandez heard horror stories about costly mistakes resulting from poor communication. Through the courses he became familiar with the different types of reports and the functions of each. He spent countless hours on the exercises assigned. All the while he suspected that professors sometimes exaggerate the importance of topics that interest them. Enrique earned a degree and took his first full-time job. There he soon learned for himself the importance of being able to write a good report. What he knew about planning and writing reports helped him to get the job and then to do it well.

As assistant purchasing director, Enrique reviewed many proposals submitted by organizations seeking to provide goods and services to his employer. He was astonished by the wide variation in the quality of the proposals he received. Some were well-planned and carefully written. Others showed a complete lack of understanding of what a proposal should be. Few of the latter were ever accepted. Enrique wondered why people would give so little thought to documents that were so important to the success of their business.

Learning Objectives

1 *To recognize the underlying purpose of informational memorandum reports.*

2 *To develop effective progress reports and periodic reports.*

3 *To develop effective justification reports and routine memorandum reports.*

4 *To identify situations for which a letter report would be appropriate.*

5 *To identify situations for which a form message would be appropriate.*

6 *To learn the purpose and strategies underlying solicited and unsolicited proposals.*

REPORTS WITH A MEMORANDUM FORMAT

Many short reports are intended for internal use, and their writers often use the memo format. Writers must be aware, however, of the differences between a memorandum and a memorandum report. A **memorandum report** is usually more structured; it will have a recognizable introduction, body, and conclusion, which a memorandum does not necessarily have. The memorandum report has the same advantages as the memorandum. Progress reports, periodic reports, and justification reports are among those that are often presented in the memorandum format. The broad purpose of all types of memorandum reports is to supply the information needed to keep the organization operating smoothly.

Progress Reports

The same format should be used for all progress reports in a series.

Progress reports are informational and are widely used throughout business, industry, and government. Depending upon the nature of the organization and the project being reported, a progress report may be made only one time or as one of a series. If there is to be a series of progress reports, the same format should be followed throughout the series for the reader's convenience.

Progress reports compare progress on a project to the schedule and also forecast future progress.

Ordinarily sent upward in the organization, **progress reports** inform management of: (1) rate of progress as compared to the schedule and (2) goals for subsequent time periods and a forecast for completion of the project. The more specifically this information is presented, the more helpful a progress report will be. In Figure 9.1, a banker describes the progress being made in a campaign through a memorandum report to upper management.

Periodic Reports

Periodic informational reports are prepared on a regular basis.

In any organization some reports must be prepared on a regular basis. Whether daily, weekly, or monthly, the purpose of these **periodic reports** is to keep others informed of some aspect of operations. Because they are ordinarily directed regularly to the same reader, the writer may assume the reader is generally knowledgeable about the subject. For that reason the writer need not provide much introductory information.

An example of a periodic report on absenteeism in a manufacturing plant is presented in Figure 9.2.

Justification Reports

You may at some time have to write a memorandum report in order to justify something—a change in procedure, an increase in budget, or perhaps reasons for resisting any new policy. For whatever reason it may be written, and there are many, the **justification report** is a common type of memorandum report.

When Bob Rollins sought to justify a change in operating procedures, he took the direct approach. He organized his memorandum report in this way:

1. Proposal
2. Description of present system
3. Advantages of the change versus its costs to the organization

FIGURE 9.1   ▪ *Progress Report*

```
                              MEMO


      TO:         Roger Davis, Director of Marketing

      FROM:       John Dartley

      DATE:       November 19, 1991

      SUBJECT:    Monthly Progress Report on Card-Bank Usage  —Oakdale Branch

      Summary

            In this reporting period, the percentage of customers using
      Card-Bank has risen from 7.1 percent to 7.9 percent.  Of customers
      with accounts for less than six months, 70 percent have used Card-
      Bank at least once.

      Present Usage

            There has been a 6.8 percent increase in the number of cus-
      tomers using Card-Bank.  Our goal for this date had been set at
      8.0 percent.  Among new customers with accounts for less than six
      months, 70 percent have used Card-Bank at least once.  The goal
      for new customer usage for this date is 50 percent.  The increased
      usage might be a result of our policy of personal instruction of
      new customers.

      Usage Forecast

            Our customer usage goal for the next period is 10 percent.
      A local media blitz is scheduled for early December. Advertisements
      will emphasize the 24-hour availability of Card-Bank.  Our surveys
      have shown that total availability is the least-known feature of
      Card-Bank.
```

Because his report is directed upward in the organization, Bob begins by reminding the reader of the problem, as shown in Figure 9.3. The remainder of the report is devoted to suggesting a change and to indicating the advantages to be derived from it.

If Bob had anticipated strong opposition to his plan, he might have taken an indirect approach. If the receiver, John Bowers, had a reputation for resisting change, Bob might have been less direct. No rigid formula exists. The writer must look closely at the situation and adapt the approach to fit it.

FIGURE 9.2   ▪   *Periodic Report*

```
                                 MEMO



          TO:        R. T. Bowen, Plant Manager

          FROM:      Bill Hughes, Assistant Personnel Director

          DATE:      February 4, 1991

          SUBJECT:   Monthly Plant Absenteeism Record

               During January the average rate of absenteeism was 6 percent.
          The average rate of absenteeism last January was 7.5 percent.
          The average rate of absenteeism during the past twelve months was
          6.8 percent.

               Here is a breakdown of absences according to shift and
          department.  An asterisk indicates those absences for which the
          absentee submitted a written excuse from a doctor.

          Shift       Production        Shipping      Yard Crew

           1st          8 of 202        1 of 28        1 of 20
           2nd         10 of 202        2 of 28        2 of 80
           3rd         19 of 200          N/A          1 of 10
                          *8               *3            *1

               Supervisors are being urged to persuade workers to call in when
          they are unable to come to work and to persuade workers to bring an
          excuse from a doctor.  Here is a breakdown of the absentees who did
          phone in advance.

          Shift       Production        Shipping      Yard Crew

           1st          6 of 8          0 of 1         0 of 1
           2nd         10 of 10         0 of 2         2 of 2
           3rd         12 of 19           N/A          1 of 1

               If you have any questions about the records, please give
          me a call.
```

REPORTS WITH A LETTER FORMAT

Many short reports intended for external communication are presented in the format of a **letter report**. As is generally true of short reports, the letter report is usually less formal than longer reports.

Just as in any letter, the nature of the message and the response expected from the reader will determine the plan to be followed. If the reader is likely to approve of the message, take the direct approach described in

FIGURE 9.3 ▪ *Justification Report*

```
                              MEMO


      TO:        John T. Bowers, Director of Personnel Research

      FROM:      Bob Rollins, Manager of Production

      DATE:      June 18, 1991

      SUBJECT:   Communication Problems at Shift Changes

      Proposal

           My proposal for improving the transmittal of instructions during
      shift changes is for the company to require a five-minute overlap of
      all production employees at shift changes.

      Present System

           At present the supervisors are responsible for communicating
      job-related information.  Much of it is done through work logs that
      each supervisor maintains.  They make entries each day regarding
      orders and equipment functioning.  At the time of the shift change,
      the incoming supervisor first reads the log and seeks any necessary
      clarification before the outgoing supervisor leaves.

           There are several problems with this system.  A supervisor will
      often forget to record vital information, and the incoming supervisor
      will not be aware of it.  Workers do not always tell their supervi-
      sors about equipment problems, so such problems cannot be recorded.
      Some supervisors are in such a rush to leave work that they are of
      little assistance to the incoming supervisor.

      Advantages of the Change

           A five-minute overlap would make the exchange of information
      at shift changes easier and more thorough.  Not only would the super-
      visors exchange work-related information, but individual production
      workers also would.  Supervisors would no longer have to depend on
      the work log for information from those on the previous shift.

           Each production employee would be paid for eight hours and ten
      minutes per day rather than for eight hours. The benefits to the
      company would be worth it.  Unclear instructions in the work log
      plus order changes that were not conveyed to the succeeding shift have
      cost the company much in terms of both dollars and frustrated workers.
```

Chapter 5. Begin the letter with the main point, because the reader agrees with it, then construct the message as a good-news or neutral letter.

If the reader is likely to disapprove of the message, you should follow the letter of refusal sequence described in Chapter 6. Rather than state your main point at the start of the letter, you should build up to it. In this type of letter a buffer and one or more reasons usually precede the main point.

A letter report is similar to a letter in appearance. Because letter reports usually are sent outside the organization, they are prepared on stationery

A letter report is similar to a letter in appearance and includes many of the same features.

with the company letterhead. Letter reports usually include many of the features of a letter: date, inside address, salutation, body, and signature. Some writers insert a subject line between the greeting and the body of the letter report.

Most letter reports are comprised of introduction, body, and close.

The body of a letter report, like the body of the business letter, has three basic parts:

1. *Introduction.* In this part the purpose of the report is described. If the report concerns a problem, the problem might be presented at this point. For longer reports a description of the way the report is organized is included in the introduction; however, a description is not necessary for most letter reports.
2. *Body.* This is the meat of any report. Here the reader's attention is directed at the findings or conclusions. If the report is somewhat involved, it may be divided into sections with headings to aid the reader in following the flow of information.
3. *Close.* In most reports this is simply an offer of additional assistance if the reader desires it. The closing paragraph may deal with the relationship between the writer and the reader rather than with the contents of the report. If the letter report is for internal use, closing comments are not necessary.

Elbert Cunningham hired National Insurance Analysts to appraise the health insurance plan provided by Falwick Industries for its employees. After investigating the plan, National responded with the letter report in Figure 9.4.

REPORTS USING PREPRINTED FORMS

Short reports perform many functions in the business organization. Listing all of the different types of short reports would be a monumental task.

The most common type of short report uses preprinted forms to transmit routine information on a regular basis.

The most common type of short report in most organizations is the informational report that is required on a regular basis. At the end of each week, for example, each sales representative for Falcon Products must send a customer contact report to the sales manager. The number of customers visited, sales made, and service problems are included in the report. Because this **form report** is submitted so frequently and by such a large number of representatives, Falcon Products provides a preprinted form for the purpose, shown in Figure 9.5. The form specifies the information needed and clearly indicates where the completed form should be sent.

From the company's perspective, the form ensures that the information provided will be uniform and hence easy to compile. From the individual respondent's perspective, it simplifies the process by indicating clearly what is to be provided. Although the number of forms that must be completed is a source of complaint for many workers, preprinted forms can save a great deal of time. If the workers had to develop and prepare individual reports instead of using preprinted forms, there would be much more complaining.

FIGURE 9.4 ▪ *Letter Report*

NATIONAL INSURANCE ANALYSTS   P.O. Box 940   Red Bank, NJ 07701

May 1, 1991

Mr. Elbert Cunningham
Director of Employee Benefits
Falwick Industries
Camden, NJ 08101

Dear Mr. Cunningham:

    Having analyzed the health-insurance plan provided by Falwick
Industries as you requested, I'm now reporting my findings, which
you may find helpful.

Forecast of the Cost of Employee Benefits

    Your concern over the spiraling cost of employee benefits is
justified. During the last decade the cost of providing employee
benefits has increased at an average rate of 14 percent each year.
Your employee benefit plan is intended to cover growing medical
costs and to replace lost job income. As long as inflation continues to reduce the real income of employees, benefit payments will
rise proportionately. In other words, this rate of increase is
expected to continue for the foreseeable future.

One Option: Pay-as-Go Insurance

    In this direct self-funding approach, the company pays claims
directly from the company's cash flow. The firm actually becomes
its own insurer and does not set aside any reserves for future
claims. Most companies using this plan purchase stop-loss insurance
to protect against unexpectedly severe claims. Since your company
does not require employee contributions to its plan, Falwick Industries is eligible, under ERISA restrictions, to initiate such a plan.

Another Option: Tax-Exempt Trust

    In this self-funding approach a plan must be drawn to meet the
unique needs of the individual company. A tax-exempt trust is then
set up, and employer and employee contributions are deposited into
it. Claims and expenses are paid from the trust, and excess funds
are invested to build up reserves. There are several tax advantages
of this trust. It may be administered so as to qualify for exemption

(Continued)

Preprinted forms constitute the greatest volume of short reports, and
they play an important role in the smooth operation of any business. Without them the routine transmitting of information would be greatly complicated. Because this kind of report requires no particular expertise to
complete, it has not been emphasized in this chapter.

FIGURE 9.4   ▪   *Continued*

```
                    Falwick Industries
                    May 1, 1991
                    Page 2



             from federal income tax.  The contributions of the employer may be
             deductible as a business expense.  Usually the benefit payments are
             not taxable to the employees who receive them.

             Administration of Self-Funding Benefit Plan

                  Either of these self-funded plans can be administered within
             the organization.  Some companies prefer to have a professional
             outside company handle the administration.  Companies that hire
             outside administrators often find that employees more readily
             accept the claims decisions.  Whether the benefit plan is admini-
             stered by an employee or by an outsider, a company such as Falwick
             Industries will enjoy considerable savings.

                  I hope that this report gives you a satisfactory picture of
             two options open to your company.  I shall be pleased to answer
             any questions that you may have.

                                             Sincerely,

                                             Roberta Simmons

                                             Roberta Simmons
                                             Employee Benefit Analyst
```

MISCELLANEOUS SHORT REPORTS

Most organizations have no shortage of short reports. These reports are very functional, and are therefore heavily used. Examples include credit reports, reports of meetings, end-of-month production reports, and some reports to stockholders. As is generally true of short reports, each one has a distinct purpose and contributes significantly to organizational operations.

FIGURE 9.5 ▪ *Form Report*

Customer Contact Report

Enter all visits with customers and potential customers each week. Indicate your time of arrival and departure as well as product(s) discussed. Describe any sale you made or service problem of which you learned. Describe any follow-up which you intend to perform.

Date	Time	Name of contact and company	Product discussed	Sales made	Service problems	Follow-up
Mon.	Arr. Dpt.					
	Arr. Dpt.					
	Arr. Dpt.					
Tues.	Arr. Dpt.					
	Arr. Dpt.					
	Arr. Dpt.					
Wed.	Arr. Dpt.					
	Arr. Dpt.					
	Arr. Dpt.					
Thurs.	Arr. Dpt.					
	Arr. Dpt.					
	Arr. Dpt.					
Fri.	Arr. Dpt.					
	Arr. Dpt.					
	Arr. Dpt.					

Signature of Sales Representative

NOTE: Complete this form at the end of each work week and mail it immediately to the Sales Manager.

PROPOSALS

A **proposal** is an attempt to persuade someone that you are especially qualified to fill one of his or her needs in exchange for compensation. Proposals are usually written documents and come in a variety of sizes and formats. A contractor may be called in to examine a house in need of remodeling. He may then submit a statement in which he identifies what will be done, the cost of labor and materials, and the date of completion. That is one example of a proposal.

Unlike propositions, most proposals are written.

Proposals vary in the degree of formality as well as in the planning that goes into them. Imagine that a man comes to your house and asks if you want any of your trees removed. When you inquire about the cost he does some quick calculations on the back of an envelope that he then gives to you.

Proposals are not uniform and vary in formality.

At the other extreme are proposals that require extraordinary amounts of preparation. The attempt by the City of Atlanta to host the 1996 Summer Olympics is one such example. The Atlanta Organizing Committee was formed early in 1987 and drafted a proposal for the U.S. Selection Committee. After many months of preparation, their proposal, approximately 100 pages long, secured for Atlanta the right to represent the United States in the competition to host the Olympics. Following their initial success they then set about preparing a proposal for the International Olympic Committee. This 600-page proposal was divided into five separate volumes. Approximately seven months after the deadline for submission, the members of the International Olympic Committee will select the winning proposal.[1] In terms of formality and complexity, most proposals fall somewhere between the one submitted to the Olympic Committee and the one prepared on the back of the envelope.

The two basic types of proposals are the solicited and the unsolicited. A **solicited proposal** is written in answer to a request. An **unsolicited proposal** is initiated by the proposer; no motivation is provided by the intended recipient. The contractor and the tree-removal specialist both provided solicited proposals. The first proposal of the Olympic Committee would be considered an unsolicited one. Its subsequent proposals were solicited.

Solicited Proposals

Changes frequently occur as a result of solicited proposals. Contracts may be awarded, funds may be dispensed, or any of a multitude of other actions may be taken. Proposals play a major role in the operation of many business organizations of all sizes.

Requests for solicited proposals may come from many different sources. Sometimes the solicitation is nothing more than a casual comment or an

---

[1]From an interview with Ginger Watkins of the Atlantic Olympic Committee, January 16, 1990.

encouraging word. Bob Reynolds, for example, had never even considered seeking a refrigeration maintenance contract with any hotel until a neighbor in the hotel business encouraged him to do so. Had his neighbor not made him aware of such possibilities, he would have continued to limit himself to the residential refrigeration market. Now Bob has contracts with almost half of the local hotels and motels.

A formal solicitation for a proposal is often called a **request for proposal (RFP)**. Many requests for proposals from various units of the federal government appear in the *Commerce Business Daily (CBD)*, a publication of the U.S. Department of Commerce. The *CBD* has been published for many years and is widely read in organizations that wish to provide goods or services to the government. An electronic edition of the *CBD* is now available for computer on-line acquisition. Here is a typical RFP as it appeared in the *CBD:*

An RFP is a request for a proposal.

> CONFERENCE FACILITIES SOL 52SBNB0C6122 DUE 030190 POC Joan Smith (301)/C.O. Pauline Mallgrave. Contractor shall supply facilities, labor, material, equipment and food to provide formal and informal meeting services for National Institute of Standards and Technology (NIST) conferences — Contractor shall be able to provide informal outdoor banquet services and facilities — Facility shall be less than 5 miles of NIST, Gaithersburg, MD — The proposed contract will be an Indefinite Delivery Indefinite Quantity type contract — The Base period will be approximately 7 months with four one-year options for renewal — Significant Evaluation Factors are: 1) experience in providing similar types of supplies/services 2) understanding the requirements in the statement of work and 3) ability to respond to last-minute changes regarding equipment and space — Please request solicitation in writing — All responsible sources may submit a proposal which shall be considered by the agency.

Most requests for proposals specifically state the goods or services that are wanted. You should therefore read the request carefully before beginning to write a proposal. Also note whether a certain kind of organizational scheme is suggested for the proposal. Solicitors often give guidelines in the RFP in order to make it easier to compare the proposals that are received. Many proposals are rejected because the writer did not specifically address all of the factors included in the RFP or did not organize the proposal as instructed. Proposals are expected to provide a rational analysis of how the writer's organization can satisfy the needs described in the RFP. Even though the writer may consider a proposal to be primarily a sales document, the persuasion should not be blatant. Solicited proposals should let the facts speak for themselves.

Unsolicited Proposals

Unsolicited proposals resemble solicited ones in most ways. The most significant difference is that, with the solicited proposal, the solicitor has already recognized a need to be filled. In contrast, the writer of the unsolicited proposal must persuade the recipient that a need exists. For that reason the sequence of ideas will be less direct, more closely resembling

Persuasion is usually more obvious in an unsolicited proposal than in a solicited one.

the sequence presented in Chapter 7. An example of an unsolicited proposal is presented in Figure 9.6.

Writing the Proposal

Whether the proposal is solicited or unsolicited, the information presented will be very similar. What will differ will be the emphasis placed on the various factors. After analyzing the needs of the solicitor or intended recipient, the writer should focus especially on the needs that appear to be most crucial.

Internal proposals are often in the form of memos.

The destination for a proposal determines the appropriate format. The proposal that is intended for in-house use is written as a memorandum. Writers usually use the letter format when preparing short proposals for external use. The long report format is used for longer proposals, whether directed internally or externally. Most proposals are relatively short.

Proposals vary greatly in such characteristics as formality, length, and format. Good proposal writers attempt to respond to the needs of the solicitor or intended recipient by tailoring the proposal to that person or organization. The characteristics of effective writing presented in Chapter 3 are all relevant for writing proposals. The use of frequent headings is especially helpful in guiding the reader through such documents, no matter how complicated. The following sections usually are included in a proposal:

- Introduction
- Statement of the Problem
- Objectives
- Method or Plan
- Materials/Equipment/Personnel Available for Use
- Cost or Budget
- Summary

An unsolicited proposal that was written in response to a problem about which the recipient had displayed no awareness or concern is shown in Figure 9.6. Two of the main challenges for such a proposal involve convincing the other party (1) that there is a problem and (2) that you are uniquely qualified to solve the problem.

✓ *CHECKLIST for Writing a Solicited Proposal*

____▪ Clearly define the problem.

____▪ Propose a reasonable approach.

____▪ Describe your company's expertise for solving the problem.

____▪ Provide a time frame.

FIGURE 9.6 ▪ *Short Proposal*

Kiddie Corral, Inc.

1812 Shady Lane   Abilene, KS 67410

July 14, 1991

Mr. Warren Downs, President
Plastic Castings, Inc.
2818 Industrial Parkway
Abilene, KS 67410

Dear Mr. Downs:

There have been several articles in The Gazette in recent
months about the high rates of employee turnover and absenteeism
in the local work force. According to authorities on the subject,
turnover and absenteeism are invariably accompanied by increased
training costs and lower employee morale. With those thoughts in
mind, I am pleased to present you with this proposal.

Problem Statement

During the past decade there have been dramatic changes in
the U.S. work force. The two-job family has become the norm, and
finding satisfactory child care is an ongoing concern. Fifty-one
percent of all mothers of infants are now in the work force. It
is expected that throughout the 1990s, fully two-thirds of all new
job recruits will be women.

Approximately 4 1/2 billion hours are lost each year due to
tardiness, sickness, and absenteeism, much of it attributable to
problems employees experience in trying to balance their jobs with
the demands of being a parent. During the last decade there was
a **3,000 percent** increase in the number of companies that provide
some form of help for employees' offspring as a means of stemming
absenteeism and turnover with its attendant skyrocketing cost of
training new employees.

Objectives

One objective of this proposal is to alert you to the wisdom
of assisting your employees in solving their child-care problems.
A second objective is to introduce you to Kiddie Corral as a

The writer provides a context for this unsolicited proposal and points out a problem in the local business community to awaken the reader's interest.

The writer documents the problem, confirms that the problem is likely to grow, and shows that a growing number of employers are addressing it.

The objectives are written from the reader's standpoint without predicting possible survey results, and focus on how both the employer and employees might benefit.

(*Continued*)

✔ *CHECKLIST for Writing an Unsolicited Proposal*

▪ **Persuade the reader that a problem exists.**

▪ **Clearly define the problem.**

▪ **Propose a reasonable approach.**

▪ **Convey expertise persuasively.**

▪ **Provide a time frame.**

FIGURE 9.6 ▪ *Continued*

Plastic Castings, Inc.
July 14, 1991
Page 2

The writer tells the reader specifically what kind of information will be sought and how it will be used, including a time frame.

possible solution. A third objective is to help you reduce the expenses incurred by such problems as absenteeism, turnover, and dissatisfied employees, as well as the expense of recruiting and training new employees.

Method

1. We will survey your full-time employees, both hourly and salaried, who have children younger than age 16, concerning their current child-care arrangements and how they think these arrangements could be improved.
2. Results of the survey will be compiled and presented to you within ten days of the completion of the survey.
3. You and any associates you select will be given a tour of Kiddie Corral to see what it has to offer to your employees.

This section justifies selecting the writer to satisfy the need described and details the resources that are most relevant for the task.

Facilities and Personnel

The newly enlarged and remodeled Kiddie Corral has the equipment and personnel necessary to provide for the comfort, security, enjoyment, and intellectual stimulation for your employees' children. We have been in business for 12 years and have earned a reputation for the highest quality in child care. We always maintain a ratio of at least 1 adult for every 8 children, and there is a registered nurse on site at all times.

The writer emphasizes the value of the service more than its cost. A detailed budget is not necessary in an unsolicited proposal.

Cost

The administration of the survey, the compilation of its results, and an extensive tour of the facility will be provided at no cost to you. Should you choose to offer our services as a fringe benefit to your employees, many options are available. Enrollment costs are $50.00 per child for five 8-hour days. Some employers offer the service to employees for free, believing that it is a fair price to pay for reduced turnover and training costs, not to mention the heightened employee satisfaction that accompanies such a benefit. Other employers share the cost of the program with their employees.

(Continued)

SUMMARY

An organization requires a great deal of information in order to function smoothly. Much of this information is transmitted in the form of various types of short reports. In some organizations preprinted forms are provided to simplify reports that must be submitted frequently.

Short reports used for internal communication are often prepared as memorandum reports, which are more structured than memoranda. A memorandum report has a recognizable introduction, body, and conclu-

FIGURE 9.6 ■ *Continued*

Plastic Castings, Inc.
July 14, 1991
Page 3

Summary

    By providing company-sponsored child care, an employer reaps
the rewards of increased employee loyalty, productivity, and satisfaction. Because Kiddie Corral is located less than one mile from
your plant, its convenience will also be appreciated.

    I am available to answer any questions you may have about this
proposal.

               Sincerely yours,

               Regina Grantham

               Regina Grantham
               President

*The writer reminds
the reader that
accepting the
proposal is the first
step to solving the
problem.*

sion; a memorandum is usually less structured. Short reports intended for
external communication are often prepared in the format of a letter.

    Proposals are documents that are especially important to many business
organizations. Proposals are used to solicit business. Some proposals are
solicited through formal requests for proposals (RFP); others are unsolicited. The information presented in both types is very similar. The unsolicited proposal, however, generally relies somewhat more on
persuasion than does the solicited one.

Key Terms

- **memorandum report**
- **progress report**
- **periodic report**
- **justification report**
- **letter report**
- **form report**

- **proposal**
- **solicited proposal**
- **unsolicited proposal**
- **request for proposal (RFP)**
- *Commerce Business Daily (CBD)*

Review Questions

1. In what ways does a memorandum differ from a memorandum report? How are they alike?
2. How do memorandum reports differ from letter reports?
3. What kinds of information might be included in a progress report?
4. What is a periodic report?
5. What are some possible purposes of justification reports?
6. Give two examples of routine memorandum reports.
7. What are the purposes of letter reports?
8. What are the advantages to an organization of providing preprinted forms for short reports? What are the disadvantages?
9. In what ways do solicited proposals differ from unsolicited proposals?
10. What is the main purpose of any proposal?

Exercises

1. You are a branch manager employed by a multinational organization. Your boss requests a short report in which you detail the involvement in the foreign culture of those of your employees who are U.S. citizens. You are manager of German Operations and you have four subordinates who are U.S. citizens. You conduct an informal survey and learn the following: (a) Bill Henry and Thornton Aldrich and their families have joined local churches; (b) Suzanne Langer belongs to a community chorus; (c) Bill and Thornton are members of a local golf club; (d) Thornton and his family and Suzanne belong to a local swimming club; (e) Suzanne and Bill and his family belong to a social club in their respective neighborhoods; (f) although Tom Nettles has not joined any formal organizations, he has volunteered his expert advice to the town council regarding two engineering problems that arose in recent months. Bill and Thornton have lived in Germany for ten months, Tom for six months, and Suzanne for four months. Prepare your report for William Fitzsimmons, manager of international production, 3T, Inc., Bangor, ME 04401.

2. As Director of Student Life you have been swamped with complaints about the lack of convenient parking for students on campus. You are seeking someone with the competence to help you solve such problems. Prepare an RFP for a consultant who is qualified to advise you on what must be done.

BOXED IN | *AN ETHICAL DILEMMA*

George Stuart has read the Request for Proposal (RFP) from Candler County and has decided to submit a proposal. The project involves the building of an addition to the county courthouse. In general, the specifications in the RFP are ones that George feels Coastal Contractors Inc. could meet. In fact, the only specification about which he is uncertain is the completion date for the project. The building has to be turned over to Candler County in 18 months.

A possible obstacle to finishing the courthouse addition in 18 months is Coastal's current major project, Mid-Iowa Mall. As George tries to calculate the likely number of days necessary to complete the mall, he recognizes that the winter weather is an unknown factor. Even if no days are lost to inclement weather, he would be cutting the time close on the courthouse project.

January and February are traditionally the worst months of the winter for lost workdays. Looking over his calendar for the past five years, George sees that in four of the years days were lost in both January and February. The average number of days lost in January was three. In February the average was two days. George has read, however, that this winter is supposed to be unusually mild with little snowfall.

From past experience with the county, George knows that Coastal will not be considered for the courthouse job if his proposal suggests any uncertainty about meeting the deadline. Always optimistic, George is inclined to accept the long-range weather forecast and assume that everything will go without a hitch. On the other hand he knows that if he gets the job and fails to meet the deadline, Coastal's reputation will be tarnished.

George feels boxed in. What would you do?

3. Imagine that you are a consultant with the necessary expertise and are responding to the RFP developed in Exercise 2. Prepare a proposal for the Director of Student Life.

4. As personnel research director of Metro Bank, a large urban bank with many branches, you were assigned six months ago to investigate why there is such high turnover among the tellers and the clerks. You implemented an exit interview program and learned that of the 60 tellers and clerks who quit during that period, 32 gave the heavy rush hour traffic as the main reason; 20 said they wanted to work part time instead; 8 others gave personal reasons.

It seems to you that a good solution would be to introduce a more flexible schedule. By altering work schedules you believe that some workers could avoid rush-hour driving. Another possibility might be to hire more part-time employees and to allow full-time employees to work part time if they wish.

The cost of training new employees is very high. Anything that can be done to reduce turnover and training costs would be worthwhile, you believe. Prepare for Willard Petrol, vice-president of personnel, a report in which you present your findings and make recommendations. Willard has a reputation for being against change. He believes that most modern personnel practices are actually harmful to the organization.

5. As head of the student activities committee you are in the process of developing a booklet for new students. You hope to include a section on free things students can do. To compile this information you plan to contact the presidents of the social, civic, and all other clubs on the campus. You hope to come up with a long list of free things to do on campus and in town. Prepare a memorandum report to be sent to the club presidents. In it you will seek as much information about free activities as possible.

6. Students and faculty alike usually believe that registration procedures could be improved at their schools. List whatever changes you consider to be desirable; then prepare a memorandum report in which you detail the steps a student must follow in registering for classes under your improved system. This memorandum report will be sent to all students who are accepted by your school. If you are pleased with present registration procedures, your memorandum report should describe them.

7. You are a management trainee in a large (4,000 employees) manufacturing plant. The plant manager, Tom Collins, has asked you to write a report on the use of quality circles in business and industry. He wants to learn what quality circles are, their uses, how widespread their use is, and their benefits. Use the *Business Periodical Index* to locate several articles on quality circles in order to gain the knowledge necessary to write the report. Tom has little patience with long reports and will not read a report longer than three pages.

8. Prepare an informational report on the "Man of the Year" selected by *Time* magazine for the past 20 years. In this report indicate the recipients, the year each was selected, the main reason each person won the award, and any trend that appears to be developing in bestowing the award. Lastly, predict the next recipient of the award and briefly defend your prediction.

9. Prepare a progress report describing the progress you are making in your education. Describe your goals, and detail your plan for accomplishing these goals. Also, describe the major obstacles to accomplishing your goals and what you are doing to overcome the obstacles. Address this report to your adviser.

10. You are a member of a professional association in your area of interest. You have been asked to suggest an appropriate topic for a 90-minute session at the national convention. You will not be responsible for giving a presentation but merely for suggesting an appropriate topic. Prepare a justification report in which you suggest a topic, and present a rationale for its being a part of the convention. Indicate clearly why you believe this topic would appeal to the members of the professional association.

11. In order to actively include as many association members in the convention in Exercise 10 as possible, it is decided that each 90-minute session will feature four presentations. Prepare a justification report in which you suggest a topic for a session. Also, explain how the topic could be divided into four parts and what each speaker would cover. Explain in what ways the topic would interest the membership and defend your suggested division of the topic.

12. Keep a time log for one week. At 30-minute intervals throughout each day stop and write down what you did during the prior 30-minute period. At the end of the week prepare a letter report in which you describe your time use.

Divide your report into sections on the basis of your major uses of time. Conclude with a list of recommendations of how you could improve your use of time. Address the report to yourself.

13. Prepare a preprinted form that could be used for keeping a time log as described in Exercise 12. Prepare this form for college students to use.

14. Locate an RFP in a copy of the *Commerce Business Daily* or in the classified section of another newspaper. (Sometimes they are listed under "Requests for Bids.") Prepare a proposal in response to it.

15. Write an RFP for some need that you consider to be currently unfilled. (Don't make it too personal.) Bring your RFP to class. Your instructor will collect all of them and redistribute them within the class. Write a proposal in response to the RFP you are given.

Selecting the Winning Proposal | CASE

Martha Andrews Nord, Owen Graduate School of Management, Vanderbilt University

Towsen Corporate Services works as an independent contractor to develop software documentation, procedures manuals, and business proposals. Starting as a one-person shop with three clients five years ago, TCS now has 25 clients, 10 contract writers, and a new full-time marketing director. Elizabeth Towson, president, is wrestling with the rapid growth. Her original five-year plan did not anticipate the current need for office space and equipment. To keep up the high-quality service to her clients, within the next quarter she must purchase additional computer equipment, office furniture, and a copy machine.

Her immediate goal is to identify a few vendors and then choose from that list. Among the steady stream of vendors with whom she has met, three sell copy machines. This past week she received proposals from all three. She knows that each offers comparable equipment and some level of support service, but she is not sure which equipment and service will best meet her needs. Feeling some pressure to make a decision, she skims the beginning of the three proposals:

Vendor One: Our Model DB4825 Copier has simple, easy-to-read digital controls that put all the copier functions at your fingertips. It makes 14 copies per minute on a variety of stock including address labels and most letterhead. For special applications, you can reduce or enlarge the copy size in one percent increments from 65% to 122%. . . .

Vendor Two: *Micshoba DB4825 System Cost*

24 Month Lease/Purchase: $189.00 plus tax per month

Micshoba DB4825 System Includes

Micshoba DB4825 Copier
Matching Console Cabinet

Paper Cassette
Reduction and Enlargement
50 Sheet Stack Sheet Bypass

Vendor Three: Although sporadic, your copying needs are complex. The nature
of your business requires that copies have a consistently high
quality and that the machine be able to
  –collate
  –duplex
  –copy in 2 colors

After her hurried review of the three documents, she quickly narrowed her
choice to one and picked up the phone to call.

Case Questions

1. Specifically, what was Elizabeth Towsen looking for in the proposals?

2. Which vendor came out on top? Why?

3. What focus did the other two proposals use that caused them to miss the
   needs of their reader, Elizabeth Towson?

CASE | *American Forged Hand Tools*

John D. Stegman, College of Business, The Ohio State University

You are pleased! Only a month out of the state university with a degree in business administration you have landed a super job. You are a new salesperson for
the Authentic Automotive Parts Company. This warehouse distributor of automotive parts for the automotive aftermarket serves the state of Indiana. Warehouse
distributors (WDs) keep large inventories of parts and accessories and serve automotive jobbers. Jobbers sell to mechanics, garages, and do-it-yourselfers. The
automotive aftermarket is quite profitable because there are always cars that
need repairs, and in most cases mechanics as well as car owners are willing to
pay top dollar for a part that is always available from the jobber. Jobbers get
overnight delivery from their WD. In addition to parts and accessories, WDs and
jobbers also carry automotive, or mechanic's, hand tools.

Your boss, Pat Sekoll, the sales manager at Authentic, wants you to go after
additional — or what she calls "PLUS" — sales in your well-established territory.
One way is to sell the jobber on stocking and displaying a line of mechanic's
hand tools. Authentic is the WD in the state for American Forged Hand Tools.
Tools are a profitable item and mechanics especially want a tool *on the spot*.
They may have a car engine torn down and discover they do not have the right
tool(s) to put it back together. Time is money for mechanics and garages.

Snappy Car Parts is a medium-sized jobber with several locations. Upon investigation, you discover that Snappy does not carry a line of tools. When they get

calls for tools they promise them for the next day and get them overnight from Authentic. They probably lose many tool sales because customers need them today, not tomorrow. The investment in inventory of tools is substantial, but it has always paid off for jobbers as well as WDs. You make a breakfast appointment for next week with Frank Kopas, the president, and Randy Jacobs, the sales manager, at Snappy. Now you begin to worry about your proposal. Perhaps you should have taken better notes in your business communication class at the university. You do not remember how to structure business proposals; should this one be an oral presentation, in writing, or both?

Case Questions

1. What are the elements in a business proposal?
2. Which would you use in this proposal to Snappy?
3. How would you structure the oral pitch to Frank and Randy?
4. How much detail would you include in the written proposal?
5. What would you emphasize, and how?

The Long Report: Planning

Stephanie McQuiston is anxiously waiting to see her boss at Atlantic Electronics, Scott Millan.

Several weeks ago she turned in a report on employee relations problems and is confident that she researched the topic well. Her solutions to the problems were, she believes, logical and desirable; she said as much in her report. But now Scott is meeting with Louise Alexander, who is his superior, and the vice president to conduct Stephanie's first semiannual review. She had known the meeting was to take place today, and she had known who would be participating. What caught her off guard was that she saw the vice president carrying her report to the meeting. It was going to be used in the evaluation.

Stephanie is worried that some parts of the report — other than her research and recommendation sections — might not be correct. Although she believes she had the right information, perhaps it could have been better organized.

In the six months she has been with Atlantic, she has written a dozen or so reports of various lengths. Scott has been gracious in guiding her to prepare the type of reports he wants. Although her business-degree background included some report-writing instruction, she quickly found that she had a lot to learn. Now she is wondering about the organization of her report, the clarity of her conclusions, and whether she should have included more visual support, such as charts, to illustrate her findings.

Well, she thinks, I'll know soon. Here comes Scott.

CHAPTER 10

Learning Objectives

1 To learn the characteristics of business reports.

2 To know the difference between informational, interpretive, and problem-solving reports.

3 To learn the steps in planning the long report.

4 To be able to differentiate between primary and secondary research methods.

5 To learn sampling techniques and how to prepare an efficient questionnaire.

6 To learn how to organize and outline a business report.

You may have had the same uneasy feeling about a term paper that Stephanie has about her business report. Of course, term papers differ from business reports, but both are used in performance evaluation; therefore, afterthoughts are likely. Chapters 10 and 11 will describe what Stephanie might have done to be more self-assured in her report preparation. An effective and appropriate report on her topic appears in Chapter 11 (Figure 11.1).

Much of the material in Chapters 11 and 12 can be applied to term paper assignments. However, several major differences between reports and term papers exist. (1) Many term paper assignments identify the specific purpose, such as an assignment to describe the influence of technology on office workers. The business report writer will often need to identify the purpose of the report. In other words, many business reports are self-initiated. (2) Most term papers are written for a single audience, usually the instructor, whereas business reports typically are written for many readers. Some reports that are written for a single reader are viewed by many more than the one intended reader. (3) Business reports typically have standard parts that are seldom used when writing term papers.

CHARACTERISTICS AND CATEGORIES OF BUSINESS REPORTS

Decisions about report characteristics are made during planning.

The characteristics of the finished report result from decisions made during the planning stage. They include:

1. *Level of formality.* Some reports, such as for government or high-level management, have an extremely formal tone and appearance.
2. *Length.* Reports may be as long as several hundred pages, depending on the topic and the purpose of the report.
3. *The time interval.* Reports may be periodic, such as annual financial reports, or they may be prepared only once.
4. *Destination.* Does the report go downward to subordinates or upward to superiors? Is the report directed internally—that is, will it be used within the organization? Is the report directed externally to an audience removed from the organization, such as a local government?
5. *Research category employed.* The presentation of information differs depending on whether primary or secondary research is used.
6. *Intent.* Is the goal of the report to justify some action, to establish progress toward an objective, or to recommend a change?
7. *Number of authors.* Team-written reports frequently have a different tone than individually prepared reports. Further, team reports may incorporate individually written sections into one package, or the team may work together, in both writing and editing, on each sentence in the document.

8. *Contribution to decision making.* Reports range from straightforward statements of fact to highly structured analyses that include recommendations and discussion of implications.

All business reports, whether short or long, can be categorized by the extent of the contribution they make to the decision-making process. The **informational report**, which presents data without interpretation, is valuable and ever present. However, it has little application in decision making. An example is a weekly absenteeism report that indicates only who was absent, when, the employee's department, and number of absences to date.

The three types of business reports differ in their contribution to the decision-making process.

A step above the informational report, the **interpretive report** adds meaning to the data. The facts presented in the informational report are examined and implications are drawn. To the absenteeism report already described, the writer would add an explanation: which employees are absentee problems, whether some departments experience higher rates than others, and what cost in time, dollars, or materials is attributable to absenteeism.

The third level of decision-making reports—and the one that makes the most contribution to the decision-making process—is the **problem-solving report**. Because the problem-solving report not only informs with data and interprets the data, but also analyzes the problem situation, reviews alternatives, examines implications, draws conclusions, and makes recommendations, it is frequently referred to as an **analytical report**. The absenteeism report already described might, for example, include a recommendation that two employees be interviewed by their supervisors to determine the cause of their extreme absenteeism.

The problem-solving report is obviously the most involved and difficult of the three types; it encompasses the other two. Thus, generally speaking, anyone who can write an effective problem-solving report can probably write the others as well. Chapters 10 and 11 therefore focus on the problem-solving report.

THE PLANNING PROCESS AND THE LONG REPORT

The first step in the planning process, as presented in Chapter 5, is to determine the objective of the message. A clear understanding of the objective, or purpose, is especially important in planning a report, which typically takes much more effort and time than a letter or a memorandum. Further, the purpose of a long report is often stated in an early section so that the reader can anticipate the direction of the report.

A clear understanding of purpose is important in planning.

Suppose that three members of the marketing department are asked to write problem-solving reports. They might define the problems in problem statements such as these:

- Sales of Product *X* have fallen 37 percent in 14 months.
- Competitors are taking approximately 1.7 percent of our market share each quarter.

▪ Sales of our best-selling products are falling because the quality of our competitors' products is better.

The purpose statements they develop to describe a desired outcome might be similar to these:

▪ This is a plan for stopping the sales decline for Product *X*.
▪ I propose this design for an aggressive advertising campaign that will recapture our market share.
▪ The purpose of this report is to propose improvements in our quality control program.

Other steps in the planning process presented in Chapter 5 are to consider the audience — expertise, interests, opinions, and hierarchical position — and to generate a list of ideas and choose the important ones. For the long report, this involves conducting research, evaluating results, and outlining the report.

CONDUCTING THE RESEARCH

Doing the research for a report means answering two questions: (1) what do I need? and (2) where can I get it? In planning her problem-solving report, Stephanie used a procedure most good report writers employ in answering the first question. She broke down her problem into three areas of need and created a checklist for herself, as shown in Table 10.1. A similar chart can help you clearly define your information needs and also serves as a feedback device — you can check items as you acquire the information.

Information may come from primary or secondary sources.

You are now ready to answer the second question, Where do I get the information? This involves choosing between two kinds of information sources — primary and secondary. **Primary sources** are generally unpublished; you get them firsthand. **Secondary sources** are publications. Here are some examples:

Primary Sources	*Secondary Sources*
Questionnaires	Newspapers
Experiments	Government documents
Interviews	Books
Personal observations	Magazines
Organization files (in some cases)	Pamphlets

Your choice of sources depends on how much time you have to complete the report, the budget, and your ability to use the sources. You should try first to use secondary research. If the information is incomplete, inaccurate, or outdated, primary research may be required. In some cases, a combination of secondary and primary research builds a stronger report.

TABLE 10.1   ▪ *A Sample Needs Chart*

Need 1: What Is the Problem?	Need 2: What's Causing the Problem?	Need 3: What Are Some Solutions?
Turnover information	Why high turnover?	More money
Absenteeism information	Why high absenteeism?	More fringe benefits
Grievance information	Why so many grievances?	Better working conditions
Morale information	Why such low morale?	What else?
Unionization information	Why talk of unionization?	

Sometimes writers assume that secondary research is easier and quicker than primary research. Although this may often be the case, it is not always true. You should not select a secondary research technique just because it appears to be the quickest method. A better rule of thumb — one that comes from scientific inquiry — is to do secondary research first. If others have already researched your topic, rely on their findings. However, you must be careful not to assume that because something is in print, it is correct or complete.

In examining secondary research, it is wise to ask: (1) Is the information complete? (2) Does it appear reasonable and logical? (3) Is it biased? (4) Is it recent? A weakness is any one of these areas may suggest the need to conduct your own (primary) research. Raise these same four questions before secondary research is included in the report.

Secondary Research

Secondary research is sometimes called library research, but this does not mean that all secondary research is done in a library. Some items, such as newspapers, magazines, or pamphlets, you may have at home or at your office. However, a thorough secondary research project will likely mean a trip to the library. Although you probably know how to use the library effectively, here are a few hints and reminders:

▪ Do not focus your search exclusively on books and neglect periodicals, or vice versa.

▪ Use the *Guide to Periodic Literature*, which may be in magazine, hardbound, or microfilm form, to find citations by title, author, or subject. The *Business Periodical Index* serves the same function but lists only articles related to business. Also consider using *The Wall Street Journal Index* and *The New York Times Index*.

▪ Remember to use computerized databases such as *InfoTrac*® or *ABC/ Inform*®, which can quickly and thoroughly search hundreds of periodicals for key words.

▪ When you find a book on your topic, use both the table of contents and the index to locate information. Skim both completely because you may not know the exact term the author uses to refer to your topic.

- Pay special attention to the footnotes in the books and articles you find to guide you to other related sources.
- Look for sources that survey your topic. Books of this type are sometimes entitled, *The Handbook of . . .* , *The . . . Manual*, or *An Analysis of. . . .* These sources often break the topic into outline form, may give its history, and frequently have many valuable footnotes.
- Watch for sources with bibliographies. Sometimes entire books are bibliographies, and these can be most helpful.
- If you become frustrated or confused, seek help from a librarian, who is an expert in locating information.
- As you locate information that you think may be of some value to you, put the information on notecards.

Notecards are better than paper for recording information obtained during secondary research.

You can save time later by taking several steps as you make notecards. At the top of the card write the complete citation of the source in bibliographic form. (The differences between footnotes and bibliographic citations, with examples of each, are found in Chapter 11.) By using separate cards instead of notebook paper, the cards can be sorted by topic, which can be helpful in developing a working outline. Further, an additional source card can easily be placed between two existing cards.

With the bibliographic citations at the top of your notecards, the bibliography at the end of your report will be easy to prepare. Alphabetize your cards by authors' last names. Put only one piece of information on a card, even if this means using several cards to represent one source, because it allows for easy sorting and cross-referencing. Make sure your handwriting is legible. If someone else types your report, that person can type the bibliography directly from your cards.

The information you write on the card may be a direct quote, your own summary, or how the information relates to other sources. You may wish to put the card catalog listing on the other side of the card so you can quickly locate the source again. A sample card may look like the one in Figure 10.1.

Be sure to relate your secondary research activity to the objective of your report. If you seek a specific person's opinion on a topic, finding a single source that gives that opinion may conclude your research. If you bring together a variety of opinions about a topic, a number of sources will need to be examined. You should continue to review sources until one of the following occurs: (1) You exhaust your search (and perhaps yourself); to be thorough is to locate everything you can find on the subject. (2) You work until what you find starts to cluster; once you reach the point where you find nothing new, you may be at the end of your search. (3) You have thoroughly answered the specific question you set out to answer; this assumes you have a specific question, such as, "How many cars for four or more passengers were imported from Japan in 1990?"

FIGURE 10.1 ▪ *Sample Notecard*

Need #3

Impact of Fringe Benefits

Smith, Carlos A. "The Usefulness of Employee Benefits in Reducing Turnover," Journal of Applied Personnel Research, December, 1990, pp. 365-372.

p. 371-"The results of most studies indicate clearly that there is no relationship between liberal doses of employee benefits and turnover rates."

p. 370- Company	*% Increase in Benefits*	*Change in Turnover*
A	*12%*	*+4%*
B	*25%*	*+1%*
C	*18%*	*-2%*

Primary Research

The primary research sources listed earlier are the most frequently used: questionnaires, experiments, interviews, personal observation, and organization files. Familiarity with primary research sources can be useful not only in writing reports but also in other activities, such as consumer behavior, research, feasibility studies, and employee attitude measurements.

Questionnaires

Properly developed questionnaires can provide an enormous amount of useful data. Improperly developed questionnaires can give misleading and often uninterpretable information. Proper use of questionnaires includes selecting an appropriate sample of respondents, carefully writing the questionnaire, administering the questionnaire in such a way as to encourage response, and accurately tabulating the results.

Sample Selection.   When you hear the results of political opinion polls, you might wonder how information obtained from as few as one thousand people can accurately reflect the opinions of sometimes millions of individuals. Because many opinion pollsters carefully select their samples, their predictions of election results are frequently accurate within several percentage points. Such accuracy occurs because these pollsters have clearly defined their population and, using scientific sampling guidelines, have chosen their sample from that population.

A **population** (also called a **universe**) is some definable group — every item, person, or thing is either in or out of the population. For national opinion pollsters in the United States, the population consists of more than 200 million citizens. On your college campus, it might be all the students or perhaps just the female undergraduate students. In an organization such as Stephanie's, the population might be all full-time employees or perhaps all hourly employees. Your first step, then, is to define your population. What group of people should the data you gather represent?

Selecting a sample involves choosing a group to represent the whole population. Ideally questionnaires would be administered to the entire population. This, however, might be time consuming and expensive. A well-conducted sample should give us similar results by contacting only a subgroup. The important assumption is that the sample represents the population.

A convenience sample is not statistically defensible.

Several types of sampling techniques exist. First, in Stephanie's report-writing problem, she might use a convenience sample. She might administer questionnaires to any available employees from the 500 employees in the company. Because she works in the operations department, she might distribute 50 questionnaires to the first 50 employees she encounters during the lunch hour. Such a sample is convenient, but Stephanie's findings would probably not represent all the Atlantic Electronics employees. She might miss employees who go out for lunch or executives who do not keep regular lunch hours. Convenience sampling generally is not an appropriate way of selecting a sample. Sampling of this type is also referred to as **nonprobability sampling** because there is a good chance the sample selected does not represent the larger population.

Probability sampling, on the other hand, assumes the elements in the population have some known chance or probability of being selected as subjects. Three types of probability sampling are random, systematic random, and stratified random sampling.

A random sample requires careful control.

Using random sampling, Stephanie would place the names of all 500 employees in a box and draw out 50 names. Employees whose names were drawn would be asked to complete questionnaires. Despite the inconvenience of having to prepare 500 names on slips of paper for the drawing, random sampling is appropriate because each member of the population (each employee) has an equal chance of being included in the sample. This chance of being part of the sample is what makes random sampling scientifically useful and defensible. With a convenience sampling, Stephanie cannot say for sure that her findings represent the opinions of all Atlantic Electronics employees. Using a random sample, Stephanie can make that important assertion.

Systematic random sampling draws from a list and takes every *n*th name. Assume that Stephanie has a list of all 500 Atlantic employees. If she randomly picks a number between 1 and 10, such as 4, and picks every fourth person from the list, she would be conducting a systematic random sample. As with random sampling, each population member has an equal chance of being part of the sample.

Stratified random sampling is the most sophisticated of the techniques. Again, random sampling is used, but sample members are also selected based on some important demographic characteristics (e.g., sex, race, or age). The sample is stratified according to some important characteristics and usually reflects the same proportions found in the population. For example, if 47 percent of the population is female, then 47 percent of the sample should be female also. Of course, not all characteristics are important. For example, in a campus political election, sample members' hometowns may not be important. Stephanie might decide to use the following stratifications: hourly or salary, management or nonmanagement, male or female, and more than five years with Atlantic or less than five years.

Stratified random sampling is a powerful sampling technique because it ensures that sample members are selected according to one or more characteristics that might influence the findings of the questionnaire. In fact, most opinion pollsters use this technique to stratify their samples by age, income, socioeconomic status, political party affiliation, and a host of other important characteristics. Such stratification adds precision to their polls and explains why their predictions are often so accurate. Generally speaking, a stratified sample uses fewer people in its sample but requires much more sophisticated development.

The terms questionnaire and, later, interview are used in this book instead of survey because of the need for clarity. A questionnaire is always a paper-and-pencil activity completed by the respondent. An interview is always oral.

Writing the Questionnaire.   A well-developed questionnaire has three basic parts: introduction, instructions, and questions. The objective of the introduction is to motivate the respondent to complete the questionnaire. If you have but a few comments to share in your introduction, you may wish to include them immediately before — or as part of — your instructions. On the other hand, as the introduction becomes lengthy or the situation more formal, you may present your introduction as a cover letter or memorandum.

A questionnaire has an introduction, instructions, and questions.

The Introduction.   The introduction identifies the purpose of the questionnaire. Unless you are concerned that stating the actual purpose for the questionnaire will bias the respondents' answers, state specifically why you are administering the questionnaire.

Second, the introduction discusses anonymity. Because you will rarely be interested in identifying individual respondents, a statement guaranteeing their anonymity will help prevent biased responses. If their names are needed, explain why. If you need to be able to identify them, but identification will not be used in the report or shared with others, emphasize this; the emphasis may be almost as beneficial as complete anonymity in gaining their response.

The questionnaire introduction covers six points.

Third, the introduction tells respondents what to do with the questionnaire once they have completed it. In the case of mailed questionnaires, for example, this section might contain instructions for returning the questionnaire through the mail.

Fourth, the introduction may explain why a response is important. If you are using a sample of 100 from a population of 1,000, you may explain that each respondent's opinions reflect the feelings of 10 people.

Fifth, particularly when questionnaires appear time consuming but actually are not, the introduction should indicate the amount of time required. "Only about two and one-half minutes of your time are required" is the type of statement that may be helpful in gaining cooperation.

Finally, the introduction should identify the sender by name and title. This humanizes the message and enhances the response rate. An example introduction, as well as the balance of a questionnaire, are found in an appendix to Stephanie's report, which is reproduced in Chapter 11.

The Instructions.   If instructions are not thorough and clear, respondents may misunderstand what they are to do. The need for clear instructions cannot be overemphasized. Assume that your reader is going to misinterpret your questionnaire — where will the error occur? Help yourself and the quality of your responses by giving clear instructions.

You may find that one set of instructions, at the beginning of the questionnaire, will guide the reader through the entire questionnaire; this is particularly true when you ask only one major category of questions, such as several rank order questions. In more complex situations, however, you may need a set of instructions at the beginning and additional instructions before each new category of questions. For example, you may need new instructions as you move from a series of rank order questions to multiple choice questions.

The Questions.   Some novices present the questions without introductory comments or instructions. Such an approach is doomed to failure. Six major categories of questions exist. Deciding when, where, and how to use these categories is both an art and a science.

Demographic questions seek information on respondents.

Each category of questions has its own purpose, strengths, and weaknesses. **Demographic questions**, which frequently appear first, seek information on characteristics of the respondents. Age, sex, income, race, department, college major, and hometown are examples of demographic questions. Demographic questions have two major values: first, they can be used to break down answers to other questions. For example, you may seek a difference by sex (demographics) in the way respondents feel toward the president's foreign policy. A second value is to test the appropriateness of a random sample. If you know that your population is 35 percent college-educated but your sample includes only 10 percent college-educated respondents, your demographic question of education indicates that your sample appears not to be random.

Dichotomous questions have two possible answers.

A second category of question is the **dichotomous question**—a question that elicits one of only two possible answers. Yes/no, male/female, and true/false are examples of responses to dichotomous questions. You may have noticed that dichotomous questions may also be demographic questions: "What is your sex?" fits both categories. Other categories of questions may overlap somewhat, too. Dichotomous questions allow respondents to branch or skip irrelevant questions. An example of a branching question and instructions is, "Have you earned a bachelor's degree as of today? _____ Yes _____ No (if yes, answer Questions 2 through 9; if no, skip directly to Question 10).

A **list question** presents a list of items and asks the respondent to select one. The selection may be the greatest or the least, the largest or the smallest, the most or least important, or the best or worst. Here is an example of a list question:

List and rank order questions are common.

Which of the following do you feel is most important in determining your job satisfaction?

_____ Money
_____ Praise from superiors
_____ Doing job well
_____ Respect from peers
_____ Fringe benefits

Similar to the list question is the **rank order question**. It too, presents a list; however, it differs because a response is given for each item in the list instead of just one item. Furthermore, the items are ranked according to some request, such as best to worst or largest to smallest. Here is an example of a rank order question:

Rank the following five items, from 1 for most important to 5 for least important, in terms of their importance to your job satisfaction:

_____ Money
_____ Praise from superiors
_____ Doing job well
_____ Respect from peers
_____ Fringe benefits

Although rank order questions can gather substantial information, be careful in analyzing the rankings. Remember the rankings determine a hierarchy among the items, but that the distances between the items is not known. That is, Selections 1 and 2 may be close to each other, but there might be a large gap between 2 and 3. The rankings are ordinal numbers rather than interval numbers.

A major category of question used in questionnaires is the **attitude question**. These questions may be direct or indirect. The direct attitude question seeks a clear or obvious attitude. Because attitudes usually are not

Attitude questions may be direct or indirect.

FIGURE 10.2 ▪ *Semantic Differential Question*

```
(Stimulus:)                    My Marketing Classes

(Scale and
 Responses:)  rewarding   ___:___:___:___:___:___:___  unrewarding
              difficult   ___:___:___:___:___:___:___  easy
              relevant    ___:___:___:___:___:___:___  irrelevant
              messy       ___:___:___:___:___:___:___  tidy
              active      ___:___:___:___:___:___:___  passive
              weak        ___:___:___:___:___:___:___  strong
              good        ___:___:___:___:___:___:___  bad
              unnecessary ___:___:___:___:___:___:___  necessary
              required    ___:___:___:___:___:___:___  elective
              illogical   ___:___:___:___:___:___:___  logical
              fun         ___:___:___:___:___:___:___  work
```

dichotomous (yes or no) but are found on a scale, a five- or seven-position type of direct attitude question is often prepared. This type of question is called a Likert question. The respondent gives a single reaction to each stimulus on a scale that most likely has five positions. Here is an example of a Likert question:

I enjoy my marketing classes.

Strongly agree	Agree	Neutral	Disagree	Strongly disagree
_____	_____	_____	_____	_____

The semantic differential question, as opposed to the direct attitude question, seeks a deeper or more indirect attitude. Figure 10.2 shows a sample question. For each stimulus there will be a number of responses, usually about 10. A scale of five or seven positions is used between bipolar adjectives or scales.

This category of question elicits responses that respondents might not have considered on their own. Semantic differential responses can be compared group against group by which side of the neutral center they fall on or by time period, such as current responses versus answers from a year ago.

The sixth and final question category is the **open-ended question**. When you are unsure about how your respondents might answer a question, when you do not want to limit them to your wording, or when you seek answers with richness and depth, consider an open-ended question. One open-ended question is, "How do you feel about your company?" The strength of such a question lies in the richness of the answers; the weakness is that it is difficult to analyze the answers statistically. You will have unique responses and therefore cannot tabulate percentages because responses may defy definite categorization.

In contrast, a closed question is one that limits the respondents' depth of answer. Thus, rank order, dichotomous, and other categories of questions can be considered closed questions.

Lack of clarity in the wording or goal of a question can lead to problems of interpretation. Here are examples of several common problems in phrasing and design:

Overlapping Answer	Age: _____ Younger than 20
	_____ 20–30
	_____ 30–40
Leading Question	You do like your boss, don't you?
Multiple Questions in One Question	Do you like ham and eggs?
Confusing-Categories Question	Marital status: _____ Widowed
	_____ Divorced
	_____ Single
	_____ Married
Multiple-Interpretations Question	Are you an honest person?

Chapter 19 presents a thorough analysis of questions used in interviews.

Experiments

A second major primary research technique is experimentation. When you use an experiment to gather primary data, there are some implicit assumptions. First, you manipulate something and pay attention to the result. Second, you start with a specific research question or hypothesis that you test. Third, you are objective and unbiased in your technique. Finally, most likely you will test your findings with well-defined statistical procedures. These major assumptions, plus many other guidelines and conditions, mean that experiments can be rigorous. However, if the experiment is to have meaning, the assumptions and guidelines must be met.

Describing important methodology in any depth is beyond the scope of this text. A few guidelines follow, and you are encouraged to seek additional direction elsewhere if you need it. The list of references at the end of this chapter offers suggestions.

- Often you will need to sample some population for your experiment. Follow the rules for sampling.
- Always try to be unobtrusive; your presence alone can affect the data you are collecting.
- Be careful not to overgeneralize your findings — the results you observe for a sample of 50 reflect only those 50 and not necessarily the balance of the population. Conditions may have changed, for

BOXED IN   *AN ETHICAL DILEMMA*

Joachim Hoang wants to measure employees' indirect attitudes toward the company's new benefits package. He is reasonably sure that the type of question he needs to ask in his questionnaire is a semantic differential question. However, he is not comfortable with the process of selecting the bipolar adjectives for his questions. His initial research has led him into an overwhelming array of complex issues. He does not understand the statistical process by which the adjectives usually fall into three main factors of evaluation, activity, and potency, nor does he know why it is important to have adjectives from each of these factors in his pilot test.

What's more, he is running out of time to complete the project.

Most discussions of semantic differential questions show adjectives such as hot/cold, friendly/unfriendly, and so on. Joachim is beginning to think he could pick up some of these common adjectives and avoid doing any more time-consuming research on how to select them. No one else in the company seems to know much about the correct use of the semantic differential. Chances are good that he would not get caught.

Joachim feels boxed in. What would you do?

example, in the time between the start of your experiment and when you draw conclusions.

- Examine the secondary literature first to see if similar research has been conducted already. The mistakes of others may help you.
- Keep your experiment simple. Try to control as many variables as possible. For example, if you wish to know the effect of raising the price of hamburgers by 10 cents in the company cafeteria, do not raise the price of other items at the same time.

Interviews

When using interviews to gather data for a business report, you are likely to use one of the following interview types: persuasive, information giving, or information gathering. Persuasive interviewing might be conducted to encourage students to take part in an experiment. Information-giving in-

✔ *CHECKLIST for Planning a Questionnaire*

___ Be sure to thoroughly define the universe and correctly select the sample.

___ Include all necessary information in the introduction.

___ Provide instructions that are thorough and clear.

___ Select the correct type of question to generate the desired data.

terviewing might be used to instruct selected subjects in how to function during an experiment. However, in terms of data gathering, you are most likely to use the information-gathering type of interview.

Two chapters in this book examine the interviewing process. Chapter 19 looks at interviewing as a management tool. Chapter 23 examines the applicant's role in the job interview. These chapters discuss types of questions, the interview structure, and styles of interviewing. The following is a summary of major concerns:

- Sometimes only one or a few individuals need to be interviewed. This is particularly true when the individuals are experts. The opinion of one dietitian may be far more valuable than the opinion of many employees about the nutrition of cafeteria food.
- If many people need to be interviewed, do you need a random sample? Must you meet the criteria of random sampling?
- If you are sampling and interviewing many people, are you conducting a scientific experiment, and are you therefore required to meet all the relevant scientific criteria? Not all studies need to be scientific.
- Because interviews are such obtrusive data-gathering techniques, should you consider an alternative collection method?
- Is interviewing, which is individualized and flexible, able to justify the sometimes extensive personnel time and effort it requires?
- Would telephone interviewing, which has its own strengths and weaknesses, serve better than face-to-face interviewing? Telephone interviewing can gather more honest answers than face-to-face interviews because the interviewee does not have to look you in the eye. But be careful—for the same reasons telephone interviewing yields honesty, it can result in dishonesty. Telephone interviewing usually takes longer to conduct than you plan. Wrong numbers, busy signals, no answers, and number changes are part of the time to account for in telephone interviewing.

Data-gathering interviewing has these strengths: flexibility, potential for uniformity, individualization, and ability to be enacted quickly. However, interviewing is expensive when many respondents are used, is obtrusive, and requires skill and training to execute properly.

The development of interviewing skills requires training and practice.

Personal Observations

A data-gathering source that is frequently overlooked is personal observation. You may be observing as you conduct an interview or run an experiment, but observation can be a formal approach to answering your research question.

Along with meeting the same rigorous guidelines as sampling and experimentation, observation must also be unobtrusive. Is your presence modifying what you are observing? Can you overcome this problem by becoming a participant within the group? Can you objectively observe the effect of raising hamburger prices in the company by joining the regular group of employees who use the cafeteria? This might have a different effect than a stranger walking about the cafeteria during lunch with a clipboard and pencil.

The benefits of observation are that it is inexpensive, quick, adjustable, and capable of individualization. On the other hand, observation is often biased, nonscientific, or incomplete.

Organization Files

Organization files can be either primary or secondary forms of research. The form of research is not so important as how to use organization files.

Sometimes you can find the answer to your research question in readily available organization files. Because you are not affecting the existing data, this technique is the least obtrusive of the primary source techniques. If you raise the price of hamburgers in the cafeteria on a certain date, are you selling more or fewer hamburgers? Records may indicate the pounds of hamburger purchased before and after the change. Did the 10 percent salary increase affect output? Look to the production reports, absentee reports, tardiness reports, or number of grievances filed for possible changes.

Frequently some ingenuity is necessary in locating the record that meets your needs. Because the information is gathered and your presence does not affect it, using organization records can provide better quality data and take less time and effort than other research methods.

EVALUATING THE RESULTS

After having determined your purpose, considered your audience, and conducted your research, the next step is to evaluate your results. To help in this evaluation — whether primary or secondary sources were used — test your data against these questions. You should be able to respond *yes* to each.

- Are my findings reasonable and logical? If not, why?
- Was my sample size adequate?
- Did I apply appropriate statistical tests to my data to make it more meaningful?
- Did I achieve appropriate depth in my research?
- Did I answer the initial research question?

OUTLINING THE REPORT

A discussion of outlining is really about the organization of the report. Organization is important and will affect how the report is received. For purposes of outlining, you need be concerned about only three of the parts of the report: introduction, body, and conclusion. Together, they make up the bulk of the report.

Arrangement of the Parts

You have three choices for presenting the introduction, body, and conclusion:

Choice 1	*Choice 2*	*Choice 3*
Introduction	Introduction	Conclusion
Body	Conclusion	Introduction
Conclusion	Body	Body

In Choice 1, the indirect order arrangement, you save the conclusion (which might contain a summary and recommendations) until last. This is appropriate when the receiver might tend to resist your conclusions or will not understand them until the rest of the report is read. However, many executives will find the conclusion, no matter where it is in the report, and read it first.

Choices 2 or 3 are direct order arrangements. Using this type of arrangement, you present conclusions either second (Choice 2) or first (Choice 3). Whether conclusions are first or second is not important. Either is appropriate when (1) the report contains good news, (2) the receiver has enough background to understand the conclusions without reading the rest of the report first, (3) the conclusions provide a framework around which to interpret the detailed information in the body, or (4) the reader needs the conclusion first.

The introduction, body, and conclusion may be arranged in direct or indirect order.

Presentation of the Body

The body of the report is almost always the longest section. You should make sure that it flows smoothly and has the kind of impact you want.

Writing the Headings

A good outline will help you write more clearly, thereby enhancing reader understanding. When you write your outline, you must use a common set of numerals and letters that many other writers use:

I. Major concept
  A. Main point
    1. Supporting point
    2. Another supporting point
      a. Additional support
      b. Additional support
  B. Another main point
II. Another major concept
  A. Main point
  B. Another main point

At each level in the outline, a minimum of two headings must occur.

A major rule of outlining is that at least two headings must occur within the same level. Thus, I requires II, and A under I must be matched with B under I.

Two types of headings are appropriate for your outline: topic and sentence. Topic headings contain single words or short phrases; sentence headings are complete sentences. Here are some examples:

Topic Headings	*Sentence Headings*
I. Employee problems	I. Atlantic Electronics has several employee problems.

A. Turnover
  1. Electronics industry rates
	A. Turnover is high.
	  1. Turnover rates in the electronics industry are decreasing.

2. Atlantic's rates	2. Atlantic's turnover rate is increasing.
a. 1986–1990	a. From 1986 to 1990 Atlantic controlled turnover.
b. 1990–present	b. Since 1990 turnover has increased dramatically.

B. Absenteeism
  1. Etc. . . .
	B. Absenteeism is at a new high.
	  1. Etc. . . .

The topic outline can be prepared more quickly than the sentence outline. However, the sentence outline will make the actual writing go faster. In fact, some of the sentences in the outline example might be good paragraph topic sentences.

Notice the importance of parallelism: equivalent parts are the same part of speech, have the same suffix, and the same structure. For example, in the sentence heading outline above, parts I-A-1 (Turnover rates in the electronics industry are decreasing) and I-A-2 (Atlantic's turnover rate is increasing) are similar in structure.

Organizing the Headings

Chronological order is often used for an informational report.

One approach to organizing the outline headings for the report body is chronological—that is, according to time. This chapter uses chronological order to describe the step-by-step procedure for planning a long report. The chronological order is especially useful for writing an informational report with a topic that can be time sequenced. Be cautious, however. The chronological approach often is not justified. So much of our lives is time sequenced that we may be tempted to force our reports into this outline as well.

A second way to organize the report body is by topic order. Using this outlining method, you organize the body around important topics. For example, if you were writing a report to help your employer choose a location for a new plant, you could organize the report around the potential sites. Some first-degree headings for such an outline are:

I. Columbus, Ohio
II. Dover, Delaware
III. Montgomery, Alabama

Or you might organize your report using the criteria your employer uses in selecting a new plant:

I. Labor market
   A. Columbus, Ohio
   B. Dover, Delaware
   C. Montgomery, Alabama
II. Community support
   A. Columbus, Ohio
   B. Dover, Delaware
   C. Montgomery, Alabama
III. Marketing and distribution benefits
   A. Columbus, Ohio
   B. Dover, Delaware
   C. Montgomery, Alabama

An advantage of the topic order is its flexibility; it can be modified to meet the organization's structure. For example, if a company has three branches, the report can be built around those branches.

Topic order has the advantage of flexibility.

A second advantage of the topic order is that the author can organize the outline in descending or ascending order of importance, as in this first-degree outline:

I. Introduction
II. Most important topic
III. Second most important topic
IV. Least important topic
V. Conclusions

Or you can reverse the order:

I. Introduction
II. Least important topic
III. Second most important topic
IV. Most important topic
V. Conclusions

The problem-solving order is a third approach to organizing the report body.

A third way to organize the body is the problem-solving order. Typically, this arrangement consists of several subparts: background, nature of the problem, solutions to the problem, and plan of action for implementing the solution. The problem-solving order is perfectly suited to Stephanie's needs because her purpose is to solve the employee relations problem. The first two major headings of her outline might look like this:

I. Background: The importance of employee relations
   A. Employee relations in the industry
      1. Effects of good relations
      2. Consequences of poor relations
   B. Employee relations at Atlantic Electronics
II. Nature of Atlantic Electronics' employee relations program
   A. Grievances
      1. Recent grievances
      2. Long-standing grievances
   B. Turnover
   C. Absenteeism
      1. By department
      2. By rank
   D. Morale
      1. Methodology
      2. Return rate
   E. Unionization

✔ CHECKLIST for Planning a Business Report

___」 **Determine the purpose of the report.**

___」 **Consider the audience.**

___」 **Gather all the necessary information.**

___」 **Analyze the information.**

___」 **Outline the report.**

SUMMARY

An important first step in report writing is the planning of the report. Planning involves figuring out the characteristics of the report, such as length and destination; determining the type of report, such as informative, interpretive, or problem solving; conducting the research; evaluating the results; and outlining the report.

The report planner must decide on primary versus secondary (or library) research. Among the many ways to gather data through primary research are questionnaires, experiments, interviews, personal observations, and company records. Questionnaires often use a variety of question types, including demographic, dichotomous, list, rank order, attitude, or open-ended.

The introduction, body, and conclusion of the report may be arranged in either direct or indirect order. A direct order places the conclusion at or near the beginning of the body whereas an indirect order places it last. Outlining main thoughts in the body helps the writer achieve better apparent organization and achieve smoother flow of ideas.

Key Terms

- **informational report**
- **interpretive report**
- **problem-solving report**
- **analytical report**
- **primary source**
- **secondary source**
- **population**
- **universe**

- **nonprobability sampling**
- **demographic question**
- **dichotomous question**
- **list question**
- **rank order question**
- **attitude question**
- **open-ended question**

References

Research

Christensen, Larry B. *Experimental Methodology.* 4th rev. ed. Boston: Allyn and Bacon, 1988.

Cozby, Paul C. *Methods in Behavioral Research.* 4th ed. Palo Alto, Calif.: Mayfield, 1989.

Dominowski, Roger L. *Research Methods.* Englewood Cliffs, N.J.: Prentice-Hall, 1980.

Emory, C. William. *Business Research Methods.* 3d ed. Homewood Ill.: Richard D. Irwin, 1985.

Statistics

Bechtold, Brigitte, and Johnson, Ross. *Statistics for Business and Economics.* Boston, Mass.: PWS-Kent, 1989.

Jarrett, Jeffrey E., and Kraft, Arthur. *Statistical Analysis for Decision Making.* Boston, Mass.: Allyn and Bacon, 1988.

Mendenhall, William. *A Course in Business Statistics.* 2d ed. Boston, Mass.: PWS-Kent, 1988.

Monks, Joseph G., and Newton, Byron L. *Statistics for Business.* 2d ed. Chicago, Ill.: SRA, 1988.

Oakes, Michael. *Statistical Inference.* Chichester, England: Wiley, 1986.

Wonnacott, Thomas H., and Wonnacott, Ronald J. *Introductory Statistics for Business and Economics.* 4th ed. New York: Wiley, 1990.

Report Writing

Baker, Sheridan. *The Complete Stylist and Handbook.* 3d ed. New York: Harper & Row, 1984.

Brusaw, Charles T., Alfred, Gerald J., and Oliu, Walter E. *The Business Writer's Handbook.* 3d ed. New York: St. Martin's Press, 1987.

Corder, Jim W. *Handbook of Current English*. 8th ed. Glenview, Ill.: Scott, Foresman, 1989.

Crews, Frederick, and Schor, Sandra. *The Borzoi Handbook for Writers*. New York: McGraw-Hill, 1985.

Review Questions

1. Why are reports prepared? Which reasons are most important? Why?

2. Describe several characteristics of business reports.

3. What are the differences between informational, interpretive, and problem-solving reports?

4. What are the steps in planning the long report?

5. Identify some primary research methods. What are the strengths and weaknesses of each?

6. Differentiate between random, stratified, convenience, and systematic random samples.

7. What are the different levels of degree headings used in outlining?

8. Discuss the development of a questionnaire.

9. What are the differences between outlining and organizing a report?

10. What are the differences between direct and indirect arrangements of the parts of the report? Describe three approaches to organizing the body.

Exercises

1. Ask three business people in your area to define *communication*. Note their answers but also pay attention to problems of nonscientific inquiry. In other words, for what reasons should you discount the answers?

2. Through personal observation of students at your school, note the differences in behavior between boyfriends with girlfriends compared to behavior between other men and women students who are not so closely associated. What conclusions can you draw regarding gathering information from personal observation?

3. Select a brief essay in a periodical, such as "My Turn" in *Newsweek*, or a feature article in *The Wall Street Journal*. Outline the essay or article.

CASE | *Planning the Report*

Kath Ralston, Chisholm Institute of Technology, Victoria, Australia

Sally Dixon is in her final year at business college. During the past two years she has worked part time at the local gymnasium and community center making appointments and scheduling classes conducted at the center. She enjoys working there, but she believes the management group is not very dynamic and does not take enough opportunities to promote the center's programs.

Recently Sally heard that the activities coordinator would be leaving at the end of the year. Sally would like to land the position and believes that with the combination of her practical work experience plus her business knowledge, she would make an excellent activities coordinator. She realizes that although the management group is pleased with her work, they would need more proof of her business ability if they were to consider her for the position of activities coordinator.

One evening when she arrived home she found a letter from her dentist reminding her of a dental checkup. This started her thinking about a promotional campaign for the community center in which each participant could be contacted in a short time after completing a class and advised of future activities at the center. This campaign would mean setting up a new record-keeping system, but she believed that the extra business the center would obtain would far outweigh any cost.

Sally decided this was her chance to show the management group that she could apply her study of business systems and marketing in a very practical way. She thought the best approach would be to present the proposal to the management group in a report.

Case Questions

1. What will be the purpose of the report?
2. What aspects of the receivers will Sally have to consider?
3. What information must Sally collect for her report? Where will she get it?
4. In outlining the report, which order do you think Sally should choose? Give the reasons for your choice.

Is This Course Really Important? | CASE

Robert J. Olney, Southwest Texas State University

As a member of the advisory board for your university's school of business, you and the school's dean are opposed to a move by other board members to remove business communication from the business curriculum. Although as a local business person and employer you are convinced of the importance of the course, you find that not all board members prioritize curriculum needs in the same way.

You have already found and reported a study in which business communication was rated very important in preparing people for leadership positions more often than any other of 13 business courses by 1,158 newly promoted executives (H. W. Hildebrandt et al., "An Executive Appraisal of Courses Which Best Prepare One for General Management," *Journal of Business Communication* 19 (Winter 1982), 5–15). However, this article wasn't enough. In order to strengthen your case, you and the dean decide to conduct your own study to see whether the 1982 findings "hold up." How do today's executives, especially in your geographic area, feel about the importance of various courses and curriculum topics in preparing business leaders? You outline a plan of attack for the project:

1. Review secondary research sources. This review will help you establish a theoretical base for your study and determine how other individuals have approached similar research studies.
2. Design a questionnaire to aid in solving the research problem. Your questionnaire will contain:
   a. An introduction that identifies the purpose of the questionnaire.
   b. Instructions that explain exactly what the respondents should do.
   c. A list of the business core from your university and a rating scale that can be used by respondents to indicate the relative importance of each course.
   d. Other questions you design to solve the research problem.
3. Select a sample of business managers in your geographic area to participate in your study and distribute your questionnaire.
4. Evaluate the findings of the questionnaire.
5. Produce a report that contains a statement of the problem of the research, the methodology, the analysis of secondary and primary data, the conclusions based on this analysis, and recommendations. Follow a report format as specified by your instructor.

Case Questions

1. Are there other steps you believe should be added to your preliminary outline of this project?

2. From your review of the literature, which procedures used in similar research projects would be effective in assuring you objective results? How have data been analyzed?

3. What types of questions or combinations of questions will allow you to achieve appropriate depth in your research?

4. What sampling technique will yield an appropriately representative response for the population? What statistical tests are appropriate to your data to make them more meaningful?

5. What graphic aids will summarize your information best and create a more interesting flow for your report?

The Long Report: Writing

Stephanie looked at the business report just delivered by its author, Bill Wells, and thought back to a report she had written almost 10 years ago — a report that had influenced her career.

As new to Atlantic Electronics then as Bill is now, Stephanie had written a problem-solving report on employee relations. Unexpectedly, that report had been viewed by her superiors in the evaluation of her work as a personnel assistant. Although she was unsure of herself at the time, things worked out fine. The vice president had been impressed with her ability and potential. He recommended a promotion to personnel specialist a full year before most personnel assistants are promoted. He had even made a point of stopping by her desk to tell her how impressed he was by the report.

Much has happened since, Stephanie thought. Louise took over the vice president's job on his retirement. Stephanie's immediate boss, Scott Millan, took a job with a competitor, and she was selected to replace him. How proud she had been to be selected as the youngest person ever to hold the job of personnel director for the company.

Well, enough reminiscing, she thought. Let's see if this report from Bill will determine *his* future.

Learning Objectives

1 *To learn the effective and correct use of headings.*

2 *To understand the correct placement of tables, graphs, and other visual matter.*

3 *To learn how to attribute information to its origin.*

4 *To understand each of the preliminary parts.*

5 *To understand each of the supplementary parts.*

6 *To know the correct order of the parts of a formal business report.*

Two characteristics of business reports, as discussed in Chapter 10, are length and formality. Report formality is determined largely by language tone, such as using third-person singular versus first-person singular *(the author* instead of *I)*, and by the number of formal parts included in the report. If the business report includes an authorization document or an abstract, for example, the report becomes more formal. The more parts, the greater the length will be. Therefore, formality and length are often related.

Chapter 10 ended with a discussion of how to outline three parts of the business report: introduction, body, and conclusion. In this chapter, they are treated together as one of the three major divisions of the report: the text. The other two major divisions, also presented in this chapter, are the preliminary parts and the supplementary parts.

THE TEXT

If the outline you have developed is thorough, writing the text should not be too difficult, although it may be time consuming. No matter in which order you have chosen to present the introduction, body, and conclusion, you should write the conclusion last. The act of writing is the first time you will think about your report material in detail, and your conclusions may change in the process.

The body is often written first. The introduction, regardless of when it is written, should conclude with a transition to the body of the report. In location as well as importance, the body is central to the report. About 75 percent of the report text should be body and the remaining 25 percent distributed between introduction and conclusion.

The body should flow from topic to topic in a logical, clear order. Use a variety of transitions, such as *next, consequently, fourth, on the other hand*, and *similarly* to function as guideposts to the reader. Give summaries periodically, such as at the end of each major section, to remind the reader where you are and where you are going.

The characteristics of effective written communication (discussed in Chapter 3) apply to long reports as they do to other forms of written communication.

1. *Tactful:* Avoid offensive language, don't insult your readers, and don't categorize them. Be especially careful to avoid sexist language.
2. *Personal:* Generally, do not use the "you" attitude when writing the text parts of a formal business report; these reports usually demand a more impersonal writing style. However, in some circumstances a report that contains formal report parts, such as an abstract or appendixes, can be made more readable by using the first or second person.
3. *Positive:* Use a positive tone whenever possible. (But remember that some ideas aren't adaptable to a positive approach.)
4. *Active:* Use the active voice as much as possible. Use passive voice only to de-emphasize an idea.
5. *Unified:* Be sure that each sentence and paragraph contain only one central idea.

6. *Coherent:* Use signposts, linking words, and enumerators to give smooth and logical transitions to the text. Proper headings help coherence.
7. *Clear:* Avoid unfamiliar words, and use jargon only if you're sure the reader can understand you.
8. *Concise:* Avoid trite expressions, wordy phrases, unnecessary repetition, and abstract words.
9. *Readable:* Consider the education level of your receiver. You might compute a readability index on your drafts to ensure that you've written them at the appropriate level.
10. *Mechanically sound:* Check and recheck for grammar errors.

Two of these characteristics, coherence and clarity, can be dramatically improved if you include headings and tables and figures in the body of the report.

Headings

A single, generic outline of **headings** and subheadings for most business reports is impossible to prepare. You should follow your outline, presenting headings and material under them in a consistent fashion. Headings serve as signposts and improve the reader's speed and ease in comprehending your ideas.

Headings serve as signposts.

Many authorities discuss the relationship between the various levels of headings. Not all authorities agree, but a few principles emerge: (1) if a heading is centered, it is more important than a heading that is flush with the left margin; (2) if a heading is flush with the left margin, it is more important than a heading that is indented; (3) if a heading is capitalized, it is more important than a heading that has only initial capital letters; (4) if a heading is underlined, it is more important than a heading that is not underlined; and (5) if a heading is placed on a line by itself, it is more important than a heading that is followed by text.

By using these principles, and intermixing them, we can develop the following hierarchy of headings and subheadings, ranging from highest to lowest:

<u>THIS IS A FIRST-LEVEL HEADING</u>

THIS IS A SECOND-LEVEL HEADING

<u>This is a Third-Level Heading</u>

This is a Fourth-Level Heading

<u>THIS IS A FIFTH-LEVEL HEADING</u>

<u>This is a Sixth-Level Heading</u>

This Is a Seventh-Level Heading

This Is an Eighth-Level Heading

This is a Ninth-Level Heading. It is indented, followed by a period, and with text starting on the same line.

You will probably never need to use all nine levels of headings. However, most reports will use at least three levels. The levels you select need not be limited to the top three. You can use the principles discussed to make obvious and helpful headings. Here is an example of picking and choosing four different levels of headings for a report:

<u>THIS MIGHT BE THE TITLE</u>
<u>OF THE REPORT</u>

<u>This Might Be a Second-Level Heading</u>

This Might Be a Third-Level Heading

This Might Be a Fourth-Level Heading

Heading levels should be obvious and logical

The important point to remember in using headings is that they must be immediately logical to your reader; which subheading is subordinate to others should be obvious.

There are other formats for headings. For example, a numerical approach uses numbers — either with or without a phrase after the number — such as 1, 3.4, and 7.5.1 for headings. The numerical approach is used more often in formal and governmental reports. The numbers are likely to occur in technical and scientific reports and in other situations as well.

As more and more reports are prepared on computers — and printed on dot matrix printers by students and on laser printers by business people — even more heading possibilities emerge. Now the report writer can use boldface, second strike, italics, expanded, condensed, or enlarged type, and even different typefaces. Be judicious in your use of type treatments and avoid the **creeping elegance** of too many divergent appearances. No matter which heading technique you use, apply it consistently and be logical in your visual differentiation.

Tables and Figures

The report text can be divided into its prose and nonprose parts; tables and figures are subdivisions of the nonprose parts. Both tables and figures are useful for summarizing a large amount of detailed information in a small space. They also break up the text material and create a more interesting flow.

Here are some guidelines for using tables and figures in the text of a business report. (An explanation of their importance and how to prepare them will be presented in Chapter 16.)

The reader should understand tables and figures without having to refer to the text.

▪ A table or figure that is one-half page or larger is placed on a page by itself. A table or figure that is less than one-half page can have text above or below it.

- A table or figure should be able to stand alone. That is, any viewer should be able to look at the table or figure and quickly understand the information. Reading the related text should not be necessary in order to understand the table or figure.
- Tables are numbered as a series, beginning with *1*. Figures are numbered in a separate series. The table number along with a descriptive phrase appears above the table body. The figure number and descriptive phrase are positioned below the figure.
- Sometimes it is unclear whether the table or figure should be located in the text or at the end of the report in an appendix. The material should be in the text if it is necessary for the reader to view it to understand the report. If the information might be helpful but is not required, it is usually placed in an appendix. If the material is lengthy — several pages or more — it is usually placed in an appendix.
- When a table or figure that was presented by someone else in published form is presented in your report, indicate that source much as you would use a footnote. The source indication, however, is part of the table or figure.
- Each table or figure should be referred to in the text. The table or figure then appears at the end of the paragraph or — if it is to appear alone on a page — on the next page. In the latter case, fill out the page on which it was mentioned with text.
- If the table must be presented parallel to the long sides of the paper, place the heading along the inside margin or spine so that it is read from the outside page margin of the report.
- In both tables and figures, the time period (years, months, and so on), is usually presented on the horizontal axis.

Documentation

The business report writer must attribute information obtained through secondary research to the source, rather than leave the reader to guess. In formal business reports, **attribution** usually appears as notes either at the bottom of the page or at the end of the text. In more informal reports, the attribution may be found solely in the text, such as, "David Fenton, our St. Louis marketing manager, said sales should increase by 37 percent this year." Internal attribution is more likely to be used when there are only a few sources mentioned. Once you reach four or five citations — or when you are writing a formal business report — you will need to use notes and a bibliography.

The footnoting approach is traditional and is widely used. With this approach, a number is placed at the end of the information you are citing in the text. The number is raised one-half line and is called a **superscript**. The first citation is numbered *1*, the next *2*, and so on sequentially through the report. Any information cited that is taken from someone else — including both direct quotations and your paraphrasing of ideas — receives a footnote number. A block of information taken from the same source in

Footnoting is the most common form of attribution.

the same publication receives one number. Thus one paragraph might be attributed to one author.

On the other hand, one paragraph might include the ideas of a variety of sources. Even a single sentence can have more than one footnote, as shown here:

> Many experts in finance agree with the point we have been discussing. Included in this group are Lewis,[1] Jones,[2] Harris,[3] and McWilliams.[4]

Each time you cite information you need to use a footnote. This is true even if you have cited the author earlier in the report. We often use *Ibid.* in a footnote to indicate we are referring to information from the same author and source as the one in the last footnote cited. *Op. cit.* in a footnote means the same author and publication as mentioned earlier but not the one immediately preceding. *Op. cit.* and, to a lesser extent, *Ibid.* are being phased out in favor of repeating the author's last name and the new page reference.

Either telephone or face-to-face interview attribution is handled as if the interview was a publication and the interviewee was the author. The observation in the text still receives a superscript number at the end of the quote or paraphrase, or by the author's (interviewee's) name.

As we use the superscript numbers in the text of the report, we must leave room at the bottom of the page for the footnote citation. If there are four superscript numbers in the text on page 7 of your report, there must be four footnotes at the bottom of the page.

Footnoting is a precise and sometimes tedious process. Considerations include the number of authors and the type of publication (book, periodical, brochure, or newspaper, for example). Footnote styles vary, and you may be directed by your organization to a particular style. The sample footnotes here follow the University of Chicago Press *The Chicago Manual of Style*, 13th edition. The first five illustrate treatment of books with varying numbers of authors. (All five books are of interest because they are manuals that discuss footnote styles.) The last three footnotes here illustrate citations of a magazine, a brochure, and a newspaper.

[1] Charles T. Brusaw, Gerald J. Alred, and Walter E. Oliu, *The Business Writer's Handbook*, 3d ed. (New York: St. Martin's Press, 1987), 194–211.

[2] Arno F. Knapper and Loda I. Newcomb, *Style Manual for Written Communication*, 2d ed. (Columbus: Grid Publishing, 1983), 32–38.

[3] Kate L. Turabian, *Student's Guide for Writing College Papers*, 3d ed. (Chicago: University of Chicago Press, 1976), 50.

[4] *The Chicago Manual of Style*, 13th ed. (Chicago: University of Chicago Press, 1982), 101–9.

[5] *The MLA Handbook for Writers of Research Papers*, 3d ed. (New York: Modern Language Association, 1988), 30.

[6] David Gabel, "Word Processing for Personal Computers," *Personal Computing*, August 1982, 82–106.

[7] *The Revolution in Software* (Berkeley, Calif.: Perfect Software, 1982), 3.

[8] James A. White, "Design, Sales Strategy Help Make IBM's Personal Computer a Big Hit," *The Wall Street Journal*, southwestern edition, 15 December 1982, 33.

This footnoting approach has both strengths and weaknesses. Besides being traditional and widely accepted, it is the most efficient approach for the reader. Attribution is made in the text, and the reader can look directly to the bottom of the page for the information. On the other hand, footnoting is tedious and time consuming for the typist. It you have ever typed a page of text and tried to leave adequate room for footnotes at the bottom only to run out of room, you know the frustration it can cause!

To avoid this frustration, a modification of the standard technique is becoming widely used. Instead of presenting the footnotes at the bottom of each page as they occur, the footnotes are lifted from each page and placed in numerical order in the first of the supplementary pages. The part containing these lifted footnotes is appropriately titled **Endnotes**. Other than their location, the endnote citations are the same as those placed at the foot of the page. A sample endnotes page appears later in this chapter (Figure 11.1).

Footnotes grouped at the end of the report are called endnotes.

In addition to deciding between footnoting or endnoting, you must also contend with different ways of preparing the note (as well as your bibliography). In some cases your employer may dictate the style. Most periodicals select one style and ask authors to use it. In other cases you may select from the various styles. Four of the most widely used are the University of Chicago style, the American Psychological Association style, the Modern Language Association style, and the Kate Turabian style. Table 11.1 illustrates these four styles for both footnotes and bibliography entries.

With the second attribution technique, there are no footnotes or endnotes. A bracketed number is placed at each location in the text where attribution is required. The numbers refer the reader to the bibliography, which is arranged alphabetically. Therefore, the bracketed numbers referring to items in the bibliography will not be sequential. Here are two sample sentences that use this attribution style:

Jones is one of the best-known authorities espousing this philosophy [6].
There are, however, other authorities who disagree with Jones [17:50], [3:63–8], [9:121].

The reader can now turn to the bibliography, find the [6] before the Jones citation, and determine the balance of the information about this source. When a specific page or pages are cited, it is customary to include this information within the brackets and after a colon. In [17:50], the 50 means page 50 in reference 17.

The third approach to formal attribution differs from the ones already described but has some similarities, too. It tends to be used in academic writing, has many variations, and is rapidly gaining application. This approach eliminates the footnoting process entirely, yet delivers the information required for the appropriate attribution.

One style of attribution eliminates numbered notes entirely.

If you choose this approach, instead of using a superscript number, you present the author's last name, the year of publication, and, if appropriate, the specific pages that were used. Citations are presented in the same fashion regardless of whether the source is an article, a book, or an interview. An exception is when the author is not known—then you present

TABLE 11.1   ▪   *Attribution Styles*

	Notes	*Bibliography*
University of Chicago Style	1. Richard C. Huseman, James M. Lahiff, and John M. Penrose, *Business Communication: Strategies and Skills,* 4th ed. (Hinsdale, Ill.: Dryden Press, 1991), 250.	Huseman, Richard C., James M. Lahiff, and John M. Penrose. *Business Communication: Strategies and Skills.* 4th ed. Hinsdale, Ill.: Dryden Press, 1991.
American Psychological Association Style	Huseman, R. C., Lahiff, J. M., & Penrose, J. M. 1991. *Business Communication: Strategies and Skills* (4th ed.). Hinsdale, IL: Dryden Press.	Huseman, R. C., Lahiff, J. M., & Penrose, J. M. (1991). *Business Communication: Strategies and Skills* (4th ed.). Hinsdale, IL: Dryden Press.
Modern Language Association Style	[1]Richard C. Huseman, James M. Lahiff, and John M. Penrose, *Business Communication: Strategies and Skills,* 4th ed. (Hinsdale: Dryden Press, 1991) 250.	Huseman, Richard C., James M. Lahiff, and John M. Penrose. *Business Communication: Strategies and Skills.* 4th ed. Hinsdale: Dryden Press, 1991.
Turabian Style	[1]Richard C. Huseman, James M. Lahiff, and John M. Penrose, *Business Communication: Strategies and Skills* (4th ed.; Hinsdale, Illinois: Dryden Press, 1991), p. 250.	Huseman, Richard C., Lahiff, James M., and Penrose, John M. *Business Communication: Strategies and Skills.* 4th ed. Hinsdale, Illinois: Dryden Press, 1991.

Sources (presented in their respective bibliographic style):

The Chicago Manual of Style. 13th ed. Chicago and London: The University of Chicago Press, 1982.

Publication Manual of the American Psychological Association (3rd ed.). (1983). Washington, DC: American Psychological Association.

Gibaldi, Joseph, and Walter Achtert. *Modern Language Association Handbook for Writers of Research Papers.* New York: Modern Language Association, 1984.

Turabian, Kate L. *Student's Guide for Writing College Papers.* 3d ed. Chicago and London: University of Chicago Press, 1976.

the publication name, the year, and perhaps the page numbers. Here is some sample text that utilizes the author's name attribution approach. Notice the information appears in parentheses after the citation, but the author's name may be part of the sentence.

As we continue to examine the effect of increased production on job satisfaction, it is necessary to consider classical management theory. Smith (1981, p. 307), for example, feels that production is all-important. Several other authorities agree with Smith (see, for example, McWilliams, 1956;

Lewis, 1961; McAllister, 1967; Harris & Woffort, 1985; or Graber et al., 1990). Probably the most sweeping comment to the opposing view is, "Smith and her cronies are absolutely wrong! Job satisfaction is so much more important than production that it can't even be mentioned in the same breath!" (Horvath, 1989, p. 227).

The reader can locate the complete citation in the bibliography. A bibliography presents much the same information as a footnote, but instead of being presented numerically, items are alphabetized by authors' last names. Thus, to find the Smith (1981, p. 307) citation, the reader would scan the bibliography to locate Smith.

If the bibliography is prepared using this attribution technique, it is the same as a standard bibliography; however, it is called references instead of bibliography.

Introduction and Conclusion

A typical introduction explains the importance of the report topic. The introduction may give a historical perspective and can discuss the organization of the balance of the body of the report. It may have sections for relevance, problem statement, scope, or purpose.

The introduction may also include a section on limitations of the study. The writer should be careful, however, not to supply ammunition to the reader to help discount the report. If relevant and defensible shortcomings exist, such as a shortage of research funds or concrete information, include them. Avoid mentioning a lack of interest in the topic, computer breakdowns at the last minute, or poor personal analytical abilities that destroy your credibility.

The conclusion section explains and summarizes what the reader has just read in the body of the report. The value of a conclusion lies in its focus and emphasis; the reader is told what were the most memorable points in the report. This section may bring together for the first time divergent ideas from the report and synthesize them. No new information should appear in the conclusion, however — only new perspectives on existing information.

No new information should be presented in the conclusion section.

The writer may wish to include recommendations as part of the conclusion or as a separate section. This should be done only when recommendations are a logical outgrowth of the material in the report and are obviously needed by the reader. For example, a lengthy analysis of safety conditions that concludes that hazards exist calls out for recommendations and perhaps even suggestions for implementation of the recommendations.

The conclusion section is much different from an abstract, although some people confuse the two.

THE SUPPLEMENTARY PARTS

The most common supplementary parts are the endnotes page, appendixes, bibliography, and the index. Supplementary parts are completed before the preliminary parts. The reason is that the page numbers for the parts at the end of the report are needed for the table of contents.

The supplementary parts include the endnotes, appendixes, bibliography, and the index.

Endnotes

Endnotes are synonymous with footnotes; the only difference is they are grouped at the end of the text. The first page is titled *Endnotes*. Endnotes are listed in the numerical order in which they are cited in the report.

Appendixes

An **appendix** contains material that is useful to the report but that might slow the reader if it appeared in the body. Items that would be part of an appendix are questionnaires, copies of interview questions, letters, memos, and other related (but not appropriate to the text) materials.

In a formal report, each appendix is preceded by a title page containing the label and the title of the appendix. Appendixes are lettered starting with *A* and placed in the order of their mention in the text. They are listed in the table of contents.

Bibliography

The bibliography is a list of the sources consulted in preparing the report, whether or not they are actually cited in the report. The bibliography assists the reader if additional information is needed; therefore, going beyond the sources cited can be useful. If all the sources are cited, the bibliography becomes a list of references.

Whether you use a bibliography or list of references, you can list your sources alphabetically either under one heading or under several subheadings. Subheadings classify your types of sources, such as books, periodicals, and government publications. The main title may be bibliography, references, or list of references.

Index

Used only in lengthy reports, the index is an alphabetical list of key topics. This list includes the page numbers for each topic. The index to this book is an example of the format. Ask yourself whether the reader would benefit from an index before deciding to include one in your report.

THE PRELIMINARY PARTS

The preliminary parts are the title page, authorization and transmittal documents, table of contents, and list of illustrations.

A variety of items can be presented in the preliminary parts; generally speaking, the more items that are included, the more formal the report is. Other items are dependent on the situation and content of the report —obviously a list of tables is used only when there are tables, for example. The following, although not an exhaustive list, includes most of the formal preliminary parts: title fly, title page, authorization document, transmittal document, table of contents, list of tables, list of figures (or a combined list of illustrations), and the abstract.

Title Fly

An optional part used in especially formal reports, the title fly contains only the report title. The title should be brief yet descriptive and should indicate either the report's depth or objective.

Title Page

Most business reports have a title page. This page contains at least the following information: the report title, the name (and perhaps the title) of the person the report was prepared for, the author of the report (perhaps with title), and the date.

Authorization Document

If your report was authorized in writing, a copy of the letter or memo authorizing you to undertake the report should accompany the report. Showing authorization will add credibility to your work. This document is likely to be found in more formal reports.

Transmittal Document

The transmittal document is also likely to be seen in more formal reports. This document—a letter or memo—transfers the report to the reader. The report recipient is likely to be the author of the authorization document; the author of the transmittal document (and the report) is probably the person authorized to do the report. These two items are closely related.

Authorization and transmittal documents are likely to be found in more formal reports.

A transmittal document should include the following:

1. The transmittal itself (first paragraph)
2. An overview of the report (second paragraph)
3. Optional acknowledgements to people who assisted in preparing the report (third paragraph)
4. A courteous closing that might discuss the next steps, express pleasure at providing the report, or indicate willingness to discuss the report in more detail (fourth paragraph)

Table of Contents

A required part of the formal business report is the table of contents. It lists all of the parts of the report except those appearing before the table of contents — list of figures, list of tables, appendixes, and bibliography, for example — as well as the first- and second-level headings in the text. Dotted lines, called leader lines, can be used to lead the reader's eyes across to the page number. The first table of contents page is titled *Contents*.

BOXED IN   *AN ETHICAL DILEMMA*

Margie learned the hard way about the supposed fair treatment of sub-ordinates at Quality Products. She recalls many occasions when she worked long and hard on reports, only to have her name removed from the title page and replaced with her supervisor's name. Even for reports in which she initiated recommendations to upper management she received no recognition or credit; her name did not appear on them. Margie is still bitter about that supervisor's getting credit for her work and ideas.

As it turns out, she realizes, she did benefit indirectly. Her supervisor was promoted to a better position and Margie has moved up to the supervisor's job.

This morning Margie received a subordinate's report to review. She sees that it proposes some much-needed changes in the manufacturing process. It is sure to catch Vice President Wilson's eye.

Now, she reminds herself, it is her turn to get some free accolades. She types a replacement title page, with her own name on it. She remembers how many times her own supervisor must have done exactly that. When it is time to take her subordinate's report to a meeting, however, she has not yet switched title pages.

Margie feels boxed in. What would you do?

List of Tables

If tables are included in the report, or even only one table, then a list of tables on a separate page should follow the table of contents. The list of tables includes table numbers, table titles, and numbers of the pages where they appear.

List of Figures

A list of figures is required if a figure or figures appear in the report. The list is not divided according to types of figures, such as graphs and charts. Rather, all figures are listed in order of their appearance in the report. The format is identical to the list of tables. The two lists are occasionally combined to create a list of illustrations.

Abstract

The **abstract**—which may also be called a synopsis, epitome, or executive summary — provides the reader with a summary of the entire text. The abstract may be considered the report in miniature; it is not simply the conclusions. An abstract (on a separate page) may help the receiver understand the text material before he or she reads it. Or it may be used as a time-saving summary after the entire report has been read. The single-spaced abstract has about a one-to-ten relationship to the text of the report, but it should seldom exceed one page.

   In writing your abstract, be informational and include some depth. Do not say, "Next we gathered some data and then analyzed them." Instead, give the reader a description with details, such as "Data were gathered by distributing by mail an anonymous questionnaire to 400 randomly selected employees. Of the 273 questionnaires returned, 63 percent ($n = 172$) were from blue-collar workers."

The abstract is normally single-spaced and should seldom exceed one page.

✓ CHECKLIST *for Writing Business Reports*

____▌ **Meet your goals in the body of the report.**

____▌ **Use headings correctly and consistently.**

____▌ **Support the text with tables and figures as appropriate.**

____▌ **Attribute sources of information.**

____▌ **Include necessary preliminary and supplementary parts.**

____▌ **Achieve an appropriate level of formality.**

____▌ **Be consistent in page treatments.**

____▌ **Produce an aesthetically pleasing product.**

THE ASSEMBLED REPORT

The chapter so far has discussed the writing of the text and preparation of the preliminary and supplementary parts. Now we are ready to put the report together. A formal report will have the following items, in this order:

Preliminary parts

Title fly*
Title page
Authorization document*
Transmittal document*
Table of contents
List of tables
List of figures
Abstract

Text (also sometimes referred to as the body)

Introduction
Body
Conclusion

Supplementary parts

Endnotes
Appendixes
Bibliography
Index*

*Especially found in formal reports.

Some additional instructions that may affect your writing and typing of the report involve pagination, spacing, and a cover.

Pagination

Briefly, **pagination** is the placement of page numbers on the pages. Knowing when, where, and which type of number to place on a page is often a problem.

Roman numerals are used for the preliminary pages.

The preliminary parts are treated differently from the balance of the report. You should count every page, but start your numbering with the table of contents. Thus, if the table of contents is the fifth page (after the title fly, the title page, the authorization document, and the transmittal document, each of which was counted but not numbered), it would be given the number *v*. This small Roman numeral is centered at the bottom of the page. The rest of the preliminary pages are numbered.

If a part, such as the table of contents, has more than one page, the page number moves to the upper right corner on the second and succeeding pages. It is always a small Roman numeral. The first page of the body is numbered with an Arabic number centered at the bottom. All pages after page 1 are numbered at the top of the page, probably in either the right corner or, less likely, centered. In any case, be consistent. An exception to this rule is when you start a major new section, such as a new chapter. The page number then is placed at the bottom, centered, on that page.

Do not use any punctuation or words with the page number. Use just the number 2, for example, and not *Page 2, -2-, 2., two*, or *"2."*

Spacing

Business reports are a combination of single and double spacing, as you will see in the complete report later in this chapter (Figure 11.1). Footnotes, for example, are single-spaced, with a space between citations. The text of the report may be either single- or double-spaced if you are consistent.

A double-spaced text promotes readability and leaves space for comments between lines. It also uses more paper, which may be important if many copies of your report will be duplicated. A single-spaced text adds an air of formality and precision while being more efficient. In reports, paragraphs are usually indented with typically five or eight spaces of indention.

Many organizations have standard formats for their reports (and letters and memoranda as well). You may be directed on which spacing is desired.

Cover

You may want to package your completed report inside a binder or prepare it with a special cover. Your organization may have printed covers for all reports. Covers can add uniformity, protection, and attractiveness.

Correct Procedures

As mentioned often in this chapter, two or more approaches may be acceptable or correct because authorities do not always agree and because organizations may have different goals for their reports. Different techniques have been presented when we thought they were important, such as the three attribution styles. There are, however, some other points on which experts differ. The bibliography is sometimes the first item in the supplementary parts. The abstract is sometimes placed before the table of contents in the preliminary parts; it is sometimes double-spaced. The table of contents does not always have leader lines and occasionally shows third- or even fourth-level headings. The page numbers for the additional levels may be given. There are other approaches to pagination, less often used, than the one described in the chapter. Some reports use numbers before headings, such as 1, 1.1, or 3.12. Other reports use a combination of numbers and letters before headings, such as 1, C, 2, a. Still other reports do not use these systems, but rely on the levels of the headings to help the reader.

Experts do not always agree on how to put together a report.

COMPUTER APPLICATIONS

With the widespread use of computers to prepare business correspondence, and especially business reports, the approach to preparing these reports and their appearance are changing. Even low-level word processing software allows authors to write sections of a report out of order and then use block moves to rearrange them. Sophisticated word processors enable the automatic generation of tables of contents, bibliographies, and indexes. The highest levels of word processors and desktop publishing packages facilitate multiple columns, varied typefaces and type sizes, and the inclusion of graphics within documents. The trend toward increasingly professional and attractive reports is sure to continue.

Computer technology is responsible for the trend toward increasingly attractive reports.

When using computers and word processors to prepare business reports, you should avoid using too many typefaces and sizes in your report. About four or five treatments is an upper limit. Make sure there is a good reason for including an element or feature. Do not include an index, for example, just because your computer system is capable of producing one.

Holding down a computer key repeats the character, making it easy to overdo characters. In preparing the leader lines in your table of contents, use period space period space rather than a series of periods, which overwhelm the viewer with unnecessary images. Use only a single question mark; more than one appears sophomoric. Use exclamation points sparingly or not at all. Running headers and footers, if used judiciously and appropriately, can improve the appearance and readability of lengthy reports. They should be unobtrusive.

If a report is to be duplicated on two sides of the paper, software can automatically modify the inside margin of varying left and right pages.

Perhaps most important of all, if you write sections of your report out of order and then rearrange them, be sure to prepare transitions for the newly sequenced items.

A SAMPLE BUSINESS REPORT

The complete business report in Figure 11.1 illustrates the writing principles discussed in this chapter. It does not present every part of a formal report, because some of them are incongruous and some duplicate others. Of the preliminary and supplementary parts, only the index — which is exemplified at the end of this book — is omitted.

Careful examination of the writing tone of the report, as well as the appearance of the parts, will guide you in preparing your business report.

This problem-solving report examines employee relations at Atlantic Electronics. Some items discussed earlier, such as outlines and tables, are used again in the report.

FIGURE 11.1 ▪ *Example of a Long Report*

EMPLOYEE RELATIONS PROBLEMS AT ATLANTIC ELECTRONICS:

NATURE, CAUSES, AND SOLUTIONS

Title Fly

FIGURE 11.1 ▮ *continued*

EMPLOYEE RELATIONS PROBLEMS AT ATLANTIC ELECTRONICS:
NATURE, CAUSES, AND SOLUTIONS

Prepared for
Scott Millan, Personnel Director
Atlantic Electronics

by

Stephanie McQuiston, Personnel Assistant

January 30, 1991

Title Page

FIGURE 11.1 ▪ *continued*

```
                                MEMO



        TO:        Stephanie McQuiston, Personnel Assistant

        FROM:      Scott Millan, Personnel Director

        DATE:      November 10, 1990

        SUBJECT:   Employee Relations Report Assignment

        As explained in our conversation this morning, I am directing you
        to research, analyze, and report on the current status of employee
        relations at Atlantic Electronics.  As members of the personnel
        office, we know there has been an increasing number of grievances
        reported to us, and the company grapevine is carrying more
        negative information than usual.

        You are to conduct research, both formal and informal, to
        adequately appraise the employee relations situation.  If the
        situation warrants it, analyze solutions to our problem and
        propose them to me.

        This matter is of major and immediate concern.  Therefore, I need
        your report by the end of January 1991.  You have a budget of
        $10,000 for supplies and can use the steno pool for duplication
        needs.  Bill Parsons, the new management trainee, is also assigned
        to you for this project.

        Do let me know if you encounter problems or have questions.
```

Letter of Authorization

FIGURE 11.1   ▮ *continued*

MEMO

TO: Scott Millan, Personnel Director

FROM: Stephanie McQuiston, Personnel Assistant

DATE: January 30, 1991

SUBJECT: Employee Relations Report

Here is the report you directed me to prepare on November 10, 1990.
The report researches employee relations problems at Atlantic Electronics, examines those problems, looks at solutions, and proposes
specific actions.

You will find that our employee relations problem is more serious
than you apparently thought when we discussed this project last
November. You'll want to pay particular attention to the implementation sections of the report for ways to overcome these problems.

This has been a most interesting project. I'll be pleased to discuss it with you, at your request.

Letter of Transmittal

FIGURE 11.1 ▪ *continued*

CONTENTS

v

Table of Contents

FIGURE 11.1   ∎   *continued*

LIST OF ILLUSTRATIONS

vi   *List of Illustrations*

FIGURE 11.1 ∎ *continued*

ABSTRACT

In the past five years, Atlantic Electronics has lost its
position of employee relations leadership in the electronics
industry. The purpose of this report is to analyze the current
employee relations situation, draw conclusions, and make recommendations for action. Investigation of the situation focused
on comparisons with companies in the industry, on our existing
records, and on an employee questionnaire. Atlantic Electronics
employees are showing an increased turnover rate internally and
as compared with the industry; they also cite a number of complaints. At the root of the discontent are inadequate rewards
and poor supervisory methods. To overcome some of its employee
disenchantment, Atlantic should offer more tangible and intangible rewards. Implementation of the recommendations would benefit
from hiring a consulting firm, starting a job rotation system,
initiating supervisor training, and planning future follow-up.

vii

Abstract

FIGURE 11.1   ▪ *continued*

EMPLOYEE RELATIONS AT ATLANTIC ELECTRONICS:
NATURE, CAUSES, AND SOLUTIONS

Problem Statement

For many years, Atlantic Electronics led the industry with its employee relations program. Recently, however, our leadership position is decaying. Our turnover rate is increasing, and many attributes associated with positive employee relationships are not being realized. The purpose of this report is to fully investigate the employee relations problem, to draw conclusions, and to recommend solutions to the problem.

Background

Atlantic Electronics is a mature and successful company. It has grown from 17 employees who produced vacuum tubes for radios to more than 2,000 employees who design and make 107 different electronics parts for home and commercial applications. Gross income has also increased dramatically: 1940 produced a gross income of only $140,000, compared to 1990's $17 million.

These increases have not been without inherent costs. President and founder Claude William Rasnor has reminisced about the good old days when the first employees were close socially as well as vocationally. Spouses of soldiers who died in World War II were voluntarily given pensions and other benefits.[1] Indeed, Atlantic Electronics was cited as a leader in the industry in low turnover rates only a few years ago.[2] As this report will show, however, employee relations are no longer at this high level.

Employee Relations in the Industry

One authority has stated that the electronics industry has led the country in positive employee relations for the last 50 years.[3] An examination of employee relations in the industry reveals the effects of good employee relations and the consequences of poor employee relations.

Effects of good relations. A company with good employee relations benefits both directly and indirectly. Direct results include higher quality,[4] harder work by employees,[5] fewer injuries and days lost,[6] and less absenteeism and tardiness.[7] Indirect benefits include cleaner work areas,[8] happier and more energetic employees,[9] and lower turnover rates.[10]

1

Page 1 of Body

FIGURE 11.1 ▪ *continued*

2

Consequences of poor relations. When a company does not have good relations, not only does it lose the positive benefits, but it also acquires negative consequences. Included among these negative consequences are employee-family problems, [11] poor public image, [12] sabotage of facilities, [13] leaks of corporate secrets, [14] and the likelihood of labor/management distrust and alienation. [15] Distrust and alienation break down the existing channels of communication. If no channels exist, a union is likely to seek admittance. [16]

Employee Relations at Atlantic Electronics

President Rasnor was always concerned with good employee relations. Since he started the company in 1940, he has maintained turnover rate records. Company records show three major clusters of turnover rates. For the 1940-1960 period, turnover was a mere 2 percent. For the 1961-1986 period, turnover rose to 6 percent, but this level was not considered especially serious.

Since 1987 our rate has been in the 20 percent and higher range. Because the rate had been creeping upward slowly since about 1973, the high level was not accurately recognized until recently. Particularly heavy demands on the company and the rapid changes in technology may have clouded the seriousness of the rate as well.

For the last seven years, under the direction of Louise Alexander, personnel manager, these rates have been compared with those of our three major competitors: Burns, Dominion, and Southern. The precise results of Alexander's record keeping are found in Table 1. Figure 1 illustrates the upward trend.

Table 1: Turnover Rates for Atlantic Electronics
and Selected Competitors, 1984-1989

Company	1984	1985	1986	1987	1988	1989
Atlantic Electronics	13	17	18	21	21	23
Burns	18	21	16	12	11	7
Dominion	15	14	17	13	12	15
Southern	17	24	18	16	15	16

Body *(Continued)*

FIGURE 11.1 ▪ *continued*

3

      Probably our fiercest competitor, the competitor closest to us in size, and the company most often compared to us, in Burns. For these reasons, we should examine our turnover rate as compared with that of Burns; this information appears in Figure 2.

      One can conclude from the information presented so far that good employee relations are to be sought, that there has been a major increase in turnover rates at Atlantic Electronics in the last six years, and that our turnover rates are rising while our major competitor's rates are constant or slightly improving.

      The balance of this report discusses the nature of the employee relations problem, examines its causes, presents solutions to the problem, and recommends implementation of specific solutions.

Body (Continued)

FIGURE 11.1 ▪ *continued*

4

<u>Nature of Atlantic Electronics' Employee Relations Problem</u>

Our immediate problem has five major components: The number of grievances is high, turnover rates are excessive, absenteeism in unacceptable, morale is low, and unionization appears imminent.

<u>Grievances</u>

The personnel office is the destination for formal employee grievances. In addition to either acting on the grievance itself or directing it to the appropriate person, the personnel office codes the severity of the grievance. For example, 1 is for a valuable and legitimate grievance, a zero denotes a neutral grievance, and a -1 is given if the grievance has no apparent value, logic, or point. The office admits this system is extremely subjective, and the office has kept the tally for only three years. However, in that three-year period, the ratio of 1-rated grievances per 100 employees per year has increased from 27 in 1988, to 41 in 1989, to 57 last year.

<u>Turnover</u>

Just knowing the rates of turnover is not enough. We also need to know the reasons for the turnover. Since the termination procedure for employees who choose to leave the company requires completion of separation forms, we know the stated reasons for turnover. The results of these inquiries are found in Figure 3. Almost three-quarters (72 percent) of the stated reasons for leaving were for one of three reasons: no job challenge, low pay, or no chance for promotion.

Body (Continued)

FIGURE 11.1 ▪ *continued*

5

Absenteeism

We define absenteeism as missing a day or more of work
without authorization by a superior on a TP-8 form or without
the knowledge or consent of the company. An employee may receive
permission to miss work, for example, in an emergency, by phoning
a superior. If an employee misses work, even for an emergency, but
does not notify a company representative, absenteeism is reported
to the personnel office.

This definition allows us to examine recent absenteeism
levels. Absenteeism rates from 1963 to 1983 did not vary from the
average for that period by more than 5 percent. In other words, in
that 20-year period, there was almost no variance in absenteeism.
Table 2 compares that rate to the last six years.

Table 2: Absenteeism Rates at Atlantic Electronics
for 1984-1989, Compared to the Preceding 20 Years

Days Lost per Employee by Year

Mean Absenteeism Rate 1963-1983	1984	1985	Annual Rate 1986	1987	1988	1989
4.4	4.6	5.1	5.4	6.0	6.8	7.2

Morale

In order to determine the current level of employee morale
and causes for employee dissatisfaction, a survey was distributed
to a random sample of 500 employees. (See Appendix A.)

Methodology. To select the 500 employees, we used our
computer file of all part- and full-time employees. The number
004 was drawn from a random number table. Every fourth name was
selected from the file.

Return rate. Surveys were mailed to employees' homes.
Of the 500 surveys distributed, 407 were returned completed, 9
were returned by the post office, and 3 were returned uncompleted.
The ratio of completed surveys to delivered surveys (407/491) is
83 percent.

When respondents were asked to rate their current morale
level on a scale of 1 to 5, with 1 being the lowest possible
score, the mean for all respondents was 1.8. One interpretation
is that any score less than 3.5, the mid-point on the scale, is
low morale. Clearly the 1.8 figure is low.

Body (Continued)

FIGURE 11.1 ▮ *continued*

Unionization

The electronics industry has relatively little unionization. There have been no overt efforts to keep unions out of the industry, and unions are most likely to emerge when conditions are poor; therefore we surmise that circumstances have not been ripe for unionization. However, in response to an open-ended survey question, 13 respondents mentioned unionization as the best way to improve working conditions and morale. Two comments stated that conversations have taken place with representatives of the Electronics Workers of America (EWA). For the first time in Atlantic's history, unionization appears a possibility. Studying the nature of the employee relations problem is not enough. Statistics about turnover and absenteeism are symptoms of more deeply rooted problems.

Causes of Atlantic Electronics' Employee Relations Problem

The employee survey focuses on the causes of employee relations problems. Two major categories of problems emerge from the survey results: inadequate employee rewards and poor supervisory methods.

Inadequate Employee Rewards

Question 2 in the survey asked respondents to check any item in a ten-item list that they believed was evident and important at Atlantic Electronics. Of the ten items, three were checked by over 50 percent of the respondents. Those three are (1) pay and benefits unsatisfactory, 71 percent; (2) work unfulfilling, 57 percent; and (3) feedback about performance nonexistent, 51 percent.

Poor Supervisory Methods

The survey also uncovered two items of major concern about supervisory methods: (1) inconsistent application of company rules and regulations and (2) lack of communication between supervisors and employees. Together they received a 50 percent notation level.

Evaluation of these survey results leads us to conclude that although pay and benefits are seen as low, nonmonetary concerns such as meaningful work, communication, and praise are also important. Our review of the nature of the employee relations problem and its causes brings us to solutions to the problem.

Body *(Continued)*

FIGURE 11.1 ▪ *continued*

7

<u>Solutions to Atlantic Electronics' Employee Relations Problem</u>

Employee concerns of unsatisfactory pay and benefits, unfulfilling work, lack of performance feedback, and inconsistent
application of company rules and poor superior/subordinate
communication are the causes of Atlantic Electronics' employee
relations problems. These problems have surfaced in increased
numbers of grievances, high turnover, high absenteeism, low morale, and discussion of unionization. The solution to employee
discontent has two parts: more intangible rewards and more
tangible rewards.

<u>More Intangible Rewards</u>

Intangible rewards are the most important aspect of the
solution package. Most of the employee complaints and concerns,
as uncovered by the employee survey, focused on the intangible
aspects of their work. This finding is not surprising, because
extensive research has shown that once a worker's basic needs
are met, the worker seeks other forms of compensation, such as
friendly working conditions, praise from supervisors, respect
from peers, and so on.[17] In improving the employees' intangible
rewards, we need to improve the jobs and provide more feedback
about employee performance.

Improving jobs. There are two aspects to improving the
employees' jobs: job enrichment and job rotation.

Improving feedback. The feedback improvement solution has
three elements: formal quarterly performance reviews, monthly
group feedback sessions, and informal daily feedback.

<u>More Tangible Rewards</u>

In addition to the improvements in intangible rewards,
Atlantic must provide increased pay and improved benefits.

Increased pay. The survey found that 71 percent of respondents checked low pay and poor benefits as major concerns. Although
the survey presents clear-cut conclusions about the concern, it
does not indicate the necessary amount of improvement. The
average pay at Atlantic Electronics is somewhat lower than the
industry average. For hourly employees, the industry average is
$11.05 versus our average of $10.45. For salaried employees, we
compare well with the industry: the industry average is $33,035
and our average is $31,985.[18]

Body *(Continued)*

FIGURE 11.1 ▪ *continued*

8

The electronics industry is highly competitive and there are many professional associations where employees can meet with peers in other companies and compare their career situations. There is also substantial pride associated with pay in the industry. We might conclude that the high level of concern over a relatively small difference between Atlantic and the industry is the result of frequent cross-industry communication and personal pride. Therefore, although we need to improve the pay scale, the increases need not be exorbitant.

Fringe benefits. The situation with fringe benefits is closely aligned with that of employee pay: frequent comparisons with the industry and personal pride account for much of the employee concern. Less than one year ago the Atlantic benefits package was compared to that of the industry in an internal report.[19] This report concluded that Atlantic is competitive with the industry in all areas except dental care, which is not included in our health insurance. About half of the companies in the industry provide dental care.

Implementation of the Solutions

Although Atlantic has a history of more than 50 years, which is relatively long in the electronics industry, it is still a newcomer to the diverse problems of rapid growth, expanded product lines, and technology. The interests of our employees, once exemplified as closeness and team spirit, have been lost recently. To regain this position, we must implement improvements in both intangible and tangible rewards. However, we need expertise from outside our company to guide us.

Hire Consulting Firm

A first step in improving jobs is to seek counsel on job-enrichment strategies. No one in our personnel office professes experience in job enrichment or formal performance review systems. Initial contact has been made with Felix Graham and Associates, the consulting firm Atlantic has retained for four years. A copy of its response to our inquiry is in Appendix B.

Begin Job Rotation System

For some time we have been contemplating a job rotation system. For the past 18 months the supervisors have met to propose how such a system would work. Their conclusion is that the system would be applied to all employees who are not classified

Body *(Continued)*

FIGURE 11.1 ▪ *continued*

9

E-3 (engineering specialist) or higher, and who wish to be rotated. All employees would spend at least one week a year in a
new job, to be determined jointly with their supervisor, and at
least one week a year in seminars, short courses, and instruction
for new jobs.

<u>Initiate Supervisor Training</u>

It is critical that we immediately initiate training sessions
for our supervisors to learn how to give effective formal and informal feedback. Amanda Lewis, a recent Ph.D. in psychology and
counseling whom we hired one month ago as an industrial psychologist, has expertise and interest in developing these sessions.

<u>Implement Follow-Up</u>

We must not allow Atlantic to come this close to disaster
again. We hope the implementation of the solutions outlined will
overcome the current crisis. But we must launch a three-part
follow-up system so we will not be caught off guard again. We
must (1) survey employees regularly, both through attitude surveys
and informally through discussions and interviews, (2) pay attention to what is happening in our industry in terms of pay and
benefits as well as other unexpected developments that might
affect the dedication of our employees to Atlantic Electronics,
and (3) stay even with — or even move ahead of — industry averages
for pay and benefits.

<u>Conclusions and Recommendations</u>

Atlantic Electronics has a proud history of employee relations. Recently, however, those relations have disintegrated as
evidenced by problems with grievances, absenteeism, morale, and
discussion of unionization. These symptoms, our employee survey
determined, are related to major concerns about intangible and
tangible rewards. To solve these problem we need to improve the
employees' jobs, provide more feedback, and enhance their pay and
benefits. Implementation of the solutions involves hiring a consulting firm, rotating jobs, training supervisors, and starting a
follow-up system.

If these solutions are implemented as outlined, Atlantic
should overcome its employee relations problems. The cost in
achieving positive employee relations will be high in dollars,
time, and effort. On the other hand, Atlantic cannot afford to
allow the situation to continue.

Body *(Continued)*

FIGURE 11.1 ▪ *continued*

ENDNOTES

1. Claude William Rasnor, <u>The History of Atlantic Electronics,</u>
<u>1940-1986</u> (New York: Executive Press, 1987), 25.

2. "A Review of the Industry," <u>Electronics Age</u>, December 1988,
134-145.

3. Mary Louise Harris, <u>Employee Relations in the Electronics</u>
<u>Industry: A Review</u> (Chicago: A. J. Smith & Sons, 1989), 421.

4. Harris, <u>Employee Relations</u>, 521.

5. Henry Rosenblum, "Work and Working Relationships,"
<u>Labor Quarterly</u>, Spring 1986, 83.

6. Sherry S. Quillan and Herman A. Quillan, "Injury in the Work
Place," <u>Labor-Management Review</u> 27 (March 1986): 330-340.

7. "Absenteeism and Tardiness," <u>Labor</u>, Fall 1987, 35-60.

8. Rosenblum, "Working Relationships," 85.

9. Harrison Smith, "An Examination of Happiness on the Job"
(Ph.D. diss., University of Texas at Austin, 1985), 221-254.

10. Harris, <u>Employee Relations</u>, 390.

11. "The Effect of Poor Employee Relations on Job Performance,"
in <u>Reflections on Employee Relations</u>, ed. Carlos S. Gonzalez
(New York: Prestige Press, 1985), 121-129.

12. "The Effect of Poor Employee Relations," 135.

13. Francis Lewis et al., <u>The New Management</u> (San Francisco:
Unicorn Publishers, 1989), 45.

14. William R. Armstrong, Vice President for Production,
Atlantic Electronics, personal interview, 12 December 1990.

15. Rosenblum, "Working Relationships," 89.

16. "When Unions Prefer to 'Make Their Move,'" <u>The Hickory</u>
<u>Times-Dispatch</u>, 18 April 1988, 3.

17. Smith, "Happiness on the Job," 207.

18. Company files and <u>U.S. Government Review of Employee</u>
<u>Income</u>, no. 114, April 1988, 1092-1107.

19. Personnel Office, Atlantic Electronics, <u>Fringe Benefits</u>
<u>Review</u> (Dover, Del., February 1990)

10

Endnotes
(University of Chicago Press Style)

FIGURE 11.1   ▪   *continued*

APPENDIX A

Employee Attitude Survey

You are being asked to respond to a few questions about
Atlantic Electronics. Only 500 employees are receiving this
survey; therefore, your response reflects the opinions of many
of your fellow employees. The survey will take about one minute
to complete, and your responses are anonymous. Use the enclosed
stamped, addressed envelope to return your survey.

The information we receive from this survey will be used to
determine employee concerns. In turn, knowing these concerns will
direct our attention to improving employee needs and benefits.
Thank you for your help.

1.   Please rate your current morale level on the following scale,
     with 1 as the lowest possible level and 5 as the highest
     possible level. Place a single check mark in one of the
     five locations. My current moral level is:

     _____ _____ _____ _____ _____
        1   2   3   4   5

2.   Listed below are ten items that relate to work conditions at
     Atlantic. Place a check mark beside any item that represents
     your feelings about your job.

     _____ Feedback about performance nonexistent

     _____ Working conditions dirty

     _____ Working conditions unsafe

     _____ Not enough training sessions

     _____ Pay and benefits unsatisfactory

     _____ No choice in shift assignment

     _____ Work unfulfilling

     _____ Plant too far from home

     _____ Poor parking situation

     _____ Uniforms not supplied

11

Appendix A

FIGURE 11.1 ▮ *continued*

12

3. Check any of the following items that you feel are current
    conditions at Atlantic.

    _____ No time to talk to supervisors

    _____ Lack of communication between supervisors and employees

    _____ Not allowed to talk to peers

    _____ Inconsistent application of company regulations

    _____ Employees don't seem to know their jobs

4. On the back of this sheet, write any comments that you think
    might improve employee relations.

Appendix A (Continued)

FIGURE 11.1 ▪ *continued*

APPENDIX B

<u>Letter from Felix Graham & Associates</u>

F E L I X *GRAHAM & ASSOCIATES*   *Management Consultants*
                                                   1414 Euclaire, Suite 100
                                                   Richardson, DE 18790

December 31, 1990

Ms. Stephanie McQuiston
Personnel Assistant
Atlantic Electronics
P.O. Box 138
Dover, DE 18717

Dear Ms. McQuiston:

As we discussed on the phone today, I am confirming our firm's interest in working with Atlantic Electronics on review, analysis, and redesign of a job enrichment program. I believe your president, Claude W. Rasnor, knows of our expertise in this area.

Our financial arrangements would follow our usual approach. Your annual retainer with us covers the first ten hours of consultation, and after that each hour is billed at $75.

We'll be pleased to visit you at the Dover location, at no cost to you, to discuss this project. Just let us know when you'd like to get together.

Cordially,

Felix Graham

Felix Graham
President

c: Claude W. Rasnor

13

Appendix B

FIGURE 11.1 ▪ *continued*

                              BIBLIOGRAPHY

"Absenteeism and Tardiness." <u>Labor</u> (Fall 1987).

Armstrong, William R., Vice President for Production, Atlantic
        Electronics. Interview, Dover, Delaware, 12 December 1990.

"The Effect of Poor Employee Relations on Job Performance."
        In <u>Reflections on Employee Relations</u>, edited by Carlos S.
        Gonzalez. New York: Prestige Press, 1985.

Harris, Mary Louise. <u>Employee Relations in the Electronics
        Industry: A Review</u>. Chicago: A. J. Smith & Sons, 1989.

Lewis, Francis, Jean Berry, and Mark Grippando. <u>The New
        Management</u>. San Francisco: Unicorn Publishers, 1989.

Personnel Office, Atlantic Electronics. <u>Fringe Benefits Review</u>.
        Dover, Delaware, February 1990.

Quillan, Sherry S., and Herman A. Quillan. "Injury in the Work
        Place." <u>Labor-Management Review</u> 27 (March 1986): 330-340.

Rasnor, Claude William. <u>The History of Atlantic Electronics,
        1940-1986</u>. New York: Executive Press, 1987.

"A Review of the Industry." <u>Electronics Age</u>, December 1988,
        134-135.

Rosenblum, Henry. "Work and Working Relationships." <u>Labor
        Quarterly</u>, Spring 1986, 71-90.

Smith, Harrison. "An Examination of Happiness on the Job."
        Ph.D. diss., University of Texas at Austin, 1985.

<u>U.S. Government Review of Employee Income</u>, no. 114, April 1988.

                                  14   ***Bibliography***
                                              (University of Chicago Press Style)

SUMMARY

This chapter examines the writing of the long business report. The report author needs to apply the characteristics of effective writing presented earlier in this text and then add headings, tables and figures, and documentation.

Once the body of the report is completed, supplementary and preliminary parts are added. The supplementary parts include endnotes, appendices, bibliography, and index. The preliminary parts are title fly, title page, authorization document, transmittal document, table of contents, list of tables, list of figures, and abstract. Only a very formal report would include all these parts; a report can be deformalized by leaving out some of these parts.

The appearance of a business report is important. The author should consider pagination, spacing, and a cover. When expertise, equipment, and the occasion permit, sophisticated computer software packages and laser printing can be used to create a professional image.

Key Terms

- **heading**
- **creeping elegance**
- **attribution**
- **superscript**

- **endnotes**
- **appendix**
- **abstract**
- **pagination**

Review Questions

1. Identify the treatments of the first four levels of headings.
2. Differentiate between the three frequently used attribution styles. What are their strengths and weaknesses?
3. What are the differences between a footnote, an endnote, and a reference?
4. What is pagination? How is it applied to a business report?
5. What are the differences between illustrations and appendixes?
6. Describe the preparation of an abstract.
7. What are some techniques for increasing or decreasing the formality of a business report?
8. What are the differences between a business report and a term paper?

Exercises

1. Working at the Grande Hotel in Miami Beach as a management trainee for the past four months has been exciting as well as educational. You enjoy your job and are pleased to be working with this hotel and in this fine location. Your business degree background and your specialization in hotel management of course helped prepare you for this position. But the on-the-job training is more beneficial than you had imagined.

One of the reasons you are optimistic about this position is that you work under the supervision of Harold Fenton, the hotel manager and part owner. He is a professional and a pleasant person as well. He gives you quite a bit of latitude in your job and is earnestly guiding you into professional hotel management. He has even told you that any area of hotel management is within your jurisdiction; you can talk to him about any problem you observe.

So far you have stayed fairly close to the problems and projects Fenton has assigned to you. Recently, however, you noticed a problem that you think should be brought to Fenton's attention.

Water is rather expensive in Miami Beach and of course your hotel uses thousands of gallons a day. Much of this water usage is from guests bathing. You know that about 88 percent of the hotel's water usage is in the guest rooms; the remaining 12 percent occurs in the hotel's kitchens, administrative offices, air conditioners, and so on. The swimming pool is not included in your analysis. At 95 percent occupancy, which is the level at which your hotel operates 10 months of the year (about 85 percent the other two months), the hotel uses an average of 70,000 gallons of water a day. There are 623 units in the hotel.

Recently, you noticed in a hotel management magazine an advertisement for a Super Water Sav'r showerhead. The showerhead is supposed to function on one-third the water of a standard unit, and it can be quickly adjusted by the user to provide a refreshing, pulsating stream of water as well. There is a sliding scale in the cost of the items:

Units	Cost per Unit
1–50	$20.00
51–100	18.50
100–500	17.50
Over 500	17.00

The hotel was built and the shower/tubs were installed 18 years ago. You assume the existing showerheads are functioning satisfactorily, because you did not uncover an unusual number of complaints about them in the hotel files.

The hotel is billed monthly for water by the city at the following commercial rates:

Gallons	Cost per Thousand
0–25,000	$1.75
25,000–50,000	1.53
50,000–100,000	1.31
Over 100,000	1.10

In appropriate report form, analyze the data and present your findings. State whether or not you recommend purchasing the Super Water Sav'r.

2. Permian Storage Tank Manufacturing Co. of Odessa, Texas, builds large oil storage tanks for oil companies in west Texas. Recently, the board of directors at Permian, under the recommendation of Jimmy Womack, president, decided to expand operations. The expansion plan encompasses building new tank-manufacturing plants in Longview, Texas, and near Carrizo Springs in south Texas. Located at the new plants will be branch offices.

Neither town is served by an airline. Permian Tank Corporation would like to purchase its own airplane to fly company executives and important customers between Odessa, Longview, and Carrizo Springs. You, as purchasing director for Permian, have been given the responsibility for conducting a survey and making a final recommendation.

For safety reasons, management would like to purchase some type of twin-engine, turboprop airplane. Because seven or more persons (not including pilots) may frequently be riding on the plane, management would like to have a cabin-class aircraft. Other required features are cabin pressurization, instrument flying capabilities, and the ability to take off and land on a runway with a length of 3,500 feet (which is the length of the strip at Carrizo Springs). The following information has been collected on various aircraft, all of which are pressurized, cabin-class, twin-engine, turboprop airplanes.

Manufacturer or Model	Maximum Number of Passengers	Maximum Cruise Speed (knots)	Takeoff and Landing Distance (feet)	Fuel Consumption (gallons per hour)	Price
Screech King Air	8	222	2261	60	$ 692,000
Pepper Indian	6	283	2480	65	707,000
Welstone Jet Prop Leader	8	290	2030	65	839,000
Screech King Air 100	13	248	2681	80	985,000
Conquest 2000	9	295	2465	80	995,000
Sakatawi Solitaire	9	321	1950	90	1,095,000
Rodgers Swift IIIB	9	309	3240	85	1,290,000

The distances between airports in nautical miles are Odessa to Longview, 370; Longview to Carrizo Springs, 340; and Carrizo Springs to Odessa, 240.

Write a report to Womack informing him of the results of your analysis. Include a recommendation of which aircraft should be purchased.

3. The National Bank of Ohio is considering adding more drive-up teller windows. Presently all 10 windows are used only during peak periods, such as Mondays and Fridays. However, at least eight of the 10 tellers are busy at all times.

Questionnaires were given randomly to 800 customers inside the bank and in the drive-up area. Of these, 411 were returned. The response was as follows:

1. How long have you been doing business with the National Bank of Ohio?

0–1 year	32	4–6 years	158
1–2 years	52	6–9 years	34
2–4 years	123	9 or more	12

2. What is the most important feature of the bank?

Location	142	Financial Service	150
Size	21	Other	19
Personnel	89		

3. How would you rate the overall performance of the bank?

Excellent	56	Poor	32
Good	135	Bad	14
Fair	174		

4. What type of account(s) do you have?

Commercial	123	Checking	190
Savings	162	Loan	56
Other	44		

5. How long does it usually take you to travel from your home to the bank?

0–5 minutes	41	13–17 minutes	104
5–8 minutes	67	17–22 minutes	20
8–13 minutes	171	More than 22 minutes	8

6. Where do you usually conduct your banking business?

Drive-up window	251	Mail	40
Inside the bank	105	Other	9

7. When you conduct your banking business, how rushed are you?

Terribly rushed	179	In no hurry	104
Somewhat rushed	128		

8. If you use the drive-up window, what is your average wait?

0–2 minutes	5	7–10 minutes	110
2–4 minutes	41	10–15 minutes	81
4–7 minutes	161	More than 15 minutes	13

9. If you see a teller inside the bank, how long is a typical wait?

0–2 minutes	7	7–10 minutes	41
2–4 minutes	43	10–15 minutes	12
4–7 minutes	65	More than 15 minutes	6

10. How often do you bank at the drive-up windows?

Less than once a month	14	Once a week	92
1–2 times a month	25	Twice a week	109
2–3 times a month	29	Three times or more	41

11. How often do you come inside the bank to conduct business?

Less than once a month	17	Once a week	41
1–2 times a month	191	Twice a week	30
2–3 times a month	101	Three times or more	31

12. How do you prefer to conduct banking business?

Drive-up window	297	Mail	14
Inside the bank	92	Other	8

13. Which day or days do you usually bank?

Monday	302	Thursday	117
Tuesday	103	Friday	383
Wednesday	88		

14. How do you rate the present drive-up window service as compared to other banks?

Excellent	61	Poor	71
Good	163	Bad	9
Fair	107		

Write a report to Baily Davis, executive vice president of the National Bank of Ohio. Your report should analyze the survey and make recommendations concerning the drive-up windows.

4. The vice president of personnel for a medium-sized firm has examined the records of the company's 50 secretaries to determine how many days each was absent on sick leave during the prior year.

The vice president needs to give the accounting department an estimate for the budget of expenses for hiring temporary help, and he has asked you to analyze the data to produce this estimate. He is interested in knowing the total number of days missed, the average number of days missed, the variation from the average, the median number of days missed, and how many days were most commonly missed. The number of days missed is as follows:

5	3	15	21	3	28	17	16	13	1
20	1	0	3	8	2	9	19	15	0
6	9	3	5	10	0	11	2	3	3
10	2	8	4	5	1	3	0	9	12
10	8	10	4	1	3	6	3	8	5

Analyze the data and prepare it for a report.

CASE | *Sunny Orange Juice*

Robert J. Olney, Southwest Texas State University

As you arrive at Bennett Food Products on Monday morning, you cannot resist stopping to look at the sign on the door of your new office. Below your name is the title Assistant Advertising Manager. While you are admiring this visible evidence of your success, Mary Poplin, advertising manager, calls you into her office to confirm a rumor you have heard: the company wants to test the effectiveness of television advertising for Sunny Orange Juice. Sunny Orange Juice is a frozen concentrate of 100 percent natural juice and has had excellent acceptance in a limited test market. You are to make a media recommendation, and it is the first opportunity to prove yourself in your new position.

From your educational background and work experience, you know that such decisions normally require extensive study, but you also realize that the relatively young company cannot afford a costly study at this time. You spend only a few minutes in thought before outlining this plan of attack for the project:

1. Contact three area television stations that represent the three national networks to determine the advertising time periods that are available.
2. Determine the viewer popularity of the shows around the available time periods.
3. Determine characteristics of the audience you want to appeal to in your television campaign.
4. Informally analyze characteristics of the audience viewing programs during each of the available times. Include age, sex, and marital status in your analysis.
5. Analyze the products currently advertised on these shows to determine the buying motives that current product advertising appeals to.
6. Produce a report that analyzes secondary and primary data that will help top management make its decision.

You call the area television stations to determine the commercial time periods that are available and discover that each station has a 30-second time period (listed as Eastern Standard Time) available in the prime viewing time: ABC, 8:15 Monday; CBS, 9:45 Friday; and NBC, 8:15 Wednesday.

Case Questions

1. Using your preliminary outline, begin your investigation.

2. Add to your preliminary outline any other factors you believe should be considered in the analysis of a time period.

3. In determining viewer popularity for the shows in the available time slots, you may want to trust the Nielsen ratings of the shows (published weekly in Wednesday's edition of *USA Today*), or you may want to conduct your own telephone survey of the households in your area. If you elect the second alternative, carefully plan your telephone interview. Be prepared for a variety of responses.

4. Determine the cost for 30 seconds at the time available at each of the networks. This information is published in *Standard Rate and Data Service*.

5. Use as many sources as possible to get other information to support your recommendations.

6. Present your problem data, analysis, conclusions, and recommendations in a report format specified by your instructor.

Breaking the Lockstep | CASE

James M. Lahiff, University of Georgia

Curriculum development is a controversial topic in many schools. Administrators and faculty members devote much time and energy to developing the curriculum, but the results rarely satisfy everyone.

You attend Midwest State, where students must take many required courses. The program, known as the lockstep sequence, has been the subject of many student complaints. Most students believe that the program should be more flexible and that students should be allowed to select more of their courses.

Midwest State has decided to seek ideas from the students regarding possible changes in the program. The idea of allowing students to structure more of their program is under consideration. You have been appointed to the program evaluation committee, a group assembled to provide student input on this matter.

As a member of the program evaluation committee, you must select eight courses you believe would make up a good program for you. Prepare a report to be sent to the chairperson of the program evaluation committee. In this report describe eight specific courses and your rationale for including each one. Indicate what you consider to be the goal of your program and how each course contributes to that goal.

Use as many sources as possible to get the information necessary for this report. Interview professors, administrators, and other students. Perhaps someone in a field in which you hope to work would have some insights on the subject. Also, review the catalogs of other colleges that may be available in your college library. Use your imagination in developing your program. The courses that you suggest need not be presently available at your school.

Case Questions

1. Why did you organize your report the way that you did?
2. Describe one other way in which you might have organized it.

Instructions, Documentation, and Policy and Procedure Statements

"Pardon me. I'm new here. I'm trying to get to the mailroom and I'm lost. Which way is it?"

"Yes, you are lost, but no problem. Take the elevator to the basement, G-2, go left down a long hallway until you get to a door with a funny poster on it, then take the next right, go until you hear the noise from the envelope sorting machine, and you're there."

"Thanks, I think I can find it now."

You did find the mailroom, of course, but only after spending 25 minutes lost and frustrated by the instructions you received. As a new employee, how were you supposed to know that not all elevators go to the basement? What did the person mean by a "funny" poster? You saw several posters in the hallway. Some were humorous and others strange. And what does an envelope sorting machine sound like? If only you had been given *good* instructions . . .

Anyone who has been frustrated by ambiguous **instructions** recognizes the importance of clearly conveying this form of information. On the job, instructions may be delivered orally from a superior on how to do a task, presented in a manual on how to use computer software, or given formally, in a policies and procedures booklet that details operations procedures. Whether written or oral, formal or informal, good instructions have common characteristics. This chapter discusses these characteristics and then relates them to two main applications: (1) documentation and (2) policies and procedures.

CHAPTER 12

Learning Objectives

1 To learn the five guidelines for giving good instructions.

2 To become aware of how instructions are used in business in documentation and policies and procedures.

3 To understand the nature of objectives, policies, and procedures.

4 To learn the five questions that a policy or procedure statement should answer.

5 To learn the correct format for writing instructions, policies, and procedures.

6 To understand the application of characteristics of effective written communication to writing instructions, policies, and procedures.

FIVE GUIDELINES FOR GIVING GOOD INSTRUCTIONS

Good instructions have five characteristics.

Good instructions are unambiguous, understandable, complete, consistent, and efficient. Each of these characteristics is a guideline for the writer.

1. Avoid Ambiguity

The more concrete your instructions, the better. Rather than "Turn at the big tree," say "Turn left at the large oak tree that has a 'House for Sale' sign on it." Writing with clarity avoids words that have multiple meanings or little meaning. Precision is an important aspect of clarity.

2. Be Understandable

Instructions should relate to the receiver. Target your audience with your message. If you are preparing computer systems documentation, you need to decide on your audience's level of familiarity with the system. Jargon and acronyms may be appropriate with some audiences and inappropriate for others. Instructions can also be made more understandable with short sentences, familiar words, and good transitions.

3. Be Complete

Instructions can be clear and understandable but still fail if they are incomplete. Leaving out an important step in a task procedure may result in failure to complete the task. In addition to identifying all central steps or elements in your instructions, anticipate possible problems or questions that may arise.

The next time you read a newspaper or news magazine, note that most stories begin by answering many of these basic questions: Who? What? When? Where? How? Why? Here is an example:

> The U.S. Census Bureau unknowingly distributed a virus-infected floppy disk to 350 research libraries, the agency revealed last week. The disk, which allows IBM PC users to read data on the Census County and City Data Book CD-ROM, contained the Jerusalem-B virus, which infects any .COM or .EXE programs, according to a warning notice from the Government Printing Office.[1]

These sentences tell us who (Census Bureau), what (distributed), when (last week), where (from the printing office to 350 libraries), and how (unknowingly), and indirectly answers why (not on purpose).

As a partial test of the completeness of your instructions, you may wish to ask yourself these six questions.

---

[1]Scott Mace, "Census Bureau Finds Virus in Research Disk," *InfoWorld*, February 5, 1990, 3.

4. Be Consistent

Much as parallel structure in sentences improves understanding, so does consistency in giving instructions. Know the different levels of your instructions and make those levels obvious to your receiver. For example, in written instructions, treat each major step similarly, each substep in a consistent fashion, and so on. Each major step might start a new page, have the same typeface treatment and white space, and start with an overview.

5. Be Efficient

Efficiency means to achieve the other four guidelines while holding the length of the instructions to an absolute minimum. Efficiency can be difficult because clear, unambiguous, understandable, consistent instructions are likely to be lengthy. Nevertheless, seek ways to minimize your instructions. For example, starting each of seven steps with the phrase, "Your next step in accomplishing your task is to . . ." is inefficient. Instead, use a similar phrase once, follow it with a colon, and then list all seven steps.

Efficiency can often be achieved through the use of overviews that give the parameters of the instructions, such as, "Installing this software involves three main steps and takes about eight minutes. Before you can install the software, however, you must know your serial number and the amount of RAM memory installed in your computer." Overviews avoid the inefficiency of getting part way through a set of instructions before learning you do not have the necessary equipment or information to complete the task.

Two types of relatively formal instructions you are likely to encounter in business are documentation and policies and procedures.

WRITING INSTRUCTIONAL DOCUMENTATION

The establishing of proof, information, evidence, or sequence, usually in written form, is called **documentation**. After a business trip, you will be asked to document your travel expenses, perhaps on an expense voucher, before you can be reimbursed. Or you may decide to protect yourself from challenges in the future by putting in writing your request to your superior for a quieter office because your clients cannot hear you on the phone, which reduces your performance.

Documentation usually is written.

The form of documentation of most interest here is instructional documentation. Instructional documentation might be computer systems operational guidelines, job or specific task instructions, or software manuals. The main purpose of instructional documentation is to teach a sequence of activities or to serve as a reference for instructions. Recent software manuals are typically divided into at least these two parts, often called "User's Manual" and "Reference Manual." In this way, information that is usually examined only once or twice during the learning process is kept separate from reference information used frequently over the long term.

As you organize your documentation assignment, in addition to applying the five guidelines, also consider how the information will be used by your audience. An airplane pilot refers to a list of necessary behaviors and conditions each time before takeoff. A word processing specialist refers to a "Quick Help" guide to refresh the memory of a seldom-used keystroke command. A computer user looks up "Fatal Error #107" only when a certain system malfunction occurs. A new employee follows a tutorial prepared by his or her predecessor to learn a complicated task. A job applicant examines a job description to evaluate interest in the position. Each of these documents has a different, focused goal based on anticipated audience use.

The quality of documentation should be checked.

In preparing documentation, you may wish to refer to this list of questions:

- What is the goal of the documentation?
- Am I writing to a single user or a group of users?
- Will the user refer to this documentation more than once?
- How long should this version of the documentation be used? (What is its lifespan?)
- Would a glossary be helpful?
- Should I pilot test the documentation on a naive user?
- Is the writing level appropriate for the lowest level user?
- Should I include an index?

The second major application of instructions in business is policies and procedures statements.

THE NATURE OF OBJECTIVES, POLICIES, AND PROCEDURES

Every business is obviously concerned about its own success. In establishing and maintaining a successful operation, the owners or managers of the business set objectives and goals. **Objectives** are generalized purposes toward which the entire organization strives. Goals are the foundation upon which the organization is based. Examples of general objectives include these:

- Maximizing net profits
- Keeping employees satisfied
- Keeping customers satisfied
- Maximizing market share
- Being of service to the community

Not all organizations — nor authorities on organizations — agree on how specific objectives should be. All seem to agree, however, on the necessity of having objectives (which are also called goals, missions, principles, or purposes). Objectives may vary from one organization to another by stability, constancy, and how well known they are.[2]

---

[2]David R. Hampton, Charles E. Summer, and Ross A. Webber, *Organizational Behavior and the Practice of Management*, 3d ed. (Glenview, Ill.: Scott, Foresman, 1978), 313–318.

Objectives perform five critical functions for the organization:

1. They provide orientation by depicting a desired future state of affairs.
2. They set down guidelines.
3. They constitute a source of legitimacy that justifies the organization's activities and its existence.
4. They serve as standards by which success can be assessed.
5. They represent a sought-after state, not one that is already available.[3]

Figure 12.1 contains an example of corporate objectives. Although they change from time to time, objectives are intended to channel the efforts of all employees toward similar ends. Yet, because they are so generally worded, objectives do not provide much guidance to employees in terms of exactly how to meet them. There are many different means to one end. Thus, policies and procedures must be written.

Policy Defined

A **policy** is a general guide to decision making and reflects the organization's attempts to achieve its goals. Policies are the framework, consistent with organizational objectives, that helps managers make decisions. Yet a policy is only a guideline, as it usually gives the manager some degree of discretion in making decisions. Here are some examples of policies as they relate to objectives:

Objective	Policy
Keeping customers satisfied	If any customer is dissatisfied with a purchase, then his or her money will be refunded.
Being of service to the community	Managers will use every opportunity to become involved in community services such as the United Way, the Heart Fund, and the American Cancer Society.
Keeping employees satisfied	All promotions to managerial positions will be from within the company.

Policies help put objectives into operation.

As you examine these policy statements, notice that they provide for discretion or flexibility in decision making. For example, the community service policy does not tell the manager which or how many community organizations to join, nor does it specify how extensively the manager should be involved in any one organization.

You'll find that the higher you move in a business, the more discretion you will probably have. Policy statements for top-level management are usually worded more generally than those that are used at lower levels.

---

[3]Amitai Etzioni, *Modern Organizations* (Englewood Cliffs, N.J.: Prentice-Hall, 1964), 3.

FIGURE 12.1 ▪ *General Motors' Mission Statement*

GENERAL MOTORS MISSION

The fundamental purpose of General Motors is to provide products and services of such quality that our customers will receive superior value, our employes and business partners will share in our success, and our stockholders will receive a sustained, superior return on their investment.

GENERAL MOTORS GUIDING PRINCIPLES

- We will establish and maintain a Corporation-wide commitment to excellence in all elements of our product and business activities. This commitment will be central to all that we do.
- We will place top priority on understanding and meeting our customers' needs and expectations.
- General Motors is its people. We recognize that GM's success will depend on our involvement and individual commitment and performance. Each employe will have the opportunity, environment, and incentives to promote maximum participation in meeting our collective goals.
- We recognize that our dealers, suppliers, and all our employes are partners in our business and their success is vital to our own success.
- We recognize that a total dedication to quality leadership in our products, processes, and workplaces is of paramount importance to our success.
- We are committed to sustained growth which will enable us to play a leading role in the worldwide economy.

- We will continue to focus our efforts on transportation products and services, both personal and commercial, but will aggressively seek new opportunities to utilize our resources in business ventures that match our skills and capabilities.
- We will offer a full range of products in the North American market and participate with appropriate products in other markets on a worldwide basis.
- We will maintain strong manufacturing resources at the highest levels of technology and be cost competitive with each manufacturing unit.
- We will operate with clearly articulated centralized policies with decentralized operational responsibilities to keep decisions as close to the operations as possible.
- We will participate in all societies in which we do business as a responsible and ethical citizen, dedicated to continuing social and economic progress.

Source: Courtesy of General Motors Corporation.

Figure 12.2 shows the amount of discretion given management levels in a small manufacturing plant.

Advantages of Policies

Policies have three main uses.

Policies help to implement objectives. There are other advantages of policies as well, especially when they are in written form. First, policies enhance consistency in decision making. Second, conflict among employees may be prevented. Finally, policies can save time. Policies keep managers from having to make the same decision over and over again.

Disadvantages of Policies

Despite the advantages of policies, they are not usually created for every decision. First, it is almost impossible to write a policy for every set of circumstances. To do so would require amazing foresight and would probably result in a policy manual hundreds of pages long (which many managers would not read). Second, although policies promote consistency in decision making, at the same time they reduce the amount of flexibility decision makers have. Exceptions to nearly every policy exist, and their existence often creates frustrated reactions.

Policies, then, are general guides to decision making. They are created to help a business accomplish its objectives. If more specific decision-making guides are wanted, then procedures are written.

Procedure Defined

A **procedure** is a specific guide to decision making, a tool for implementing a policy. While the general wording of a policy allows discretion in making decisions, procedures provide little or no discretion. When procedures give discretion, they are called **guides**. If no discretion is allowed, then the procedure is a **rule**. The example below shows this distinction.

Guides differ from rules.

Objective	Policy	Procedure (Guide)	Procedure (Rule)
Keeping customers satisfied	If any customer is dissatisfied with a purchase, then his or her money will be refunded.	Check the returned merchandise carefully to see if it has been misused.	The customer must sign the refund slip.

For this one objective we could develop a long list of both guides and rules. However, notice first that the guide listed gives the employee discretion, whereas the rule does not. Second, notice how the chart moves from the general (the objective) to the specific (the rule). The farther we go toward the right side of the chart, the more control we exert over the behavior of our employees.

Not all businesses have written policies and procedures.

You may have worked for a company that had no written policies or procedures: many businesses do not. The larger a firm is, the more written

FIGURE 12.2   ■   *Example of Differing Amounts of Discretion Allowed by a Policy Statement*

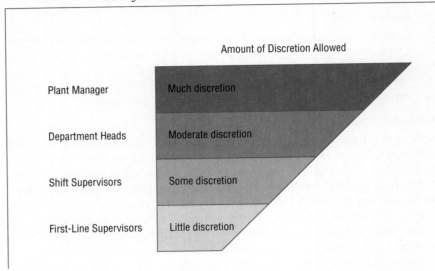

BOXED IN   *AN ETHICAL DILEMMA*

"Ralph, it's company policy," said Paul, leaning back in his chair. "I can't help what they do in other departments."

"But, Paul, I've got a lot of unhappy people down there," Ralph responded. "When they called in, I told them we'd pay them only for the hours they put in. And Jean is paying all of her people for a whole day. Some of her folks didn't get here till three o'clock."

"I know," Paul replied. "Look, Ralph, this happened once before — long before you got here. Must have been 15, maybe 16 years ago. We had a terrible storm. Ice on the roads . . . hanging from the trees. Believe me, the whole town was just dead. But you know, we had 10 or 15 faithful employees show up, some of them after lunch. And that's when the man upstairs decided to give a full day's pay in circumstances like this. Jean knew about it because she was one of those people who got paid."

"Is that written down somewhere?" Ralph asked.

"The policy?"

"Yeah."

Paul shook his head. "I doubt it. We've got enough company policy, rules of conduct, standard operating procedures, and the like in writing as it is. Look, Ralph, I'm sorry you didn't get the word. But it's simple. Your people stayed home. They get paid nothing. If they'd shown up at even four o'clock, we'd have paid them for the whole day. But they didn't. Now you're going to have to work this out with them as best you can."

Ralph feels boxed in. What would you do?

policies and procedures (sometimes called standard operating procedures, or SOPs) the firm usually will have. You will also find that if the business has unionized employees, then no matter how large or small it is, most policies and procedures will be contained in what is called the labor agreement or contract.

Figure 12.3 shows part of a policy statement that includes procedures. Other terms than objectives, policies, and procedures may be used in corporate statements, and these three items may be written in a single statement, but the final test of the statement is whether it is clear, understandable, and ultimately followed.

WRITING POLICIES AND PROCEDURE STATEMENTS

As you pursue your career in business, you will most likely be involved in writing policies and procedures in one of three instances: (1) when a new business is formed; (2) when a new policy or procedure is needed; or (3) when old policies or procedures are being rewritten. You will probably have a chance to write policies and procedures on a variety of topics, including promotion and pay policies, actual work procedures for performing a task, and employee grievances and discipline.

Many organizations have policies and procedures for hiring new employees, ensuring employee safety, disciplining employees, hearing employee grievances, handling customers, dealing with employee absences, and evaluating employees. You can see from this list that most policies and procedures affect the internal operation of a company.

As you write your policies and procedures, apply the five guidelines presented earlier. Note how this partial policy–procedure is concrete, understandable, complete, consistent, and efficient:

Sick Leave Policy. As an employee of Burns Chemical Company you are allowed time off with pay when you are unable to work because of illness. Pay for sick leave is for the sole purpose of protecting you against loss of income when you are ill.

Procedure

1. If you are sick and unable to work, you should call your supervisor at least one hour before your shift begins.
2. If you are unable to work for three or more days in a row, then you must bring a note from your doctor on the day you return to work. This note should be given to your supervisor.

Although this example is only part of a sick leave policy and procedure, it clearly tells the employee *who* is involved (the employee, the supervisor, and possibly a doctor). *What* is a telephone call and bringing a physician's note. Two *whens* are in the procedure — one hour before the shift begins and the day the employee returns to work. The *how* is implicit in this procedure because it links the answers to the first three questions. *Why* is answered in the policy statement. Note also that the statement is consistent.

An effective policy/procedure answers five basic questions.

FIGURE 12.3   ▪   *Administrative Order*

STATE DEPARTMENT OF HIGHWAYS AND PUBLIC TRANSPORTATION	
Administrative Order No. 17-86	
SUBJECT	Department Written Communications
TO	Deputy Directors, District Engineers and Division Heads
REFERENCE	A.O. No. 35-81

Par. 1. Purpose
2. Effective Date
3. Supersedes
4. General Information
5. Engineer-Director Communications
6. Department Correspondence
7. Motor Vehicle Information Circulars
8. Attachment

AO 17-86
June 1, 1986
D-7

1. Purpose

To establish policy governing the format, intent and use of Department administrative written communications.

2. Effective Date

Administrative Orders — June 1, 1986; Other - July 1, 1986

3. Supersedes

Administrative Order No. 35-81.

4. General Information

Intradepartment communications transmitting policy, procedures or instructional/informational data are to be prepared in the style used in this order. It will not apply to technical data changes or legal documents.

Correspondence of a personal nature and Department external communications will be prepared in letter format.

With exception of correspondence prepared for the Engineer-Director's signature, documents should bear the typed initials of the originator.

5. Engineer-Director Communications

The documents listed below are published over Engineer-Director signature and are used to communicate directives and information within the Department. They are prepared on white paper stock with preprinted headings as shown on the Attachment and printed on the colors of paper described below. Detailed formatting guidance for the preparation of the documents shall follow by Administrative Circular.

(Continued)

Source: Texas State Department of Highways and Public Transportation, Austin, Texas, June 1, 1986.

Engineer-Director Communications	• Administrative Orders are for use by the Engineer-Director to communicate Department directives and policies. Orders shall be typeset after approval and prior to Engineer-Director signature. Printing is on white paper stock.
	• Administrative Circulars are used for communicating procedures and guidance and are printed on pink paper.
	• Manual Change Transmittals are used to transmit revisions to Department and Division manuals and are printed on buff paper. A summary of changes is included in the text and/or as an attachment.
	• Newsletters are used by the Engineer-Director to communicate items of interest to employees of the Department such as personnel matters, promotions, retirements, etc. Printing is on green paper.
	• Department Management by Objectives documents are printed on yellow paper and are transmitted by Administrative Circular.
6. Department	The signature level for Department correspondence should be determined by the position or level of authority of the receiver. Consideration may also be given to the significance, impact or sensitivity of the subject matter on Department operations.
	Correspondence between Deputy Directors/Districts/Divisions shall be addressed to and carry the signature of the respective Deputy Director, District Engineer or Division Head. Exception is made when signature authority for such correspondence has been delegated or the correspondence is addressed below the executive manager level. The signature block on all correspondence should be that of the signer.
	Courtesy copies of correspondence addressed to ALL Districts and/or Divisions shall be provided the Engineer-Director, the Deputy Directors and the Internal Review and Audit Section.
7. Motor Vehicle Information Circulars	Instructions to county tax assessor-collectors are published and distributed by the Director, Division of Motor Vehicles.
8. Attachment	Preprinted headings.

M. G. Goode

M.G. Goode
Engineer-Director

The two characteristics of a policy and procedures statement format are (1) policies appear first, then procedures, and (2) procedures are listed step by step.

As you write policy and procedure statements, you will often find that more than one policy is covered by a given procedure. If this is the case, you will want to list all those policies first, then follow them with the procedures. The following example expands the sick leave policy we used earlier:

Sick Leave Policies. As an employee of Burns Chemical Company, you are allowed time off with pay when, because of illness, you are unable to work. Pay for sick leave is for the sole purpose of protecting you against loss of income when you are ill.

✔ CHECKLIST *of Indications That an Organization Would Benefit from Policy/Procedures Statements*

___ Does the organization have frequent personnel changes between jobs?

___ Is the turnover rate of employees high?

___ Do supervisors realize that people have memory limitations?

___ Are many activities complex and often repeated?

___ Do supervisors tend to formalize communication by "writing things down"?

___ Do supervisors or trainers have to repeat instructions?

___ Do employees forget important steps in complex tasks?

___ Do employees complain they did not know certain steps were required as part of a procedure?

1. You are allowed 18 paid sick days per calendar year.
2. If you do not need all of your sick leave days during a year, then you may add the days you don't use to your next year's total. A maximum of 90 paid sick leave days can be saved.

Procedures
1. If you are sick and unable to work, you should call your supervisor at least one hour before your shift begins.
2. If you are unable to work for three or more days in a row, then you must bring a note from your doctor on the day you return to work. This note should be given to your supervisor.

In this example the first policy may seem to be a procedure because it appears to be a rule. However, remember that procedures are specific guides to decision making. They tell us how to take action to implement a policy.

When writing procedures, you should organize them step by step. Often, following procedures results in an end product of some kind. Therefore, to be sure that the product is correct, you should organize and label the steps clearly:

Customer Refunds Policy. If any customer is dissatisfied with a purchase, then his or her money will be refunded.

Procedures
1. Check the customer's sales slip. Only the store manager may authorize returns on merchandise the customer has had for more than 30 days.
2. Fill out the customer refund slip, making sure that you enter:
   a. Customer's name and address
   b. Date of purchase
   c. Stock number and description of merchandise

      d. Sales number of salesperson who sold the merchandise

      e. Your sales number

      f. Reason for return

  4. Take the customer refund slip to your immediate supervisor, who will approve the refund.

  5. Have the customer sign the customer refund slip.

  6. Refund the customer's money:

      a. If the purchase was by credit card, then tell the customer his or her account will be credited with the amount of purchase. Do not make cash refunds on credit card purchases.

      b. If the purchase was by cash, then refund the customer's money from your cash register drawer. Place the audit copy of the credit refund slip in the drawer.

  7. Take the remaining copies of the credit refund slip and the returned merchandise to the customer service department.

Each step in the procedure requires a different action. Ideally, no two acts (unless they are closely connected, as in 6b) should be described in one step.

    Typically, policies and procedures should follow this format:

- General policy
- Specific policies (1, 2, 3, etc.)
- Procedures (1, 2, 3, etc.)

    As a business person, you will likely be aware of your organization's goals, will be required to align with its policies, and may take part in formulating its procedures. The better you understand the roles and interrelationships of these statements, the better you will respond to their purposes.

SUMMARY

Giving good written and oral instructions in business is crucial. These instructions should achieve the guidelines of avoiding abstract language, being understandable, being complete, achieving consistency, and being efficient. Business instructions can be divided into two main categories: documentation and policies and procedures.

    Documentation is typified by software manuals, job instructions, and task instructions. Policies and procedures are guides to decision making. They are intended to help a business meet its objectives by providing guidelines for more consistent decision making. Few people want to consult a policy or procedure manual, but they will be more inclined to do so if, when you write your policy and procedure statements, you apply three specific guidelines:

1. Answer every possible question about the behavior wanted.

2. Follow an appropriate and consistent format.

3. Give careful attention to your receiver as you apply the qualities of effective written communication.

Key Terms

■ **instructions**   ■ **procedure**

■ **documentation**   ■ **guide**

■ **objective**   ■ **rule**

■ **policy**

Review Questions

1. What are the guidelines for giving good instructions?

2. What questions might you ask as you write documentation?

3. Explain the differences among an objective, a policy, and a procedure.

4. What is the role of discretion in writing policies and procedures?

5. Describe two basic kinds of procedures.

6. What questions does an effective policy and procedure statement answer?

7. What is the proper format for a policy and procedure statement? Describe it in detail.

Exercises

1. Locate some software instruction manuals that are five or more years old. Compare them to some recently written manuals. Is there a difference? Have manuals improved over time? How?

2. Locate a software instruction manual that gives poor instructions. Why is it poor? How would you rewrite it to improve it?

3. Find a policy and procedure statement in the student handbook for your college or university.
a. Evaluate the statement using the guidelines in this chapter.
b. If the statement does not meet all the guidelines, rewrite it so that it does.

4. You work for a company that has decided to begin an employee suggestion system. Employees who submit useful suggestions will receive cash awards. Write a policy and procedure statement for all the hourly employees to follow in participating in the new system.

5. Write a set of instructions about one of the following:
a. How to change an automobile tire.
b. How to change a typewriter ribbon.
c. How to fold and place a letter in an envelope.

6. Write a policy statement for each topic:
a. Employee vacations.
b. Employee coffee breaks.
c. Employee safety.

7. Choose one of the policy statements you wrote in Exercise 6 and write a set of procedures for it.

8. Write a set of instructions for some simple task one of your classmates might perform in class (for example, folding papers, working with columns of

numbers). Give the procedures to a classmate and see how well that person can follow your instructions.

What Is the Policy? | CASE

David B. Parsons. Lakehead University, Thunder Bay, Ontario, Canada

Varsity Sports Inc. is a local sporting goods store. During the last week of July, it was selling baseball equipment for half price. Grady Cowan stopped by the store after work to buy a catcher's mitt for his son. Cowan normally pays cash for everything he buys.

This time, however, he paid by check. He asked the cashier whether he could return the mitt for refund if it was the wrong size. Being assured that he could return the mitt as long as he had the receipt, Cowan wrote a check for $69.95.

When he returned the mitt the next day, a new cashier was on duty. She told Cowan that he would have to wait 10 days for his check to clear the bank before he could get a refund. Cowan told her that he would return in 10 days, and the cashier confirmed the date.

Ten days later, Cowan was told that the store policy required that 10 banking days had to elapse before he could get his refund. Rather upset, he asked why this policy had not been specified earlier. The reply was a shrug of the shoulders. The cashier did say, however, that if he returned on Monday, he would get his refund.

On Monday, Cowan returned for the third time, only to be told that the 10 banking days were not officially over until Tuesday morning. His subsequent appeal to the manager fell on deaf ears.

On his fourth visit to the store, Cowan finally received his $69.95. He vowed never to shop at Varsity Sports again. He also decided to write a letter of complaint to the owner of the store.

Case Questions

1. Who was at fault for the communication breakdown?
2. Assuming the role of Cowan, write the letter of complaint.
3. Assuming the role of the owner, write a reply to Cowan's complaint. Concentrate on selling Varsity Sports as a good place to shop.
4. What should have been done to avoid this situation?

Policy Changes from the Treasurer's Office | CASE

William C. Sharbrough III, The Citadel

Ralph, the controller, and John, the treasurer, the company's two top accounting officers, were discussing a problem that had just developed with employee accounts.

Ralph: We've had a real problem with employees not paying their employee accounts on time. These are the credit accounts that they use to buy our products for personal use. Some of them have run up bills of more than $300. To combat this problem, we did the same thing we do to customers. We implemented a $10 late fee.

John: To make sure the employees knew about this policy change, we made an announcement in the August company newsletter telling them it would go into effect on the October bills. Then we added the announcement to both the September and the October bills. Several employees still paid their October bills late. Now, here we are. The November bills have had the late charges added to them, and employees are screaming, "When did you make this change? You didn't notify us!" When we told them we had put the announcement in the newsletter, they responded, "We don't read the official announcements in the newsletter. They never apply to us." Further, they said that they didn't read the notice on the bills. They read only the amount owed.

Ralph: Well, we solved one problem. Employee accounts are paid on time now. But now we have another problem. We've got angry employees, and some of them had very small bills — less than $10 — that were doubled by this first late penalty. How could something so simple develop into such a big problem?

Case Questions

1. What communication problems occurred here?

2. What could Ralph and John have done to prevent this whole set of problems from occurring?

3. What can they do now?

PART THREE

STRATEGIES FOR ORAL COMMUNICATION

Listening as a Communication Tool

"It just isn't fair, Beth. I'm as good a listener as anyone else and George really tore into me for messing up that letter I wrote about the company stationery. I admit I had some things wrong but I could swear that George said them that way when he gave me the assignment."

"I was there too, Erin, and I didn't get the same impression of the details as you did. I wasn't taking notes but I do remember he said *44* cases of #10 envelopes and *60* reams of watermarked letterhead, instead of the other way around. And I'm sure he said the order had to go out by the tenth, even though you don't remember that."

"I took good notes. I don't understand it. It's the same as when my notes in school didn't agree with what the instructors said. They'd never believe me when I insisted I was paying attention. It's not as if I have a hearing impairment or am dumb or anything. I think I am a good listener."

Erin may be a good listener and may not be. Looking at the speaker and taking notes is not the same as really listening. Just because people spend much of their lives hearing other people speak does not mean they are good listeners.

Surveys indicate that managerial people in organizations spend up to 80 percent of their workday in face-to-face conversations, in meetings, on the phone, or writing.[1] Others have

Learning Objectives

1 *To understand the amount of time spent listening.*

2 *To examine the potential relationships between effective listening and various individual characteristics.*

3 *To become aware of major perceptual barriers to effective listening.*

4 *To understand the valuable concept of active listening.*

5 *To learn how concentration, objectivity, questioning, and feedback can improve listening behavior.*

6 *To understand the difference between good listening behavior and poor listening behavior.*

---

[1]Sylvia Porter, "Now Hear This: Americans Are Poor Listeners," *Tampa Tribune,* November 15, 1979, 15-A.

Managers may spend as much as 80 percent of the workday in some kind of communication.

suggested that approximately 60 percent of the workday is spent listening,[2] yet less than 50 percent of the oral messages used in a day may be fully understood.[3] A study of communication preferences by first-line managers and supervisors has found that the predominantly used communication skills are listening and speaking, and that listening is perceived as the most important communication skill.[4]

Many organizations offer employee training in listening, sometimes built around learning packages such as those of Nichols[5] or Spectra.[6] Employers are becoming increasingly aware that listening relates to almost all forms of business communication. It is a necessary skill, for example, in gathering information for a business report, in working in a small group, in interviewing as a management tool or to get a job, and in communicating effectively across cultures.

CHARACTERISTICS OF LISTENING

People retain 50 percent of what they hear, and 48 hours later that drops another 50 percent.

The average listener who hears a 10-minute presentation will hear, understand, and retain only half of what was said. Forty-eight hours later that portion drops another 50 percent. Put another way, we retain about 25 percent of what we hear.

Part of the reason for poor listening ability is the educational system, which emphasizes the speaker at the expense of the listener. The system focuses major attention on reading, writing, and speaking skills — not listening skills. Yet one study shows that 45 percent of total working hours are spent listening, 30 percent speaking, 16 percent reading, and 9 percent writing.

You have no doubt found yourself in the situation of talking to another person and suddenly becoming aware that the other person is not listening. Not a very good feeling, is it? The fact is that most people have no fundamental hearing deficiency, but they still do not listen very well. How can people become better listeners?

Several researchers have examined the potential relationships between effective listening and other individual characteristics. The research suggests several conclusions.

Sex

Although some research has shown that females comprehend slightly less from lectures than do males, the discrepancy is probably caused by the manner of testing, not inherent sex differences.

---

[2]"The Act of Listening," *Royal Bank of Canada Monthly Letters*, January 1979.

[3]Eric H. Nelson and Jane Gypen, "The Subordinate's Predicament," *Harvard Business Review* (September–October 1979): 133.

[4]Martha Eaton Maddox, "First-Line Managers/Supervisors/Perceptions and Business Communication Faculty's Perceptions of Communication Skills Needed by First-Line Managers/Supervisors," unpublished dissertation, University of Georgia, 1989.

[5]Ralph G. Nichols, *Successful Listening* (St. Paul, Minn.: Telstar, 1985).

[6]*We Are Listening!* (New Orleans: Spectra, 1989).

Personality

Generally speaking, researchers have discovered no marked relationship between listening comprehension and personality characteristics; that is, a good listener does not possess a certain type of personality.

Intelligence

Obviously, intelligence can be a determining factor in listening (aural) comprehension, but it is not the only element that affects aural proficiency. Intelligence alone does not produce listening skills.

Scholastic Achievement

Moderately positive correlations exist between listening ability and cumulative grade average. Such findings indicate that those who listen well get higher grades. Furthermore, because listening and reading have similar correlations with grade point average, it is reasonable to conclude that scholastic excellence depends equally upon aural and reading skills.

Verbal Ability and Vocabulary

Verbal competence is an important part of listening comprehension. An adequate vocabulary aids listening and word retention. In fact, the effective use of words, through both listening and speaking, is a definite business and social asset.

Note Taking

Because most listeners take poor notes, note taking does not have a noticeable effect on listening comprehension and retention. However, if you listen carefully and synthesize as you write, you will probably perform better on examinations.

Motivation

Motivation is one of the most significant elements of listening proficiency. Specifically, motivation — in terms of interest, emotional appeals and attitudes, and mind set — determines the level of aural competence. A listener's comprehension improves if there is interest in the topic before the speech, if interest is created during the speech, or if the listener is to be tested after the speech. Comprehension is also determined by the intensity of the listener's emotional reaction to what is being said. Finally, a listener's level of understanding is influenced by various methods of producing an anticipatory mind-set. For example, if you introduce your point by stating that it is going to be critical of, say, tax increases, your listeners are more apt to remember your criticisms. You have created, in the minds of your audience, a mind-set to anticipate criticisms.

Organizational ability

Listening comprehension is directly related to the ability to organize and structure a message. The better organized the message, the higher the comprehension will be. This applies to speakers as well as listeners.

Environment

Research findings show that environmental factors influence comprehension. Good listeners will learn to allow for or adjust to distracting elements, such as poor lighting or extraneous noises, distance from the speaker, or other environmental shortcomings that the listener cannot control.

Hearing Ability

Many think that those who suffer some hearing loss therefore are not good listeners; actually just the opposite is true. Those with moderate hearing loss usually are better listeners than those who have normal hearing.

Usage

Writing skills and, to a lesser extent, speaking skills, improve with use, but this is not necessarily the case with listening. Just because people have been hearing the spoken word all their lives does not mean they are good listeners. Instruction and practice in effective listening are needed for listening improvement.

Listening ability depends on a complex combination of factors. No particular personality trait or intelligence level excludes anyone with a stable personality and average intelligence from being a good listener. Listening is a skill that can be learned; all of us can become better listeners and better teachers of listening skills.[7]

BARRIERS TO EFFECTIVE LISTENING

Major barriers to effective listening are perceptual in nature.

In order for listeners to improve their listening skills, they need to be aware of the major barriers to effective listening.[8] Some barriers are perceptual in nature; others are more general.

Perceptual Barriers

Frame of Reference

People perceive stimuli according to their individual frames of reference. "Meanings are in people" means a message is composed solely of aural and visual stimuli. Although the speaker (message sender) may want to

---

[7]"The Act of Listening."

[8]The review of listening research is based on the following work: Charles R. Petrie, Jr., "Informative Speaking: A Summary and Bibliography of Related Research," *Speech Monographs* 30 (January 1963): 79–91. See also Sam Duker, *Listening Bibliography*, 2d ed. (Metuchen, N.J.: Scarecrow Press, 1968); Sam Duker, *Listening Readings*, vols. 1 and 2 (Metuchen, N.J.: Scarecrow Press, 1966, 1971); Larry Barker, *Listening Behavior* (Englewood Cliffs, N.J.: Prentice-Hall, 1971); Carl Weaver, *Human Listening* (Indianapolis: Bobbs-Merrill, 1972); C. William Colburn and Sanford B. Weinberg, "An Orientation to Listening and Audience Analysis," *Modcom* (Chicago: Science Research Associates, 1976); Malra Treece, *Successful Business Communication* (Newton, Mass.: Allyn & Bacon, 1987), 389–396; Rose V. McCullough, "Fight the Spread of Pessimism," *Rough Notes* 125 (January 1982): 48–50; and Lyman K. Steil, Larry L. Barker, and Kittie W. Watson, *Effective Listening: Key to Your Success* (Reading, Mass.: Addison-Wesley, 1983).

convey a particular meaning, it is the listener's individual frame of reference — that is, total life experience up to that point — that determines the actual meaning assigned to the message. As discussed in Chapter 2, the speaker and listener may share similar but never identical meanings through a given message.

Many aspects of culture determine our frame of reference and how we apply it to our listening behaviors. These cultural differences increase in importance as we expand into international markets and employ global trade. For example, the belch after a meal that is considered a compliment in Arabia is socially unacceptable in the United States.

Expectations

People perceive stimuli according to their own expectations. Expectations are based on experiences in similar situations. For example, picture two Americans in the headquarters of a large business in a Middle Eastern country. This is their first visit to the region, and they felt it was appropriate to arrive 15 minutes early for their appointment with a local executive. They have been waiting an hour and 15 minutes. They are frustrated and upset. Finally, the executive appears and says, "Oh, there you are. Won't you please come in?"

The Americans think, "How rude to not even apologize for the delay."

The executive thinks, "Perhaps I should have kept them waiting a bit longer to emphasize even more my position above them."

What occurred is a mix of cultural differences and forceful experiences that probably overrode much of what took place in the meeting. In this case, the listeners' past climate of communication determined their perceptions of the immediate listening situation, the speaker, and the messages being sent.

Particularly when position in a formal hierarchy is highly defined, vantage point may determine expectations. You may approach a situation in which you communicate with a superior differently than when communicating with a subordinate or a peer. For example, if you are a line person, you may communicate in a different tone with a manager than with another line person.

Attitudes and Beliefs

People perceive stimuli according to individual attitudes and beliefs. Most people have an almost innate ability to distort information so that it fits into their model of the world. This process is called **selective perception** and is relevant to listening activity. For example, some employees may conveniently filter out criticisms from a supervisor to support the belief that their work is acceptable. They refuse to hear negative comments about their work, thus avoiding an unpleasant confrontation with reality. Selective perception serves as a protective device against unwelcome aural stimuli.

People selectively remember certain experiences (selective retention). They selectively pay attention to those things they find of value (selective

Our communication behavior is selective.

attention). They have comprehension skills in some areas and weaknesses in others (selective comprehension). Awareness of these attitudes is important if you are to overcome them.

Relationship with Speaker

The continuing relationship between speaker and listener plays an important role in perception. The relationship between superior and subordinate is the most relevant case in point. Subordinates will pay close attention to a respected, credible supervisor's comments and will be more conscious of how they perceive communication from that supervisor. However, subordinates are likely to attach minor importance to the comments of a supervisor with low credibility or little power.

Nonverbal Cues

Ineffective listeners are unaware of nonverbal cues, although they dramatically affect how people listen. As Chapter 14 shows, as much as 93 percent of people's attitudes are formed by nonverbal cues. Knowing this should help you avoid undue influence from nonverbal communication.

Influential Words

"Signal" words can cause anxiety or raise emotions. People have certain words that affect them in either a positive or a negative way. Check yourself and create an inventory of these influential words. Do not let specific words get in the way of effective listening.

✔ CHECKLIST for Overcoming Perceptual Barriers

___ Avoid perceiving stimuli according to your own frame of reference.

___ Avoid perceiving stimuli according to your own expectations.

___ Avoid perceiving stimuli according to your own attitudes and beliefs.

___ Do not allow your relationship with the speaker to detract from effective listening.

___ Be aware of nonverbal cues.

___ Watch out for "signal" words that can cause anxiety or raise emotions.

General Barriers

In addition to perceptual barriers, other barriers exist that are of a more general nature:

▪ *Faking attention.* All too many people know how to appear as though they are listening. Outward appearance and actual listening may be quite different.

- *Listening only for facts.* Although individual facts are important, check yourself to ensure that you are also clear on the overall goal of the message.
- *Avoiding difficult listening.* Difficult topics vary with individuals and depend on other circumstances such as the listener's physical alertness and the context. Be sure you do not turn off your listening when you encounter a topic that is difficult.
- *Dismissing the topic as uninteresting.* "I've heard it all before," is an attitude that is certain to affect listening detrimentally; so is the assumption that a topic is beneath you or beyond your sphere of interest.
- *Criticizing physical appearance on delivery.* If you have ever not listened to an individual because the speaker's looks, dress, age, mannerisms of speech, or slight speech defects bothered you, you will realize that this is a common barrier to effective listening.
- *Yielding easily to distractions.* People listen for many reasons. They listen for information, to evaluate the speaker, for esthetic appreciation of the voice, and to empathize with the sender. Research indicates that when they are not listening, they are likely to be daydreaming (about something totally unrelated to what is being said), detouring (from what was said to their own thoughts), debating (against what was said), or planning (what to say when it's their turn). To overcome distraction you need to concentrate.

Having considered some of the major barriers to effective listening, you are ready to examine ways to improve your listening ability.

✓ CHECKLIST for Overcoming General Barriers

——▪ Do not fake attention.

——▪ Listen for the overall message as well as facts.

——▪ Be receptive when topics require difficult listening.

——▪ Do not dismiss a topic as uninteresting.

——▪ Do not criticize physical appearance or delivery.

——▪ Avoid yielding to distractions.

THE ACTIVE LISTENING CONCEPT

When you think of a person listening, do you picture a passive activity? To improve your listening behavior, you must modify this view. The preferred approach pictures a good listener as actively involved in the listening process.

Active listening entails grasping the speaker's point of view.

Several years ago Rogers and Farson introduced a concept of **active listening**.[9] Basically, it requires the listener to grasp, from the speaker's point of view, just what is being communicated. More than that, listeners must convey to the speaker that they are seeing things from the speaker's viewpoint.

Listening for Total Meaning

Any message a person attempts to convey usually contains two important and meaningful elements: content and the attitude or feeling underlying this content. These two components make up the total meaning of the message, which is what listeners try to understand. To illustrate, machine operator Alan Morrison tells his foreman, "I have finished the production run." This message has definite content and may be interpreted as a request for another work assignment. Suppose, instead, that Alan says, "Well, I've finally finished that damned production run." The basic content is the same, but the total meaning of the message is quite different.

The difference in the meanings of the two statements has important implications for both the foreman and the machine operator. Listening sensitivity on the part of the foreman will determine whether this conversation is a successful exchange between the two parties. Suppose the foreman's reaction is simply to assign another production run. Would Alan believe that he had successfully communicated his total message? Would he feel free to talk to his foreman? Would he have a positive feeling about his work and be anxious to perform even better on the next job assignment?

On the other hand, the foreman could respond with such statements as "Worked under a lot of pressure, right?" Or "Glad to have it over with, huh?" or "Guess I couldn't get you to do that again!" In this instance the foreman's listening sensitivity reacts in line with Alan's attitude or feeling about the completed task. In other words, the foreman responds from Alan's point of view. Such supportive replies do not mean that the next work assignment need be changed or that the way is open for the employee to complain about the pressure of the job. Listening sensitivity is simply a way to transform an average working climate into a more positive one.

Responding to Feelings

In some situations the message content is far less important than the feeling that underlies it. To interpret the full meaning of the message accurately, listeners must respond to the feelings or attitude component. For example, if Alan had told his foreman, "I'd like to disassemble the production machine and sell its parts to our competitor," responding to content would obviously be absurd. The meaning of any message contains

[9]Carl Rogers and Richard Farson, "Active Listening," in *Readings in Interpersonal and Organizational Communication*, 3d ed., eds. Richard Huseman, Cal Logue, and Dwight Freshley (Boston: Holbrook Press, 1977), 561–586.

various degrees of feeling; each time the listener must be sensitive to possible variations. What is this person trying to tell me? What does this mean to him or her? What is this person's view of the problem?

Noting All Clues

Communication is made up of verbal and nonverbal cues. Words alone do not reveal everything that the speaker is communicating. Sensitive listening requires an awareness of several levels of communication besides verbal. Voice inflection is one factor: a speaker may stress certain points loudly and clearly and only mumble others. The way a speaker hesitates reveals a great deal. The speaker's facial expressions, posture, hand gestures, eye movements, and breathing also help to convey the total message.[10]

OTHER CONCEPTS RELATED TO LISTENING ABILITY

The concept of active listening has to do with the mental attitude that we should bring to the listening situation. In addition, several other basic concepts relate directly to our listening ability.

Concentration

People are motivated to listen in varying degrees to a variety of messages. Simultaneously, they are demotivated from listening for many of the same kinds of reasons. Effective listeners are continually and consciously motivated to listen. From the effective listener's viewpoint, whatever other individuals wish to communicate is important. Though it sometimes appears that nothing of great value may be gained through listening, effective listeners consciously strive to disprove this expectation. They become selfish listeners who look for potential economic benefits, personal satisfaction, or new interests and insights. In brief, each listener needs to say, "What is that speaker saying that I can use?"

Motivation and demotivation affect the listening experience.

A significant differential exists between average speaking rate (100 to 200 words per minute) and an average listener's ability to process messages (400 words per minute). Such a differential provides opportunities for mental tangents. Average listeners tend to tune in and out of conversations. As a consequence, they often fail to grasp what the speaker deems the important contents of a message.

Concentration is the key to avoiding such counterproductive tangents. The listener should be aware of the difference between the rate of speech and the rate of thought and should use the time lag effectively rather than let it destroy the listening process.

Concentration is an important determinant of listening ability.

[10]Sherman K. Okun, "How To Be a Better Listener," in *Readings in Interpersonal and Organizational Communication*, 3d ed., eds. Richard Huseman, Cal Logue, and Dwight Freshley (Boston: Holbrook Press, 1977), 582–586.

BOXED IN | *AN ETHICAL DILEMMA*

Connie: I'm going to reward Jennifer with the promotion.

Bill: It's clear your mind is made up, but why didn't you pick Marie? She came to the company in the same training class as Jennifer and has been doing well, too.

Connie: Yes, Marie is doing well. The difference is that I don't have to go over instructions with Jennifer two or three times the way I do with Marie. It's nice to go over things just *once* with Jennifer and know that she will get them right.

Bill: Nice enough to give the promotion to Jennifer instead of Marie?

Connie: You make it sound as if I should feel guilty for rewarding Jennifer because she is a better listener. Is that what you think?

Bill: The question is, what do *you* think?

Connie feels boxed in. What would you do?

Several tactics can be used both to maintain attention to the speaker's message and to aid retention. One of them is to anticipate what the speaker will say next. Whether or not the anticipations are confirmed, this activity focuses the listener's attention on the subject at hand. Another tactic is to focus the message. Weighing the speaker's evidence and searching for the speaker's deeper meanings, particularly connotative ones, will help bridge the time gap created by the speech–thought differential. A third tactic is to review previous points. This involves mentally summing up the major points already covered. Reviewing points can help to reinforce the ideas the speaker is explaining.

✔ CHECKLIST For Listening Concentration

___ Anticipate what the speaker will say next.

___ Focus on the message.

___ Review previous points.

Questioning

The use of questions is an effective listening strategy.

In dyadic or paired communication, such as between a superior and a subordinate, asking questions may often be an effective listening tactic. Such activity serves two purposes: it encourages the speaker by demonstrating that the listener is, indeed, actively listening, and it can clarify and develop points, thereby enhancing the listener's chances of clearly understanding the speaker's message.

To improve listening capabilities, **probing questions** are highly useful types of questions. The listener simply asks questions that build on a speaker's words. Probing and other types of questions are discussed in Chapter 19.

Objectivity

Objectivity is a critical element in effective listening. Not only can lack of objectivity result in assigning distorted meanings to messages, but it may also jeopardize the relationship between speaker and listener. An effective listener knows how to overcome barriers to objectivity.

Objectivity is crucial to effective listening.

Emotion-Laden Words

Effective listeners minimize the impact of emotion-laden words. Quite often a listener's perceptual process goes awry simply because the speaker arouses an automatic emotional response. Words and phrases such as *sexism*, *reduction in force*, *strike*, and *grievance* can sometimes engender feelings of hostility or anxiety in a listener. When such feelings arise, the ability to think clearly and logically may be severely hampered.

Delivery

Effective listeners judge content, not delivery. Listeners often discount messages largely because of some distracting characteristic in the speaker's tone of voice, delivery, or pronunciation. Subjective impressions of the value of messages seriously endanger listening efficiency. An effective listener, therefore, focuses on what is said, not on how it is communicated.

Unfair Reaction

Effective listeners react fairly and sensibly. One of the most difficult listening functions is to avoid reacting too soon to what is heard. For example, a department head was informed by the plant manager that her staff must be reduced by two people. Rather than wait for an explanation or justification from her superior, she immediately responded defensively. She plunged right in, offering every reason imaginable for not cutting back the number of people in her department. Her defensiveness resulted only in the plant manager's defensive behavior and hostile feelings between them.

Effective listeners follow the timeworn advice, "wait your turn." They allow others sufficient opportunity to satisfactorily communicate their position or ideas. By adhering carefully to the rule of taking turns, the listener becomes a more effective communicator.

Distractions

Effective listeners overcome distractions. Listeners should not let environmental factors affect their listening. For example, you should turn down a stereo or television that keeps you from hearing.

Isolated Facts

Effective listeners detect the central message. Isolated facts are not allowed to get in the way of the total meaning. You should ask for clarification or rewording if you are unsure what is being said.

✔ CHECKLIST for Objective Listening

___| Minimize the impact of emotion-laden words.

___| Judge content, not delivery.

___| React fairly and sensibly.

___| Overcome distractions.

___| Detect the central message.

Note Taking

The usefulness of note taking depends on the situation.

Note taking may be useful in some situations; it may be unnecessary in others; in some cases it may even be distracting. Your purpose in listening should determine whether or not you need to take notes. If you think you will need to refer to the information in the future, notes are probably necessary. If the information is for immediate use, you are probably better off to listen carefully and omit notes.

Appropriate note taking may nonverbally convey to the speaker that you are paying close attention to what he or she is saying. Such note taking shows respect for the speaker and earnestness on the part of the listener.

Feedback

Feedback is important in the listening process.

Although feedback is important to listening, it is frequently overlooked. Listeners should provide feedback at appropriate points to a speaker, who is sometimes unsure what is actually getting through to the listener. The speaker may start repeating the same ideas if the listener does not appear receptive. At this point the listener shows even less interest and comprehension, the speaker repeats even more, and the entire communication process quickly deteriorates. This problem can be alleviated when the listener provides appropriate and timely feedback to let the speaker know that an idea has been understood.

Appropriate feedback may be verbal or nonverbal. Examples of nonverbal response include nodding the head in agreement, appearing involved with the conversation, and maintaining eye contact. Verbal clarifiers might be "What you're saying is . . ." or "Let me see if I have this right. . . ."

KEYS TO EFFECTIVE LISTENING

Ten keys to effective listening demonstrate the major differences between good listeners and bad listeners. Lyman Steil, a well-known authority who serves as a listening consultant to major corporations throughout the country, has summarized these differences, as shown in Table 13.1.

TABLE 13.1 ▪ *Ten Keys to Effective Listening*

Keys	The Bad Listener	The Good Listener
1. Find areas of interest.	Tunes out dry subjects	Opportunizes; asks "what's in it for me?"
2. Judge content, not delivery.	Tunes out if delivery is poor	Judges content, skips over delivery errors
3. Hold your fire.	Tends to enter into argument	Doesn't judge until comprehension complete
4. Listen for ideas.	Listens for facts	Listens for central themes
5. Be flexible.	Takes intensive notes using only one system	Takes fewer notes. Uses four to five different systems, depending on speaker
6. Work at listening.	Shows no energy output; attention is faked	Works hard, exhibits active body state
7. Resist distractions.	Distracted easily	Fights or avoids distractions, tolerates bad habits, knows how to concentrate
8. Exercise your mind.	Resists difficult expository material; seeks light, recreational material	Uses heavier material as exercise for the mind
9. Keep your mind open.	Reacts to emotional words	Interprets color words; does not get hung up on them
10. Capitalize on the fact that thought is faster than speech.	Tends to daydream with slow speakers	Challenges, anticipates, mentally summarizes, weighs the evidence, listens between the lines to tone of voice

Source: Lyman K. Steil, Larry L. Barker, and Kittie W. Watson, *Effective Listening: Key to Your Success,* pp. 72–73, © 1983, Addison-Wesley Publishing Co. Reprinted with permission of Random House, Inc.

SUMMARY

Ample research supports the view that listening is a critical business skill. Although people spend most of their communication time listening, it is the communication skill in which most are deficient. To sharpen and develop their listening skills, they must overcome major perceptual barriers such as relying too much on their frame of reference, having faulty expectations, using their own attitudes and beliefs, not evaluating their relationship to the speaker, disregarding nonverbal cues, or being too influenced by "signal" words.

Various personality traits are associated with effective listening. Although personality factors are related to the ability to communicate, effective listening is a skill that can be learned. Hints for better listening are to listen for total meaning, respond to feelings, note all cues, take notes, and give feedback.

Key Terms

■ **selective perception**   ■ **probing questions**

■ **active listening**

Review Questions

1. On the average, how much of the workday do people spend in some type of communication? How much of that time is spent listening?

2. On the average, how much of what someone tells us do we remember immediately after we have heard it? Forty-eight hours after we have heard it? What do these facts tell you about the average person's level of listening retention?

3. Select what you believe are the six or seven more important individual characteristics that affect your ability to listen. Explain your selections.

4. Give an example in a business setting of each of the major perceptual barriers to listening.

5. What is active listening? Why is it so important?

6. What is a selfish listener?

7. What are the tactics a listener can use to facilitate concentration? In turn, how does concentration facilitate listening?

8. Is the use of questions an effective listening strategy? Explain.

9. Why is objectivity a critical element in effective listening? In terms of objectivity what should an effective listener do?

10. What are the major differences between good listeners and bad listeners?

Exercises

1. You and a classmate each choose a topic of considerable personal interest. Take turns discussing your topic for three minutes. After each discussion have the listener convey the content of the message and the attitude or feeling underlying the content.

2. As a variation of Exercise 1, the class can be divided into triads consisting of a speaker, a listener, and a referee who will evaluate the feedback by the listener and make suggestions for more active listening.

3. If some memorable event is scheduled and if all class members have access, each member should attend or watch. An appropriate event might be a presidential address on television, a presentation by a campus speaker, or an organization meeting. Students should listen but not take notes. The next day the instructor will quiz the class on what they heard.

4. Present a five-minute speech on a business-related topic to a friend majoring in the liberal arts. Ask your friend (the listener) to provide feedback at any point the speech is unclear. Reverse the roles so that you become the listener providing feedback to your friend's speech on some aspect of the liberal arts.

5. Which of your friends or classmates is a good listener? What makes you think so? Explain to that person that you are interested in knowing more about

how he or she became a good listener. Try to improve your own listening skills by applying the same techniques.

6. Visit the library and search out information on listening improvement. Which skills are consistently perceived as important? Try to apply those techniques, even for a short period of time, such as for five minutes. See how much you can recall.

Do You Know the Way to Midway? | CASE

Anji K. Roy, University of Wisconsin — Oshkosh

Sandy, a sophomore at Marquette University in Milwaukee, planned to visit her cousin in San Jose during the spring break. She checked all of the airlines and found that Popular Airlines offered the lowest fare. She would, however, have to change planes in Chicago and Los Angeles.

On the afternoon she was to leave, her 3:15 flight from Milwaukee to Chicago was canceled because of fog. Even if she were able to take the next flight to Chicago at 5:25, she could not make connections the rest of the way. She would have to stay overnight in Los Angeles before going on to San Jose the next day.

Sandy decided that she might as well stay in Milwaukee and leave the next morning. She was disappointed, because her cousin had already made special plans for the next day.

Sandy's sister, Simone, volunteered to drive her directly to Midway Airport in Chicago. Sandy might still make the earlier flight from there to Los Angeles.

The Popular Airlines agent gave Simone instructions to Midway. "Take I-94 East from Milwaukee to the 294 bypass south around Chicago. Leave the bypass at I-55. Take that to Cicero Avenue and exit south. Midway Airport is right on Cicero."

Simone followed the directions, but realized that they were headed south toward St. Louis on I-55. She turned around at the next exit and went back north on I-55. They reached Midway Airport five minutes after the flight had left.

Sandy had to take a later flight from Chicago to Los Angeles after all, and she stayed overnight in Los Angeles at her own expense.

Case Questions

1. Why did Simone take I-55 South instead of I-55 North?

2. What could Simone have done to be reasonably sure that Sandy would catch the flight?

3. What were the wrong assumptions on which this miscommunication was based?

4. What could the Popular Airlines agent have done to avoid the situation that Sandy found herself in?

Nonverbal Communication

Guest Speaker: Thanks for inviting me to speak to you today about effective strategies for enhancing long-term growth of your stock market portfolio. I welcome the opportunity to talk with you members of the South Side Rotary Club and always enjoy sharing my financial expertise.

Tyler: That speaker is lying. Lying like crazy.

Henry: What are you talking about? He's a well-known expert on investments and what's more, he's barely starting talking.

Tyler: He's barely started talking but he's lying. His voice is trembling. He's wringing his hands when he's not white-knuckling the podium or jingling the change in his pocket. He won't look us in the eyes and he's nervously pacing behind the podium. Henry, that speaker is scared stiff, even if he did say he was pleased to be here.

Tyler's observations are examples of the many ways that nonverbal communication influences people every day.

Learning Objectives

1 *To understand the importance of nonverbal behavior in the communication process.*

2 *To learn how paralanguage can affect the message.*

3 *To improve your perception of body movement in nonverbal communication.*

4 *To learn how space is used to communicate.*

5 *To recognize the impact of dress and appearance, color, and time on those around you.*

6 *To understand that different cultures assign different meanings to various nonverbal behaviors.*

More and more writers on the subject of business communication stress the importance of nonverbal communication. For example, in your resumé you communicate not only with words that describe your education and experience, but also with the quality and color of paper your resumé is typed on, the neatness of the typing, and similar nonverbal qualities. Although this text separately analyzes several aspects of nonverbal communication, in practice the verbal and nonverbal aspects of the message together comprise the total message that is communicated.

Chapter 2, on the nature of communication, was primarily concerned with **verbal communication**—the transferring of information through messages encoded in words. This chapter focuses on **nonverbal communication**—the transferring of information without relying on word meaning. Many authorities maintain that the nonverbal aspects of communication are the key to most ordinary communication. However, verbal and nonverbal communication usually occur together.

THE IMPORTANCE OF NONVERBAL COMMUNICATION

More than 90 percent of the message may be communicated nonverbally.

One authority, Albert Mehrabian, believes that words convey a very small part of the message. He argues that 93 percent of the total impact of any given message consists of nonverbal factors, as shown in Table 14.1 If you carefully analyze the messages that others communicate, it may surprise you how much emphasis is placed on the nonverbal aspects of communication.

Nonverbal communication usually occurs *with* verbal communication and always as part of a situation that gives context. Listeners should be cautious of placing too much importance on a single, isolated nonverbal cue until they have compared it to other nonverbal cues, to the verbal message, to the immediate situation, and to the larger environment and culture.

THREE MAJOR CATEGORIES OF NONVERBAL COMMUNICATION

Researchers divide nonverbal communication into three major categories. The first involves voice qualities. The other two are communication through body language and communication through space.

Paralanguage — How You Say It

Paralanguage can reinforce or undermine the verbal message.

Of the three major categories of nonverbal communication, **paralanguage** is most akin to verbal communication. Language deals with what is said; paralanguage deals with how it is said. To realize the importance of paralanguage you can perform a simple test. The next time a friend asks you to do something—for example, to go to a movie or to a particular restaurant for dinner—respond, "Sure, I would love to go," but let your tone of voice betray your words and convey that you have little or no interest in going. Watch the reaction of your friend to your response.

At times people mean to communicate a particular message through the use of paralanguage. For example, the phrase "I would like to help you" can convey several meanings, depending upon the paralanguage employed. Note the following types of emphasis:

▪ *I* would like to help you.
▪ I would *like* to help you.

TABLE 14.1 ▪ *Comparison of Verbal and Nonverbal Communication*

Message Impact	Type of Communication
7 percent	Words
38 percent	Tone of voice and inflection
55 percent	Facial expression, body position, gestures

Source: Adapted from Albert Mehrabian, "Communication without Words," *Psychology Today* 2 (September 1968): 53–55.

▪ I would like to *help* you.
▪ I would like to help *you.*

In each case the emphasized word changes the meaning of the message.

Paralanguage can be better understood by looking at voice qualities, including volume, rate, rhythm, pitch, and resonance. Everyone at one time or another has been made aware of the quality known as rate — how fast or slow someone is speaking. Depending on the other messages that are being communicated, an increase in rate could indicate anger, impatience, or anxiety from the person sending the message. A decrease in rate can indicate thoughtfulness or a reflective attitude; on the other hand, it can indicate boredom or lack of interest.

Paralanguage voice qualities include rate, volume, rhythm, pitch, and resonance.

Volume is another voice quality that frequently conveys meaning, especially in conjunction with rate. If a supervisor said softly, "I would like to talk with you in my office," you might feel somewhat at ease. But if your supervisor said loudly, "I would like to talk with you in my office," you would feel disturbed and ill at ease.

The qualities of rhythm, pitch, and resonance are more difficult to understand than rate and volume. When you consider voice qualities, the major point to note is a change or deviation from the speaker's normal voice quality. Noting differences in the sender's rhythm, pitch, and resonance can often increase your understanding of the message.

The voice qualities of rate, volume, pitch, and resonance in combination with vocal qualifiers cause paralanguage to become most apparent. Vocal qualifiers include intensity (overloud to oversoft), pitch height (overhigh to overlow), extent (extreme drawl to extreme clipping), and accent.[1] Accent was demonstrated earlier by changing the emphasis on words in a sentence. Consider the effect of accenting different words in this sentence: "I am going to the boss's house for dinner tonight."

The major function of paralanguage is to express emotions. Several researchers have demonstrated that it is possible to communicate various emotions solely with paralanguage. Actors who read the following am-

Paralanguage conveys emotion.

[1]Mark L. Knapp, *Nonverbal Communication in Human Interaction*, 2d ed. (New York: Holt, Rinehart and Winston, 1978), 19.

biguous text made sure that the meanings communicated were solely the result of vocal cues rather than vocabulary.

> You've got to believe it in time to keep them from hanging me. Every night you ask me how it happened. But I don't know! I don't know! I can't remember. There is no other answer. You've asked me that question a thousand times, and my reply has always been the same. It always will be the same. You can't figure things like that. They just happen, and afterwards you're sorry. Oh, God, stop them . . . quick . . . before it is too late![2]

The actors repeated the statement to 64 student judges and attempted to convey contempt, anger, fear, grief, and indifference. The study concluded that all those emotions could be communicated. Average accuracy of identification for the five emotions was 88 percent for indifference, 84 percent for contempt, 78 percent for anger and grief, and 66 percent for fear.

Several more recent studies have demonstrated that paralanguage—how we say something — does convey emotions. These studies indicate that some emotions are more accurately transmitted than others. Frequently, it is easier to convey impatience, fear, and anger than satisfaction and admiration.

Kinesics — Communicating through Body Movement

The face and eyes convey 10 different types of meaning.

The second major category of nonverbal communication is **kinesics**, which means communicating through body movement. The face and eyes are the most expressive means of body communication. Dale Leathers has found that 10 basic classes of meaning can be communicated by facial expression.[3]

1. Happiness
2. Surprise
3. Fear
4. Anger
5. Sadness

6. Disgust
7. Contempt
8. Interest
9. Bewilderment
10. Determination

The ability to interpret facial meaning is an important part of communication, because facial expressions can facilitate or hamper feedback. Leathers developed the Facial Meaning Sensitivity Test (FMST). Part I of the FMST contains photographs representing the 10 basic classes of meaning. To test your ability to perceive facial expression, study the 10 photos in Figure 14.1, which were originally used in facial research many years ago, and match them with Leathers' list.[4]

[2]G. Fairbanks and W. Pronovost, "An Experiment Study of the Durational Characteristics of the Voice during the Expression of Emotion," *Speech Monographs* 6 (1939): 88.

[3]Dale Leathers, *Nonverbal Communication Systems* (Boston: Allyn & Bacon, 1976), 24.

[4]These facial expressions portray: I, disgust; II, bewilderment; III, happiness; IV, determination; V, fear; VI, anger; VII, surprise; VIII, interest; IX, contempt; and X, sadness.

FIGURE 14.1 ■ *Facial Meaning Sensitivity Test, Part 1*

Source: Reprinted by permission from Dale Leathers, *Nonverbal Communication Systems* (Needham Heights, Mass.: Allyn & Bacon, 1976).

Eye Contact

The eyes play an especially important role in facial communication. Eye contact is one of the most powerful forms of nonverbal communication. Authority relationships as well as intimate relationships are frequently initiated and maintained with eye contact. Looking directly at your listener is usually thought to convey openness and honesty; people usually believe it is easier to trust someone who looks right at them. On the other hand, they tend to distrust those who don't look directly at them; less confidence is attributed to those who avoid eye contact. Prolonged eye contact can signal admiration, while brief eye contact usually means anxiety. On the other hand, direct eye contact of more than 10 seconds can create some discomfort and anxiety. The especially unusual behavior most people exhibit on elevators — being quiet, avoiding physical and eye contact, and concentrating on the floor-indicator numbers—can be fascinating to study.

Eye contact is one of the strongest forms of nonverbal communication.

Gesture

Another important element of kinesic communication is the use of gestures. The language of gesture is usually thought of as hand and arm movements, but the entire body is capable of gesture. Ekman and Friesen have identified five types of body gesture.[5]

Emblems.   Emblems are thought of as sign language and are the equivalent of words or phrases. For example, the thumb and forefinger held in a circle say *OK*. The index and middle fingers held up in the form of a *V* indicate victory.

Illustrators.   Directly tied to verbal language, these gestures illustrate the words a speaker is saying. When a speaker says, "My third and final point is . . ." and holds up three fingers, this gesture is an illustrator. When a baseball umpire calls someone out at home plate, he uses an illustrator as he points his thumb up and quickly jerks his hand upward.

Regulators.   Regulators control oral communication by alerting the sender to the need to hurry up, slow down, or repeat something. Examples are frequent glances at your watch or drumming your fingers on the table when someone is talking with you.

Affect Displays.   These indicate emotional states, such as anger or embarrassment, and usually occur in facial expressions. Affect displays differ from the three previous types in that people have far less control over them. Many people, for example, have felt their faces turning red because they were angry or embarrassed, but there is little they can do to control this affect display.

Adaptors.   These are another type of gesture over which people have little control. Frequently people are not conscious of performing such gestures. Stifling a yawn or clasping the hands to the face in fear are adaptor gestures.

Posture

Posture of superiors and subordinates conveys meaning.

A person's general posture, even without specific gestures, communicates meaning. Posture frequently gives clues to self-confidence or status. For example, superiors usually take a more relaxed posture than their subordinates.[6] Posture is also a way to demonstrate interest in another person. Several writers have concluded that when you lean forward to the person you are speaking with, you demonstrate interest in that person. Sitting back, on the other hand, may communicate a lack of interest (see Figure 14.2).

Movement Analysis

It is difficult to assess exactly how important gesture and posture are as modes of communication. Apparently gesture and posture are assuming more importance in organizational life. A London-based management con-

---

[5]Paul Ekman and Wallace V. Friesen, "The Repertoire of Nonverbal Behavior: Categories, Origins, Usage, and Coding," *Semiotics* 1 (1969): 63–92.

[6]Randall Harrison, *Beyond Words: An Introduction to Nonverbal Communication* (Englewood Cliffs, N.J.: Prentice-Hall, 1974), 132–133.

FIGURE 14.2 ▪ *Nonverbal Communication of Interest Level*

sultant, Warren Lamb, has developed his business based on the idea that a person's posture and gesture can tell much about how effectively the person will perform in an organization. Lamb claims that his program, called **movement analysis**, represents a new branch of applied behavioral science.[7] Corporations hire Lamb to help in the selection and promotion of managers. He conducts his work by holding an interview session and watching for three types of body movements.

Some firms make selection decisions primarily on the basis of posture and gesture.

Side-to-side Movements.   These are most evident when a person shakes hands. This person moves the arm in a sideways, circular motion and occupies a lot of space when talking. Such an individual is an effective informer and listener—in short, an effective communicator. According to Lamb, this individual is best suited for companies seeking a sense of direction in their business ventures.

Forward and Backward Movements.   These movements occur when an individual extends the hand straight forward when shaking hands and leans forward during an interview. The person using these forward and backward movements is described as an operator. Lamb would assign this type of person to an organization that needs a dramatic change or an infusion of energy.

Vertical Movements.   These take place during the handshake, when the person using vertical movements draws himself or herself up to the tallest posture possible. According to Lamb, this individual is the master salesperson or presenter, an expert at selling himself or herself or the company.

---

[7]Jean Ross-Skinner, "Those Telltale Executive Gestures," *Dun's Review*, March 1970, 66–67.

BOXED IN | *AN ETHICAL DILEMMA*

Recruiter: I'm not inviting Harold back for another office interview. There's something about him that isn't quite right. I don't trust him.

Manager: How can you say that? He has the best credentials of any of the applicants so far. In looking over your notes, you will surely find that he said the right things in the interview, too. What's the problem?

Recruiter: I can't pinpoint anything he said or did but I know he's not right for us. I've been a recruiter for 17 years and I can tell when there's something wrong. Harold made me uncomfortable by sitting too close, looking at me too much, things like that. I think he's a con man who's going to take advantage of us.

Manager: Is it ethical to reject an applicant simply because he makes you uncomfortable?

Recruiter: I gave you my reason — his behavior. We are going to call back only three candidates for the position, and I think at least three others are more deserving of a second look.

Manager: It's your decision, of course, but. . . .

The recruiter feels boxed in. What would you do?

No single gesture can always be accurately interpreted. However, Lamb asserts that the three categories of gesture — side to side, forward and backward, and vertical — enable him to identify and place executives where they will function most effectively.

Classification of Body Movements

Most people will not make their living the way Lamb does, but on a daily basis they need to understand what other people are communicating with their posture and gestures. Knapp has provided a useful scheme for classifying major types of body movements.[8] The following classifications are based primarily on Knapp's work.

Attitudes. Everyone likes or dislikes particular elements in the environment. Many times these attitudes are reflected in body movement. The degree of like or dislike can be seen in terms of general body orientation by noting if the communicator's legs and shoulders are turned toward or away from the other person. When the body is turned fully toward the other person, it may indicate liking, whereas the body turned away may indicate a degree of dislike.

Status. Individuals in superior roles or positions have status. They frequently keep their heads raised when communicating with others. Those in lower or subordinate roles often lower their heads and shoulders when speaking.

[8]Mark Knapp, *Nonverbal Communication in Human Interaction*, 2d ed. (New York: Holt, Rinehart and Winston, 1978), 220–232.

Affective States of Moods. These occur in various degrees of emotional conditions and are associated with body movements. The head and face convey information about anger, joy, and happiness; other body movements convey the intensity of the particular emotional state.

Approval Seeking. People may nod their heads and smile to secure approval from another person. In general, their bodies are more active than when they are not seeking approval. Frequently, this type of bodily activity can be observed by watching a subordinate present an idea to a superior.

Inclusiveness. Inclusiveness involves cues as to whose side you are on. The positioning of the body, especially the way the legs are pointed, will communicate, "I am on your side and not on their side." It can also indicate whether someone is open-minded or closed-minded to the other person's ideas.

Interaction Markers. Certain body movements naturally accompany particular oral language. Frequently, at the end of a statement a person will move the head, eyelids, or hands downward. At the end of questioning statements, these movements will tend to be upward. Other types of interaction markers include leaning back when listening and leaning forward when speaking.

   Although it is easy to oversimplify the classifications, you should realize that kinesic behavior affects the communication process. Having some basic understanding of how people communicate with their bodies will make you a more effective communicator.

Proxemics — Communicating with Space

The third major category of nonverbal communication is **proxemics**, or how people communicate with space. How close or far they stand in relation to another person, where they sit in a room, or how they arrange the office furniture has a real impact on communication. One of the major writers on this type of communication is anthropologist Edward T. Hall. He has identified three major types of space: feature-fixed space, semifixed feature space, and personal space.[9]

People use the space around them to communicate.

Feature-Fixed Space

Feature-fixed space refers to buildings and other fairly permanent structures, such as walls. The manner in which buildings are laid out and the sequence of rooms and offices have a considerable influence on communication. You will probably communicate more with those individuals whose offices are closer to rather than farther from yours.

Semifixed Feature Space

The placement and arrangement of movable objects, such as desks and chairs, is referred to as semifixed feature space. Currently a great deal of emphasis is placed on how business offices are arranged. Frequently, the

[9]Edward T. Hall, *The Hidden Dimension* (New York: Doubleday, 1966).

superior person will come from behind the desk and sit face-to-face with the subordinate to make it easier to communicate.

Personal Space

Communication zones determine social interaction.

The physical distance people maintain in their encounters with others is known as personal space. Hall has suggested four different zones or distances for different types of social interaction:

- *Intimate distance* ranges from actual physical contact to about 18 inches from another person. Communication and interaction within this distance are intimate activities. In organizations confidential information is often communicated within the intimate distance. The major form of intimate contact in business organizations is, of course, the handshake. Most people respond positively to men who give a firm handshake and negatively to men who give a limp handshake. Men respond positively to women who have either a firm or limp handshake. Many women, however, do not respond positively to a firm handshake from another woman.
- *Personal distance* ranges from 18 inches to four feet. Interaction in this zone includes casual and friendly conversation.
- *Social distance* ranges from four feet to about eight feet. Communication in this zone often occurs in the business setting. Much of the communication in organizations is done at social distance. The attention a teacher gives primarily to the front and middle section of the classroom is a unique form of interaction.
- *Public distance* ranges from 12 feet to the limits of visibility and hearing. Communication at public distance is considered public speaking. A good deal of communication within and outside an organization takes place at this range.

The space people occupy in the organization communicates much about their status in the organization.

Everyone is aware of some of the ways space is used to communicate in business organizations. Goldhaber has identified three basic principles about the use of space as it relates to status within the organization.[10]

First, the higher people are in the organization, the more and better space they are allotted. In many organizations the president has the most attractive office, while the vice president, the department heads, and lesser employees have succeedingly smaller offices. The number of windows in the office and the way the office is furnished are also commensurate with rank or position.

Second, the higher people are in the organization, the better protected their territory is. Many times the more status a person has in the organization, the more difficult it is to see that person. Outer offices and secretaries often are used to protect the high-status person.

Third, the higher people are within the organization, the easier it is for them to invade the territory of lower status personnel. The supervisor

---

[10]Gerald M. Goldhaber, *Organizational Communication*, 4th ed. (Dubuque, Ia.: William C. Brown, 1986), 202–206.

usually can enter the subordinate's office at will. The supervisor also has the ability to phone the subordinate at almost any time. However, the subordinate usually does not have this same access to the supervisor.

Photographs illustrating these principles are reproduced in Figure 14.3.

OTHER CATEGORIES

Some areas that receive less attention than the three major categories of nonverbal communication nevertheless play an important role in communication.

Dress and Appearance

Everyone has heard the cliché, "Clothes make the person." However, many people are not aware of the impact that clothing has on those around them. John Molloy, a consultant on executive dress with major corporations, has conducted several experiments to see what various types of clothing communicate.[11] In one of his studies Molloy compared the impact of black and beige raincoats. He took a set of twin pictures with only one variable: the pictures showed the same man in the same pose dressed in the same suit, the same shirt, the same shoes, the same tie. The only difference was the raincoat—one black, the other beige. Participants were told the pictures were of twin brothers and were asked to identify the more prestigious of the two brothers. Over 87 percent of the 1,362 people in the study chose the man wearing the beige raincoat as the more prestigious.

Clothing communicates much about the wearer to others.

In another set of experiments Molloy found a group of 27 restaurants in New York where ties were not required. In each restaurant he asked the headwaiter to divide the dining room into the most preferred seating areas and least preferred areas. Those areas near the street door and near the kitchen door were considered to be the least preferable. Invariably there was a disproportionate number of men who were not wearing ties in the less preferable areas; in fact, almost no men without ties were seated in the more preferable areas.

Although these experiments are interesting, the basic question remains: does the way a person dresses communicate something to others in the organization? The impact of dress is placed in perspective by Molloy in his book, *The New Dress for Success*:

Top executives have an unwritten code for corporate dress.

> Twelve years ago I surveyed one hundred top executives in either medium-sized or major American corporations about their attitude toward corporate dress. With updated pictures I reran the survey for this version of the book.
>
> The first series of questions was designed to establish the most up-to-date attitudes on corporate dress.

[11]John T. Molloy, *Dress for Success* (New York: Peter Wyden, 1975).

FIGURE 14.3   ▪   *Nonverbal Communication of Status*

I showed the executives five pictures of men, each of them wearing expensive, well-tailored, but high-fashion clothing. I asked if this was a proper look for the junior business executive. Ninety-two of the men said no, eight said yes.

I showed them five pictures of men neatly dressed in obvious lower-middle-class attire and asked if these men were dressed in proper attire for a young executive. Forty-six said yes, fifty-four said no.

I next showed them five pictures of men dressed in conservative upper-middle-class clothing and asked if they were dressed in proper attire for the young executive. All one hundred said yes.

I asked them whether they thought the men in the upper-middle-class garb would succeed better in corporate life than the men in the lower-middle-class uniform. Eighty-eight said yes, twelve said no.

I asked if they would choose one of the men in the lower-middle-class dress as their assistant. Ninety-two said no, eight said yes.[12]

Uniforms — such as bankers' clothes, nurses' outfits, or your interviewing outfit — transmit special messages. Outside the business world, clothing communicates as well. For example, *T*-shirts, which have been called the graffiti of the 1980s, often are used to show allegiance to a favorite rock group, to identify where the wearer spent a vacation, to publicize college, club, or fraternity affiliation, or just to say something to the world.

Clothing styles and appearance change with time and depend on context. You might guess a man's military vocation, even out of uniform, by

[12]John T. Malloy, *The New Dress for Success*, rev. ed. (New York: Warner Books, 1988), 27–28.

his short haircut. The jeans worn by working people for years took on a new and almost universal appeal with the advent of designer jeans in the early 1980s. Not too long ago businesswomen, particularly in executive roles, were encouraged by both fashion and some experts to wear the corporate uniform of the three-piece suit. Shortly afterward, the three-piece suit was no longer recommended, because the appearance was perceived as an invasion of the man's world, rather than an effort by women to be accepted in the corporate world. Furthermore, the look was unnecessarily and inappropriately unfeminine.

Whether or not people are correct in their evaluation of the wearer, certainly most of them are aware of other's clothing. Most clothing decisions are not made on exclusively functional grounds.

You can test your "image IQ" by answering the following questions:

1. What is the most effective raincoat color?
2. For which professionals are bow ties acceptable — and often preferred — attire?
3. What tie color makes men look sexy?
4. Should today's executive wear pants with cuffs — or without them?
5. Are shirts with contrasting collars acceptable in conservative companies?
6. "Old money" Americans are most likely to distrust a man who (a) has disheveled hair, (b) is wearing a wrinkled suit, (c) is wearing shoes that are unshined or worn at the heels, (d) drives an old car.
7. Should suspenders always have button fasteners?
8. Should you wear stripes or solids if you are going to appear on television?
9. If you are a small man, will a dark, pinstripe suit make you look smaller and ineffective?

The answers appear at the bottom of the page.[13]

Color

The communication involved in the choice of color can be related to dress because color in clothing affects communication. Some evidence indicates that a relationship exists between specific moods and color. This relationship, in terms of color, mood, and frequency of times chosen, is illustrated in Table 14.2.

Color is related to particular moods.

The colors around people affect them. In rooms with warm or hot colors, such as reds or oranges, people are likely to be more creative, stimulated, and prone to quick decisions. Rooms with cooler colors, such as blues,

Warm or hot colors engender quick decisions.

[13]John T. Malloy, *The New Dress for Success*, rev. ed. (New York: Warner Books, 1988), i. Reprinted with permission.

Answers: 1. beige 2. waiters, clowns, college professors, and commentators 3. bright red 4. with cuffs 5. Yes, Lee Iacocca made them acceptable. 6. (c) 7. yes 8. solids 9. No, with the right accessories it will do the opposite.

TABLE 14.2 ▪ *Matching Colors with Moods*

Mood Tone	Color	Frequency of Times Chosen
Exciting, stimulating	Red	61
Secure, comfortable	Blue	41
Distressed, disturbed, upset	Orange	34
Tender, soothing	Blue	41
Protective, defending	Red	21
	Brown	17
	Blue	15
	Black	15
	Purple	14
Despondent, dejected, unhappy, melancholy	Black	25
	Brown	25
Calm, peaceful, serene	Blue	38
	Green	31
Dignified, stately	Purple	45
Cheerful, jovial, joyful	Yellow	40
Defiant, contrary, hostile	Red	23
	Orange	21
	Black	18
Powerful, strong, masterful	Black	48

Source: L. B. Wexner, "The Degree to Which Colors (Hues) Are Associated with Mood-Tones," *Journal of Applied Psychology* 38 (1954): 432–435. Table from Mark L. Knapp, *Nonverbal Communication in Human Interaction*, 2nd ed. (Ft. Worth, Tex.: Holt, Rinehart and Winston, Inc., 1978).

will likely engender solitude; slow, deep and methodical thinking; and detachment.

Men and women often describe colors with different language. Men may describe objects as purple, blue, and yellow, whereas women might describe the same objects as fuchsia, robin's egg blue, and canary yellow.

Check the colors of a fast-food establishment, a church, and a classroom. There's a good chance that colors enhance the desired image or mindset. If your classroom is devoid of color, that absence is probably not an accident but a carefully planned effort.

Time

Being early, on time, or late communicates much in our society. Setting and meeting deadlines is also important. The employee who is habitually late for work and misses deadlines communicates very little interest in the job. Another observation about time is that individuals with high status are usually able to get appointments sooner and their meetings with superiors usually last longer. They wait less in the waiting room. High-status people usually have more flexible work hours. We even hear about banker's hours as the working day for individuals with higher status. Today, of course, bankers no longer keep banker's hours.

Another way in which time communicates is the amount of time it takes to provide or receive feedback. For example, someone who responds too quickly to a written request may not have carefully considered the request. On the other hand, if a long period of time elapses with no response, the person who made the request may believe it is because of a lack of interest even though formal communication has not taken place.

The amount of time taken to provide or receive feedback communicates a message.

THE IMPACT OF COMBINED CATEGORIES

So far this chapter has looked at categories of ways that nonverbal information is communicated. There are also occasions when categories are grouped and create nonverbal impact.

Power

Nonverbal indicators of power are prevalent in the business world. How you perceive others' indicators, react to those indicators, and pick indicators for yourself may have substantial impact on your business career.

In addition to using clothing for power, people adorn themselves with other power indicators, some of which may serve as clues to wealth or judgment as well. These three clues—power, wealth, and judgment—may stand alone but they often overlap and reinforce one another. For example, while you may be aware of a man's expensive cologne, you may also be offended by it. Conversely, you are likely to be impressed by a person in well-coordinated attire, with expensive but not gaudy accessories.

Examples of power indicators can be found in all of the nonverbal categories, such as standing tall, using expansive gestures, speaking in a loud voice, taking large strides, using a firm handshake, and looking away or walking while others talk. Physical examples of power with which people surround themselves are recognition plaques, memberships in honorary or exclusive organizations, photos of powerful people, large and well-appointed offices, and a private secretary.

Often people are only slightly aware of power symbols, but they are still cognizant of the presence of power and adjust their behavior. The high-status individual who does not have to face you but whose eyes you try to contact, even if you must back out of the person's presence, is establishing or exercising power.

People who know when, where and with whom to use power symbols and actions can positively affect how others see and react to them. At all levels in the business world power is present; clearly some use it and others abuse it. Skillful understanding of the intricacies of nonverbal power can pay rich rewards.

The Professional Image

Some business people stand out in a crowd. They appear confident, attractive, well-dressed, personable, and in control. In short, some people transmit a professional image. They accomplish this through careful manipulation of what they write and say supported by effective nonverbal behavior.

In Control

People who are confident and in control are not afraid to look others in the eyes. Whether men or women, they often initiate firm handshakes. They speak up, aware that a strong voice suggests authority. They have something to say and, when opinions are sought, share theirs. Studies suggest that those who initiate conversations and who talk the most are seen as leaders, even when the content may be weak.

Well-Dressed

Traditional and conservative clothes are safe for most jobs.

Business people with a professional image dress meticulously, making sure that clothes are clean, pressed, and fit well; shoes are shined; and jewelry is tasteful. They avoid both fads and the appearance of being out-of-date. Traditional and conservative clothes are safe for most jobs, and a professional image requires the best clothes the wearer can afford. Colors should enhance body color and size and, if possible, suggest power.

Attractive

A professional image demands good posture. It means avoiding negative images from perspiration, from too-strong perfume or after-shave cologne, or from strong foods. Conversely, appropriate perfumes and after-shave lotions, fresh-smelling hair, or the imagery brought about by the smell of a leather briefcase can be positive. A professional image may require enlisting help in caring for hair and nails.

Personable

Those with a professional image know that gestures suggest vibrancy and activity and that positive facial expressions are noticed — and are usually desirable.

THE MODIFYING OF NONVERBAL COMMUNICATION

People are taught, over many years, how to manipulate verbal communication. Some become quite adept at lying with words. However, few can manipulate their nonverbal behavior much beyond such obvious changes as clothing or the surrounding environment. If they are experiencing stage fright, for example, they find it hard to turn off nonverbal messages of perspiration, white knuckles, or a cracking voice.

People receive little practice or instruction in how to modify nonverbal communication, which makes the application of nonverbal communication to public presentations and speech making very important. Although

✔ *CHECKLIST for a Professional Image*

—❙ **Look people in the eyes.**

—❙ **Give a firm handshake.**

—❙ **Speak with a strong voice.**

—❙ **Avoid reticence.**

—❙ **Dress meticulously.**

—❙ **Do not slump or slouch.**

—❙ **Pay attention to cleanliness and neatness.**

—❙ **Allow yourself to gesture.**

—❙ **Smile.**

speakers have little control over emotions that present themselves in recognizable nonverbal patterns, they can modify their behavior somewhat.

Here are some nonverbal behaviors associated with effective oral presentations, with some suggestions for overcoming nonverbal problems:

▪ A relaxed speaker tends to gesture, but not too much. A nervous speaker either avoids gestures and movement or tends to overdo it.
▪ The confident speaker does not show perspiration. The nervous speaker might consider dressing in lightweight clothes so as not to start out too warm.
▪ Visual contact with the audience enhances a presentation. This visual contact also scares many speakers. One well-known approach is to avoid direct eye contact by looking just above the eyes of your audience. Then, as you become more confident, you can work to effective direct eye contact. A similar technique for eye contact is to try to talk to and look at the audience one by one. Try not to think of the large group, but rather engage a person on one side of the room for a few seconds, then look at a person in the middle, and then one on the other side of the room. Most effective speakers use this technique not so much to overcome nervousness, but more for a personal touch.
▪ Effective voice control affects the impact of a speech greatly. An over-rehearsed speech often comes out in a monotone no matter how enthusiastic the speaker. On the other hand, an ill-prepared speaker is likely to exhibit the cracking voice, gasping, or swallowing that we associate with nervousness. Try to pace yourself in terms of speed. A speaker who is unconfident is likely to change delivery speed by either speeding up or slowing down. Aim for a normal delivery rate.
▪ Hands and fingers are not obtrusive for the confident speaker; they tend to shake for the nervous speaker. This shaking is amplified many

An over-rehearsed speech is often delivered in a monotone.

times over if you point with a pencil at a transparency during overhead projector use. If you plant your pencil solidly on the film, you won't shake.

∎ Some effective speakers move around behind the podium somewhat, but usually not much. Beware of the speaker's shuffle. This side-to-side balancing often can be overcome if you remember to put one foot forward and one backward diagonally.

THE MEASURING OF NONVERBAL FEEDBACK

Many instruments measure nonverbal communication and nonverbal behavior, but they are usually focused on a specific category, such as the FMST to measure facial expressions. An approach to measuring a larger portion of the nonverbal experience — and even the verbal message — is Leathers' Nonverbal Feedback Rating Instrument (LNFRI).[14] This instrument uses 10 semantic differential scales to measure a person, event, or behavior. Photographs may be used to depict the ends of the scales and to guide the novice evaluator, as shown in Figure 14.4. The LNFRI "provides the user with detailed information about the feedback to his own communication that suggests (1) whether any corrective action should be taken and (2) what types of corrective actions should be taken."[15]

The semantic differential approach yields a wealth of information. For example, a person's nonverbal behavior can be viewed as predominately positive or negative depending on which half of the scale is checked. The behavior can also be compared to similar evaluations from another time period, thus showing change over time.

Three dimensions in a grouping of semantic differential scales are evaluation, potency, and activity. A person might be measured as being good (evaluation), offering potential (potency), and being passive (activity). When respondents react to a series — usually at least 10 — of semantic differential scales, they will probably note that some of the scales are similar and that they answer those scales in about the same way. Using the LNFRI, we might evaluate an individual similarly on the attentive/unattentive scale, the responsive/unresponsive scale, and on the interested/disinterested scale. The grouping of these three scales broadens our understanding of the evaluation. Even clearer conclusions can be drawn through application of various statistical techniques.

SUMMARY

People transmit and receive much more information through nonverbal channels than verbally. The major categories of nonverbal communication are paralanguage, kinesics, and proxemics. Paralanguage involves such

---

[14]Leathers, *Nonverbal Communication Systems*, 214–220.
[15]*Ibid.*, 215.

FIGURE. 14.4 ■ *Nonverbal Feedback Rating Instrument*

Confident 7 : 6 : 5 : 4 : 3 : 2 : 1 Uncertain

Pleased 7 : 6 : 5 : 4 : 3 : 2 : 1 Displeased

Involved 7 : 6 : 5 : 4 : 3 : 2 : 1 Withdrawn

Deliberative 7 : 6 : 5 : 4 : 3 : 2 : 1 Spontaneous

(Continued)

Source: Adapted from Dale Leathers, *Nonverbal Communication Systems* (Boston: Allyn & Bacon, 1976), 24.
Photo source: John M. Penrose, Jr.

FIGURE. 14.4 ■ *Continued*

Responsive 7 : 6 : 5 : 4 : 3 : 2 : 1 Unresponsive

Analytical 7 : 6 : 5 : 4 : 3 : 2 : 1 Impulsive

Interested 7 : 6 : 5 : 4 : 3 : 2 : 1 Disinterested

Attentive 7 : 6 : 5 : 4 : 3 : 2 : 1 Unattentive

Clear 7 : 6 : 5 : 4 : 3 : 2 : 1 Confused

Friendly 7 : 6 : 5 : 4 : 3 : 2 : 1 Hostile

voice qualities as rate, pitch, rhythm, volume, and resonance. Kinesics is the study of communication through body movement. The movements of the face and eyes are especially important in transmitting information, though gestures and postures also send much information. Proxemics is the study of communication in spatial ways. One expert breaks space into fixed, semifixed, and personal space. Personal space is further divided into intimate, personal, social, and public distances.

Other categories of nonverbal communication important in business are dress and appearance, color, time, power, and the professional image. The chapter concludes with a discussion of an instrument that facilitates measuring nonverbal communication.

Key Terms

- **verbal communication**
- **nonverbal communication**
- **paralanguage**
- **kinesics**
- **movement analysis**
- **proxemics**

References

Leathers, Dale G. *Successful Nonverbal Communication Principles and Applications.* New York: Macmillan, 1986.

Malandro, Loretta A., and Larry L. Barker. *Nonverbal Communication.* Reading, Mass.: Addison-Wesley, 1983.

Review Questions

1. Why do nonverbal messages play such a critical role in communication?
2. How can paralanguage reinforce or undermine the verbal message?
3. Cite examples of how facial expressions attach emotional meaning to our messages.
4. In what ways is gesture an important means of kinesic communication?
5. How can posture provide clues to the self-confidence or status of a person in a business organization?
6. How is space used as a communication device?
7. In what ways might your dress and appearance and the way you handle time impress your business colleagues?
8. Can you think of an example of nonverbal business behavior from each of the following categories — music, kinesics, posture, proxemics, time, paralinguistics, animal communication, clothing, body beautification, tactile communication, taste, smell, man–machine communication?

Exercises

1. Identify some nonverbal rules, such as books and coat in a library chair marking a person's territory. Then break the rule, in this case by moving the books and coat and sitting in the chair.

2. Observe and record people's behavior in elevators. List as many nonverbal behavior patterns as you can. Compare these patterns to those of people using escalators. What are the differences? Why do you think these differences exist?

3. Most of us feel comfortable in a classroom and think little about its nonverbal aspects. Identify the nonverbal patterns of students and instructors in typical classrooms.

4. What is the appropriate dress and appearance in a typical business setting? How much can you vary from this standard without being penalized?

5. What are the nonverbal aspects of music? Does music create different moods in different people at different times? How? Give examples. How is music used in business?

6. Observe the proxemic behaviors of people in a room, such as a classroom or cafeteria. Do some sit or stand closer together than others? Why do you think this is? Can you categorize those people who are alone? Are there proxemic behavior differences by age or sex?

7. Observe members of another culture. What nonverbal things do they do differently from you? Are there differences in tone of voice (even if you don't understand the language), clothing, spacial differences between sender and receiver, or eye contact?

8. Many speakers of a romance language, such as Spanish or Italian, prefer to be closer to their listener than is comfortable for Americans. Test this theory by visiting with a person whose primary language and culture are from a romance country.

CASE | *The Telephone Answering Machine*

Marcia Mascolini, Western Michigan University

Andy Smith runs Andy's Plumbing Service out of his home. His business is small, and he does not have a secretary. Instead, he uses an answering machine on the family telephone to accept messages from customers when he is out on a call and his wife is at work. Andy believes that the answering machine is a necessity for anyone who runs a one-person operation like his; however, he is not happy with the recorded customer calls that he has been receiving.

This is the greeting, recorded by Andy's wife, that customers hear when they call Andy's number: "Hello. You've reached the Smiths'. When you hear the tone, please leave your message. We'll get back to you as soon as we can."

These are 10 typical calls recorded on the answering machine:

▪ Hi, Andy. This is Dave. Call me back when you get a chance.

▪ (no message)

▪ Hello. . . . Um. I'm having trouble. . . . You know that new pipe you put in the basement last week? The cold water pipe? Well, I think something's wrong with it. It looks sort of funny. I'm really worried. Should I shut off the water? I can't shut off the water because I just put a load of clothes in, and the kids are all home from school sick. I don't know what to do. It's getting wet, sort of dripping. I'm over on Main Street, the white house on the corner. Please come over as soon as you can.

▪ (no message)
▪ (no message)
▪ (no message)
▪ Hello? Andy's Plumbing? Please call me at 555–1212. Thanks.
▪ –2325. Please call this evening after 6 p.m.
▪ (no message)
▪ Hi, Andy. You were right about the faucet that you said was going to go out on me. It went. Give me a call when you get a chance. It's Charlie Ensminger. Call me at work if it's before five.

Case Questions

1. Analyze the greeting on Andy's phone. What specific suggestions could you give for improving it?

2. What do you think accounts for the large number of calls that people place without leaving messages?

3. Analyze the messages people have left on Andy's answering machine. Why would each one cause Andy additional work?

4. If you had a plumbing problem that you wanted Andy to fix, what specific message would you leave to ensure his speedy response?

Body Language │ CASE

Mildred W. Landrum, Kennesaw College

Mike Thornton was seething. Every time it looked as if he had finally straightened out his production supervisor, Steve Perkins, Steve managed to blow another situation with one of the workers. This time the worker had walked out, and the line had to be slowed down while a replacement was found.

This was a critical time for Mike. The vice president in charge of production was coming from New York for an inspection tour of the southeastern plant, and Mike wanted everything to go right. His future with the corporation depended on it.

For the third time he called in Steve to talk with him. Steve had better understand this time that he was really in trouble. Twelve years with the corporation gave Steve seniority, and the union would be difficult to handle if Mike fired Steve. Mike had to be sure Steve was impressed with the seriousness of the situation.

When the secretary buzzed Mike that Steve was in the waiting room, Mike said, "Let him cool his heels." Fifteen minutes later he asked Steve to come into the office. Mike did not raise his head and greet Steve nor did he rise to shake hands as he would normally have done. Steve stood at his desk several moments before Mike looked up and said, "Sit down." The telephone rang, and Mike talked five minutes before putting down the receiver. He then turned to Steve, folded his arms, leaned back, and said, "Well, tell me about this one."

Steve was upset by the extremely negative attitude he felt from Mike. He dropped his eyes, lifted his hands in a hopeless gesture, and said, "Well, what can you do with some of these guys who think they know everything?"

Case Questions

1. Describe the negative nonverbal messages Mike sent to indicate his displeasure with Steve.

2. Describe the submissive nonverbal messages Steve sent to Mike.

3. Give a positive movement for each negative movement named in this interaction.

Public Presentations

Brian Cox recently graduated from the state university with a B.B.A. degree. He had majored in management information systems and belonged to a student organization called SMIS. While at the university he had achieved a high grade point average, but he had acquired little practice giving presentations. In fact, he had always avoided making speeches because the prospect of speaking in front of a group frightened him.

After graduation, Brian accepted a position with a leading computer firm. He was enjoying his job, and his supervisor, Sherry Phillips, had complimented him several times on his performance. The one concern that she had voiced was his lack of presentation skills. Because Brian lacked confidence in his speaking ability he felt unsettled about his future.

Sherry wanted to offer Brian every opportunity to improve his speaking skills. Recently, such an occasion had presented itself. The advisor for Brian's former SMIS group had contacted her about the possibility of providing a speaker from her company for the next dinner meeting. Sherry encouraged Brian to make the presentation for two reasons: first, it would provide him with additional experience and, second, it would look good on his next performance evaluation.

As usual, Brian's primary concern was his ability to hold the group's interest. To calm his fears Sherry suggested that he choose a topic that would have interested him when he was a student. Focusing on her recommendation he decided to discuss how his education had prepared him for his current position.

CHAPTER 15

Learning Objectives

1 *To recognize the value of developing exceptional public presentation skills.*

2 *To understand the necessity for developing a general and specific purpose for each speech.*

3 *To appreciate the significance of establishing credibility with the audience while meeting their needs.*

4 *To learn the advantages of using various methods of organizing and delivering speeches.*

5 *To identify techniques that minimize the impact of stage fright on the speaker.*

6 *To practice the systematic approach and thus learn to give a superior public presentation.*

Once Brian began preparing the notes for his speech he realized that he did have something important to say. This recognition began to ease some of his apprehension. Rehearsing his speech, and listening to the final version he had taped on his cassette recorder, further reduced his anxiety. He was convinced he was ready to perform.

However, by the night of the dinner his old fears were beginning to resurface. Worst case scenarios kept racing through his head. What if he forgot the words? What if the audience thought he was boring?

As he started to speak, he felt very self-conscious, but as the speech progressed he began to gain confidence. The group was obviously interested in his ideas because they were making eye contact with him and laughing at the appropriate places. In conclusion he encouraged the students to seize every opportunity to practice public speaking. He honestly communicated that following his own advice would have saved him years of uncertainty about his own presentation skills.

Brian recognized the benefits of his hard work. The speech had been a success, and he had gained more confidence in his public speaking abilities. He now knew that he could apply these same principles to improve his presentations at work. Improving his communication skills had enhanced his value to the company and ensured him a brighter future.

A survey of 2,500 Americans indicated that over 40 percent of those surveyed feared speaking before a group.[1] All 2,500 were shown a long list of items and asked to indicate which ones they were afraid of. The 10 items picked most often were:

Speaking before a group	40.6%
Height	30.0
Insects	22.1
Financial problems	22.0

[1]David Wallechinsky and Irving Wallace, *The Book of Lists* (New York: William Morrow, 1977), 469–470.

Deep water	21.5
Sickness	18.8
Death	18.7
Flying	18.3
Loneliness	13.6
Dogs	11.2

The surprise is not that many people fear giving public speeches, but that the fear is so widespread. Such fear can be overcome by learning to apply a systematic approach to the process of public speaking. Approaching the problem systematically removes much of the apprehension by replacing the uncertainty with a plan.

A systematic approach may reduce some of the uncertainties associated with public speaking.

THE ROLES OF THE SPEAKER

Public speaking encompasses many aspects of people's lives. Over the years your public presentation skills will influence how well you function in your roles as an individual, an organization person, and a member of society.

The Individual

When you apply for a job, the employment interviewer evaluates you on the basis of certain characteristics. Your ability to communicate is one characteristic, and it comes across clearly in an interview. Employers realize that the ability to communicate often separates an exceptional employee from the average ones.

Being able to organize and present your thoughts is a significant determinant of your personal and professional success. When you speak and others listen and respond to your comments, it affects the way you see yourself and how others see you. Being able to give an effective public speech enhances your self-esteem; you feel good about yourself.

Public speaking ability has a major influence on personal and professional success.

Your message is more likely to be accepted if you have credibility with your audience. Source credibility pertains to both oral and written communication. Your credibility as a speaker and as a person will be recognized to the extent that you are perceived as expert, trustworthy, dynamic, objective, and well-intentioned.

The Organization Spokesperson

An organization, it has been said, is only as good as the individuals who comprise it. It might also be said that an organization communicates only as effectively as its individual members do. Business needs people who can effectively present the organizational viewpoint to the public. The average business organization does a poor job of acquainting the public with its contributions to society.

✔ CHECKLIST for Establishing Credibility

___**|** Be knowledgeable about your subject and well-prepared to speak. (expertise)

___**|** Develop and maintain a reputation for telling the truth. (trust)

___**|** Display an urge to communicate through your genuine involvement with both subject and audience. (dynamism)

___**|** Be open-minded to the views of others. (objective)

___**|** Be considerate of the feelings of others. (goodwill)

There have always been exceptions. For example, when Robert Blake entered a management training program 24 years ago, very little set him apart from the other trainees in terms of educational background and technical ability. However, he soon displayed a superior ability to organize his thoughts and to express himself. At the end of the training program he was awarded the choicest job assignment ever given to a trainee. Today he is president of the company. He recognizes the importance of technical ability, but as he sees it, "Unless a person is able to transmit information to others in a well-organized and convincing way, that person is likely to remain a technician — and a mediocre one at that."

From a communication standpoint it does not matter how pure the motives of the organization are. What does matter is what the public knows about such things and how the public responds to this knowledge. Unless the public is made aware of what business is doing and why, the best intentions of business will be to no avail.

Only through effective external communication can business present the information that is most likely to result in a desirable image. One of the most important and effective formats used to present that information is the public speech.

The Member of Society

The free expression of ideas is not merely tolerated but is encouraged in the United States. Issues are analyzed and points of view are presented in many different formats. Newspaper editorials, listener call-in shows on radio, town hall meetings, and barroom discussions (or arguments) are a few ways in which opinions are shared.

A democratic society thrives on the free expression of ideas, for it is through such interchange that a balanced perspective is maintained. When a certain point of view ceases to be expressed, perhaps for the lack of someone willing and able to speak out, that viewpoint no longer influences society.

Through pubic speaking ideas are presented for public evaluation. This was as true in the preliminaries to the Declaration of Independence as it is today in election campaigns. It is as evident at an annual meeting of stockholders as at the monthly meeting of a local union.

For lack of an effective speaker a good idea may fail to be considered. A lack of articulate opponents may result in the passage of legislation of little merit. Our free society requires willing and articulate people of every viewpoint.

THE PURPOSES OF THE SPEECH

Many speakers seem unable or unwilling to determine in advance the purposes of their speech. Consequently, the response of listeners is likely to be:

- "I'm not sure exactly what he meant."
- "I couldn't find any point to the speech."
- "I don't know what she was getting at."
- "What was the purpose of the speech anyway?"

In planning a speech you should first decide what its purposes will be. This is a two-step process: first determine the general purpose and then the specific purpose.

General Purpose

Most authorities recognize three general purposes in public speaking: to inform, to persuade, and to entertain. Although the three general purposes are usually considered as if they were separate and distinct, that is not actually true. Very few speeches are entirely informative, persuasive, or entertaining. Most speeches are a combination of two or more.

The three general purposes of public speaking are to inform, to persuade, and to entertain.

Informative

When you try to teach your listeners or to explain something to them, your general purpose is to inform. The classroom lecture is an example of an **informative speech**. Some informative speeches are intended to acquaint the listeners with something completely new to them. When Brenda White, a personnel director, explains to a group of new employees the company's benefits program, she is doing just that. Some informative speakers try to update listeners who are already somewhat knowledgeable about a subject. To give another specific example, when officers of credit unions attend the regional meeting of their trade association, they hear many informative speeches.

Persuasive

The second general purpose is to persuade the listener. **Persuasive speeches** range from those that seek to change the listener's beliefs or attitudes to those that attempt to get the listeners to act in a certain way.

The purpose for giving a persuasive speech is to elicit a covert response or an overt response. A **covert response** is, as the word implies, not readily apparent to the speaker nor to an observer. When a union leader seeks to convince the members that the union has their interests at heart, the speaker is seeking a covert response, acceptance of an idea. It is usually difficult to evaluate a speaker's effectiveness when the response being sought is covert.

Measuring effectiveness is easier with an overt response than with a covert response.

Evaluating a speaker's effectiveness is easier when the speaker is seeking an **overt response**, one that is observable and measurable. The manager who tries to get billing clerks to reduce their errors can check future error counts for evidence of effectiveness. The production manager who urges increased output from production workers can also measure results easily. In each of these specific examples, the speaker is seeking an overt response.

Entertaining

The third general purpose is to entertain — the response sought from the listeners is enjoyment. Many persons consider entertainment and humor to be synonymous, but that is not the case. Humor is certainly a common ingredient of entertainment, but it is not the only one. Perhaps you have had a teacher who thoroughly entertained and captivated the class with little or no humor. Some speakers who are enthusiastic about their subjects entertain their listeners. Others are able to entertain through their flair for drama or through their picturesque language.

Specific Purpose

The number of specific purposes for making a presentation is virtually infinite. The specific purpose of a speech is constructed with both the subject and the audience in mind.

The following examples suggest the relationship among subject, audience, general purpose, and specific purpose.

- *Subject:* The collection of delinquent accounts
- *Audience:* A class of undergraduate students of business administration
- *General purpose:* To inform
- *Specific purpose:* To explain techniques commonly used by business organizations to collect past-due bills from customers

- *Subject:* The collection of delinquent accounts
- *Audience:* Professional association of collection officers
- *General purpose:* To inform
- *Specific purpose:* To explain the latest approaches for collection of delinquent accounts

- *Subject:* Use of nuclear energy for generating electrical power
- *Audience:* Approximately 100 members of a neighborhood homeowners association
- *General purpose:* To persuade

> ## BOXED IN   *AN ETHICAL DILEMMA*
>
> Bill Johnson sits quietly in his plush, corner office reflecting on his history with Dynacon Inc. When he started with the company, management was producing one high-quality product. Bill learned to value product quality early in his career because it increased his credibility and contributed to high sales.
>
> Over the years the company expanded rapidly. The growth seemed positive but, in retrospect, Bill has some major doubts. As the product line expanded, quality became much more difficult to control. Bill's major concern is declining research dollars. He feels Dynacon is releasing its latest product, XG-15, prematurely. Some of the people in research and development still have questions about health hazards related to the product's use. In his opinion management has not ordered adequate testing.
>
> Bill feels his frustration mounting. His last official assignment, before retiring, is to introduce XG-15 to a group of clients he has worked with very closely. He values these associations. Bill knows his endorsement will sell the product, and conceivably problems will not surface for years. All Bill has to do is give the presentation and walk away.
>
> Bill feels boxed in. What would you do?

- *Specific purpose:* To persuade listeners to write their senators and representatives to express their opposition to increased reliance on nuclear energy.

These examples indicate that, while the general purpose may remain the same, the specific purpose will vary according to the audience.

RESEARCH FOR THE SPEECH

Audience Analysis

The more the speaker can learn about the audience in advance, the more appropriate the speech should be. To illustrate, Congressman Lilburn was invited to address the Wilbanks Employees Association. Seeking reelection, he was happy for the opportunity to promote his campaign theme, which was economy in government. He arrived at the auditorium barely in time. He spoke with vigor and emotion about the Social Security system and the absurdity of it. The audience numbered nearly 200, but only two people asked questions, and both were hostile. Had the congressman bothered to do research on the association in advance, he would have learned that most of the active members are retired employees.

A common shortcoming among speakers is a tendency to assume that what they find interesting will also interest their listeners. To be a good speaker you must adopt a **listener orientation**. When preparing a speech, ask yourself how you would feel if you were in the listener's place. Before being able to answer that, you must learn as much about your listeners as possible. This necessitates asking some basic questions immediately:

▪ How large will the audience be?
▪ How educated are the listeners?
▪ What occupations will be represented?
▪ What is the age range represented?
▪ To which social, political, or religious groups do the listeners belong?

The best way to analyze an audience is to talk personally with the prospective audience. Ideally, you would accomplish this far enough in advance to give you ample time to tailor the material to the listeners. Unfortunately, this is an unrealistic approach to audience analysis — in most cases it would be difficult, time consuming, and impractical.

A satisfactory alternative is to talk to several people who are likely to be in the audience. Assuming that they are similar to the rest of the audience members, you will get accurate insights into the interests of your listeners. When it is not possible to talk with a likely member of the audience or even to talk with anyone familiar with the audience, you face a challenge. You will have to make some inferences about the audience from the information that is available.

The more similar your listeners are in terms of such factors as educational level, occupation, age, and group memberships, the easier it is to predict their attitudes toward you and your message. The more heterogeneous or diversified the audience is, the fewer inferences you can make about your listeners.

The audience for a business presentation is generally knowledgeable about the speaker's topic. Because the audience members are similar in interests, knowledge, and background, the speaker can make certain assumptions about the audience. As in any speaking situation, however, advance audience analysis is also important in making a business presentation.

Topic Research

Much more time should be devoted to preparing a speech than to giving it.

Just as an athlete spends much more time practicing than actually competing, you will devote more time to preparation than to speaking. After determining the general purpose and the specific purpose, and after analyzing the audience, you should then take inventory of the sources of information available on the topic.

In recent years many business organizations have developed speakers' bureaus comprised of employees who volunteer to speak before local community organizations. In most cases these employees speak on subjects related to their areas of specialization. For speeches of this nature the speaker is probably his or her own best source of information.

To illustrate, when Randall Best, assistant purchasing manager, was asked to speak to a civic club on purchasing and its effects on the local community, he spent hours in the library preparing his speech. Yet he was disappointed with the audience's response. At the end of the speech he offered to answer questions, but no one asked any. There was courteous applause. The next day his boss was sympathetic but bluntly pointed out Randall's mistake: "As a purchasing agent you are recognized by these local groups as an expert. They want to learn what you think on the subject. They don't want some list of figures. They want your opinion."

Business speakers may be their own best source of information.

Businesspeople who need more specific information for a speech can usually call on someone else in the organization for help. Either through personal observations and knowledge or with the assistance of colleagues, most business speakers can prepare an appropriate speech.

Most students do not have the appropriate personal experiences for source material so the research process is complicated by the need to go beyond themselves for suitable ideas. This approach is not limited to students, because business speakers often look to outside sources for support of their ideas or to clarify knowledge of the subject. Students particularly, however, need to be aware of printed sources of information. These were described in Chapter 10, along with a discussion of the research process.

A knowledge of information sources will facilitate smooth and systematic progress from preparation to presentation of the speech. Throughout the preparation process keep in mind these questions that your listeners will be seeking answers to:

▪ How do you know?
▪ Is this an accurate statement?
▪ Does it agree with other sources?
▪ What does it have to do with the subject?
▪ What does it have to do with me?[2]

Of particular interest to speakers is a magazine called *Vital Speeches* devoted to significant recent public speeches. By reading it you can gain insights into the positions being taken by prominent speakers.

ORGANIZATION OF THE SPEECH

Speakers often make the mistake of believing that they are ready to speak once they have completed their research. What usually results is a speech that is unclear in purpose and inconsistent in direction. Such speakers have overlooked the necessity of organizing their material.

Speakers should have an overabundance of materials from which to select the most appropriate. Inexperienced speakers often question the value of doing more research than is absolutely necessary; however, after they have presented several speeches, the reasons will be obvious. It is

[2]Robert T. Oliver, Harold P. Zelko, and Paul D. Holtzman, *Communicative Speaking and Listening*, 4th ed. (New York: Holt, Rinehart and Winston, 1968), 104.

uncomfortable to a speaker and obvious to the listeners when a speech is short on ideas, for a speaker is then likely to include digressions, redundancies, and irrelevant statements.

The Body

A speech is made up of three main parts: the introduction, body, and conclusion. Although the body follows the introduction, most speakers develop the body first. The body of a speech presents its actual message and has three main components: central idea, main ideas, and supporting materials.

Central Idea

The central idea is the major theme of a speech; the speaker wants the listeners to remember it even if they forget all else. A campaigning politician may present many ideas in a campaign speech. The central idea, however, is usually "vote for me." Although central ideas are generally longer, they should be limited to one sentence. A training director recently gave an informative speech in which the central idea was this: a person should not be made a supervisor until he or she has satisfactorily completed a course in interpersonal communication. A good central idea is, like the example, brief and clear. The central idea represents the minimum that you want the listeners to remember.

Main Ideas

Several main ideas support the central idea.

After determining the central idea, you seek ideas to support it; these are the main ideas. The main ideas are secondary in importance only to the central idea, and speakers hope that the listeners will retain the main ideas, too. For that reason there should be many; four or five are sufficient for most speeches.

Supporting Materials

Once the main ideas have been selected, look for ways to support them. Because an argument that convinces some listeners will not necessarily convince others, you should seek enough supporting materials to reach all of the listeners.

Among the methods of support most frequently used are quotations, examples, analogies, and statistics. In deciding the appropriateness of a given form of support, the speaker should consider these questions:

1. *Quotations (or testimony)*
   a. Will the person being quoted be recognized by the listeners?
   b. Will the listeners regard the quoted person as an authority?
   c. Does the person being quoted have credibility with the listeners?
2. *Examples*
   a. Can the example be understood by the listeners?
   b. Is the example clearly related to the main point?

3. *Analogies*
   a. Is the analogy appropriate for the subject being considered?
   b. Will the listeners be able to grasp the relevance of the analogy?
4. *Statistics*
   a. Will the statistics be understandable to the listeners?
   b. Will the listeners recognize the relationship between the statistics and the main point the statistics are intended to support?
   c. Are the statistics recent and reliable enough to be acceptable to the listeners?

Sequence of Main Ideas

Once the central idea, the main ideas, and the supporting materials have been selected, the speaker must decide the sequence in which the main points will be presented. Some of the most common organizational patterns are the chronological, topical, spatial, and logical sequences. The sequence that will be most appropriate depends on the topic, the purpose, and the listeners' interests. Effective speakers are equally adept in using any one of these sequential arrangements.

Chronological Sequence.   In the **chronological sequence** the speech progresses from one given point in time to another. This sequence is regularly used when explaining a process. For example, when a plant manager explained papermaking to a class of undergraduates, he started by explaining how the lumber is purchased and what is done to it in the wood room. He described the entire process for the listeners up until the time when the paper is packaged and shipped out of the mill.

The chronological sequence might be used to describe the evolution of an idea or to explain how to do something.

Topical Sequence.   When a topic is divided into several different parts, it is arranged according to the **topical sequence**. The more natural the divisions, the easier it is for the listeners to understand and retain what the speaker is presenting. To illustrate, a company president spoke at the annual meeting of stockholders on the declining productivity of employees. He first spoke about the causes of this problem as perceived by management, then he presented the causes as perceived by labor. He concluded by discussing those causes perceived differently by the two sides.

The topical sequence seems to be the one used most frequently. Some speakers tend to use it even though another sequence would be more effective.

Spatial Sequence.   As the name **spatial sequence** implies, the use of space determines the arrangement of ideas that the speaker presents. In the spatial sequence the speaker arranges the material according to physical location. One approach to the spatial sequence might involve describing something directionally, from east to west; another might be to describe a building from its first floor to the top floor. For example, when the city planner presented recommendations for a mass transit system, she talked

The spatial sequence involves presenting material according to physical location.

about the unique ways each suburb would be affected by the system. She described the location of the main stations in the inner city and the system's accessibility to downtown office workers and shoppers. She also described the major northern, southern, eastern, and western routes and the terminus of each route.

Speakers who use the spatial sequence describe the physical location of certain points and the relationship between them. The spatial sequence should enable the listeners to visualize what the speaker is telling them.

The causal and the problem–solution patterns are examples of the logical sequence.

Logical Sequence.   Several different arrangement patterns are included within the logical sequence. Among the most common are the causal and the problem–solution patterns.

In using the causal approach, speakers have two options. One is to point out certain forces and the results that follow from them. For example, when a state chamber of commerce official spoke, he described the organized efforts made to attract new business to the state. He listed organizations that have moved to the state as a result of the efforts. In the presentation the efforts of the chamber were the forces and new business organizations the results.

The other option using the causal approach is to describe events and then to explain the forces that caused them. To illustrate, a representative of the Sierra Club discussing water pollution pointed out the growing health problems associated with it. She listed discharges from manufacturing plants and lax sewage control as the causes. In her argument she presented the results first, then the causes.

The problem–solution approach is quite similar to the causal approach because the speaker presents two main points. For example, in discussing an increase in customer complaints about sales personnel (the problem), the personnel director urged that greater emphasis be placed on employee training (the solution).

Introduction and Conclusion

Until you have decided what you will present in your speech, it is difficult to know how to get the listeners involved in it. For that reason the body of the speech should be developed before the introduction and the conclusion.

There are some speakers, however, who develop their ideas in the order they will present them. These speakers believe that by developing the introduction, body, and conclusion in that order, they will achieve better continuity between ideas.

An introduction should establish rapport with the listeners while gaining their attention.

The manner in which you introduce your speech will greatly influence the listeners' initial impressions. There are two purposes of the introduction: to establish rapport with the listeners and to gain the listeners' attention.

Among the approaches commonly used in the introduction are these:

1. Make a startling statement.
2. Refer to the audience.
3. Refer to the occasion.
4. Quote a recognized authority.
5. Ask a rhetorical question.
6. Use humor that is relevant.

Regardless of the approach you use, you should remember the purposes of the introduction and of the speech: to indicate your subject and to gain the acceptance of the listeners.

In concluding a speech you should, at a minimum, restate the central idea of the speech. A good conclusion indicates to the listeners that the topic has been thoroughly covered. These are some of the most common ways a speaker may conclude a speech:

1. Summarize the main points.
2. Propose a solution.
3. Quote a recognized authority.
4. Challenge the listeners to accomplish some specific goal.
5. Visualize the future if your proposal is or is not accepted.

OUTLINE FOR AN INFORMATIVE SPEECH

In outlining an informative speech, arrange its different parts into a sequence that allows an orderly presentation of ideas. Through the use of an outline you can determine whether the relationship between ideas is clear. An outline also helps the listener follow your train of thought. This is the outline of an informative speech given by a training director to an undergraduate professional management society:

By outlining a speech, the speaker is able to clarify the relationship between ideas.

    I. Introduction
      A. Brief history of the training function within the business organization
      B. Increased specialization and automation changes as stimulants for training
   II. Central idea: The job of the training director is varied enough to be challenging and very important to the organization
  III. Body (main ideas)
      A. The training director must learn the training needs of the organization
         1. Through observation of operations
         2. Through interviewing upper management
         3. Through interviewing line workers
      B. The training director must develop training programs to meet organizational needs
         1. Determine the target audience for the program
         2. Locate and schedule competent instructors for the program
      C. The training director must evaluate the effectiveness of the training programs
         1. Test participants on the subject matter
         2. Interview superiors of the participants and use other criteria to measure improvement
  IV. Conclusion
      A. Summary of speech body

1. Training director must learn training needs
2. Training director must develop appropriate training programs
3. Training director must evaluate the effectiveness of the programs
   B. The job of the training director is important to the organization and challenging to the individual

OUTLINE FOR A PERSUASIVE SPEECH

Although the outline of the persuasive speech is similar to that of the informative speech, the two types are not developed in the same way. The informative speech is usually factual and not controversial, and so gaining the listeners' acceptance is usually not difficult. To the persuasive speaker, however, gaining the listeners' acceptance is a challenge. The more a persuader's ideas conform to the way people think, the more likely it is that successful persuasion will occur.

In the motivated sequence ideas are presented in a natural order.

The **motivated sequence** is a method of speech organization based on analysis of the thought process.[3] If you follow this sequence, you will present your ideas in the natural order that people follow when thinking through to a problem solution. Listeners who are led through these steps will be motivated to accept your proposition. The motivated sequence consists of five steps:

1. Getting attention
2. Showing the need
3. Satisfying the need
4. Visualizing the results
5. Requesting approval or action

Just as readers become oblivious to magazine and newspaper advertisements, listeners also become oblivious when speakers try to persuade them. This is certainly not surprising; during an average day most of us are bombarded by numerous attempts to persuade. For these reasons a persuader must first get the attention of the listeners. There are a number of options available. The most appropriate approach depends on many factors, including the occasion and the nature of the audience. The opening least likely to get the attention of the listeners is, "My topic today is. . . ."

In showing the need to the listeners, you describe a problem. Besides a mere description you may clarify the problem by using examples. The examples will be effective if they illustrate the seriousness of the problem. Listeners are more likely to recognize the need if you point out how the problem affects them.

In satisfying the need you present a solution to the problem raised in the previous step. You show how the solution will satisfy the need of which the listeners are now aware. At this point you clearly state the attitude or action the listeners are being asked to adopt. By using examples or other

[3]Alan H. Monroe and Douglas Ehninger, *Principles of Speech Communications*, 8th ed. (Glenview, Ill.: Scott, Foresman, 1978), 252.

supporting materials, show that your proposal will work. As you explain how the solution will meet the need, you should anticipate likely objections and address them during this step.

By describing future conditions you help the listeners to visualize the results of the proposed solution. Some speakers describe the results likely if the solution is accepted. Others approach it negatively and describe future conditions if the solution is not accepted. The intended result of the visualization step is to intensify the desire of the listeners.

In requesting approval or action you focus the thoughts of the listeners on the theme developed in the speech. The speaker's request should be brief, to the point, and unmistakably clear.

This is the outline of a persuasive speech given by a production manager to a group of supervisors. In addition to the ideas presented, the steps of the motivated sequence are also indicated:

I. Introduction (*attention*)
   A. You have within you the power to grant yourself a pay increase.
   B. You are in a position to generate more business for the company.
II. Body (main ideas)
   A. Industrywide research shows that we trail competitors in two significant factors. (*need*)
     1. We have the highest rate of lost-time accidents in the industry.
     2. We have a worse than average rate of consumer complaints about product defects.
   B. There are some actions you can take that will increase your earnings and improve the company's position within the industry. (*satisfaction*)
     1. Always enforce all safety regulations.
     2. Stress constant quality control and make more spot checks yourself.
   C. If you follow our supervisory manual to the letter, lost-time accidents will be reduced by 50 percent and consumer complaints will be reduced by at least 30 percent. You will benefit directly in two ways. (*visualization*)
     1. Your earnings will increase.
     2. You will have less unproductive paperwork to complete concerning accidents.
III. Conclusion (*action*)
   A. Report all violations of safety regulations.

THE DELIVERY OF THE SPEECH

Many speakers believe if they have attended to all of the preliminaries leading up to a speech, the delivery will take care of itself. The advice they most likely give beginning speakers is, "Be natural." They tell speakers, "Imagine that you are carrying on a conversation with the audience and act accordingly." Such advice, although well-intended, is not helpful, because it is difficult to be natural in what is an unnatural situation.

Bodily changes usually occur when you are about to give a speech. Blood pressure and pulse rate increase, digestive processes slow down, perspir-

✔️ *CHECKLIST for Reducing Stage Fright*

___❚ Select a topic that genuinely interests you.

___❚ Analyze your audience and the setting in advance.

___❚ Prepare thoroughly; use a notecard for your main points.

___❚ Practice, practice, practice — but do not memorize.

___❚ Go through the entire speech on six or seven consecutive days.

___❚ Always keep your main purpose in mind.

___❚ While waiting to speak, sit in a relaxed, even limp, position and breath deeply.

___❚ Know your introduction especially well.

___❚ Refer to the notecard as necessary, but do not read.

___❚ Focus on your message and the response, not on yourself.

___❚ Use gestures and movement for emphasis.

ation increases, and breathing becomes irregular. These are some of the many different signs of anxiety that speakers may experience when facing an audience. Other signs are trembling hands, dryness in the mouth, and butterflies in the stomach.

Some nervousness is to be expected in giving a public speech, but much of it can be overcome.

Feeling nervous in a public-speaking situation is to be expected — it is completely normal. As you become more experienced, such signs may become less apparent, but they never completely disappear. Even extreme nervousness — which you may be so aware of — is not nearly as noticeable to the listeners as you may think.

Nervousness has a positive aspect. It gives you a slight edge, which is evident in greater alertness and sensitivity to the listeners. In fact, speakers who are more anxious very often give better speeches than do speakers who are less anxious. All in all, delivering a speech is a challenge that can provide satisfaction.

Voice Qualities

Since noise pollution has become an issue in society, people have grown increasingly aware of loudness, or volume. Speakers addressing a group should adjust their volume according to such factors as room size and background noises.

A speaker who regularly speaks more softly toward the end of each sentence is probably practicing improper breath control. Fred Rosen, for example, is a well-organized and an articulate speaker with one overriding fault that greatly reduces his effectiveness. He begins each sentence with enough volume to be easily heard, then reduces his volume until many of the listeners are unable to hear the end of each sentence. This practice has led his subordinates to call him Half-a-Sentence Rosen. If you have this problem, use shorter sentences or else consciously pause at natural breaks in the expression of your ideas to take a breath.

The speed, or rate, at which you speak influences the way others respond to you and your message. Inexperienced speakers sometimes speak too quickly due to nervousness, and this causes other problems. Speaking too rapidly results in breath-control difficulties and a tendency to give all ideas equal emphasis. Your main ideas should leap out at the listener, but this will not happen unless you slow down—but not to extremes. By speaking much too slowly some people err in the opposite direction.

Rate of speech and pitch contribute to the impression made by a speaker.

The high or low sound level of the voice is referred to as pitch. No one pitch is correct, but individuals have a certain pitch level at which their voice is most effective.

Variety is the key to the successful use of these voice qualities. By varying your volume, rate, and pitch you will become more interesting to hear, and your message will be more memorable.

Modes of Delivery

The four main modes of delivery used in public speaking are (1) impromptu, (2) extemporaneous, (3) memorized, and (4) manuscript. The impromptu speech is delivered with little opportunity to prepare. Its main virtue is that it is spontaneous; its main shortcoming is that it is usually not well planned. When you are urged to say a few words without any advance warning, what results is an impromptu speech.

Extemporaneous speaking is somewhat more formal than impromptu speaking. You have an opportunity to plan, and the resulting speech is better organized than an impromptu speech. You will usually rely somewhat on notes, but you will not read to the listeners. Most public speeches are delivered extemporaneously.

A memorized speech allows for a well-planned expression of ideas. When presenting a speech from memory, however, speakers tend to lose a certain amount of naturalness and sometimes sound and look quite wooden. The possibility of forgetting the speech is another negative aspect of the memorized speech.

Manuscript speaking is relied on for more formal occasions. Speaking from a manuscript, you are able to be very precise, and you can carefully control the exact message the listeners receive. Of course, it takes longer to develop a manuscript speech, and frequently the manuscript becomes a barrier between you and the audience.

Visual Support

Visual support, which will be discussed in Chapter 16, can help the communicator in at least four ways: by crystallizing vague ideas, by helping listeners remember information, by overcoming boredom and day-

Visual aids help keep the speaker and listeners on track.

✔ *CHECKLIST for Delivery*

___ Record your speech at least once while practicing and carefully evaluate it.

___ Vary your rate, pitch, and volume so that you emphasize your main points.

___ Avoid vocalized pauses: silence is preferable to unnecessary *uhs*.

___ Maintain eye contact with your listeners.

___ Develop an urge to communicate by selecting a topic in which you are interested.

___ Lessen the distance between yourself and your listeners.

dreaming, and by serving as signposts to keep the listener and speaker on track.[4]

Photographs, charts, graphs, handouts, chalkboards, bulletin boards, and overhead projectors are frequently used by the speaker as visual aids. However, they are also frequently misused. Visual support is not a substitute for the speech itself. The burden is still on you to convey the message. Very good support material will not compensate for a mediocre speech.

Team Presentations

Although individual presentations are much more frequent, presentations by teams of individuals are not unusual. Continuity is especially important in a team presentation. The presentation should appear as a unified whole rather than as a series of individual presentations. Through careful planning the team members should avoid repetition and should structure the presentations so that each speaker paves the way for the succeeding speaker.

To illustrate, a chamber of commerce that sought to attract a major league baseball team assembled a group to present the city's case to the owners of the ball clubs. The first speaker described the area from which the team would draw spectators. Through the use of flip charts the makeup of the population according to educational level was described. The second speaker presented the findings of a wage survey done in the community. The various income levels were described, and the amount of discretionary income at each level was estimated. Transportation facilities were described by the third speaker. Information about the airport and flight

[4]Paul R. Timm, *Functional Business Presentations* (Englewood Cliffs, N.J.: Prentice-Hall, 1981), 131.

✔ *CHECKLIST for Team Presentation*

____⌐ Plan the team presentation as a group, and divide the topics into logical and well-balanced divisions.

____⌐ Anticipate questions and be prepared to respond to them.

____⌐ Unless you are the first speaker, begin by referring to the previous speaker.

____⌐ Direct your speech primarily to the larger audience rather than to the other speakers.

____⌐ Refer where appropriate in your speech to the speeches of those who preceded you.

____⌐ Do not infringe on the time of the speakers who follow you.

____⌐ Do not lose sight of the goal of the team.

schedules was presented, as was a description of the city bus system. The urban freeway system was also shown with graphics. The fourth speaker described the sports complex where the team would play and listed the specific financial incentives and tax benefits the city would provide the team that accepted its offer. After agreeing to move to the city, the team officials cited the attractive package and persuasive presentations as major reasons.

The team presentation contains all the burdens of an individual presentation, and it also requires coordination with your colleagues. Planning, therefore, is especially important. Be sure to practice with visual aids and to time each speaker's presentation, because a limited amount of time often is scheduled for team presentations.

Planning and coordination are especially important in team presentations.

People react differently to the stress of public speaking, making it difficult to know exactly how much time each speaker may take. In their anxiety, some speakers speed up their delivery rate by as much as one-third or more. Others do just the opposite; they slow down and therefore put pressure on other members to cut their presentations so that the team ends on schedule. Some system, such as placing a watch on the lectern or signaling the time remaining, can help keep the presentation from continuing too long.

All of the principles of effective communication by individual speakers pertain to the team presentation as well.

SUMMARY

The fear that many people express at the prospect of giving a speech can be overcome through careful preparation. Public speaking is important not only to the professional growth of the individual but to the organization the individual represents and, in our free society, to the democratic process.

The three main general purposes for public speeches are (1) to inform, (2) to persuade, and (3) to entertain. The numerous specific purposes depend on what the individual speaker wishes to accomplish.

The first step in planning a speech is to decide what the purposes will be. The speaker should then learn as much as possible about the audience. The more that is known in advance about the listeners, the more likely that the speaker will be able to appeal to their interests. The next step is to research the topic fully, which may require library research.

A speech is made up of three main parts: introduction, body, and conclusion. The body, which is the most important part, should be prepared first. It includes a central idea, several main ideas, and supporting materials. Quotations, examples, analogies, and statistics are among the most common methods of support. A speaker can choose from several different sequences of ideas. The topical sequence is used most frequently. Some other common sequences are chronological, spatial, and logical.

After the body of the speech has been prepared, the speaker will develop an introduction and a conclusion. Outlining the speech enables the speaker to examine the relationships between ideas and to provide for continuity.

The motivated sequence is a series of steps that a persuasive speaker can use to carry listeners along to the desired solution.

The primary message of a speech is the verbal one, but the speaker provides much additional information through other channels. The four modes of delivery are impromptu, extemporaneous, memorized, and manuscript. Through the use of visual support or team presentations, a speaker may attract greater interest in a subject.

Key Terms

- **informative speech**
- **persuasive speech**
- **covert response**
- **overt response**
- **listener orientation**

- **chronological sequence**
- **topical sequence**
- **spatial sequence**
- **motivated sequence**

Review Questions

1. Why is public speaking so important to the individual, the organization, and society?

2. Describe the two-step process used to arrive at the purpose of a speech.

3. What are the differences between a covert response and an overt response? Give three examples of each.

4. What is audience analysis?

5. What are the five basic questions you should consider when analyzing an audience?

6. Explain the relationship between the central idea, the main idea, and supporting materials in a speech.

7. What are four commonly used forms of support?

8. What are four commonly used sequences of main points?

Exercises

1. Select a speech from *Vital Speeches* magazine and analyze it to determine its general purpose, main ideas, and supporting materials.

2. Develop a five-minute informative speech to present to your class. Encourage comments and questions from the class members. Write a one- or two-page paper in which you describe the changes you would make in the speech if you gave it again.

3. Do a written audience analysis of your communication class. Detail the ways in which class members are similar and ways they are different.

4. Develop a five-minute persuasive speech on a subject about which you feel strongly. Describe those factors from your audience analysis (as in Exercise 3) that most influenced your approach.

5. Give a one-minute impromptu speech on a topic selected by someone else in your class. Try to present one main idea and support it as well as you can.

6. Tape-record one of your speeches and write a two-page evaluation of it.

7. In groups of four or five prepare a team presentation to be given before the class. Select a subject, and divide it among the team members. Each team member should have a specific role, and the other class members should be told the kind of group they are to represent. Following each team presentation ask the class to do an evaluation.

8. Name two public figures whom you have seen give a speech (either in person or on television). Describe what you think each should do to become a better public speaker.

Central Telephone Company | *CASE*

John D. Stegman, The Ohio State University

Central Telephone (CTC) is an independent communications company, not con-nected with any of the Baby Bells. It is large enough to maintain a profitable enterprise and provide the service that is required by the state's Public Utilities Commission (PUCO). The company provides telephone service to homes and businesses. Like all utilities, CTC must obtain the approval of the PUCO for a rate increase. The reason for a recent request for a 2 percent increase in rates is that CTC's previous increases have not been enough to keep pace with inflation. CTC, like most other companies, has shareholders to please. In addition to the requested rate increase, CTC has proposed an aid package for those who are below the federal poverty level and therefore cannot afford local phone service.

In order to sell the proposed rate increase, CTC is sending spokespersons to give free ''coffee and donut'' sessions to the opinion leaders of various towns. The towns are not picked at random. They are those that the company expects to oppose the increase. The company spokespersons are usually local service reps, and so the townspeople know them well. Unfortunately, the service that CTC provides is not always good. Many complaints have been made about noisy lines, billing problems, and high rates. The company will use the welfare proposal as an argument against the complaint about high rates. Recent advances in service levels and office improvements (digital conversion of central offices) should help CTC to counter other complaints.

One of the meetings is scheduled at the Hillyerds Grade School. You represent CTC as the local service representative and spokesperson. Jerry Neal, your division manager, will also attend the meeting. In the audience will be the Hillyerds mayor and council members plus several extremely disgruntled local customers. You know that anyone who favors a telephone rate increase will not likely attend such a meeting. You realize that this is a crisis communication situation. Accordingly, your planning must include speaking to a hostile audience.

Case Questions

1. What is your purpose for this presentation to this particular audience?
2. What elements of the audience makeup are important to you and how you tailor your message?
3. What tone and style should you use to speak to this group?
4. Will you involve your boss, the division manager? If so, how?
5. How are your strategies different from normal speaking situations?

CASE | ***The City Council Meeting***

Julie C. Burkhard, Charlottesville, Virginia

Jeffrey Faught is the director of the chamber of commerce in Eastman. The town has a population of approximately 3,000 but is growing.

Jeffrey has been working for about two years to bring industry to Eastman. Presently the town has no industries at all. Most of the people in Eastman are local business people or farmers. Jeffrey believes the town needs some industry. It would not only strengthen the economy but would also create more jobs. With jobs come people, and people need homes to live in; therefore, real estate would gain from the industry as well.

Jeffrey has been talking with someone who might be interested in moving a light-manufacturing branch to Eastman. The problem is that many townspeople want a park and recreational area where the plant would be built. The city council must decide whether to grant a zoning change for the new industry or the new park.

The second Tuesday night of every month, the city council meets. The public is invited, and so anyone may attend. This particular Tuesday Jeffrey decides he must make his stand known to both the town council and the people who want the park. He has not given many speeches, but he knows this presentation must be very persuasive.

Many townspeople have wanted a park for their children for years. They believe the town is doing just fine without industry. In the past, the town council has shared this view. Jeffrey is faced with the job of convincing both the council and the people to change their views.

Case Questions

1. What should Jeffrey take into consideration when analyzing his audience?

2. How might he organize his presentation to accomplish his persuasive purpose?

3. Knowing that Jeffrey has to overcome the objections of the council and the people, what modes of proof should he attempt to employ?

Visual Support

Learning Objectives

1 *To know the correct format for a table.*

2 *To learn when to use visual support.*

3 *To be able to correctly choose the type of figure that best supports a written or oral report.*

4 *To learn how to prepare different forms of figures.*

5 *To know the major media that support oral presentations.*

"I'm worried about this presentation, Henry. My research is thorough and my conclusions are solid, but there's so much data that the managers may not be able to follow my analysis or they may get bored. I'd really like to use some flashy 3-D pie graphs. Can you help me?"

"That's our job in Media Services — to help employees who are writing reports or making oral presentations. We all know that visual support can add interest, precision, and clarity to the presentation. On the other hand, we have to be careful not to mislead the audience or obscure important information. And too much 'flash' can call undue attention to the visual support itself.

"Our job, Jeannie, is to apply solid principles of visual communication to enhance primary messages. I need to find out from you the goals, the main points, and areas of potential confusion in your presentation. We might ultimately use a 3-D pie graph, but there are many important steps to take first. Visual support is a process, not just an end result."

Jeannie's request for a specific form of visual support, without knowing the underlying principles, is not unusual. Many finished reports and presentations are weakened by this approach.

Chapter 11 was devoted to the writing of effective reports, and Chapter 15 discussed the effective delivery of oral presentations. This chapter examines how to make them more effective through the use of carefully executed visual support.

PREPARATION OF TABLES AND FIGURES

Tables provide a relatively large amount of precise data.

Most types of **visual support** can be incorporated in a written report or delivered as part of an oral presentation equally well. In fact, written reports often precede oral reports on the same topic, and written information is often distributed as part of the oral presentation. Of the two categories of visual support, tables are more likely to be used in written reports because of the amount of precise data they contain. On the other hand, the category referred to as **figures** — which includes graphs, charts, maps, drawings, and photographs — has at least as many applications in oral presentations as in written reports.

Tables

Their tabular format gives **tables** a rather standard appearance, as discussed in Chapter 11. Tables are valuable for delivering precise data. Organizations that use computers to store, retrieve, and analyze data use database and spreadsheet software, and the initial output from this software is usually in tabular form.

The appearance of tables may vary somewhat, but they typically have these parts: title, spanner head, stub head, column heads, rules, and data. They may have totals, footnotes, source information, and a caption in addition to the title. A series of tables may be numbered. Figure 16.1 shows the position of typical elements. Although not shown in the figure, data that include decimals should be aligned vertically on the decimal points. Rules are lines that separate portions of the table. A double line or bold line separates the title from other information. A single line of normal weight separates spanner heads from column heads. Data is then placed in rows and columns.

When used in oral presentations, tables need to be simple enough so that the main concept can be quickly grasped. Adding shading or a change in color to important columns or rows, such as subtotals, can dramatically improve the speed of comprehension. Note in Figure 16.2 how shading, italics, and different type sizes improve the appearance of the same information as in Figure 16.1.

Figures

The data available in table form from your spreadsheet or database can be entered into presentation graphics software to produce graphs, charts, maps, drawings, or other visual support forms. Use these treatments to summarize information, add clarity, illustrate relationships, or to add vividness. Among the most popular types of figures you might use in a long report are graphs, charts, and maps.

Graphs

Graphs can sometimes present information more effectively than tables.

Like tables, **graphs** are used to present quantitative data. You will often discover that information you intended to put into table form can be shown more effectively in a graph. Graphs show trends, comparisons, or some-

FIGURE 16.1 ▪ *Parts of a Table*

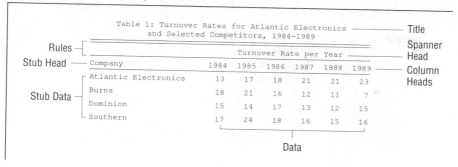

FIGURE 16.2 ▪ *Table Using Shading, Italics, and Different Type Sizes*

Table 1: Turnover Rates for Atlantic Electronics and Selected Competitors, 1984-1989						
	Turnover Rate per Year					
Company	**1984**	**1985**	**1986**	**1987**	**1988**	**1989**
Atlantic Electronics	13	17	18	21	21	23
Burns	18	21	16	12	11	7
Dominion	15	14	17	13	12	15
Southern	17	24	18	16	15	16

times both trends and comparisons. Four basic kinds of graphs are pie graphs, line graphs, bar graphs, and pictographs.

Pie Graphs.   Pie graphs, also called circle graphs, show comparisons only. They contain a comparison of parts to a whole. You will recall the pie graph in the long report in Chapter 11, reproduced here as Figure 16.3. These simple rules should help you construct a good pie graph:

1. Always begin your pie graph at the 12 o'clock position.
2. Enter the largest percentage first, and work clockwise around the graph entering the remaining percentages in descending order according to size. If there is a "miscellaneous" or "other" category, it may appear last, regardless of size.
3. To compute the exact space needed for each percentage, multiply 360 (the number of degrees in a circle) by the percentage. Your product is the number of degrees the percentage should represent. (For example, 360 × 29% = 104 degrees.)
4. Use a protractor and ruler to draw the graph.

Line Graphs.   Single line graphs show trends. Double line graphs show both trends and comparisons. Double line graphs usually contain no more than three or four lines; too many will confuse the reader. One line — usually the lowest, the primary, or the earliest — should be a solid line.

FIGURE 16.3   ■   *Sample Pie Graph*

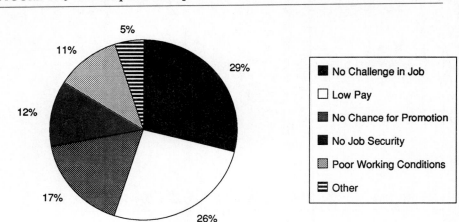

Figure 3: Reasons for Employee Separations at Atlantic Electronics

Other lines, added above the solid one, are often dotted and dashed. Another option is to use colors for the lines. In any case, the treatment selected should allow quick differentiation. Figures 16.4 and 16.5 are line graphs reproduced from the long report in Chapter 11.

Bar Graphs. The third kind of graph, the bar graph, best shows comparisons. Again, the example (Figure 16.6) is from Chapter 11.

In preparing a bar graph, make the bars wider than the space between them. If the *x*-axis has a logical progression, such as time units, use that progression and plot the bars as the data dictates. If no logical sequence exists, however, arrange the items so the bars either increase or decrease in height.

Grid lines and tick marks can be helpful to the viewer. Grid lines are light horizontal, or occasionally vertical, lines that lead the eyes from the value on the *y*-axis across to—and behind—the bars. Tick marks on either the *x*- or *y*-axis appear at major divisions of the axis, such as at 500, 1,000, 1,500, and 2,000 units.

If the bars extend from left to right, the graph is called a horizontal bar graph. Another type, the subdivided bar graph, can be used if you have more specific information about the contents of each bar. For example, in Figure 16.7, we see that the information about turnover rates has been subdivided by sex.

A final type of bar graph can show both positive and negative qualities. This graph is called a bilateral bar graph. If the information in Figure 16.7 for 1989 (23 percent turnover rate) is broken down by plant location, we develop the bilateral graph shown in Figure 16.8.

FIGURE 16.4 ▪ *Sample Line Graph*

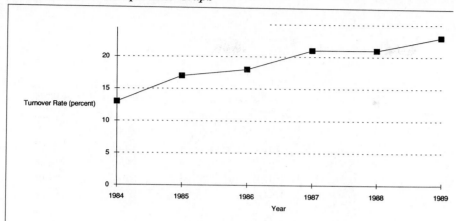

Figure 1: Atlantic Electronics Turnover Rates, 1984-1989

FIGURE 16.5 ▪ *Double Line Graph*

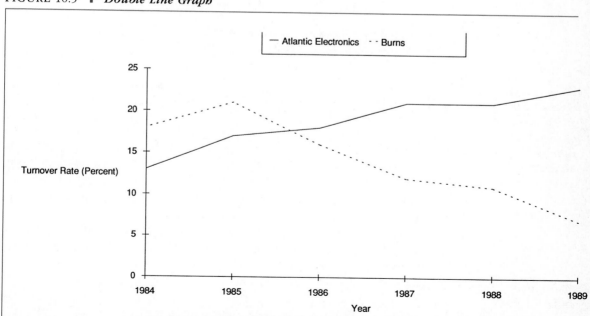

Figure 1: Turnover Rates for Atlantic Electronics and Burns, 1984-1989

FIGURE 16.6 ▪ *Sample Bar Graph*

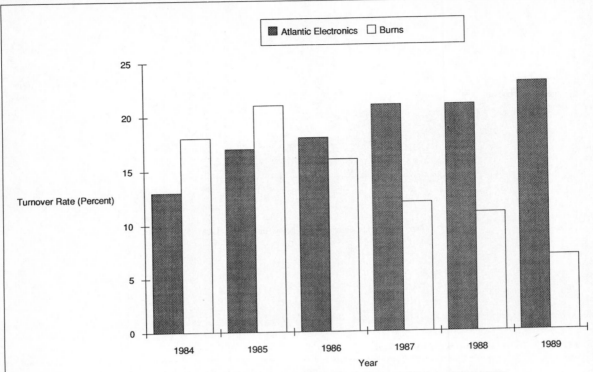

Figure 2: Turnover Rates for Atlantic Electronics and Burns, 1984-1989

Three special types of bar graphs are horizontal, subdivided, and bilateral.

On a bilateral bar graph, the zero point is drawn through the middle of the graph. Positive quantities are entered first, beginning with the largest positive quantity. Negative quantities are on the right side of the graph, with the smallest negative quantity shown first. An exception to this arrangement is when the *x*-axis has an inherent order, such as years from 1988 to 1992. In that case, the bars would be plotted in year order regardless of positive or negative order.

Pictographs.   Another type of graph is the pictograph. This is similar to the bar graph except symbols rather than bars represent the quantities shown. The symbols can vary widely, from coins representing money to tractors representing farmers. See the color insert following page 422 for an example of a pictograph.

Charts show nonquantitative information.

Charts

Unlike graphs, which contain quantitative data, **charts** and diagrams show nonquantitative information. The differences between charts and diagrams are not always clear-cut. However, most diagrams show some kind of process, whereas charts contain static information.

FIGURE 16.7 ▪ *Subdivided Bar Graph*

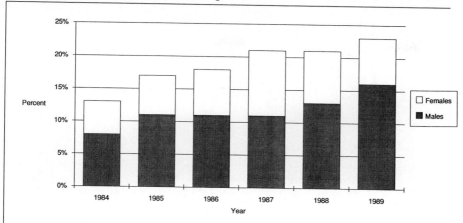

Figure 1: Comparison of Male Versus Female Turnover Rates
at Atlantic Electronics, 1984-1989

The organizational chart many businesses have is a picture of the organization. It shows (1) the various positions in the hierarchy and (2) the lines of authority among these positions. An organizational chart for a small construction firm with five functional areas might be very simple, as shown in Figure 16.9.

The variety of charts and diagrams you might use in long reports is unlimited — although all of them would not appear in a single report, of course. During the planning stage for a report, you might even put together a kind of checklist, called a needs chart, for your own use. A sample needs chart was shown in Chapter 10 (Table 10.1).

BOXED IN *AN ETHICAL DILEMMA*

Marie: **I'm not too comfortable about submitting this bar graph to George. I think it's misleading.**

Paul: **It looks fine to me. I really like the vivid red for our company. It makes us look better than our competitors with the drab-colored bars.**

Marie: **That's my point. The graph is supposed to reflect the actual data. But using a bright color for us—and drawing the three-dimensional graph so that we have more area than the competitors—seems as if we're tricking the viewer. The graph makes us look much bigger and better than we are.**

Paul: **I like it. George will like it. What's your problem?**

Marie feels boxed in. What would you do?

FIGURE 16.8   ▪   *Bilateral Bar Graph*

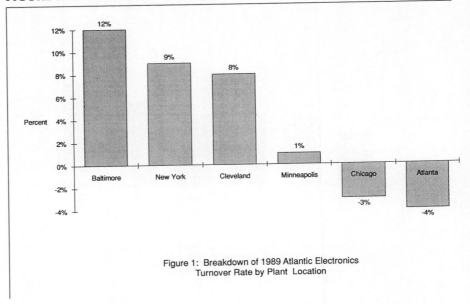

Figure 1: Breakdown of 1989 Atlantic Electronics
Turnover Rate by Plant Location

FIGURE 16.9   ▪   *Organizational Chart*

Prepared with MORE II software courtesy of Symantec Corporation.

These brief guidelines should help you prepare charts and diagrams:

▪ Keep the chart or diagram as simple as possible. Do not slow your readers down by forcing them to spend unnecessary time trying to understand your drawing.

▪ Label each important part of a chart or diagram in capital letters.

▪ If you are diagramming a process, add arrows between steps or stages in the process. Arrows will help readers follow the process itself.

▪ Give the chart or diagram a number and a title. Place this information directly beneath the drawing (for example, Figure 1: Steps in Computing Compound Interest). Typically, an Arabic number is used.

▪ Place the chart or diagram on the page as you would a table. Introduce it, present it, and interpret it.

▪ Do not rule out the use of color. If you only have one copy of the report to prepare, it is easy to add color, which itself adds clarity, understanding, and interest.

Maps

In writing long reports, maps are used less frequently than graphs, charts, and diagrams. However, maps are an interesting way to present the geographical distribution of a variety of information. For example, you might use a map of the United States to show the dollar sales for a particular company in each state. You might also break the map into territories or regions and show increases or decreases in sales for each region. Generally, you can use any map of a city, state, region, country, or larger area if it fits your report material. See the color insert following page 422 for a computer-prepared map.

Drawings and Photographs

Occasionally, a report can be improved by adding a drawing or photograph. Drawings could include floor plans, artistic illustrations, or medical and anatomical drawings. Figure 16.10 is an engineering drawing prepared with computer-assisted design and drafting software. Photographs are used for much the same purposes as drawings, but photographs add realism and precision because they are pictures of the actual item. Both drawings and photographs, of course, can be presented in color.

Computer-Generated Visual Support

As business increasingly relies on computers for text editing and data analysis, it will also integrate special graphics tools. Besides saving time and money, computer-generated visual support can be produced in color. The report writer or oral presenter processes, examines, and manipulates the data, prepares and edits the text, and designs the maps, graphs, and drawings, all at the same computer terminal.

Microcomputer-generated graphics are created in four ways: from statistical packages, from spreadsheets, from graphics packages, and from packages that are combinations of other packages. One of the major types of combination packages is the presentation graphics software group. Fig-

Savings in both time and money result when visual support material is computer generated.

Computer graphics are created in four ways.

FIGURE 16.10 ▪ *Sample Drawing*

Source: Prepared in Drafix® CAD Ultra, courtesy of Foresight Resources Corporation,™ Kansas City, Missouri.

ure 16.11 shows 16 categories of typical output. These packages usually import data from the database or spreadsheet of a personal computer and produce graphic output. Figure 16.12 depicts this process. The more expert the user and the more powerful the software, the more impressive the results will be. Vivid colors and combinations of visual support categories are possible, as seen in the color insert following page 422. This shows a 3-D pie graph, a 3-D bar graph, an area and drawing combination, a color world map, a bar and line graph combination, a bar and map combination, and a computer-prepared color map.

✔ CHECKLIST for Preparation of Visual Support[1]

▬▪ Present the correct amount of precision.

▬▪ Avoid misleading the viewer through poor choice of support form or color.

▬▪ Select the correct support form for showing comparison, trends, or relationships.

▬▪ Plan for an esthetically pleasing appearance.

▬▪ Make sure the major point is immediately clear and obvious.

▬▪ Do not allow visual support to draw too much attention to itself.

[1]Paul R. Timm, *Functional Business Presentations* (Englewood Cliffs, N.J.: Prentice-Hall, 1981), 136.

FIGURE 16.11 ▪ *Typical Graphics Output of a Combination Software Package*

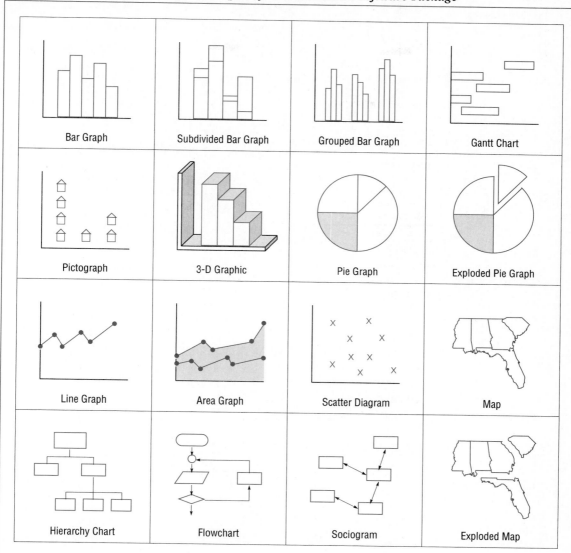

Source: Figure 13-12 from *Understanding Computers and Information Processing: Today and Tomorrow,* Third Edition, by Charles S. Parker, p. 426, copyright © 1990 by The Dryden Press, a division of Holt, Rinehart and Winston, Inc., reprinted by permission of the publisher.

FIGURE 16.12 ı *Graphics Package Process*

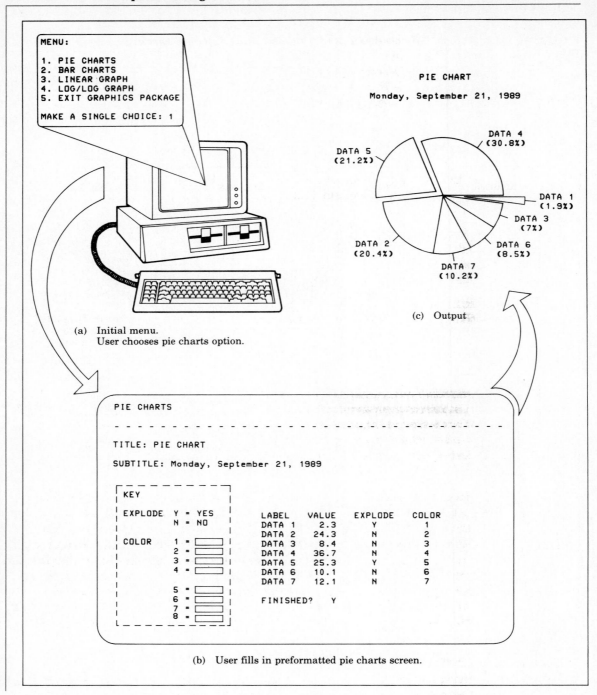

(a) Initial menu.
User chooses pie charts option.

(c) Output

(b) User fills in preformatted pie charts screen.

Source: Figure 13-13 from *Understanding Computers and Information Processing: Today and Tomorrow,* Third Edition, by Charles S. Parker, p. 427, copyright © 1990 by The Dryden Press, a division of Holt, Rinehart and Winston, Inc., reprinted by permission of the publisher.

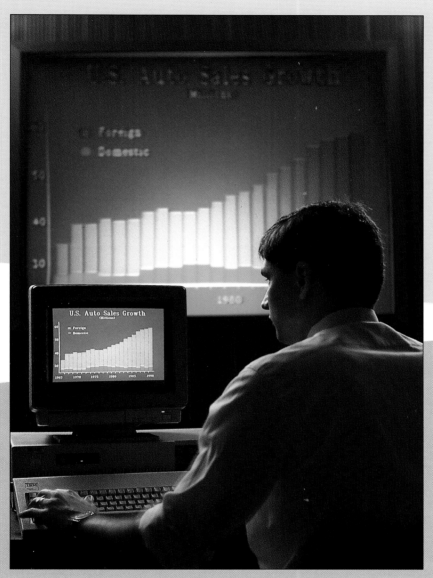

Source: Courtesy of The University of Georgia, Department of Management.

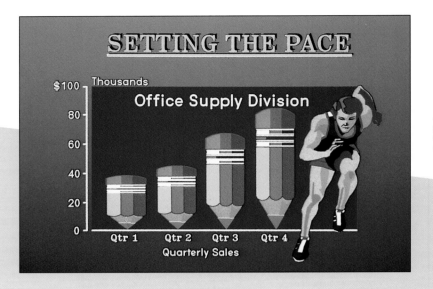

Pictograph
Source: Courtesy of
General Parametrics
Corporation.

*Computer-Prepared
Map*
Source: Prepared with
Pixie Software, courtesy
of Zenographics.

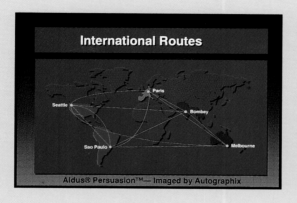

Color World Map
Source: © Aldus
Corporation 1988-1990.
Used with the express
permission of Aldus
Corporation. Aldus
Persuasion® is a
registered trademark
of Aldus Corporation.
All rights reserved.

*Area and Drawing
Combination Chart*
Source: Image created by
SlideWrite Plus, courtesy
of Advanced Graphics
Software, Inc.

3-D Bar Graph
Source: Image created by
SlideWrite Plus, courtesy
of Advanced Graphics
Software, Inc.

Bar Graph and Map Combination
Source: Prepared with Pixie Software, courtesy of Zenographics.

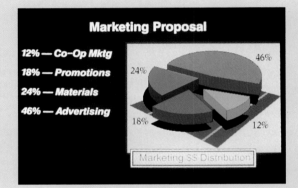

3-D Pie Graph
Source: Prepared with MORE II software, courtesy of Symantec Corporation.

Bar and Line Graph Combination
Source: Prepared with Pixie Software, courtesy of Zenographics.

FIGURE. 16.13   ▪   *Summary of Visual Communication Principles*

Primary Objective	Best Support Form	Primary Application Concerns	Secondary Application Concerns
Deliver Precision	Table	Accuracy, heads, rules, totals	Spacing, placement on page or in report
Deliver Complex Documentation	Table	Thoroughness of information	Spacing, placement on page or in report
Achieve Retention	Combine oral and visual messages	Balance of oral and visual	Timing
Enhance Comprehension: Show Trends	Line graphs	Differentiating lines	Grid lines, tick marks, legend
Enhance Comprehension: Show Comparisons	Bar graphs	Selection of correct type of bar graph	Grid lines, tick marks, legend
Enhance Comprehension: Show Relationships	Pie graphs, Venn diagrams	Avoiding too much complexity	Showing secondary relationships
Illustrate Technical Detail	Engineering drawing	Accurate representation	Avoiding too much detail
Create Interest	3-D graphics, colors, pictures, drawings	Avoiding inappropriate emphasis of items	Creating too much interest in support
Maintain Continuity	Text selections, icons	Achieving consistency	Producing too much information

MODES OF DELIVERY

The placement of visual support in a written report was discussed in Chapter 11. For oral reports, the media used to deliver the images include transparencies, 35mm slides, flip charts, and blackboards.

Business is placing increasing emphasis on high-quality, visually supported presentations, and the design of conference rooms is changing accordingly. Computer and photographic equipment is available in increasing variety for the preparation of images. These developments underscore the importance of mastering techniques for the delivery of high-quality, well-executed visual support.

Transparencies

Transparencies are widely used in academic settings and for quick, informal presentations. The overhead projectors for transparencies are easy to use, inexpensive, work well for small and large audiences, and do not require a totally darkened room. Black-on-white original images can be transferred to transparencies as black-on-clear, black-on-color, or color-on-clear film. Several transparencies can be made for a dollar and preparation requires only a few minutes. Most laser printers can provide black-

Laser printers can provide black-on-clear transparencies.

on-clear transparencies instead of paper originals. Color images can be transferred to color transparencies for a higher cost, but the quality of the output varies.

When using the overhead projector, avoid leaving the projector on with no image showing, leaving an image on longer than necessary, standing in front of the screen, looking at the screen rather than the audience, and relying too heavily on the visual portion of your presentation. Instead, use transparencies to add continuity and interest to your presentation and to clarify data. Consider covering part of the transparency and disclosing items as you discuss them. Also consider using pens with either permanent or removable ink to add to transparency images. For example, you may wish to have a prepared x- and y-axis grid to which you add, with different colors, the lines of a line graph as you discuss each one.

35mm Slides

Slides tend to be used in more formal situations with larger audiences than transparencies. The recent marriage of photography and computer text and images is increasing the quality and speed of preparation of 35mm slides. A color photograph on a slide can be sent to a computer screen, where text or graphics can be added or the photograph modified, and output sent to an on-the-spot processing machine. Another machine can print a sequence number and title on the slide carrier to ease slide show organization. The total time required is only a few minutes.

For most preparers, several days are needed for film processing, and slides cost more to prepare than transparencies. The projection of slides requires an almost dark room.

Flip Charts

Speakers may write on flip charts during the presentation — or prepare the pages in advance.

Widely used for small business presentations because of their flexibility and low cost, **flip charts** are large tablets of plain or gridded paper fastened to an easel. Information can be added with a marking pen during the presentation and pages can be flipped or removed as clean sheets are needed. Another approach is to place packaged presentations on tablets for repeated use.

Use flip charts only for informal presentations and be sure each member of the audience can see the chart. Write legibly. Use various colors of markers to add interest and variety.

Blackboards

The reasons why blackboards have been used in educational settings for so many years are that they allow spontaneous sharing of information, are inexpensive, and are easy to use. Businesses today are moving more to whiteboards that are marked on with erasable, colored pens. Some portable whiteboards can electronically capture the image on the screen and provide a photocopy immediately. Modern conference and presentation

✔ *CHECKLIST for Delivery of Visual Support*

⎯⎤ Make sure everyone can see the visual.

⎯⎤ Don't talk to the visual; look at your audience.

⎯⎤ Display the visual only when you refer to it; for example, turn off an overhead projector when you have made your point.

⎯⎤ Learn in advance the most appropriate time to use a visual.

⎯⎤ Be familiar with your equipment; practice beforehand if you need to.

⎯⎤ Be sure the equipment is operable.

⎯⎤ Have a back-up machine if the aid is integral to your presentation.

rooms often are equipped with built-in boards, screens, projectors, lighting control, and even computer image projectors.

SUMMARY

Both written reports and oral presentations benefit from visual support, which can enhance comprehension and retention, clarify and simplify, and add interest. Almost all forms of visual support fall into one of two categories: tables and figures. Tables are tabular presentations of precise data. Figures include such subcategories as graphs, charts, maps, drawings, diagrams, and photographs. Graphs may be line graphs, which are useful for showing trends, or bar graphs, which are effective for showing comparisons. For illustrating relationships, pie graphs are also valuable. Special situations and more complex data may require stacked, clustered, or bilateral bar graphs.

Personal computers and presentation graphics software have become highly effective in helping produce top quality output for written and especially for oral presentations of information. A nonprofessional user can prepare professional quality transparencies and slides with this software.

Oral presentations usually rely on one of four media for support: transparencies, 35mm slides, flip charts, and blackboards. Whatever the medium of support, the presenter should keep in mind that visual support must not call undue attention to itself.

Key Terms

▌ **visual support**	▌ **graph**
▌ **figure**	▌ **chart**
▌ **table**	▌ **flip chart**

References

Hoadley, Ellen D. "Investigating the Effects of Color," *Communications of the ACM* 33 (February 1990): 120–125.

Spear, Mary Eleanor. *Practical Charting Techniques* (New York: McGraw-Hill, 1969).

Tufte, Edward R. *The Visual Display of Quantitative Information* (Cheshire, Conn.: Graphics Press, 1983).

Review Questions

1. What is the difference between tables and figures?

2. What are the major types of figures?

3. What are the categories of graphs?

4. Which type of graph is best for comparison of parts?

5. Which type of graph is best for showing trends?

6. What are the major media employed in business to support oral presentations? Describe the strengths and weaknesses of each.

Exercises

1. As an accountant at Briggs Manufacturing, you have been able to isolate the utilities costs incurred in the operation of the research building that was completed and occupied four years ago. Your superior, Henrietta Starling, has asked you to gather this information so that she can analyze it. You know this information will be part of a report she is preparing for the board of directors, and you want to present as clear and understandable a report as possible. If you can take some of the burden of the report preparation off Starling, so much the better.

You have decided that you will present the information in a variety of ways. You will supply both charts and tables; in some cases this will be a duplication so that Starling may choose between alternatives. The data are as follows:

Monthly Electricity Usage in Kilowatt Hours

	1987	1988	1989	1990
J	2,500	2,575	2,495	2,600
F	2,500	2,600	3,000	3,200
M	3,000	3,100	3,200	3,500
A	3,800	3,800	3,700	4,000
M	4,800	4,775	4,975	5,000
J	5,025	5,000	5,600	5,250
J	5,100	5,200	5,750	5,200
A	5,600	5,500	6,000	5,800
S	4,800	4,800	4,900	5,000
O	3,900	3,700	3,700	3,800
N	3,000	3,000	3,200	3,200
D	2,400	2,275	2,700	2,700

Fuel Oil Usage in Gallons

	1987	1988	1989	1990
J	4,900	4,800	5,000	5,010
F	4,500	4,550	4,600	4,750
M	2,500	2,250	2,500	2,000
A	1,000	1,100	950	1,100
M	600	750	600	550
J	200	210	190	200
J	210	195	200	195
A	850	1,000	900	1,000
S	3,000	2,950	1,500	2,500
O	4,200	4,000	3,250	3,950
N	4,500	4,500	4,350	4,275
D	4,950	4,775	5,010	5,040

Water Usage in Thousands of Gallons

	1987	1988	1989	1990
J	100	110	105	101
F	98	100	101	104
M	102	100	97	102
A	88	90	103	100
M	97	100	102	98
J	100	101	96	94
J	89	92	96	100
A	91	102	107	100
S	103	100	98	98
O	92	94	94	93
N	101	93	100	98
D	97	95	102	104

a. Prepare, for insertion in a report, a single table showing a year-by-year unit total (gallons, kilowatt hours) for electricity, fuel oil, and water.

b. Prepare one line graph showing month-by-month electricity, fuel oil, and water usage fluctuations for a 12-month period. (Sum the four Januaries, the four Februaries, and so on.)

c. Prepare one pie graph for electricity that indicates the percentage of the whole for each of the four years.

d. Prepare a bar graph for fuel oil only that shows the percentage of change from the preceding month for all four years. That is, compare the total of four Januaries to four Februaries, and so on.

e. Combine electricity (at a constant $.08 per kilowatt hour), fuel oil (at a constant $.80 a gallon), and water (at a constant rate of $1.00 per 1,000 gallons) into a segmented (or subdivided) bar graph that has four bars — one for each of the four years.

2. As the student member of the president's building committee at your university, you have been given a report from the building's architects. The report shows the sizes of the existing and the proposed classrooms for Jefferson Hall and the adjoining Sloane Hall. Additionally, the report presents the proposed numbers of classrooms for the small addition that will be built between, and connecting, Jefferson and Sloane Halls.

The committee will meet tomorrow, and you must be prepared to interpret the data.

Classroom Capacity	Jefferson Hall Existing	Jefferson Hall Proposed	Sloane Hall Existing	Sloane Hall Proposed	New Construction	Total Existing	Total Proposed
1– 19	10	1	13	13	0	23	14
20– 39	14	2	11	15	4	25	21
40– 59	28	2	4	11	8	32	21
60– 99	7	0	9	9	6	16	15
100–199	3	3	2	2	18	5	23
200+	1	0	0	0	2	1	2

a. Decide how much visual support is needed to deliver this information.

b. Prepare the visual support for the meeting.

CASE │ Memorable Graphics

Lecia Archer, University of Colorado, Boulder

"Hi Al."

Al Wyborg turned around to see Mary Flannery, a friend and classmate from college, entering the cafeteria. "Hi Mary. Are you eating alone?"

"Not if you join me. What looks good today?'

Al and Mary worked for companies located in the same building and occasionally ran into each other at lunch. Mary's company, Barker, Carroll & Associates Architects, designed commercial buildings in the fast-growing southern California market. Al's company, Seismic Simulations Inc., conducted complex computer simulations to test the effects of earthquakes on commercial buildings. This very rigorous testing was required to ensure that new buildings conformed to state code and, although most architectural firms conducted their own preliminary testing, an independent firm was required to conduct simulations also.

Because of the need for technical expertise and expensive computer equipment, only six firms in the area competed for testing contracts. They submitted proposals outlining the type of tests they planned to conduct as well as individuals' and corporate technical expertise. The proposals were often quite technical as a result, offering a great deal of complex, quantitative information to readers.

Seismic Simulations had recently submitted a proposal to test a new building design for Barker, Carroll & Associates. Al had been part of the proposal writing team for this contract and was disappointed to learn that a competitor, Blake & Company, had been awarded the contract.

Al decided to ask Mary why. "I understand Blake got the contract for your new design. What made you decide to go with them? Was it their price?"

"Their price was on a par with most," Mary replied. "I can't quite put my finger on it, Al. All I know is that everyone that read Blake's proposal understood the explanations of the proposed analyses, and it seemed to stand out in our minds."

"Our proposal was written in an easy-to-read style with several visuals to ease understanding. I wonder what they did that was different," said Al.

"I remember yours, Al; it was easy to read. But so were several others. Maybe it was Blake's color graphics," suggested Mary. "I can't say that Blake had more graphs than others, but they certainly were easy to read, and memorable."

On the way back to his office, Al thought about the conversation. Was it possible that the use of color graphics in proposals could give his company a competitive edge? He decided to investigate.

Case Questions

1. Conduct an experiment: Find a high quality color graphic and a similar black and white graphic. Show both to a group of people. Which seems easier to understand? Which will be remembered?

2. Prepare a report on the following problem statement: Readers perceive reports with color graphics to be more professional looking or of higher quality than their black and white counterparts.

3. Determine whether Al's company should buy a color plotter or an ink-jet type color printer. Write a report on your finding.

4. Prepare a report analyzing the use of color. Specifically, address the issue of clutter and distraction caused by color in a graphic aid. How many colors are too many? Which colors are best? Should some color combinations be avoided? Which? Why?

Marketing Presentation for the Board of Directors | *CASE*

Marie Flatley, San Diego State University

As the marketing director for an expanding shoe company, you formulate market forecasts and expansion recommendations. This year you've been asked to present your report orally to the board of directors. For this presentation, you've decided to use a variety of graphics to supplement both the written and oral reports.

You've determined that you need three different types of graphics for this report. The first will be a world map; it will show through the use of colors or shading and hatching where you are doing business now, where you propose to be doing business five years from now, and where you recommend to be doing business ten years from now. The second graphic will be line graphs. In these graphs you'll show the estimated population trends in the countries where you are proposing to do business in the next five years and the next ten years. The third graph will be a stacked bar graph showing the components of income and income projections for ten years ago, five years ago, current, five years ahead, and ten years ahead.

Choose any countries you like for this report. Use your library and references such as almanacs for the population data and population growth rates projections for your countries. Then use statistics from the shoe industry along with your company's current market share to determine income projections. You'll find spreadsheet software helpful in creating the data-generated line and bar charts, and drawing or clip art software will be helpful in creating the world map. Be sure to include all the components necessary for each graphic as discussed in the chapter.

Case Questions

1. Do your illustrations clearly show the data?

2. Have your illustrations met all the principles presented in this chapter?

3. Could any of your illustrations be challenged as misleading?

Meetings: Small Group Communication

"I've got a million things to do today," Tim was thinking as he entered the conference room. "The last thing I need is another meeting." The purpose of this meeting was to explain to the supervisors the new worker involvement program the company was about to implement.

Ron Ryan, the plant manager, conducted the meeting with the assistance of an outside consultant. In the first part of the meeting the consultant described the benefits other companies experienced through worker involvement programs. After that the consultant explained the process and the critical role that the supervisor played. Tim found the concept of worker involvement interesting. He was skeptical, however, about its working in his company.

Following through on what he had been taught, but with considerable apprehension, he called a meeting of the people in his unit. He explained the worker involvement program and described how everyone stood to benefit from the program's success.

"Concentrate on quality control," he told the workers. "What are some things you think should be done to improve quality control?" After an awkward silence a few members made halfhearted suggestions. Fortunately, the time had come to end the meeting. "Same time next week," Tim reminded his people, all the while dreading the prospect of another such meeting. "Between now and then, keep thinking of ways to improve quality control," he said.

At the next meeting, Tim realized that his fears had been unfounded. The group members required no

Learning Objectives

1 To understand the role of small group communication in organizations.

2 To become aware of the advantages and disadvantages of reaching decisions in small groups.

3 To know the purposes of various types of meetings and the alternatives to meetings.

4 To examine the various styles of group leadership and gain the skills necessary to lead in small group situations.

5 To recognize the important roles played by participants.

6 To study the relationship among meeting planning, conduct, and follow-up.

7 To examine the use of electronic meetings.

prodding to participate. The members obviously had given some thought to quality control, and they were no longer hesitant about expressing their thoughts.

Tim was pleasantly surprised by the transformation of a collection of individuals into a group. As a result of his experience with the worker involvement program, Tim began to recognize the many values to be derived from working with groups.

THE ROLE OF GROUPS IN TODAY'S BUSINESS ORGANIZATION

Groups have played a major role in U.S. society since the nation's inception. The Declaration of Independence and the U.S. Constitution were forged through painstaking discussion and debate, which is also true of virtually every piece of legislation at both state and national levels.

Business management, also, traditionally has made extensive use of groups. In the past, however, the makeup of such groups was exclusively managerial; that its, only managers and staff participated in the meetings designed to find facts and make decisions. Plans were developed and policies were determined by groups that rarely included any of the individuals affected by them. Business leaders considered these activities to be the province of management alone.

In modern organizations decision making involves people at all levels.

Today the use of groups pervades all levels of the organization. In the quest for greater productivity and employee satisfaction, many companies have moved toward **participative management**. This means that employees at every level become involved in job-related decision making.

The growth of the quality circle movement in Japan, the United States, and many European nations, mirrors the growing emphasis on participative management. **Quality circles** are small groups of workers (and managers) that meet regularly to discuss and resolve problems of productivity, quality, and the workplace in general. The impact of quality circles appears to be significant in terms of employee commitment to the organization as well as in organizational productivity and development.

Whatever job you eventually assume in a business organization, you will become a part of various work groups. Your ability to work and to interact effectively in groups will significantly determine your occupational success. A knowledge of the contents of this chapter will not in itself turn you into a polished team player, but it will help you move in that direction.

BASIC CHARACTERISTICS OF SMALL GROUPS

Imagine that you participated in two groups today. The first group gathered in the plant cafeteria 30 minutes before starting work. It consisted of you and five friends who meet most mornings and discuss such topics as sports and politics. The second group was the plant grievance committee, consisting of seven members who meet weekly to consider employee grievances. You represent the shipping department. Only one of these groups meets all of the criteria necessary to be designated a small group for our purposes.

A Common Purpose

The members of the plant grievance committee gather with a common purpose to consider the grievances of employees. The individuals who meet in the cafeteria do not share a common purpose. Some enjoy talking about sports, some like to talk about current events, and others have their own interests. They enjoy each other's company and so they continue to meet.

Group members must share a common purpose.

A Small Number of Participants

The size of a group has a significant impact on productivity as well as on the satisfaction of group members. A group that is too small will be limited in the quantity of information it can generate. Individual members may, however, have greater opportunities to participate because of the small size of the group. The increased opportunities will often result in more satisfied members.

With greater size a group can generate more ideas. There will be fewer opportunities for individual participation, however, and members may be less satisfied with their groups. Although there is no magic number at which groups automatically achieve greatest effectiveness, groups of five members are often regarded as the ideal.

Interdependency among Members

Groups are assembled with the intent of capitalizing on the combined efforts of the members. Members not only influence one another, but they also rely on one another for information and support. A bond develops between the members that leads to an interdependence that facilitates communication within the group. Members remain aware of the collective nature of the group.

Face-to-Face Interaction

Interaction among group members is traditionally face-to-face.

Another characteristic of a small group is that the members interact face to face. The members meet and exchange information verbally and nonverbally. To an extent, this characteristic has been modified by the introduction of computer conferencing and other types of electronic meetings.

Roles

The type of group as well as members' individual characteristics determine their roles.

The roles that group members assume are a function of the type of group as well as the characteristics of the individual group member. If group members belong to a command group of superior and subordinates, the roles they play will depend on their organizational position as well as their relationship with the group's formal and informal leaders. If the group were a friendship group, the role and role expectations would be entirely different.

In any group, individuals can choose whether to play a task or a maintenance role. A **task role** focuses on accomplishment of the task set before the group. Conversely, a **maintenance role** centers around the emotional and psychological needs of the group members. Both roles are essential for effective group functioning.

A **small group** may therefore be defined as a collection of a few individuals who interact face-to-face, verbally and nonverbally, for a common purpose, and with interdependency among the members. The grievance committee possesses all of the characteristics. The cafeteria group does not, because it lacks both a common purpose and interdependence among its members.

ADVANTAGES OF GROUP DECISIONS

The complaints most often voiced against group meetings are that there are too many meetings, that meetings take too much time, and that most meetings do not achieve any worthwhile results. The obvious question is, therefore, why do managers schedule so many meetings? The answer is that a decision made at a small group meeting has several potential advantages.

Higher Quality of Decisions

A group decision is usually superior to the decision of an individual, provided the members of the group have appropriate knowledge and expertise. Obviously a group of sales managers cannot be expected to deliver a quality decision regarding the implementation of a new computer system for the accounting department. In general, however, groups will bring a greater sum of knowledge and a greater number of approaches to a given problem. This is especially true when no one is an acknowledged expert.

Acceptance

Subordinates' being involved makes decisions easier to accept.

Subordinates who are included in the decision-making process will usually accept the decision more readily than if it is simply handed down. By getting people together to discuss an issue or problem you may expect there to be a greater understanding of others and their ideas and a greater involvement in the arrival at an acceptable solution. For example, suppose that the clothing manager in a retail store is faced with requests from three full-time salespeople for the same week of vacation. One of the three must be asked to reschedule so that the business can function normally. This is not a decision about quality — any one of the three salespeople could perform adequately alone. If the department manager makes the decision, the unlucky salesperson will be upset and may become hostile. However, if the three salespeople are asked to work out a decision among themselves, each has the opportunity to discuss his or her own viewpoint. A group decision in this instance improves the chances that all the salespeople will accept the final agreement.

Commitment

The elements of acceptance and commitment are closely related. Commitment, however, goes beyond acceptance. When individuals are directly involved in analyzing and solving a problem, they become more committed to the effective implementation of the decision. Greater enthusiasm is likely for the broader group goals. Thus, a company considering such motivational tools as job enrichment, wage incentives, or profit sharing might benefit from involving employees in selecting the appropriate program.

Status

Participants gain a sense of heightened status and recognition from the responsibility and interaction in group decision making. This advantage is often one of the keys to effective participatory management in that it gives group members the very real sense that they share an active role in the management of the organization.

DISADVANTAGES OF GROUP DECISIONS

Decision making by small groups has several potential disadvantages.

Time

The typical manager may spend 69 percent of his or her daily communication time in meetings.[1] In addition to the time spent in each meeting, the leader and the participants need time to prepare for it. All of this is time taken away from other duties.

Cost

Surveys indicate that business meetings cost the organizations that sponsor them more than $8 billion a year. A manager's time may be worth over $50 an hour if allocated overhead costs are included. A two-hour meeting of 10 such managers would cost the company more than $1,000. When you consider that business people spend more than 1.5 billion hours a year in meetings, you can see what is at stake. Table 17.1 gives an easy

Meetings are expensive.

---

[1] Henry Mintzberg, *The Nature of Managerial Work* (New York: Harper & Row, 1973).

TABLE 17.1 ∎ *Meeting Costs per Hour*

Number of Participants	Average Annual Pay			
	$50,000	$40,000	$30,000	$20,000
10	$240	$192	$144	$96
8	192	154	115	77
6	144	115	87	58
5	120	96	72	48

way to calculate how much a meeting might cost just in terms of participant salaries.

Unclear Individual Accountability

Group decisions blur individual accountability.

When an individual is assigned a task, that person is accountable for its satisfactory completion. When a group is assigned a task, accountability is less clear. **Accountability** means the expectation that someone will do some specific things to accomplish a specific goal. When a group pursues a task, accountability is blurred.

Someone once said, "Success has a thousand fathers; failure has none." Although it was not meant to refer specifically to groups, the quotation suggests a disadvantage of groups. When a group effort is successful, individual members will often try to take credit for the success. When a group effort is unsuccessful, individual members will often seek to disassociate themselves from the results. From the standpoint of individual members, unclear accountability may be viewed as an advantage of small groups. From the standpoint of group productivity, unclear accountability is a definite disadvantage.

Undue Conformity

The mere gathering of different people into a group does not guarantee an ideal result. Sometimes, a group is dominated by one individual and the other members acquiesce in order to speed the decision or to avoid conflict. At other times, a group may perceive a member as more knowledgeable than is actually the case and, therefore, go along with that person's opinions. Less outgoing group participants may hesitate to speak out, especially when a supervisor is in the room.

A related problem has to do with a phenomenon called **group polarization**.[2] In some instances, a group may take a riskier position on an issue than any one individual would take working alone. In other cases, the group might be inclined to a more cautious position. These extremes are

[2]Marvin E. Shaw, *Group Dynamics*, 3d ed. (New York: McGraw Hill, 1981).

typically dependent on the decision to be made and the nature of the participants themselves.

Finally, there is the problem of excess cohesion. The more often a group meets or interacts, the greater the pressures on members to conform. Peer pressure — the influence of the other members — is likely to ensure conformity. The greater the conformity, the less likely a group will benefit from all members' expertise. At the extreme, such conformity is called groupthink, which is discussed later in the chapter.

TYPES AND PURPOSES OF MEETINGS

Small groups are used in a wide variety of situations. However, the two basic purposes of small groups are to share information and to solve problems. Frequently, these purposes are combined within the same group; for example, a group usually exchanges information before it reaches a decision about a problem.

Information-Sharing Meetings

The major purpose of information-sharing meetings is to transmit information, ideas, programs, or decisions from one person or group to another person or group. Specifically, these meetings might be held for any one or more of the following purposes.

A major purpose of some meetings is to transmit or share information.

Report Presentation

The report presentation is an uncomplicated meeting. For example, you may have asked the sales manager of a new territory to give an update on efforts to break into the new market. The marketing staff is gathered to hear this report and perhaps to give feedback that might be useful in the development of the new area.

Training Session

The overall purpose of a training session is to see that essential information is transmitted to an appropriate group. As an example, assume that you are the supervisor of safety and training for a medium-sized manufacturing firm. Your company has just purchased $8 million worth of highly sophisticated, numerically controlled, metal-working lathes. The operations manager for the firm asks you to coordinate a number of hands-on training sessions for the operators of the new machine. Another use for this type of meeting would be to demonstrate a new product for the current sales force.

Brainstorming Session

The purpose of this type of gathering is to generate new ideas or concepts. The discussions are necessarily freewheeling, with the exchange of information among group members as a major goal. When brainstorming is the sole function of a group meeting, a problem-solving meeting often follows. Brainstorming will be discussed in more detail in the section on special techniques for conducting a meeting.

Problem-Solving Meetings

Another major purpose of meetings is to solve problems.

The problem-solving meeting reaches a group judgment or decision or solves a particular problem. Sometimes this type of group may be designated as a committee or task force. In any event, problem solving groups may come together for any of the following purposes.

Decision Making

In the business setting a wide range of strategic decisions require group attention. A bank or savings and loan, for example, might need to decide whether to open a branch in a large new shopping center. An automobile manufacturer may be faced with deciding whether to discontinue a product line when sales decline.

Problem Analysis

Perhaps the group's most difficult task in reaching an appropriate solution is to determine the real problem. Groups have often decided on a course of action that, once taken, leaves the problem still there. A number of techniques to help analyze and define the question are discussed later in the chapter.

Conflict Resolution

In any organization, various personalities or issues come into conflict. The issues may involve overlapping authority, unequal workloads, impending layoffs, company policies, and the like. The object of bringing together appropriate parties in a group setting is to try to make decisions that will placate the opposing factions. Disgruntled employees need the opportunity to air differences and come to a better understanding of other points of view.

Alternatives to Meetings

A phone call or memorandum might take the place of a meeting.

The manager's prime obligation in terms of small group communication is to call a meeting only when absolutely necessary. Managers should take advantage, whenever possible, of all alternatives to meetings. For instance, a phone call to the right person or persons (perhaps a conference call) can often resolve a problem, generate an idea, or ratify a decision. For simple information sharing, a memo to all concerned parties can be used to provide the facts and solicit comment. Managers should approach the calling of a meeting with the same concern for cost that they show for the purchase of new equipment or supplies.

PREPARATION FOR THE MEETING

Both the group leader and group participants must assume significant roles in getting ready for a meeting.

Leader Responsibilities

Meeting leaders may find the 4 Ws — who, when, where and why — to be useful in making basic decisions about their meetings. They must determine who will attend, inviting only those necessary to make the meeting productive. They must decide when the meeting will be held so that time is allowed for adequate preparation and there is minimum conflict with other activities. Where the session will convene must be considered in terms of convenience to participants and isolation from disturbances. Finally, and most important, leaders must come to grips with the why of the meeting — the most important purpose, the singular issue, or precisely what is to be accomplished.

The 4 Ws for meeting planning are who, when, where, and why.

Defining the Objective or Purpose

Clarity of purpose is the key ingredient in determining a meeting's success. If you have any doubt about what you wish to accomplish, you are unlikely to accomplish it. Look ahead to the conclusion of the meeting and what it is you wish to have achieved. Are you looking for a final decision? Are you wanting key people to be informed about a policy change? Once defined, this purpose should be conveyed to all invited participants.

Studying the Issues to be Discussed

Leaders should thoroughly study the general subject area on which group help is sought. Such study will better equip them to guide the group process and ask questions of a reasonable quality.

Selecting the Participants

Careful study of the issues will go a long way in helping leaders determine the composition of the group that they plan to convene. Only those who have something to share or those who have a stake in hearing what is shared should be invited to attend. You may occasionally want to include someone who is likely to oppose a decision reached by the group simply because he or she was not invited. However, as the number of participants increases, the opportunity for quality discussion decreases. You should also be aware of Wolf's law of decision making:

> Major decisions are rarely decided by more than four people. If you think a larger meeting you're attending is really "hammering out" a decision, you're probably wrong. Either the decision was agreed to by a smaller group before the meeting began, or the outcome of the larger meeting will be modified later when three or four people get together.[3]

Setting the Date and Time

If leaders cannot get together with everyone they need, they may not attain the purpose of the meeting. They should therefore set both date and time for the convenience of participants. The date should be far enough in

[3]Paul Dickson, *The Official Rules* (New York: Delacorte Press, 1981), 187.

advance so that group members can prepare for the meeting and adjust their schedules as needed. When planning a meeting, the leader should establish an ending time as well as the starting time. This allows participants to budget appropriately the time block needed for the session.

Notifying the Participants

Notice of the meeting should include the time and place, a complete agenda, specific preparation guidelines for the group members or key participants, the purpose or objective of the meeting, perhaps a list of participants, and any necessary background information. The more you can tell group members prior to the meeting, the more thoroughly they will be able to prepare for it and the more likely they will be to contribute to the desired outcome.

Writing the Agenda

The leader will probably find it useful to furnish each participant with an order of business or list of things to be done. This is the agenda. Most often, business meetings call for the consideration of only one topic. In that case, the meeting notice will likely suffice as the agenda. In a multi-item gathering, however, invited participants should have a list of the topics in the order in which they will be approached. You may want to arrange your agenda so that complex topics are taken up at the most appropriate point in the meeting. Following John E. Tropman's "rule of the agenda bell" illustrated in Figure 17.1, the group moves through discussion items in ascending and then descending order of complexity so that group energy and intensity can be properly focused.[4] Because the best meetings last no more than 1 or 1½ hours, however, an extremely complex or controversial item might be best relegated to a separate meeting.

Setting up the Meeting Room

Given a choice of meeting rooms, the leader should select a room that is as far away as possible from noise and interruptions. However, the choice of location should not make it difficult for group members to attend. The room should be well lighted and equipped with comfortable chairs and sturdy tables.

The table and seating arrangement should be based, to some degree, on the nature of the meeting. In all cases, the ideal layout provides for eye contact among all participants. In a general discussion session that calls for equal participation on the part of each person present, a square, round, or wide-oval table is best (see Figure 17.2). If, on the other hand, you are leading a problem-solving meeting that requires rather strong leadership to help the group stay on task, you might consider an arrangement that provides a dominant position. Typically, this may be achieved

---

[4]John E. Tropman with Gersh Morningstar, *Meetings: How to Make Them Work for You* (New York: Van Nostrand Reinhold, 1985).

FIGURE 17.1 ▪ *Tropman's Agenda Bell*

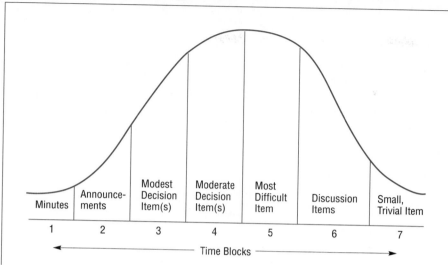

with a rectangular or narrow-oval table (see Figure 17.3). Whichever layout is selected, you should always ensure ample elbow room for each participant. For more on the importance of this arrangement, you might review the section on personal space in Chapter 14.

At least a day or two before the meeting the leader should make the necessary arrangements for any special audiovisual aids that may be used in the meeting room. Generally, an overhead projector and screen, chalkboard, and flipchart will cover most group needs.

Finally, the leader must check just prior to the meeting to make sure that the meeting room is neat, clean, and orderly and that all audiovisual equipment is in good working condition. Pads and pencils for participants should be in place before they arrive.

FIGURE 17.2 ▪ *Seating Arrangement to Promote Discussion*

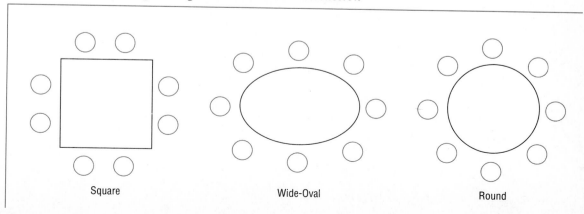

FIGURE 17.3   ▪   *Seating Arrangement to Provide Strong Leader Position*

Rectangle   Narrow-Oval

● = Leader Position

Naming of the Recorder

The recorder should have some knowledge of the subject.

An often overlooked aspect of meeting preparation is the naming of an individual to take notes. The recorder's function is very similar to that of a club secretary. In appointing the recorder, the meeting leader should select a person who knows enough about the subject to summarize rather than record word for word what takes place. The recorder should note who is in attendance and the decisions that were made. The information summarized by the recorder will provide the basis for all follow-up activities.

Participant Responsibilities

Participants should carefully review the agenda and study any other pre-meeting materials or background materials, keeping in mind the precise objective or purpose of the meeting. They should make careful notes on

✔ CHECKLIST for Leader Preparation Responsibilities

___▪ Define the meeting's objectives or purpose.

___▪ Study the issues to be discussed.

___▪ Select the necessary participants.

___▪ Choose an appropriate date and time for meeting.

___▪ Notify all participants.

___▪ Prepare and distribute a complete agenda.

___▪ Set up the meeting room.

___▪ Appoint a recorder.

ideas, comments, questions, or suggestions as they occur in addition to gathering information and sources related to their own area of expertise. Participants who plan to propose a certain solution or strongly support a certain position should make clear and concise notes in order to be prepared to articulate their side of the argument. If the presentation will include visual support (see Chapter 16), the group leader should be alerted to the need for a projector or other equipment.

Overall, the leader selects a group member for a particular reason. It has to do with the individual's role in the organization and how that role may affect the outcome of the group's efforts. Therefore, when you are asked to participate in a group, in all your preparations you should look for ways to support the leader's stated purpose or objective.

✔ *CHECKLIST for Participant Preparation Responsibilities*

— Review the agenda.

— Study all premeeting materials and background.

— Write down ideas, comments, and questions on the topic.

— Gather necessary information to present at the meeting.

— Prepare any position statement carefully.

— Look for ways to support the group's purpose and objective.

THE GROUP LEADER'S ROLE DURING THE MEETING

A key role in every group is that of the group leader. Because of the importance of leadership, a great deal of research has been done on it.

Styles of Leadership

Researchers have identified four styles of group leadership.

Authoritarian Leadership

Authoritarian leaders usually determine the specific task for each participant because they often believe that group participants are limited in ability and need strict guidance and control. This style of leadership, therefore, is rigid and inflexible. Authoritarian leaders often dominate discussion and are usually reluctant to acknowledge those who disagree with them. Such leaders discourage member participation, causing members to resign themselves to the fact that the leader will make all the decisions no matter what anyone else might have to contribute. Leaders who employ the authoritarian style may very quickly reach the solution they want, but in terms of group morale the costs are high.

Authoritarian leaders exercise strong control.

The emotional consequences of authoritarian leadership are serious. You might wonder, why would any group leader use this style of leadership? In many situations, leaders want the group to know beyond any doubt that they are in control. Because they so completely dominate their groups they remain unaware or unconcerned about the members' perception of them as leaders.

Authoritarian leadership would be appropriate for some situations—for example, in a crisis or when time is extremely limited or when the matter under discussion is trivial. Authoritarian leadership, however, is overused and counterproductive.

Supervisory Leadership

Supervisory leaders are slightly more flexible than authoritarian leaders.

Supervisory leadership, which stops short of autocratic control, is useful when efficiency is critical. Supervisory leaders almost always introduce the problem for discussion with a lengthy description. They usually decide the problem that will be discussed in the meeting and frequently summarize what has taken place in the group. Such leaders are not as formal or as rigid as the authoritarians, but they give little attention to the needs of the group.

Participative Leadership

Participative leaders relinquish some control and encourage group participation.

Both authoritarian and supervisory leaders depend on methods that limit the participation and freedom of other group members. Participative, or democratic, leaders encourage group members to participate actively in discussion. Rather than restrict group members, this style of leadership has a positive effect. Meetings conducted in the participative style can be characterized as follows:

- All group members participate freely.
- Communication is directed to all members, not just the leader.
- Group decisions are perceived as group achievements.
- Group members are able to satisfy some personal needs in the group environment.
- Group members are able to identify with the group.

Employing the participative style is difficult. The leader must balance the need to achieve the desired task with the aim of encouraging uninhibited group interaction. This type of leadership is the most frequently used because it promotes a high degree of group cohesion and at the same time spurs the group toward accomplishing the task.

Group-Centered Leadership

Group-centered leaders are permissive.

Group-centered, or laissez faire, leaders expect group members to be self-directed. They refrain from structuring the group in any way. They listen but do not show approval or disapproval, and although they may clarify on occasion, they are careful not to inject their own thoughts. The group atmosphere is extremely permissive. The leader of a group-centered group always tries to view the discussion from the frame of reference of the member who is speaking.

Relationship between Styles

The relationship between the styles of leadership can be seen on the continuum in Figure 17.4. Participative leadership is usually desirable. Although the group usually takes longer to reach a consensus, member satisfaction is highest. Each group has its own needs, however, and each leader will want to select a style that is in keeping with these needs and with his or her personality.[5]

Basic Duties of the Group Leaders

Regardless of the leadership style, several basic duties are essential to attaining the group's purposes. They can be most easily understood by dividing the meeting into three parts.

The Beginning. Arrive early. As leader, you should make sure that the room is set the way you want and that all necessary equipment and materials are on hand. Start on time. Keep in mind the high costs associated with meetings. If you respect participants' time, you are more likely to gain respect for your time in return. Make your opening count:

A responsibility of the group leader is to start and end the meeting on time.

- Establish the right tone — usually serious and positive.
- Be sure to identify any participants unknown to the group.
- Offer any background comments that might prove useful to the group.
- Review the objectives of the meeting in terms of items on the agenda.
- Identify any time constraints not already expressed on the agenda — for example, when the meeting must end.[6]

The Principal Task. The actual conduct of the meeting should reflect your primary purpose (or purposes) for calling it. Keep to the planned agenda. As leader, you will probably have to prod the group, from time to time, to return to the task at hand. You may want to periodically restate the purpose of the meeting. Ask the recorder to summarize points made or decisions completed as you progress through the agenda. Above all, you will want to balance the discussion between those who tend to dominate meetings and those who are always reluctant to speak. This will help you remain impartial and diffuse controversies to the end that all of the individuals you have gathered will have the opportunity to express their thoughts. Finally, you will want to set a good example by listening attentively to all speakers and thus take advantage of the expertise they bring to the meeting.

The Closing. As leader, you should make every effort to end on time. Nothing can more easily destroy the atmosphere of a well-run meeting than to have people get up to leave because they have another commit-

---

[5]This discussion of leadership styles is adapted from Charles R. Gruner, Cal M. Logue, Dwight L. Freshley, and Richard C. Huseman, *Speech Communication in Society*, 2d ed. (Boston: Allyn & Bacon, 1977), 258–260.

[6]John M. Penrose, Jr., et al., *Advanced Business Communication* (Boston: PWS-Kent, 1989), 234.

FIGURE 17.4 ▪ *Styles of Leadership*

Minimum Control	Leaderless Group	Group-Centered Leadership	Participative Leadership	Supervisory Leadership	Authoritarian Leadership	Maximum Control

ment. As you approach the ending time, you should summarize all the decisions made. Emphasize specifically the action that should be taken, by whom, and when.

Special Techniques for Meeting Conduct

Maximum and proper participation on the part of all group members produces the most useful results. Toward this end, the leader can employ a number of skills and techniques for encouraging and channeling participation.

Problem-Participant Methods

Timid participants must be treated differently from overtalkative ones.

In any group setting you, as leader, may encounter individuals whose behaviors are counterproductive to the overall mission. You should know some of the methods for dealing with them. The timid participant, for example, may be brought out with an occasional question or by soliciting

✔ *CHECKLIST for Leading a Meeting*

___▪ Arrive early and start on time.

___▪ Make your opening count. Be sure to define the purpose and state the timetable for the meeting.

___▪ Keep to the planned agenda.

___▪ Remain impartial.

___▪ Balance the discussion.

___▪ Restate the purpose/objectives periodically.

___▪ Listen attentively to other group members.

___▪ Summarize the group's decisions or progress at intervals during the meeting.

___▪ Diffuse hot controversies.

___▪ End with a summary of decisions made.

___▪ Highlight the action that should be taken, by whom, and when.

information that he or she holds exclusively. At the opposite extreme is the person who always seems to have too much to say about everything. Appropriate actions include interrupting the person at the end of a sentence and asking for comments from another member, changing the topic to consider another point, or reminding the group of the need to move on because of a crowded agenda.

The private conversationalists are a special problem because their talking among themselves makes it difficult for other participants to hear the discussions on the topic at hand. You might ask them to continue their conversation after the meeting or invite them to share their comments with the rest of the group. In all cases, you should try to remain calm, understanding, and tactful and maintain a good sense of humor.

The Dewey Reflective Thinking Process

Nearly every small group brought together to solve a problem finds it useful to follow a set format or agenda. The most widely used format is based on John Dewey's Reflective Thinking Process.[7] These six steps are based on Dewey's work:

The most widely used format for problem solving is the Reflective Thinking Process.

1. Defining and Analyzing the Problem.   During the initial meeting the precise nature of the problem should be specified and its underlying causes investigated. Consider, for example, a small retail firm that has low employee morale, a decline in sales, and an unusually high rate of employee turnover. The conference leader might begin by describing these problems and delineating them with available facts. By concisely depicting the present state of affairs, the leader is defining the problem.

Once each conference participant understands the nature and scope of the problem, the group can investigate potential causes. This is the crux of the first step in problem solving. In the example, group members would offer their perceptions of what might be causing the morale, sales, and turnover problems. These perceptions are discussed, modified (if necessary), and recorded by a leader or appointed group member. Suppose the group perceives the following four possible causes: (1) lack of communication between superiors and subordinates; (2) poor motivational programs; (3) conflict between the sales and delivery departments; and (4) insufficient advertising. After analyzing information from attitude surveys or grievance and exit interviews, the group might decide that inadequate motivation is the major cause of the problem. When the problem is defined and the suspected cause is identified, the group can move to Step 2.

2. Establishing Criteria for a Solution.   The criteria step in the problem-solving sequence is optional and may be postponed until solutions are actually evaluated. Suppose, however, that this group determines the criteria that any potential solution must meet. The criteria might be that the solution: (1) must include all nonmanagement employees; (2) must be-

[7]John Dewey, *How We Think* (Boston: D.C. Heath, 1933).

come effective within two months; and (3) must cost no more than 2 percent of the company's gross profits.

These criteria are derived from discussion among the conference members. Some proposed criteria were altered slightly, while some were rejected. In any event, the group has arrived at three criteria and is ready to begin Step 3 of the problem-solving process.

3. Proposing Possible Solutions.   In this step participants suggest as many potential solutions as possible. Each participant attempts to propose solutions that meet the specified criteria. Although members may amend the solutions offered by others, no solutions are evaluated at this time. The third step is essentially brainstorming.

Suppose that the group suggests the following five potential solutions: (1) better fringe benefits; (2) increased commissions; (3) profit sharing; (4) a sales contest; and (5) wage incentives. The group can now move to Step 4.

4. Evaluating Possible Solutions.   In Step 4 the conference members evaluate each of the proposed solutions. Each solution is weighed against any criteria outlined in Step 2 as well as against other proposed criteria. The group's aim is to identify the advantages and disadvantages of each solution. For example, the wage incentives might be pertinent to all non-management employees and easily set up within two months but, nevertheless, too costly and irrelevant to the needs of the commission salespeople.

Once the advantages and disadvantages have been assigned to each solution, the group can proceed to Step 5.

5. Selecting a Solution.   A critical point to keep in mind is that the group is not obligated to select only one of the proposed solutions. The most effective decision might combine two or three proposed solutions or an altered version of only one solution. Whatever the outcome, during Step 6 a final decision must be made concerning the best possible solution. The precise details of the solution should also be decided. Suppose, in this example, that the group chooses to increase commissions by one percent across the board. In addition, the group decides on a three-month sales contest between hard- and soft-line divisions, and the winners are to receive cash bonuses and gift certificates. The participants are now ready for the final step in the problem-solving sequence.

6. Plotting a Course of Action.   This final step concentrates on how best to execute the solution. Before the conference can end, the participants must agree on a specific, detailed method for enacting the solution. Conference members may volunteer to assume responsibility for certain aspects of the program, or the leader may assign specific tasks to group participants. Whatever approach is chosen, agreement must be reached before the problem-solving process can terminate.

For the sake of illustration, suppose that two department heads have volunteered to direct the sales contest. Together they will work out the details and report to the store manager within one week. Finally, the store manager announces that the one percent commission increase will become effective at the beginning of the next month.

The Ideal Solution Format

Although Dewey's six-step format is the best known and most widely used approach to problem solving, there are other formats in use. One is the ideal solution format, which was developed from observing the problem-solving process followed by many business groups. In the ideal solution format, group discussion follows this sequence of questions:

- Are we all agreed on the nature of the problem?
- What would be the ideal solution from the point of view of all parties involved in the problem?
- What conditions within the problem could be changed so that the ideal solution might be achieved?
- Of the solutions available to us, which one best approximates the ideal solution?

The ideal solution format for solving problems originated in business.

The Single Question Format

The single question format is another approach to group problem solving. Groups that follow the single question format focus on a single objective and thereby are less likely to pursue digressions. In the single question format this sequence of questions is followed:

- What single question will yield the answer that is all the group needs to know to accomplish its purpose?
- What subquestions must be answered before this single question can be answered?
- Do we have sufficient information to confidently answer the subquestions? (If yes, answer them. If not, continue.)
- What are most reasonable answers to the subquestions?
- Assuming that our answers to the subquestions are correct, what is the best solution to the problem?

The single question format for problem solving discourages digressions.

The ideal solution format and the single question format appear to be more direct and to the point than the Dewey approach. The Dewey approach, however, is more thorough and is more likely to develop the group members' analytical skills. As a group matures and remains intact over long periods of time, it adopts a more abbreviated approach to problem solving. Its new approach may be the ideal solution format or the single question format, or the group may adopt another approach specifically tailored to its environment and needs.

The Nominal Group Procedure

Sometimes groups are dominated by individuals with powerful personalities. These individuals often keep others from actively participating in the group process. You may encounter a group member who digresses and consumes valuable group time talking about unrelated topics. On

*The nominal
group procedure
avoids problems
caused by
aggressive or
unfocused
members.*

other occasions, individuals in the group may press for a quick decision before all the important aspects of the problem have been thoroughly considered. In numerous other ways, also, individuals can dilute the decision-making potential of groups. One way to overcome some of these problems is to employ the nominal group procedure. The nominal group procedure can be briefly outlined in three stages, which are discussed in terms of analyzing possible problem causes.[8]

In the first stage, the members who are going to participate in the small group session are brought together and are asked not to speak to each other; thus the term **nominal group** is used because the members are in a group setting but no verbal interaction is permitted. After the participants are seated, they are asked to write on a piece of paper what they believe are the major causes of the problem under consideration. This task should take approximately 10 to 15 minutes. For example, if the problem-solving group has been brought together to discuss a high rate of absenteeism, each group member would be asked to list as many causes for the absenteeism as possible. Throughout this first stage it is important that individuals in the nominal group not talk to each other.

In the second stage, after the members of the nominal group have had enough time to list the causes of the problem, the group leader asks a member to read one of the items he or she listed. As the person reads the cause aloud to the group, the leader writes the cause on a large pad of paper or blackboard so that all group members can read it. The group leader proceeds to the next person and asks for another cause, continuing around the group until everyone's list has been read. When a cause is put on the master sheet that other members have also included on their lists, they cross that item off their lists. In this way each cause is listed only once on the master list. If there is a question whether an item overlaps with an item already on the list, that item should be placed on the master list.

In the final stage, all members examine the master list carefully and rank order the causes of the problem. If the list is long, the group members are asked to select the top five by secret ballot. After all individuals have completed their rankings, the information is collected and tabulated.

All three stages of this process can be completed in about one hour. When employed this way, the nominal group process can identify the major causes of the problem. The procedure also allows for the establishment of the most important causes. Because individuals rank the causes by secret ballot, the probability is high that the priority causes of the problem are accurately established.

When used as described here, the nominal group format enhances the advantages and minimizes the disadvantages of the interacting group format. The following are some major advantages of the nominal group:

---

[8]Richard C. Huseman, "The Role of the Nominal Group in Small Group Communication," in *Readings in Interpersonal and Organizational Communication*, eds. Richard C. Huseman, Cal M. Logue, and Dwight L. Freshley (Boston: Holbrook Press, 1977), 493–502.

- Members' influence is more equal.
- Members accept ideas more readily.
- Members need not be acquainted for the group to be productive.
- Premature evaluation of ideas is avoided.
- Time is spent more effectively.
- The format can be used to involve very large groups.

Brainstorming

This is a well-known technique for reaching creative solutions to a variety of problems. In the brainstorming session, the leader states the problem. The recorder writes down the ideas for solving the problem as fast as the group members can call them out. The main purpose of this method is to generate as many novel solutions as possible. Participants are encouraged to be creative without regard to whether what they propose is actually feasible. No group member may explain or criticize any proposal. This activity continues as long as group members have ideas. The theory is that creativity will build as one idea triggers another. Only when participants have exhausted their ideas on the subject is evaluation allowed. The basic rules of brainstorming are these:

- Ideas are expressed freely without regard to quality. The emphasis is on quantity.
- Criticism of ideas is not allowed until the brainstorming session is over.
- Elaboration and combinations of previously expressed ideas are encouraged.

A record of the ideas generated is kept by the recorder or other appointee.

Circular Response Method

This technique is an ideal way of seeing to it that all participants are given the opportunity to speak on the given subject. As the topic is announced, the leader begins by soliciting a comment from one member of the group. The next person on the right or left is then directed to comment, and so on around the entire group. This pattern continues until everyone has spoken. The basic rule is that no one can speak a second time until every member of the group has had the opportunity to comment at least once. Like the nominal group procedure, this technique is useful in reducing the dominance of one strong participant.

The circular response method ensures that everyone contributes to the meeting.

Groupthink Avoidance

Groups that are overly cohesive suffer from **groupthink**.[9] Groupthink occurs when agreement becomes more important than critical thinking. Under conditions of groupthink, a group may make decisions that the individual group members, acting alone, would probably not have made.

Groupthink hampers decision making.

[9]Irving L. Janis, *Groupthink*, 2d ed. (Boston: Houghton Mifflin, 1982).

A sentiment that often prevails in groups beset by groupthink is expressed by the cliché, "Don't make waves."

Here are the symptoms of groupthink:

- An illusion of invulnerability, shared by most or all the members, which creates excessive optimism and encourages taking extreme risks
- Collective efforts to rationalize in order to discount warnings that might lead members to reconsider their assumptions before they recommit themselves to their past policy decisions
- An unquestioned belief in the group's inherent morality, inclining the members to ignore the ethical or moral consequences of their decisions
- Stereotyped views of opposition leaders as too evil to warrant genuine negotiations or as too weak and stupid to counter whatever risky attempts are made to defeat their purposes
- Direct pressure on any member who expresses strong arguments against any of the group's stereotypes, illusions, or commitments, making clear that dissent is contrary to what is expected of all loyal members
- Self-censorship of deviations from the apparent group consensus, reflecting each member's inclination to minimize the importance of any doubts and counterarguments
- A shared illusion of unanimity concerning judgments conforming to the majority view (partly resulting from self-censorship of deviations and augmented by the false assumption that silence means consent)
- The emergence of self-appointed mindguards — members who protect the group from adverse information that might shatter their shared complacency about the effectiveness and morality of decisions[10]

Groupthink is prevalent and is destructive to genuine group efforts. Its presence defeats the main reason for assembling groups — critical thinking.

Decision-making groups can take measures to prevent groupthink.[11] As a first step, the leader should assign the role of critic to each member. Doubts and objections are thus more likely to be exposed and discussed rather than suppressed. Group leaders must set an example by accepting criticism of their ideas and thoughts. Acceptance of criticism does not often come naturally; it may have to be learned by group members.

Second, when assigning a decision-making mission to a group, the leader should be impartial rather than state preferences. When executives in an organization give guidance to decision-making groups, many times they introduce bias unwittingly by being too specific in outlining what they want accomplished. If the time is short, more guidance will hasten the decision. However, less guidance will lessen the chance that the ex-

---

[10]Ibid., 197–198.
[11]Ibid., 198–199.

BOXED IN	*AN ETHICAL DILEMMA*

Claire Watson is in her 10th year as director of management information systems (MIS) for a major firm headquartered in Charlotte, North Carolina. Although she holds an important position, she feels that she has not always received recognition for her efforts. She has built what is, perhaps, the most comprehensive MIS division in the industry. For the past year, Claire has responded to overtures from one of her company's top competitors to become vice-president for MIS.

This morning Claire accepted the competitor's job offer by phone. Her calendar shows a marketing meeting scheduled after lunch. She decides that, immediately after the meeting, she will get together with her boss and discuss her transition out of the company. She has kept him apprised of negotiations regarding the new position, but she is confident that he will be surprised.

The company president himself called the special marketing meeting, which is held in his luxurious conference room. Shortly into the meeting, he announces a significant change in marketing strategy—a change based primarily on the firm's strategic advantage of having a state-of-the-art MIS division and a dynamic MIS director. Claire squirms uncomfortably as the meeting seems to focus on how critical she will be to the success of this new venture. Her boss is beaming because his best division head is finally being recognized in grand fashion. As Claire looks at the timetable for implementation, she knows that the changes in marketing thrust cannot be effected on schedule if the company must search for a new director of MIS.

Claire feels boxed in. What would you do?

ecutive's preconceived notions will unduly influence the group's decision. Certainly the leader should not be so specific as to indicate which of several alternatives is personally preferable. A delicate balance is needed between enough guidance to get the job done and so much guidance that group members believe they have been manipulated. A good group leader should strive for that balance.

Third, members of the decision-making group should seek advice and counsel from trusted associates in their own departments within the organization. Fresh perspectives on a problem can be gained by introducing thoughts from outside the group. When the decision involves highly confidential planning of goals or policies, discretion must be used in implementing this suggestion, of course.

Finally, the tendency to seek consensus could be thwarted effectively by using a devil's advocate at each group meeting. The role of devil's advocate, to be most effective, should be rotated among the group members, and in some cases more than one may be desirable. Criticisms by the devil's advocate should be taken seriously and discussed to the satisfaction of all present.

PARTICIPANTS' ROLES DURING THE MEETING

You may not always be cast in the role of leader in a small group situation but, rather, as a participant who is present because of a certain expertise you possess. In that role, you should take equal responsibility for the attaining of the group's purpose. Several behaviors of participants contribute to the group's success.

Arriving on Time

Participants have a primary responsibility to arrive at a scheduled meeting at the appointed time, perhaps even a little before. By arriving late, you disrupt the proceedings and extend discourtesy to those who arrived on time.

Following the Agenda

You should make every attempt to restrain yourself from making comments that do not relate to the items on the agenda. The objectives and purposes of the meeting must be regarded as uppermost in importance.

Contributing Information

The problem-solving group needs information to reach a decision. Effective group members bring information they have gathered about the topic. Some participants have a tendency to divulge all their information the first time they have the opportunity to speak; this leads to disorganization. People need to develop the ability to see where their information on the topic applies. Timing is a critical element in presenting information.

Evaluating the Information

Group participants need to bring several critical skills to the problem-solving situation. One of the most important is the ability to carefully examine all information presented to the group. Participants should offer additional supporting evidence when they have it and contradictory evidence when it is available. Fallacious reasoning and unsupported assertions should be exposed. Good reasoning and accurate information are essential to the problem-solving process. Participants should resist the tendency to accept everything that is said during the discussion.

Asking Questions

Group participants perform an important function by asking pertinent questions at appropriate times. Such questions help to expose inaccurate information or to clarify a point that one of the other members is attempting to make. The use of questions encourages feedback, aids the understanding of all group members, and helps keep the participants on the main subject of the discussion. The attention of the entire group can be focused on the central issue of the discussion by a well-phrased, pertinent question.

Listening Empathetically

Effective group participants listen to the content of what other members are saying and also "listen between the lines." The empathetic listener tries to see the topic from the other members' frames of reference as they speak. The listener should be sensitive to the attitudes and feeling of other group members.

Avoiding Side Discussions

A participant may on occasion be stimulated to discuss a topic with the group member in the adjacent seat. Such discussions obviously disrupt the deliberations of the rest of the group. The best action to take is to simply make note of the side issue and plan to bring it up in another setting after the meeting is over.

Thinking as the Group Thinks

The group member needs to be aware that thinking as the group thinks is different from individual thinking. Participants need to relate their comments to the group's thinking. People should refer to what their fellow group members have said and what has already been agreed on. The more often people participate in a group, the more skilled they usually become in group thinking. To try to move ahead too quickly is not a good idea. For the group to function effectively, the group must think together.

Encouraging Others

Equal to your responsibility to share your expertise is your obligation to encourage others to share theirs. You may stimulate the reticent participant

✓ CHECKLIST for Participating in a Meeting

— Be on time.

— Follow the agenda.

— Contribute information.

— Evaluate information.

— Ask questions.

— Listen empathetically.

— Avoid side discussions.

— Think as a group member.

— Encourage others to participate.

— Keep your comments brief.

— Take notes to retain specific information.

by simply stating, "We haven't heard from Susan on this issue. Susan, what do you think about this proposal?" Try to follow up by positively reinforcing the suggestions of your fellow group members.

THE MEETING FOLLOW-UP

A successful meeting requires a successful follow-up.

Follow-up activities are often as important as the preparation for the meeting. At this stage the decisions, suggestions, and solutions are implemented. Both leaders and participants share the responsibility for the implementation.

Leader Activities

Follow-up activities should be swiftly executed. A coordinated effort by the group leader and the recorder is necessary to assemble and reproduce copies of the meeting record, or minutes. The record should not be long or formal. It should, however, include the date and place of the meeting; the names of the group leader, the recorder, and all participants; the purpose of the meeting; the alternatives considered; the decisions made; and the action required, by whom, and when. Ideally, the record is in the hands of all participants within two or three days after the meeting.

The leader is responsible for following up with individuals regarding implementation of the solutions generated at the meeting.

Participant Activities

Basic follow-up activities for the participants are twofold. First, group members who have been appointed to do special tasks should immediately plan and move on the implementation. Any uncertainty about these tasks should be cleared up in the meeting record. The second responsibility of each participant is to review the meeting record and forward to the leader any corrections or clarifying comments. The meeting has not been a success until all follow-up activities are completed.

THE ELECTRONIC MEETING

Electronic meetings break with tradition in that participants are not face-to-face.

One of the traditional characteristics of small groups is that members interact face-to-face. To this extent, electronic meetings differ from what is customarily considered to be small group communication. The individuals involved may, at best, see only images of faces.

One useful form of electronic group interaction involves the linking of compatible personal computers at either local or distant sites. To illustrate, James Cox is international materials manager for a large manufacturer of parts for the aerospace industry. His company has eight regional manufacturing facilities located in various parts of the United States, Spain, and Brazil, all linked by computers. Lately, several of the plants have been experiencing erratic, unexplained fluctuations in spare parts inventories.

James uses his desktop computer to transmit a message to all eight regional managers. Before long (accounting for the widespread time zones involved), all eight managers have read the message and are inputting their own suggestions as well as comments on suggestions made by others. By the end of the next day, as his supporting managers have dropped in and out of his electronic meeting and back in again, James Cox is ready to decide on a solution to the inventory problem.

Computers may be employed in other unique ways. A relatively recent development is known as Collaborative Work Support Systems (CWSS), or sometimes alternatively as Group Decision Support Systems. The possibilities that result from merging of CWSS and the traditional group session are virtually unlimited.

Suppose, for example, that a group of managers is linked electronically to a local CWSS. A meeting is called for a week in the future. The managers begin brainstorming ideas into their office computers, entering information at random times prior to the meeting. These ideas may or may not be attributed to the respective sources. When they convene for the face-to-face meeting, a compiled list of all the ideas is retrieved from the networked computer in the meeting room. They are available for all of the group members to view, discuss, and evaluate — perhaps projected onto a larger screen.

Savings in travel costs and time have been mentioned as an obvious advantage of electronic meetings. Electronic conferencing can work well when routine decisions are made among managers located some distance from one another. A disadvantage is the lack of a sense of interpersonal interaction among participants. Doubt still exists as to whether the quality of decisions produced can match the quality of those produced in a face-to-face encounter.

A comparison of face-to-face meetings with various types of electronic meetings is shown in Table 17.2. In simplest terms, electronic meetings can be classified as audio, commonly via telephone; audiographic, which adds a device for transmitting diagrams, maps, charts, and sketches; video, or telecommunicating; and computer conferencing, represented by the James Cox example. Chapter 20 is devoted to electronic equipment used in business.

SUMMARY

Small groups play an essential role in the management of virtually every organization. Making decisions through the small group, or meeting, process has significant advantages and disadvantages. Several alternatives to calling a meeting are available, but at times a meeting will result in a better decision, wider acceptance of the decision, or stronger commitment to the decision.

Meetings are typically either problem solving or informational. For the problem-solving meeting, a number of methods and techniques can be used that may enhance the quality of solutions generated, considered, and

TABLE 17.2 ▪ *Meeting Comparison Chart*

Features	Type				
	Audio	Audiographic	Video	Computer Conferencing	Face-to-Face
Does everyone have to be on line at the same time?	Yes	Yes	Yes	No	Yes
Can graphics be exchanged?	No	Yes	Yes	Yes	Yes
Can facial expressions and other nonverbal clues be exchanged?	No	No	Yes	No	Yes
Is a written record immediately available?	No	No	No	Yes	No
Does everyone have to be in the same location?	No	No	No	No	Yes

Source: Adapted from Robert Johansen, Jacques Vallee, and Kathleen Spangler, *Electronic Meetings: Technical Alternatives and Social Choices* (Reading, Mass.: Addison-Wesley, 1979).

determined. Before, during, and after the meeting both leader and participants have essential responsibilities to ensure the desired outcomes are achieved.

Modern business people should be aware of the role of computers and other electronic devices in the conduct of meetings. Overall, these aids hold the promise for significant savings in both time and money for many organizations.

Key Terms

- **participative management**
- **quality circle**
- **accountability**
- **group polarization**
- **task role**

- **maintenance role**
- **small group**
- **nominal group**
- **groupthink**

Review Questions

1. Discuss the major advantages and disadvantages of reaching decisions in small groups. Give an example of each.

2. What are the basic identifying characteristics of a small group?

3. Define and discuss the two basic types of small group meetings. Give examples of each.

4. What are some of the most useful alternatives to the calling of a meeting?

5. Describe some of the duties required of the leader in preparing for a meeting.

6. Discuss the basic principle underlying Tropman's "rule of the agenda bell."

7. Why is the simple arrangement of tables and chairs important in the conduct of a meeting?

8. What are the major styles of group leadership? Which style best fits your personality? Why?

9. Most of the time, the participative leadership style is the most desirable. Why?

10. Describe some of the basic leader duties essential to the conduct of each part of a successful meeting.

11. Discuss the six steps involved in the Dewey Reflective Thinking Process.

12. In what ways is the nominal group approach to problem solving superior to the interacting group approach?

13. What is brainstorming and why is it useful in the problem solving process?

14. What is groupthink? How does it contribute to irrational and poorly formulated decisions? What are some of the ways of avoiding groupthink?

15. Describe some of the behaviors that group members can exhibit that can contribute to a meeting's success.

16. Why is follow-up important to a group process?

17. What are some of the advantages and disadvantages of the various types of electronic meetings?

Exercises

1. As a class, divide into groups of five or six and use the brainstorming technique to generate solutions to a problem that confronts your school.

2. Attend a meeting of the local city council and observe the interaction of council members. Record your observations.

3. Critically evaluate a meeting connected with your interests at school — student government, fraternity or sorority, professional honor society, or the like. Include both pros and cons of the proceedings in your evaluation.

4. Select a problem that you have in common with a peer group. Reach a decision on your own, then discuss it with the group. Record any new viewpoints that the group brought up that you overlooked in your original decision.

5. Lead a group discussion about a pertinent issue such as job placement or course curriculum degree requirements. How did your role as a group leader differ from that of a participant? Rotate the leadership role among other group members and describe how individual styles produced various types of interaction.

6. Assemble two groups of four to six people. Discuss an issue. How did the conclusions and decision-making procedures differ between the two groups?

7. Form a group with 12 classmates. Split up into two subgroups of four and eight, then attempt to resolve the same problem as in Exercise 6. Did the size

of the two groups affect the communication process and the eventual outcome? How?

8. As a class, divide into three groups and select a single problem in which the participants are interested. Assign each group a different approach to solving the problem. One group uses the steps of reflective thinking; another uses the single question format; the third uses the ideal solution format. Following the exercise, discuss the differences and similarities of the three approaches.

9. Each person in the class should make a list of the problems experienced as a new member of an established group. As a class, divide into groups of five or six and construct a master list for each group using the individual lists. Each group should then identify ways in which group members can overcome these problems.

10. Using the problem lists generated in Exercise 9, identify ways that group leaders can assist members in overcoming those problems.

11. One half of the class should design and implement a Delphi technique and the other half should use the focus group approach to decide whether condoms should be advertised on television. Compare and contrast the results from these two approaches.

CASE | ***The Realty Tangle***

Doris D. Phillips, University of Mississippi

Kilgore and Mitchell, Realtors, is a Mississippi real estate firm that has been in business for 15 years and has a strong local and regional reputation. Partners James J. Kilgore and Donald O. Mitchell are assisted by six full-time salespeople, two part-time salespeople, and two full-time secretaries. Until recently they had enjoyed a harmonious office atmosphere.

Virginia Bolt has been with the firm in part-time sales for about five years and has built a reasonably large clientele. Before joining Kilgore and Mitchell she worked a total of 25 years in various clerical positions in banks and with governmental agencies. She had excellent clerical skills but was unable to remain long in any job because of an inability to get along with people.

Her recent actions indicate a renewal of the old people problem. In addition to antagonizing other salespeople in the firm by undercutting and backstabbing, she has allegedly violated an important point in realty ethics by advertising property in her own name with no reference to Kilgore and Mitchell as her employers.

Mitchell wants to release Virginia from her position with the firm. He believes that her unethical actions could damage the firm's good name. He also thinks that her personality is disrupting an otherwise smooth operation.

Kilgore wishes to give Virginia another chance. His reasoning is that her successful record in sales outweighs her shortcomings in other areas.

Case Questions

In groups of five, analyze the case.

1. Make the management decision about Virginia's future with the firm.

2. Decide how to communicate the decision to Virginia and to others in the office so as to provide the greatest degree of acceptance and harmony.

3. Draft messages to Virginia and to the other employees informing them of the decision reached.

The Springwood Drive Plaza | *CASE*

Judith V.A. Dietrich, R.N.M.S.N., formerly Sessional Lecturer, University of British Columbia, Vancouver

The United States is facing new problems related to a phenomenon called the "graying of America." A decrease in infant mortality and improvements in the diagnosis and treatment of disease have helped reduce mortality rates and extend life expectancy. Greater numbers of Americans are living longer. Some 28 million people, or 12 percent of the population, are 65 or over; at least 21 percent, or 66 million people, will be 65 or over by the year 2030.[12]

As people age, they often become less able to care for themselves. The elderly frequently must either obtain help within the home or move into some type of institutional setting. Society has the responsibility of ensuring that the home help services and care facilities are available. Presently they are inadequate, however, and a definitive plan for meeting the needs of the year 2030 still must be addressed.

The Springwood Drive Plaza is one facility that offers a unique approach to these problems. It provides apartments for the elderly individual or couples, support services on site, and supervision by caring, skilled personnel.

The Plaza is managed by Marie, Susan, and Dennis. Marie and Susan are registered nurses; Dennis is a social worker. The three of them have worked extensively with the aged population in a variety of settings. Their combined skills and backgrounds provide the expertise required to accurately assess, plan, carry out, and evaluate strategies designed to meet the needs of the tenants. In addition, they are familiar with and know how to cope with the type of stress generated from caring for the elderly.

Marie, Susan, and Dennis have maintained an effective and satisfying working relationship during the three years their business has been in operation. Though they consider themselves to be partners, Marie is considered to be the leader of the group and is officially recognized as the administrator of the organization.

[12]Joseph A. Califano, Jr., *America's Health Care Revolution — Who Lives? Who Dies? Who Pays?* (New York: Random House, 1986), p. 177.

The relationship has been characterized by the use of open communication lines. The three of them chat over coffee and meet informally during the week to discuss any problems that arise. Once a month, they and their families get together for a supper or barbecue. There is also a formal meeting once a month to review major problems and the success of the program in helping the elderly tenants retain independence and meaning in their lives.

Eight months ago, an additional service was added to the package offered to the tenants. Tom, a massage therapist and physiotherapist, had convinced Marie, Susan, and Dennis that a program of massage and exercise would help the tenants feel better and maintain the physical strength needed to carry out the activities of daily living. The results of the program have been positive in both of these areas.

Gradually, Tom began to spend more time talking to Dennis. He had mentioned to Dennis over coffee one day how satisfying it was to work independently and not have to deal with the restrictions of a hospital bureaucracy. The fact that Dennis had two women for partners and that one of them was the administrator of the Plaza seemed to surprise Tom.

During Tom's fourth month at the Plaza he asked Dennis if he could participate in the monthly meetings. Dennis discussed the request with Marie and Susan, and as a group they made the decision to include Tom in the meetings.

Tom has attended two of the meetings. At the first meeting he contributed little to the discussion. When he did speak, it was to boast about the success of his massage program. At the second meeting, he spoke in an authoritarian manner when addressing Marie and was openly critical of how the status of the tenants was assessed.

Case Questions

1. What factors fostered the cohesiveness within the small group consisting of Marie, Susan, and Dennis?

2. What type of leadership style would you use with a group member such as Tom?

3. What are the different types of individual roles a group member may play?

4. What can be done when a group member has adopted an individual role that hinders the progress of the group?

Communication and Conflict

Ken McBride gazed blankly at the softly rolling hills as he traveled the short distance to the plant. His mind was working double time. During his many years with the company he had learned to dread Fridays. Every week ended with a planning session. Ken was the firm's production scheduler. His decisions caused constant clashes with the marketing manager, Pat Francis.

Pat's staff did a good job, but frequently the salespeople promised customers delivery dates the production department found difficult to meet. The success of the firm's latest line was compounding the problem. For the first time he was finding it absolutely impossible to juggle the production schedule to meet delivery dates. Ken needed to state his case emphatically.

Ken dreaded the upcoming confrontation. He knew previous arguments about the same subject would serve to intensify the current conflict. As the guard waved him through the gate he felt his stomach tighten; another week was going to come to an uncomfortable close.

Learning Objectives

1 *To identify the role conflict plays in organizational behavior.*

2 *To recognize the characteristics of conflict.*

3 *To examine the role of perception in conflict situations.*

4 *To recognize the difference between valuable and unproductive conflict.*

5 *To identify the various styles of conflict management.*

6 *To learn guidelines for communicating in conflict situations.*

All of us experience some type of conflict in our daily lives. Tensions, antagonisms, and frustrations always occur when people work together. Think about any part-time or summer jobs you have held. You will probably remember disagreements, perhaps even fights, between employees and the supervisor or between coworkers. Aside from personality clashes, people simply have different viewpoints about the way things should be done.

*We become aware
of conflict
through some
form of
communication.*

Conflict is an appropriate topic for a business communication text because it relates directly to communication. Although we can have communication without conflict, we cannot have conflict without some form of communication. More important, through communication we can minimize the impact of conflict when it occurs. Both verbal and nonverbal communication can soothe tempers, settle misunderstandings, and get the organization back on a normal work schedule.

THE NATURE OF CONFLICT

When conflict occurs, the adrenal glands deliver extra energy. The individual is in a state of tensed readiness in which hearing and vision become more acute. Properly channeled, this type of stress can stimulate a person to put forth superior effort. In fact, conflict is an inevitable by-product of an interesting and challenging job. Many active people thrive on conflict, and it can have a beneficial effect on physical and mental health. For example, competition between two companies can be healthy for the members of both organizations and beneficial to the companies as well.

On the other hand, conflict can be damaging. Too much conflict can be harmful when your overstimulated body refuses to relax and assume normal activity. Your blood pressure remains high, your back muscles develop spasms, and your judgment is impaired. Excessive conflict over time could make you unable to work.

Competition within an organization is potentially dangerous because it can divide loyalties and hamper cooperation. Even competition as apparently harmless as an interdepartmental bowling league should be examined carefully.

*Conflict can be
constructive or
destructive.*

Conflict is like one of the modern miracle drugs: the correct dosage can be good for you, but too much can bring damage. One level of conflict may key you up for superior performance — that is, moderate conflict can be **constructive conflict**. Too much conflict may cause worry or fear, hamper your work performance, and in some cases lead to ulcers and other forms of physical and mental illnesses. Thus intense or prolonged conflict is **destructive conflict**.

Conditions Leading to Conflict

Certain social relationships characterize various kinds of conflict behavior. Each one could occur in your work area. As future managers, the more aware you are of these conflict settings, the better your chances of correcting them and running a smooth operation.[1]

---

[1]These nine characteristics of conflict are adapted from Alan C. Filley, *Interpersonal Conflict Resolution* (Palo Alto, Calif.: Scott, Foresman, 1975), 9–12. Reprinted by permission.

Ambiguous Jurisdictions

Conflict is greater when the lines that set forth each employee's jurisdiction (area of job responsibility) are unclear. When two people have related job tasks with ambiguous boundaries, the potential for conflict between them increases. For example, consider the case of a department head to whom three first-line supervisors report. Each of these supervisors should have clearly defined job responsibilities so that the potential for overlap among the three is reduced. Otherwise, confusion and conflict result as each of the supervisors tries to do all of the jobs. The boundaries between the department head and the supervisors must also be clearly spelled out; otherwise the supervisors may resent the department head's interference in their work responsibilities. The result is a department full of discord and conflict over unclear limits of authority. Such an antagonistic situation can be avoided if job descriptions are clarified so that all employees know the extent of their work responsibilities.

Conflict of Interest

Conflict will be greater when people's interests diverge. For example, consider the conflict between the marketing manager and the plant production manager of a leading producer of chocolate. Each manager would like to have more control over the factors that affect the company's profitability. In the face of fierce competition from other chocolate manufacturers, the marketing manager occasionally wants to run a sampling campaign to support a new candy bar. This manager needs to act fast before competitors match the new product. However, when the marketing manager asks for sharply increased production capacity during the sampling campaign, the plant production manager refuses. The hiring and training of new workers would only be temporary. After the sampling campaign is completed, the company would lay off the new workers. The results is a conflict of interest between the marketing and plant production managers, and a competitive edge for rival chocolate manufacturers.

Communication Barriers

Conflict will be greater when barriers to communication exist. If parties are separated from each other physically or by time — for example, the day shift versus the night shift — the opportunity for conflict is increased. To illustrate, suppose a company employs only one plant supervisor, who works the day shift and leaves orders at the beginning of each week for the workers on the night shift. By the end of the week, however, these orders have been only partially carried out. The supervisor cannot figure out why. Obviously, the supervisor's absence from the night shift has posed a communication barrier, which in turn causes decreased output. Space or time separations can promote isolated group interests rather than advance a common effort toward joint goals.

Dependence of One Party

Conflict will be greater when one party is dependent on another. When parties are dependent, they must rely on each other for performance of tasks or for provision of resources. For example, a supervisor who depends on the preparation of a cost-effectiveness report by a subordinate in order to make a marketing decision may monitor the subordinate's progress. The subordinate resents this close supervision and in retaliation takes a long time to prepare the report. The supervisor, in turn, reminds the subordinate of a forthcoming performance evaluation. The interdependence of supervisor and subordinate fuels the potential for serious conflict.

Differentiation in Organizations

Conflict will be greater as the degree of differentiation, or the division of labor, in an organization increases. When people work together in a complex organization, there is evidence that conflict is related to the number of organizational levels, the number of distinct job specialties represented, and the degree to which labor is divided in the organization. For example, consider the administrators in your college: most likely there is a dean, an associate dean, department heads, program advisors, and secretaries. All of these people administer some aspect of your curriculum and other educational needs. However, they are at different levels of the organizational hierarchy and handle specialized tasks. Although these university employees share a common focus, their different positions and job concentrations can lead to overlap and conflict.

Association of the Parties

Conflict will be greater as the degree of interaction of the parties increases. As used here, degree of association, or interaction, refers both to the parties' participation in decision making and to informal relations between them. When parties make decisions jointly, the opportunity for conflict is greater, which may explain why some managers are reluctant to involve others in decision making. These managers would prefer to make decisions on their own rather than risk a difference of opinion with a colleague. However, there is a trade-off between the possibility of gaining valuable suggestions and the possibility of an argument. The association of parties has constructive and destructive possibilities.

Need for Consensus

Conflict will be greater when consensus between the parties is necessary; that is, when all parties must agree on a decision so that no individual believes the decision is unacceptable. It is possible to avoid conflict by having mechanisms such as voting to make decisions without the confrontation of consensus. However, such mechanisms themselves may have undesirable consequences. They may offer an easy way out of the immediate conflict but may not solve the problem. Settling the matter by majority rule may only postpone the conflict until a true crisis occurs. When consensus is difficult to achieve, the resultant conflict should not be avoided but used in a constructive manner.

Behavior Regulations

Conflicts will be greater when behavior regulations are imposed. Regulating mechanisms, which include standardized procedures, rules, and policies, seem to do two things at once. On the one hand, they reduce the likelihood of conflict because they make relationships predictable and reduce the need for arbitrary decisions. Some individuals need specific guidelines explaining how to perform their jobs. They are only comfortable making routine decisions about their work. Other individuals have a greater need for autonomy and self-control. Regulating mechanisms that increase the degree of control may be resisted by some workers and welcomed by others. For either type of individual, if the adherence to or the imposition of rules becomes discretionary, further sources of disagreement are created. If behavioral regulations fail to match individual needs of employees, conflict is bound to occur.

Unresolved Prior Conflicts

Conflicts will be greater as the number of unresolved prior conflicts increases. That is, the longer problems are ignored or postponed, the worse new conflicts become. Suppression of conflict through the use of power or compromises to which the parties are uncommitted creates conditions and expectations that may lead to further conflict.

Suppose the people in an office want to streamline operating procedures and rearrange desks and other office furniture to fit this new office reorganization. The workers are not content with the present office organization and their lack of input into office policy. For some time their complaints have been ignored by the division manager, who hoped they would tire of asking for changes and drop the matter once and for all. Together with their supervisor, the employees seek permission from the division manager to draw up reorganization plans. In an effort to placate them, the manager approves their request. The office members and their supervisor earnestly devise new guidelines for office rearrangement. They submit the guidelines to the division manager, who rejects their proposals because he lacks sufficient time to review the plans properly and he fears unsatisfactory changes. The staff becomes very angry and seeks outside help in organizing a union. The manager's attempt to suppress conflict by the use of power has increased the original conflict to a crisis point. This example underscores the idea that unresolved prior conflicts are active breeding agents for future crises.

The conditions that can lead to conflict need not always do so. However, these conditions create the opportunity for conflict to occur. Being aware of the conditions for discord will help you to avoid some potential conflicts and to understand other conflicts once they become apparent.

The Conflict Episode

When people experience a particular conflict, they may feel frustration or even anger. Sometimes it is difficult for them to know exactly why they experience this conflict. Furthermore, they are not sure exactly how to remedy the situation.

| BOXED IN | *AN ETHICAL DILEMMA* |

Tim Fields is leaving his office to start his daily round of sales calls when the phone rings. His morning's plans go awry as the angry voice on the other end of the line demands to know the status of an order. The order represents Tim's biggest sale to date and the first his company has made with a major franchise.

Tim quickly contacts Ken McBride. Ken feels his breath catch in his chest. As he had predicted earlier in the month, production has fallen behind schedule. Now he has a unique part on hand that is needed for two different orders. He has to decide whether to use it to fill a regular customer's order, which is legitimately far ahead of the one in question and urgently needed—or to honor Tim's frantic request.

Ken could reduce his immediate stress level and save Tim's day by bumping the regular customer's order. This move would cause serious problems for the valued old customer, however. No business would be lost, of course, because the old customer would have no way of knowing that its order had been set aside to accommodate a new customer in the hope of generating future sales.

Ken feels boxed in. What would you do?

The conflict episode provides a perspective for viewing the conflict situation.

A convenient perspective for examining conflict is what Pondy has termed the conflict episode, which consists of five distinct stages.[2]

Latent Conflict Stage

Latent conflict has underlying sources. In an organizational setting, these sources include competition for scarce resources (such as materials, money, and labor), drives for autonomy, and differing subunit goals within the organization.

As an example of latent conflict on a personal level, assume you attend a university that has a very limited number of tennis courts. During the past few years more and more students have started playing the game. You have become an avid tennis player and two or three nights a week you try to play.

Perceived Conflict Stage

Perceived conflict can occur whether or not latent conflict is present. When no latent conflict exists but conflict is nevertheless perceived, it is said to be the result of the parties' misunderstandings of one another's true positions. When latent conflict exists but fails to reach the level of awareness,

[2]L.R. Pondy, "Organizational Conflict Concepts and Models," in *Management of Change and Conflict*, eds. John M. Thomas and Warren Bennis (Middlesex, England: Penguin Books, 1972), 360–366.

it is not because such conflict is not actually perceived, but because certain individual defense mechanisms tend to suppress it.

To continue the personal conflict episode, on Monday evening you and a friend decide to play tennis. As the two of you take your rackets and get in the car, your friend remarks, "Boy, I sure hope we can get a court." You glance at your watch and notice that it is almost 6:30 — a time when the few tennis courts are likely to be in use. Suddenly, you perceive a conflict situation.

Felt Conflict Stage

Felt conflict may also be termed personalization of conflict, because at this stage the conflict actually affects the individual directly. Felt conflict is normally a function of either (a) individual anxieties created by organizational demands that the individual perceives as limiting personal growth or (b) total involvement in a relationship, making an individual necessarily more aware of the occurrence of conflict.

To continue the example, as you approach the tennis courts you observe that all the courts are occupied. Then you notice that the group on the last court has apparently finished and the players are leaving the court. Just then another car speeds into the parking lot. Two players quickly jump out and rush toward the court. You and your partner make a dash for the court.

Manifest Conflict Stage

Manifest conflict is identified simply as the actual occurrence of conflicting behavior. It may range from aggression to apathy or even extremely rigid adherence to rules with the intention of frustrating another party to the relationship. So long as both parties perceive a specific behavior to be conflicting, and so long as the party indulging in the behavior persists, a clear case of manifest conflict has developed.

Again to continue the example, your partner wins the race and secures the court. As you and your partner begin play, the two players that lost the footrace come onto the court and sit down close to the playing area. During the match the two other players make comments when you or your partner misses a shot. Your match stands one set to one set. As you begin the third set, the two unwanted visitors stand up and start bouncing tennis balls with their rackets. On your first serve you double fault. You eventually lose the set 6–4.

Conflict Aftermath Stage

Conflict aftermath is a function of how well the entire episode or sequence of episodes has been resolved. Perhaps this stage will reveal that bases for a more cooperative relationship have been established; or it may suggest how newly perceived problems might be handled; or, if the latent conditions were merely suppressed instead of resolved, they may emerge at this time to foster more serious difficulties. The aftermath stage suggests the dynamic nature of conflict; that is, a conflict between or among two or more individuals in an organization is not likely to consist of only one episode, but it is made up of a sequence of such episodes. Each one results from the resolution of conflict in the previous episode.

To conclude the personal conflict episode, you and your friend discuss the possibility of trying to play tennis again on Thursday. Neither of you display much interest as you both recall the conflict that frequently results from the limited number of courts available. Early the next morning your tennis friend calls you and excitedly tells you that his parents have just given him a birthday present — a membership in a new tennis club. The membership guarantees six hours of court time each week. Suddenly your interest in the game of tennis is renewed.

PERCEPTION AND CONFLICT

The adage, "beauty is in the eye of the beholder," makes the point that what one person perceives as beauty may not be thought beautiful by another. You have no doubt watched two people observe the same event, yet later describe two different situations. People do not behave according to the facts as other people interpret them. The behavior of individuals is based on their unique perceptions of themselves and the world in which they live. Indeed, all behavior is completely determined by the way people perceive the events around them.

Conflict must be perceived for it to exist.

In conflict situations perception also plays a major role. In some cases perception may be the cause of conflict. Whatever the cause of a conflict situation, those involved must be aware of the conflict in order for it to exist. Perception as it relates to conflict can be illustrated by five conflict levels.

1. *Intraindividual conflict* occurs when the perceiver experiences conflict within himself or herself. Such conflict may arise from personal or job responsibilities and may influence, either directly or indirectly, job performance.
2. *Interindividual conflict* exists between the perceiver and another individual within the organization. Although the other person need not be aware of the conflict, the perceiver of the conflict situation recognizes the present or future impact the conflict can have on job performance.
3. *Intragroup conflict* occurs between the perceiver and his or her immediate group within the organization. The immediate group can consist of a work team, department, or union. Whether fully or only superficially aware of the conflict issue, the perceiver realizes that the conflict can directly or indirectly affect job performance.
4. *Intergroup conflict* arises between the perceiver's immediate group and another group within the organization. Again, the perceiver's involvement may not be critical, but he or she must be aware of the situation and the potential impact the conflict can have on work performance.
5. *Organization-environment conflict* arises between the perceiver's organization and the environment it is part of. Environment may refer

to the city, country, or world in which the organization exists. For example, if the environment consists of a home office and a number of branches, each branch may be viewed as a single entity within its local environment or as part of the entire organization within a state, nation, or worldwide setting. Whatever the context, the environmental boundary should be defined so that the conflict situation is accurately understood. As with the other four conflict circumstances, the perceiver may be acutely or only casually aware of the conflict and its effect on job performance.

To illustrate these five levels of perceiving conflict, take the case of a second-year business student at a leading two-year college. Jan has worked hard throughout her college career and maintained a high grade point average. As she nears graduation, she is anxious about getting a good job. She has recently received a very low grade in one of her courses and is worried that the grade will lower her overall average. Furthermore, she believes that the grade is unfair because she always completed her assignments on time and had worked hard to write an excellent term paper. Jan wants to discuss with her professor the possibility of a grade change, but she wonders if she dares take the time away from job hunting (intraindividual conflict). Furthermore, her professor is known to be an insensitive person who reacts poorly to any student's request for a grade change (interindividual conflict). If Jan gets her grade changed, then her classmates might start squabbling about who else deserves a raise in grade (intragroup conflict). If several grades are changed and word gets back to students from previous semesters, they might complain about unequal grading standards among the different classes (intergroup conflict). Finally, if word of the discrepancy gets to the board of examiners that accredits the college's business program, the business department risks having its accreditation reviewed (organization–environment conflict).

Table 18.1 provides an analysis of the five levels of conflict involved in Jan's deciding whether to ask the professor for a grade change. Although Jan's case does not provide entries for each column of the table, it is easy to imagine other cases that would illustrate those areas.

An example in a business setting involves the assistant manager of production for a medium-sized company that makes pleasure sailboats. Jeff, although not a yacht designer, sees a modification to the keel of his company's top-of-the-line boats as an idea with potential. He prepares a proposal and submits it to his immediate supervisor.

Jeff receives no response to his proposal for four months. Then he hears through the grapevine that some major modifications are to be made to the larger boats. The production line is halted for those models.

When Jeff asks about what is going on, his supervisor is evasive. The following week, the company announces a breakthrough in keel design for its large offshore boats. This design will be incorporated immediately in selected models. At the same time the company announces that Jeff's boss will be promoted to vice president.

TABLE 18.1   ∎   *An Analysis of Conflict as Perceived by a College Student*

| | Perceived Impact of Source of Conflict | | | |
| Perceived Source of Conflict | Direct (Impact on Student) | | Indirect (Impact on Extra-Organizational Concerns) | |
	Current (Operating Now)	*Potential (Likely to Operate)*	*Current*	*Potential*
Intraindividual	Student wonders whether to spend time getting grade changed.			Student loses time for job search.
Interindividual		Student and professor disagree over grade change.		Student's relationship with professor is strained.
Intragroup	Furor erupts in class over changing only one student's grade.	Students argue among themselves about who deserves a higher grade, and the conflict becomes worse.	Low ticket sales to end-of-school party result from tension caused by grade controversy.	
Intergroup	Class groups from previous semesters quarrel over why their grade changes weren't granted.	Class groups from different semesters may complain to dean about unfair grade distribution.		
Organization–Environment	Board of examiners has the power to investigate irregular grading policies.	Angry students contact board of examiners.		Business department loses accreditation by board of examiners.

Jeff is unsure whether to do or say anything about his report (intra-individual conflict). He is tempted to speak to his boss, who is the only person to whom he had given his report. Jeff knows there is potential here for interindividual conflict because he believes his idea has been stolen.

Jeff doesn't want to let others in the department know of his anger for he realizes it could create unrest (intragroup conflict). He also is wary of talking to acquaintances in the yacht design department, which has been mentioned as deeply involved in the keel design project (intergroup conflict). Jeff considers going to the editor of the employee newspaper, the trade journal, or even the local daily newspaper, but reconsiders (organization–environmental conflict).

CONFLICT MANAGEMENT

Managers need to distinguish between conflict that is useful and conflict that should be reduced or eliminated. The objective of conflict management is to see that conflict remains creative and productive. Besides requiring managers to be able to distinguish between functional and dysfunctional conflict, conflict management requires that managers develop individuals who can work under conflict and tension and still be productive members in the organization.

Conflict management can improve performance.

Method for Analyzing Conflict Situations

In deciding how to handle a particular conflict situation, the manager first needs to understand it. The following suggestions comprise a method for analyzing conflict situations.

Analyzing conflict situations can aid in conflict management.

1. *Assess the importance and impact of the conflict.* Is the conflict useful and motivational in nature and likely to improve the performance of one or several members of the organization? Or is the conflict damaging and in need of resolution? If the conflict is harmful, the remaining steps of analysis should be used.

2. *Identify the type of conflict.* Intraindividual conflict is conflict individuals experience within themselves. Interindividual conflict is conflict the individual experiences with another. Intragroup conflict is conflict between the individual and his or her immediate group within the organization. Intergroup conflict is conflict between the individual's immediate group and another group within the organization. Organization–environment conflict is conflict between the individual's organization and the larger outside environment.

3. *Select an overall strategy for dealing with the conflict.* Controlling the conflict may be preferable — perhaps at this time it is either impossible to resolve completely or it would take too much time and energy to do so. Resolving the conflict is another strategy — if the conflict is serious, you will want to resolve it.

4. *Identify methods for reducing the conflict.* Decide on the basic approach to conflict resolution. Select particular communication strategies.

Styles of Conflict Management

In every conflict situation there are at least two major concerns. The first is the extent to which an individual wants to meet personal goals. The second is the extent to which the individual wants to maintain a relationship with another individual or group or wants to be accepted by the individual or group.[3] The way these two concerns interact is demonstrated

Two major concerns exist in every conflict situation

---

[3]The remainder of this section is based on Robert R. Blake and Jane Srygley Mouton, "The Fifth Achievement," *Journal of Applied Behavioral Science* 6, no. 4 (1970): 413–426, and Jay Hall, *Conflict Management Survey* (Houston: Teleometrics, 1968).

in Figure 18.1. Concern for personal goals is scaled from 1 to 9 representing the increasing degree of importance in the mind of the individual (1 = low concern; 9 = high concern). The concern for relationships is also scaled from 1 (low concern) to 9 (high concern). Given this scale, Blake and Mouton identify the following styles: high concern for personal goals and low concern for relationships (9, 1); low concern for personal goals and high concern for relationships (1, 9); low concern for personal goals and low concern for relationships (1, 1); moderate concern for personal goals and moderate concern for relationships (5, 5); and high concern for personal goals and high concern for relationships (9, 9). With this overview, each style can be examined in more detail.

- *Tough Battler Style:* The win–lose style (9, 1) is the trademark of the tough battler who seeks to meet goals at all costs without concern for the needs of others. For this type of individual losing means the loss of self-image. This type of person is willing to sacrifice individuals or groups to be a winner.
- *Friendly Helper Style:* The yield–lose style (1, 9) involves the friendly helper who overvalues relationships with others and undervalues the achievement of personal goals. People of this type desire acceptance by others so much that they given in to the desires of others almost all the time. They always avoid conflict in favor of harmony.
- *Loser Style:* The lose–leave style (1, 1) is used by the person who sees conflict as a hopeless and useless experience. Rather than be a part of any conflict, this type of person simply withdraws, either physically or mentally, from the conflict.
- *Compromise Style:* The compromise style (5, 5) is exemplified by the middle-of-the-roader who takes the position that half a loaf is better than none. The person using this style looks for a position that allows each side to gain something. This individual always looks for the middle ground when confronted with a conflict situation.
- *Problem-Solver Style:* The integrative (9, 9) style is the approach of the problem solver, who seeks to satisfy his or her own goals as well as the goals of others.

The individual who takes the problem-solving approach has the following views: (1) Conflict is natural and helpful and can even lead to a more creative solution if handled properly. (2) The attitudes and positions of everyone need to be aired when attempting to resolve conflicts. (3) No one is ever sacrificed simply for the goal of the group.

Filley reports on research that shows the relative effectiveness of three different conflict styles. He cites the work of Cummins, who identified three types of bargainers: the tough bargainer, the soft bargainer, and the equalizer. Filley points out that the tough bargainer is equivalent to the tough battler (9, 1); the soft bargainer equates to the friendly helper (1, 9); and the equalizer is like the problem solver (9, 9).

Interaction of conflict styles results in various consequences.

Filley also describes the consequences when the tough battler, the friendly helper, and the problem solver interact with one another. This is his summary of the interaction of these conflict styles:

FIGURE 18.1 ▮ *The Conflict Grid*

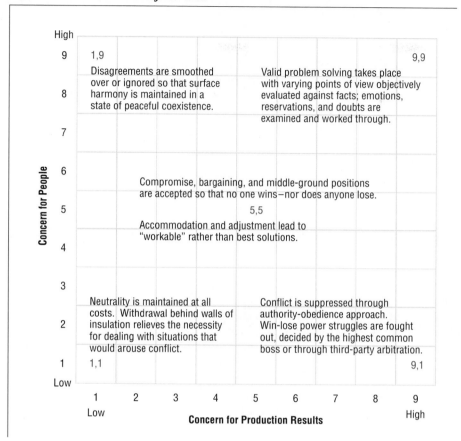

Source: Reprinted by special permission from Robert R. Blake and Jane Srygley Mouton, "The Fifth Achievement," *Journal of Applied Behavioral Science* 6, No. 4 (1970): 418, NTL Institute for Applied Behavioral Science.

- When one tough battler meets another tough battler, a stalemate results 80 percent of the time.
- When the tough battler meets the friendly helper, the battler wins 90 percent of the time.
- When the tough battler meets the problem solver, the battler wins over 50 percent of the time.
- Strangely enough, when two friendly helpers meet, a stalemate results 80 percent of the time.
- When a friendly helper meets a problem solver, the problem solver usually wins.

▪ When two problem solvers interact, they frequently arrive at an agreeable solution.[4]

Filley concludes that the problem-solving style of conflict resolution is the preferred style in that it provides advantages relative to possible agreements reached through the use of other styles.[5]

A problem-solving approach is the preferred style.

Given that the problem-solving approach has the greatest potential for resolving conflict, we can now offer some specific suggestions for communicating in conflict situations. The suggested pattern for communication in conflict is based on Rapoport's Region of Validity Technique.[6] It is illustrated by a common scenario that you may have experienced as a college student. Whether you communicate orally or in writing, the following is useful as an overall approach to communicating with someone in a conflict situation.

Step 1. Communicate to the other people that they have been carefully heard and that understanding exists. If misunderstanding still exists, ask the other party to express his or her position again. Keep in mind that it is important that the other people are convinced that you understand their exact positions.

As an example, suppose you have spent hours writing a term paper for your favorite class. You are expecting a high grade for your extra effort, hence you are very upset when the paper is returned with a low mark. You decide to communicate to the professor that you would like him to reread your paper and raise the grade or at least provide a critique. The professor thinks you are criticizing his grading standards and reacts defensively. To clear up this misunderstanding, you reiterate that you are asking the professor simply to reread the paper and change the grade only if he feels it is justified. The professor relaxes and is more open to discussion about your paper.

Step 2. At this point you enumerate the valid points in the other person's position. Concentrate on the valid points, not the inadequacies of the position.

To continue the example, you explain your paper's content. You want to make sure the professor understands that you followed his instructions. You avoid criticizing the inadequacies of his assignment and concentrate instead on enumerating his instructions and the corresponding points in your paper.

Step 3. At this stage in the process you invite the other party to participate in the process, as you did in Steps 1 and 2.

To conclude the example, you hope that you have convinced the professor of your sincere scholarly interest. You ask if you correctly understood

---

[4]Filley, *Interpersonal Conflict Resolution,* 55–56.
[5]Ibid., 56.
[6]Anatol Rapoport, *Fights, Games, and Debates* (Ann Arbor: University of Michigan, 1960).

his instructions. After he answers this question, ask him to discuss the valid points of your paper to make sure he understood your explanation. The conflict is resolved through open communication about both parties' perceptions of the term paper.

You should be able to differentiate these same three stages in this incident:

> You have been called to the director of personnel's office, and you know that several others in your department have also been called in. They were reprimanded for making personal calls on the company's long-distance telephone line. They had to reimburse the company, and a disciplinary letter was placed in their personnel files.
>
> You have never used the telephone system for personal calls. Once you did find a colleague using your extension for a private call and although you made it clear he was not to use your extension again, you let the matter slide because other employees were taking advantage of the system.
>
> The personnel director brings you into the office, points to a chair, and coldly states, "I'm sure you're aware of the policy statement of November 12 about inappropriate use of the company phone system. That policy is the subject of this conversation." You volunteer your position regarding personal use of the system and explain that you have never misused the system. Indeed, you believe in the policy and support it.
>
> You mention that you know of the disciplinary actions taken on the others and that on one occasion you found someone misusing your extension. You don't volunteer the person's name.
>
> You then say, "I suppose you want to discipline me, too, because an inappropriate call showed on my extension. Is this the purpose of this meeting?"
>
> "Yes and no," is the response. "Alicia told me last week that she misused your phone. To get to the bottom of this situation, I asked the others who were involved about your participation. I'm pleased to report that they all verify your story. Congratulations—you're one of the few in the department to follow company policy. I just wanted you to know we appreciate your honesty and loyalty. I'm sorry I don't sound more enthusiastic with my praise. I've got a toothache that's killing me!"

The accompanying checklist can be applied to a number of communication situations that you will face using both written and oral formats. It is essential to understand how the other party perceives the conflict situation. After this perception, communication needs to be directed openly and honestly in a manner that promotes trust and confidence from the receiver.

SUMMARY

Conflict is present to some degree in all organizations. A certain amount of conflict can actually make us perform better, while too much conflict can hamper our work. While we cannot always prevent conflict, we can become aware of conditions that are likely to lead to conflict. We examine various interpersonal settings that characterize different kinds of conflict behavior. A convenient perspective from which to examine conflict, the conflict episode, will give you a more thorough understanding of the na-

✓ *CHECKLIST for Analyzing Conflict Situations*

____ Assess the importance and impact of the conflict.

____ Identify the type of conflict.

____ Select an overall strategy for dealing with the conflict.

____ Identify methods for reducing the conflict.

ture of conflict. The role of perception in conflict is emphasized, and five conflict situations are presented to illustrate this point.

Finally, we present major steps to help you analyze a conflict situation when it occurs. Several basic styles of conflict management are identified and described. We give particular emphasis to the friendly helper, the tough battler, and the problem solver styles. In most cases the problem-solver style is most appropriate. This style promotes the climate that everybody wins, which is most helpful in airing differences that contribute to conflict situations. Regardless of the style you select to manage conflict, you can use Rapoport's Region of Validity Technique as a suggested pattern for communicating in conflict situations.

Key Terms

▪ **constructive conflict**   ▪ **destructive conflict**

References

Nye, Robert D. *Conflict among Humans*. New York: Springer, 1973.

Scherer, Klaus R., Ronald P. Abeles, and Claude S. Fischer. *Human Aggression and Conflict*. Englewood Cliffs, N.J.: Prentice-Hall, 1975.

Smith, Clagett G., ed. *Conflict Resolutions: Contributions of the Behavioral Sciences*. South Bend, Ind.: University of Notre Dame Press, 1971.

Swingle, Paul, ed. *The Structure of Conflict*. New York: Academic Press, 1970.

Review Questions

1. Comment on the statement, "All conflict is harmful and should be reduced or eliminated whenever possible."

2. You manage a large department of employees with different backgrounds, skills, and job responsibilities. Within the context of the nine characteristics of social relationships associated with conflict behavior, provide an example of each kind of conflict situation that could arise in your department.

3. Discuss the five distinct stages of a conflict episode.

4. How does perception play a major role in conflict situations? Provide original illustrations of the five possible conflict circumstances that could occur in a business organization.

5. What is conflict management? What steps might a manager take to analyze a particular conflict situation?

6. Describe the different styles of conflict management. Which style is preferred? Why?

Exercises

1. The next time you have a disagreement with a friend, see if you can identify the various stages of the conflict. Does this identification process help you better understand how the conflict arose?

2. Conflict can occur in student work groups. The next time you observe group conflict, see if you can help resolve that conflict by following the guidelines presented in this chapter.

3. Identify as many situations from your experience as you can in which conflict was beneficial. Are there similarities among these positive experiences? What are they?

4. Of the various styles of conflict management, which would be easiest for you to assume? The most difficult? Why to you lean in the direction you do? Will this learning hinder your ability to be an effective conflict resolver?

5. Review recent articles in a local newspaper and identify an article dealing with a conflict between two or more parties. How many underlying causes of the conflict can you identify?

The Hemphill Company | CASE

Elizabeth Plunkett, West Georgia College

One of the nation's leading shirt manufacturers, the Hemphill Company, a moderate-sized, family-owned business, has recently acquired a highly sophisticated Japanese pressing system. Because Hemphill's purchase represents the introduction of this technology into the United States, the Japanese electronics manufacturer will provide specialized training for Hemphill's mechanics. The Japanese firm will assume all costs — except for transportation to and from Japan — for an unlimited number of Hemphill's mechanics to participate in a three-week program.

The company president called a meeting to determine who should attend this training program. Present at the meeting are: Jim Hemphill, the company president/general manager; Tom Cates, the production manager, who assists the president with many management decisions (he is ambitious to become general manager and considered by Mr. Hemphill to be capable); Dave Day, the personnel manager, whose responsibilities uniquely but appropriately include overseeing maintenance personnel, equipment needs, and small parts procurement; Susan Miller, the research and development manager, who is responsible for managing training programs; and Jackie Lee, the chief engineer, who is responsible for setting rates and payback figures on new equipment.

The management group considers six employees to be possible candidates. Brian Finch, the mechanics' foreman, respected by his subordinates, has refused previous training opportunities, believing that they required too much personal time. Joan South was stationed in Japan in the military, and her familiarity with Japan is considered an asset. Even though Joan is highly skilled on manual equipment, electronic machines under her supervision have not performed well. Ed Crawford has consistently been Hemphill's top performer in training programs, and while extremely successful with electronic equipment, he appears to be negligent in routine maintenance of equipment. Karlene Miles has previously received additional training to become the company specialist on one piece of electronic equipment. Bill Hatfield works exceptionally well with Karlene Miles, and the electronic machinery under their joint supervision has attained optimal productivity. A dedicated employee, Bill has had personal problems with drug addiction and marital difficulties. Although he appears to have conquered his drug problem, his marital situation still conflicts with his job. Recently, his wife objected to his absence while he attended a two-day training session. Despite this conflict, he excelled in the course. All of the above candidates are from 28 to 34 years of age, except Finch and Hatfield, who are 40 to 42 years old.

The managers agree that Brian Finch should be included in the program, in spite of his previous reluctance to accept training. They feel that he needs updating in this technology and that his leadership could influence the success of this program. Brian enthusiastically accepts the challenge of this important project. When asked for his suggestions regarding the other candidates, Brian responds that he has no preference among them and that he has no additional names for consideration.

After much deliberation, the managers reach a standstill in the decision-making process. Jim Hemphill is adamant that performance and teamwork are essential factors in candidate selection. Karlene Miles and Bill Hatfield meet these particular requirements. Faced with the issue of Bill's marital conflict, Jim Hemphill emphasizes that management must be careful about making decisions for subordinates based on how the managers judge subordinates' nonwork environment. He feels that Bill Hatfield should have the opportunity to choose whether or not to accept the assignment.

Tom Cates supports Joan South and Ed Crawford, believing that Joan's knowledge of Japan is invaluable and that Ed's proficiency and success with electronics equipment make him a natural choice. On the other hand, Dave Day suggests that the foreman should make the final decision but that personally he would eliminate Ed Crawford and Karlene Miles from consideration. He objects to Ed's maintenance record and stresses that Karlene, with her specialized training, could not be spared. Dave also indicates that a company's extensive investment and dependence on any single individual could create unnecessary vulnerability.

Conversely, Susan Miller proposes that Ed Crawford and Karlene Miles are the only logical selections based on their strong training performance records. Jackie Lee, however, firmly believes that all the candidates should attend the course because this solution not only would assure the payback on this expensive system but also would resolve the deadlock in this discussion.

Case Questions

1. What could be done to facilitate the decision-making process?

2. What interpersonal factors influence the decision makers in their selections?

3. Which candidates would you select to participate in the training program? Support your recommendations.

A Touchy Situation   CASE

Margaret Fitch-Hauser, Auburn University

Ellen Jones is an attractive woman in her mid-30s. She has worked for 14 years in public relations. Six months ago she began a new job that represented a major career advancement for her. She began work for a large industrial firm as their chief public relations officer. During the brief time that she has been on the job, she has worked very hard to establish a sound image for the company and a reputation for herself. The reactions to her efforts have been very favorable. Much of her success has been due to the fact that Ellen finds the job both challenging and rewarding. However, a situation has arisen that she feels threatens her job performance and may force her to resign.

The situation involves the behavior of Rex Dycus, a senior vice president with the firm. On a number of occasions he has made comments or behaved in a manner that Ellen perceives to be condescending or to contain obvious sexual overtones.

Several times when she went to get a cup of coffee, Rex was also at the coffee maker. On two of those occasions, he placed his hand on her back as if to pat her on the back but then let his hand slide on down until it brushed her seat. Not knowing exactly what to do, she simply stepped away and returned to her office as soon as she could. Lately, she has begun to avoid the coffee room.

On other occasions, Rex has come into her office to talk about certain projects of mutual interest. For the most part, Ellen has enjoyed their conversations because Rex is a good problem solver. She has found him to be very insightful about the company's various public relations problems. In fact, several times she has been able to more clearly understand a particular situation because of his observations. Clearly, he is a valuable information resource for her. Unfortunately, he nearly always manages to drop a comment or two about helping her advance in the company if she is willing to do some favors for him. He has even suggested that the two of them get together after work some evening for dinner and "whatever" so they can discuss how they might be of mutual benefit to one another. On these occasions Ellen has been embarrassed and angry but has managed only to stammer some type of joking response. However, she does not feel that Rex is joking. She is afraid that if she responds in anger, she will come across as a pushy, defensive woman and consequently undermine her hard-earned credibility as well as lose a valuable information source.

Ellen has also become aware that Rex seems to go out of his way to be in the corridor when she arrives at work in the mornings. On these occasions he always compliments her appearance. Although the attention is flattering, the content of his compliments disturbs Ellen. He has said things like, "What a lovely suit. It really shows your womanly build." On another occasion he commented that a particular garment was especially attractive as she walked down the hall because it moved with her hips. Not wanting to appear ungrateful for the compliments, Ellen has simply said thank you and walked quickly away. On at least two occasions she heard some of the other men in the hall snicker as she left.

The entire situation has really disrupted Ellen's ability to work. She finds that she is spending much of her time trying to avoid Rex or trying to figure out how to handle the situation without damaging either one of their positions with the company. The problem is compounded by the fact that she is currently working on a major project for Rex's division and has to consult with him regularly on several matters. These meetings are always in one of their offices, and she feels especially vulnerable when she is in either office alone with him. At this point Ellen is so frustrated that she is ready to tender her resignation.

Case Questions

1. What type of conflict is described in this case?

2. Should Ellen report Rex's behavior to her superiors?

3. Should Ellen confront Rex about his behavior?

4. What is the best approach Ellen can take in handling this problem?

5. Should Ellen resign, or can the situation be resolved?

Interviewing as a Management Tool

One of Susan Marsh's first tasks as a new department supervisor was to conduct a disciplinary interview with Jim Johnson, who had been late for work on a number of occasions recently. Looking through his employment record, she noted that he had always been punctual in the past.

Susan felt uncomfortable disciplining an older employee who had been with the company for years. She planned to start the meeting on a positive note. She felt the best approach was to recognize Jim's good work record. She wanted to emphasize that she was willing to work with him if he was having a temporary problem but that he needed to correct the situation.

After the interview, Susan felt drained. It had certainly started out well, but she had fallen into the trap of making too many complimentary comments. Somehow, despite her intentions, she had difficulty broaching the topic of tardiness. She was positive she had failed to make her expectations clear to Jim. She realized he had probably left her office confused. Aware that she needed help, Susan made an appointment with her supervisor to discuss interviewing strategies.

PURPOSES AND CHARACTERISTICS OF INTERVIEWS

As used by management, the interview has a wide variety of purposes. Job applicants are hired on the basis of interviews. Employees who experience personal problems may be counseled in an interview. In many organizations man-

CHAPTER 19

Learning Objectives

1 To recognize the importance of the interview as a business communication technique.

2 To know the types of questions asked by interviewers and the advantages and disadvantages of each.

3 To understand the structure of interviews.

4 To learn how to conduct effective employment, performance appraisal, and correction interviews.

5 To understand other types of interviews conducted in the business environment.

6 To know the differences among interviewing styles.

agers evaluate the performance of their workers in regularly scheduled appraisal interviews. Disciplinary interviews are conducted with workers who are involved in job-related problems. Through an exit interview program a company seeks to learn the reasons why employees leave the company. New employees are often oriented to their duties through an interview. Through the interview management acquires and transmits much of the information necessary for efficient operations.

Business people no longer believe that anyone who can carry on a conversation can conduct an interview. To understand the need for trained interviewers, they need only look within their organizations. A large number of employment interviews have resulted in the selection of unsuitable individuals. Counseling interviews often do not resolve problems and disciplinary interviews may not result in changed behaviors.

An interview is a purposeful exchange of information for a predetermined purpose in a structured situation.

Some characteristics of an interview clearly differentiate it from a conversation. An interview is purposeful, whereas a conversation may not be. Interviewers must draw out the desired information while motivating the interviewee to cooperate. Because the interview has a predetermined purpose, it is more formal than a conversation. Interviews are clearly structured. They are comprised of an opening, a body, and a closing, and the participants have specific roles. In contrast, many conversations appear formless. Conversations may involve an exchange of information, but the exchange is a universal characteristic of the interview.

TYPES OF QUESTIONS USED BY INTERVIEWERS

Generations of schoolchildren have been taught that the verb is the motor of the sentence. Without a good verb, a sentence will wander rather than move purposefully. An interview also has a motor—the question. Without appropriate questions an interviewer accomplishes little. Unless they are able to recognize and use the variety of questions available, they will not utilize the full potential of the interview.

Open and Closed Questions

Open questions allow the interviewee more freedom to respond.

Questions fall into two general categories–open and closed. **Open questions** allow the interviewee much freedom to respond. An open question is broad in scope and usually requires more than a few words in response. When you ask an open question, you are often merely specifying the topic to be covered. The interviewee may decide on the quantity and the type of information to provide.

Open Questions

Open questions are not all alike. They may differ in their degree of openness. The following questions are very open:

- Tell me about yourself.
- What are you seeking in a career?
- How do you feel about the present candidates?

Other questions are less broad. Although still open, they restrict the interviewee's response somewhat:

- What do you like about your present job?
- Tell me how you feel the problem developed.
- Why did you apply for this job?

Open Questions	
Advantages	*Disadvantages*
Provide interviewer greater opportunity to observe	Take more time
Are considered nonthreatening because they are usually easy to answer	Are often difficult to record or the information is difficult to quantify
Suggest interest by the interviewer	Make controlling the interview more difficult

Closed Questions

Closed questions are somewhat restrictive in nature and generally call for a brief and limited response. By using closed questions you limit the answer options available to the interviewee. The following questions are moderately closed as they call for only a brief bit of information:

Closed questions are more restrictive than open questions.

- Who is Peter Drucker?
- What is your main duty on your present job?
- For what reason do you wish to leave?

Questions may be very closed in that the interviewer has few answer options. These are some very closed questions:

- Rank the following courses in terms of their value to you: business mathematics, English composition, American history.
- How would you rate the present governor in terms of his concern for the unemployed: very concerned, neutral, or unconcerned?
- Do you drink alcoholic beverages?

Closed Questions	
Advantages	*Disadvantages*
Require less training of interviewers	Provide too little information
Take less time	Sometimes inhibit communication
Make it easier for the interviewer to exert control	Provide little opportunity for the interviewee to offer additional information
Make tabulation of the answers easier	

Neutral and Leading Questions

Neutral questions are completely unbiased.

When you ask a neutral question, you make no attempt to direct the interviewee's response. Because neutral questions do not exert any pressure, they may elicit more accurate responses. **Neutral questions** are phrased so that possible responses are not indicated, and alternatives are presented in a balanced fashion. These are typical:

▪ How would you feel about work that requires a considerable amount of traveling?
▪ Why are you leaving the company?
▪ Who do you think is responsible for the problem?
▪ Which one of the following sports do you enjoy participating in most — baseball, football, basketball, tennis, or soccer?

Through leading questions an interviewer can guide the interviewee in a certain direction.

On the other hand, **leading questions** enable the interviewer to obtain accurate information quickly by guiding the interviewee in a certain direction. They are especially useful when trying to verify factual information. Leading questions are sometimes regarded negatively because, when used carelessly, they may result in biased responses. These are some leading questions:

▪ You have a driver's license, don't you?
▪ You are at least 16 years of age?
▪ You have a telephone, don't you?
▪ Do you believe, as most students do, that you are overworked?

Loaded Questions

Loaded questions are strongly directional.

A **loaded question** is even stronger in direction than a leading question, which may be somewhat subtle. A loaded question tends to be hard-hitting. Some interviewers use loaded questions to create stress by using language likely to draw an emotional response or by inquiring into topics about which the interviewee feels strongly. No need exists in most interviews for loaded questions. They should be left to skilled interviewers for the exploration of emotional issues. These are examples of loaded questions:

▪ What do you think of the government's foolish waste of the tax dollar?
▪ Do you mean to tell me that you have no work experience? (asked of a new college graduate who has been rejected by other interviewers for lacking experience)
▪ How do you like the company's ridiculous policy about vacations?

Mirror Questions

A mirror question can get an interviewee to elaborate.

A **mirror question** reflects an interviewee's previous answer with the intent of drawing out additional information. Through the use of mirror questions more information can be obtained without biasing the interviewee's responses. When you believe a response is incomplete, you may draw the interviewee out more by simply restating that response. This is called mirroring a response. When you do it, you are trying to get the interviewee to elaborate on a particular topic. Mirror questions are employed in these examples:

Interviewee:	I like my last job a lot. It was interesting and the pay was good. I'd still be there if it weren't for my problems with my supervisor.
Interviewer:	Problems with your supervisor?
Interviewee:	You'll see that I do good work so long as people don't hassle me.
Interviewer:	Hassle you?

Probing Questions

A **probing question** is stimulated by the interviewee's previous response. Some interviewers prepare a schedule, or list of questions, in advance. No probing questions could be included in such a list, for probing questions are unplanned. For example, if a job applicants says, "In my present job I had to learn how to assume responsibility," the interviewer might then ask probing questions such as these:

Probing questions are stimulated by the interviewee's previous response.

▪ Exactly how did you assume responsibility?
▪ How much responsibility did you assume?
▪ Why did you have to learn that?

Through probing questions the interviewer may elicit important information that had not been anticipated.

Pauses

Although it is not actually a question, the **pause** may serve the same purpose. When you want the interviewee to elaborate, you may simply remain silent. The pause is the most neutral approach of all, because it does not structure the answer or even suggest a topic for discussion. At some point your pause may turn into an embarrassing silence, which the interviewee will find threatening. With experience, however, you will become comfortable and proficient in the use of pauses to stimulate the interviewee.

By pausing, the interviewer can draw out the interviewee.

THE INTERVIEW STRUCTURE

Although they differ in purpose, all interviews are very much alike in structure. Awareness of this structure makes interviewing more productive and more pleasant. The interview process is continuous, with no apparent separation between phases. An interview has five distinct phases, however, and your strategy should be different for each one.

Planning

*Planning is vital
to the success of
most interviews.*

Planning is vital to the success of the interview. It should include the following steps:

1. Determine the purpose or purposes of the interview.
2. Identify the type of responses being sought from the interviewee.
3. Learn as much about the interviewee and about the subject in advance as possible.
4. Determine the amount of structure to employ, and on that basis develop whatever questions are necessary.
5. Select an appropriate setting for the interview and communicate this information to the interviewee.

The extent of planning to be done depends on the purpose of the interview. Before a performance appraisal interview some managers spend several hours familiarizing themselves with the interviewee's work records. An employment interviewer should read the completed application form. In contrast, the clerk in a clothing store may have no advance information about a customer — but will be prepared to discuss the merits of the clothing.

Establishing Rapport

*Establishing
rapport should
result in a better
climate.*

For many individuals an interview is an infrequent occurrence and as such is a cause of tension. In order to reduce the tension and make it easier to exchange information, the interviewer should strive to establish rapport with the interviewee. Rapport is simply a harmonious relationship. Greeting the interviewee graciously and extending simply courtesies will help to establish rapport. Many interviewers engage in small talk at the start about topics of mutual interest.

More time for establishing rapport is needed in some types of interviews than others. The success of a counseling interview, for example, depends on the climate established. The relationship between the interviewer and the interviewee is also a factor. People who work together ordinarily have little need to devote attention to establishing rapport.

Even after an interview has started smoothly, the interviewer should remain aware of the importance of rapport. Differences of opinion may surface, or tension may increase for other reasons. In any case, through rapport, a climate conducive to open communication can be developed and maintained.

Stating the Purpose

*The interviewer
should clearly
state the purpose
of the interview.*

Interviewers often assume that they and the interviewee have the same understanding of the purpose of the interview. An employment interviewer, for example, may explain the duties of a level-1 secretary at great length to an applicant for a level-2 job. Such problems could be prevented by establishing the purpose of an interview at the outset.

Even when people work together, the purpose of an interview may not be clear. To illustrate, in her job as a programmer Jan Rowan has had the same boss for two years. A couple of weeks ago he asked her to reserve an hour so he could talk with her. At the end of the hour Jan left without knowing what the purpose of the interview had been. He asked questions about how she liked her job, problems in the organization, the conditions of the lunchroom, and even her vacation plans. As Jan said, "It's nice to have a boss who is interested in you, but it would also be nice to know what he is getting at."

Asking Questions

The nature of the interview will determine the type of questions chosen as well as the strategy the interviewer will employ. If control of the interview is very important, then the interviewer may choose to ask primarily closed or even loaded questions and to employ a directive strategy. This strategy involves a highly structured question-and-answer format and allows the interviewer to control the direction the interview takes. This strategy is most appropriate when the interviewer has a purpose to accomplish (such as correcting an employee about a particular behavior) and does not want the interview to deviate from that purpose.

The purpose of the interview will determine the strategy and the types of questions asked.

On the other hand, if the interview is a device for fact finding, the interviewer would ask more open questions, probes, mirror questions, and neutral questions to employ a nondirective strategy. Counseling interviews, complaint handling, and problem solving are situations in which these types of questions and this strategy are most appropriate. The use of these questions in the nondirective strategy underscores the interview's need for freedom of exchange and the interviewer's desire not to control the direction of the interview.

This phase constitutes the largest part of the interview. The interviewer comes into it having already determined the types of questions to ask and the sequence in which to ask them.

Summarizing

During the questions phase, interviewer and interviewee usually exchange a considerable amount of information. Some of the information may be highly relevant, and some may be less so. Irrelevancies, redundancies, and unanticipated interruptions may blur some of the conclusions, with the result that the interviewer and the interviewee may not perceive the conclusions identically. The interviewer should clarify what he or she considers these conclusions to be. Without such a summary the interview may end with the parties unaware that differences exist.

At the end of an interview the interviewer should summarize the conclusions that were reached.

ALLOCATION OF INTERVIEW TIME

The amount of time appropriate for a particular phase of the interview structure varies with the type of interview. In a 30-minute employment interview, for example, the first two phases—establishing rapport and stating the purpose — are vitally important to the success of the interview. Together, they should consume only 4 to 5 minutes, or about 13 percent of the interview time. In all types of interviews the third phase — asking questions — should take the majority of the time available. In the employment interview applicants should have some time to ask questions of interviewers in order to determine if the organization is the one best suited to meet their needs. This step of the employment interview should take approximately 24 minutes, or 80 percent of a 30-minute interview.

Asking questions will consume approximately 80 percent of an employment interview.

Summarizing is a critical last step in the actual interview, but it should consume proportionally little of the employment interview time. In fact, summarizing what has occurred during the interview and any further actions either party will take as a result of the interview should take only about 2 minutes, or 7 percent of a 30-minute interview.[1]

TYPES OF INTERVIEWS

Interviews are often classified as information getting, information giving, or problem solving. However, they can be more clearly identified on the basis of specific purpose. This section will review the types of interviews conducted most frequently in business organizations.

The Employment Interview

The interview is used more than any other method for selecting employees.

The employment interview is an important tool in the selection process of most organizations and is, in fact, the basis of most selection decisions. Yet top management often fails to realize the importance of the interviewer's job. The way applicants feel about a company is influenced by their impression of the company's representative. As far as most applicants are concerned, the interviewer is the company.

As an example, Wanda Metcalf had met with 20 employment interviewers by the time she graduated from college. Most of them represented large national organizations. Some were well-organized and businesslike: others were not. A recruiter for a paper company said little beyond "Tell me all about yourself." A chemical company recruiter must have asked 100 questions, all of them of the yes or no variety. Several interviewers did not seem to know anything about the job they were trying to fill. Although none was actually unfriendly, a few interviewers did not seem to be at all interested in Wanda. She wondered why they had bothered with the interviews.

Employment Interview Goals

As an interviewer your main goal should be to determine an applicant's suitability for the job. You should also tell interviewees enough about the job so that they will clearly understand its scope and duties. Usually the

[1]John D. Drake, *Interviewing for Managers* (New York: American Management Association, 1972), 146–157.

applicant's knowledge of the job is slight, probably based on a newspaper ad or a brief job description posted on a bulletin board. Therefore you must educate the applicant about what the job actually entails. The more thorough you are in performing this function, the less likely it is that new employees will quickly grow disillusioned with their jobs.

You should also be aware of the importance of good public relations. Seek to create and maintain goodwill for the company. Often numerous applicants are interviewed before anyone is hired. You have the opportunity to influence how the applicant, whether successful or not, will view the company and its products or services in the future.

As an employment interviewer you should have three goals: (1) principally, to determine a person's suitability for employment; (2) to present an accurate description of the job to the applicant; and (3) to create and maintain goodwill for the company.

Topics usually covered in an employment interview are:

▪ Work experience, emphasizing jobs recently held
▪ Educational background, including both formal and informal training
▪ Outside interests, especially those that might affect the individual's job performance
▪ Physical characteristics, if such factors are important for the job

In order to comply with the guidelines of the Equal Employment Opportunity Commission you should ask questions that are directly related to the job being sought and ask the same main questions of all the applicants.

Throughout the interview you should encourage the applicant to ask questions, and you should respond to the questions with as much detail as necessary. In closing the interview you should briefly summarize the main points covered as well as clearly indicate to the applicant what will follow. At the end of the interview the applicant should know exactly what to expect. If the applicant will be expected to take further tests, you should explain that. If some organizational policy dictates the next step in the selection process, you should make the applicant aware of that. It is an interviewer's responsibility to remove as much of the applicant's uncertainty as possible.

In closing the employment interview the interviewer should tell the interviewee what to expect next.

After the Employment Interview

Interviewers often meet many applicants in a single day and should therefore record the findings from each interview as soon as possible after the interview. Many companies provide forms on which interviewers rate applicants. If forms are not available, you should develop one of your own so that you are sure to note your reactions immediately following the interview.

The Performance Appraisal Interview

In many organizations **performance appraisal interviews** are conducted on a regular basis, often annually or semiannually. The interview is conducted by a worker's immediate superior. It is intended to provide the worker

Performance appraisal interviews are usually conducted by a worker's immediate superior.

✔ CHECKLIST for an Employment Interview

___⌐ Learn the applicant's background by reading the completed application form and the applicant's resume (if it's available).

___⌐ Know enough about the job so that its most important requirements are clear to you.

___⌐ Schedule the interview so that sufficient time is available and so that there will be no interruptions.

___⌐ Scan the topics to be covered early in the interview, and proceed through each topic in an organized manner.

___⌐ Determine that the interviewee is aware of the most important aspects of the job.

___⌐ Relate your questions to the job the interviewee is applying for, and ask the same questions of each applicant.

___⌐ Summarize what has been accomplished at the close of the interview and indicate specifically what the interviewee can expect next.

with feedback concerning how the company thinks the worker is performing.

The performance appraisal interview is strongly evaluative in nature and is sometimes difficult to conduct. Adding to the sensitivity of the situation is the effect that the appraisal could have on the subordinate's pay. The specific goal of each performance appraisal interview depends on how the interviewee has been performing on the job.

To illustrate, Werner Nelson is required to conduct 10 performance appraisal interviews a year. Evaluating 10 subordinates is a difficult and a time-consuming process. No two workers are exactly alike, and the goals of each interview differ according to the nature of the individual worker.

As Werner sees it, this year he conducted three different types of appraisals. In interviewing five of the subordinates he believed his main task was to recognize their good work and to express the company's appreciation. At the same time he attempted to point out ways they could improve. He was trying to develop two other subordinates for higher level jobs, and he used the appraisal interviews with them mainly for that purpose. The other three subordinates were still on probation and had been performing poorly. Werner warned each one of them that some improvement was necessary. These appraisals consisted of discussing specific ways each interviewee could improve.

Werner said of the appraisal interviews, "My people seem to think that I like evaluating them, but they're dead wrong. I don't like it any better than they do. No one likes to play God, but it's a method of developing people, of helping them become better at their jobs."

Before the Performance Appraisal Interview

You must decide what the specific purposes of a performance appraisal will be on the basis of what the interviewee's performance has been.

After determining the purposes, you decide the extent to which the interviewee should participate in the preliminaries. In some organizations employees are given copies of the evaluation forms in advance and are requested to evaluate themselves. They bring their completed forms to the interview so there can be discussion of how the supervisor's rating differs from their own and the possible reasons for the differences. At the very lest, workers are told well in advance of the pending appraisals so they can organize their thoughts.

During the Performance Appraisal Interview

The evaluation form should certainly not be the sole focus of the performance appraisal interview. Emphasis should be on involving the subordinate in two-way communication rather than telling the subordinate what is to be done. If the discussion of problems is to be meaningful, the subordinate must first acknowledge that problems exist. In setting goals for the future there must be agreement between the superior and the subordinate. The main strength of the performance appraisal process lies in human interaction.

Goal setting is an important aspect of the performance appraisal interview.

In closing the performance appraisal interview you should summarize the main points covered. By now there should be agreement on (1) the areas in which the subordinate is performing well; (2) the areas in which the subordinate needs improvement; and (3) what the subordinate must do to attain that improvement. If disagreement exists between the parties after the summary, the interview should not end until the points of disagreement are resolved.

After the Performance Appraisal Interview

You must follow up the interview in whatever way has been agreed upon. In some organizations the subordinate is given a copy of the final evaluation form. If additional paperwork is to be completed, you should do it immediately. If the subordinate complained during the interview about the standards used for measurement, you should look into the matter immediately rather than wait for it to surface again in the next appraisal interviews.

The Correction Interview

Managers who dislike conducting performance appraisal interviews react even more negatively to the **correction interview**. In this type of interview the superior seeks to get the subordinate to substitute some desirable behavior for behavior that is undesirable. Even though negative information might be presented to the interviewee in the performance appraisal interview, at least it is a regularly scheduled event in which all employees routinely participate. The correction interview, however, is not a part of

✔ CHECKLIST for a Performance Appraisal Interview

——❙ Notify subordinates well enough in advance to allow them to prepare for the interview.

——❙ Encourage written or oral self-evaluation by the subordinates.

——❙ Involve the subordinates in every aspect of the discussion.

——❙ Separate salary matters and discussion of promotional possibilities from the appraisal itself.

——❙ Identify and solve, together with the subordinate, any performance problems.

——❙ Set specific, short-term objectives with the subordinate and discuss methods of attaining them.

every employee's schedule. The irregular nature of the correction interview adds to the suspicion and hostility that usually accompany it.

Before the Correction Interview

Correction interviews deal with sensitive matters. For that reason before the interview the supervisor should collect as much information as possible concerning the employee's alleged infraction. The supervisor should also be aware of what corrective measures might be appropriate and should then schedule the interview as soon as possible.

During the Correction Interview

Openness and candor are vital for an effective correction interview.

A correction interview is a serious matter, and both parties know it. Little time need be devoted to establishing rapport, because both parties, especially the subordinate, are anxious to get on with it. The interviewer should state the interview's purpose and describe the violation in as much detail as necessary. The subordinate should be encouraged to describe his or her version of the problem, and both parties should work together to arrive at a solution. In closing the correction interview, the interviewer should summarize what has been accomplished and restate the corrective action to be taken.

To illustrate, Ellen noticed that George's productivity was dropping and began to observe him more closely. George did not manage time well. When he arrived at work at exactly 8:00 a.m., he would devote 15 or 20 minutes to straightening up his desk. Each afternoon he quit work 15 minutes early to prepare to leave. For several weeks Ellen kept records of all her subordinates' time usage habits. She concluded that the misuse of time was causing George's decreased productivity.

Following her research Ellen conducted a correction interview in her office with George. At first George disputed Ellen's findings; however, her carefully kept records soon convinced him that a problem existed and that

✓ *CHECKLIST for a Correction Interview*

___◢ Obtain all of the relevant facts in advance and get verification when possible.

___◢ Conduct the interview out of earshot of others.

___◢ Concentrate on the subordinate's behavior in describing the problem, and avoid any discussion of personality traits.

___◢ Encourage the subordinate to describe the infraction as it occurred.

___◢ Discuss possible corrective actions with the subordinate.

___◢ Summarize what has occurred during the interview and the corrective action that will be taken.

his misuse of time was the cause. Ellen and George agreed that George would become more aware of how he used time. Within three weeks George had regained his previous high level of productivity.

After the Correction Interview

If a description of the violation should be put in the employee's file, this should be done immediately. The manager should ascertain not only that corrective action is being taken, but also its apparent effect. This might be accomplished through any or all of the following: observation, judicious discussion with the associates of the subordinate, or discussion with the subordinate.

The Counseling Interview

Because **counseling interviews** are directed at personal problems, many people believe that only social workers and psychologists conduct them. Although counseling is not always recognized as a manager's duty, most managers do counsel their subordinates. Even if a problem is personal or family related, it will have some effect on the employee's job performance.

To illustrate, when Bob Wiggins became a supervisor he assumed that on-the-job problems would mainly involve equipment, raw materials, and the manufacturing process. He had not expected the high incidence of personal problems among workers. Bob found that personal problems make many workers less effective than they would otherwise be. He estimates that he devotes 10 percent of his work week to counseling employees with problems. "It's time well-spent if it results in a more productive worker," he has said.

Because of the personal nature of the subject, the climate that is established is very important. The interviewer should try to create a situation that will allow a free exchange of information. Such a climate is more likely if the interviewer does the following:

BOXED IN   *AN ETHICAL DILEMMA*

While checking the monthly reports Susan Marsh notices that the employee she counseled earlier, Jim Johnson, is still arriving late for work. Following her supervisor's recommendations on strategies for successfully conducting disciplinary interviews, she prepares to meet with the employee. This time Susan designs open-ended questions with the intention of resolving the problem.

Susan does a much better job than before of conducting the interview, but the information Jim confides puts her in an uncomfortable position. He is working a night job to pay for medical treatment that one of his children desperately needs. Jim is clearly doing his best, but the extra burden is taking a toll on his daily performance. Moreover, the company has a very strict policy about working second jobs. Should the situation become known Jim could be terminated, and Susan would not be viewed in a very favorable light.

Susan empathizes with Jim's problem and wants to do all she can to help reduce his anxiety. He assures her that the situation is temporary, but she feels very uncomfortable with the prospect of knowingly violating company policy to cover for him.

Susan feels boxed in. What would you do?

1. Secures the trust of the interviewee, possibly by assuring that what the interviewee says will remain confidential
2. Creates an atmosphere in which the interviewee will feel free to bring up any subject without fear of offending or alienating the interviewer
3. Maintains a nondirective approach so that the interviewee, rather than the interviewer, determines the subjects to be considered
4. Refrains from evaluating, either verbally or nonverbally, what the interviewee is saying

The Orientation Interview

The purpose of **orientation interviews** is to acquaint new employees with their jobs and with the range of duties involved. A good orientation interview will provide the new employee with a desire to learn and an interest in succeeding. This type of interview is unique because the interviewer's primary role is that of information giver. The interviewer tells the new employee about the job and the company. Organizational policies and procedures may be discussed, as will any other subject that is pertinent to orienting a new worker to the environment. Initial opinions, attitudes, and expectations are formed, at least partly, as a result of orientation interviews.

The orientation interview can profoundly affect the way a new employee views the job and the organization.

The initial expectations formed at the orientation interview can significantly influence the behavior of the new employee. As an example, the most memorable of a dozen or so typist jobs Bob Porter has held was the one with Allied Industries. On his first day, Mae Rosen, his supervisor, told him that she hoped Bob would like his job. "The only really bad thing about this work," she said, "is that it is so repetitive. You do the same thing from nine until five. Until you learn how to think about other things while typing, you'll be pretty bored." Bob soon discovered what Mae had meant. He probably never gave the job a chance because he was led to expect to be bored and he immediately was bored. He quit the job after the longest two weeks he could remember.

The Exit Interview

An **exit interview** is conducted in order to learn why employees who leave voluntarily are doing so. The interview is usually conducted by a personnel specialist, who also may use the opportunity to explain the organization policies on such matters as letters of recommendation and continuation of insurance.

The exit interview can yield information that is useful in improving the organization.

The exit interviewer intends to discover if the employee's reasons for quitting indicate some organizational problem that merits investigation. For example, if several departing employees cite the supervision on the night shift as their reason for leaving, an actual problem exists.

This is a difficult interview to conduct because of several obstacles to frank disclosure of the true reasons for leaving. Interviewees are often suspicious of the company's sudden show of interest. The chance always exists that the employee may want to return to the organization and therefore is unwilling to speak negatively of it.

The exit interviewer must overcome such obstacles by securing the interviewee's trust. The suggestions for creating an appropriate climate for the counseling interview are equally pertinent to the exit interview. A good exit program can be the source of information that leads to significant organizational improvements.

Rarely a week goes by that Charlie Bennings, as assistant personnel manager, does not conduct several exit interviews. Some of these interviews last for an hour or more. "After doing several exit interviews, I have a tendency to stick to the company interview form and rush through it. If I take my time in establishing rapport and keep the interview conversational, I get more helpful information," he has observed.

The Information-Getting Interview

Many of the interviews conducted in organizations do not fall into any of the major categories. Instead, they are conducted to elicit information for a specific purpose. An interviewer from the news media would conduct an information-getting interview with witnesses to an accident. An interviewer for a public opinion poll would conduct an information-getting interview, as would an automobile service manager when talking with the owner of a care that requires service.

Numerous such interviews are routinely conducted, many of them so unstructured that they resemble conversations rather than interviews. Jerry Sloan, for example, is a project coordinator who is currently responsible for keeping three construction projects on schedule. Most of his time is spent talking to each of the three site managers to ensure that deadlines will be met. When bottlenecks seem likely, Jerry talks with the subcontractor responsible and tries to solve the problem. "I'm a coordinator," says Jerry, "and coordination is communication; I'm also an interviewer, because I get most of the information I need through interviews."

Styles of Interviewing

The three styles of interviewing are highly directive, directive, and nondirective.

Styles of interviewing can be thought of in terms of two concepts: freedom and control. The extent to which these two concepts are balanced determines interviewing style. The three distinct styles of interviewing are (1) highly directive, (2) directive, and (3) nondirective. They are not unique and separate; rather they should be thought of as existing on a continuum. The differences among styles are matters of degree and are determined by the extent that the interviewer emphasizes freedom and control. This continuum is illustrated in Figure 19.1.

In the **highly directive interviewing style** the interviewer exerts strong control. Typically little time is devoted to establishing rapport. Most of the questions are closed, and the responses elicited are often recorded. The highly directive style is frequently used for gathering factual information. Many, if not all, of the questions asked by the highly directive interviewer may be prepared in advance.

The **directive interviewing style** is characterized by the interviewer's balance between freedom and control. A more flexible approach allows the interviewer more leeway in terms of approach. Directive interviewers usually prepare their main questions in advance and they rely on a balance of open and closed questions.

In the **nondirective interviewing style**, open questions are used almost exclusively. The nondirective interviewer may list in advance some topics for discussion, but the style is mainly an unstructured one. Considerable control of the interview is given to the interviewee, who does most of the talking. This style is appropriate only for skilled interviewers; otherwise it takes much time and the results are largely unclear.

SUMMARY

Unlike conversations, interviews are characterized by a predetermined purpose and a clear structure; they are conducted to exchange information.

Many different types of questions are available to a skilled interviewer. Questions fall into one of two general categories, open and closed. Open questions allow the interviewee more freedom to respond; closed questions call for narrow, restrictive answers. Neutral questions, which are completely unbiased, are usually desirable. Leading questions are stronger

FIGURE 19.1 ▪ *Interview Styles as Related to Freedom and Control*

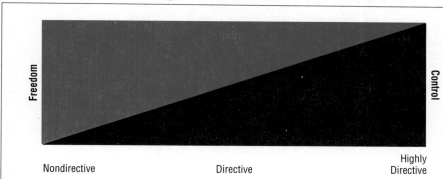

in direction and draw an emotional response. A mirror question reflects a previous answer in order to draw additional information. Interviewers should also use probing questions and pauses to attain their goals.

The way an interviewer handles control and freedom in conducting an interview determines the interviewer's style. There are three distinct styles of interviewing: highly directive, directive, and nondirective.

An interview may be divided into five phases: (1) planning, (2) establishing rapport, (3) stating the purpose, (4) questions and answers, and (5) summarizing.

The major types of interviews are employment, performance appraisal, and correction of subordinates. The main goal of the employment interview is to select the best applicant for the job. Secondary goals are to describe the job accurately to the applicants and to maintain goodwill for the company. Performance appraisal interviews are intended to let a worker know how the worker is performing on the job. A key to successful performance appraisal is the involvement of superior and subordinate. The purpose of a correction interview is to get the interviewee to substitute desirable behavior for undesirable behavior.

Key Terms

▪ **open question**

▪ **closed question**

▪ **neutral question**

▪ **leading question**

▪ **loaded question**

▪ **mirror question**

▪ **probing question**

▪ **pause**

▪ **performance appraisal interview**

▪ **correction interview**

▪ **counseling interview**

▪ **orientation interview**

▪ **exit interview**

▪ **highly directive interviewing style**

▪ **directive interviewing style**

▪ **nondirective interviewing style**

Review Questions

1. What is an interview?

2. How does an interview differ from a conversation?

3. How do open questions differ from closed questions?

4. How do leading questions differ from loaded questions?

5. What are the five phases of the interview structure?

6. What must you do when planning an interview?

7. Why does the importance of rapport vary with the purpose of the interview?

8. What are the four main topics usually covered in an employment interview?

9. In what types of interview would the time allocation differ from that of the employment interview? Give reasons for your answer.

10. By the end of the performance appraisal interview there should be agreement between interviewer and interviewee regarding three main points. What are these three points?

11. What are the three main styles of interviewing? Describe each style.

Exercises

1. Interview someone who has a job in which you are interested. In the interview emphasize such aspects of the job as qualifications necessary to do the job, opportunity for growth and advancement, and likely starting salary and future earning potential. Describe your findings in a letter report for the director of the placement office at your school.

2. Conduct two interviews, one with a person who works primarily with his or her hands and another with someone who mainly uses his or her mind. Determine what they like and dislike about their respective jobs. Prepare a report in which you compare and contrast your two interviewees.

3. Conduct an interview with a person in business concerning that person's letter-writing practices. Find out the kind of writing that your interviewee does most. What is the purpose of it? What are the most important principles in doing that kind of writing? Prepare a brief informational report for your professor. Prepare an oral report to present before your business communication class.

4. Interview someone who graduated within the past three years. Find out what your interviewee considered the strengths and shortcomings of his or her college program. Find out any changes that your interviewee would suggest. Prepare a short informational report for your professor.

5. Your business communication professor has a policy of conducting performance evaluation interviews with each student midway through the term. Prepare a form that would ensure that the same topics are covered with every student.

6. Form a pair with another student. Participate in two interviews, once as interviewer and once as interviewee. Each interview should last five minutes. Each interviewer should try to learn as much as possible about the other person's background and interests. The first interviewer should ask only closed

questions; the second interviewer should ask only open questions. Write a one-page report on the interview you conducted and the effect of asking only one type of question.

7. Interview someone who conducts employment interviews. Try to learn the interviewing techniques that your interviewee uses. Compare what your interviewee says to what is presented in this chapter. Write a one-page report.

8. Visit a factory or office in your community and learn the performance appraisal techniques used. Interview someone who conducts performance appraisal interviews and write a report on the approach used.

9. Keep a diary for one day of all your contacts with others. How many of these were interviews? How many were conversations? Write a report explaining what made you label some interviews and others conversations.

10. Select a national figure and make a list of 20 questions you would like to ask this person.

11. Have another student role play the part of the interviewee in Exercise 10. Ask that person your 20 questions. After each response, ask two probing follow-up questions.

12. Select a topic about which people are concerned. Write two lists of closed questions—one of 10 neutral questions; the other, 10 leading questions. Ask five persons your 10 neutral questions and record their answers. Ask five other persons your 10 leading questions and record their answers. Write a one-page report in which you compare the responses to the neutral questions with the responses to the leading questions.

13. Interview someone in a personnel office who conducts exit interviews. Find out the purpose of the exit interviews and the kinds of information obtained from them. Prepare a report on this topic.

A Hair-Raising Situation | *CASE*

Amanda Copeland, Southwestern Oklahoma State University
Kathy B. White, University of North Carolina at Greensboro

Jean entered a nationally franchised hair-care center in a town of approximately 30,000 population and asked for the owner.

Marie, who was at the desk, noted the young woman's self-confident and poised manner. "I'm the owner," she said, "What can I do for you?"

Jean explained that she was new in town and was looking for a job. She offered proof of her ability and previous employment by producing check stubs from a hair-care center of the same franchise in a large city. Substantial earnings, as shown on the stubs, indicated that Jean was a good hairdresser. As the conversation continued, Marie became more and more favorably impressed with Jean's personality and apparent skill.

Although impressed, Marie decided to defer any positive commitment. She told Jean that she had no immediate opening, but that things looked promising and that she would let her know in a week's time whether business would let her afford another hairdresser.

The next morning Jean returned to the shop and asked for Marie. Sue, the shop manager, came forward and told Jean that Marie would not be in that day and asked if she might help.

Jean drew some papers out of her purse and asked Sue to complete them for her so that she could return them immediately. The papers were from a local apartment complex, asking for confirmation on Jean's employment date and salary.

Sue told Jean that she could not complete the papers, because she knew nothing of the hiring. Jean insisted that she had to have the papers, that she had talked with Marie the day before, and that she was going to work there. She was so insistent that Sue felt inept; she did not know what to do about the papers or how to handle the situation. Finally she told Jean that she really was sorry but that she could do nothing except take the papers and ask Marie to take care of them when she returned to the shop the following day. Plainly perplexed and exasperated, Jean left and left the papers for Marie.

The following day, Sue gave Marie the papers and told her about the incident. Marie was dumbfounded. She could not imagine what had gone wrong or why Jean would think that a job offer had actually been made.

Case Questions

1. What do you think went wrong?
2. Who failed to communicate what properly or adequately and to whom?
3. What could be done to ensure that no similar incident occurs again?

PART FOUR

STRATEGIES FOR TODAY'S BUSINESS CLIMATE

The Electronic Office

The owner of a travel agency in Smyrna, Georgia, used to spend a lot of time on the telephone answering routine questions and playing telephone tag. "I used to feel like a machine, giving out the same information over and over again," she recalls. She now enthusiastically endorses the voice mail system that has taken over some of her work. It "handles information requests, takes messages for me, and never takes a day off."

She has programmed the system to answer her customers' most frequent questions. For example, a vacation shopper can browse through the agency's most popular packages just by listening to directions and pressing the correct buttons on a touch-tone phone. Regular customers are now surprised when the owner picks up the phone herself. Many of them prefer to "talk" with the unhurried voice mail system.

The agency also has dial-up mail boxes assigned to frequent customers so they can get quick, confidential answers to questions about reservations and travel arrangements, even if the office is closed or staff cannot answer the phone when the customer calls for information.[1]

Learning Objectives

1 To recognize the importance of the electronic office.

2 To understand the components of the electronic office and how each contributes to effective and efficient communication.

3 To identify the advantages and disadvantages of different methods of communication.

4 To become familiar with the terminology used in the office.

The modern office, regardless of the size of the organization, is fast being equipped with complex electronic machinery. The luxuries of the past decade—word processors, personal

---

[1]Claude Whitmyer and Daniel Ben-Horin, "Getting the Tools to Make the Office Hum," *Working Woman,* January 1989, 54–56.

FIGURE 20.1 ▪ *Traditional Method of Originating and Sending a Written Message*

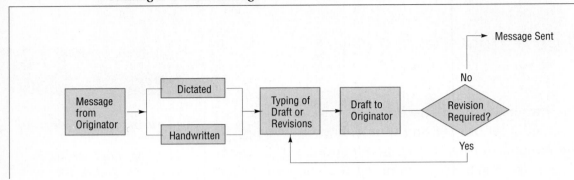

computers, facsimile machines, multipurpose phone systems, and color copiers—are relatively commonplace now. Technology increases the efficiency of communication. The ultimate effectiveness of communication remains a human responsibility, however, and the challenge of the 1990s is one of integrating human skills and electronic technology.

THE EVOLUTION FROM TRADITION TO TECHNOLOGY

The paperwork explosion, ever-increasing costs, and the declining availability of skilled employees have combined to exert heavy pressure for higher productivity rates in the office. The office has been called the most labor-intensive and least cost-effective domain.[2] The percentage of information workers versus the combined total in agriculture, services, and industrial classifications in the United States has grown steadily since the turn of the century. Information workers have been the largest group since 1955 and their numbers are still rising.

Electronic equipment is becoming easier to use and less expensive.

Business must use electronic technology to remain competitive. Fortunately, this technology is becoming easier to use and less expensive to purchase.

The Traditional Office

In the traditional office, one manager employed one secretary who performed a variety of duties. They included answering the phone, greeting visitors, taking dictation, typing, running errands, filing, arranging meetings, and keeping records. Desktops were cluttered with file folders, loose papers, calendars, and telephone message reminders. The office supply cabinet held a large quantity of typewriter erasers, corrections paper, white correction fluid, carbon paper, file folders, and labels, along with several different types of office paper.

---

[2]"Stepping into Tomorrow's Office," *The Office,* November 1981, 119.

FIGURE 20.2 ▪ *Generations of IBM Typewriters*

Source: Courtesy of International Business Machines Corporation.

At times, work piled up. As the secretary typed a report, the manager often found information to add or change. The revise-and-retype cycle might go on through many revisions. In any case, the secretary had to totally retype the text, use correction fluid on the typed copy, or cut-and-paste the text for each revision. In most cases, at least the final copy was retyped for quality. (See Figure 20.1.)

The old term cut-and-paste is used when editing a document stored in word processing equipment.

In the mid-1960s storage was added to office typing systems. IBM developed the MT/ST (Magnetic Tape Selectric Typewriter), a very specialized, and expensive, typewriter-based system. The characters keyed in were stored on a cassette tape and later on a magnetic card. (See Figure 20.2.) Meanwhile companies such as Lanier were developing stand-alone word processing systems designed especially to capture and store words, revise them, and print them. These systems were specialized **computers** that could do only one task, word processing.

New Divisions of Duties

The evolution to word processing has had interesting effects on the nature of office duties—for example, the development of typing pools, in which people with excellent typing skills utilized those skills eight hours a day. This was primarily an efficiency move, as experts believed that the office, like the factory, could benefit from separations of duties based on skills. Before long the emotional effect of such separation became apparent. Changing a secretary's job to two jobs—office assistant and clerical typist—was received enthusiastically by some people and less enthusiastically by others. With time, and with the decline in equipment price, it became obvious that the word processor could support both tasks, making each more interesting.

FIGURE 20.3   ■   *NBI OASys 4000S Stand-Alone Word Processing System*

Source: Courtesy of NBI, Inc.

Many managers now operate computer systems rather than use support staff.

Every day computer companies introduce new hardware and software with ever-increasing capabilities. For example, the movement away from special computer languages means the new electronic tools are easier to operate. Many managers now operate their systems directly rather than use support staff. In the electronic office, all employees are responsible for and take part in improving office productivity.

With the introduction of so-called **laptop computers**, which weigh about 9 to 15 pounds, more managers began carrying computers to use on business trips. As an example, Terry Hoffman, who is president of Universal Title Agency in Atlanta, carries a laptop computer. His firm closes real estate loans for mortgage companies. Often customers want last-minute changes and, as he has explained, "If the customer doesn't like the terms, I can print out a new contract right there." When he returns to the office, he transfers the data from his laptop computer back to his microcomputer.[3]

Even smaller portable computers, called notebook computers, weigh only about 6 pounds. They fit easily into a briefcase and run on the same IBM-compatible software as desktop computers.

[3]Jon Pepper, "Office Machines: More, Better, Cheaper," *Nation's Business,* February 1989, 30–34.

FIGURE 20.4 ▪ *Microcomputer System*

The system unit contains the microprocessor, primary memory, and secondary storage devices—two floppy disk drives and a hard disk drive.

WORD PROCESSING

The word processor has evolved from a stand-alone system, such as the one shown in Figure 20.3, to a software package on a **microcomputer**.

The microcomputer system has a keyboard, a **video display terminal** (monitor), disks for storage, a printer, and a microprocessor to serve as a "brain," as shown in Figure 20.4. System software, such as DOS, drives the total system, and word processing software provides the word processing capabilities.

The microcomputer can be used for other functions, such as spreadsheets and graphics, as well as for a variety of word processing software. See the color insert following page 518 for examples of these microcomputer systems.

Input

In both the electronic and the traditional office, input is the beginning step in the creation of a business communication. The most often used method of input is longhand. The writer drafts the communication in longhand and gives it to the word processing specialist to keyboard. A more efficient method of input is machine dictation. A recent development is that some writers prefer to do their own keyboarding.

Machine Dictation

Dictating usually means speaking directly into a recording device, although dictators can often use the telephone to connect to an automated

✔️ *CHECKLIST for Machine Dictation*

___▎ Plan to dictate rush items first.

___▎ Gather information pertaining to the correspondence.

___▎ Jot down an outline for each message for which you think it will be helpful.

___▎ Begin by identifying yourself, your title, your department, and your phone number.

___▎ Indicate the type of document—letter, memo, report, and so on.

___▎ Be sure to specify whether the document is to be a rough draft or in final form.

___▎ Indicate when the document is required and how many copies are needed.

___▎ Specify special stationery or paper if necessary.

___▎ Give an estimation of the length of the document whether it is a short one-page letter or a long report.

dictating machine system. By pressing codes on the phone they can play back the recording for review and editing. (See Figures 20.5 and 20.6.)

Dictation skill increases with practice.

Dictation requires skill, because no immediate copy exists to review for continuity. The dictator can quickly record thoughts but will most likely revise the first draft extensively. Skill at dictation increases with practice.

Direct Keyboarding

Writers who compose first drafts at the computer cite a gain in independence and control. Lee Cummings, executive vice president of a medium-sized firm on the American Stock Exchange, has explained: "With my PC and soon my laser printer, I can, myself, produce a document with higher quality in terms of content, formatting and appearance, in less time than I could with a secretary. . . . For the manager who isn't afraid of it, the computer means greater and greater control over his or her life. It means the security of less and less dependence on other people."[4]

Optical Character Recognition

Another type of input is **optical character recognition (OCR)**. OCR equipment when used in combination with word processing equipment can be a rapid means of input. It reads pages of previously typed documents, converts them to electronic information, and places that information on

[4]Barbara Garson, *The Electronic Sweatshop* (New York: Simon and Schuster, 1988), 201–202.

FIGURE 20.5 ▪ *Sony BM-550 Portable Dictation Unit*

Source: Courtesy of Sony Corporation of America.

a magnetic medium, usually a disk. The disk can then be placed in a word processing machine; the document is called onto the screen and is edited.

For example, you receive a report from another branch of your company. You are asked to update the report, and you write the changes directly on the report. The report is scanned by the OCR equipment, and the information is transferred to a disk. The word processing specialist inserts the disk in the word processing machine, views the document on the screen, incorporates the changes you have indicated, and prints a revised copy of the report.

The advantages to using OCR are these: (1) Previously typed documents do not have to be rekeyed. (2) Any typewriter could be used to keyboard information, the document is scanned, and then word processing equipment is used for subsequent editing. (3) Word processing equipment is better utilized because it is used solely for editing purposes. (4) OCR equipment can read 350,000 to 450,000 characters an hour while operators key 10,000 to 15,000 characters hourly.

Use of the OCR reduces keyboarding time.

Boilerplate and Form Communications

Not all of the advances in office efficiency occur with the purchase of expensive and sophisticated equipment. Often, we can dramatically affect office productivity simply by changing how we do our jobs.

A former president of Bell & Howell related an incident that demonstrates this point. When he first went to work as an entry level office employee, his job was to dictate letters to customers who had complained about products. At the end of the first day, he had dictated a large number of individual letters. As he was carrying the glass dictation records to the typing pool, he tripped and broke the entire day's efforts. As he had been dictating the letters, he recognized that strong similarities existed among the complaint situations. The accident caused him to find a better, and

Productivity can sometimes be improved at little expense.

FIGURE 20.6   ▪   *Dictaphone Desktop Dictation Unit*
Featuring Electronic Cuing

Source: Courtesy of Dictaphone Corporation, Rye, New York.

safer, way to fulfill his duties. He cataloged the 137 letters and gave each a number. Then, when he had to respond to a complaint, he simply wrote the number of the response on the bottom of the letter and gave it to the clerk to type. He had created a supply of letters, each of which was well worded and could be reused, saving time and mental energy. His colleagues quickly determined that he had thought his way out of employment, which of course he had, right to the top of the corporation.

His story illustrates reusable communications are a way to improve content and save time. With word processing equipment, you can create individual paragraphs, possibly with missing words, and then instruct the word processing specialist to use the paragraphs in the order specified and insert the proper special words. Standard paragraphs of text that are reusable are called **boilerplate**. They are stored on the word processor and called into memory in the order used. With such a system, a letter that appears to be unique can be created in a short time.

Taking this a step further, form communications are composed with blank spaces onto which the person sending them handwrites the unique words. For form letters these include the addressee's name, the date, and

BOXED IN   *AN ETHICAL DILEMMA*

Susan has worked in the corporate office for seven months and is comfortable with the equipment and systems. She has her own microcomputer that is everything she could hope for. The computer contains enough storage to hold all of her work, a color monitor, and a variety of software packages. She has WordStar word processing, Lotus 1-2-3 spreadsheet, the latest version of MS-DOS, and a fancy printer. Susan has become so knowledgeable about the software that she is asked questions by coworkers almost every day.

Jim and Susan are at lunch discussing the computer Jim is thinking about ordering. He has a catalog of computer equipment and software and is trying to put together a system with software and stay within his budget of $2,500. "It's amazing what they offer," Jim tells Susan, pointing to a system like hers for $2,500. "I wish I could afford that, but there would be no money left over for software. If I get the software, I will have to drop the color monitor and either the hard disk or printer."

All of a sudden Jim's face lights up. "Susan, if I get the $2,500 system, is it all right for me to copy your software? That would save me a lot of money and you would still have the original software. In fact, no one is hurt."

Susan thinks about Jim's question. If she says yes, she will be agreeing to let Jim violate the software copyright and place both their jobs in jeopardy. She has seen other people copy software from their machines for their computers at home and has not really thought about it much. But this is her software on her machine. What if she is caught? In any case, is it right to let Jim make a copy of software that cost several hundreds of dollars, even if no one knows?

Susan feels boxed in. What would you do?

the sender's name. (See Figure 20.7.) Interoffice memos often use this approach to save typing time and costs. (See Figure 20.8.) A less personal approach is to simply place checkmarks beside the appropriate items on a printed list. (See Figure 20.9.)

Text Editing

Some text editing features commonly available on software include the following:

- *Delete/insert* allows characters, words, sentences, paragraphs, and so forth to be deleted or inserted anywhere in the text.
- *Copy/move* allows any amount of information to be copied or moved anywhere within the document or to any other document that is on the system. For instance, a paragraph that appears in one document but needs to be repeated in another document can easily be moved or copied.

FIGURE 20.7 ▪ *Fill-in-the-Blank Letter Form*

```
                              A B C  COMPANY
                              Main Street Office
                              Anywhere, State




Date:  _____

Dear Valued Customer:

     This office recently received correspondence from you
concerning your difficulty with our product:

_____.

     We strive to sell products that work and are easy to use.
I have sent your letter to our office at _____
for action.  You should be hearing from the manager there within
____ days.

     Please excuse this form of communication; we have found it
to be the fastest way to support our valued customers and hold
costs to a minimum, allowing us to keep our prices the lowest in
the industry.

     Please don't hesitate to write again if our solution is not
adequate and timely.

Sincerely,




Manager, Customer Relations
```

▪ *Pagination/repagination* allows the selection of the number of lines to appear on each page. The operator keys in the desired number, and the system counts the lines and indicates the page breaks. When a document has been edited and text has been added or deleted, new page breaks can be automatically inserted and the revised document printed rapidly.

▪ *Format change* allows the line length and tabs to be reset at any time. The system automatically adjusts all lines to the requested format.

FIGURE 20.8　▮ *Interoffice Memo Form*

INTEROFFICE MEMO
A B C COMPANY

TO: _____

FROM: _____

DATE: _____

SUBJECT: _____

REFERENCE: _____

ACTION REQUIRED: _____
_____
_____
_____
_____
_____
_____
_____
_____

Vertical spacing can also be changed; single, double, triple, one-and-a-half, and quarter spacing are among the options.

▮ *Justified right margin* directs the system to produce a document with a straight right-hand margin. This feature is especially useful in newsletters and manuals.

▮ *Document assembly* allows previously keyed paragraphs to be assembled in any order to create a new document. Boilerplates would be used with this function.

▮ *Merge* allows the combining of previously keyed text, such as form letters and lists of names, to create repetitive letters that appear to be originals. Form letters containing variables that change with each name are also produced by use of the merge function.

▮ *Columnar interchange* allows columns to be switched around. For example, when a statistical report needs to be updated, one column

FIGURE 20.9 ■ *Select-from-the-Menu Form*

The Quality Restaurant

Sandwiches

___ Chicken Salad ($1.89)   ___ BLT ($1.69)
___ Tuna Salad ($1.89)   ___ Egg Salad ($1.69)
___ Ham ($1.89)   ___ Pimento Cheese ($1.69)
___ Turkey ($1.89)   ___ Grilled Chicken ($2.59)

___ Bacon, ___ Swiss, or ___ Cheddar on above is 40 cents extra.

Garnishes   (Complimentary)

___ Mayonnaise ___ Mustard ___ Lettuce ___ Tomato

Breads   (Choose 1)

___ Wheat   ___ White   ___ Croissant (75 cents extra)
___ Sourdough   ___ Rye   ___ Pita

could be deleted entirely, the other columns moved left, and new information added in a far right-hand column.

■ *Global search and replace* locates a specified character string wherever the string appears in the document. The characters can then be replaced with another set of characters. For example, if a proposal has been composed for the ABC Company and the same proposal later is made to the XYZ Company, the global search and replace function will find each occurrence of *ABC Company* and replace it with *XYZ Company*. A new customized document is created, but the costly rekeyboarding and proofreading are held to a minimum.

■ *Headers and footers* allow, for instance, section titles to be placed automatically at the top of each page and consecutive page numbers to be placed at the bottom of each page.

■ *Glossary/phrase library storage* allows the storing of frequently used words or phrases. These phrases are coded so that they appear fully spelled out in the document, but the input is accomplished with just two keystrokes. The date, company names, and frequently used words or phrases can be stored in the glossary and called on when needed.

■ *Dictionary* allows spelling to be checked automatically. When a page has been keyed, the dictionary function can be accessed. The keyed words are automatically checked. Incorrect words are highlighted, and the operator can correct errors. This function is not to be used as a replacement for proofreading the document. For example, the dictionary does not know that *their* was used when the correct word was *there*. Neither can it check for word omissions or transpositions.

The dictionary function takes care of a great deal of the proofreading, but it does not check for errors in agreement of nouns and verbs and other grammar or syntax errors.

- *Thesaurus* allows the writer to ask for alternative words. The writer identifies the word that he or she would like to change, and the computer supplies a number of choices. The writer makes a selection, and the new word automatically replaces the previous one.
- *Subscripts and superscripts* allows numbers to be placed slightly above or below lines for use in footnoting or keyboarding formulas, for example, 2^4 CO_2.
- *Footnote tie-in* automatically allows space at the bottom of the page for the footnotes indicated in the text. Some systems keep the footnote number and footnote together automatically. For instance, if the footnote number is transferred to another page, the footnote will be transferred automatically to the bottom of the new page.
- *Table of contents update* automatically updates the table of contents of a document when new sections are added, deleted, or moved. Outline update and index update work in the same manner.
- *Forms* allows a form, such as an invoice, to be created on the system. A *forms mask* is called up on the screen, and the operator fills in the blanks. The mask is used over and over as many times as needed and is stored for future use. Masks for multiple forms may be stored on a central processor and accessed by terminals or personal computers in other locations both to streamline processing and to avoid the cost of preprinted forms.

With such programs as RightWriter and Grammatik IV, you can compute readability as well as check for split infinitives, run-on sentences, and other grammar problems. Figure 20.10 shows typical output from RightWriter.

A thesaurus feature of word processing software enables the writer to ask for alternate words.

Storage

Internal Storage

Text is stored in the computer in the **semiconductor (chip) memory**. This main, or primary, memory is expensive, allows the computer to work at high speeds, but is lost when power is removed from the machine. Thus, to permanently store the text, external, or secondary, storage is required.

External Storage

The least expensive form of secondary storage is magnetic tape, similar to an audiocassette tape. This medium, however, is very slow. The medium of choice for current work is a **hard disk**—a round device resembling a 45 rpm record that records computer data on its magnetic surfaces. Hard disks can store from 10 million to over 100 million characters in a quick-to-retrieve form. For storage of text or other data that is not currently being utilized, and backup (safety) copies of current work, **floppy disks** are better because they are much less expensive and can be easily removed from

FIGURE 20.10 ∎ *Output from RightWriter Text Style Check Program*

```
                        <<** SUMMARY **>>

            OVERALL CRITIQUE FOR:  p:hospital.TXT

            READABILITY INDEX:  11.33
            Readers need an 11th grade level of education to understand.
                    Total Number of Words in Document:  1671
                    Total Number of Words within Sentences:  1579
                    Total Number of Sentences:  86
                    Total Number of Syllables:  2843


            STRENGTH INDEX:  0.15
            The writing can be made more direct by using:
                          - the active voice
                          - shorter sentences
                          - fewer weak phrases
                          - less slang


            DESCRIPTIVE INDEX:  0.56
            The use of adjectives and adverbs is within the normal range.


            JARGON INDEX:  0.27

            SENTENCE STRUCTURE RECOMMENDATIONS:
                        1. Most sentences contain multiple clauses.
                           Try to use more simple sentences.
                        14. Consider using more predicate verbs.

                        <<  WORDS TO REVIEW  >>

            Review the following list for negative words (N), colloquial
            words (C), jargon (J), misspellings (?), misused words (?), or
            words which your reader may not understand (?).
```

the computer for external protective storage. Figure 20.11 illustrates a removable-pack disk system.

The latest entry for high-volume secondary storage is the CD-ROM, meaning **compact disk-read only memory**. CD-ROM plastic disks store very large amounts of data using lasers to read back into the computer. A single disk can hold from 200 million to 800 million characters, depending on the mode and density used. This form is used for **archival data**, that is, data that you want to keep but will not update back to the same disk. When this medium is connected to the microcomptuer for storing data as well as reading it,

Source: Courtesy of Covia.

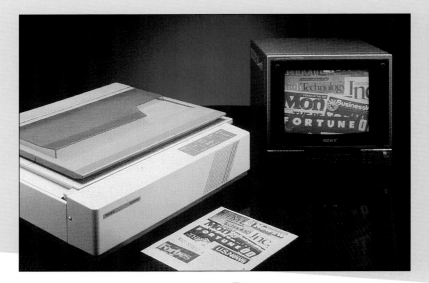

An Image Scanner

Image scanners such as this Howtek color scanner are used to digitize images of photographs, drawings, and documents into computer memory. Some scanners are also equipped with software that enables them to recognize text.
Source: Courtesy of Howtek, Inc.

Fingerprint Recognition

No match, no entry.
Source: Courtesy of Thumbscan, Inc.

1

2

3

4

5

6

A Variety of Display Devices

1

A Color Monitor
Source: Courtesy of International Business Machines Corporation.

2

Monochrome, Flat-Panel Display Terminal
Source: Courtesy of International Business Machines Corporation.

3

Two-Page, Gray-Scale Monitor
Source: Courtesy of Moniterm Corporation.

A Variety of Printers for Microcomputers

4

Thermal-Transfer Printer
Source: Courtesy of Tektronix, Inc.

5

Laser Printer
Source: Courtesy of Hewlett-Packard Company.

6

Impact Dot-Matrix Printer
Source: Courtesy of NEC Technologies, Inc.

How Much is One Million Mice?

63 miles
One million mice end-to-end would stretch 63 country miles (over hill and dale).

104,167 ft.
A stack of one million mice would reach an altitude three and one half times that of Mt. Everest (this is no tall tail).

2739 years
If you used a different mouse every day, it would take 2739 years to use one million mice (nearly three mouse millennia).

When its famous mouse broke the million-unit sales barrier in 1988, Microsoft used presentation graphics to publicize the event.

This graphic uses seductive trivia to create a memorable impression.
Source: Reproduced with permission from Microsoft Corporation.

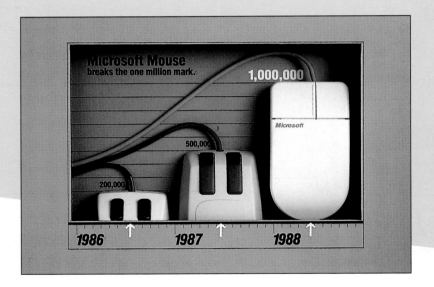

Microsoft Mouse breaks the one million mark.

1,000,000

500,000

200,000

1986 1987 1988

This graphic uses a photograph with a combination bar-chart and pictograph format.
Source: Reproduced with permission from Microsoft Corporation.

FIGURE 20.11 ▪ *Removable-Pack Disk System*

Disks are assembled into disk packs, which are mounted in the disk unit.

Source: Figure 5-3 from *Understanding Computers and Information Processing: Today and Tomorrow,* Third Edition, by Charles S. Parker, p. 132, copyright © 1990 by The Dryden Press, a division of Holt, Rinehart and Winston, Inc., reprinted by permission of the publisher.

it is called a WORM, meaning *w*rite *o*nce, *r*ead *m*any times. As with the CD-ROM, data is written to the disk once and read many times. CD-ROMs cannot be altered once written. New CD storage devices appearing on the market can be altered and they act much like a hard disk, but the price is higher and the data delivery may occur at a slower rate.

Micro-Media Storage

The secondary storage media just discussed have the advantage that the data are computer readable. If the output of the computer is printed and the paper or its image is stored, the computer cannot access or use the data unless it is input back into a machine-readable form. Thus paper reports, although desired by the users, take a lot of storage space and are not longer usable by the computer. Very small images of the paper copy can be stored on **microfilm** (reels) or **microfiche** (sheets). The film and fiche images are not available to the computer for processing, however.

Currently, the preferred form of storage is on magnetic disk. Until recently, microfilm/fiche was the medium for storing checks and credit card receipts. American Express Company now stores the images of credit card receipts on disk and prints them on bills with laser printers. Because the

Paper reports may be reduced to very small images for storage on film reels or sheets.

disks are connected to the computer, the receipts are also available to the service representative on his or her computer terminal.

Printed Output

The best-known relatively inexpensive option for letter-quality printed output is the daisy-wheel printer, which has raised characters that strike a carbon ribbon, much like a typewriter. The rate of output of this type of printer is too slow, however, for most business uses.

The dot matrix printer, when slowed down, produces near-letter-quality printing.

The low-to-medium priced printer of choice for computers is the **dot matrix printer**. It strikes the ribbon with tiny pins in the shape of the character to be printed with the result that characters are made up of tiny dots. Quality ranges from characters that do not have quite enough dots—and are therefore obvious computer output—to near letter quality (NLQ) printing. The printer hits more dots per character when slowed down. Even in NLQ mode it is faster than a typewriter. When cost, speed, and high-quality finished product are all important, a good dot matrix printer is the printer of choice. To maintain quality, however, ribbons must be reinked or replaced.

The laser is the printer of choice when variety, quality, and speed are more important than cost. The **laser printer** uses the same principle as the plain paper copier; that is, light beams make marks for printing. Dots are placed on a film, black carbon toner is added, and the result is heat fused onto paper. Laser printers reproduce at rates of 4 to 13 pages per minute, use a variety of type fonts in many different sizes, and can include graphics on the same page with text.

DESKTOP PUBLISHING

Desktop publishing is extremely high-quality word processing.

The user of desktop publishing can be highly creative and obtain typeset quality at a lower cost and in less time. **Desktop publishing** is extremely high-quality word processing, made possible by the faster general purpose microcomputers and lower cost, high-quality laser printers.

If your only communication is letters and memos, word processing is adequate. If, however, you create brochures, newsletters, advertisements, programs, and the like, and you work within tight budgets and time constraints, desktop publishing is a possibility. This technology allows you to use the power of words, graphics, pictures, and style to create high communication impact. As noted in Aldus Corporation's manual, Page-maker does in minutes what it formerly took hours to do with traditional typesetting, layout, and pasteup methods.[5]

Input of text is either directly into desktop publishing files through the computer keyboard or by importing text from other word processing files. Of special interest is the ability to use any one of a number of character

[5]*Getting Started, Aldus PageMaker* (Seattle, Wash.: Aldus Corporation, 1988).

fonts, by itself or in combination on a page, and to use the fonts of several different sizes. Thus, you can create a paragraph with your word processing software, import it into your desktop publishing file, and create a section title of larger, more ornamental type than the text.

Unlike most word processing packages, desktop publishing allows you to include nontext forms such as graphics and pictures. These images are included in the file by scanning printed copy and storing the light patterns along with the text or by creating graphics in such applications as PC-Paintbrush and importing them into the file.

ELECTRONIC MAIL

Suppose you could take stored text from the word processor and send it electronically without ever printing it on paper. This procedure would eliminate the cost of the paper and envelope as well as the postage, and, most important, would reduce the delay in delivering the message. This is the objective of **electronic mail** (E-mail), the process of capturing text on an electronic device and transmitting it to another electronic device.

Conceptually, electronic mail connects two word processors by means of a telephone line. If electronic mail worked exactly like the telephone— that is, if both sender and receiver had to be connected to transfer a message—the sender would likely miss the receiver most of the time. However, it is designed so that the sender can send messages at any time and the receiver views them at a convenient time. Figure 20.12 illustrates the electronic mailbox system.

The first corporate electronic mail systems were installed in the 1970s. Users soon began to notice a downside: unwanted mail. Walter Ulrich, a partner at Coopers & Lybrand, monitored ways to cope with the problem of overuse while serving as chairman of the privacy and security subcommittee of the Electronic Mail Association. He described a typical case of information overload in a private corporate electronic mail system: "Someone in a branch office hires a new salesman and sends a message to everyone in the company, including the chairman. That clutters everyone's mailbox. It is so simple to address the message to 'everyone' that there is abuse. Without electronic mail that branch manager would never think of making the same announcement, running off 10,000 Xerox copies and mailing it out."[6]

Coopers & Lybrand predicted that the number of messages over public electronic mail systems would reach 2 billion in 1992 and on private, corporate systems, over 10 billion.[7]

---

[6]David Churbuck, "Prepare for E-Mail Attack," *Forbes,* January 23, 1989, 82–87.
[7]Ibid.

FIGURE 20.12   ▪   *Electronic Mailboxes*
Using an electronic mailbox system, an employee can send messages or work to others
without leaving his or her desk.

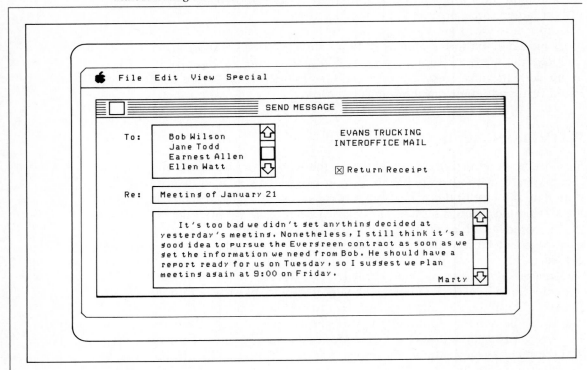

Source: Figure 16-8 from *Understanding Computers and Information Processing:
Today and Tomorrow,* Third Edition, by Charles S. Parker, p. 514, copyright © 1990
by The Dryden Press, a division of Holt, Rinehart and Winston, Inc., reprinted by
permission of the publisher.

FACSIMILE MACHINE

A technology that is not new, but only recently has become widely used
because of cost reductions, is the facsimile machine. **Facsimile** (or fax) is
used to send copies of a document from one place to another electronically. While electronic mail requires that actual characters be input or
stored in the system for transmittal, fax can transmit anything. You can
send copies of pictures, graphics, handwritten notes, or a signed contract.
What is received in E-mail can be treated as a document for further processing; that is, you can add a note to a received E-mail message or even
change the wording and send it to someone else. What you receive with
fax is a picture. Although fax is quite useful for sending nontextual information quickly over a distance, the received document generally cannot
be reprocessed. Fax is like two copy machines connected by means of a
telephone line. (See Figure 12.13.)

FIGURE 20.13 ▪ *Facsimile Machine*

With a facsimile (fax) machine, hard-copy documents can be sent from one location to another—perhaps thousands of miles away—within seconds.

Source: Courtesy Canon U.S.A., Inc.

COPY MACHINE

Found in traditional offices for several decades, the copy machine makes duplicate copies of a page of text, drawings, or pictures. Its purpose is to make copies of paper documents for storage, use, or transmittal to other people for storage, use, or transmittal to still other people. Secretaries of the 1950s remember less than fondly going home with black and blue arms and stained clothing after having used spirit duplicating machines and carbon paper. These were the only ways to make copies at that time, other than retyping the document. Although Xerography was invented and patented in the late 1930s, it was not until the late 1950s and early 1960s that use of Xerox machines became routine. This was the plain paper copier, still in use today. With expiration of the Xerox company's patent, the plain paper copier is now available from dozens of companies and is even used in many homes.

Dozens of companies began producing copiers when Xerox's patent expired.

Toner cartridges are available in several colors for some copier models. This equipment will produce the entire document in one color. Some copiers will even produce full-color copies.

VOICE MAIL

If you have recently called a large corporate office, an airline reservation office, the IRS during April, or a company that takes orders on the phone, you most likely encountered a machine before a human. The phone system that answered either held the call or directed it to the person who would talk with you. In some cases, no person was available and you had the chance to leave a voice message. In this situation, the phone system had a dictation capability available to store a message for the person you were calling. The simplest form of voice mail is the telephone answering machine many of us have in our homes. For a business, the system is somewhat more complex and expensive and provides many more features. Like the phone answering system, **voice mail** has an outgoing message that is repeated to each caller. Both systems record incoming messages and store them. Voice mail systems can also forward the message to one or several other people and can send an original message to a list of receivers.

Voice mail is the most natural form of communication, but the speaker has no chance to revise and resubmit.

Voice mail contains more information than written mail—loudness, inflection, tone, and so on—has the least time delay, is the easiest to create, and requires no intermediary person or paper. As with dictation, it initially requries practice to use competently. In any case, voice mail will increase speed and reduce cost of communication.

ELECTRONIC WORKSTATION

In the traditional office, many objects vied for space on the desk, among them a telephone, calendar, notepad, and calculator. These helped people to remember, analyze, schedule, and communicate. The electronic office has more support items but occupies relatively little space. The **electronic workstation** is an area for a single worker equipped with a microcomputer and telecommunciation lines.

To call a colleague or customer, you would bring up a telephone database—an electronic directory—on the workstation and highlight the individual's name. The system then places the call. While the call is in progress, you could bring up an **electronic notepad** (a stored file) to make a note about the subject, activate the internal calculator or make a spreadsheet to compute mileage for a trip, place the name and address of a new vendor in the database, place your next meeting with your colleague on your electronic calendar, and send an E-mail message to your boss about the meeting.

TELECOMMUNICATIONS

Communication by electrical or electromagnetic means, usually over a distance, is called **telecommunication**. When you talk on the telphone, use the fax machine, or upload a text file from your computer to another, you are using telecommunications. This technology allows large organizations to share resources and communicate as if they had a single location.

The telephone is considered vital and central to organizational functioning. Audio, however, is but one form of communication, and the telephone is but one form of telecommunications. We also want to communicate text, data, graphics, and video. We have fax networks for graphics; direct connect data communications networks for text and data; and cable TV, satellite radio, and microwave radio for video.

It is possible, and routine, to convert all of the communication forms mentioned into a **digital format** (sending the message, even voice conversations, as ones and zeros). AT&T, MCI, and Sprint convert all telephone calls that they carry over distances to digital forms. In fact, they all use optical fiber telecommunication channels and therefore have to convert to digital, because optical fiber carries only digital codes. Computer-stored text and data are already in digital form, and graphic and video can be converted much like audio telephone calls. When we place all of these data forms in a digital mode, we not only can carry them on any digital network, but can intersperse them and the network cannot tell the difference.

The reason we care about telecommunications in general and **analog-to-digital conversion** (changing the continuous wave to a digital wave for transmission) in particular is that we need to send communications to a distant place, in a hurry, at a low cost. As noted with electronic mail, using networks and deleting paper achieves all of these objectives. Because many networks send the data in packets (a group of characters at a time), we can send any non-time-sensitive information anywhere the network goes, worldwide, quickly and cheaply.

If we can, indeed, communicate electronically between remote sites and can send all forms of data—numbers, text, audio, graphic, and video—then we can hold a meeting by using television cameras and monitors instead of attending in person. As discussed in Chapter 17, these electronic meetings are called **teleconferences**. At the same time, increasing numbers of people **telecommute**; that is, they stay at home and work on an office computer. These two activities are having a strong effect on the location and form of the workplace, the manner in which meetings take place, and the way we interact and communicate.

A form of telecommunication used most directly in the electronic office, other than the telephone system, is a **local area network (LAN)**. This is a small telecommunications network for connecting computers that are located close together. (See Figure 20.14.) A LAN uses telephone-like wires, coaxial cables, or optical fiber to connect computers or workstations in a work group, department, area, building, or campus. The people so connected work together and share common interests.

The LAN network has three basic configurations. In the star configuration, individual computers or workstations are all connected to a central switching station or computer. In the ring configuration, they are all connected in a closed loop or circle and information is passed along the loop until it reaches the receiver. In a bus configuration, they are all connected

The forms of telecommunications include fax networks and cable TV.

FIGURE 20.14 ▪ *Local Area Network (LAN)*

The surge in microcomputer usage has made local area networking a particularly attractive solution for sharing resources.

Source: Figure 7-13 from *Understanding Computers and Information Processing: Today and Tomorrow,* Third Edition, by Charles S. Parker, p. 236, copyright © 1990 by The Dryden Press, a division of Holt, Rinehart and Winston, Inc., reprinted by permission of the publisher.

to the main line so that additions can be made at the end of the network without interruption.

The LAN may be further connected to other LANs and to WANs (wide area networks). This allows resource sharing and communications. For example, all members of a LAN can use the applications stored on a single disk (file server) instead of having individual copies, use data from a single up-to-date source, and share a single high-quality laser printer.

SUMMARY

Businesses must use electronic technology to be competitive. Fortunately, this technology is becoming easier to use and less expensive to purchase. The traditional office relied on revise-and-retype cycles to produce documents. This system gave way to use of word processors in the late 1970s. The word processor has evolved from a stand-alone system to a software

✔ *CHECKLIST for Equipping a Small Office*

——◖ Choose a basic copier designed to accept options that you might need as the business grows.

——◖ Consider selecting a brand-name fax machine, which is much more likely than a "no-name" to provide long-term satisfaction and reduce the worries of servicing and dependability.

——◖ Remember that electronic typewriters with some memory and storage options still make a lot of sense as workstations for those whose output generally consists of short letters, memos, proposals under 10 pages, and executive correspondence.

——◖ Add a notebook computer to the basic three—copier, fax machine, and electronic typewriter or microcomputer—if your executives are always on the go.

*Jon Pepper, "The Basic Tools for Today's Office," *Nation's Business,* February 1990, 42–45.

package used on a microcomputer. The steps of word processing are inputting, text editing, storage, and output. Desktop publishing is extremely high-quality word processing, made possible by the faster general-purpose microcomputers and lower cost, high-quality laser printers.

Electronic mail connects two word processors by means of a telephone line. It is a more efficient, cost-effective alternative to communication through letters or telephone calls. The sender can send messages at any time and the receiver can view them at a convenient time. Facsimile machines send documents from one place to another electronically. Copy machines reproduce documents for storage, use, or transmittal. Voice mail systems repeat an outgoing message to each caller and record, store, and forward messages to receivers.

Key Terms

- computer
- laptop computer
- microcomputer
- video display terminal
- optical character recognition (OCR)
- boilerplate
- semiconductor (chip) memory
- hard disk
- floppy disk
- compact disk-read only memory
- archival data
- microfilm
- microfiche
- dot matrix printer

- laser printer
- desktop publishing
- electronic mail
- facsimile (fax) machine
- voice mail
- electronic workstation
- electronic notepad

- telecommunication
- digital format
- analog-to-digital conversion
- teleconference
- telecommute
- local area network (LAN)

Review Questions

1. Name the various kinds of equipment found in the electronic office and the function of each.

2. Compare the equipment of the electronic office and the equipment each replaced.

3. Which equipment in the electronic office do you consider of the greatest importance? Which is the easiest to learn to use? Which is the most difficult to learn to use?

4. If you were opening a new office with three people, what equipment would you purchase first? If the office has 12 people, would you purchase additional equipment?

5. When would electronic mail be of the greatest value?

6. When would facsimile be of questionable value?

7. Of what value are preprinted or form letters?

8. Discuss telecommunications in the office. Why should you understand the engineering principles?

9. Is the electronic office a lot of hype to sell more equipment, or is it real?

10. Would you consider the electronic office a competitive advantage for a business?

Exercises

1. You are starting a new office supplies business with one employee and have a very limited amount of money. You will need to prepare correspondence, invoices, and receipts. What equipment do you need? Where would you find out about this equipment? Call sources for the equipment and document information for three alternatives, giving a final price for each. Be prepared to present this to your class for discussion.

2. You have received in the mail a request for proposal on a large quantity of supplies. Unfortunately, the request arrived late and the bid is due to the customer tomorrow. Explain how you would get the bid to the customer on time.

3. You have opened a business to do typing for students. Determine how you can be sure that the student receives a disk copy of the output as well as a

paper copy that is ready to turn in to the professor. Describe the equipment you will need and find out the price of it.

4. You have just been hired by a company as a documentation text editor. That is, other people in the firm will create the documentation and you will review it for correctness and content. What equipment should the originators of the text have and what equipment should you have? Will you perform your task manually or electronically, and what are the implications of each of these modes?

Miscommunication in an Electronic Office | *CASE*

Carolena L. Smith, San Diego State University

AMS College is a nationwide, home-study computer literacy school headquartered in California. AMS has sales representatives in 50 states. The home-study course enables students to work at home with textbooks, study guides, computers, and software and then mail completed lessons to the college. Students can receive assistance over the telephone by calling a toll-free 800 number.

The AMS school, when it opened, had neither computers nor personnel with experience in using computers. A student from a nearby university was hired to direct the company's efforts to computerize. Initially, computerization included only the creation of a student record database on a microcomputer. The person who was hired did not stay with AMS long enough to write documentation for the operation of the database system he created.

The owner of AMS decided on an even more ambitious plan for using computers in the business office. He hired another university student with experience in computer networking. Given the title of technical service support director, this student was instructed to "computerize AMS." Unfortunately, he went about this task without analyzing the environment or consulting with any of the staff. Instead, he relied solely on his previous experience installing a local area network (LAN). The LAN he installed at AMS College consisted of a 386 network file server with workstations attached in a star topography using coaxial cable.

Two programmers were also hired to assist in the creation of application software. Under the supervision of the technical service support director, the programmers wrote programs that allowed the workstations to access the students' record database stored on the network file server. Once this task was completed the director resigned from AMS to take a job with another company. He departed without leaving documentation or anyone knowledgeable enough to supervise and to maintain the LAN.

Case Questions

1. Discuss the computerization pitfalls at AMS.

2. Are the problems at AMS technical problems or communication problems?

3. What written communication should have taken place at AMS with the implementation of the new system?

4. As the newly hired technical service support director, what would you do to get AMS on track?

5. What are some questions the owner should have asked before hiring the other director?

CASE | *Computing Needs of a Documentation Support Group*

Carolena L. Smith, San Diego State University

Carolyn Felton is the head of the publications and briefing production group at the Impact Communications Personnel Research and Development Center. Her group consists of seven people whose main function is providing documentation support for publications and briefings.

About 80 percent of the group's work is done using a Xerox Star 810 Workstation Electronic Publishing System. The software for the workstation is proprietary to Xerox and is not compatible with microcomputers. The system includes one printing server, which also acts as a backup; one communication server; and a file server, which also serves as the major clearinghouse and mail server. Included in the system configuration is a stand-alone U.S. Link Media Conversion System used to convert data on an 8-inch floppy disk to a 5¼-inch floppy disk, or visa versa. The maintenance contract for the system is $60,000 a year.

For a large project, 100 pages or more, the project may be split among three or four people in the group to hasten completion. Each person receives an equal portion of the document. When the individual portions are completed, the lead person may put the portions of the document together into final form. Another method used by the lead person to complete the final document is to send each individual assigned to the project, via electronic mail, a copy of each portion of the document for final edit.

Carolyn is not happy with the system. It is expensive to maintain, and her customers would be better served if her group used a system compatible with the other systems in the center. A compatible system would allow customers to send their work request directly to Carolyn's group via electronic mail. This procedure would eliminate the need for media conversion.

After assessing present and future computing needs, Carolyn proposes the following system to replace the Xerox 810 workstation:

- 6 SUN 386i workstations
- 1 Apple LaserWriter
- 1 Scanner
- 1 DocumentPro Desk Top Publishing Software
- Ethernet Communication Link

The new system will be faster and more expandable, and its Unix operating system will communicate with the center's main computer.

Case Questions

1. How can desktop publishing assist the group?

2. What are alternatives to delegating the large projects received by the group?

3. What type of report should Carolyn Felton write to management to present her ideas on a new system to replace the Xerox 810 workstation?

4. Write the report needed to present Carolyn's ideas to management. Provide any additional information necessary to complete the report.

Internal Communication at a Large Insurance Company | **CASE**

Glenn B. Dietrich, University of Texas at San Antonio

Midwest Insurance Company has experienced rapid and steady growth for the past 10 years. The company began business as a casualty insurance company that restricted its customers to one segment of the population that the founders considered to be a low-risk group. Until 10 years ago, the organization had one office, and its customers were required to communicate with this office for all business activities, including claims adjustments. Business transactions were conducted through the mail or by telephone.

Changes in the policies of the company resulted in the expansion of the population segment that Midwest considers to be its primary market segment. Additionally, the number of insurance products was increased to include life and health insurance. As a result of these changes, along with an aggressive marketing campaign, Midwest has become one of the 20 largest insurance companies in the country. Midwest has 476 offices throughout the United States, Europe, and the Far East. Customers now conduct most of their business with a Midwest employee at a local office.

The impact on internal communication has been significant. No longer can a document be delivered to another employee in a matter of minutes; in fact, overseas memos frequently require a week or more for delivery. Fred Marshall, the manager of information systems, estimates that internal communication has increased twentyfold in the past 10 years and sees this as the most important problem facing the company in the immediate future.

Fred formed a task force to study the internal communication requirements of Midwest. This group concluded that many of the intraoffice and interoffice communication requirements could be satisfied if an electronic mail system was installed, with all of the offices included in the system. Essentially, anyone with access to a computer terminal would be on the electronic mail circuit.

Fred thought that the electronic mail system could be used to satisfy the internal communication requirements of Midwest. However, before committing the organization to the investment required to implement this recommendation, he requested that the task force determine answers to the following questions.

Case Questions

1. How would the ability to send memos electronically affect communication traffic?

2. Would the ease of sending memos result in information overload to key managers?

3. Would there be a shift in the work associated with answering a memo? For example, would the person viewing the memo type a reply while sitting at the keyboard rather than compose the reply and have a secretary type it?

4. Would there be a saving of clerical personnel?

5. Is there any way in which the recipient of the electronic mail could be affected negatively?

6. Would the proposed system be enhanced if other technologies such as voice recognition were included?

International Business Communication

Jim Bradford graduated with the class of 1980. His friend Robby Wiggins still had a year of course work left. When Robby learned that the language requirements for graduation were being changed, he cursed his luck, because he would have to fit in two quarters of a foreign language. Jim laughed.

Hired by G&P Global Construction corporation, Jim was assigned to a three-month training program and then transferred to the European division. His assignments took him to Spain and France, where he struggled to communicate with clients. Even in England, although language was not a problem, Jim sometimes alienated clients by his lack of understanding of local customs.

Meanwhile, Robby found that he enjoyed learning German. After graduating and going to work for Kinney Trading Inc., he took additional language courses at night. His company quickly discovered how useful Robby was to them. His first assignment was to Bonn, West Germany. Because the language presented no major barriers, he was able to concentrate on developing his understanding of local customs and, consequently, his rapport with clients. As his influence and circle of foreign friends grew, Robby hoped he would never have to leave the exciting arena of international business.

Jim returned to the United States and accepted a managerial position on a construction project in Los Angeles, where he had grown up. He was astonished at the changes that had taken place during his years abroad. As he observed, "It's no longer necessary to go

Learning Objectives

1 *To know the importance of cultural awareness and foreign language skills.*

2 *To understand the major components of culture.*

3 *To recognize how people from other cultures perceive Americans.*

4 *To recognize significant cultural differences among the geographic areas in which U.S. multinational corporations are most active.*

5 *To understand the interaction between culture and communication.*

6 *To learn how to increase the probability of understanding and being understood.*

overseas to encounter major cultural differences because they're all around you right here."

Parents bemoan their children's inability to recognize life for what it is. Students complain about unreasonable teachers. Management views labor as unresponsive to changing conditions. Labor lodges a similar charge against management. Most misunderstandings such as these involve people who are much alike in background, education, and general experience. Obviously, as the differences between individuals increase, so also does the range of possible misunderstandings. The following brief quiz illustrates.[1]

1. Smiling fish is a:
    a. term used by Middle Easterners to describe American tourists.
    b. French chef working in a Japanese kitchen.
    c. dish served in China in which the fish is still alive.
2. In England, to table an issue or motion means to:
    a. put it aside until later.
    b. send it to arbitration.
    c. bring it up and discuss it.
3. Allah is the Supreme Being of which religious group?
    a. Shintoists
    b. Buddhists
    c. Moslems

The answers are at the bottom of the page. How you performed on this quiz may not be significant to you personally, but the implications of not understanding foreign customs and languages have enormous ramifications for business. According to Harry Obst, director of the Department of State's Office of Language Services, the United States lost over $50 billion in sales and opportunities in 1988 because of ignorance of foreign languages and culture.[2]

Poor communication skills cost U.S. business billions of dollars.

CULTURAL FOUNDATIONS

The **culture** is a function of a society's values, religious traditions, decision-making patterns, and language. It includes everything that the society thinks, says, does, and makes. When different cultures are represented in a business transaction, the barriers to communication increase.

---

[1]Rose Knotts, "Cross-Cultural Management: Transformation and Adaptations," *Business Horizons,* January–February 1989, 29–33. Answers to quiz: 1.c, 2.c, 3.c.

[2]Natasha Wolniansky, "We Do (Do Not) Accept Your Offer," *Management Review,* December 1989, 54–55.

Values

In the United States, managers are expected to calculate what must be done in order to accomplish their job-related goals and then to act on the calculations. They are trained to remain conscious of the goals at all times. Goal orientation is not such a significant part of many foreign cultures, however; individuals commonly allow nonurgent family matters to take precedence over business. Efficiency and productivity, which are common goals of American managers, are alien notions in many foreign cultures.

Not all cultures produce managers who are as goal-oriented as Americans.

American values are not readily transferable to other cultures. For instance, Jane Scarborough accepted an assignment as compensation consultant to a mid-sized textile producer in South America. She convinced management that more generous pay would increase employee loyalty and reduce absenteeism. Pay was increased by 25 percent. Jane returned to the United States. Absenteeism worsened as many workers discovered that the increased pay enabled them to subsist on an even shorter workweek. Some workers began to take every Wednesday off and others left at noon on Wednesday.

Many American managers define themselves by their jobs, but this is seldom true in foreign cultures. Foreign managers frequently place a high priority on getting to know individuals before doing business with them. Small talk and socializing routinely precede getting down to business. This dismays American representatives, who regard such use of time to be wasteful, if not pointless.

Religious Traditions

Many early colonists came to America in search of a sanctuary in which religion would be a matter of personal choice. Regular or semi-regular attendance at weekly religious services is the most obvious evidence of membership in an organized religion. Americans assume that religious beliefs influence their morals and ethics in everyday matters. Little additional tangible evidence exists of the practical impact of religion.

In many countries businesses follow religious dicta.

In many foreign countries, however, religion directly influences the manner in which business is conducted, including business communication. In Muslim countries, for example, everything stops five times a day for prayers. Non-Muslims, though not expected to pray, are expected to honor the practice, despite delays in business matters.

Every culture has its own holy days. Business travelers need to refer to a calendar that includes, for example, Ramadan, Lady of Guadalupe Day in Mexico, and Chinese New Year.

Decision-Making Patterns

In the goal-oriented, time-is-money culture of the United States, decisions are usually made and implemented as quickly and efficiently as possible. Often this efficiency depends on the accepted strategy of delegation of authority. In other countries, approaches vary; some are more participative than the United States and others are less so.

In many countries, companies are run from above, with all decisions, even on routine matters, made at or near the top of the organization. French, German, and Italian executives tend to make most decisions themselves rather than to delegate, and they direct rather than persuade.

Arab executives rely on one-to-one consultation rather than on committees or on simple delegation of decision-making responsibility. Decision-making patterns in Arab culture are unstructured and informal.

Japanese managerial principles emphasize the role of the group in decision making. In this **bottom-up style**, subordinates are actively involved in all phases of arriving at decisions. There is much give and take between top management and subordinates. This approach is time consuming but, once made, decisions are implemented quickly because all of the details have already been considered.

The most successful managers assume the decision-making patterns of the host culture.

Patterns of decision making vary throughout the world. A manager who considers his or her own approach to be superior and attempts to mandate its use in another culture is unlikely to succeed. American managers can work toward maximizing their effectiveness by accepting and employing the decision-making patterns of the **host culture**—that is, the culture of the country in which they seek to do business.

To illustrate, Jeff Turner strongly believed in letting workers make as many decisions as possible. When transferred to Germany, he continued to ask workers to make group decisions. He soon learned, however, that they simply polled the group and reported the findings. The German workers expected Jeff, as manager, to make the decision.

Language

Many Americans justify their lack of a second language by pointing out that English is rapidly becoming the language of international business. This attitude can lead to problems, as Holly Norton learned during a 30-day assignment abroad. She had been unconcerned about going to West Germany, because everyone there must study English in school. She soon discovered that the English language requirement did not necessarily mean overall fluency or that American English was being taught. The night she drove 60 miles in the wrong direction in a heavy rain before realizing that she had misunderstood directions, Holly vowed to acquire a second language.

Foreign nationals are likely to nod in agreement over this old joke:

Q: What do you call a person who can speak two languages?
A: Bilingual.
Q: How about three?
A: Trilingual.
Q: Good, how about one?
A: Hmmmm . . . American![3]

---

[3]Phillip R. Harris and Robert T. Moran, *Managing Cultural Differences* (Houston, Tex.: Gulf, 1979), 61.

Even while depending on English-speaking foreigners to transact business in English, Americans tend to use jargon in their speaking and writing that is intelligible only to other Americans. Those who assume that their English will always be understood as intended are in for a shock.

CHARACTERISTICS ATTRIBUTED TO AMERICANS

The United States is an insulated country, sharing borders with only Canada and Mexico. Because of the country's huge size, many of its citizens, especially those in the heartland, are unaware of the significant differences that exist among cultures. This lack of cultural awareness will gradually subside as dealings with other countries become more routine. Meanwhile, non-Americans tend to attribute certain characteristics to Americans, and some behaviors of Americans tend to validate these perceptions.

Individualistic

Diverse people have immigrated to America for religious, economic, and political freedom throughout the country's history. U.S. citizens have always valued their independence. Strength is often measured by the ability to stand alone; for many years actor John Wayne was viewed as the epitome of rugged individualism. Today Lee Iacocca is widely admired for his individualism and for his drive for self-realization through the American business process.

In keeping with this heritage, the United States sets global standards for human rights, particularly as related to employment. Foreign companies operating within U.S. borders are likely to encounter difficulties in following American laws written to protect women, minorities, older citizens, and the handicapped. They often perceive these laws as unreasonable, counterproductive, and contrary to their own views of social order.

Arrogant

Many American business people tend to act as if they believe everyone wishes he or she were American. As a result they deal with foreign nationals in a manner perceived as offensive. By conveying an attitude of superiority and displaying an unwillingness to accept the worth of others, Americans construct obstacles that hamper their intercultural effectiveness.

Americans tend to act as though they are members of a superior culture.

The enthusiastic patriotism of Americans stems from certain basic beliefs. For example, Americans assume that all people—male or female, rich or poor, regardless of race or creed—can become successful if they work hard enough. Americans also view with pride the system of advancement based on merit. Their confidence in the free enterprise system is a topic that Americans expound on to an extent that may alienate others.

Aggressive

Americans respect the ability to confront problems head on. They are taught to answer challenges directly through clever and quick verbal exchanges. Consider that there are 15 times more lawyers per capita in Amer-

America is considered a litigous society because of the number of lawyers and lawsuits.

ica than in Japan. Given the Japanese' mistrust of the legal system, particularly the U.S. legal system, the presence of lawyers can severely disrupt negotiations between Japanese and American business people.

American business operates in an environment of high pressure. Successful business people in the United States are able not only to cope with the pressure but to flourish under stress. When they are assigned to a foreign country, however, these same abilities often become dysfunctional. The aggressiveness that leads to accomplishment in the United States may contribute to failure abroad. An aggressive and direct communication style will be viewed as unmannerly and inappropriate in many foreign countries.

Intolerant of Silence

Americans tend to be overly talkative in the eyes of many foreigners.

As children, Americans are frequently put on display and are taught by their parents to entertain and to show other adults what they have learned. They are instructed to focus on external communications and how these communications move them toward predominantly materialistic goals. Contrast this with Eastern cultures that hold spiritual growth in higher regard and stress the mastery of inner communication. Rather than view periods of silence as an opportunity to reflect on the situation at hand, Americans feel uncomfortable with silence and feel pressured to fill the void with conversation. This puts them at a significant disadvantage when negotiating with many foreign executives, especially Asians, who are comfortable with the silence.

Money Oriented

American business people are commonly viewed as having a bottom-line mentality, that is, they base their actions primarily on the effect the actions will have on the finances of the operation. When a choice must be made between people and profits, Americans are expected to opt for profits. Indeed, U.S. companies often view their people and social institutions as resources to be cultivated. An American manager based in an undeveloped country may strive to mechanize as a means of reducing labor costs; foreign managers may view such an action as contrary to good business practice because it will take away jobs. Any business communicator whose messages focus solely on money will enjoy little credibility in many foreign countries.

Preoccupied with Time

A race with the clock is how many Americans spend every business day.

American business people tend to view time as a scarce natural resource, as something not to be wasted. For that reason they set deadlines for themselves and operate to meet them. In many other parts of the world, however, time is viewed as the servant rather than the master. The expression "laid back" describes many cultures' attitudes toward time. Signs of impatience by a U.S. sales representative kept waiting for a scheduled appointment reduce the probability of success.

The focus of Americans is often criticized, too, as being too narrow and present oriented. Rather than develop broad strategies, which requires recognition that organized change takes time, Americans act to bring about rapid change. The long-term results of this approach are being questioned by Americans themselves. In a study of nearly 1,000 U.S. managers, 76 percent felt that there had been a damaging overemphasis on quarterly earnings and present budget.[4]

Obsessed with Talking Shop

Americans, it is alleged, do not discriminate between appropriate and inappropriate settings in which to transact business. Instead, they are likely to violate the norms of a host country by talking about business matters in settings in which social conversation is expected. Good business communication practices dictate that message content be appropriate for the situation.

Informal

Although highly structured with their time and goal-oriented behaviors, Americans tend to be relaxed in dress and in their relationships with others. Picture the stereotypical California talent agent as characterizing this position at an extreme. His clothing is casual, faddish, and gaudy. He delights in calling people by their first names and may tack on a "sweetheart" or "my man." He leans back in his chair with his feet on the table in front of him. When meeting people for the first time, he is likely to vigorously clasp their hand and shoulder as though being reunited with a long-lost buddy.

Few American businessmen carry informality to this length, but in the eyes of foreigners they are still too unceremonious. No other country tolerates such relaxed exchanges between superiors and subordinates, nor do many of them accept the use of first names in business. In Japan, for example, first names are used only among family members and close friends. Even long-time business associates and coworkers are hesitant to use first names.

Unwilling to Learn Host Language

Many foreign nationals are fluent in several languages. In contrast, American managers historically have expected business communication to be conducted in English. Unwillingness to take the time to learn a host language reinforces the negative impression Americans make.

As early as 1958 a book called *The Ugly American* indicted representatives of the United States, both official and unofficial, for their behavior

In today's business environment Americans need to speak the language of countries in which they do business.

[4]Knotts, "Cross-Cultural Management," 29–33.

✓ *CHECKLIST for Changing the Way Americans Are Perceived Abroad*

____▪ Tone down the image of rugged individualist.

____▪ Resist the temptation to feel that American ways are superior.

____▪ Learn the art of patient compromise.

____▪ Be aware that silence can be a strategy.

____▪ Understand the impact on other cultures of putting money before people.

____▪ Do not press for immediate action or decisions.

____▪ Restrict shop talk to appropriate settings.

____▪ Avoid excessive informality.

____▪ Learn to speak the language of the country in which you are doing business.

abroad.[5] The negative impressions created by their behavior, according to the authors, would ultimately damage the image of the United States. Many of the allegations made in that book are still relevant. With inappropriate behavior and questionable communication practices, American business representatives abroad damage themselves, their employers, and their country.

PROFILES OF FOREIGN CULTURES

English is spoken by only about 10 percent of the world's population. Even if a global language were to exist, cultural differences would preclude complete understanding among people. The more business people can learn about a foreign culture, however, the more effectively they will operate within it. This section focuses on the cultures in which readers are most likely to find themselves doing business.

Canada

Canada and the United States are the world's largest trading partners. The 1988 merchandise trade between the two countries totaled more than $152.4 billion compared with $127.5 billion between the United States and Japan.[6] The Canada–U.S. Free Trade Agreement signed in 1990 re-

---

[5]William J. Lederer and Eugene Burdick, *The Ugly American* (New York: Norton, 1958).
[6]*U.S. Foreign Trade Highlights 1988* (Washington, D.C.: Department of Commerce, 1989).

moved all tariffs on products traded between the countries, with the result that more and more U.S. companies are becoming involved in business with Canada.

When measuring cultural diversity, the differences between Canada and the United States seem slight, but they are noteworthy. The similarities between the two countries lead many U.S. business people to view Canada as identical to the United States. Although most Canadians live close to the U.S. border and are familiar with American ways, they do not necessarily like the American way of doing things.

The close proximity of the United States to Canada is both an asset and a liability. We tend to take Canada for granted, and this often weakens relations between the two countries at all levels—government, business, and interpersonal. Business people who display an awareness of Canada's uniqueness are better able to communicate with Canadians.

Two primary cultures dominate Canada: English and French. Canada is officially designated as a bilingual nation and many of its citizens are truly bilingual. This bilingualism contributes to the cosmopolitan atmosphere of the Canadian business community. French is recognized as the official language in the province of Quebec. Anyone who is able to conduct business in French when in Quebec holds a definite advantage over a competitor who lacks that ability.

The ability to speak French is an aid to doing business in Quebec.

The Canadian business culture is more formal than that of the United States. European styles and manners prevail and people are more aware of etiquette than in the United States.

Canadians appreciate business communication that is direct and to the point. Presentations that are both clear and thorough are likely to be well received. In the traditional business culture, a conservative approach to communication is appropriate. Gimmickry and showmanship will go unrewarded; decorum is expected.

In Canada the system for dating correspondence is like that in Europe. May 1, 1991, is written 5/1/91 in the United States; it is 1/5/91 in Canada and Europe. Business relationships have soured as a result of this difference. Imagine discovering that the order expected to arrive on January 5 would not arrive until May 1.

Canadians have long felt that most people from the United States are both ignorant of and indifferent toward Canada. They will be more receptive to the U.S. manager who communicates a knowledge of Canadian current events, political units, and geography.

Mexico

Like Canada, Mexico sometimes seems to exist in the shadow of the United States. This proximity sometimes causes identity problems for Mexicans, who do not like for their country to be compared to the United States. Even implied comparisons should be avoided in business communication.

Neither Canadians nor Mexicans like to hear U.S. citizens referred to as "Americans." They share this sentiment with the citizens of most of the other nations in Central and South America, all of whom rightfully consider themselves to be Americans as well.

The first step in doing business with Mexicans is to develop sincere interpersonal relationships and trust.

The warmth and personalism of the Mexican people pervade all areas of that culture, including the business community. Anyone who fails to devote attention and time to personal relationships will not do well in this culture. U.S. business people should get to know the people with whom they are dealing and establish a rapport with them.

Until trust is developed, little business will be transacted in the Latin culture. Developing trust is a gradual process, and Mexicans do not like being rushed. Hard-sell approaches are not effective.

> Doing business in Latin America is like getting married in a formal, old-fashioned way. First there's a period of courtship. It's a time of testing, a proving ground. If the two of you can manage to fall in love with each other, the rest becomes easier and things take on a logic and momentum of their own. If you don't take the time for a romance, the wedding will probably be called off. The business will to go a competitor who has the patience to cultivate a relationship first.[7]

Friendships are important in this culture, although they may take considerable time to cultivate. Casual conversation and sociability, likely to be perceived as unprofessional and inefficient in some cultures, is an important dimension of any business relationship in Mexico.

Mexicans like to make people happy and they show deference to those of higher status. This tendency results at times in their saying what they think the other person wants to hear. This same tendency also sometimes results in oral agreements that are subsequently broken in writing. Written agreements are necessary in business dealings in this type of culture.

Mexicans, and Latins in general, disclose much about themselves in their dealings with others, and they expect others to reciprocate. Hard-driving U.S. executives who attempt to avoid such rituals are rarely effective in this culture. The best strategy is to reveal your personal side. Latin businessmen strive to develop a *simpatico* relationship—characterized by a sincere empathy such as old friends might share—before doing business together. The most effective U.S. business communicators recognize the value of empathy and work to develop it.

For individuals who manage foreign nationals in this culture, the style that seems most effective is one that demonstrates **machismo**—a strong sense of power and pride. Machismo is conveyed through forceful and self-confident dealings with others.

Germany

East Germany operated for years as a police state with tightly controlled information and media and limited free enterprise. West Germany, on the other hand, has closely resembled the United States in its manner of trans-

[7]Neil Chesanow, *The World-Class Executive* (New York: Rawson, 1985), 268.

acting business, the main difference being that the German business environment is more formal. A united Germany with a market-oriented economy can be expected to resemble West Germany in its culture.

In Germany, as in most of Europe, people are introduced by their last names and titles. Referring to a person by first name is considered impolite unless you have been invited to do so. Individuals who have known each other, perhaps worked side by side for many years, still often address one another by title.

Unlike Latin Americans, Germans devote little time to developing relationships with business associates. A social conversation may precede business dealings, but it will be kept brief. German business executives tend to get down to business quickly.

To be well received, a business presentation should be factual, explicit, and thorough, yet concise. A business presentation that is perceived as infomative will be viewed more positively than one seen as being mainly persuasive. Logical appeals are more effective in this culture than emotional appeals. Jokes, a part of many presentations in the United States, should be excluded for two reasons: (1) cultural differences make it unlikely that jokes told by a U.S. representative will be understood and (2) business communication, including whatever small talk accompanies it, is regarded as serious.

Germans prefer logical rather than emotional arguments.

One German proverb defines America as "a place where an hour is 40 minutes." This may suggest that the pace in the United States is much faster than in Germany, but there is not much difference between the two, especially in urban areas. Punctuality is as important to German executives as to their U.S. counterparts. Appointments should be made well in advance, and business calls should not be made without appointments.

Northern European nations in general take pride in their longevity and admire it in other institutions. The date of the founding of any older firm should be included on the business cards of the representatives of the firm. Holders of advanced educational degrees also receive high esteem. Business representatives' advanced degrees should be indicated on their business cards.

Currently, pride in native languages is growing in many countries. This pride is sometimes reflected in an insistence that the local language be used. In West Germany, for example, government contracts must be written in German; this policy has significant implications for any organization seeking to do business with any unit of the German government.

Although few U.S. executives may become fluent enough to write contracts in a second language, a basic knowledge of the language of the host nation is invaluable. Most European languages distinguish between a familiar and a polite form of "you." Learning to distinguish between the two forms and mastering the use of the polite form, which would ordinarily be used in business communication, are important so as to avoid embarrassment.

In the past it was important to distinguish between West and East Germany and to use the formal names of the two countries: the Federal Republic of Germany (West Germany) and the German Democratic Republic (East Germany). Travelers to Germany should now determine the current attitudes of the people with whom they will be interacting.

The West German workforce is comfortable with an authoritarian management style. Communication is direct and managers who are most effective in this culture direct rather than persuade. In Germany, policy, decisiveness, and breadth of knowledge give a manager stature.

Business communication should be direct and task-oriented, but hard-sell approaches are rarely effective. Logical, rather than emotional, messages are more likely to be successful.

China

China covers a land area the same size as the United States, but its population of one billion is approximately four times that of the United States. From 1949 until the mid-1970s the Chinese government kept the nation isolated from the rest of the world. Since then the doors have been open to foreign trade, and organizations in the United States, as well as in other nations, have been transacting business with the Chinese. In 1989 some sanctions were placed on China by countries that disapproved of China's action during the Tiananmen Square incident. Thousands of students and citizens of the Republic of China who were peaceably striking, calling for democratic social and economic reform, were killed in Tiananmen Square by soldiers of the People's Liberation Army.

The United States has become China's third largest trade partner, after Japan and Hong Kong. In 1988 China exported approximately $8.5 billion worth of goods to the United States while importing $5 billion.[8]

In the Chinese business community, organization and punctuality are important. Directness, however, is one characteristic on which the Chinese culture differs from those of the United States and northern Europe. In fact, the prevailing communication sytle is indirect, extremely polite, and bordering on the evasive. This evasiveness can be both frustrating and charming. In their book *Going International*, Copeland and Griggs tell of a rejection slip that a Beijing publication sent to a British journalist:

> We have read your manuscript with boundless delight. If we were to publish your paper, it would be impossible to publish any work of a lower standard. And as it is unthinkable that, in the next thousand years, we shall see its equal; we are, to our regret, compelled to return your divine composition, and beg you a thousand times to overlook our short sight and timidity.[9]

Obviously, the Chinese tend to use hyperbole in their communication.

---

[8]*U.S. Foreign Trade Highlights 1988* (Washington, D.C.: Department of Commerce, 1989).

[9]Lennie Copeland and Lewis Griggs, *Going International* (New York: Random House, 1985), 109.

Formality is another significant characteristic of the Chinese culture. Etiquette is more important than in most cultures in which U.S. business operates. A very reserved people, the Chinese do not like to be touched. A brief handshake and bow is the usual greeting or farewell. The stereotypical backslapping U.S. salesperson would be met with quiet disdain.

The Chinese are very formal, reserved, and slow in developing business relationships.

The Chinese are very slow in establishing business relationships with outsiders. They are willing to devote inordinate amounts of time to social relations before getting down to business, much to the dismay of U.S. executives. Salespeople from the United States who have done business with the Chinese will attest that it seems to take forever to reach a decision. Once the decision is made, however, the Chinese may become as impatient to implement it as a North American.

A group orientation pervades every aspect of the Chinese culture. A Chinese business person uses "we," even when talking about himself or herself. U.S. business executives should do likewise and avoid the use of "I," which is viewed as evidence of self-centeredness, a characteristic the Chinese view with contempt.

Involving the worker is a key to effective management. Senior and middle-level employees are encouraged to make suggestions, and in the process management seeks to develop some common goals. Because an authoritarian style of management is likely to succeed, managers should seek to establish a cooperative work environment.

Japan

Japan is a small country, destitute of natural resources, a part of Asia but not like Asia. Indeed, Asia is still hostile toward Japan because of Japan's cruelties during World War II.

In Japan contrasts abound, both visually and idealistically—for example, the modern Seto Ohashi bridge stands in sharp contrast to ancient Shinto shrines. The furious pace of technological development seems to contradict the fervent attempts to preserve centuries-old customs, rituals, and social structure. The conflicting desires of the Japanese people are causing their culture to change haltingly. Foreign visitors still find Japan to be one of the least accommodating of all the industrialized nations.

The Japanese have actively sought to prevent outsiders from becoming part of their society. They value conformity—in dress, education, roles, language, and values. Japan's education system is considered to be one of the best in the world, with well-qualified teachers commanding high respect and significant salaries. Students in Japan attend school 240 days a year compared with 180 days in the United States.

The Japanese, like the Chinese, focus on conformity, group values, and harmony.

Japanese children are taught that they must develop inner strength and peace in order to be able to use these values to benefit society. Meditation is encouraged. The Japanese people believe that communication can occur through sensory channels other than hearing, seeing and physically touching. Silence can therefore be used as a means of communication. Japanese parents value this "silent rapport" with their children. Adults in group

A cardboard box on the corner of the desk holds photographs and other personal possessions John will take with him after 16 years with the company. The memories are rich and bring a smile to his face. But, like many companies today, Lovecraft Importers is having to downsize, and many long-term employees are being let go. After 2 years of wondering when his number would come up, John is glad the waiting is over. He is ready to start a new career that will renew his passion for work.

He picks up a document from Jiang Silk Inc., a Chinese exporting firm, and quickly scans its familiar contents. This document represents over six months of negotiations on a project that John has personally supervised and that has resulted in a substantial contract for Lovecraft. He takes pride in a job well done and also recalls with pleasure the foreign friends he has made in the process.

He discovers that this final contract, complete except for his signature and that of his superior, contains a major error. Despite care to ensure that the communications between the two companies were clear and exact, the agreement drawn up by Jiang Silk reflects a translation error that would cost the Chinese company thousands of dollars in fees. John knows that if he points the misunderstanding out to his superior, he will be told to sign the contract anyway—his company cannot afford another delay. John is weary of the rat race. He knows that all he has to do is sign his name, pick up his box, and walk out the door, and these hassles will be behind him.

John feels boxed in. What would you do?

situations feel no need to self-disclose or use space-filling conversation in order to be at ease.

The primary unit of value in Japan is the group. Attention to the individual is required only for its value to the group. Identity is found, not through individual virtue, but through collective excellence and strength. The Japanese support consensus decison-making and group responsibilities and rewards. Managers do not single out individuals for recognition because outstanding individual effort is considered to be a necessary part of group participation.

Communication patterns are very different from those seen in most other cultures. In a conflict situation, Japanese will typically choose silence as their response. As conflict increases, their withdrawal becomes even more pronounced. Their primary goal is harmony and they will allow as long as necessary for the relationship to develop in order to support this goal.

Europe 1992

The Common Market—a coalition of France, West Germany, Italy, Belgium, the Netherlands, Luxembourg, and later Denmark, Great Britain, Ireland,

International business will change dramatically as a result of Europe's combined economic power.

Greece, Portugal and Spain—was founded in 1958. It was formed to improve economic activities and political relationships between the member countries. Now known as the European Community, or EC, it has evolved into a combined market of 323 million consumers with a potential combined output of $4.5 trillion in goods and services.[10]

Member nations recognized, however, that many trade barriers continued to stand in the way of effective business communication and inhibit the movement of people and products within the EC. They agreed to dissolve the remaining barriers and form a true international common market by 1992. The EC hope is to enhance Europe's global competitiveness and improve the citizens' standard of living.

Specific communication obstacles that interfere with smooth operations between EC countries have included seven different languages and hundreds of different cultures and subcultures. Each country and many communities have had their own conflicting regulations that affect trade. Additionally, telecommunication in the EC is archaic, inefficient, and expensive.

Although the diversity in people and customs will not be affected by the transformation in 1992, business strategies certainly will. The increased business activity will require other nationals to have greater international communication skills.

CLEAR COMMUNICATION IN ENGLISH

Communicating effectively in English with people who do not share your culture or for whom American English is a second language requires careful use of the language.

Idioms, Acronyms, and Jargon

When you tell a friend from Dubuque that it is "raining cats and dogs," the news is likely to be greeted with a yawn. When you make the same statement to an associate from Caracas you may see a look of astonishment, and perhaps, a dash to the window. Such an expression is an **idiom**. Although each word may be understood by an English-speaking foreigner, the intended meaning may not be. Idioms complicate international communication.

Technical writing often relies heavily on jargon. Consider this printed information that accompanied a hair dryer manufactured in China:

> Choosing subferalle high temperature and hard plows materials, it cannot be easily broken more thom its inner part has heatproof equipment and not change the sapl of outride for a long time ure[sic].

---

[10]James A. Senn, "The Evolution toward Europe in 1992: A Summary of Progress," *SIM Network,* Fall 1989, 1.

The message, which was meant to attest to the durability of the hair dryer, was lost in the translation into English.

An **acronym** is a word comprised of the first letters from each of a series of words in a phrase. Using acronyms allows people to save time in their writing or speaking, provided everyone is familiar with the acronyms. Anyone employed in a U.S. business organization knows what a CEO is, for example, but foreign nationals would not. Acronyms should be avoided in international communication.

Semantic Traps

Recent marketing history is rich with examples of advertising campaigns that backfired because of problems with semantics, "Come alive with Pepsi" went over well in the United States. The German version, "Come out of the grave with Pepsi," and the Asian interpretation, "Pepsi brings your ancestors back from the grave," understandably failed to increase sales in those countries. On the other hand, Braniff's slogan "Travel on leather" was translated into an alluring "Travel naked" in Spanish. Incidently, the phrase "The spirit is willing but the flesh is weak" becomes "The Ghost is ready but the meat is rotten" in Russian. All ads, speeches, slogans, and important letters should be checked with a local translator.

Rapid Speech

All languages sound like gibberish if spoken too rapidly for the listener to understand.

Anyone listening to a conversation in a foreign language marvels at the participants' ability to understand such rapid speech. You may recall hearing an unfamiliar language and thinking it sounded like gibberish. Rapid English sounds the same way to those for whom it is not a primary language. For that reason, speak slowly. When the other person is speaking in English, never interrupt. He or she may need time to think about how best to express a thought.

INTERCULTURAL DIFFERENCES IN BODY LANGUAGE

Only 7 percent of what is communicated between people is transmitted through words. As discussed in earlier chapters, the bulk of what is communicated is a function of interpreted physiology, both body language and tone of voice. Individuals who are skilled at observing and interpreting the physiology of others, and who can adjust their viewpoints of the world in such a way as to accommodate the perspectives of others, will find that they are able to communicate rather effectively with people with whom they have no common language. However, this task is complicated not just by the absence of a shared vocabulary, but also by the radically different meanings that common body movements can have. Drawing primarily on the work of Peter Marsh, this section will explore some of these differences in terms of distance, eye contact, facial expression, and time.

Distance

Each individual varies in the size of the bubble of personal body space that surrounds him or her, but cultural patterns can be seen. The people of the **contact cultures** of Latin America, Southern Europe, and the Arab states touch more often and stand much closer than do Northern Europeans. North Americans fall somewhere between these two extremes. Marsh reported a study done on the differences:

> One researcher observed 180 touches on average between pairs of acquaintances spending an hour together in San Juan, Puerto Rico, and 110 in Paris, France. In Gainesville, Florida, the average was less than twice. In London, England, it was 0. When people touch each other during conversation, their contact commonly includes control touches such as tapping your listener on the arm to emphasize a point, as well as touching on the arm or shoulder to amplify expression of support and appreciation.[11]

Visitors to foreign cultures can also be startled by the different types of touches. In the Middle East or Southern Europe, two men might walk with their hands clasped or with their arms around each other's shoulders. Westerners would regard this behavior as acceptable for women but effeminate in men, preferring to greet each other with a handshake. Mexicans embrace companions upon meeting them, Japanese bow, and Malaysians press their noses against each other's cheeks. Without knowing what is acceptable distance in a culture, business people can easily violate a social norm or misinterpret the behavior of others as being either distant and cold or as being overly aggressive, depending on their point of view.

Eye Contact

Culture influences what is considered acceptable or expected eye contact. People in the contact cultures not only stand physically closer; they also tend to exchange more eye contact. Although Americans view direct eye contact as a sign of power and honesty, they feel that unbroken eye contact is too aggressive to be used in normal business dealings and personal interactions. They may interpret the directed gaze of Latin Americans as being threatening or insulting. At the same time, a Southern European may view a North American's broken eye contact as insincere or impolite.

People of the contact cultures touch more often, stand closer, and have more eye contact.

Even more extreme eye contact customs were reported by Marsh to exist in some cultures. Members of the Lua tribe of Kenya are forbiddent to look directly at their mother-in-law. Some Nigerian tribesmen do not make direct eye contact with superiors, and natives of some South American Indian tribes do not look at each other when conversing.[12]

---

[11] Peter Marsh, *Eye to Eye* (Oxford: Andromeda Oxford Ltd, 1988), 90.

[12] Ibid., 76.

Facial Expressions

Cultural differences in smiling are found even within the United States. The highest incidence of smiling is in the Southeast, specifically in Atlanta, Louisville, Memphis, and Nashville. A Southerner smiling and walking down a New England street may be seen as crazy or scorning. On the other hand, a New Englander, who typically smiles the least, might be seen as annoyed or dejected in the South.[13]

Even something as subtle as raising eyebrows can have different connotations in different cultures. According to Marsh:

> Darwin reported that if (eyebrow raising) accompanied a head-toss it meant "yes" in Ethiopia and Borneo. In Greece and Turkey, however, a similar gesture means "no." The difference between the two expressions may lie in the eye opening wide for "yes," resembling the pleasure of a surprise; narrow, resembling a supercilious expression, for "no." In Japan the eyebrow flash has sexual connotations and decency requires its avoidance in Japanese meetings.[14]

Time

Each culture has its own timetable.

Each culture has its own timetable and own level of importance attached to keeping on schedule. In the relaxed atmosphere of Eastern Europe, people eat when they feel like it and are relaxed about events starting on time. Contrast that with the Far East, where people can go for hours without eating or breaking from their activities. Americans and Western Europeans structure their day around their meals. Groups of individuals from different cultures may therefore have difficulty setting up work patterns that meet the needs of all participants.

Three attitudes associated with time were identified by anthropologist Margaret Mead: postfigurative, configurative, and prefigurative.[15] Each culture relies predominantly on one approach. For example, picture a middle-aged businessman reflecting on the small business that he started 30 years earlier. In a **postfigurative culture** he would think about how his child is moving into the business and—having learned the father's ways—will make no major changes in the business in the future. In a **configurative culture** the man would dream of great undefined changes in the future for his child and business. Finally, in a **prefigurative culture** the man is riddled with doubt about his future; it is more than he can comprehend. Depending on the attitude to time, substantially different meanings are attached to deadlines, emergencies, forecasting, meetings, and schedules.

[13]Ibid., 87.

[14]Ibid., 86.

[15]Margaret Mead, *Culture and Commitment: A Study of the Generation Gap* (Garden City, N.Y.: Doubleday, 1970), 1.

AMERICAN MANAGERS ABROAD

In the past several decades, the volume of international business has increased greatly. In 1984 more than 93,000 U.S. firms were involved in international business, and approximately 25 percent of them maintained offices or other facilities abroad.[16] Employees of multinational organizations are routinely transferred to foreign countries. Two million U.S. citizens were employed abroad in 1986, and the volume of international business operations will continue to expand.[17] Each successive year's college graduates are increasingly likely to spend time living and working in foreign cultures.

Researchers have identified two skills they think contribute most to intercultural effectiveness. They are (1) the ability to establish interpersonal relationships and (2) the ability to communicate effectively. Individuals who possess these skills cope better in foreign environments than do those who lack them. Unfortunately, U.S. companies may send these employees abroad with no intercultural or language training and with no consideration for how the individual employee will fit in with the cultural expectations of the new setting.

Growing numbers of graduates are likely to spend time living and working in foreign cultures.

Preparing for Travel Abroad

Prior to departing for a foreign assignment, managers should learn as much about the culture as possible. No matter how rigorously they have prepared for the foreign assignment, however, they will experience some culture shock. This shock will be cushioned in proportion to the extent of their preparation.

Some business organizations provide intercultural training for employees anticipating overseas transfers. Such programs are intended to reduce the uncertainty the employee experiences on being thrust into a different environment. Whether or not you have access to such formal training, you can do much to reduce your degree of culture shock. In learning about a country's culture, you will gain the ability to anticipate patterns of behavior to which you will be exposed abroad as well as the reasons for the behavior. Equally important, you will learn the sort of behavior that will be expected of you in unfamiliar surroundings.

Some U.S. businesses provide employees with intercultural training before sending them abroad.

Using Foresight in Planning Negotiations

Business people who negotiate international business in their own country have the home-court advantage. When planning critical meetings on foreign ground, they should visit the country and their business counterparts

---

[16]Copeland and Griggs, *Going International,* xix–xx.

[17]*Statistical Abstract of the United States* (Washington, D.C.: Department of Commerce, Bureau of the Census, 1987).

ahead of time. This visit can facilitate their understanding of the people and reduce uncertainty surrounding the issues.

Indeed, the term issues points up a crucial cultural difference in negotiations. Westerners negotiate issues. From their perspective, each issue is to be discussed and agreed upon individually before moving on to the next issue. In the Soviet Union and Japan, however, agreement comes only after all issues have been discussed. No issue is settled in and of itself. This presents a problem to the Western negotiator.

American negotiators, for example, may become frustrated by what they perceive as a lack of progress when meeting with the Japanese and may be tempted to make concessions. The Japanese perspective, however, may be that negotiations are moving appropriately and the stage for making demands or concessions has not been reached. The Americans can easily lose power and respect by not recognizing the Japanese viewpoint.

Attending to Details

Meetings and telephone contact among business people from diverse cultures are more likely to be successful if these suggestions for planning and follow-up are observed:[18]

1. *Use of interpreters.* Be sure that all interpreters are familiar with both languages and both cultures so that they will be able to offer an interpretation that conveys the meaning of what you are saying and not just a translation of the words. These interpreters should also be familiar with the business to be discussed and should know the terminology or language of the business.
2. *Use of visuals.* During a presentation, make maximum use of clear, understandable visuals. Sometimes a picture really is worth a thousand words.
3. *Written summary.* Follow up every meeting with a written summary. Include in this summary what was discussed and what was agreed to.
4. *Use of confirmation.* To be sure that meanings and not just words have been communicated, use the telex to confirm the content of telephone conversations and to have a backup written statement of the communication.

MAINTAINING PERSPECTIVE

The competitive spirit between countries and cultures can be assumed to be an inherent part of the human drive. This does not mean, however, that all or even many business negotiations are win–lose situations. The emphasis should be on understanding and communicating for the purpose

---

[18]Nina Streitfeld, "How to Communicate in Other Cultures," *Public Relations Journal* 42 (February 1986): 34–35.

of satisfying mutual goals. Both parties in international business transactions should strive for win–win outcomes.

The U.S. population is heterogeneous and is, itself, comprised of multiple cultures. Business people, therefore, need not go abroad to interact with foreign cultures. Some 600,000 legal immigrants arrive in the United States yearly, many more than go anywhere else in the world. These people restore national energy and enthusiasm and bring new talents. The flexibility and perspectives gained by growing up with and interacting with diverse cultures on a daily basis become the foundation for developing the needed skills for international business.

SUMMARY

The globalization of the world economy has created an environment in which business people must be skilled in communicating with individuals from different cultures in order to compete effectively in the marketplace. Americans are better able to interact with foreign nationals when they understand how Americans are perceived abroad. Characteristics that Americans value such as individualism, assertiveness, and informality may appear illogical or inappropriate to other cultures. Each country has its own set of traditions that influence the business practices with which they operate. Communication competency is increased not only by understanding these environmental differences but also by understanding nonverbal communication. Body language varies between countries just as verbal language does. Individuals can be taught both to understand others more effectively and to enable others to understand them. Organizations that do not provide these skills to their employees find that communication errors result in both monetary and strategic losses to their companies.

Key Terms

- **culture**
- **bottom-up style**
- **host culture**
- **machismo**
- **idiom**

- **acronym**
- **contact cultures**
- **postfigurative culture**
- **configurative culture**
- **prefigurative culture**

Review Questions

1. What are four significant components of culture?
2. Do you feel that foreign nationals' perceptions of Americans are accurate?
3. Discuss the difficulties English-speaking natives of other countries would have working in the United States.
4. Choose a country discussed in this chapter and describe how you would prepare for a year-long assignment to that country.

5. Are there industries within the United States in which strict adherence to timetables is not as important? When foreign business people set up business in the United States, do they necessarily have to adapt to American time standards?

6. What two skills contribute most to intercultural effectiveness?

Exercises

1. Your company is sending you to Japan to negotiate a contract for importing art objects to the United States. Although you speak no Japanese, the representatives from the other firm speak limited English. What steps should you take in preparing for this meeting?

2. Ask an international student what kinds of things Americans do that make it harder for him or her to understand and fit into the American culture. What kinds of things are helpful?

3. Form groups of two to four people and experiment with different distances and eye contact. At what distance do you feel as if someone is too close to talk to? Too far away? Vary the topic of conversation from something impersonal (such as the weather) to something personal (for example, what you find embarrassing) and note whether eye contact changes.

CASE | *Lou's New World*

Chun-Sheng Yu, Hangzhou University, Hangzhou, Zhejiang, P.R. China

Lou got off the airplane and stood near the exit of the International Airport in Atlanta. It was 8:55 p.m., the arrival time Lou told his uncle in his letter. This was Lou's first visit to the United States. He continued to wait for his uncle to come and pick him up.

Lou had graduated from Beijing University in China and received his master's degree in management. Having been a university instructor for two years, he recognized that it would help in his professional development to do additional study abroad. Fortunately, Lou had an uncle who had been living in the United States almost 40 years. Because of his uncle's support, Lou was accepted by a university located in the city where his uncle lived.

Nearly an hour passed and Lou's uncle still had not appeared. Lou was wondering whether his letter had reached his uncle. Finally, he decided to telephone. To his surprise, his uncle told him over the phone that he had arranged with a Chinese restaurant to hire Lou and also provide Lou a place to live. Lou's uncle told Lou to go directly to the restaurant.

Lou was puzzled. He was the only nephew of his uncle. According to Chinese tradition, he would be warmly welcomed into his uncle's home and attend a big banquet in his honor his first night in the new country. Looking at the two big pieces of baggage, he felt lonely and helpless. He could not imagine carrying them with him and searching for the location of the restaurant in a large city that was totally new and strange to him.

Three weeks after his arrival, Lou was busy working as a waiter in the restaurant. He had made some friends in the city. One of them was Tom, a graduate student in the same business school where Lou was soon to begin his studies. Both of them worked in the same restaurant. That day Lou saw several professors come in to the restaurant. As he quickly approached them, one of them leaned toward him and said politely: "If you don't mind, I would like my son, Tom, to come and serve us." Tom came up, smiling. Lou heard the professor introduce Tom to his friends proudly and later saw that they put a tip on the table when they left. Lou spoke to Tom about it. "It's unimaginable in China, a father should bring his friends to the restaurant where his son was a waiter and pay a tip to his son!" Tom took Lou's comment quite casually and said it was common in the United States. Lou told him people in China would look down on a waiter. Certainly nobody would let his or her friends know that his son was a waiter. Tom responded, "Maybe you would be even more surprised if you know who my father is. He is president of your university!" Lou was utterly at a loss for words.

Lou's first quarter began. Within a few days, he noticed several things he could not understand. Students in the United States were very active in class. They seemed to have an endless number of questions every day. Some of the questions sounded facetious or silly. Lou thought, "Why are they not afraid of losing face before others?" Even more puzzling, a student raised a question and the professor simply said, "You've got me there. I cannot answer it right now. That's a really insightful question." In China it was unacceptable for a professor to admit his or her ignorance so openly, and students would despise such a professor. A professor should know everything.

What Lou found even stranger was that another professor took his dog into the classroom and introduced himself as a single man. Many students were enjoying soft drinks and snacks during the class. Soon Lou's advisor called him into his office and asked why he was so silent in class. He told Lou his lack of participation in class activities might affect his grade.

Lou was frustrated. He had been in the United States only a month and many strange things had happened in that short period of time. Lou wondered what else he would encounter.

Case Questions

1. What do you think of Lou's uncle? Why do you think the uncle introduced Lou to the restaurant owner instead of having Lou stay with him?

2. What is the hidden reason for Tom's work in the restaurant?

3. Why was Tom's father proud of his son?

4. Is there any relationship between the class behavior and culture? Please explain.

5. What suggestion could you make to Lou to help him adjust to his new world?

CASE | *Business is Business Wherever You Are*

Susan Tucker Kinney, University of Georgia

The weather in Minneapolis was a frigid −3 degrees as Jennifer opened the massive doors at Old World Spice. She was insensitive to the cold, however, as she thought about her new appointment. Imagine! She was soon to be Jennifer Sanders, regional manager, for the district office in Kerala, India.

She had worked hard for this level of responsibility and this assignment. In the seven years she had been with the organization, she had accepted all assignments without complaint. Admittedly she was tired from working 60-hour weeks and taking work home on weekends and on vacation. She could not say that she had made many friends in the company but that was not important to her. She had proven to management that she was a "company player" and willing to sacrifice her personal life for the good of the company.

For a while Jennifer had been worried that she would not get the Kerala post. She was in competition with a relatively new member of the firm. John Kirshner, a 1988 graduate of the University of Minnesota, had majored in international business and spoke four languages fluently. Although he did not have much of a track record with the company, he was well liked and was quickly gaining respect for his ability to communicate with the increasing number of foreign suppliers the company worked with. Apparently management had decided to reward Jennifer for her dedication to the company.

The day after the appointment was announced, she found on her desk a folder labeled *India: A Study of the Culture and the People.* The author was John Kirshner. The index listed such topics as traditions, religion, languages, dress, climate, and industry. "What nerve," she thought. "Does he believe I need to read one of his old essays?" She threw the report into the trash together with a packet of information on company training programs. Her time before leaving for India would be taken up with paperwork and reports. Besides, she had got by quite well so far on her own resources. "Business is business no matter where you are and I am a proven winner," she thought. She began to set an agenda for making the move.

Case Questions

1. Compile a list of criteria Old World Spice might use in selecting employees for overseas assignments.

2. Given the selection instrument you designed in response to Question 1, how might John and Jennifer compare?

3. You are Jennifer's immediate supervisor. What action will you take at this time to ensure that she is prepared for the move?

4. Assuming that Jennifer goes to India with no real understanding of the society, what kind of problems is she likely to encounter?

5. Find a recent article on India and note the ways the culture is different from your own.

A Rough Start | CASE

Margaret Fitch-Hauser, Auburn University

Sandra Lewis had been with Takabishi USA for a week when it was announced that the chairman of Takabishi Inc. would be coming from Japan to visit the U.S. locations. Sandra's boss, Jackie, needed every available minute to do the paperwork involved and asked Sandra to coordinate and schedule the events for the visit. She told Sandra to check the company's library for information on Mr. Takabishi, on the parent company, and on Japanese social and business customs. This trip would be Mr. Takabishi's first visit to the new plant and it was crucial that everything go smoothly.

Sandra found the material in the company library that Jackie had recommended. After carrying it to her office, she decided to begin by making a list of the tasks that she needed to complete in order to be ready for Mr. Takabishi's visit. This done, she picked up a book on Japanese customs and glanced at the table of contents. She noticed a section on gift giving. Oh yes, she thought, I remember that the Japanese like to exchange gifts. Immediately, Sandra put the book down and added gifts to her list.

Once Sandra had made all of the arrangements for Mr. Takabishi's visit, she wrote him a letter and enclosed the itinerary. She signed her letter "Sandra."

On the big day Sandra was undecided about what to wear. Finally satisfied with her appearance, she hurried to her car. If she caught all of the lights just right, she would be only a fashionable five minutes late.

Unfortunately, finding a parking place took longer than she had expected and she was 20 minutes late. Near the arrival gate she saw a group of Japanese men talking with some American officers of the company. They were all waiting for her, because she had scheduled herself to escort the party to the first stop on the itinerary.

Sandra wished she had taken more time to look at the company reports so that she would know which man was Mr. Takabishi. Unfortunately, she had not, and so she approached the nearest of the blue-suited men and shook hands and introduced herself. She failed to notice that the young man seemed embarrassed as he bowed to her. Sandra, not accustomed to bowing, decided not to return the bow. She did notice that a distinguished-looking man at the end of the line appeared to be shocked at her behavior.

After introductions, she opened her briefcase and gave each member of the party one of the gifts that she had selected for the occasion. As she handed each unwrapped box to a recipient, beginning with the guest standing nearest to her, she noticed they all looked uncomfortable. In an attempt to put everyone at ease, she urged that they open the boxes. Inside each box was a shiny pen with a digital clock near the clip. On a band around the pen were the words "made in Japan."

Sandra then gave them all a copy of the day's schedule of events and led them to cars waiting to take them to the hotel. As soon as they were settled, Sandra returned to her office. There Jackie was waiting for her, clearly unhappy.

Case Questions

1. Why did Jackie suggest that Sandra read about Mr. Takabishi, the company, and Japanese customs?

2. What mistakes might Sandra have avoided if she had taken the time to read the material Jackie suggested?

3. Why do you think the young man that she first shook hands with was uncomfortable?

4. Of what significance are the words "made in Japan" on the gift pens?

5. Of what significance is Sandra's late arrival at the airport?

PART FIVE

CAREER STRATEGIES

Writing a Resumé

Doug Mills has been a successful recruiter for one of the Big Six accounting firms for 12 years. He prides himself on his ability to screen college students, based on their resumés, and to select good candidates for introductory interviews. Doug knows that accounting is a profession built on accuracy and precision. He believes resumés need to reflect those characteristics. He therefore looks for high grades—at least a 3.0 overall. He also seeks indications of involvement in the profession beyond majoring in accounting, such as membership in an accounting club. Finally—and he applies this rule rigorously—if he sees a misspelled word or uncorrected typo, he discards the resumé immediately and does not even send an acknowledgment letter.

Learning Objectives

1 *To understand the components of an effective resumé.*

2 *To learn several ways to compile a resumé.*

3 *To learn how to package the resumé.*

Whether you are a student about to finish school, a person reentering the job market after a period of time, or someone simply wanting to find a more attractive position than the one you have now, you will find that people use a variety of techniques to find a job:

- Personal contacts through family and close friends
- Personal contacts through acquaintances
- Employment agencies
- College placement centers
- Mass mailings
- Newspaper advertisements
- Unannounced visits to businesses
- Community surveys of employers

No matter which technique you use, your success in convincing a company to hire you instead of someone else depends on three factors: your background, your effectiveness in presenting that background, and your performance in the job interview.

THE USES AND CHARACTERISTICS OF RESUMÉS

The resumé and the cover or application letter that accompanies the resumé are usually the first contact between you and the organization; therefore, you will be evaluated through these documents. In reading a resumé and letter of application, the recruiter seeks three types of information: (1) Do you have the basic credentials for the job, such as a business degree for a business job? (2) Do you have background that elevates you beyond the basic qualifications, such as related job experience? and (3) Are you good at what you do?

Recruiters are particularly interested in whether applicants are good at what they do.

This third type of information is the most important to most recruiters. Many recruiters prefer an applicant who is good at ditch digging, for example, to one who is only mediocre in a job. The enthusiasm, leadership, or responsibility that emerges when you hold a job indicates your effectiveness. This effectiveness is sometimes referred to as your track record. If you can show a history of winning, recruiters will anticipate your continued success. Most resumés transmit the first type of information; many transmit the second type. Few, however, take full advantage of the third type.

Three characteristics define resumés: they are factual, categorized, and tabulated. The information in resumés can be substantiated and is not opinion. The location of your high school and the date of your graduation, for example, can be verified. Your belief that you are enthusiastic cannot be verified. The information is categorized or grouped under headings, such as education or job experience. The headings tend to be mutually exclusive. Information in a resumé is not presented in sentence form; it is tabulated much like a balance sheet, with headings and subheadings and responses to queries, such as *Interests: writing programs for home computer, playing tennis.*

Whether or not you use a resumé to obtain interviews, you will need one at some time during the job hunting process. Interviewers refer to the resumé during the interview. Resumés are used later to compare applicants for a position or for further evaluation.

COMPONENTS OF AN EFFECTIVE RESUMÉ

The order of the components in a resumé may determine the image or tone of the message. Just as we organize persuasive letters differently from positive letters, we need to plan the organization of the resumé. It will benefit from moving stronger components to positions of strength and emphasis and playing down weaker components by either omitting them or placing them near the end.

The most effective resumé is one that presents factual data in an enticing, clear, positive, and individualized fashion. The effective resumé writer does not think in terms of just filling in blanks on a form; instead he or she decides which information has the most value and how it can be phrased for maximum effect.

Heading

A required part of every resumé, the heading should contain your name, address, and telephone number. The word *resumé* is an optional part of the heading, although it is being included less often than in the past. If you have two addresses, one at school and one at home, put both in the heading. Listing your home address will help an employer contact you when you are no longer in school. Here is an example:

ROBERT J. ANDERSON

(until June 1, 1991)	(after June 1, 1991)
134 Ansley Street	1897 Clearwater Road
Atlanta, GA 30324	Duran, IA 52242
(404) 863-2717	(319) 422-5799

If you have only one address, place it either to the far left or directly beneath your name.

You may wonder why no photograph is used with a resumé. In times past pictures were usually included. However, federal laws now prohibit employers from discriminating on the basis of several factors, including race, sex, and age. If you put your picture on your resumé, someone at the company that receives it will likely feel obliged to obscure it. Rather than put a potential employer in an embarrassing position, omit the picture.

Resumés should not include a photograph.

Availability Date

Companies budget many of their entry-level openings to coincide with graduation dates. For example, Doug Mills' organization at the beginning of this chapter might have five openings beginning July 1 (for May and June graduates), two September 1 openings (for August graduates), and two January 1 openings (for December graduates).

Openings may occur in every month of the year, of course. As a convenience to the potential employer, however, place your date of availability on the resumé. This will enable the employer to more easily fit you into a budgeted position. Give both the month and year and, if possible, the specific day:

AVAILABLE: June 1, 1991

If you are available for a position at the time you complete your resumé, you might write the availability component like this:

AVAILABLE: Immediately

If you know that the availability date is not important to the company, place this information near the end, perhaps with personal data.

Objective

The impression you make on your potential employer is due in large part to how clearly defined your goals are. As Chapter 23 explains, interviewers will normally ask about both your short-term and your long-term goals. To many interviewers applicants with clear-cut goals show more maturity and readiness to pursue a profession than applicants who have no clear goals in mind. This is an example of a goal statement:

OBJECTIVE: Responsible career position in accounting or finance

Choose your words carefully. The word "responsible" says that you want and are willing to assume responsibility.The word "career" says that you want to stay with the company. Employees are expensive to replace. In some organization the cost of hiring and training a replacement could be $2,000 or $3,000. Therefore, at the front of every interviewer's mind will be the question, how long will this applicant stay with this company?

Be sure that the position you mention in the goal statement is as specific as you can make it. Accounting and finance are fairly closely related. Try to avoid general statements (for example, general business) or statements that represent you as the proverbial jack of all trades (for example, accounting or real estate). On the other hand, when using one resumé for many openings, some generality may be necessary. Perhaps you will even omit this component.

Are you willing to relocate or to travel? If so, state your willingness along with your objective:

OBJECTIVE: Responsible entry-level position in personnel management
with opportunity for advancement. Willing to relocate and
travel.

The reason for placing relocation and travel information with your objective is that every reader will notice it.

This information is tremendously important to some businesses. In recent years many managers in large companies have turned down promotions and salary increases simply because relocation was involved. If you are willing to relocate, let the reader know as soon as possible. Such willingness is critical for many sales positions. No matter what position you seek, however, some traveling may be involved, especially during the training and orientation period.

Education

The education section of your resumé should contain these important items:

1. When you received your degrees or diplomas
2. Where you earned your degrees or diplomas
3. Your major or field of concentration
4. Relevant course work
5. Your grade point average, if appropriate

Where you place the education component in your resumé will depend on which format you decide to use. However, most students just finishing school place education directly beneath the objective.

If you have or are expecting to receive a four-year degree, you might write your education component like this:

EDUCATION:

June 1990   Bachelor of Business Administration, Southern University, Atlanta, Georgia. Major in personnel management. Minor in marketing. Course work included wage and salary administration, personnel selection, personnel administration, EEO, and ERISA. GPA of 3.8 on a 4-point scale. Graduated summa cum laude.

June 1986   Graduated with honors from Southwestern High School, Roanoke, Virginia.

If the location of your college or university is well-known, then omit the city and state, but always include the city and state for your high school entry.

The course work you list should be related to the objective stated in your resumé. Be careful about listing courses by name, as often the name of a course is misleading or ambiguous. For example, if a course called Human Resource Management focused primarily on such topics as Equal Employment Opportunity (EEO) and the Occupational Safety and Health Act (OSHA), then your course work statement should read "EEO and OSHA."

Finally, list your grade point average (GPA) only if you want to call attention to it. Many employers are more interested in your major, work experience, and activities than in your GPA. Be sure to show the scale on which your GPA is computed (for example, 3-point scale, 6-point scale). Also, if your overall GPA is not high but the GPA in your major is, then state, "GPA in major of 3.6 on a 4-point scale."

Grade point averages are listed only if the applicant wants to call attention to them.

If you are a graduate of a two-year college, then you might use this format for your education component:

EDUCATION:

June 1991   Associate of Arts in Business Administration, Atlanta Junior College, Atlanta, Georgia. Concentration in general business. Forty hours of business course work, including Administrative Practices, Business Communication, Marketing Principles, and Accounting Theory. GPA of 3.4 on a 4-point scale.

June 1989   Graduated with honors from Central High School, Atlanta, Georgia.

Finally, if you have a four-year degree but also attended a two-year school during your college career, you can work both colleges into your resume like this:

EDUCATION:

June 1991 (expected)	Bachelor of Business Administration, Southern University, Atlanta, Georgia. Major in personnel management. Minor in marketing. Course work included wage and salary administration, personnel selection, personnel administration, EEO, and ERISA. GPA of 3.8 on a 4.0 scale. Graduated summa cum laude.
September 1987 to June 1989	Attended Wolfson Junior College, Roanoke, Virginia. Concentration in general business. GPA of 3.9 on a 4.0 scale.
June 1987	Graduated with honors from Southwestern High School, Roanoke, Virginia.

If you write your resumé before you receive your final degree, you can place "expected" beneath the date shown. If that date is only two or three months away, however, most potential employers reading your resumé will understand that the degree is expected.

High school information is often omitted from the resumé.

If you are short of space — and especially if you do not have high school honors — consider omitting or reducing the high school information.

Work Experience

For every full-time or part-time job that you list, include the following information:

1. When you held the job
2. Your job title
3. Who your employer was
4. Your responsibilities
5. Your accomplishments

Here is an example:

WORK EXPERIENCE:

| September 1989 to present | Part-time Registration Clerk, Holiday Hotel, Atlanta, Georgia. Responsibilities include registering hotel guests, making reservations, processing checkouts, and handling guest problems. Earned approximately 30 percent of college expenses. |
| Summer 1989 | Sales Representative, Eastern Book Company, Baltimore, Maryland. Responsibilities included calling on potential customers, processing orders, and delivering merchandise. Was top salesperson in 12-person territory. Earned 70 percent of college expenses for 1989–1990 year. |

The applicant who has held a number of part-time jobs might list only the goal-related ones.

First, notice that the jobs are listed in reverse chronological order — most recent job first. Second, if you held a number of jobs during college and high school, you may not want to list them all. Choose those most related to your objective. Remember that no matter how menial the job seemed to you, to a potential employer your having worked says two things: (1) this applicant has been out in the real world and therefore has actual business experience and (2) this applicant shows initiative and responsibility.

Dates of Employment

The dates in the example are not exact—you do not need to list the actual days you began and ended your employment. If you held the same job at different times, you can state "Summers 1988, 1989" or "Summers 1988, 1989 and Christmas 1989."

Job Title

Some jobs do not have specific titles. If you had such a job, simply make up a descriptive title for it. For example, if your job was serving customers at the counter of a fast-food restaurant, then you can call your position "counter clerk." Each job title is underlined so that it stands out.

Name of Employer

When you list employers, show their names and locations. If your potential employer wants to call for a reference or verify your employment, this will make it easier to do so.

Responsibilities

The key word is responsibilities, not duties. Again, your purpose is to show that you are capable of assuming responsibility. You need not list all of your responsibilities, just those you think are the most important.

Accomplishments

Any accomplishment that your potential employer can verify belongs in your list of accomplishments. The work-experience example illustrates two kinds of accomplishments: earning money to attend school and succeeding as a salesperson. Other types of accomplishments you can list include supervising other people or training your replacement, both of which show leadership skills to many potential employers. If you assumed your supervisor's duties while he or she was absent, include that information. Perhaps you made some suggestion that was adopted by your employer. If so, then list it. Even seemingly minor accomplishments, such as an employee-of-the-month award, being placed in charge of other student summer help, or being assigned security or cash-handling duties, can impress the person who reads your resumé.

The accomplishments section — also called results — spotlights your track record, the third and most important type of information found in a resumé.

Accomplishments help set the applicant apart from others.

Honors

Any school-related honor you received belongs in an honors section of your resume. If you have only one honor, however, you should consider including it in the activities section and renaming that section honors and activities. You can look outside school activities for honors as well. Here is a sample honors section:

HONORS: College
Sigma Iota Epsilon (National Management Honorary, 1990
Phi Kappa Phi (Scholastic Honorary), 1990
Cardinal Club (Freshman Honorary), 1989
High School
Beta Club (Scholastic Honorary), 1988
National Honor Society (Languages), 1988
Others
Selected social director of neighborhood bicycling group.
Chosen to represent senior high-school students from area
at national church convention.

A brief explanation of each honor is provided as well as the year the honor was received. Never list your honors in paragraph form. An interviewer is likely to forget which honors you have received. If you list them as in the example, the interviewer might at least remember how many honors you have received.

Activities

The activities in which you have been involved constitute an important part of your resumé. Activities differ from honors in that honors are bestowed upon you by others; activities are things you yourself decide to do. To most potential employers, activities you list show interest in other people, practice in developing interpersonal relationships, and social skills. If you have served as an officer in some organization, you may also have leadership skills. Include organizations at school as well as church, volunteer, and other outside activities.

ACTIVITIES: College
Society for the Advancement of Management (vice president, 1988–1990).
Member, Democrats in Action, 1988–present.
Chairperson, Red Cross blood drive on campus, 1989.
High School
Spanish Club, 1987–1988 (president, 1988).
Tennis team (lettered three years).

Interests

You may have wondered, when filling out an application for a job, why you were required to list your hobbies or interests. To many potential employers your interests are as important as your activities. Many employers seek a person who has a balance of individual and group interests. Consider the following:

INTERESTS: Reading, jogging, skiing, photography.

Some interviewers will perceive a person with interests like these to be an isolate. There are no real group activities listed. Other interviewers will have an equally negative perception of:

INTERESTS: Tennis, basketball, chess, backgammon.

Interests such as these might depict a total group orientation. The interviewer may perceive you as too dependent upon others.

Your interests should include a mix of group and individual activities. However, do not list interests that you do not actually have. An interviewer will ask you to discuss the most recent book you have read or how often you jog. If you do not actually read or jog, you have placed yourself in an embarrassing predicament.

The resumé should show a mix of group and individual interests.

You may include hobbies instead of interests, if you wish, or you may combine the two. Interests are things that interest you, even though you may not do them often. Hobbies are usually done with some regularity or frequency.

In presenting hobbies or interests, keep these points in mind:

- Seek a balance between individual and group activities. For example, include "read science fiction" with "play intramural football."
- Seek a balance between athletic and more cerebral activities. Contrast "avid jogger" with "enjoy classical piano concertos."
- Avoid items that appear average, or make you appear average, such as "watch TV" or "go to football games."
- Try to find job-related items, such as writing programs for a home computer or charting marketing trends in some industry.
- Be specific in your description if possible. "Sorority tennis team cocaptain" is better than just "tennis."
- Job-oriented organizations, such as a business fraternity or a real estate club, are valuable assets. Volunteer work, such as blood drive worker, or hospital candy striper, also carries a positive message.
- Do not overdo it. A list of too many items suggests you may not have enough time or interest for the job. A total of about six hobbies, interests, or activities is probably the maximum.

Achievements

If you have at least three major achievements, consider illuminating them. These achievements might be found in more depth elsewhere on your resumé but are highlighted here.

Make sure your items are true achievements. To emphasize achievements and then present weak items is quite negative. Similarly, having only one or two items under the heading shows a weakness in achievements, not a strength. Five or six items should be the most you present, however; more tend to diminish your entries.

Here are some sample achievements entries:

ACHIEVEMENTS: Earned 90 percent of college expenses.
                  Achieved 3.8 GPA (on 4.0 system) for four-year
                  period.

Elected president of Finance Club.
Dean's list (three semesters).
Re-employed each of four summers by same
company.
Selected by (college/dean/fraternity/sorority/busi-
ness organization/church group, etc.) as representative at (convention, meeting, seminar, etc.)

Personal Data or Background Information

Personal data are an optional component of the resumé.

Businesses are prohibited from making selection decisions based on your age, race, sex, marital status, and other personal data unless the data are bona fide occupational qualifications. Thus, this section of your resumé is optional. You should include personal data only if you think it will help you get the position.

With ongoing pressure to keep resumés brief, constant concern by companies to avoid making discriminatory hiring decisions, and a hesitancy by many applicants to disclose personal details, clearly the trend is away from including the personal data section—or at least from including much information in it.

A personal data section may be helpful in some instances. For example, if you are an unmarried female who is also willing to relocate, then your marital status might help you although legally it should not. You may wish to check with your placement office for guidance on local or regional approaches to this component.

Personal data on a resumé usually includes the following:

PERSONAL: Age: 22   Birth Date: August 15, 1968
              Health: Excellent

With both age and birth date provided, you do not need to update your age if a birthday occurs during the job-seeking process.

Other items sometimes included as background information are the following:

- Geographic preference
- Date of availability
- Percentage of college expenses earned
- Hometown
- Social Security number
- Physical characteristics (height, weight)
- Religious preference
- Family background (number of children, information about spouse or parents, etc.)
- Preference for nonsmoking environment

Many of these items are inconsequential to the job—you would only include items you believe might reflect favorably on you. You should also be aware that you are volunteering this information. Current laws are clear

BOXED IN	*AN ETHICAL DILEMMA*

"George, you're misrepresenting yourself on your resumé and you're going to get caught."

"People stress their best qualities on resumés, Juanita. It's assumed you're going to try to make yourself look good."

"That's probably true up to a point, but it's dishonest to say your grades are 3.0 and that you have related job experience."

"I just rounded 2.86 to a 2.9 and 2.9 is almost 3.0. Besides, by the time I graduate I'll probably have a 3.0. And who's to say that my work serving hamburgers doesn't have managerial overtones? Companies want people who have an optimistic outlook and who can see the bright side of things. I'm just improving the perception they'll have of me."

"You're pushing the 'facts' too far. You're being unethical."

"And you're confusing me. I wish you had kept your ideas on business ethics to yourself."

George feels boxed in. What would you do?

that you are not required to give information about such items as religion or family background.

Military Service

An entry pertaining to your military service is appropriate only if you received an honorable discharge. Also, persons with military service receive bonus points on aptitude tests when applying for many civil service positions.

If your military service is extensive (more than two years) and relates closely to your objective, you might enter it as part of your work experience component. Otherwise, the entry should be brief:

> <u>MILITARY SERVICE</u>:   U.S. Navy, 1984–1986. Served as supply officer on a destroyer. Discharged as lieutenant (junior grade).

Licenses and Other Accreditations

Possessing a license or some professional certificate may be important to your getting a position. For example, if you are applying for a real estate salesperson's position, having a real estate license should help. Other examples of licenses or accreditations that might be entered on your resumé are licensed practical nurse, registered nurse, certified public accountant, certified nuclear safety engineer, certified life underwriter, and any teaching certificate relevant to your objective. An entry for this component can appear like this:

PROFESSIONAL LICENSES:	Licensed Practical Nurse, State of Illinois Certified Nurse–Midwife, State of Illinois

Special Skills

Special skills include computer languages and foreign languages.

Some jobs you may apply for require special skills. For example, many computer programmers are expected to know several computer languages as well as different types of computer systems. Their special skills component might appear as follows:

COMPUTER SKILLS:	Languages:	COBOL, FORTRAN, SYSTEX
	Systems:	IBM 4381 and AS/400; CYBER 380 VAX VMS; Sun VME System

Many applicants for positions in international business must know one or more foreign languages. These special skills can appear on the resumé in the same format as the computer skills:

FOREIGN LANGUAGES:	Speak and read German and Spanish fluently. Read and write Italian.

Any special skill you possess that is relevant to your objective should be entered on your resumé.

Professional Memberships

Many college students are members of campus chapters of professional organizations. Your membership in such organizations can be listed under the activities component, unless you would like to draw special attention to it, as in this example:

PROFESSIONAL MEMBERSHIPS:	American Marketing Association, 1989–present American Society for Personnel Administration, 1985–present

References

Unless you are changing jobs and want to keep your decision private as long as possible, consider listing your references on your resumé. Phrases such as "references available upon request" are inconvenient to the personnel specialist, who must either call or write you, ask for your references, and then contact them. You'll save the specialist time if references are on the resumé. If your references are easy to check, he or she may be more inclined to consider you.

Categories of references are professional, character, and educational.

References are supplied for possible verification of the facts you have presented on the resumé or for additional information. References fall into three main categories: (1) professional references, who can speak about your professional ability for this job, such as your knowledge of accounting or computer science; (2) character references, who know your personality, such as your industriousness or ambition; and (3) educational references, who can respond to questions about your scholarly achievements and background, such as your performance in a management class.

Former employers are frequently used as professional references; friends, neighbors, or colleagues are used as character references; and teachers are used as educational references. Keep in mind, though, that how they know you determines the category of reference. A boss may be a friend (character reference), for example. Of course, one reference may be found in several categories. Never list a person as a reference until you have obtained permission to do so.

Some types of people should generally be avoided as references. Family members, clergy, or students are assumed to be biased in your favor. Their opinions, therefore, are discounted.

You may wish to categorize your references under subheadings in the references component. Because educational references are close to professional references in the type of information they supply, the two can be combined under the professional references subheading.

When you use references subheadings, supply an equal number of references under each subheading for balance. That is, supply two professional references to equalize two character references. Here is an example of a reference section from a resumé:

REFERENCES (with permission)

Professional	Character
Dr. Lillian Patterson	Ms. Betty Weatherford
Department of Business	Department of English
Southern University	Southern University
P.O. Box 3561	P.O. Box 3561
Atlanta, GA 30723	Atlanta, GA 30723
(404) 731-8265	(404) 731-8143
Mr. William Lucey	Dr. John L. Harper, D.D.S.
Distribution Manager	Harper Dental Center
Eastern Book Company	Maguire, GA 30703
4324 Brownsboro Road	(404) 737-2245
Baltimore, MD 13426	
(301) 926-5333	

Be sure each of your references has a title (for example, Dr., Mr., Mrs., or Ms.) so that the personnel specialist who telephones them will know how they are to be addressed. Give the complete business address and telephone number. Never list the reference's home address unless the reference prefers it.

What your references say about you will not — unless it is negative — have a great impact on your evaluation. Some potential employers will not even contact your references, although others will. Employers expect that anyone you list as a reference will support your application. Nevertheless, you will be required normally to submit at least three names of people who are willing to recommend you.

Should you decide not to list your references on the resumé, you might use one of the following statements:

REFERENCES: Excellent references available upon request.
REFERENCES: Excellent references available at:
Career Planning and Placement Center, Southern
University, Atlanta, GA 30723.

You can choose from among the 15 components those that you think will best show your accomplishments. The balance of the chapter will be devoted to packaging these components in a compelling format.

RESUMÉ FORMATS

From a variety of formats, you can select the one you think presents your resumé components in the best way. The formats presented here will meet most needs, but creating your own format for a specific company may be even more effective. Keep your resumé balanced, clean, and esthetically pleasing.

Resumé Format for New Graduates

A resumé format tailored to a student about to receive an associate degree and enter the job market with little work experience is shown in Figure 22.1.

In this example most section headings are capitalized, underlined, and set apart in the left-hand margin. A reader can quickly find the information that is most important. For example, some will want to read about work experience first; others, about education. The information is blocked attractively, several spaces in from the section headings. The appearance of a resumé is almost as important as its contents.

Another example, this one for a graduating senior, is shown in Figure 22.2. It has several additional components and carries over to a second page. Note that the references are listed across, not down, the page to save space and to make them easier to identify.

Chronological Resumé Format

Both the chronological and the functional resumé formats are typically used by people with extensive work experience. In the **chronological resumé** the work experience component appears early and describes each position in detail. An example appears in Figure 23.3.

Chronological or functional resumé formats are appropriate when work experience is extensive.

With this resumé format the individual's work experience consumes the most space. Work experience also precedes education, because it is more important.

Functional Resumé Format

The **functional resumé** emphasizes kinds of work. Using the functional format, you can choose the qualifications you think are important for the position you want, list them separately, and show how you possess each

FIGURE 22.1 ▪ *Typical Resumé for a Graduating Student*

```
                        HOLLY M. CLARK
                      1554 Westside Drive
                      Atlanta, GA 30110
                        (404) 638-2176

AVAILABLE:       July 1, 1991

OBJECTIVE:       Responsible entry-level position in computer
                 programming.  Willing to relocate.

EDUCATION:       Associate of Arts in Computer Sciences, Northrup
June 1991        Junior College, East Point, Georgia. Concentration
(expected)       in Computer Analysis and Design. Course work
                 included Computer Design, Computer Programming,
                 COBOL, and FORTRAN.  GPA in concentration of 5.4
                 on a 6-point scale.

June 1989        Graduated from Southwest High School,
                 East Point, Georgia.

WORK             Part-Time Computer Programmer, Northrup Junior
EXPERIENCE:      College Computer Center.  Responsibilities include
September 1987   programming, checking system malfunctions, assisting
to present       students with computer jobs, keeping time-sharing
                 records on all users.

Summer and       Salesperson, Annette's Dress Shop, East Point,
Christmas        Georgia.  Responsibilities included assisting
Vacations        customers, stocking merchandise, creating
1987 to 1988     displays, and inventory.  Trained replacement at
                 the end of Summer 1988.

ACTIVITIES:      Baptist Student Union, 1990 to present
                 Staff writer, The Blue and Gold (Northrup Junior
                 College newspaper)

COMPUTER         Languages:  COBOL, FORTRAN
SKILLS:          Systems:  IBM PS/2 Model 80, Apple Macintosh

PROFESSIONAL     National Computer Science Association, 1989 to present
MEMBERSHIPS:     Computer Users of America, 1990 to present

INTERESTS:       Writing computer programs for home computer
                 Singing in church choir
                 Playing intramural tennis (doubles)

PERSONAL:        Age: 20   Birth Date: August 15, 1971
                 Health: Excellent

REFERENCES:      Available on request
```

of the qualifications. In Figure 22.4 an individual with little formal education and work experience was able to show himself to be highly competent.

There are five dimensions in effectively preparing your resumé that set you apart from — and above — the crowd.

1. Present positive information with positive phrasing.

2. Order your components and the items under the components with most important (to the reader) information first.

FIGURE 22.2 ▪ *Typical Resumé for a Graduating Senior*

ROBERT J. ANDERSON

(until June 1, 1991)   (after June 1, 1991)
134 Ansley Street, Apt. 4-B   1897 Clearwater Road
Atlanta, GA 30723   Duran, IA 63217
(404) 863-2717   (612) 422-5799

AVAILABLE:

 June 1, 1991

OBJECTIVE:

 Responsible career position in accounting or finance.

EDUCATION:

 Bachelor of Business Administration, Southern University,
 Atlanta, Georgia. Major in Accounting. Minor in Finance.
 Course work included Accounting Principles, Tax Accounting,
 Accounting Law, Financial Analysis, and Financial Planning.
 GPA of 3.7 on a 4-point scale (4.0 in major).
 Graduated summa cum laude, June 1991.
 Graduated with honors from Southwestern High School,
 Roanoke, Virginia, June 1987.

WORK EXPERIENCE:

 Part-Time Registration Clerk, Holiday Hotel, Atlanta, Georgia.
 Responsibilities include registering hotel guests, making
 reservations, processing check-outs, and handling guest
 problems. Have earned approximately 30 percent of college
 expenses. September 1990-present.
 Sales Representative, Eastern Book Company, Baltimore, Maryland.
 Responsibilities included calling on potential customers,
 processing orders, and delivering merchandise. Was top
 salesperson in 12-person territory. Earned 70 percent of
 college expenses for 1990-1991. Summer 1990.

HONORS:

 College
 Beta Alpha Psi (National Accounting Honorary), 1991
 Phi Kappa Phi (National Scholastic Honorary), 1991
 Cardinal Club (Freshman Honorary), 1988
 High School
 Beta Club (Scholastic Honorary), 1987
 National Honor Society (Languages), 1987

(Continued)

3. Show your track record. Indicate that you're good at what you do, whatever it may be.
4. Avoid being average or saying average things. Look for information that sets you apart from the crowd.
5. Aim for consistency and balance. Try to present equal numbers of items or to handle items similarly.

FIGURE 22.2 ▪ *Continued*

```
        Robert J. Anderson, p. 2



        ACTIVITIES:

            College
            Alpha Kappa Psi Business Fraternity
            (Vice President, 1987-1988, 1989-1991)
            Member, Democrats in Action, 1989-present
            Chairperson, campus Red Cross blood drive, 1990
            High School
            Spanish Club, 1986-1987 (President, 1987)
            Tennis team (lettered three years)

        INTERESTS:

            Reading, tennis, basketball, photography


        REFERENCES:

        Professional
        Dr. Lillian Patterson            Ms. Betty Weatherford
        Department of Business           Department of English
        Southern University              Southern University
        P.O. Box 3561                    P.O. Box 3561
        Atlanta, GA 30723                Atlanta, GA 30723
        (404) 731-8265                   (404) 731-8143

        Character
        Mr. William Lucey                Dr. John L. Harper, D.D.S.
        Distribution Manager             Harper Dental Care
        Eastern Book Company             Maguire, GA 30703
        4324 Brownsboro Road             (404) 737-2245
        Baltimore, MD 21426
        (301) 926-5333
```

Resumé Formats for Unusual Backgrounds

Each individual should try to transmit his or her unique personality when writing a resumé. Some people, however, have especially unusual backgrounds that may affect resumé preparation. Among them are the older-than-average student and the international student.

For the older-than-average student, the resumé should emphasize maturity, judgment, and drive. Because this person may have large gaps between high school and college graduation, some explanation may be

FIGURE 22.3   ▪   *Chronological Resumé Format*

WILMA G. PETERSON

4255 Tufts Road
Troy, IL 62234
(316) 614-8432

OBJECTIVE: Responsible and challenging management position in
                  health-care administration.

EXPERIENCE:
May 1990   Assistant Administrator, Cowans County Medical Center,
to present   Troy, Illinois
                  Responsibilities
                  - Directly responsible for hiring all hourly
                    employees to staff 100-bed hospital
                  - Administer wage and salary program for all staff
                    members
                  - Write policies and procedures for employee
                    handbook
                  - Supervise four department heads, two clerical
                    workers
                  Accomplishments
                  - Implemented technical training program for all
                    health-care employees; received highest possible
                    rating from Hospital Accreditation Board
                  - Implemented employee suggestion system that has
                    resulted in net savings to hospital of $75,327

September 1989   Nursing Supervisor, Cowans County Medical Center,
to April 1990   Troy, Illinois
                  Responsibilities
                  - Scheduled working hours for all nursing staff
                  - Supervised three shift supervisors
                  Accomplishments
                  - Promoted use of paraprofessionals to assist
                    nursing staff
                  - Awarded the Illinois Nurses' Association
                    "Supervisor of the Year Award," 1989

June 1986 to   Nurse, Groveland Hospital, Chicago, Illinois
August 1989   Responsibilities
                  - Patient care and medication, intensive care unit
                  - In charge of 12 other nurses on night shift
                    (June-August 1989)
                  Accomplishments
                  - Promoted to nurse-in-charge after three years
                  - Recommended changes in patient care were
                    implemented
                  - Salary increased 110 percent in 39-month period

(Continued)

necessary. If the void is filled by job experience, the reason for returning for the college degree may be given. Other activities, such as unemployment while raising a family, form a desirable rationale. Figure 22.5 is an example of a resumé for an older-than-average student.

The international student studying in the United States, graduating, and seeking a job here, faces some concerns different from native students. Prospective employers will want to know the answers to the following questions:

FIGURE 22.3 ▪ *Continued*

```
Wilma G. Peterson, p. 2


EDUCATION:
1990 to          Working toward a Master's Degree in Hospital
present          Administration, Acton College, St. Louis, Missouri.
                 Have completed 35 hours of course work.

June 1986        Bachelor of Science Degree in Nursing, St. Mary's
                 School of Nursing, Chicago, Illinois.  Graduated
                 with high honors.

PROFESSIONAL
MEMBERSHIPS:     - National Association of Hospital Administrators
                 - Illinois Association of Health Care Administrators
                 - National Association of Nursing Administrators

COMMUNITY
ACTIVITIES:      - American Cancer Society
                 - American Red Cross
                 - United Way (Campaign Chairperson, 1989)

INTERESTS:       - Collecting antiques
                 - Playing golf
                 - Listening to light opera

REFERENCES:      - Available upon request
```

▪ Are you seeking permanent, full-time employment (or will you have to leave the country in several years)?

▪ What is your language ability, especially with English? How are your writing and speaking abilities?

▪ What is your citizenship situation? Do you hold dual citizenships? Do you hold a visa? What kind? Do you plan to apply for American citizenship? When?

FIGURE 22.4   ▪   *Functional Resumé Format*

```
                              HAROLD D. WILLIAMS

        25 Clarkston Place
        Salem, OR 80135
        (817) 236-5926

        OBJECTIVE:        Responsible general management position in textile
                          or related field.  Willing to travel or relocate.


        EXPERIENCE:
        General           Supervised more than 100 hourly workers in two
        Management        textile plants.  Responsible for scheduling and
                          employee-relations problems.


        Quality           Met or exceeded quality standards 95 percent of
        Assurance         the time.  Helped establish quality standards for
                          new product.


        Production        Assisted in introduction, set-up, and operation of
                          new machines.  Am familiar with Crossland and
                          Weaveright equipment.


        Motivation        Used MBO, goal-setting, and piece-rate systems.

        WORK HISTORY:     1987 to present: Production Manager, Bostick Mills,
                          Salem, Oregon
                          1983-1987: Production Supervisor, Quality Fabrics,
                          Inc., Salem, Oregon


        EDUCATION:
        June 1983         Graduated from Owen Technical School, Salem, Oregon
                          (two-year program).  Concentration in Textile
                          Management.  Course work included Production
                          Planning, Quality Control, Supervision, Machine
                          Design, and Human Factors Engineering.


        June 1981         Graduated from Northside High School, Salem.

        COMMUNITY
        ACTIVITIES:       Lion's Club, 1988 to present
                          Toastmaster's International, 1983-1986


        SPECIAL
        QUALIFICATIONS:   Four years' related job experience
                          Supporting technical eduation
                          Record of achievement

        INTERESTS:        Hunting with bow and arrow, Pente, old movies

        REFERENCES:       Available on request
```

▪ Does your country expect you to serve some obligation, such as in the military? Have you served yet?
▪ Is there any reason to be concerned about security clearances? Have you been cleared before? By whom?
▪ Do you have family in your country? How often do you visit them? Do you have relatives in this country?

✓ *CHECKLIST for an Effective Resumé*[1]

____▮ **Forget the fancy stuff.** The person reading the resumé wants information pertinent to the job vacancy, not an elaborate format or colored paper.

____▮ **Keep it simple and hard-hitting.** Flowery language and literary affectations are a waste.

____▮ **Lead off with work experience,** going back from your current job. Education comes next. It's the easiest kind of resumé to write — and read.

____▮ **Stick to two pages.** A single page is even better.

____▮ **Customize.** Emphasizing one job experience over another depending on the position you're seeking.

____▮ **Don't blow your horn too loud.** When you accomplished something as part of a team, say so.

[1]Mark Silver, "Selling the Perfect You," *U.S. News & World Report,* February 5, 1990, 70–72. Reprinted with permission from U.S. News & World Report.

The international student may wish to address these questions in the resumé or in the letter of application. Figure 22.6 illustrates an international student resumé in which some of these issues are confronted.

THE PRINTED RESUMÉ

Traditionally the final versions of resumés were prepared on a typewriter. Copies were then made by professional offset printers. Now more and more resumés are being written on a computer and the finished product is output from a laser printer. The computer makes corrections and updates easier and provides design options that can be used to improve appearance. An inexpensive dot matrix printer is useful for draft copies, but you should always prepare the resumé you send to a prospective employer with a high quality printer.

A variation on using the computer is to prepare the resumé with desktop publishing software or advanced word processing software. The packages often can slightly increase or decrease a typeface size to expand or contract text to fit better on the printed page. Although you must be careful of overdoing the visual treatments, goals of an esthetically pleasing, balanced, and neat final product are more approachable with this software. See Figure 22.7 for an example of desktop publishing treatment applied to a resumé.

A third option is to use software that prepares the resumé, usually with a choice of formats, on the basis of your responses to questions. You can

FIGURE 22.5   ▪ *Resumé of Older-than-Average Student*

JUDITH KASTON BERRY

Bachelor of Business Administration
May 1991

<u>Permanent Address</u>
1717 Royal Court
Chicago, IL 60681
(312) 771-1003

<u>EDUCATION</u>:   Roosevelt University, 1983-1991
Degree: Bachelor of Business Administration
Major: Dual major in accounting and finance
Grades: Overall, 3.71/4.0; accounting, 3.6/4.0;
finance, 3.75/4.0
Honors: Dean's list (seven semesters); graduation
with honors anticipated; highest score ever achieved
on mock CPA exam

<u>RELATED</u>
<u>EXPERIENCE</u>:   Treasurer, Church of the Good Shepherd
Accountant/bookkeeper, part-time, Lion's Club
Women's Auxiliary
Treasurer, Cub Scout Pack #214
Bookkeeper and tax work, part-time (in home) for
Green Laundry, 10 months

<u>VOLUNTEER</u>
<u>WORK</u>:   St. Margaret's Children's Hospital, Chicago, work in
cafeteria
Church of the Good Shepherd, teach Sunday school
American Heart Association, fund-raiser
KCHI, public broadcasting station, auction volunteer

<u>PERSONAL</u>
<u>BACKGROUND</u>:   Age: 46
Family: Husband is employed in city transportation
department; three children (one senior in high
school, one junior at Roosevelt University, one
employed in St. Paul)

<u>OTHER</u>:   Geographic requirement: Chicago or northwest suburbs
Position sought: full-time job in accounting or
finance with an established company

<u>REFERENCES</u>: References available on request

---

*Resumé software
is available for
both IBM and
Macintosh
computers.*

accept the output or modify the spacing, typefaces, or content, or make other adjustments with your word processor. Resumé software for both IBM and Apple Macintosh computers often includes additional elements, such as a word processor, spelling checker, database for tracking contacts, mail-merge of network names and form letters, calendars for scheduling interviews, questionnaires for self-assessment, help with developing weekly action plans, lists of major companies, and extensive how-to manuals.

FIGURE 22.6 ∎ *Resumé of International Student*

```
                        CARLOS LUIS RODRIGUEZ

      Present address:                  Permanent address:
      1324 Halfhill Court               Monterrey 893 Col. Mexico
      Phoenix, AZ 60990                 Nuevo Laredo, Tamps., Mexico
      (602) 691-8891                    Phone: 7.27.21

                             OBJECTIVE

      Full-time position in data processing or systems management

                             EDUCATION

      Arizona State University 1987-1991, Bachelor of Business Administration
      Majors: Data Processing and Analysis, General Business
      Grades: Overall GPA, 3.31/4.0; DPA, 3.5/4.0

      Saltillo Escuela Preparatoria, Saltillo, Mexico  1985-1987

                             EMPLOYMENT

      Arizona State University  1990-1991
      Registration supervisor for university registration; in charge of 15
      student workers; responsible for security and student traffic flow.

      College of Business Administration  1988-1990
      Computation center PC laboratory assistant and mainframe computer
      operator; proctored lab; distributed printed mainframe output.

                          COMPUTER SKILLS

      Languages:              COBOL, FORTRAN, BASIC
      Software Familiarity:   PC WRITE, LOTUS 1-2-3, dBASE IV
      Hardware Familiarity:   IBM PS/2, Apple Macintosh, Novell networks

                             ACTIVITIES

      Data Processing Management Association
      Delta Sigma Pi National Professional Business Fraternity
      Chicano Business Students Association

                               OTHER

      Speak and write fluent English and Spanish
      Mexican citizen; hold student visa (since 1987); plan practicum and
      then application for U.S. citizenship
      Brother, a Chicago banker and legal alien; rest of family is in Mexico
      Geographic preference: Southwest United States

                             REFERENCES

      Available on request
```

SUMMARY

An important first step in the job-getting process is the development of an effective resumé. Many components may be used in a resumé: the heading, availability date, objective, education, work experience, honors, activities, interests, achievements, personal data, military service, licenses, special skills, professional memberships, and references.

Resumés may be prepared in a variety of formats: the format for new graduates that emphasizes education, the chronological format that fo-

FIGURE 22.7   ▪   *Resumé Prepared Using Desktop-Publishing Computer Program*

Samuel G. Toliver   1569 West College Avenue
                                         San Diego, CA 92183
                                         (619) 594-3241

Summary of Qualifications

Worked for four years as assistant manager of shoe department for a major San Diego retailer; joined Retailing Club at San Diego State University in 1988, maintained high grades for full college experience; applied retailing experience with social fraternity at SDSU as part of fund-raising campaign to help homeless people of the community.

Experience

Assistant Manager, Softstride Shoe Department of Federated Stores, San Diego, 1987-present.
Shift Supervisor, Homer's Hamburgers, 25 hours a week, Summer 1987.
Held following part-time jobs while in high school: paperboy, gas station cashier, cut grass for neighbors, worked in family grocery store.

Education

Bachelor of Business Administration, San Diego State University, May 1991.
Majored in marketing (GPA: 3.2) and minored in communication. Overall GPA: 3.0/4.0.
Took elective marketing courses in advanced retailing principles.
Internship in retailing under Dr. Ron Carruth, national retailing expert.

Honors

One of top ten marketing students in class of 1991 on the basis of grades.
"Best Salesperson," Shoe Department at Federated, May 1990.

Special Skills

Computer skills (Macintosh, VAX minicomputer): word processing, spreadsheets, and database.
Oral presentations: class and on-the-job experience making business presentations supported by graphics.

Activities

Retailing Club, San Diego State University: vice president (1990-91), head of sales force selling light bulbs in community to raise money for homeless people (Fall 1990), head of speaker selection committee (Spring 1990).
Sigma Phi Nu Social Fraternity: president of pledge class (1988), vice president for ceremonies (1989), assistant house manager (1990).

Hobbies and Interests

Intramural athletics with fraternity, mountain bicycling, reading Retailing News and Advertising Age.

cuses on experience, and the functional format that stresses skills. Whatever the format, the appearance of the resumé is important, too. Laser printers and computer desktop publishing software can enhance the delivery of the factual information.

Key Terms

▪ **resumé**

▪ **chronological resumé format**

▪ **functional resumé format**

Review Questions

1. What does the education component of a resumé contain? The work experience component?

2. What is meant by a balance of interests on the resumé? Why is this balance important?

3. Describe and differentiate among three different resumé formats.

4. What are special skills on a resumé?

5. Briefly discuss the final printing and copying of a resumé.

Exercises

1. Write a draft of your own resumé using the format for recent graduates. Exchange resumés with a classmate. Evaluate one another's drafts, suggesting changes you think will help.

2. Rewrite your resumé using either the chronological or the functional format. Do you see any advantages in this format for your resumé?

3. Make an appointment to interview a personnel officer in a company in your community. Your purpose is to find out the following:
a. What does he or she consider to be most important in a resumé?
b. How does he or she use the resumé in making selection decisions?
c. What does he or she not like in a resumé?
Write a brief report summarizing your interview findings.

4. Visit the placement center at your school. Ask to see the resumés of students who have left them for distribution to companies or that are otherwise available for public viewing. What things about these resumés are well done and what are some common mistakes?

5. Ask the placement office director at your school to speak to your club or business organization about effective resumé techniques. What inside advice can that person share to help your group?

Why Larry Can't Get an Interview | CASE

Anita S. Bednar, Central State University, Edmond, Oklahoma

Your friend Larry is despondent because he is unable to get an interview in his chosen career field of accounting. He has asked you to take a look at his resumé and accompanying cover letter and tell him what is wrong. Looking at them, you cannot find much that is right. You have learned in your business communication class how to write an effective resumé. Larry's cover letter and resumé (Figures 22A.1 and 22A.2) are not only ineffective; they are unacceptable.

FIGURE 22A.1 ▪ *Cover Letter of Larry Gray*

116 Walnut Street
Stinnett, TX 78903
September 1, 1991

Dear Sir,

My name is Larry Gray. I am interest in the Accounting position
you advertise about in the Amarillo Daily Globe.

I graduated this past May from North Central University in Big
Foot, Texas. I major in accounting and graduated with a 2.98
grade point in my accounting subjects and a 3.01 overall grade
point.

I am 23 years old and single. I am a hard worker and willing to
learn. I have no experience in accounting, becuase all of my
spare time during college was taken up by football.

I am very interested in accounting and would like an opportunity
to grow in this field. I hope you will consider me for the job.

Cordially yours,

Larry Gray

Larry Gray

Case Questions:

1. List everything in both the resumé and the cover letter that might keep Larry from getting a job interview in accounting.

2. Think about a better approach for Larry to use. He is from a small town, attended a small college on a football scholarship, and wants to work as an accountant in a mid-sized city. With no experience in accounting, what can he do to emphasize the positive and present himself in the best light?

FIGURE 22A.2 ▪ *Resumé of Larry Gray*

```
                              PERSONAL SATA

        Name:                      Larry Gray
        Address:                   116 Walnut St.
                                   Stinnett, Tex.   78903

        Phone:                     806-943-9345
        Marital Status:            Single
        Age:                       23

        High School

        I graduated from Stinnett High in Stinnett, Texas in 1987.
        I had a grade point average of ab about 3.4 upon graduation.

        College

        I graduated from North Central in May of this Year.  My degree was
        in accounting.  I had a 2.98 grade point average in my accounting
        subjects and a 3.01 overage grade point average.

        My only activity in college was football.  I recieve a scholarship
        upon graduation from high school from North Central. I was a four-year
        starter at fullback.  I earned several honors while playing:

            2nd-team all-conference fullback as a sophomore
            2nd-team all-conference fullback as a junior
            1st-team all-conference fullback as a senior
            1st-team all-distrist fullback as a senior

        Here are a list of my summer jobs I had during college.
        They were all in the oilfield and had nothing to do with accounting.

        company                    address              phone
        Jefferson Tool & Supply    N of town            229-1430
                                   Stinett, Tex. 78903
        ─────────────────────────────────────────────────────────
        Riley & Marshall           5 A Sw               223-8311
                                   Borger, Tx.   78110
        ─────────────────────────────────────────────────────────
        Hank's Wldg & Mch Shop     201 E. Vine          229-1167
                                   Stinnett, Tex. 78903
```

Resumé for an Average Student | CASE

Richard Pompian, The University of Texas at Austin

When a student has a good academic and work record, writing an effective resumé is often just a matter of not making a mistake. By definition, most students are average, however, and they need special help in presenting themselves honestly but effectively. Generally, techniques center around emphasizing the positive and deemphasizing the negative.

John Demetrius Smith is a senior at Washington College. He expects to graduate next May with a Bachelor of Business Administration degree in management. John wants to work for a large automobile manufacturer. National Motor Company will have a representative on campus and has invited potential interviewees to submit a resumé for prescreening. John decides to apply even though his 2.8 grade point average is below the "preferred" 3.0; it puts him just barely in the upper half of his class. He also knows that many other students with higher GPAs will apply. His current resumé shows that he has considerable experience with cars; in fact, he calls himself a car psychologist because he is quite good at diagnosing car problems and buyers' needs even when the customers are unclear about them.

However, John has been involved with little else except cars (except for some mechanical drafting and building construction). Academically, the best he can offer is a 3.05 in his major, though he is fluent in modern Greek and can converse in Spanish. Outside of management, his grades were best in personnel management, organizational behavior, and marketing. His extracurricular activity has been limited by the need to work. He plans to marry soon after graduation.

Knowing that you are majoring in business communication, John asks for your opinions and suggestions concerning his resumé, which appears in Figure 22B.

The purpose of the resumé is to get an interview, not the job itself. Accordingly, John should focus on presenting himself as a person who is interesting enough for the interviewer to want to meet. That means that he should emphasize qualifications, deemphasize negatives, and avoid looking like just another (in this case, weak) applicant. An analysis of his resumé reveals the following:

- *Graphics:* John's resumé is satisfactory overall but could benefit from some bold type for headings and main ideas, or at least from some underlining.
- *Name:* Should John use a middle name that reflects a possible ethnic origin? That could be an advantage in some circles, and in any case plain John Smith is not very exciting. A reasonable compromise might be to use the middle initial.
- *Address:* Fine, but will the reader know where to reach John when? A phrase such as "through June 3" will be helpful to the recipient.
- *Objective:* Improvements would be "Entry-level management position" and "major automobile manufacturer" rather than "car company." John should probably say what area of the company is of interest to him.
- *Education:* The positioning of this item is a mistake. John has nothing special to offer here: his degree is similar to that of his competitors (fellow applicants), and he has no special honors, GPA, or class standing. John's experience should come first because it establishes greater relevance and a high degree of interest in automobiles.

  Within the education section, items should begin with the credential earned. Lack of this specific mention may make the reader wonder if John successfully completed the program.

  John was wise not to mention his grade point average because it was below the 3.0 mentioned by the recruiter. To show that he is not totally lacking

FIGURE 22B ▪ *Resumé of John Demetrius Smith*

```
                            JOHN DEMETRIUS SMITH

         Local Address: 422 Fourth St., Rydal, PA 19046 / (215) 998-0405
         Permanent Address: 312 Ford Rd., Falls, NY 14303 / (919) 245-0090




     OBJECTIVE:      Management position with major car company;
                     eventual move into senior management.

     EDUCATION:      Washington College, School of Business Administration,
                     major in management, 1979-1983

                     Glen Sigforce High School, Falls, New York, 1975-1979

     EXPERIENCE:     Night manager, Mel's Auto Parts,
                     Rydal, Pennsylvania, 1989-1990

                     Bought, repaired, and sold wrecked cars,
                     Falls, New York, 1985-1988

                     Salesman, Good Deal Used Cars,
                     Falls, New York, 1983-1985

                     Mechanic's helper, Al's Service Station,
                     Falls, New York, 1977-1979

     ACTIVITIES:     High school varsity baseball
                     Lettermen's Club
                     Auto Club (treasurer)

     INTERESTS:      Sports, cars, hunting and fishing, rock music

     HONORS:         Mechanical Arts Award, Auto Club
                     Employee of the Month, Good Deal Used Cars

     AVAILABILITY:   June 1990

     REFERENCES:     On request
```

academically, he could and probably should add: Grade point average in major: 3.0+

Experience: John needs to be a bit less modest. He should tell what he did and what he accomplished in each position. He will achieve greater credibility by mentioning specific facts and numbers: number of cars and dollar value sold, skills learned, and so on.

Activities: John should mention at least one college activity to round out the list. He should put his titles, if any, first. Some interviewers will want to know which sport he lettered in.

▪ *Interests:* This list is satisfactory, but John might want to find out a little about his reader. Will this reader be impressed (positively or negatively) by entries such as "rock music"? John may want to delete one or more items, depending on what he finds out about the interviewer.

▪ *Availability:* Satisfactory, but "Available June 1990" could be placed at the end of the objective entry unless other items are added under the availability heading.

▪ *References:* John needs credibility, and his references should be listed in order to help achieve that. His references should be as impressive as possible — ideally, one or two each of the best business, academic, and personal references. John should get permission first.

▪ *Other Items:* Does John have location needs or preferences? Is he willing to travel? Unless he is inflexible, these items should be mentioned tactfully; for example, "New York or Northeast preferred; up to 30 percent travel acceptable." These items too can be placed under objective or availability.

John appears to have participated very little in extracurricular activities during college. If this is because he worked his way through, he could include the entry, "Percentage of college expenses earned: 65 percent." This emphasizes his commitment and at least partially explains his lack of extracurricular activities. John could also join a professional association or two and list them in an affiliations section.

Case Question

1. What could be done to improve Smith's resumé? Be specific.

CASE | ## *The Resumé: Path to an Interview – and a Job*

Richard J. Barnhart, San Francisco State University

Now that you are familiar with the theory of resumé writing, you should be able to pinpoint the devices that distinguish an acceptable resumé from a truly effective one.

Figures 22C.1 and 22C.2 show two resumés prepared by a young marketing graduate with a few years of business experience who set for himself the goal of landing a job in sales with IBM.

He updated the resumé he had used in his senior year in college and mailed it directly to IBM's San Francisco area marketing manager. When he received no reply after two weeks, he phoned and learned from the secretary that the company had no sales openings.

Using his marketing experience — he was, after all, selling himself — he revised his resumé and resubmitted it. This time he received a phone call from the marketing manager asking him to come in for an interview. And he did get the job he wanted.

FIGURE 22C.1 ▪ *Original Resumé of Wilson Paray*

```
                          Wilson Paray

                         140 Crossroads
                    Hayward, California  81001

                        (415) 775-0179


  EXPERIENCE:
  1986 to        American Greetings Corporation
  present        Hayward, California
                 Accounts Manager: Promoted from sales representative
                 in supermarket division to accounts manager of a top
                 national drug chain.  Maintain customer satisfaction
                 with successful sales through the development of
                 innovative merchandising techniques and analysis of
                 market trends.  Supervise six employees.
                 Accomplishments
                 Over forecast in 1988 by 32 percent and in 1989 by
                 71 percent with 11 new accounts opened. Percentage of
                 new stores successfully prospected is up 40 percent
                 in 1989 over previous two years.

  1980 to 1986   Magic Chef Delicatessen
                 Daly City, California
                 Night Manager: Worked up from apprentice clerk to
                 night manager with responsibilities for preparing and
                 closing the store.  Paid for all school and traveling
                 expenses with money earned.

  EDUCATION:     Bachelor of Arts in International Business from
                 San Francisco State University, June 1986.  Member
                 of the Student World Trade Association.

  AWARDS:        Earned Business Achievement Award from the Bank
                 of America in 1984 on the basis of scholastic accom-
                 plishments and debating skills.

  INTERESTS:     Building fine furniture, playing golf and racquetball.


  REFERENCES:    References available upon request
```

Case Questions

1. Place yourself in the marketing manager's position. You do not have a current opening, but you can make room for an exceptional applicant. Which version would arouse your interest enough to call the applicant for an interview?

2. Why? Defend your selection with specific examples.

FIGURE 22C.2   ■ *Revised Resumé of Wilson Paray*

```
              Wilson Paray                    Telephone
              140 Crossroads                  (415) 775-0179
              Hayward, CA 81001


Occupational
Objective:    To be an active participant in sales with a
              progressive company

Experience
Highlights:
1986 to       American Greetings Corporation
present       Hayward, California
              Accounts Manager: Initially employed as a sales
              representative in the supermarket division. Promoted
              to accounts manager, requiring supervision of merchan-
              disers, sales analysis, development of innovative
              merchandising techniques and customer relations.

1980 to 1986  Magic Chef Delicatessen
              Daly City, California
              Night Manager: Worked up from apprentice clerk to
              night manager with responsibilities for preparing and
              closing the store.  Paid for all school and traveling
              expenses with money earned.

Education:    B.A. in International Business from San Francisco
              State University, June 1986.
              Played on college golf team.  Member of the Student
              World Trade Association.  Earned Business Achievement
              Award from the Bank of America in 1984.

Military
Service:      Completed six years of service in the California
              National Guard

Personal
Interests:    Building fine furniture, playing golf and handball

Personal
Data:         Age 26; married, no children, height 6'0";
              weight 170 lbs.; excellent health

References:   Personal and business references available upon request.
```

Interviewing for a Job

About to graduate with a degree in business, Phil Parton does not yet have a job. He has been through three interviews at the campus placement center, each of which he thought had gone well. Yet in the past week he has received rejection letters from all three companies. The letters said much the same thing: "You have fine qualifications, but at present you don't fit the position we are filling. Please keep us in mind in the future."

"So much for a college degree," Phil thought, as he packed his now huge collection of textbooks in boxes for shipment home. "Here I am, a 3.5 average, and I can't even get a job. Maybe I should go to graduate school."

Each years thousands of junior college and senior college students have an experience like Phil's. Desperation sets in as graduation approaches and no job offers appear.

Some students find jobs easily because they majored in a field in which jobs are abundant. Most students, however, find attractive entry-level positions in business because they carefully plan and carry out a strategy to find the best possible job. Their primary goal is to schedule as many job interviews as they possibly can. There are two reasons for this strategy: experience and probability.

Most students have little or no experience in interviewing for a career position. Such interviews can be ego threatening and even traumatic, especially when an interviewer asks a question the applicant is not prepared to answer (for example, "What is your major weakness?"). As applicants progress through a number of interviews, however, they will become

Learning Objectives

1 *To learn different techniques for getting job interviews.*

2 *To learn how to write job search letters.*

3 *To learn how to write interview follow-up letters.*

4 *To learn how to plan for the job interview.*

5 *To understand the kinds of questions job interviewers typically ask.*

6 *To learn how to improve performance during a job interview.*

The more interviews an applicant has, the greater the chances of finding an attractive position.

more confident and be able to sell themselves because they have learned from practice and from their own mistakes.

The more interviews they have, the greater the probability that they will be offered a job. Phil, in our story, had only three job interviews. He will be offered a job only when his qualifications match the position being filled and he is better qualified than all the other individuals who have applied for that position.

STRATEGIES IN GETTING INTERVIEWS

Job interviews come from many sources. Perhaps someone you know tells you about a job opening or you may apply to a company for which you have worked before. Most job openings, however, are found through direct-mail approaches, newspaper advertisements, or college placement offices.

Direct-Mail Campaigns

The **direct-mail approach** most often involves writing unsolicited letters, which are also called surveying or prospecting letters. They are sent to companies without known job openings. This is in contrast to the letter of application — a solicited letter — sent to a company with a known job opening.

The direct-mail approach is a "shotgun" approach. Even though you may write to many companies, your chances of actually acquiring an interview are not particularly good. Nevertheless, if jobs are scarce in your major or if you wish to maximize your chances for acquiring interviews, a direct-mail campaign might be explored.

Direct mail is a "shotgun" approach.

The three steps in the direct-mail campaign are these:

1. Select the companies.
2. Prepare and mail a cover letter and resumé.
3. Follow up as necessary.

You cannot mail your resumé to every existing company, and so in Step 1 you should narrow your list of prospects down to companies that fit your job objective and, if important, your geographic preference. For example, if you want to work for an insurance company in Chicago, you might search the yellow pages in the Chicago telephone directory for the names of prospective employers. Should you want a personnel position, you might consult *Personnel Administrator.* Published by the American Society of Personnel Administrators, this journal prints an annual directory of its membership. Other key sources for selecting companies are:

▪ *College Placement Annual.* Contains a list of companies in both the United States and Canada that are seeking college graduates. Published by the College Placement Council.

- *Dun & Bradstreet Million Dollar Directory.* Provides information about more than 30,000 companies whose net worth exceeds $1 million.
- *Dun & Bradstreet Middle Market Directory.* Similar to the *Million Dollar Directory,* but information is about more than 30,000 companies whose net worth is between $500,000 and $999,999.
- *Moody's Manual of Investment.* Contains information about a variety of companies, including banks, public utilities, insurance firms, and industrial firms.
- *Standard & Poor's Register of Corporations, Directors, and Executives.* Contains an alphabetical listing of more than 35,000 corporations in the United States and Canada. Provides listing of products and services, officers, and telephone numbers.
- *Thomas' Register of American Manufacturers.* Contains a list of manufacturers under headings of 70,000 products. Information includes addresses and telephone numbers of manufacturers.

Some students select as many as 500 companies for their direct mail campaign; more typically, 100 or fewer key prospects are chosen. If you send your application to 100 such firms, you can expect a rejection rate of approximately 85 percent. You will not hear at all from some of the other companies. However, should you get six or seven job interviews from such a campaign, your strategy has been successful.

Much of the reason for the low number of positive responses in a direct-mail campaign lies in the breadth of the approach. The more you narrow the focus of your campaign, the greater your success. You can do this in a number of ways: (1) Pick companies that offer the type of job in which you are interested. (2) Select companies with jobs for which you are qualified. (3) Locate companies that are known to provide advancement in your field. (4) Find companies that are centered or have branches in geographical locations of interest to you. (5) Omit companies where you are sure you would not accept a job. In the direct-mail campaign, your **cover letter** is just as important as the resume. First, get the name and address of the person to whom you intend to mail your letter. Never send campaign letters to *Dear Sir or Madam* or *To Whom It May Concern.* A personal touch is critical in your campaign. Usually, the person whose name you want is the personnel officer of the company. Often you can obtain this name by consulting the sources already listed or by calling the firm and asking for the name and title of the personnel officer (for example, personnel manager, vice president for personnel, or recruiting officer).

Preparing an effective cover letter is essential in a direct-mail campaign.

Second, decide on a reason for applying with each specific company. You can include this reason in your cover letter as a way of showing interest in the firm. You can also get this type of information from the sources listed earlier.

Third, write the actual letter. Because it is a persuasive letter, you might use the format discussed in Chapter 7. Make the reader want to check your written personality (the cover letter) and your factual background (the resumé) against your face-to-face persona. As always, you should use the "you" attitude as well as the other strategies for effective communication.

One authority suggests that the cover letter used in a direct-mail campaign should accomplish these things:

1. Ask for a job; be specific about what you want.
2. Explain how your experience, as outlined on your resumé, relates to the desired job and to the company.
3. Tell how you were attracted to the company.
4. Ask for the interview. Tell the reader you would like to arrange a meeting at a time and place convenient for the employer.[1]

An example of a cover letter is shown in Figure 23.1.

Usually responses from your prospects arrive about two weeks after you mail your letter and resumé. If you do not hear from a company after about 14 days, you might consider following up by phone or letter. The phone call is quicker, but it may be perceived as too aggressive. If you decide to call, try to reach the person to whom you addressed the letter. Ask about the progress of your application. With the letter, you can organize your thoughts to achieve your goal.

A sample follow-up letter is provided in Figure 23.2. Notice first that the writer uses tact by mentioning the earlier contact without placing blame for inaction. Second, another resumé is enclosed in case the original is misplaced. Third, another summary of relevant qualifications is provided. New information can be added at this time as it is another opportunity to emphasize your qualifications. Finally, available times for receiving phone calls are repeated.

Response to Newspaper Advertisements

A convincing cover letter and resumé are essential when responding to newspaper ads.

When you respond to a help wanted advertisement in a newspaper, be assured that scores of other applicants are responding to the same ad. You must prepare a most convincing cover letter and resumé. Cover letters about known job openings differ somewhat from letters in a direct-mail campaign. You need to accomplish six things:

1. Identify the job opening, tell where you learned of it, and state that you are applying.
2. Describe the job opening as you understand it. This description clarifies your immediate aspirations and allows the reader to correct misunderstandings. It also sets up item 3. In writing item 2, try to show a void in the company that you (and your abilities and skills) can fill, with item 3. This combination can have a strong persuasive effect.
3. Pick selected items from your background to show how you meet the qualifications outlined in item 2.

---

[1]"Goof-Proof Your Resumé," *Changing Times,* September 1983, 43–46.

FIGURE 23.1 ▪ *Campaign Cover Letter*

```
                                        1065 Locust Drive
                                        Fayetteville, AR 72701
                                        March 12, 1991

        Ms. Patricia Markham
        Personnel Manager
        Able Computers, Inc.
        P.O. Box 1511
        Columbus, OH 43216

        Dear Ms. Markham:

        The reputation and growth of Able Computers have led me to apply
        for a position in your management trainee program.  Information in
        the University of Arkansas Placement Annual indicates that you hire
        college graduates with business degrees.  The Annual states you
        prefer computer, management, and sales or marketing majors.

        The fact that you were rated number one in a poll as the most
        promising company of the 1990s by Electronic Industry Magazine is
        impressive.  The challenge of helping you maintain your position
        of leadership in the volatile computer industry is especially
        exciting.

        My BBA degree from the University of Arkansas incorporates a major
        in management and a minor in marketing.  Further, my two years of
        part-time work for the Bank of New England in the data processing
        department utilized capabilities acquired in my three college
        computer classes.

        As you will note on my attached resumé, I am willing to accept
        challenges and carry them through to successful completion. Grover
        Jefferson, of the Bank of New England, has offered to support this
        view.  His address, and the names and addresses of other
        references, are on the resumé.

        May I have an interview at your convenience?  I am available at
        the phone at (501) 555-4567 between 2 p.m. and 6 p.m., weekdays.

                            Sincerely,

                            Jules Steiner

                            Jules Steiner

        Encl.
```

4. Enter some human interest information. You may include details about why you are interested in this company or industry. Consider telling the reader of your enthusiasm or belief that you are a valuable asset. This is the only location in the letter (or the resumé) where you should express any opinions.

5. Mention one of your references as a source of verification of your credentials and abilities. Mention that you have enclosed a resumé.

6. Ask for the interview. Make it easy for the reader to respond to your request: offer to meet at the reader's convenience, give hours you can

FIGURE 23.2 ▪ *Follow-Up Letter*

                                        1065 Locust Drive
                                        Fayetteville, AR 72701
                                        April 1, 1991

Ms. Patricia Markham
Personnel Manager
Able Computers, Inc.
P.O. Box 1511
Columbus, OH 43216

Dear Ms. Markham:

Several weeks ago I wrote you applying for a management traineeship
with Able. I do wish to ensure that you know of my enthusiasm for
Able. As my March 12 letter stated, I am impressed with your
position of leadership in your industry.

You are interested, I understand, in recruits with computer, management, and marketing abilities. My management major, marketing minor,
and data processing job experience meet those qualifications. Last
week I was honored as the most promising senior in the University of
Arkansas Management Club, a group of over 120 students.

The enclosed resumé presents more information about how my education, job, and extracurricular activities well prepare me for your
traineeship.

An interview with you, at your convenience, is still my goal.
My schedule remains the same; I am available by phone weekdays from
2 p.m. until 6 p.m.

                                        Sincerely,

                                        Jules Steiner

                                        Jules Steiner

Encl.

be reached by phone, mention your address, or volunteer to travel on certain days.

An example of an expanded cover letter is shown in Figure 23.3.

Again, be sure to follow up if the firm does not respond to your letter within two weeks.

If a firm grants you an interview as a result of your direct-mail campaign or your response to a newspaper advertisement, then you might write a letter confirming the date, time, and place for the interview and expressing

FIGURE 23.3 ▪ *Expanded Cover Letter*

```
                                    1065 Locust Drive
                                    Fayetteville, AR 72701
                                    March 12, 1991

      Ms. Patricia Markham
      Personnel Manager
      Able Computers, Inc.
      P.O. Box 1511
      Columbus, OH 43216

      Dear Ms. Markham:

      Please consider me an applicant for the management trainee position
      you advertised in the March 11 issue of  The Wall Street Journal.

      The ad states you seek a person with a college degree and that you
      prefer a business major and some related experience.  The job would
      include a six-month training period in Columbus and then placement
      in one of your three Ohio offices.  The training class starts July 1.

      My May 1991 BBA degree from the University of Arkansas, with a
      management major and marketing minor, meets your requirements.
      Having worked each summer for the last six years, I have acquired
      some related experience.  This last summer I sold computers and
      did some hardware trouble-shooting for Computek.

      Your job is especially interesting to me since it would allow me
      to make use of my management and marketing knowledge and pursue my
      personal interest in computers.  Here at the university I was co-
      founder of the Computer Users Group and am just finishing my term
      as president.  My skills, interest, and proven enthusiasm for hard
      work would serve me well as your management trainee.

      Professor Paul Jarston, the club's faculty adviser and a member of
      the data processing faculty, has agreed to serve as a reference.
      Other references are found on the enclosed resumé.

      May I have an interview at your convenience?  Reach me by phone
      most afternoons at (501) 555-4567.  I can travel to Columbus at
      most any time.

                                    Sincerely,

                                    Jules Steiner

                                    Jules Steiner

      Encl.
```

your appreciation for being given the interview. Here's an example of the body of such a letter:

Thank you for scheduling an interview with me about opportunities in Able Computers' manager trainee program. I am looking forward to our meeting.

As you requested during our telephone conversation [or As you requested in your letter], I'll be in Room 117 of the Able Building at 10:00 a.m. on Thursday, August 9.

I appreciate your interest in my application. If you need additional information, please let me know.

The direct-mail campaign and responding to newspaper advertisements are only two approaches to getting job interviews. Other strategies you might consider, especially if the job market in your particular field is tight, include: (1) calling personnel officers directly and asking for an interview; (2) making unannounced visits to the firms where you seek employment; (3) placing your own ad in a newspaper; (4) attending conventions or trade shows of industries you have selected as potential employers, and (5) networking. **Networking** is contacting friends, fraternity or sorority members (including recent graduates), family members, former employers, and others who may know of job openings. Some experts estimate that as many as 90 percent of positions are filled through word-of-mouth announcements. Networking is likely to increase in importance as you move through your career and make more business contacts. Nevertheless, networking can be a valuable technique even for entry-level positions.

Use of the College Placement Office

Using the placement office in acquiring interviews is much different from direct mail or newspaper advertisement techniques. The direct mail and newspaper advertisement approaches are general in tone, frequently cannot be personalized, and are used on the assumption that if you apply to enough companies, you will receive some interviews.

The college placement office sometimes leads directly to an interview.

The placement office, on the other hand, is more individualized and, in some cases, leads directly to an interview. The placement office is a valuable location to find the latest publications. Often recent publications on how to interview or write resumés are available. Many companies send placement offices their annual reports and other recruiting literature. In addition to the library function, workers in the placement office often can help you with career decisions or know the most recent trends in industries. They may also know of the latest job openings. Some placement offices maintain your records, including letters of reference and resumé. The workers can even review your resumé or application letter.

A second major activity of the placement office is scheduling on-campus job interviews. Companies frequently visit the campus to interview 13 to 15 students a day in a series of 30-minute interviews. The placement office coordinates room scheduling and time-period assignments, makes company literature available, and gathers interviewees' resumés.

Signing up for an interview through the placement office is far easier than having to use the letter of application to schedule an interview. For this reason, as well as the other benefits mentioned, regular communication with your placement office is usually wise.

INTERVIEW PLANNING

Throughout this text we have emphasized planning in every business communication situation. Planning is of paramount importance to the job interview.

FIGURE 23.4 ▪ *Matching Process during the Job Interview*

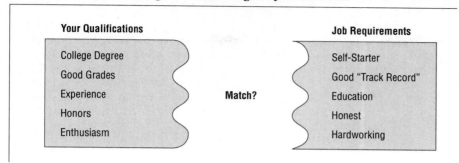

Source: Pizza Hut.

Reviewing Your Qualifications

Your job search will be successful when the employer's representative realizes that there is a match between your qualifications and the requirements of the position being filled. The question, "Is this person qualified?" is always uppermost in every interviewer's mind. Your goal is to show this match during the interview, to demonstrate that the pieces of this job-selection puzzle do fit together. Figure 23.4 suggests the complexity of the matching process.

The interviewer looks for a match between company and job applicant.

Your qualifications for a job include not only your previous applicable work experience, education, and extracurricular activities, but also any salable personal characteristics you have. Figure 23.5 provides a list of qualities that employers consider to be important. As you rate yourself on each quality by placing a check mark in the appropriate column, do not forget to consider all of your work and school-related experiences.

You should be able to justify clearly any high rating you have given yourself. Trained interviewers are not interested in statements, such as "I am a self-starter," unless you can give evidence of your initiative. Be prepared to show that you are dependable, adaptable, mature, and so on.

Be able to document your best qualities.

Any activity in which you have been involved can provide the necessary evidence. For example, playing basketball or any other team sport requires the ability to work with others. Earning part or all of your college expenses shows initiative. A clear and logical explanation of why you changed majors or transferred from one school to another can indicate decision-making ability and, perhaps, adaptability. Leadership skills can be shown through various activities, including offices in organizations, working as a counselor in a summer camp, or training your replacement for a job you left.

In short, pick your major qualifications, document them, review them, and be prepared to talk about them during the interview.

Researching the Company

One of the most important steps in preparing for an interview is to research the company. You need to know the size of the company, its products or services, position in the industry, some historical perspectives, locations

The applicant should know as much as possible about the company.

FIGURE 23.5 ▪ *Qualifications Checklist*

Am I Qualified?	Superior	Above Average	Average	Below Average	Poor
Leadership Skills	____	____	____	____	____
Initiative (self-starter)	____	____	____	____	____
Decision-Making Abilities	____	____	____	____	____
Written Communication Skills	____	____	____	____	____
Oral Communication Skills	____	____	____	____	____
Adaptability	____	____	____	____	____
Professional Appearance	____	____	____	____	____
Working with Others	____	____	____	____	____
Enthusiasm	____	____	____	____	____
Dependability	____	____	____	____	____
Self-Confidence	____	____	____	____	____
Maturity	____	____	____	____	____

from which it operates, financial considerations, employment situation, types of jobs being filled, the subsidiary situation, and its plans for the future. Articles by or about recruiters that discuss major problems or errors in interviews inevitably point to the interviewee's lack of knowledge about the company as a serious shortcoming. One recruiter for a nonprofit institution received comments about his company's products. Another recruiter was startled that an $80,000-a-year executive did not bother to read a prospective employer's annual report.[2]

In addition to the sources mentioned earlier in the direct-mail campaign, look also to *The Wall Street Journal,* the company annual report, recruiting literature, and the *Business Periodicals Index.*

Anticipating What Will Happen in the Interview

Knowing what to expect will help you prepare for the interview and reduce your anxiety as well.

Interviews fit into one or more of eight classifications.

Types of interviews.   Most interviews or interview situations fit into one or more of these classifications: (1) screening interview, (2) open-ended interview, (3) panel interview, (4) group interview, (5) stress interview, (6) office visit interview, (7) videotape interview, and (8) computer interview.

The **screening interview**, as its name implies, screens prospects into groups to interview further, to reject, or to hold for future decision. These interviews usually occur before other categories of interviews and typically last about 30 minutes.

[2]*Ibid.*

| BOXED IN | *AN ETHICAL DILEMMA* |

This morning Shawna received a phone call about a second interview. "We're quite interested in you," the personnel assistant explained, "but we need more information. We'd also like you to meet Annette Mead. She was unavailable during your first visit. Will 10 a.m. Friday be acceptable?"

"Yes, of course," Shawna said.

She begins thinking about how to make a great impression. "Let's see," she muses, "Last time they seemed interested in my accounting and bookkeeping skills. I can probably get away with saying that I'm the accountant rather than the bookkeeper at Wilson's Grocery. Instead of saying I worked there from late June to the end of July, I can say I have been there all summer. And I can say that at Happy Lanes Bowling Center I was in charge of all other part-time college students. There was only one, but it will sound impressive."

That should do it, she decides. They are sure to hire someone with more experience than she really has.

She wonders if employers check references even for little part-time jobs. If it turns out that they do, then she is not being very smart after all — and not very honest either. "If you have to worry about getting caught, what you're doing can't be right," she reminds herself. However, she is sure she will do well if she can only get the job.

Shawna feels boxed in. What would you do?

An **open-ended interview** (or unstructured or nondirective interview) follows no discernible pattern. Your answer to an initial question may determine the next question. The interactions and responses form the direction of the interview.

A **panel interview** involves one interviewee and more than one interviewer. Occasionally you may feel outnumbered when there is only one interviewer; imagine the pressure you might feel with several people questioning and observing you. On the other hand, if the company believes an interview with you is important enough to justify the time of two or more recruiters, perhaps they are already impressed with you.

The **group interview** is the antithesis of the panel interview — several interviewees are presented with one interviewer. You are likely to encounter a group interview in a social setting, such as a party to which many job prospects are invited, or a mass screening when there is a large number of applicants for few positions. Because these interviews may not last long, each interviewee seeks to make a quick and positive impression — often at the expense of other applicants. Do try to impress your interviewer, but avoid direct comparison to others in the room if possible.

The **stress interview**, probably the most unpleasant of the eight categories, places the interviewee in a stressful situation that the interviewer

The stress
interview is
meant to be
unpleasant.

then carefully observes. Inviting you to smoke but not supplying an ashtray or putting you in a lengthy business simulation full of tricks and pitfalls are examples of stress activities. Questions the interviewer knows to cause stress may also be used. At one time stress questions and stress interviews were fairly common. Today they are less frequent. For high-level, high-stress executive jobs and positions (high-pressure sales, for example) you are more likely to encounter stress interviews.

The **office visit interview** (or plant or headquarters visit), is not a single interview but a series of interviews that may incorporate many of the other categories. Some interviews may be stressful, others may be conducted by a panel, and still others may be open-ended. A six-or seven-hour day, including lunch and coffee breaks with company officials, is not unusual. Although the day will range from formal interviews to casual, informal discussions, you are constantly being evaluated; never let down your guard. Other activities you may encounter include psychological or ability testing, building tours, discussions with potential peers or subordinates, and completion of application or travel reimbursement forms.

The **videotape interview** occurs in one of two ways. In some cases, the job applicant, on his or her own initiative, may submit a videotape showing performance, describing personal characteristics, interest in the field, background strengths, and perhaps some personal data. In other cases, companies ask applicants to respond to a list of questions while being taped, either at the company or at a place of the applicant's choosing. The videotape can reduce recruiter time, allow replays, save travel expenses, and still transmit important applicant characteristics, such as preparation, enthusiasm, and communication ability.. As with other forms of interviews, videotape interviews require thorough preparation.

The **computer interview** requires the applicant to complete a survey of direct and indirect questions. The computer interview may be part of a lengthy interview sequence or it may be an initial screening device. It allows development of a database and statistical analysis and minimizes costly face-to-face interaction. Computer ability and careful self-assessment before the computer interview are valuable attributes.

Most interviews
are conducted by
a practitioner or
a personnel office
specialist.

Types of Interviewers.   Just as there are many types of interviews, there are also different types of interviewers; the major categories are the practitioner and the personnel office representative. These categories may be encountered in either a screening interview, which is usually the first interview, or the office visit, which is usually the culmination interview.

The practitioner is a person who is currently doing the type of job for which you would be hired. The term field interviewer is also used. For example, an accountant interviews prospective accountants, and so on. The practitioner may be the person who would be the immediate superior of the new hiree. The practitioner is not likely to have formal training in interview procedures; therefore, it is difficult to predict the course of the interview. The area of expertise and background about the job are likely to be discussion topics. Because of their naivete, practitioners are more likely to ask stress questions at inappropriate times or ask questions deemed illegal by Equal Employment Opportunity Act guidelines.

The representative of the personnel office or personnel recruiter probably has, as part of his or her job description, the role of recruiter. Training in selection methods, appraisals, and interviewing prepare these people for this role. Because of their training, representatives of personnel offices are difficult to read. They will be pleasant and courteous, but seldom will you be certain what impression you have made.

Flow of the Interview. A description of a typical screening interview will help you prepare for it. The interview may last from 15 to 45 minutes, but 30 minutes is traditional. A typical 30-minute period might be broken down as follows:

A typical screening interview lasts 30 minutes.

First 5 minutes:	Introductions, small talk, questions of low priority
Next 10 minutes:	Focus on interviewee's abilities and responses to interviewer's questions
Next 10 minutes:	Responses by interviewer to interviewee's questions and description of company and job
Last 5 minutes:	Closing comments, explanation of next steps

A full-day office visit depends on the organization and type of job. However, a visit to an office for a management job might proceed through these steps:

9–10 a.m.:	Breakfast with the interviewer who conducted the screening interview
10:15–11 a.m.:	Introductions to other personnel office employees
11 a.m.–12 p.m.:	Meeting with vice president of related area
12–1:30 p.m.:	Lunch with two members of personnel office and prospective immediate superior
1:30–2:30 p.m.:	Meeting with prospective immediate superior
2:30–4 p.m.:	Half-hour meetings with three potential peers
4–5 p.m.:	Completion of company forms and tour of facilities with personnel office representative
5 p.m.:	Depart with screening interviewer for the airport for flight home

As you can see, by the time you get home, you will have had a long, tiring, and eventful day.

Types of Questions. Four types of questions may be asked during an interview—inconsequential questions, important-answer questions, stress questions, and inappropriate questions. Most interviews start off with questions to which the answers—that is, the content per se—are really inconsequential. Their purpose is to break the ice and get the interview moving. Trained interviewers know that you will be anxious about the interview. After all, much rides on how you perform in a short period of time; you

Most trained interviewers begin by asking a few ice-breaking questions.

will be in a strange and perhaps bleakly appointed interview room; you are meeting a total stranger and talking, in some cases, about personal thoughts and feelings.

For these reasons questions about the weather or last Sunday's football game occur first. The recruiter does not care much about what you say but rather about how you say it. Your enthusiasm for a certain football team is more impressive than which team you prefer.

Shortly after you start to relax, the questions will focus on your interests, knowledge of the company or the job, and why you think you can do the job. The recruiter will listen carefully to your responses to these important-answer questions and is likely to build on your answers with related follow-up questions. You are evaluated on the speed, depth, and quality of your answers, as well as other ingredients.

Stress questions may occur at any time in an interview, but they are most likely to follow some important-answer questions. Planning on how to respond to a stress question is difficult; their intent is to catch you off guard. Still, just knowing they may occur should help you.

Inappropriate questions are either illegal or unrelated to the job. Rules keep interviewers from asking questions that might discriminate against you. For example, questions about your age, marital status, or religion are seldom allowed. Exceptions occur when this or other information is directly related to the job, such as hiring a parent instead of a childless person for a child-care center. Other questionable topics include race, political affiliation, club memberships, handicapped status, national origin, and veteran status.

What should you do when you are asked one of these questions? You have several options. If you do not find the question offensive or the answer potentially damaging, you can answer it. If the answer to the question is personal or you think it is not related to the job, politely tell the recruiter so. Perhaps you will wish to ask the purpose of the question; there may be a good reason for it that you did not anticipate.

The interviewee is usually allowed time to ask questions.

Most interviewers allow time for the applicant to ask questions about the job and the organization. Two reasons exist for asking truly valuable questions: the better the question, the better its reflection on you; and you should have some questions to which the answers are important. Prepare yourself before the interview with five or six questions. The interviewer may answer some of them in the company or job description segments of the interview. Then, when given the opportunity, you can raise several probing questions. Avoid trite or shallow questions. Aim for open-ended questions rather than those that yield only a yes or no answer. Consider questions about the extent of responsibility you would be given, the types of assignments encountered, and even queries about the negative aspects of the job. Here are some example questions you might ask:

1. What positions do your typical manager trainees hold after five years with the company?
2. How important are advanced degrees, such as an M.B.A. or a law degree, to advancement?

3. Do you normally promote from within the company?
4. What kind of orientation program or training do you provide for new employees?

Be sure to avoid questions that might threaten the interviewer's ego or cause other negative feelings. For example, "Are you having much trouble with EEOC?" is inappropriate unless you are interviewing for a personnel job. "Will I have to work much overtime?" might categorize you as having little initiative. You should avoid questions about salary unless starting salaries are the same for all incoming employees (for example, some teaching positions, government jobs, and even management trainee programs).

As part of interview planning you will also find it valuable to review three categories of interview questions discussed in Chapter 19: open-ended questions, direct or closed questions, and indirect questions.

Listed in Figure 23.6 are 23 questions that are frequently asked by college recruiters. Examination of the questions will give you the flavor of an interview. Some of these questions are likely to be asked of you, and you may want to think of answers to them. As you read the questions you will notice that many seek your opinions and others ask for facts. Most interviewees have much more difficulty with the opinion questions because a correct answer is not clear.

College recruiters often ask similar questions.

Here are some suggestions for dealing with two of the questions that students have found difficult:

What percentage of your college expenses did you earn? How? A paradox of our society is that most of us envy the wealthy, such as a college student who does not need to work during the summer or after school hours. However, job experience and indications of industriousness are paramount in employee selection. All things being equal, the recruiter is more impressed with the student who works to pay education expenses, even doing menial work or activities that are not job related, than with the wealthy student who does not indicate a willingness to work. Therefore, the stronger a case you can build for yourself in percentage of expenses earned, the better your evaluation. If your parents give you all your expenses, you earned 0 percent. If your spouse is paying the expenses, you can claim 100 percent. If you are using a loan that you will repay, claim that as a percentage from you.

Can you forget your education and start from scratch? Your goal in answering this question is to underline the importance of your education but at the same time to show a willingness to learn new things. Thus an answer such as this might be appropriate: "I can't really forget my education, because I think I've learned some things that will be helpful to me in my work. However, I know that my education isn't completed yet. I'm willing and eager to learn new things."

Knowing What the Recruiter is Seeking

You can prepare for an interview better if you have some feeling about how and on what you will be evaluated. Many students are surprised to learn that often they are not evaluated for what they know. Instead, recruiters assume that your college degree has given you some basic information and shows you have the ability to learn. It also indicates an interest

FIGURE 23.6   ■   *Questions Most Frequently Asked by Recruiters Interviewing College Students*

1. What are your future vocational plans?
2. In what school activities have you participated? Why? Which did you enjoy most?
3. How do you spend your spare time? What are your hobbies?
4. In what type of position are you most interested?
5. Why do you think you might like to work for our company?
6. What jobs have you held? How were they obtained? Why did you leave?
7. What percentage of your college expenses did you earn? How?
8. Why did you choose your particular field of work?
9. What courses did you like best? Least? Why?
10. How did you spend your vacations while in school?
11. What do you know about our company?
12. Do you feel that you have received a good general training?
13. What qualifications do you have that make you feel that you will be successful in your field?
14. What extracurricular offices have you held?
15. What are your ideas on salary?
16. How interested are you in sports?
17. If you were starting college all over again, what courses would you take?
18. Can you forget your education and start from scratch?
19. Do you prefer any specific geographic location? Why?
20. How much money do you hope to earn at age 30? 35?
21. Why did you decide to go to this particular school?
22. How did you rank in your graduation class in high school? Where will you probably rank in college?
23. Do you think your extracurricular activities were worth the time you devoted to them?

Source: New York Life Insurance Company.

in specific areas. If the recruiter hires you, the company supervisor will teach you, in depth, the specifics that he or she wants you to know. Therefore, few questions are asked about your knowledge of subjects, such as the difference between municipal bonds and corporate bonds or the application of Maslow's theory to a management trainee job. Questions are asked to determine such characteristics as tact, enthusiasm, industriousness, maturity, human relations skills, leadership ability, motivation, congeniality, or communication ability. How directed you are and your initiative, competitiveness, and intelligence will be scrutinized as well.

Most companies use an interviewee evaluation form that the recruiter completes after the interview. Because attributes of importance differ by company, no standard form exists. To understand better the content of these forms, visit your college placement office. The sample form in Figure 23.7 is typical in the type of attributes evaluated and the length and depth of response requested.

FIGURE 23.7 ■ *Interview Appraisal Form*

Name _____ School _____

Campus Address _____ Phone Number _____

Post Graduation
Mailing Address _____ Phone Number _____

Availability _____ Geographical   Career
Date _____ Preference _____ Interests _____ G.P.A. _____

Selection Standard	Observations	Exceeds	Meets	Does Not Meet
	Relates to selection standards and to information reported by applicant or			
Presentation	Forcefulness, Organization, Conciseness—ask related questions.			
Achievements	Academic, Technical, Professional Contributions to previous employers. Do they relate to our needs?			
Ambitions	Career Goals, Financial Goals—are they realistic?			
Contributions	Long- and short-term, what can the candidate add to the organization?			
Is Candidate Sold on Pizza Hut	Understands Career Opportunity.			
Overall Reaction				

_____
Recruiter's Signature

Highly Recommended _____
Recommended _____
Reject _____

Source: Pizza Hut.

Considering Your Appearance

One survey of practicing interviewers found that in a 20-minute interview the average interviewer had made a selection decision within the first four minutes of the interview.[3] Some interviewers claim that they can decide whether an applicant is suitable for a job the very instant that applicant enters the room. Obviously, these early decisions are based in large part on physical appearance.

Generally, you should dress as you would in the job for which you are applying. This guideline means that, as graduates of a two- or four-year college, males wear a coat and tie and females a dress or suit and appropriate shoes. If you are not sure how to dress, it is probably better to dress simply in business attire, giving consideration to what is socially acceptable in the area.

Preparing for the Unusual

Stories abound about tricks that interviewers use to catch an applicant off guard. Although it is unlikely that you will be confronted with any of these tricks, you should nevertheless be aware of and be prepared for them. Examples are:

■ *Silence:* The interviewer says absolutely nothing at the beginning of the interview. Instead, he or she simply looks at you. You, therefore, must begin the interaction.
■ *Sell me:* If you are interviewing for any kind of sales or marketing position, the interviewer slides an ashtray or pencil across the desk to you and says, "Here. Sell this to me."
■ *Turnabout:* The interviewer says, "I've been interviewing people all day. I'm tired. Why don't you interview me?"
■ *No smoking:* You are a smoker. You are nervous. The interviewer asks, "Would you like to smoke?" You light a cigarette and discover that there is no ashtray in the room.
■ *Choose a chair:* When you enter the interviewer's office, two chairs are available from which to choose. One is near the interviewer's desk, the other is several feet away from the desk. The interviewer says simply, "Have a seat," but does not tell you which chair.

If these examples seem frightening to you, remember that very few interviewers use such tricks. Most contemporary interviewers are highly trained, competent businesspeople who want to evaluate your qualifications in a straightforward manner.

INTERVIEW PERFORMANCE

For many years companies used two basic approaches to selecting new employees: the job interview and psychological testing. Now, however, many companies no longer use psychological testing because of federal

---

[3]Robert L. Dipboye, Richard D. Arvey, and David E. Terpotra, "Equal Employment and the Interview," *Personnel Journal* 55 (October 1976): 521.

laws; a company must be able to provide evidence that a psychological test can differentiate between good and poor performers on the job. Because gathering such evidence is difficult, especially for smaller companies, the job interview is now the major selection tool for most organizations.

Your actual, face-to-face interaction with a representative of the company is the most critical step in your job search process. Be sure to arrive on time — or even a little early. Being late for a job interview shows lack of dependability (one of the qualities discussed earlier). If you must be late, call the interviewer and explain why. Consider making a trial run prior to the interview to determine travel time, parking facilities, and exact location of the interview. Arriving late will put unneeded pressure on you.

Successful interviewing begins with being on time.

Shake hands with the interviewer. A handshake is a sign of acceptance and greeting in a business situation. Have a firm handshake. A weak fishlike handshake is perceived by some interviewers to be characteristic of a similarly weak personality. Do not be afraid to offer your hand first. The job interview is not a social situation steeped in rules of etiquette. Many interviewers have expressed the same uneasy feeling about the handshake as you might experience: Do I shake hands first? You can relieve much interviewer uneasiness and show some assertiveness if you simply extend your hand as you approach the interviewer.

Establish and maintain eye contact with the interviewer. Like the weak handshake, an absence of eye contact connotes a weak personality to many interviewers. To a few of them it also indicates that the interviewee may be lying. Interviewers will also sometimes unconsciously form negative perceptions of applicants who slouch in a chair, cross their arms or legs, and face away from them. Sit erect, facing the interviewer. Do not cross your legs and arms at the same time. Some interviewers believe that people who sit in such a closed position are trying to shut the other person out.

Playing with objects (for example, a pen or pencil) during the interview communicates unusual nervousness to many interviewers. Often they will translate nervousness during the interview to mean that you cannot perform well in stress situations on the job. Particularly do not pick up objects on the interviewer's desk.

An interviewer can interpret your criticism of past employers as an indication that you are a complainer who criticizes all your employers. Also, such criticism can be interpreted as a rationalization for the real (and damaging) reasons you left your previous employers. Similarly, do not evaluate previous jobs — simply describe them. Because many college students have work experience they consider to be simple or menial, they are often inclined to communicate that perception during the interview: "Well, really all I did was fry hamburgers," or "The job really wasn't much — I just waited on people." No matter how unimportant you think a job might have been, an interviewer will ask questions about it in order to assess a number of qualities, among them dependability, leadership skills, working with others, and initiative.

Two common mistakes are to criticize previous employers and to belittle menial jobs.

✔️ *CHECKLIST for Interview Performance*

▢ Arrive on time.

▢ Shake hands firmly.

▢ Use effective eye contact.

▢ Be attentive to posture.

▢ Avoid playing with objects.

▢ Refrain from criticizing former employers.

▢ Describe but do not evaluate previous jobs.

▢ Ask questions about the company.

▢ Remain honest.

▢ Express appreciation for the interview.

During interview planning you prepared questions about the company. Remember to ask them before the interview ends.

Do not try to be someone or something you are not. Allow your true personality to emerge and try to make a good impression, but avoid developing an image that is inaccurate. Recruiters are making hiring decisions on what they see in the interview. Problems may occur if the real you who shows up for work is substantially different.

As the interview closes and you are about to leave, remember to thank the interviewer for discussing employment opportunities with you. If possible, express appreciation for any constructive suggestions the interviewer has made, especially if you think you will not be considered for the job.

Interviewing requires polished, professional behavior. You can gain the needed skills by practicing with anyone (classmates, friends, relatives) who will take the time with you.

INTERVIEW FOLLOW-UP

Immediate Follow-Up

Follow-up should occur within one to two days after your interview.

As soon as possible after the interview, write the interviewer a follow-up letter. Basically, this letter consists of three paragraphs. In the first paragraph express appreciation for the interview and your continued interest in the position. In the second paragraph add any important information about yourself that you failed to mention during the interview. Or emphasize one of your qualifications that the interviewer stressed as being important, especially if you feel personally confident about the qualification. Or emphasize some information you learned about the company

FIGURE 23.8　∎　*Follow-Up Letter to an Interview*

```
                                    1065 Locust Drive
                                    Fayetteville, AR 72701
                                    May 12, 1991

          Ms. Patricia Markham
          Personnel Manager
          Able Computers, Inc.
          P.O. Box 1511
          Columbus, OH 43216

          Dear Ms. Markham:

          Thank you for the time you spent with me on Thursday discussing
          employment opportunities in Able Computers' manager trainee
          program.  You description of Able's program is impressive and
          reinforces my serious interest in the position.

          You mentioned during the interview that Able is interested in
          individuals who can assume responsibility.  Both my work experi-
          ence (where I trained new employees and replaced the manager when
          she was out of town) and my extracurricular activities (where I
          assumed leadership positions in three different campus groups)
          show the kind of responsible experiences you might be seeking in
          an applicant.

          If you wish to further discuss my qualifications for the manager
          trainee position, please call.  I look forward to hearing from you.

                              Sincerely,

                              Jules Steiner

                              Jules Steiner
```

during the interview which impressed you. Finally, in the third paragraph, communicate your willingness to answer further questions about your qualifications. Assume a positive attitude toward hearing from the interviewer.

Try to say something in the follow-up letter that will remind the reader of you and the interview; pick something that would not have been discussed with other interviewees. You may mention also, as appropriate, that you have completed and enclosed an application form. An example of such a follow-up letter appears in Figure 23.8

Most companies use their own standard application forms that ask for much of the same information supplied on your resumé. Your resumé is used to catch the recruiter's eye and to achieve an interview. You may be asked to complete the organization's form before a screening interview, immediately after the screening interview, or at the office visit. Frequently, at the completion of a successful screening interview, you will be asked to take a form with you and return it by mail. This is an indication that you are proceeding through the hiring process. As you complete the form, keep in mind that neatness, spelling, grammar, and punctuation are important. A sample application form appears in Figure 23.9.

Delayed Follow-Up

Most interviewers will close a job interview by telling you how soon a selection decision will be made: "We'll let you know something by the 15th of next month." If you do not hear from the company by the deadline they specify, then telephone the interviewer to check on the progress of your application. If a decision has not yet been made, you will have gained the advantage of immediate follow-up. If a decision has been made and you have not been chosen, you will at least know where you stand.

If you are turned down, you have little to lose by remaining diligent. Perhaps you can revise your application to a different area of the company, ask for a reevaluation, or seek to have your file remain active in case another position opens. Recruiters sometimes talk about the employee they hired whom they could not shake — who would not take no for an answer.

Whether by letter or telephone, the follow-up serves two purposes. First, it is a public relations device designed to enhance your relationship with the interviewer. Second, it is a means of bringing your name back to the interviewer's attention. Many interviewers, especially those who visit your school's placement center, will interview as many as 15 applicants in one day. You will want your name to stand out among the applicants as a qualified person who is genuinely interested in the position.

Follow-Up to Letters of Acceptance or Rejection

Letters of acceptance and rejection both require response.

You will probably get both of these kinds of letters — some offering you a position and others turning you down. You should respond to both. If made an offer, either accept or refuse the position.

Letter of Acceptance

A letter of acceptance should formally accept the position, express appreciation for the offer, and confirm the details of the offer, including salary, starting time, location, and the name of the person to whom you will be reporting. In addition, it should show anticipation of doing good work. Here is an example of such a letter:

> Your offer of a position in Able Computers' manager trainee program is enthusiastically accepted. Thank you for your confidence in my potential to perform well in the program.

FIGURE 23.9 ■ *Application Form*

PLEASE PRINT

Personal Data

Print Name in full

(Last)   (First)   (Middle)   Social Security Number

Home address

(Street)   (City)   (State)   (Zip Code)   Telephone

Temporary Address

(Street)   (City)   (State)   (Zip Code)   Telephone

If hired, can you furnish proof of age? ☐ YES ☐ NO   Licensed to drive car? ☐ Yes ☐ No   Is license valid in this State? ☐ Yes ☐ No
(Answer only if position for which you are applying requires driving.)

Are you a U.S. Citizen ☐ YES ☐ NO   or Resident Alien ☐ YES ☐ NO

Have you ever been employed by Sears? ☐ Yes ☐ No   If so, when and where last employed?

Former employes of Sears and certain subsidiaries may be entitled to service credit under the Pension Plan based on prior employment with Sears, Roebuck and Co., Homart Development Co., Sears Investment Management Co., Sears Roebuck Acceptance Corp., Sears, Roebuck de Puerto Rico, Inc., Sears, Roebuck Oversea, Inc., Terminal Freight Handling Co., Allstate Insurance Company and their subsidiaries, Lifetime Foam Products, Pacific Installers, and Sears, S.A. (Central America).

Position _____

Are any of your relatives employed by Sears in the unit(s) where you want to work?

Type of position desired?   Date available for work   State salary you will consider

Are you willing to relocate?   What initial location would you prefer?

Have you been convicted during the past seven years of a serious crime involving a person's life or property? ☐ NO ☐ YES

If yes, explain. _____

Physical Data

A PHYSICAL DISABILITY OR HANDICAP WILL NOT CAUSE REJECTION IF IN SEARS MEDICAL OPINION YOU ARE ABLE TO SATISFACTORILY PERFORM IN THE POSITION FOR WHICH YOU ARE BEING CONSIDERED.

Do you have any physical condition which may limit your ability to perform the job applied for? If so, please give details. _____

To protect the interests of all concerned, applicants for certain job assignments must pass a physical examination before they are hired. Alternative placement of an applicant who does not meet the physical standards of the job for which he/she was originally considered is permitted.

Education

	No. of Years	Name of School	City and State	Course or College Major	Average Grades	Did you Graduate?	Type of Degree
Senior High School							
College							
Graduate Studies							
Other— Give Type							

Military Service

	Branch of Service	Date Entered Service	Date of Discharge	Highest Rank Held	Service Related Disability	Service-Related Skills and Experience Applicable to Civilian Employment
					YES ☐ NO ☐	

Activities

Professional Organizations _____

What are your hobbies or special interests? _____

Experience

Please give a detailed account of your previous experience and training. Specify the type of work done and the type of work you would prefer to do. If more space is needed, continue on a supplementary page.

RECORD OF EMPLOYMENT AND REFERENCES

LIST BELOW YOUR FOUR MOST RECENT EMPLOYERS, BEGINNING WITH THE CURRENT OR MOST RECENT ONE. IF YOU HAVE HAD LESS THAN FOUR EMPLOYERS, USE THE REMAINING SPACES FOR PERSONAL REFERENCES. IF YOU WERE EMPLOYED UNDER A MAIDEN OR OTHER NAME, PLEASE ENTER THAT NAME IN THE RIGHT HAND MARGIN. IF APPLICABLE, ENTER SERVICE IN THE ARMED FORCES IN THE REVERSE SIDE.

☐ It is satisfactory to contact my present employer.   ☐ It is not satisfactory to contact my present employer.

NOTE: State reason for and length of inactivity between present application date and last employer.

1   Name   Tel. No.
Address
City   State   Zip Code

What kind of work did you do?   Starting Date (Month / Year)   Starting Pay $ ☐ Mo. ☐ Wk. ☐ Hr.   Date of Leaving (Month / Year)   Pay at Leaving $ ☐ Mo. ☐ Wk. ☐ Hr.   Nature of Employer's Business   Why did you leave? Give details   Name of your Supervisor

NOTE: State reason for and length of inactivity between last employer and second last employer.

2   Name   Tel. No.
Address
City   State   Zip Code

What kind of work did you do?   Starting Date (Month / Year)   Starting Pay $ ☐ Mo. ☐ Wk. ☐ Hr.   Date of Leaving (Month / Year)   Pay at Leaving $ ☐ Mo. ☐ Wk. ☐ Hr.   Nature of Employer's Business   Why did you leave? Give details   Name of your Supervisor

NOTE: State reason for and length of inactivity between second last employer and third last employer.

3   Name   Tel. No.
Address
City   State   Zip Code

What kind of work did you do?   Starting Date (Month / Year)   Starting Pay $ ☐ Mo. ☐ Wk. ☐ Hr.   Date of Leaving (Month / Year)   Pay at Leaving $ ☐ Mo. ☐ Wk. ☐ Hr.   Nature of Employer's Business   Why did you leave? Give details   Name of your Supervisor

NOTE: State reason for and length of inactivity between third last employer and fourth last employer.

4   Name   Tel. No.
Address
City   State   Zip Code

What kind of work did you do?   Starting Date (Month / Year)   Starting Pay $ ☐ Mo. ☐ Wk. ☐ Hr.   Date of Leaving (Month / Year)   Pay at Leaving $ ☐ Mo. ☐ Wk. ☐ Hr.   Nature of Employer's Business   Why did you leave? Give details   Name of your Supervisor

Source: Reprinted with permission from Sears, Roebuck and Co.

✔ CHECKLIST for Interview Follow-Up

____▪ Complete and return application forms or other requested materials.

____▪ Write a letter of appreciation for the interview.

____▪ Write notes to yourself regarding what was covered, names of people you met, and upcoming deadlines.

In confirming your letter offering the position, I understand that the starting salary is $19,150 per year to be paid monthly. I will report to Room 236 of the Able Building at 8 a.m. on Monday, January 4, and ask for Phillip Slone, who is to be my training coordinator.

As we discussed earlier, I am impressed with the opportunities Able Computers provides qualified applicants. I will do all I can to justify your trust in my potential.

Letter of Refusal

If you refuse a position offered by a company, your letter should express appreciation for the offer, compliment the interviewer or the company offering the position, clearly refuse the position and explain your refusal, and repeat your appreciation for the offer. Here is an example of a letter refusing a job offer:

Thank you for your letter of September 23 offering a position in Able Computers' manager trainee program. I am sincerely impressed by both your confidence in my potential and the opportunities Able offers to qualified applicants.

Just this morning Stover Chemicals offered me a training position in its employee relations department. Because of Stover's closeness to my home and the immediate opportunity to work directly in the employee relations field, I have decided to accept their offer.

Your interest in me and your consideration of my application are appreciated.

Response to a Rejection Letter

If you receive a letter rejecting your application for a position, you should follow it up, especially if you might reapply with the company in the future. Such a letter should express appreciation for considering your application, express appreciation for the learning experience the application process has provided you, and introduce future application possibilities. Here is an example of a response to a letter of rejection:

Your letter of September 23 indicating that I will not be offered a position in Able Computers' manager trainee program arrived today.

Your time and effort in considering my application are appreciated. Interviewing with you has also been a learning experience that provided me with valuable insight into my qualifications and opportunities for improvement.

As we discussed earlier, I am genuinely impressed with the opportunities Able provides qualified applicants. Therefore, as my qualifications you mentioned in your letter become better, I intend to reapply for a position with Able. Please keep my application on file.

THE DELAYED JOB DECISION

Sometimes you may receive a job offer from one company but will want to wait to see if you receive other, better offers. When this is the case, you may wish to write a letter seeking a delay in your decision. Recruiters assume you are interviewing elsewhere and are not embarrassed nor disconcerted by a request for a delay. On the other hand, they often have deadlines to meet or other applicants to whom they would like to offer the job. Therefore, your request must be tactful:

Recruiters will sometimes allow the applicant a little extra time to consider a job offer.

1. Express appreciation for the offer.
2. Indicate that your goal is to select the company in which you can be of the most benefit and your career will be most enhanced.
3. Explain that your interviewing process is not quite complete and you wish an extension of the decision date (state when you will be able to make a decision).
4. Do not explain that if forced into an immediate decision you would turn the offer down; this is better left unsaid.
5. Reaffirm your interest in the job and the company.

Here is a sample delay request letter:

> Last week you offered me a position at Able computers as a management trainee, starting June 1, at a salary of $19,150. I am very pleased to receive this offer and am giving it much thought. With your offer, you asked that I decide by February 1.
>
> As discussed during my visit to Columbus, I am seeking a position where I can make a valuable contribution while moving toward my career goal of high-level management. To be fair to myself and the company I will work for, I need to explore the job market fully. My exploration is not quite complete.
>
> Would it be convenient to delay my decision about your offer from February 1 until February 20?
>
> Your job offer impresses me and I am excited by it. This delay will enhance the quality of my decision — a decision that is important to both of us.

We hope that you will have the opportunity to compare many job offers, although it is sometimes difficult to weigh the organizations evenly. One company, realizing this, supplies a form for comparison. Its form is shown in Figure 23.10.

SUMMARY

The job interview is the occasion for the company recruiter and the applicant to evaluate each other. The interview thus is an important element in the job-getting process. The more interviews an applicant has, the more experience gained and the greater the probability of landing an offer. To

FIGURE 23.10 ■ *Form for Recording Comparative Data on Prospective Employers*

The Main Hurdman
Career Guide

Despite the fact that accounting opportunities are expanding rapidly, there are many accounting graduates who never fully examine the range of options which are open to them.

From a student's viewpoint, the major accounting firms bear a striking resemblance to each other. Most of the well-known firms were founded within a decade of each other. All have a number of appealing but similar qualities—a record of growth, expanding opportunities, and attractive clientele.

Sorting it out.
A key to effectively planning your career lies in developing a systematic approach to assessing a variety of firm attributes. Certainly, this is no easy task. The Main Hurdman career guide on the next two pages should help you place into perspective various firms and to compare career options.

Before you begin.
The Main Hurdman career guide suggests several important variables, and provides space for applying these variables to different accounting firms. One column, which contains facts about Main Hurdman, has been completed.

Answers in many of the categories will require subjective judgments based upon your own experiences. When you are finished, you will have a set of organization profiles for comparison, analysis and further consideration.

It's Your Decision
If you have made an effort to use this guide, you will have organized some of your thoughts about the firms which you are considering. But there are many variables which cannot be compared objectively. Such qualities as reputation and leadership in the profession are difficult to assess on your own. Speak with your professors, your career counselors, or friends in the profession. They may be able to provide you with specific insights into the firms you are considering.

There is not a great deal of advice we can give you about analyzing the profiles you have developed. You must compare your own goals, values, and abilities with what a firm has to offer,

and then make your own decision. This is an intensely personal process and one that can never be accurately structured, except on an individual basis.

Each firm has a distinctive personality which will become evident to you during the recruitment process as you talk with various firm representatives. If you feel comfortable and interface well with these representatives you will probably be able to achieve maximum self-development in that firm's environment. In the final analysis a firm is nothing more or less than its people.

KMG Klynveld Main Goerdeler International firm

(Continued)

Source: Main Hurdman.

FIGURE 23.10 ■ *Continued*

	Main Hurdman	Firm A	Firm B	Firm C	Firm D	Firm E
Firm image	Recognized for its high quality work and leadership in the profession.					
Professional environment	Staff accountants are highly visible members of their local offices. They work directly with partners and managers. Firm stresses individual development and judgment.					
Firm growth	Dramatic growth over the last decade. Outstanding opportunities available as firm attains its growth goals.					
International scope	Services are provided throughout the world. Opportunities are available for international assignments at advanced levels.					
Firm size	An international accounting firm, but not so large as to lose sight of the individual.					
Client orientation	Main Hurdman provides professional services to a wide range of organizations, from "Fortune 500" multinational firms to small businesses, unions, governmental bodies and other entities.					
Career development	Staff members at all levels participate in an active career counseling and development program. Specialization is available.					
Evaluation and advancement	Promotion solely on merit. Comprehensive written evaluations after assignments.					
Professional education	Formal national professional education programs, regional and local office seminars and intensive on-the-job training.					

acquire interviews, the applicant can use a direct-mail campaign, respond to newspaper advertisements, or use the college placement office.

Once an interview is scheduled, the applicant should plan the interview by evaluating his or her qualifications, researching the company, anticipating what will happen in the interview, knowing what the recruiter is seeking, and preparing for the unexpected. In the interview, the applicant should be on time, and make a positive impression through appropriate nonverbal cues and by saying the right things. The interview should be followed up with a letter of appreciation. Later, the applicant may need to write a delayed follow-up letter that determines his or her standing. Ultimately, a letter of acceptance or rejection will need to be written in response to a job offer.

Key Terms

- direct-mail approach
- cover letter
- networking
- screening interview
- open-ended interview
- panel interview

- group interview
- stress interview
- office visit
- videotape interview
- computer interview

References

Bolles, Richard Nelson. *What Color Is Your Parachute?* Rev. Ed. Berkeley, Calif.: Ten Speed Press, 1990.

Djeddah, Eli. *Moving Up: How to Get High-Salaried Jobs.* Berkeley, Calif.: Ten Speed Press, 1978.

Einhorn, Lois J., Patricia Hayes Bradely, and John E. Baird, Jr. *Effective Employment Interviewing.* Glenview, Ill.: Scott, Foresman, 1982.

Medley, H. Anthony. *Sweaty Palms: The Neglected Art of Being Interviewed.* Berkeley, Calif.: Ten Speed Press, 1984.

Rogers, Edward J. *Getting Hired.* Englewood Cliffs, N.J.: Prentice-Hall, 1982.

U.S. Civil Service Commission. *Career Planning Handbook; A Guide to Career Fields and Opportunities.* Washington, D.C.: Government Printing Office, n.d.

Review Questions

1. What steps are involved in the direct-mail campaign? Describe them.

2. What are the steps in planning for a job interview?

3. Describe five nonverbal behaviors you should be conscious of during the job interview.

4. Discuss the importance of follow-up as it applies to job interviews.

5. What are three situations in which you would be likely to use a follow-up?

Exercises

1. You are a campus recruiter for Goldwin's, a chain of department stores with locations in Dallas, Atlanta, Chicago, and New York. You are looking for an applicant who shows three major qualities: dependability, initiative, and willingness to assume responsibility. The chosen applicant will become a manager trainee at Goldwin's in Atlanta.

a. Interview one of your classmates for this position.

b. Write a brief (no more than two pages) report that summarizes the following:

  i. How you assessed your classmate against the three qualities.

  ii. What your classmate said that made you believe that he or she possessed each of the qualities.

  iii. How your classmate's nonverbal communication affected your perception of him or her.

2. Form a trio with two of your classmates. Person A is the interviewer, Person B is the interviewee, and Person C is the observer. A should interview B for approximately 10 minutes, asking any of the 23 interview questions in Figure 23.6. A and C should give feedback to B about both his or her answers and nonverbal communication. Allow B to practice answering difficult questions. Then switch roles for the next 20 minutes, making sure that each member of your trio plays each person in the exercise.

3. Fill out the qualifications checklist presented in Figure 23.5. Then write a brief report justifying your rating on each qualification. Use your work experience, activities, honors, and interests as evidence.

4. Make an appointment to interview the personnel officer of a local company. Your purpose in this interview is to find out the following:

a. The kinds of questions the person likes to ask in job interviews

b. The role this person thinks nonverbal communication plays in the job interview

c. The most difficult problem this person has in selecting among applicants

d. What qualities this person looks for in people with your level of education

Write a brief report or make a short oral presentation to the class summarizing your findings.

Multiple Offers | CASE

Mary Debner, University of Georgia

John Behn, a senior at State University, put down the phone and let out a loud "Yahoo." He had just received his first job offer. The salary wasn't as high as he had hoped, and the firm wasn't his first choice; but it was a real job. And he would finally be able to get a decent car and get on with his life. He had accepted the offer on the phone and planned to start in June.

The next day, the company that had been John's first choice telephoned with a job offer. The job was in Tampa, right near the beach. The salary was higher, and the company offered a signing fee of $2,000. The recruiter even suggested that if he accepted immediately, he could get an extra $500. John was tempted to accept right away, but he told the recruiter he would have to think about his decision.

John called the company whose offer he had accepted and said, "I know I accepted your offer, and I am very excited about working with you. Something has come up, however, that I would like to discuss with you. Another firm has made a very attractive offer that I feel I must seriously consider. This firm offers a management career track that would put me in charge of a small operating unit right away. As you may recall from our interview, this is just the kind of opportunity I've been looking for."

John paused, waiting for an indication from the other end of the phone that he hadn't gone too far out on a limb. None came; he plunged ahead. "I will be happy to honor my commitment with you, yet if you would feel comfortable with my making another choice, I would accept the offer from the other company. While I am very excited about the opportunity to work with your firm, the other offer also represents strong challenges that are closely aligned with my career interests in marketing and management."

The manager of the original firm said that he was impressed with John's presentation of the problem, but he still expected John to honor his acceptance. It looked like the dream job was down the tubes.

Case Questions

1. What do you think John should do?

2. Was John's phone call to the original firm appropriate?

3. How could John have prevented this problem?

4. Why do you think the manager was impressed with John's presentation of the problem? What characteristics did John communicate to the manager about himself? How would these characteristics be productive if John were a manager?

CASE | *Who's Interviewing Whom?*

Jim Stull, San Jose State University

Carla Chavez landed an interview with Tom Coates, regional sales manager for Nirvana Computers. During the interview, he asked, "Why do you want to work for Nirvana?"

Carla replied, "Well, Mr. Coates, that's why I asked for the opportunity to meet with you. I want to be sure that Nirvana *is* the right company for me. I've read a great deal of literature about Nirvana. I've met a few of your employees. I listened to a presentation by one of your campus recruiters. Everything that I've heard and read has been extremely positive. I'm especially impressed by your concern for employees and service to customers.

"But I need to see some of this for myself. I'm not sure that I can get a true feeling for the Nirvana culture without visiting and finding out how I would fit the profile of a Nirvana sales representative. I have a few questions that I need answered before I can be sure."

Tom said, "Go ahead and ask."

Carla had specific questions about Nirvana policies, and she probed until she was satisfied that she had received the information she needed.

Tom leaned back in his chair. "I like your style, Carla, and I think you've got the making of a top-notch Nirvana sales representative."

Case Questions

1. What do you think it is in Carla's verbal behavior that Tom likes? Be specific and identify some of Carla's words that you believe were particularly effective in winning Tom over.

2. Some interviewers might perceive Carla's statement, "I want to be sure that Nirvana *is* the right company for me," as threatening. Why do you think that they might?

3. Carla used an information-getting technique called probing. Explain why this is effective when used by the interviewee. Why is this technique especially effective for Carla, in view of her objective to be a sales representative? Write a brief dialogue between Carla and Tom showing how Carla would use the probing technique.

Lost Opportunity | CASE

Michael T. O'Neill, Personnel Finders of Arlington, Inc.

On the advice of his college placement center, Sid Flaccus called Data Preparation Associates to set up an interview for the entry-level technical writing position DPA advertised in the placement center's *Job Hot Line*.

Flaccus is 22 years old and has a B.A. in English. He works part-time for Personnel Service of Arlington, Texas, where he writes manuals, letters, memos, and reports.

Sid arrived 15 minutes early for his interview with Betty Boman, the chief editor at DPA. He had dressed in a suit and tie and had even shined his shoes. Two days earlier he had had his hair styled and cut short.

Betty was dressed casually and appeared relaxed. Sid could see that she was an experienced interviewer. She let Sid do most of the talking, but interrupted his digressions about his writing experiences to ask pointed questions about Sid's knowledge of computers and computer software.

Sid knew a little about computers from his required course in computer science, and he added that he "didn't see much difference between journalism and tech writing." He even recommended a recent article to Betty that took computer software writers to task for their jargon. Sid quoted several humorous examples from it.

When the conversation turned to Sid's writing, he quickly pointed out that he had published a short story in the campus magazine and was writing a scholarly paper on poetry. He also mentioned that his English professors had praised his writing and encouraged a writing career.

The interview lasted nearly an hour; for the last half hour Betty asked no questions. She and Sid discussed the novels of William Faulkner, in whose work they shared an interest. The interview ended cordially, and Betty told Sid to call in about a week.

When Sid called a week later, he was surprised to find that another applicant had been offered the job.

Case Questions

1. What do you suspect caused Betty to turn Sid down?

2. What would you have done differently at the interview that might have changed its outcome?

3. Would you tell Sid to do anything differently at his next interview? What?

Recognizable Patterns of Language

RECOGNIZABLE PATTERNS

A knowledge of grammar is necessary in order to communicate efficiently. Grammar provides the logical, mutually recognizable patterns in which the language operates.

Consider the following two sequences of numbers:

a. 5   3   9   1   4   0   8   2   7   6.
b. 9   8   7   6   5   4   3   2   1   0.

Which sequence puts less burden on the reader? Which sequence is easier to remember? Why? Sentence b is the answer, of course, because it follows a recognizable pattern. People look for such patterns in every aspect of life—in their daily schedules, in professors' lectures, in the music they listen to, in the way they drive cars, in certain matters of social protocol, and in the grammar of language.

Take a look at the following two sentences:

c. audited accountant ledger The the.
d. The accountant audited the ledger.

Which of these sentences communicates more efficiently? Which is easier to remember? Why? The answer is sentence d, because it follows the grammar (recognizable patterns) of the English language, whereas sentence c is nonsense.

Of course, not all the problems discussed in this chapter are as flagrant as those in the nonsense sentence, but readers do look for recognizable patterns. Further, the burden is on the writer (or speaker) to adopt the "you" attitude, that is, to identify with the reader's (or listener's) interests and concerns and to make the grammar everything that it should be for the reader's (or listener's) ease.

As it is actually used, the language has four levels of formality:

- *Standard.* This is what the textbooks teach, the highest level. You should use this level in contexts like job interviews and written reports.

Learning Objectives

After reading and understanding this section, you will be able to write a correct sentence. More specifically, you will be able:

1 *To identify grammatical patterns.*

2 *To follow the formal guidelines for usage.*

3 *To punctuate in accordance with established guidelines.*

4 *To spell correctly.*

- *Informal.* This is the level of most conversations around the office.
- *Colloquial.* This is the level of the company picnic or fishing trip.
- *Substandard.* This is the level of small children and others who have yet to learn the rules.

You should try to use the level appropriate to the situation. The grammar of the fishing trip will keep you from getting a job in an interview; the grammar of the interview will seem stilted on a fishing trip. Learn the standard rules so that you can rise to them when the occasion demands. A basic assumption is that the audience in business is usually literate; that is, the audience will be most favorably disposed toward the message and the product if the message follows the recognizable patterns (guidelines) of standard English. There are times when educated business people break some of these guidelines; they should do so deliberately, not ignorantly. For example, the writers of a widely circulated advertising campaign were well aware that *we*, not *us*, is the proper pronoun to serve as a subject of a verb, but still they used, "Us Tareyton smokers would rather fight than switch." Perhaps the writers reasoned that an audience of fighters wouldn't really care about grammatical formalities.

UNITS IN GRAMMAR

"Give me a place to stand," said the Greek mathematician Archimedes, "and I will move the world." By analogy, the writer might say, "If I can write a sentence, I can move the world." A complete sentence has at least one clause, a clause has at least one phrase, and a phrase has at least one word.

Complete Sentence

A sentence may be of any length provided that it contains the following:

- A capital letter on the first word
- An independent clause
- A period or other appropriate ending punctuation mark

Clause

A clause must contain both of the following:

- *A subject.* In commands, the subject is often understood, as in "[*You*] type this letter."
- *A verb.* This must be a full verb, such as *audit*, not an infinitive, such as *to audit.*

Clauses may be of two kinds, independent or dependent.

Independent Clause

An independent clause can stand alone. It does not depend on another thought to make a statement. *The accountant audited the ledger* is an example.

Dependent Clause

A dependent clause begins with a subordinating word. It may function as an adverb, an adjective, or a noun within a sentence. In this sentence, the dependent clause functions as an adverb: *When the accountant audited the ledger*, the judge dismissed the lawsuit. In this sentence it functions as an adjective: The accountant *who audited the ledger* is Laurie Sosebee. In this sentence it serves as a noun: The judge could see *that the accountant had audited the ledger*. In the dependent clause used as a noun, the "subordinating word" is often understood and omitted: The judge could see *the accountant had audited the ledger*.

Phrases

A phrase is a cluster of words that work together grammatically and that function as a single word might serve, if available. Some of the more common types of phrases are as follows:

- **Noun** (nominal). Noun phrases always function as nouns; for example: *The accountant* audited *the ledger*.
- **Verb**. Verb phrases always function as verbs; for example: The accountant *is auditing* the ledger.
- **Infinitive**. An infinitive phrase may function as a noun; for example: Laurie decided *to audit the ledger* (infinitive plus object of infinitive). An infinitive phrase may function as an adjective; for example: The accountant *to audit the ledger* is Laurie. It may function like an adverb; for example: *To audit the ledger*, you will need to see the bursar.

  Sometimes the *to* preposition does not appear in front of the infinitive; the most common instance is an infinitive after a modal verb (*can, may, must, shall, will*): I can pass the CMA examination; not, I can to pass the CMA examination.
- **Participial**. Participial phrases always function as adjectives (modifiers of the meanings of nouns or pronouns). The present participle always ends in *ing*; for example: *Auditing the ledger*, the accountant had difficulty with some entries. The past participle of most verbs ends in *ed*; for example: *Audited in accordance with the specifications*, the ledger was returned to the file.
- **Gerundive**. A gerundive phrase always contains an *ing* word formed from a verb and used as a noun; for example: *Working late* is something that accountants often do during the first two weeks of April. Compare this with the present participle, which is used as an adjective. The gerund (*ing* word used as a noun) is identical to the present participle in form but not in function.
- **Prepositional**. A prepositional phrase may function as an adverb; for example: The accountant testified *on the witness stand*. Alternatively, it may function as an adjective; for example: The accountant *on the witness* stand is Laurie Sosebee.

Words

Words serve various functions. Some of the most common of these functions are the following.

Substantives

Nouns and pronouns are classified as substantives.

1. *Nouns* serve as subjects and complements of verbs and as objects of prepositions. Nouns generally form the plural by adding an *-s* to the singular (*girl→girls*), but a few are irregular (*woman→women, datum→data, series→series*).
2. *Pronouns* are stand-ins for nouns. There are at least four common pronoun types.
   a. *Personal pronouns* are summarized in Table 1. Note the three forms (cases). The nominative case is used for the subject of the verb (*I* saw John), the objective case for the object of the verb (John saw *me*). The possessive case denotes possession.
   b. *Relative pronouns* appear in clauses used as adjectives, to relate the clause to the noun antecedent. There are five relative pronouns: *that*,[1] *which*, and *who*, plus a possessive form, *whose*, and an objective form, *whom*. (Can you find the relative clause you are now reading?)
   c. *Interrogative pronouns* ask questions: *who, whose, whom*, and *which* appear here as well as in the list of relative pronouns. Another interrogative pronoun is *what*.
   d. *Indefinite pronouns* include *one, anybody, anyone, everybody, everyone, somebody*, and *someone*. They are the only pronouns that use the apostrophe to form the possessive (*one's, anybody's*, and so on).

Verbs

Verbs express action or states of being. Each verb has three parts: the stem *(audit/write),* the past *(audited/wrote),* and the past participle *(audited/written).* Verbs have two basic tenses—present *(audit)* and past *(audited).* With the use of auxiliaries, verbs can express future time *(is going to audit, will audit)* as well as shades of present time *(is auditing)* and past time *(has audited, had audited).* Most verbs have a passive form *(is audited),* which differs from the active in that the passive contains (a) some form of be *(be/am/is/are/was/were/being/been)* plus a past participle and (b) directs its action toward the grammatical subject *(the ledger was audited).*

If a verb ends its past tense in *ed* and uses the same form for its past participle, the verb is regular *(audit→audited).* Any other verb is irregular

---

[1] Additionally, *that* may function to introduce a clause used as a noun or may be used as a demonstrative adjective. In this sentence, *that* is a relative pronoun: The ledger *that I audited* is on the desk. In this sentence, it introduces a noun clause: I saw *that the ledger was audited.* In this sentence, it is a demonstrative adjective: *That* ledger is the one I audited.

TABLE 1 ▮ *Personal Pronouns*

	Singular			Plural		
	Nominative	*Objective*	*Possessive*	*Nominative*	*Objective*	*Possessive*
First Person	I	me	my/mine	we	us	our/ours
Second Person	you (thou)	you (thee)	your/yours (thy/thine)	you[a] (ye)	you[a]	your/yours
Third Person						
Neuter	it	it	its	they	them	their/theirs
Feminine	she	her	her/hers	same as neuter		
Masculine	he	him	his	same as neuter		

[a]Common regional variants in speech are *y'all* (contraction of *you all*), *yous* (pluralizing *you* like a noun), and *you guys,* all of which have possessive forms as well: In speech these forms compensate for the distinction lost several centuries ago when *you*, historically plural, replaced *thou* and *thee*, which have always been singular.

(write→wrote, written). A verb that takes an object is called transitive, because its action goes across to the object. (The Latin prefix *trans* means across.) A verb that takes no object is intransitive. *Raise* and *lay* are transitive; their intransitive cognates are *rise* and *lie*. You raise the desk [object]. The desk rises [no object]. Only transitive verbs can go into the passive voice.

Modifiers

Adjectives and adverbs are classified as modifiers.

1. *Adjectives* modify or clarify nouns and pronouns.
   a. *Descriptive* adjectives often precede the word they modify; for example: I audit *red* ledgers. However, they can take a position far from the noun or pronoun modified; for example: Ledgers I audit are *red*. Descriptive adjectives can usually be compared (*red, redder, reddest*).
   b. *Demonstrative* adjectives (*this, that, these, those*) must always precede the noun they modify. They also differ from descriptive adjectives in that they must agree with the noun in number. (*These book* is not grammatical English.)
   c. *Articles* (*an, an, the*) follow the same rules as demonstrative adjectives. They must always precede the noun and agree in number. (*A books* is not grammatically correct.)
2. *Adverbs* modify verbs, adjectives, and other adverbs, as illustrated in these examples:

   I wrote *fast*. (The adverb *fast* modifies the verb.)

   I wrote *unusually* fast. (The adverb *unusually* modifies another adverb.)

   He is *unusually* tall. (The adverb modifies the adjective *tall*.)

Some analysts put *very* into a separate category, intensifiers. The reasons are that *very* is historically an adjective, is often used as an adjective (the very idea), and is not a pure adverb in that it cannot modify verbs (you can run fast, but you can't run very).

Prepositions

Prepositions are the headwords in prepositional phrases. They always connect a substantive to the rest of the sentence. The combination of preposition with substantive is a prepositional phrase (I went *into my office* to audit the ledger).

Conjunctions

The most important class of conjunctions is the coordinating conjunction, so named because it conjoins two or more units that are grammatically equivalent (two prepositional phrases, two verbs, two nouns, and so on). The coordinating conjunctions are *and, or, nor*, and *but*. When used to combine two independent clauses, the coordinating conjunction should be preceded by a comma; for example: The ledger contained mistakes, *and* the accountant had to work overtime to find them.

Expletives

The two common grammatical expletives are *it* and *there*. Both serve merely to get a clause moving:

It is raining.
There is one ledger on the table.
There are two ledgers on the desk.

Note that *there* can never be the subject of a sentence.

Interjections

These include *oh* and *well* used at the beginning of a clause.

QUIZ

This quiz may help you ascertain how well you apply specific guidelines for use of the English language. For each of the 25 sentences, indicate the type of error that you find, if any, by entering in the blank one letter from the following list. Correct each sentence in which you find an error.

A. Error in grammar or usage
B. Error in punctuation
C. Correct, no error
D. Error in spelling or capitalizing
E. Erroneous statement about grammar or punctuation
  1. _____ The chapter on loans was entitled "Principal and Interest".
  2. _____ The ledger was kind of illegible.

3. _____ A comma should appear before the coordinating conjunction joining two independent clauses.

4. _____ According to Mark Lester, "Grammar is a way of talking about how words are used to make units that communicate a meaning." (*Introductory Transformational Grammar of English*, 2d ed. [New York: Holt, Rinehart and Winston, 1976], 13).

5. _____ The city's four industries, Unisys, Data General Datapoint, and Halliburton, were expanding rapidly.

6. _____ The financial planner applied the new formula and the long-term forecast became much more optimistic.

7. _____ John's writing 32 instead of 23 in the last column caused the total to be $9 too high; however, he found the error quickly.

8. _____ B. F. Skinner was born in Susquehanna, Pennsylvania in 1904.

9. _____ Susan B. Anthony and Carrie Nation both supported womens' suffrage.

10. _____ Rensselaer Polytechnic Institute is a technological university. The oldest one in the United States.

11. _____ Metathesis is when someone transposes or reverses the letters in a word.

12. _____ The speaker's habit of inserting "You know" into virtually every sentence of the presentation weakened it's overall effect.

13. _____ I would urge you to sell that stock now and you should reinvest the money in a computer company.

14. _____ A worker must pay their union dues by payroll deduction.

15. _____ The accomodations were inadequate.

16. _____ On Sunday the "Daily Star" had a circulation of 35,003.

17. _____ Attending the class, a cadaver was used for experiments.

18. _____ Jill claimed, in her resumé, that she had taught at the University of Leeds, England, from 1989–1990.

19. _____ The passive voice in grammar is a combination of some form of *be* plus a past participle.

20. _____ After recieving fair warning from the instructor, George finally learned to separate *a lot* into two words.

21. _____ The contract is to expire at noon on July 1, 1994 when the new contract takes effect.

22. _____ You should remember to add in the deposits that have arrived by mail, you should never send out notices of bad checks until you have considered all deposits for the day.

23. _____ Attending the meeting were Joseph Biggs, Laramie, Wyoming, president, David L. Carson, Troy, New York, secretary, and Allen White, Duncan, Oklahoma, treasurer.

24. _____ Laurie felt badly about the erroneous entries in the ledger.

25. _____ Now that we have finished the quiz, is there any questions?

Answers and Corrections

  1. **B.** The chapter on loans was entitled "Principal and Interest."

  2. **A.** The ledger was rather illegible.

  3. **C.**

4. B. According to Mark Lester, "Grammar is a way of talking about how words are used to make units that communicate a meaning" (*Introductory Transformational Grammar of English*, 2d ed. [New York: Holt, Rinehart and Winston, 1976], 13).

5. B. The city's four industries—Unisys, Data General, Datapoint, and Halliburton—were expanding rapidly.

6. B. The financial planner applied the new formula, and the long-term forecast became much more optimistic.

7. B. John's writing <u>32</u> instead of <u>23</u> in the last column caused the total to be $9 too high; however, he found the error quickly.

8. B. B. F. Skinner was born in Susquehanna, Pennsylvania, in 1904.

9. B. or **D.** Susan B. Anthony and Carrie Nation both supported women's suffrage.

10. B. Rensselaer Polytechnic Institute is a technological university—the oldest one in the United States.

11. A. Metathesis is the transposing or reversing of the letters in a word. *Or* Metathesis occurs when someone transposes or reverses the letters in a word.

12. B. or **D.** The speaker's habit of inserting "You know" into virtually every sentence of the presentation weakened its overall effect.

13. A. I would urge you to sell that stock now and to reinvest the money in a computer company.

14. A. Workers must pay their union dues by payroll deduction. *Or* A worker must pay his or her union dues by payroll deduction.

15. D. The accommodations were inadequate.

16. B. On Sunday the *Daily Star* had a circulation of 35,003.

17. A. Attending the class, I used a cadaver for experiments. *Or* When I attended the class, a cadaver was used for experiments.

18. A. Jill claimed, in her resumé, that she had taught at the University of Leeds, England, during 1989 and 1990. *Or* from 1989 to 1990.

19. C.

20. D. The correct spelling is *receiving*; the other frequently misspelled expressions—*separate* and *a lot*—are correct as given.

21. B. The contract is to expire at noon on July 1, 1994, when the new contract takes effect.

22. B. You should remember to add in the deposits that have arrived by mail; you should never send out notices of bad checks until you have considered all deposits for the day.

23. B. Attending the meeting were Joseph Biggs, Laramie, Wyoming, president; David L. Carson, Troy, New York, secretary; and Allen White, Duncan, Oklahoma, treasurer.

24. A. Laurie felt bad about the erroneous entries in the ledger.

25. A. Now that we have finished the quiz, are there any questions?

GUIDELINES

These guidelines, if followed, will enhance your ability to communicate, especially in writing, so that the reader can understand you more easily. Remember that the "you" attitude minimizes the burden on the reader (or listener).

Proofreading Symbols

The following symbols are often used in proofreading to correct various errors:

⌒ ⌣	Close up, as in *partner⌒ship*.
⌿	Delete material slashed and close up, as in *judg⌒ment*.
✗	Delete the material circled, as in *July⃝1974 was President Nixon's last full month in office*.
¶	Start a new paragraph.
No ¶	Do not begin a new paragraph.
∨ ∧	Insert missing material, as in *The TVA began during the Franklin Presidency of∧ Roosevelt*.
⊦[	Move the item to the left.
]⊢	Move the item to the right.
Sp	Correct the spelling error.
⑤p	Spell out the abbreviation in the text. (This notation usually appears in the margin.)

The rest of this Appendix is in three sections: "Guidelines for Usage," "Guidelines for Punctuation," and "Guidelines for Spelling and Capitalization." Usage has to do with choice of words in speaking or writing. Punctuation and spelling and capitalization are issues only in writing.

Guidelines for Usage

A/An Confusion

Use *a* before consonant sounds, *an* before vowel sounds: *A/An*

Colloquial:	The company requested *a* audit.
Standard:	The company requested *an* audit.
Standard:	The word begins with an *f*.

Adjective/Adverb Confusion

Do not misuse an adjective for an adverb or an adverb for an adjective.   *Adj/Adv*

Misleading:	Laurie felt *badly* about the erroneous entries in the ledger.
True:	Laurie felt *bad* about the erroneous entries in the ledger.
Colloquial:	You did *real good*.
Standard:	You did *really well*.
Nonstandard:	I could *sure* use a new calculator.
Standard:	I could *surely* use a new calculator.

Some of the pairs of words that are often confused, cited later in guidelines for Word Misuse and for Spelling, are adjective/adverb confusions (for example, *because of/due to* and *all together/altogether*).

Adverbial Noun

Do not use an adverb clause where a noun clause is needed. The words *if* and *because* are adverbs and in standard English should not be used to introduce noun clauses. *When* and *where* are also subject to this error when they are used in definitions.

Instead of:	I'll see if she is here.
Use:	I'll see whether she is here.
Instead of:	The reason is because I'm penniless.
Use:	The reason is that I'm penniless.
Instead of:	Metathesis is when two letters are transposed.
Use:	Metathesis is the transposition of two letters. *Or:* Metathesis occurs when two letters are transposed.

Dangling Expressions

DglP   Make sure that a participle has a substantive logically to modify. Participles are verbal forms ending in *ing* (present) and *ed* (past) and used as adjectives. If the substantive that the participle is to modify is not actually named, the participle is said to dangle. See also guidelines for Misplaced Modifiers.

Dangling participle:	Rejected by management, a strike began at midnight.
Correct:	Rejected by management, the union went on strike at midnight.

The most vexing problem is with a present participle at the beginning of a sentence (often passive). Here is how such a dangling participle develops:

> I attended the class.
> I used a cadaver for experiments.

> Attending the class (*present participle*).
> A cadaver was used for experiments.

The passive sentence, in eliminating the need to mention the doer of the action, simultaneously eliminates the word that *attending* needs to modify. See the guideline on Passives, Needless.

Dangling participle:	Attending the class, a cadaver was used for experiments.
Correct:	Attending the class, I used a cadaver for experiments.
Correct:	When I attended the class, a cadaver was used for experiments.
Correct:	In one of my classes, a cadaver was used for experiments.

Name the doer of the action of a gerund.

Dangling gerund:	By standing on the riverbank, a steamboat could be seen.
Correct:	By standing on a riverbank, I could see a steamboat.

DglG

Double Negative

To express a negative concept, use *one* negative word. Observe that *hardly* and *merely* are negative in effect.

Colloquial:	I can't hardly sleep well, because of the money I lost in the canal.
Standard:	I can't sleep well, because of the money I lost in the canal.
Standard:	I can hardly sleep well, because of the money I lost in the canal.

Double negatives can be used in standard English if the intent is to express a positive concept. This behavior, technically known as litotes, is in fact *not uncommon.*

Incomplete Constructions

Do not leave out any word that is necessary to make a statement or a comparison logical and complete.

IC

Incomplete:	Richard wanted to pass not only the CPA examination but the bar examination.
Complete:	Richard wanted to pass not only the CPA examination but also the bar examination.
Incomplete:	Be specific as possible.
Complete:	Be as specific as possible.

Misplaced Modifiers

Position a modifier and the word modified as close together as possible. See also guidelines for dangling expressions.

MM

Misplaced:	It is unwise to carry an electromagnet into a computer center that is activated.
Better:	It is unwise to carry an electromagnet that is activated into a computer center.
Better still:	It is unwise to carry an activated electromagnet into a computer center.

A particular problem arises with the use of certain words such as *almost, just, nearly,* and *only.* Observe how *only* effects a different meaning in each of the following positions noted by the caret (�‿):

1   2   3   4   5
˘ The ˘ house ˘ cost ˘ $90,000 ˘ .

1. You'll pay an additional fortune for the garage!
2. There's no other house on the block.

3. The house really isn't worth that much.
4. The house doesn't cost any more than that.
5. There's no additional charge in pesos or yen.

Mood

Use the moods of verbs correctly. English verbs have three moods: indicative, subjunctive, and imperative. The indicative, used for statements and questions about facts, is by far the most common.

1. Use the subjunctive mood for statements contrary to fact and for resolutions under parliamentary procedure. (You look as if I *were* from Mars. I move that the budget *be adopted.*)
2. Use moods consistently. A common problem occurs when an untrained writer shifts needlessly from the indicative to the imperative (command); this shift usually involves a simultaneous shift in person, because the imperative mood can by definition be only in the second person.

Parallelism, Faulty

// Make concepts that are parallel in thought parallel in grammatical form. In particular, because a coordinating conjunction must coordinate, be careful to keep coordinate elements on either side of it.

Faulty:	Keyboarding the data and to write the program might take all week.
Parallel:	To keyboard the data and to write the program might take all week.
Parallel:	Keyboarding the data and writing the program might take all week.

Also, be sure to follow each member of correlative pairs (*both. . .and, either. . .or, neither. . .nor, not only. . .but also*) with the same grammatical structure as the other member of the pair.

Faulty:	Both in cost and size, this computer is best.
Parallel:	In both cost and size, this computer is best.
Parallel:	Both in cost and in size, this computer is best.

Passives, Needless

PX Avoid needless use of the passive voice (which may sound stilted) when the active voice (which is specific and often dynamic) will do the job. Use of the passive may also contribute to the construction of a sentence that begins with a dangling participle (see Dangling Expressions).

Passive:	The audit was conducted.
Active:	The accountant conducted the audit.

Preposition at End of Sentence

PrepX Prepositions at the end of a sentence are native to the English language; avoid them only if you gain some rhetorical advantage by doing so.

Flat:	This is the desk our best accountant worked herself to death at.
Better:	This is the desk at which our best accountant worked herself to death.

If nothing will be gained by a change, this is a rule that you can just forget *about*.

Pronoun Problems

Give each pronoun a specific noun (antecedent) to refer to. The problem occurs most often with *it, that, this, they,* and *which*.   *PRef*

Vague:	The accounts had not been audited. This brought about many problems with the Internal Revenue Service.
Proper:	The accounts had not been audited. This failure brought about many difficulties with the Internal Revenue Service.
Proper:	Failure to audit the accounts brought about many difficulties with the Internal Revenue Service.

Make each pronoun agree with its antecedent in number and gender.   *PAgr*

1. Use a plural pronoun to refer to a plural noun and a singular pronoun to refer to a singular noun (see also guidelines for Subject–Verb Disagreement).
2. If the antecedent is two substantives joined by *and* (as in *X and Y*), make the pronoun plural (such as *they*), unless X and Y form a single unit, as in *bacon and eggs* (*it*).
3. If the antecedent is two substantives joined by *or* or *nor*, make the pronoun agree with the nearer antecedent.
4. Use a singular pronoun (such as *it*) if a collective noun antecedent is unitary.[2]

Unitary:	It [the committee] agrees with the union about the need for a stock option plan.

[2]British standards differ from American standards in some pronunciations and in several other ways. A few examples:

a. British collective nouns (such as *committee, government*) are always plural.
b. British occasionally exercises different syntactical choices (*Have you got the time?* and *Is our policy different to yours?* as opposed to American *Do you have the time?* and *Is our policy different from yours?*).
c. Certain vocabulary items in British are unknown in American, and vice versa. Examples are *bloke* and *zebra crossing* (crosswalk) in British and *sidewalk* and *automobile* in American.
d. Words have different meanings in the two dialects. In American *to table a motion* usually means, in effect, to kill it; but in British *to table a motion* means to schedule it for a vote.
e. British punctuation uses single quotation marks where American uses double quotation marks, and vice versa.
f. Spelling is often different (*civilization/civilisation, color/colour, connection/connexion, maneuver/manoeuvre*).

We should be aware of these and other differences and exercise special care in international business communications. Multinational managers should be particularly careful to design advertising slogans that can be used throughout the English-speaking world.

Individual: They [the committee] are going to the meeting in separate cars and airplanes.

If the use of a plural pronoun with a collective noun antecedent is awkward, you may wish to recast the sentence.

5. Avoid sex bias in the use of pronouns. See Chapter 3 for examples of how to avoid sexist language.
6. Treat words following *every* (*everybody, everyone*) as singular (*every man, woman, and child* has *his or her* problems).
7. Treat foreign plurals (*data, memoranda*) as plural in English, too.

PCase Use the proper case of pronoun.

1. Remember that a pronoun takes the case it has in its own clause.

Instead of: Give the file to whomever asks for it.

Use: Give the file to whoever asks for it. (*Whoever* is the subject of *asks;* the object of the preposition *to* is the entire clause *whoever asks for it.*)

Instead of: This is her you're speaking with.

Use: This is she you're speaking with. (The object of *with* is an understood *whom* or *that.*)

2. In the formal context use nominative pronouns for all nominative uses.

Say: Susan and I wrote the program.

Say: This is he, speaking.

3. Use objective pronouns for all objective uses.

Say: The secretaries gave a party for John and me.

Say: Between you and me there is an understanding.

4. Use the possessive case before a gerund.

Don't say: I was displeased with him resigning so abruptly.

Say: I was displeased with his resigning so abruptly.

5. Be conscious of courtesy in sequence of pronouns; if you can put yourself last, do so.

Say: Janice and I are the top salespersons.

Split Infinitive

SInf A split infinitive is often awkward; if it is, try to avoid it.

Awkward: Virginia decided to, at the last minute, take the CPA review course.

Better: At the last minute, Virginia decided to take the CPA review course.

Subject–Verb Disagreement

Make each subject and verb agree in number and person. See also guide-lines for Pronoun Problems. *SVAgr*

1. Use a singular verb with a singular subject, a plural verb with a plural subject.
2. If the subject is two substantives joined by *and*, as in *X and Y*, make the verb plural unless *X and Y* forms a single unit (for example: *Ham and eggs is a common breakfast*).

Don't say:	Dallas and Houston is the largest cities in Texas.
Say:	Dallas and Houston are the largest cities in Texas.

3. If the subject is two substantives joined by *or* or *nor*, make the verb agree with the nearer substantive. For verbs, this rule applies to agreement in person as well as to agreement in number.

Don't say:	Either the accountants or the manager have objected to the new policy.
Say:	Either the manager or the accountants have objected to the new policy.

4. Use a singular verb (such as *is*) if a collective noun subject is unitary. If a collective noun subject is acting as individuals and a plural is awkward, you should recast the sentence. Instead of *The committee have*, say *The committee members have*.

Unitary:	The committee has remained firm in its resolve.
Individual:	The committee have argued all morning. *Or:* The committee members have argued all morning.

5. In sentences beginning with *there* or *here*, be careful to make the verb agree with the logical subject.

Colloquial:	There is too few accounting professors.
Formal:	There are too few accounting professors.

6. Treat words after *every (everybody, everyone)* as singular; for example: *Every man, woman, and child was present.*
7. Treat foreign plurals (*data, memoranda*) as plural in English, too.

Don't say:	This data is...
Say:	These data are...

8. Make the verb agree with the real subject, not with the object of an intervening prepositional phrase.

Not this:	Yesterday's balance of the accounts were correct.
But this:	Yesterday's balance of the accounts was correct.

Tense Problems

1. Use English tenses properly with regard to time. *Tns*
   a. The present tense describes current happenings (*I am studying ac-counting*), facts that are always true (*Only women can give birth*),

or historical events discussed in present time (*Hildebrand goes to Canossa and begs for mercy*).

   b. The past tense describes events in past time.

   c. English expresses future time by using the present tense with an adverb of time (*I study accounting tomorrow*), with modal *will* or *shall* (*I will study accounting*), or through other means, usually the present participle of *go* (*I am going to study accounting*).

2. Use tense consistently.

Don't say:	Geraldine adds up the columns and advised her supervisor about the overrings.
Say:	Geraldine added [or adds] up the columns and advised [or advises] her supervisor about the overrings.

3. If events happen at different times, use auxiliary verbs logically.

Not this:	Peri has been a good skier before she has broken her leg.
But this:	Peri had been a good skier before she broke her leg.

Word Misuse

WL   **1.** Use logical comparisons. Some adjectives and adverbs are absolute in meaning and do not logically submit to comparison. Examples are *complete, full, perfect*, and *unique*. Instead of saying *fuller/fullest* or *more/most unique*, use *more/most nearly full* or *unique*.

Wordy   **2.** Avoid wordiness.

Don't write:	Due to the fact that. . .
Write:	Because. . .
Don't write:	Fill the tank up.
Write:	Fill the tank.
Don't write:	Utilize
Write:	Use
Don't write:	The ledger that was returned to me was Tom's.
Write:	The ledger returned to me was Tom's.
Don't write:	Consensus of opinion
Write:	Consensus
Don't write:	Whether or not
Write:	Whether
Don't write:	And etc.
Write:	Etc.

3. Use standard expressions.

WW   **a.** There is no *s* in *anywhere, nowhere*, or *a long way*.

   b. The adverbial *kind of* and *sort of* (or *kinda, sorta*) should be omitted or changed to a standard expression such as *rather, somewhat*, or *a little. Kind of* and *sort of* are correct if the *of* preposition has an object (*Jane is the best kind of consultant*). *Kind of* and *sort of* are correct if you can use *type of* in the same position.

c. The infinitive sign *to* is preferable to *and* after *try* (*try to come*, not *try and come*).

d. Some words in colloquial speech are out of place in business situations where you are expected to use standard English.

Colloquial	*Standard*
Complected	Complexioned
Enthused	Enthusiastic
Irregardless	Regardless or irrespective
Yourn, Yous	Yours
Illiterate past tenses and past participles, such as brung, clumb, knowed, have went, and have wrote	*Correct past tenses and past participles, such as brought, climbed, knew, have gone, and have written*

e. Some words are more specific than others. Use exact language.

Inexact	*Exact*
Contact	Communicate with, telephone, visit
Good	Delicious, effective, fitting, pious, well-behaved, wholesome
Great	Famous, large, wonderful
Nice	Attractive, congenial, easygoing, thoughtful

f. Some expressions that seem alike in some way are actually different. Learn to discriminate between the following pairs:

Almost	Most
Among	Between
Amount	Number
An	And
As . . . as (*with positive comparison*)	So . . . as (*with negative comparison*)
Because of	Due to
Can	May
Continual	Continuous
Each other	One another
Fewer	Less
Farther	Further
Imply	Infer
In	Into
Lay (*transitive verb* meaning to put or place)	Lie (*intransitive verb* meaning to recline)
Oral	Verbal
Set (*transitive verb* meaning to put or place)	Sit (*intransitive verb* meaning to seat oneself)
Shall	Will
Whereas	While

Many people have difficulty with the difference between *lay* and *lie*. No native speaker misuses *raise* and *rise*, where the issue is the same. Observe the following:

	Transitive	*Intransitive*
Stem	raise/lay	rise/lie
Past Tense	raised/laid	rose/lay
Past Participle	raised/laid	risen/lain

Guidelines for Punctuation

Apostrophe

Apos

1. For all nouns, use the apostrophe to indicate possession. If a noun ends in *s*, add only the apostrophe. If the noun does not end in *s*, add *'s* for the singular possessive or end the word with *s'* for the plural possessive.

Singular		*Plural*	
Nominative	*Possessive*	*Nominative*	*Possessive*
Thomas	Thomas'	Thomases	Thomases'
Jane	Jane's	Janes	Janes'
company	company's	companies	companies'
woman	woman's	women	women's
attorney general	attorney general's	attorneys general	attorneys general's (*or* of the attorneys general)

2. Use the apostrophe with only the last noun in a series citing joint ownership.

   Individual ownership: John's and Mary's clothes

   Joint ownership: Derrill and Suzanne's advertising agency

3. Use the apostrophe with indefinite pronouns to indicate possession (*everybody's, one's*).
4. Use the apostrophe to stand for the missing elements in contractions (*doesn't, don't, y'all*).
5. Do not use needless apostrophes. The most flagrant violation of this rule is the confusion of the contraction *it's* (for *it is*) with the possessive pronoun *its*. Although some educated people use apostrophes in simple plurals of letters or numbers, the following is acceptable: *1920s* or *CPAs*.

Brackets

1. Use brackets to insert material into a quotation, as in the following example. See also guidelines for Ellipsis Marks.

   > Senator Fogbound claimed that "unemployment is no longer an anecdote [*sic*, antidote] to inflation."

2. Except in mathematics and in computer languages, substitute brackets for parentheses used inside parentheses, as in this example:

   > According to Mark Lester, "Grammar is a way of talking about how words are used to make units that communicate a meaning" (*Introductory Transformational Grammar of English,* 2d ed. [New York: Holt, Rinehart and Winston, 1976], 13).

Colon

1. Use a colon to introduce an enumeration, explanation, list, or long quotation (particularly one that contains commas).
2. Use a colon in the following particular places:
   a. Between title and subtitle, as in Grinder and Elgin's *Guide to Transformational Grammar: History, Theory, Practice.*
   b. Between place of publication and publisher in a citation, as in *New York: Holt, Rinehart and Winston, 1973.*
   c. Between hours and minutes, as in *11:05 a.m.*
   d. Between sentences, if there is a cause–effect relationship. (This situation is similar to guidelines for the Semicolon and should be used sparingly.)
   e. After the salutation in a business letter—except when an open style of punctuation is used.
3. Do not use a colon that interrupts the syntax.

Unnecessary colon:	We sent technicians to: Birmingham, Leeds, and Manchester.
Correct:	We sent technicians to Birmingham, Leeds, and Manchester.
Correct:	We sent technicians to the following: Birmingham, Leeds, and Manchester.

Comma

1. Do not use a comma to join two independent clauses unless the comma is followed by a coordinating conjunction. This error, called a *comma splice* (or *comma fault*), is one of the most serious in punctuation. The comma splice, in other words, misuses the comma as if it were a period or semicolon.

Wrong:	John did not study, therefore he did not pass.
Right:	John did not study, and therefore he did not pass

2. Do not use a comma merely because it "feels good." There are rules that govern the use of commas. In particular, do not use a comma needlessly between subject and verb or between verb and complement (object, predicate nominative, etc.).

Not this: Anne and Tyrone, studied together.
But this: Anne and Tyrone studied together.

3. Do not use a comma before an indirect quotation or before a direct quotation that runs on with the sentence:

Indirect quotation: Eleanor said that she would not go.
Running text: Paul urged the Romans to be "Not slothful in business" (Rom. 12:11 KJV).

4. Use a comma before a coordinating conjunction (*and, or, nor, but*) JOINING TWO INDEPENDENT CLAUSES. For example:

The financial planner applied the new formula, and the long-term forecast became much more optimistic.

Rule 4 is especially useful when the subject of the second independent clause may momentarily be confused as an object of the verb in the first independent clause. The comma in the sentence above presents this problem. Remember to adopt the "you" attitude and make things easy for the reader.

5. Use a comma after any verbal material that precedes an independent clause.

Correct: When Bonnie finished the examination, she forgot to hand in the answer sheet.
Correct: In preparing this form, you should write everything in ink.

6. Use the comma to set off an appositive—a noun explaining or defining another noun. See also guidelines for the Dash.

Correct: Kimberly Shipman, our last supervisor, transferred to Alaska.

If the appositive is essential to the sense, the commas are not used. This type of appositive is called an "identifying appositive."

Correct: The futurist Alvin Toffler wrote *Future Shock* and *The Third Wave.*

7. Use the comma to set off a nonrestrictive clause—that is, a clause not essential to the meaning of the sentence.

Correct: Thomas Darden Willis, who sits in the back row, gave an excellent presentation.

8. Use the comma to separate words in a series.

Correct: Mark wrote the COBOL program quickly, neatly, and accurately.

Do not be confused by newspaper style, which usually eliminates that last comma. Most business writers retain it to ensure absolute clarity.

9. Use the comma to separate adjectives that independently modify a noun.

Correct: Gretchen became involved in a long, expensive lawsuit.

10. Use the comma to set off a noun of address.

    Correct: What do you think, Trevor, about this solution?

11. Use the comma before a short direct quotation.

    Correct: John Paul Jones said, "I have not yet begun to fight."

12. Use the comma to separate contrasted elements.

    Correct: Take the blue form, not the red one, to the bursar.

13. Use the comma for the following purposes:
    a. To set off *yes* or *no* from the rest of a sentence.
    b. To set off conjunctive adverbs—particularly *however.*
    c. To set off tag questions. (*Thaddeus is stupid, isn't he?*)
    d. To separate certain items in dates.

    > **Correct:**   July 1994 is the termination date.
    > **Correct:**   July 1, 1994, is the termination date.

    e. To separate items in addresses (except state and zip code) when they are run in a sentence.
    f. To stand for nonrepeated elements. (*The red form goes to the registrar; the blue one, to the bursar.*)
    g. To aid clarity as needed.
14. Remember that a comma on one side of an item to set it off generally requires a complementary comma on the other side of the item.

    Correct: Baton Rouge, Louisiana, is the capital.

Dash

1. Use the dash to set off an appositive that (a) has commas inside it or (b) is separated from the substantive to which it refers.   *Dash*

    Correct: John's book was widely read—a bestseller for months.

2. Use dashes, instead of parentheses, if the material set off is to be emphasized.
3. Remember that a dash on one side of an item to set it off requires a complementary dash on the other side of the item, unless the sentence ends there.
4. Observe that the dash and the hyphen are two different marks of punctuation, with no uses in common. On a keyboard, the dash is formed by typing two hyphens, with no spaces before, between, or after.

Ellipsis Marks

1. Use ellipsis marks (spaced periods) to show an omission within a   *El* quotation. See also guidelines for Brackets.
2. Type ellipsis marks to conform to the following:
   a. Three spaced periods show an omission within a sentence.

b. Four periods show an omission that crosses over a sentence boundary; one period marks the end of the sentence, and it is followed by three spaced periods.

c. An entire line of spaced periods indicates the omission of at least a paragraph.

Exclamation Point

Excl Use the exclamation mark only occasionally to show strong emotion.

Hyphen

Hyph

1. Use the hyphen to separate the whole number from the fraction in a mixed number, as 3-5/16.
2. Use the hyphen in compound words, such as *self-actualization.*
3. Use the hyphen between compound (unit) modifiers (*36-inch pointer* or *computer-scored answer sheet*).
4. Use a "suspension" hyphen after each item in a hyphenated series (*The company needs fewer mid- and upper-level managers*).
5. Do not use the hyphen between words that merely follow each other:

Compound modifier:	20-dollar bills (= $20 × quantity)
Separate modifiers:	20 dollar bills (= 20 × $1)
Compound modifier:	A deep-dredged canal
Adverb and adjective:	A deeply dredged canal

6. Do not hyphenate words at the ends of lines in these instances:
The entire word is less than seven letters.
The division does not occur between syllables.
The word is part of a proper name.
The line is at the end of a page.
The hyphenated word comes immediately after or before another hyphen or dash.
There are several other hyphenated words on the page.
(Hyphenation is at best a privilege to be used sparingly.)
The manuscript is to be submitted to a publisher.

Parentheses

Paren

1. Use parentheses for supplementary remarks or for references in the text (Joseph N. Ulman Jr. and Jay R. Gould, *Technical Reporting*, 3d ed. [New York: Holt, Rinehart and Winston, 1972], 197–198).
2. If the sentence element before the parentheses requires a mark of punctuation, place the mark of punctuation after the closing parenthesis. Ulman and Gould (page 197), while discussing parentheses, also cite this rule.
3. Use parentheses to enclose the area code for a telephone number: (504) 345–2063.
4. Use parentheses in pairs.

Not this:	1)
But this:	(1)

Period

1. Use the period at the end of a statement or a polite *would you please* request.   *Pd*
2. Use the period with certain abbreviations (*U.S., f.o.b., I.O.O.F., P.D.Q.*), but not with others (*CIA, CYA, GAAP, NCR, TVA*). Most dictionaries include frequently used abbreviations. There are dictionaries of abbreviations that include less common abbreviations. If use of the period is optional, then be consistent (if *AM*, then *PM*; if *a.m.*, then *p.m.*).
3. Use the period for a decimal point.

Question Mark

1. Use the question mark for a direct question, but not for an indirect question.   *QM*

   Correct: Judy asked, "Did I hurt someone's feelings yesterday?"
   Correct: Judy asked whether she hurt someone's feelings yesterday.

2. Use the question mark in parentheses to express doubt about the material preceding the parentheses.

   Correct: John's new (?) car was a Model T.

3. Do not follow the question mark immediately with a comma, a period, or a semicolon.

Quotation Marks

1. Use quotation marks to enclose a speaker's or writer's exact words.   *Quo*
2. If a quotation extends over more than one paragraph, use opening quotation marks before each quoted paragraph, closing quotation marks only at the end of the quotation.
3. Use quotation marks to enclose the title of a work that is published as part of a book—for example, the titles of short stories, chapters, and poems. See also guidelines for Underlining.
4. Position the closing quotation marks as follows if there is an immediately adjacent mark of punctuation:
   a. The comma or the period always goes inside (to the left of) 'the closing "quotation marks."
   b. The colon or the semicolon always goes outside (to the right of) the closing "quotation marks":
   c. The exclamation point or the question mark goes inside if part of the quotation and outside if part of the sentence surrounding the quotation.

   Correct: Mary said, "When will I see you again?"
   Correct: Did Mary say, "I will see you again tomorrow."?
   Correct: Did Mary say, "When will I see you again?"?

5. Use single quotation marks for quotes within quotes; inside the single quotes revert to double quotation marks.

Correct: John said, "Bill claimed, 'I have read the section entitled "Recognizable Patterns of Language." ' "

6. Use quotation marks sparingly to indicate words used in a special (sometimes satiric) sense; do not use quotation marks as decorations.
7. Do not use quotation marks as an abbreviation for *inches* and *feet*. Spell the words out or use the standard abbreviations *in.* and *ft.*
8. Do not use quotation marks to surround blocks of quoted material that are separated from the text, indented, and single spaced unless these quotation marks are in the original quote. (The layout by itself indicates that the material is being quoted; quotation marks are therefore redundant.)

Semicolon

Semi

1. Use the semicolon to separate independent clauses that are intimately joined in logic.

Correct: Semicolons are one thing; commas are another.

2. Use the semicolon to join clauses or items that have internal commas.

Confusing: Attending the meeting were Joseph Biggs, Laramie, Wyoming, president, David L. Carson, Troy, New York, secretary, and Allen White, Duncan, Oklahoma, treasurer.

Clear: Attending the meeting were Joseph Biggs, Laramie, Wyoming, president; David L. Carson, Troy, New York, secretary; and Allen White, Duncan, Oklahoma, treasurer.

This guideline sometimes works together with guidelines for the Comma (item 4):

Correct: Suzanne, afraid of the final examination, studied frantically while drinking tea, coffee, and Royal Crown Cola; and, in the end, she fell asleep during the test.

3. Use the semicolon only between grammatically equal units. Do not use it, for example, between a dependent clause and an independent clause:

Wrong: While Sara studied to be a CPA; her boyfriend found a new lady.

Right: While Sara studied to be a CPA, her boyfriend found a new lady.

Sentence Fragment

Give each sentence a subject and verb that do not have any initial subordinating word to prevent them from forming a complete sentence.

Fragment: Because the bookkeeper was drunk.
Sentence: The bookkeeper was drunk.

Many times a fragment is actually a clause or phrase that belongs with the preceding sentence but has erroneously been punctuated as a sentence by itself. The dash is useful in correcting the problem.

Not this:	Rensselaer Polytechnic Institute is a technological university. The oldest one in the United States.
But this:	Rensselaer Polytechnic Institute is a technological university—the oldest one in the United States.

Sentence Punctuation Error

Use only a period, a semicolon, a colon, a dash, a question mark, an exclamation point, or a comma plus coordinating conjunction between two independent clauses. See also guidelines for the Comma.   *SPE*

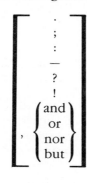

S_1
This is the first
independent clause

S_2
This (or this) is the
second independent
clause.

Slash (Virgule)

Use the slash to indicate alternative possibilities.   *Slash*

Correct:	One may telephone the message to Richard at (504) 345-3682/2063.

Spacing

In typewritten work be careful to use spaces as follows: #
1. Space twice at the end of a sentence.
2. Insert spaces between the dots in ellipses.
3. Space twice between the state and ZIP code (or postal code) in an address.

Correct:	The vendor is The Bible Shop, Post Office Box 2491, Hammond, LA 70404-2491.
Correct:	W. R. O'Donnell lectures in the Department of Linguistics and Phonetics, The University of Leeds, Leeds, West Yorkshire LS2 9JT, England.

4. Do not space before or after the dash.

Underlining

Use underlining (underscoring) for the same functions as italicizing in print.   *Und*
1. Underline the titles of separately published works such as books and periodicals. See also guidelines for Quotation Marks.
2. Underline expressions used as themselves.

Correct:	The word <u>word</u> should be underlined when used as a word.
Correct:	John's writing <u>32</u> instead of <u>23</u> in the last column caused the total to be $9 too high.

3. Underline foreign words and expressions that have not become fully anglicized.

   Correct: The evaluator claimed that Ian's argument was <u>post hoc, ergo propter hoc</u>.

4. Underline the names of vehicles, particularly ships.

   Correct: David received valuable business experience while serving as disbursing officer aboard the USS <u>Berkeley</u>.

   Correct: Charles Lindbergh's <u>Spirit of St. Louis</u> is now in the Smithsonian Institution.

Guidelines for Spelling and Capitalization

Spelling

Sp   1. Spell words in accordance with the dictionary. English spelling is more or less regular, but rules to describe it usually become submerged in exceptions. People who read a lot tend to spell well; the reason is partly a matter of pattern recognition. Some of the most troublesome words are listed in Table 2.

2. Differentiate between expressions that are alike in pronunciation but different in meaning or syntactic function (role in the structure of the sentence). The following similar-sounding words or expressions are sometimes confused:

▪ Accept/except	▪ May be/maybe
▪ Affect/effect	▪ Passed/past
▪ All ready/already	▪ Principal/principle
▪ All together/altogether	▪ Right/write
▪ Any one/anyone	▪ Some one/someone
▪ Capital/capitol	▪ Some time/sometime
▪ Cede/seed	▪ Stationary/stationery
▪ Cite/sight/site	▪ Their/there/they're
▪ Every one/everyone	▪ To/too/two
▪ Faze/phase	▪ Who's/whose
▪ Its/it's	▪ Your/you're
▪ Led/lead	

3. Spell out expressions that, in the situation, may be misunderstood. Pronounce expressions in full if the audience is unfamiliar with the acronyms (*Students in Free Enterprise* instead of *SIFE*). The problem is particularly likely to occur in multinational business, where Americanisms like *ID* (for *identification*) are meaningless or misleading (*Idaho*). Spell out all words in international correspondence, especially addresses (*LA* may mean *Los Angeles*, not *Louisiana*, to foreigners answering your letters).

4. Spell out the words for symbols unless you really need to save space.

   Not this: @, ¢, #, %.

TABLE 2 ▪ *Potential Spelling Difficulties*

a lot	convenience	interest	performance	repetition
absence	coolly	interface	permissible	rhythm
accessible	cylinder	interpret	persistent	ridiculous
accidentally	decision	irresistible	personal	schedule
accommodate	definitely	irritable	personnel	seize
accommodation	definition	laboratory	picnic	sense
accurate	define	ledger	picnicking	separate
achievement	describe	leisure	possession	separation
acquaintance	description	license	possible	sergeant
acquire	desirable	lose	practical	sheriff
among	despair	loose	precede	shining
analogous	development	losing	predictable	similar
analyze	disappear	maintenance	preference	studying
apparent	disappoint	maneuver	preferred	succeed
appropriate	disastrous	marriage	prejudiced	succession
arguing	discriminate	mere	prepare	suddenness
argument	drunkenness	misspelling	prevalent	superintendent
assistant	efficiency	moral	privilege	supersede
attorneys	embarrassment	morale	probably	supposed
balloon	environment	mortgage	procedure	surprise
beginning	equipped	necessary	proceed	technique
belief	exaggerate	newsstand	profession	than
believe	exceed	ninety	professor	then
beneficent	excellence	noticeable	prominent	thorough
beneficial	existence	occasionally	pronunciation	through
benefited	existent	occurred	propeller	tragedy
carburetor	experience	occurrence	psychology	transferred
category	explanation	occurring	ptomaine	tries
changeable	fascinate	offered	pursue	truly
choose	forty	offering	quantity	undoubtedly
chose	government	omitted	questionnaire	unnecessary
coming	grammar	opinion	quiet	until
committee	grievous	opportunity	realize	using
comparative	guarantee	original	receipt	vacuum
conscience	height	paid	receive	varies
conscientious	holiday	pamphlet	receiving	vicious
conscious	imagine	panicky	recommended	villain
consensus	immediately	parallel	referred	weird
consistent	incidentally	paralyze	referring	woman
controversial	indispensable	part-time	relevant	writing
controversy	insistent	pastime	renowned	written

Note: Thirty of the most troublesome words are underlined.

But this: At, cent or cents, number (or pounds), percent.

The # symbol has different meanings and in any case is often redundant before a number. Why write *Apartment #B727* when *Apartment B727* will suffice?

5. Leave the name of an organization exactly as it is officially—for example, *Texas Tech University*, not *Texas Tech. University* and not

Texas Technological University. (This guideline also applies to punctuation—for example, *Holt, Rinehart and Winston*, not *Holt, Rinehart, and Winston.*)

6. Use apostrophes correctly in spelling of possessives (singular possessive *woman's*, plural possessive *women's*). See also the guideline for Apostrophe.

Numbers and Numerals

Num Use numbers and numerals according to the business writing conventions. The following guidelines are arranged in increasing power or importance.

1. Write as numerals all numbers of two digits or more (10 and up) whether positive or negative.
2. Express all numbers containing decimals as numerals.
3. Use a cipher (even if *0*) to fill decimal notation (that is, write 1.0, not 1., and 0.1, not .1).
4. As a general rule use numerals with any unit of measure, even if below 10. Units of measure include money, time, dates, addresses, age, volume numbers, and arithmetic calculations, in addition to bushels, inches, meters, and so on.
5. Differentiate series running together. (*George had five 12-column ledgers and twelve 9-column ledgers.*)
6. Spell out any number coming immediately at the beginning of a sentence. (There are no capital numerals.)
7. Be consistent. For example, if you type a paper that has the fractions 1/2 and 3/16, you must type the 1/2 as 1/2, and not by using the ½ key on the typewriter, because there is no ³/₁₆ key.

See also guidelines for the Hyphen.

Capitalizing

1. In material to be capitalized, except in headings and other situations in which you will use all capitalization (ALL CAPS), capitalize the first letter of nouns, verbs, adjectives, and adverbs.
   a. Capitalize the first letter of the first word in such material even if the word is not a noun, verb, adjective, or adverb.
   b. You may capitalize prepositions longer than four letters, if you wish, but be consistent.

Inconsistent:	*Communicating through Letters and Reports* was written after the War Between the States.
Consistent:	*Communicating through Letters and Reports* was written after the War between the States.
Consistent:	*Communicating Through Letters and Reports* was written after the War Between the States.

2. Capitalize the following:
   a. Names of deities and of titles of scripture books.
   b. Works such as books, articles, poems, and stories.
   c. Important documents (*the Magna Carta, the Declaration of Independence.*)

d. Days, holidays, months, and historical periods (*the Industrial Revolution*).

e. First word in a sentence.

f. Languages.

g. Organizations (*IBM, Rotary International, European Community*), but preserve the capitalization that the organization uses officially (for example, *E. I. Du Pont De Nemours & Co., Inc.*, not *E. I. DuPont De Nemours and Company*).

h. Places and regions (*the Sahara, the South*).

i. Names of streets and other thoroughfares.

j. Title when followed by a name (*Miss Alice Young, Professor Yaney*).

k. *President* when referring to the chief executive of the United States of America.

l. Certain nouns if followed by numbers, as in *Apartment B727*.

3. Be consistent in capitalization of comparable words.

Wrong:	The officers present were President Elizabeth Carter and treasurer Pat Underwood.
Correct:	The officers present were President Elizabeth Carter and Treasurer Pat Underwood.
Also correct (consistent):	The officers present were Elizabeth Carter (president) and Pat Underwood (treasurer).

4. Use lowercase (small) letters for

a. Seasons of the year (*winter*).

b. Academic subjects not otherwise capitalized.

Correct:	Brenda, Dee, and Terry respectively studied management, Roman history, and English.

c. Simple directions, as on a compass.

Correct:	When John worked in the North, his office was on the south side of a busy street.

When you have finished studying this appendix, you may want to return to the quiz to see how much you have improved.

GLOSSARY

abstract Summary of the entire body of a report, presented idea by idea in the same order and with the same emphasis.

accountability Expectation that an individual will do specific things to accomplish a specific goal.

acronym Word formed from the initial letters of each of a series of words in a phrase.

active listening Approach to listening with the goal of accurately receiving and retaining information.

advertising Form of highly structured external communication including television commercials, printed ads, and direct mail.

AIDA sequence Sequence of four steps to follow in persuasive writing (Attention, Interest, Desire, and Action).

analog-to-digital conversion Changing the continuous wave to a digital wave for transmission.

analytical report See problem-solving report.

announcement memorandum Memorandum used to announce a personnel transfer, meeting, policy change, or other organizational news.

appendix Information placed at the end of the report that may be helpful to the reader but not required by the reader.

archival data Data to be kept but not updated back to the same disk.

attention line Line in a business letter that specifies the person who should read it.

attitude question Question in a research questionnaire that seeks a respondent's attitude toward a statement.

attribution Use of endnotes, footnotes, or other sourcing technique to indicate the origin of information.

bad-news letter Letter with a message that the receiver will consider bad news; a letter of refusal.

blaming style Style of communication that focuses on finding fault or discovering who is to blame for a problem.

blind copy Copy of a letter sent out without the receiver or addressee being made aware that this is being done.

boilerplate Standard paragraphs of text that are reusable; also called form paragraphs.

bottom-up style Style of management in which ideas originate at lower levels and move upward through the organization.

burnout Exhaustion caused by excessive demands on one's energy or strength.

central selling point Primary reason why a potential buyer would want what a seller is offering.

chart Type of figure that shows trends or relationships for nonquantitative information.

chronological resumé format   Style of resumé that presents information by date with most recent first.

chronological sequence   Progression from one point in time to another.

closed question   Type of question that is restrictive and generally calls for a brief and limited response.

configurative culture   Culture in which both children and adults learn from their peers.

coherence   Logical connection between ideas.

Commerce Business Daily (CBD)   Publication of the U.S. Department of Commerce containing requests for proposals from various units of the federal government.

compact disk–read only memory (CD–ROM)   Plastic disk that stores a vast amount of data using lasers to read back into the computer.

computer   Electronic device that can store, retrieve, and process data.

computer interview   Interview in which the interviewee types responses to questions posed on a computer screen.

conciseness   Expression of an idea in the fewest possible words; opposite of wordiness.

constructive conflict   Moderate conflict that may key the individual up for superior performance.

contact culture   Culture in which individuals tend to touch often and to stand close together when conversing.

copy machine   Photocopier for reproducing paper documents.

correction interview   Type of interview in which a superior seeks to get a subordinate to substitute some desirable behavior for undesirable behavior.

counseling interview   Type of interview directed at personal problems of the subordinate.

cover letter   Letter that accompanies an item being mailed, such as a resumé.

covert response   Response that is not readily apparent to either the speaker or an observer.

credibility   The quality of inspiring belief.

creeping elegance   Overuse of typefaces, fonts, and emphasis treatments, such as boldface or underlining.

culture   Everything a society thinks, says, does, and makes; a function of a society's values, religious traditions, decision-making patterns, and language.

decisional roles   Manager activities focused on the essential managerial activity of decision making.

decoding   Process of translating a message into an idea.

deductive arrangement   Order of presentation of ideas that begins with the main idea and then gives secondary details.

demographic question   Question in a research questionnaire that seeks information on characteristics of respondents, such as age or sex.

desktop computer   Microcomputer.

desktop publishing   Extremely high-quality word processing.

destructive conflict   Intense or prolonged conflict that may cause worry or fear, hamper work performance, and in some cases lead to physical and mental illnesses.

dichotomous question   Question in a research questionnaire that has only two possible answers.

digital format   Sending of a message as ones and zeros, even voice conversations.

direct-mail approach   Letter-writing campaign aimed at achieving a particular goal, such as securing job interviews at companies where no known openings exist.

direct sequence   Arrangement of points from specific to general.

directing style   Style of communication that focuses on telling others how to do their jobs or solve problems.

directive interviewing style   Style of interviewing characterized by the interviewer's balance between freedom and control.

director of communication   Person responsible for managing the flow of information within an organization and for solving communication problems.

documentation   Establishing of proof, information, evidence, or sequence, usually in written form.

dot matrix printer   Printer for computer output that strikes the ribbon with tiny pins so that printed characters are made up of tiny dots.

draft   Version of a written message (e.g., first draft, second draft, final draft).

electronic mail (E-mail)   Generic name for noninteractive communication of text, data, image, or voice messages by systems using telecommunication links.

electronic notepad   Computer-stored file of notes formerly kept on a pad on the desk.

electronic workstation   Area for a single worker equipped with a microcomputer and telecommunication lines.

emotional appeal   Appeal directed to the receiver's emotions or feelings.

encoding   Process of translating an idea into a message.

endnotes   Notes grouped at the end of the report body, usually giving attribution to an original source.

enumerating   Assigning a specific numeric or chronological label to each of the points being made.

exit interview   Interview conducted for the purpose of learning why an employee is voluntarily leaving the organization.

external communication   Communication with individuals or groups outside the organization.

facsimile (fax) machine   Form of electronic mail that uses an electronic scanner to transmit graphic images.

feedback   Reaction that the receiver has to the sender's verbal and nonverbal message.

figure   Visual support in any form except tabular.

flip chart   Large tablet fastened to an easel for use during informal oral presentations.

floppy disk   Record-shaped sheet of mylar used for secondary storage for computer data; also called diskette or floppy.

form letter   Very general letter that may be sent to many people without change.

form report   Short report presented on a preprinted form; the most common type of short report.

formal communication   Messages sent through channels developed by management.

full-block format   Format for business letters in which every line begins at the left margin.

functional resumé format   Style of resumé that emphasizes job functions.

good-news letter   Letter with a message that the receiver will perceive as good news.

graph   Type of figure that simplifies numerical data to show trends or relationships.

group interview   Interview in which multiple interviewees are interviewed at the same time.

group polarization   Concentration of opinion around a more extreme position than would be taken by group members individually.

groupthink   Tendency of group members to conform rather than to think independently and critically.

guide   Type of procedure that allows discretion; compare with rule.

hard disk   Round device resembling a 45 rmp record that provides secondary storage for computer data.

heading   Words or phrases used in written reports to inform the reader about the content to follow.

hierarchy of needs   Progression of needs from lower to higher levels, ranging from survival needs to self-actualization.

highly directive interviewing style   Style of interviewing in which the interviewer exerts strong control.

horizontal communication   Communication between peers (people on the same level in an organization).

host culture   Culture of the foreign country in which a firm is doing business.

idiom   Expression whose meaning cannot be derived from the combined meanings of the words.

indirect sequence   Arrangement of points from general to specific.

informal communication   Exchanges between individuals who are not formally connected.

information explosion   Proliferation of paperwork made possible by computer technology.

information overload   Having too much information to make intelligent use of it.

informational report   Report that presents data without interpretation.

informational roles   Manager activities focused on the receipt and dissemination of information.

informative speech   A speech with the general purpose of teaching or explaining.

instruction   Form of information that may be written or oral.

internal communication   Messages sent and received within an organization.

interpersonal roles   Manager activities focused on interpersonal relationships.

interpretive report   Report that presents and examines data.

jargon   Verbal shortcut that allows specialists to communicate among themselves more easily.

justification report   Short report to justify a particular action or lack of action.

laptop computer   Portable, battery-powered computer that weighs about 9 to 15 pounds.

laser printer   Printer for computer output that uses a laser beam to form images on a light-sensitive drum.

letter report   Short report using a letter format.

kinesics   Relationship between body motion and communication.

leading question   Question phrased so as to guide the response in a certain direction.

letterhead   Printed heading on business stationery.

linking words   Words that serve as transitions or bridges between ideas.

list question   Question in a research questionnaire that asks the respondent to select from a list of answers.

listener orientation   Focus by a speaker on the interests of listeners.

loaded question   Question phrased so that it is strongly directional.

local area network (LAN)   Small telecommunications network for connecting computers located close together.

logical appeal   Appeal directed to the receiver's rational thinking.

machismo   Strong sense of power and pride.

maintenance role   Role played by a group member who focuses on the emotional and psychological needs of group members; compare with task role.

management by walking around (MBWA)   Management technique that enables managers to increase their contact time with subordinates, suppliers, and customers.

mass emphasis   Technique of using repetition for emphasis.

memorandum   Message written for use within the organization.

memorandum report   Report using a memorandum format but usually more structured in that it has an introduction, body, and conclusion.

microcomputer   Small computer with a keyboard, a monitor, disks for storage, a printer, and a microprocessor to serve as a "brain"; also called desktop computer or personal computer.

microfiche   Sheet film on which very small images of paper documents are stored.

microfilm Reels of film on which very small images of paper documents are stored.

mirror question Question that reflects a previous response with the intent of drawing out additional information.

modified-block format Format for business letters in which all lines begin at the left margin except the date, the close, and the signature; these begin at the center of the page.

motivated sequence Progression based on an analysis of the thought process.

movement analysis Warren Lamb's effort to determine how a person will perform in an organization based on his or her kinesic behavior.

networking Exchange of information or assistance among individuals or groups.

neutral letter Letter with a message that the receiver will perceive as neither good nor bad.

neutral question Question phrased so that possible responses are not indicated and alternatives are presented in a balanced fashion.

nominal group Group that meets to solve a problem without engaging in verbal interaction.

nondirective interviewing style Style of interviewing in which open questions are used almost exclusively.

nonprobability sampling Collecting data when there is a good chance that the sample selected does not represent the larger population.

nonverbal communication Transferring of information without relying on word meaning.

objective Generalized purpose toward which an organization strives.

office visit Day-long series of interviews and discussion as part of the job-getting procedure; also called plant visit or headquarters visit.

open-ended interview Interview with no apparent structure.

open-ended question Question in a research questionnaire that sets no limit on the time or space the respondent may use in answering.

open question Type of question that allows much freedom in the response received.

optical character recognition (OCR) Equipment that can scan a printed page and read, digitize, and enter the information directly into a computer.

orientation interview Interview intended to acquaint a new employee with the job and the company.

overt response Response that is observable and measurable.

pagination Placement of the page number on pages of a report following standard rules.

panel interview Interview in which a single interviewee is interviewed by more than one person at a time.

paralanguage Nonverbal component of the spoken message that includes such voice attributes as pitch, volume, rate, and resonance.

parallel structure Repetition of grammatically equal words, phrases, or sentences.

participative management   Management style in which employees at every level become involved in job-related decision making.

pause   Temporary silence intended to encourage elaboration on a response in an interview.

perception   Individual's unique understanding of the way things are.

performance appraisal interview   Type of interview conducted on a regular basis for the purpose of providing the worker with feedback about his or her performance.

periodic report   Short report issued on a regular basis (daily, weekly, or monthly) to keep others informed about some aspect of operations.

personal computer   Microcomputer.

persuasion   Art of getting people to do something that they would not ordinarily do if not asked.

persuasive letter   Letter that seeks to modify the thought and action of the receiver in a certain direction.

persuasive speech   A speech with the general purpose of eliciting a response, either covert or overt.

persuasive style   Style of communication that employs information sharing and acceptance techniques.

place emphasis   Emphasis achieved by placing an idea at the beginning or end of a message (locations of maximum emphasis).

planning   Prewriting process that involves determining objectives, considering the audience, choosing the ideas to include, and selecting the appropriate medium.

policy   General guide to decision making.

population   A definable group from which a sample will be taken in order to conduct primary research; also called universe.

postfigurative culture   Culture in which children learn primarily from their forebears.

prefigurative culture   Culture in which adults learn also from their children.

primary source   Source of data that involves original research.

probing question   Question stimulated by the response to the previous question.

problem-solving report   Report that presents and interprets data and makes recommendations; also called analytical report.

problem-solving style   Style of communication that seeks mutual acceptance from both sender and receiver of the final action.

procedure   Specific guide to decision making.

progress report   Short report that gives the rate of progress on a project as compared to the schedule and also gives goals for subsequent time periods.

proposal   Written attempt to persuade the management of one organization that the writer's organization is especially qualified to fill a need in exchange for compensation.

proxemics   Spatial relationships between speakers and listeners.

quality circle Small group of workers (and managers) that meet regularly to discuss and resolve problems.

rank order question Question in a research questionnaire that asks the respondent to place a list of items in some order, such as most important to least important.

request for proposal (RFP) Formal solicitation for a proposal.

resumé Factual, categorized, tabulated information about an applicant that is used in obtaining a job interview.

reversal word Word that changes the direction or tone of a message from positive to negative or from negative to positive.

revision Altered version of the draft of a written message.

rule Type of procedure that allows no discretion; compare with guide.

salutation Word or phrase of greeting that usually precedes the body of a letter.

salutopening First few words of the opening paragraph and the recipient's name, used in place of the traditional salutation in business letters.

screening interview Brief interview used to eliminate job applications who are not well qualified.

secondary source Research source, such as a newspaper or magazine, that gives the findings of others.

selective perception Process of selectively hearing only parts of a message and thus distorting the information.

semiconductor (chip) memory Small devices that can store data or instructions used by computers; the main, or primary, memory.

signature block Writer's name and job title as they appear in a business letter.

signpost To assign brief headings to major ideas.

simplified format Format for business letters in which all lines begin at the left margin, a subject line replaces the salutation, and no close is used.

small group Collection of a few individuals who interact face-to-face, verbally and nonverbally, for a common purpose, and with interdependency among the members.

solicited proposal Proposal written in response to a request.

spatial sequence Progression from one physical location to another.

stress interview Interview in which questions or conditions are used to create stress in the interviewee.

superscript Number or letter typed a half line above normal text.

table Visual support consisting of tabular presentation of data.

task role Role played by a group member who focuses on the task; compare with maintenance role.

telecommunication Communication by electric or electromagnetic means, usually over a distance.

telecommute To work at home on the office computer.

teleconference Meeting held by using television cameras and monitors rather than by convening in person.

topical sequence Progression from one part of a topic to another.

traditional format Format for business letters that is identical to the modified-block format except that paragraphs are indented five spaces.

transmittal memorandum Memorandum that introduces the reader to a longer, accompanying message.

turnaround time Amount of time it takes for business firms to provide customers with goods or services.

universe See population.

unsolicited proposal Proposal initiated by the proposer.

verbal communication Transferring of information through messages encoded in words.

vertical communication Communication between superior and subordinate in an organization.

video display terminal Computer monitor; also called cathode ray tube (CRT).

videotape interview Interview in which an interviewee is taped either describing his or her qualifications or answering specific questions as part of the job-getting procedure.

videotext Interactive two-way system for sending and receiving graphic or textual information through a computer interface.

visual support Tables and figures used to support written or oral presentations.

voice mail Form of electronic mail that processes voice messages rather than text messages.

workaholic Person obsessed with work to the point that other aspects of life suffer.

writer's block An inhibition preventing a writer from writing.

INDEX